Why Do You Need this New Edition?

If you're wondering why you should buy this new edition of *Drugs and Behavior: An Introduction to Behavioral Pharmacology*, here are 15 good reasons!

1. Addition of many new figures, tables, and images to help students master the material.

2. New data on prevalence trends in drug use.

3. Coverage of newly emerging club drugs, including salvia and mephedrone (bath salts).

4. Extensive coverage of new research studies, their findings, and implications has replaced older material.

5. New information on a variety of topics, including the placebo effect, energy drinks, and stimulant and club drugs.

6. Greatly expanded content on neurophysiology, neurotransmitters, and the nervous system.

7. Greater detail and coverage of neurobiological theories of substance use and addiction.

8. Inclusion of treatment approaches for drug addiction and the latest evaluations of their effectiveness.

9. Updated information on the neurophysiology of drug effects, much of which was previously unknown.

10. Updates on currently available and most prescribed drug treatments for anxiety disorders, depression, and schizophrenia.

11. Updates on the status of mood, anxiety, and psychotic disorders on the cusp of a new version of the DSM.

12. Expanded coverage of neurobiological theories of schizophrenia and depression.

13. Expanded coverage of mechanisms of action of many drug classes, including opioids, antidepressants, antipsychotics, stimulants, and others.

14. Newly included MySearchLab, providing engaging experiences that personalize, stimulate, and measure student learning.

15. A complete eText—just like the printed text, you can highlight and add notes, listen to audio files, and more.

D1091780

DRUGS AND BEHAVIOR

AN INTRODUCTION TO BEHAVIORAL PHARMACOLOGY

Seventh Edition

DRUGS AND BEHAVIOR

AN INTRODUCTION TO BEHAVIORAL PHARMACOLOGY

William A. McKim

*Memorial University of Newfoundland
and
Queen's University*

Stephanie D. Hancock

Memorial University of Newfoundland

Boston Columbus Indianapolis New York San Francisco Upper Saddle River
Amsterdam Cape Town Dubai London Madrid Milan Munich Paris Montréal Toronto
Delhi Mexico City São Paulo Sydney Hong Kong Seoul Singapore Taipei Tokyo

BH

Editorial Director: Craig Campanella
Editor in Chief: Jessica Mosher
Executive Editor: Susan Hartman
Editorial Assistant: Shiva Ramachandran
VP, Director of Marketing: Brandy Dawson
Senior Marketing Manager: Wendy Albert
Director of Production: Lisa Iarkowski
Managing Editor: Denise Forlow
Project Manager: Shelly Kupperman
Senior Manufacturing and Operations Manager for Arts & Sciences: Mary Fischer

Operations Specialist: Diane Peirano
Digital Media Director: Brian Hyland
Digital Media Editor: Peter Sabatini
Digital Media Project Manager: Pam Weldin
Full-Service Project Management and Composition: Revathi Viswanathan/PreMediaGlobal
Printer/Binder/Cover: Courier/Westford
Cover Designer: Suzanne Behnke
Cover Image: MacX/Fotolia
Text Font: 10/12 Adobe Jenson Pro

Credits and acknowledgments borrowed from other sources and reproduced, with permission, in this textbook appear on the appropriate page of appearance and on pages 392–395.

Many of the designations by manufacturers and seller to distinguish their products are claimed as trademarks. Where those designations appear in this book, and the publisher was aware of a trademark claim, the designations have been printed in initial caps or all caps.

Library of Congress Cataloging-in-Publication Data
McKim, William A., 1945–
    Drugs and behavior: an introduction to behavioral pharmacology.—7th ed./William A. McKim, Stephanie D. Hancock.
        p. cm.
    ISBN-13: 978-0-205-24265-8
    ISBN-10: 0-205-24265-0
    1. Psychopharmacology—Textbooks.   2. Psychotropic drugs—Textbooks.   I. Hancock, Stephanie D.   II. Title.
    RM315.M36 2012
    615.7'8—dc23
                                                                                            2012016040

10 9 8 7 6 5 4 3

Student Edition
ISBN-10: 0-205-24265-0
ISBN-13: 978-0-205-24265-8

Instructor's Review Copy
ISBN-10: 0-205-92035-7
ISBN-13: 978-0-205-92035-8

PEARSON

6/26/15

To Alyssa, Jacob, Nicholas, James, Jillian, Sarah, Aiden, and Petra
and
Darron and Cole

CONTENTS

Preface   *xvii*

Chapter 1   **SOME BASIC PHARMACOLOGY   1**
What Is a Drug?   1
Names of Drugs   1
Describing Dosages   4
Potency and Effectiveness   6
Primary Effects and Side Effects   6
Drug Interactions   7
Pharmacokinetics   7
Routes of Administration   8
Absorption from Parenteral Sites   10
Inhalation   12
Oral Administration   13
Transdermal Administration   16
Distribution of Drugs   16
Elimination   18
Factors that Alter Drug Metabolism   21
Combining Absorption and Excretion Functions   23
The Therapeutic Window   23

Chapter 2   **BEHAVIORAL ANALYSIS OF DRUG EFFECTS   25**
History of Behavioral Pharmacology   25
Research Design   27
Measuring Unconditioned Behavior of Nonhumans   30
Measuring Conditioned Behavior of Nonhumans   31
Stimulus Properties of Drugs   33
Reinforcing Properties of Drugs—Abuse Liability   34
Measuring Behavior of Humans   35
Development and Testing of Psychotherapeutic Drugs   38

Chapter 3   **HOW WE ADAPT TO DRUGS—TOLERANCE, SENSITIZATION, AND EXPECTATION   40**
Tolerance   40
Mechanisms of Tolerance   42
Withdrawal   43

Conditioning of Drug Effects   46
Sensitization   52
Expectancy and Context   53

Chapter 4 NEUROPHYSIOLOGY, NEUROTRANSMITTERS, AND THE NERVOUS SYSTEM   56
The Neuron   56
The Synapse   63
The Nervous System   67
Development of The Nervous System and Potential for Disruption   78
Neurotransmitters   79
Brain Imaging of Drug Effects   91

Chapter 5 SUBSTANCE USE AND ADDICTIVE DISORDERS   96
Defining Addiction   97
History of Research on Drug Use and Addiction   100
Addiction as Physical Dependence   102
Modern Behavioral Explanations of Drug Use   104
The Neuroanatomy of Motivation and Reinforcement   114
Incentive Sensitization Theory   121
Hedonic Dysregulation and Adaptation   123
Disruption of Brain Control Circuits   125
Treating Drug Addiction   126

Chapter 6 ALCOHOL   132
Source of Alcohol   132
Origin and History   133
Measuring Alcohol Levels in the Body   135
Route of Administration and Pharmacokinetics   136
Absorption   136
Distribution   137
Elimination   139
Neuropharmacology   139
Alcohol Antagonists   142
Effects of Alcohol   142
Effects on Human Behavior and Performance   143
Effects on the Behavior of Nonhumans   146
Discriminative Stimulus Properties   146
Tolerance   147

Withdrawal   148

Self-Administration in Nonhumans   148

Self-Administration in Humans   149

Alcoholism   150

Harmful Effects of an Acute Administration   152

Harmful Effects of Chronic Consumption   154

Benefits of Alcohol Consumption   156

Treatments   159

Chapter 7 ANXIOLYTICS AND SEDATIVE-HYPNOTICS   162

The Nature and Neurophysiology of Anxiety   162

Introduction to Anxiolytics and Sedative-Hypnotics   163

History of Anxiolytic and Sedative-Hypnotic Drug Development   164

Neurophysiology   167

Route of Administration and Absorption   169

Distribution and Excretion   170

Effects on the Body   170

Effects on the Behavior and Performance of Humans   171

Effects on the Behavior of Nonhumans   173

Discriminative Stimulus Properties   173

Tolerance   174

Withdrawal   175

Self-Administration in Humans   177

Self-Administration in Nonhumans   178

Harmful Effects   180

Treatment   181

Chapter 8 TOBACCO AND NICOTINE   182

Preparations   182

History   183

Route of Administration   186

Distribution   189

Excretion   189

Neurophysiology   189

Effects of Nicotine   191

Effects on the Behavior and Performance of Humans   192

Effects on the Behavior of Nonhumans   194

Drug State Discrimination   195

Withdrawal Symptoms   196
Self-Administration in Humans   198
Harmful Effects   202
Treatments   205

Chapter 9   CAFFEINE AND THE METHYLXANTHINES   209
Sources of Methylxanthines   209
History of Methylxanthine Use   213
Extent of Methylxanthine Use   214
Route of Administration   215
Absorption   215
Distribution   215
Excretion   216
Neurophysiology   216
Effects of Caffeine and the Methylxanthines   217
Discriminative Stimulus Properties   220
Withdrawal   221
Self-Administration in Nonhumans   223
Self-Administration in Humans   224
Harmful Effects   225
Beneficial Effects   227
Epilogue   227

Chapter 10   PSYCHOMOTOR STIMULANTS   228
Sources   228
History   229
Routes of Administration and Absorption   231
Distribution   232
Excretion   232
Neurophysiology   232
Effects of Psychomotor Stimulants   235
Effects on the Behavior and Performance of Humans   236
Effects on the Behavior of Nonhumans   241
Dissociation and Drug State Discrimination   242
Tolerance   242
Withdrawal   243
Self-Administration in Humans   244

Harmful Effects   249
Treatment   251

Chapter 11 OPIOIDS   254
Origins and Sources of Opioids   254
History   256
Routes of Administration   258
Distribution   258
Excretion   259
Neurophysiology   259
Effects of Opioids   262
Effects on Human Behavior and Performance   262
Effects on the Behavior of Nonhumans   264
Drug State Discrimination   265
Tolerance   265
Self-Administration in Humans   267
Laboratory Studies   268
Self-Administration in NonHumans   269
Harmful Effects   270
Pharmacological Treatment of Opioid Addiction   273

Chapter 12 ANTIPSYCHOTIC DRUGS   277
The Nature of Schizophrenia   277
Theories of Schizophrenia   280
Discovery of Antipsychotic Medications   285
Comparing Typical and Atypical Antipsychotics   286
Routes of Administration   289
Absorption and Distribution   289
Excretion   289
Effects of Antipsychotics   290
*Effects on the Behavior and Performance
of Humans   291*
Effects on the Behavior of Nonhumans   291
Drug State Discrimination and Dissociation   292
Tolerance   292
Withdrawal   292
Self-Administration in Humans and Nonhumans   292

Harmful Effects   293

Other Therapeutic Effects of Antipsychotic Drugs   293

Chapter 13 ANTIDEPRESSANTS 294

The Nature of Depression   294

Theories of Depression   296

History of Antidepressant Medications   300

Neurophysiology   302

Absorption   303

Distribution   303

Excretion   303

Effects of Antidepressants   304

Effects on the Behavior and Performance of Humans   306

Effects on the Behavior of Nonhumans   307

Discriminative Stimulus Properties   308

Tolerance   308

Withdrawal   308

Self-Administration in Humans and Nonhumans   308

Harmful Effects   309

Other Treatments for Depression   310

Chapter 14 CANNABIS 312

History   312

The Cannabinoids   314

Absorption   315

Distribution   316

Excretion   317

Neuropharmacology   317

Effects of Cannabis   319

Effects on the Behavior and Performance of Humans   320

Effects on the Behavior of Nonhumans   323

Dissociation   324

Drug State Discrimination   324

Tolerance   325

Withdrawal   325

Self-Administration in Humans and Nonhumans   326

Epidemiology   326

Harmful Effects   327

Chapter 15 HALLUCINOGENS, PHANTASTICANTS, AND CLUB DRUGS   332

LSD and the Monoamine-Like Drugs   332

Ecstasy and Synthetic Mescaline-Like Drugs   339

Salvia   342

Dissociative Anesthetics: Phencyclidine and Ketamine   343

Dextromethorphan   346

GHB   347

Mephedrone   349

References   350

Credits   392

Index   396

PREFACE

Like most modern scientific endeavors, the field of behavioral pharmacology is ever changing. Each day brings exciting new developments and insights, and a great many discoveries have been made since the first edition of this book in 1987. These discoveries intrigue people who use drugs both as medicines and for recreation. It is an ongoing challenge to keep current with these new developments and decide what to include in each succeeding edition. At the same time, we believe that it is important to tell the stories of the pioneers, to describe their groundbreaking research and insights, and to provide the context in which these new discoveries were made. In addition, new drugs and new fashions in drug use, both recreational and medicinal, come on the scene as others go out of style. As students ask new and different questions, it is important to be able to provide answers. While every edition of this book has attempted to keep up with these rapid changes, it is sometimes difficult to keep pace, and any book in the field is apt to be a bit behind the times. As such, we count on course instructors to supplement the text content with up-to-date material on new trends and developments, with the text providing background in which the significance of new developments can be understood.

NEW TO THIS EDITION

The following changes have been made to the seventh edition.

- This edition welcomes a coauthor, Dr. Stephanie Hancock. Stephanie is an experienced teacher and researcher. In the sixth edition, she contributed to the chapter on neurophysiology. Now, she has brought her energy, enthusiasm, and fresh new insights to the seventh edition, making it a completely revised text.
- We have expanded the discussion of the neuroscience behind each class of drugs, the area of research in which the most new developments are taking place.
- We have also expanded the chapters covering psychotherapeutic drugs—anxiolytics, antipsychotics, and antidepressants—and updated the descriptions of the related disorders.
- We have updated the chapter on addictions, detailing the most recent theoretical and neurophysiological developments.
- We have also increased the amount of visual material–graphs, tables, drawings, and figures–in order to make the information more accessible to students.
- **MySearchLab:** Included with this edition, MySearchLab provides engaging experiences that personalize, stimulate, and measure student learning. Pearson's MyLabs deliver proven results from a trusted partner in helping students succeed. Features available with this text include: **A complete eText**—just like the printed text, you can highlight and add notes, listen to audio files, and more. **Assessment**—chapter quizzes, topic-specific assessment, and flashcards offer and report directly to your grade book. **Chapter-specific learning applications**—ranging from videos to case studies, and more. **Writing and Research Assistance**—a wide range of writing, grammar, and research topics including access to a variety of databases that contain academic journals, census data, Associated Press newsfeeds, and discipline-specific readings. MySearchLab can be packaged with this text at no additional cost—just order using the ISBN on the back cover. Instructors can also request access to preview MySearchLab by contacting your local Pearson sales representative or visiting www. mysearchlab.com.

SUPPLEMENTS

The following supplements are available to qualified instructors.

Instructor's Manual with test materials (0205913571): Written by Dr. Anna Hicks, the instructor's manual is a wonderful tool for classroom preparation and management. The manual contains a brief overview of each chapter of the text with suggestions on how to present the material, sample lecture outlines, classroom activities and discussion topics, ideas for in-class and out-of-class projects, and recommended outside readings. The test bank contains multiple-choice, short-answer, and essay questions, each referencing the relevant content pages in the text.

PowerPoint Presentation (0205920926): Created by Dr. Anna Hicks, the PowerPoint Presentation is an exciting interactive tool for use in the classroom. Each chapter pairs key concepts with images from the textbook to reinforce student learning.

MySearchLab (0205924824): MySearchLab provides engaging experiences that personalize learning and comes from a trusted partner with educational expertise and a deep commitment to helping students and instructors achieve their goals. Features include the ability to highlight and add notes to the eText online, or download changes straight to the iPad. Chapter quizzes and flashcards offer immediate feedback and report directly to the grade book.

ACKNOWLEDGMENTS

This book would not have been possible without the assistance of many people. These include all of the individuals acknowledged in the earlier editions whose contributions are still reflected in the text. In this edition, we would like to further acknowledge the help of our spouses, Edna McKim and Darron Kelly, who tolerated our frequent and prolonged absences, both physical and mental, while the manuscript was being revised.

We would also like to acknowledge the contribution of many of our colleagues at Memorial University and at other institutions around the world who have made helpful suggestions, read drafts, and corrected our errors. We also want to acknowledge the many students who have used earlier editions and contributed helpful suggestions and criticisms that have helped shape this most recent edition. We acknowledge the help of Brent Turner and Cam Rempel, two young men with very bright futures, who researched and contributed particularly to the chapters on alcohol, cannabis, and hallucinogens.

We would like to acknowledge the helpful comments of the reviewers of the seventh edition and thank the people at Pearson for their excellent professional help with the editing and production. These include, but are not limited to, Susan Hartman, Jessica Mosher, Shivangi Ramachandran, Wendy Albert, Shelly Kupperman, Revathi Viswanathan, and Sathya Dalton.

Apart from taking credit where it is due, none of these people can be held responsible for errors or problems in the book. Please direct all complaints to us so we can make the eighth edition even better.

William A. McKim
Brighton, Ontario

Stephanie D. Hancock
Medicine Hat, Alberta

1

Some Basic Pharmacology

WHAT IS A DRUG?

Most people understand what is meant by the term *drug*, but, surprisingly, coming up with a precise definition is not all that easy. The traditional way is to define a drug as any substance that alters the physiology of the body. This definition, however, includes food and nutrients, which are not usually thought of as drugs. Consequently, a drug is sometimes defined as a substance that alters the physiology of the body but is not a food or nutrient. This definition usually works, but it still leaves a lot to be desired. To begin with, the distinction between a drug and a nutrient is not at all clear. Vitamin C, for example, alters physiology, but is it a drug? If it is consumed in the form of an orange, it is clearly food, but if taken as a tablet to remedy a cold, it could be thought of as a drug.

Similarly, some substances that alter the physiology of the body may best be thought of as toxins or poisons rather than as drugs and may not be deliberately consumed. Gasoline and solvent vapors are examples. If they are consumed deliberately to get high, they might be drugs, but when inhaled unintentionally in the workplace, they may be called environmental toxins. The exact distinction between a toxin and a drug is not clear.

One element that complicates the definition appears to be the intention of the drug user. If a substance is consumed to get high or to treat a disorder, it is clearly best to think of it as a drug, but if it is consumed for taste or sustenance, it may not be useful to think of it as a drug. Such a debate has been waged about caffeine. As you will see in Chapter 9, caffeine clearly alters human physiology, but it also has been used as a flavoring agent in products such as soft drinks. If consumers prefer a soft drink that contains caffeine because they like the drink's taste, perhaps caffeine should not be thought of as a drug in that context. If the soft drink is consumed because of the effect caffeine has on the nervous system, then it is appropriate to think of it as a drug. A similar debate has been waged about the role of nicotine in tobacco (see Chapter 8). In these cases, the consequences are important to government regulatory agencies and various manufacturers. Fortunately, it is not necessary for us to form a precise definition of the term *drug*. An intuitive definition will serve our purposes. However, we should never lose sight of the fact that any one definition may not be appropriate in all circumstances.

NAMES OF DRUGS

One of the more confusing things about studying drugs is their names. Most drugs have at least three names—a chemical name, a generic name, and a trade name—and it may not always be apparent which name is being used at any given time. In addition, recreational drugs have an assortment of street names.

Chemical Name

All drugs have a *chemical name* stated in formal chemical jargon. A chemist can usually tell by looking at the name what the molecule of the drug looks like. Here is the chemical name of a drug:

7-chloro-1,3-dihydro-1-methyl-5-phenyl-2H-1, 4-benzodiazepin-2-one

As you can see, it is full of chemical terminology, letters, and numbers. The numbers refer to places where different parts of the drug molecule are joined. To make things more complicated, there are different conventions for numbering these parts of molecules. As a result, the same drug will have different chemical names if different conventions are used.

Generic Name

When a drug becomes established, its chemical name is too clumsy to be useful, so a new, shorter name is made up for it—a *generic name* or *nonproprietary name*. The generic name for the drug whose chemical name we just struggled through is *diazepam*. A drug's generic name bears some resemblance to its chemical name. The conventions for making up generic names are handy to know because they are clues to the nature of the drug. Initially, the generic name was derived by combining parts of the chemical name, and these names are still in use, but more recently, a system has been adopted that uses a *stem* to indicate the class or function of the drug. The stem is usually the last part of the generic name, although it could be at the beginning or in the middle. For example, *oxetine* is a stem that indicates an antidepressant drug. Thus, if you see the name *fluoxetine* or *duloxetine*, you know what type of drug it is, even though you may never have heard of it before. Table 1-1 shows stems for some behaviorally active drugs you may come across.

Generic names are established in the United States by the United States Adopted Names Council (USANC) and are called United States Adopted Names (USAN). Similarly, the British Approved Name (BAN) is established by the British Pharmacopoeia (2012). Internationally, the World Health Organization establishes the International Nonproprietary Name (INN). Attempts are made to harmonize all these names so that the same

generic name is used throughout the world. In spite of these attempts, there are still a few cases where different names are used for the same drug. For example, the USAN *amphetamine* is still widely used in Britain and the United States, but many other parts of the world are now using *amfetamine*, the INN. Most scientific journals and textbooks published in North America (including this book) use USANC generic names.

There is a type of unofficial generic name you might also encounter. Because establishing a generic name is a costly and time-consuming process, new drugs created by drug companies may be used extensively before generic names are officially awarded by the official naming agencies. But instead of using their clumsy chemical names, these drugs are sometimes referred to by a code using letters and numbers established by the company. For example, you may see a name like *SKF 10,047*. The letters refer to the drug company (in this case, Smith, Kline, and French), and the numbers are a unique code for the drug. SKF 10,047 has now been assigned the generic name *alazocine*.

Trade Name

When a drug company discovers and develops a new drug, often at a cost of millions of dollars, it can patent the drug for a number of years so that no other company can sell it. Even though it must use the generic name somewhere in its advertising and documentation, the drug company does not sell the drug under its generic name. Instead, it makes up a new name called the *trade name*, *proprietary name*, or *brand name*. The trade name is the property of the company that sells the drug, and no other company can use that name (hence, the name is proprietary). Generic names, on the other hand, are nonproprietary and can be used by anyone. The trade name for diazepam is Valium. After the patent expires, which typically occurs in 5 to 7 years, other companies can sell the drug or they can make it under license from the owner of the patent, but they frequently sell it under a different trade name. Therefore, one drug can have many different trade names.

Because drug companies sell their products under trade names, people in the medical profession are most familiar with trade names and are most likely to use those names. If a physician gives you a prescription for a drug and you are told the name of the drug, you may not

TABLE 1-1   Generic Name Stems of Behaviorally Active Drugs

Generic Drug Name Stem	Definition	Examples
-adol or -adol-	Analgesics (mixed opiate receptor agonists/antagonists)	taz**adol**ene; spir**adol**ene; levonant**radol**
-anserin	Serotonin 5-HT2 receptor antagonists	alt**anserin**; trop**anserin**; adat**anserin**
-axine	Antianxiety, antidepressant inhibitor of norepinephrine and dopamine reuptake	radaf**axine**
-azenil	Benzodiazepine receptor agonists/antagonists	bret**azenil**; flum**azenil**
-azepam	Antianxiety agents (diazepam type)	lor**azepam**
-azocine	Narcotic antagonists/agonists (6,7-benzomorphan derivatives)	quad**azocine**; ket**azocine**
-barb or -barb-	Barbituric acid derivatives	pheno**barb**ital; seco**barb**ital; etero**barb**
-caine	Local anaesthetics	dibu**caine**
-caserin	Serotonin receptor agonists, primarily 5-HT2	lor**caserin**; vabi**caserin**
-clone	Hypnotics/tranquilizers (zopiclone type)	pago**clone**
-dopa	Dopamine receptor agonists	levo**dopa**
-erg-	Ergot alkaloid derivatives	p**erg**olide
-fenine	Analgesics (fenamic acid subgroup)	flocta**fenine**
-fylline	Theophylline derivatives	enpro**fylline**; bami**fylline**; cipam**fylline**
nab- or -nab-	Cannabinol derivatives	**nab**azenil; dro**nab**inol
nal-	Narcotic agonists/antagonists (normorphine type)	**nal**mefene
-nicline	Nicotinic acetylcholine receptor partial agonists/agonists	alti**nicline**
-orphan	Narcotic antagonists/agonists (morphinan derivatives)	dextro-meth**orphan**; dextr**orphan**
-peridol	Antipsychotics (haloperidol type)	halo**peridol**
-peridone	Antipsychotics (risperidone type)	ris**peridone**; ilo**peridone**; oca**peridone**
-perone	Antianxiety agents/neuroleptics (4'-fluoro-4-piperidinobutyrophenone derivatives)	duo**perone**
-serod	Serotonin receptor antagonists and partial agonists	pibo**serod**
-spirone	Anxiolytics (buspirone type)	zalo**spirone**; tio**spirone**
-stigmine	Cholinesterase inhibitors (physostigmine type)	quilo**stigmine**; teser**stigmine**

Prefixes are shown as "stem-," middle syllable as "-stem-," and suffixes as "-stem."

Source: Adapted from United States National Library of Medicine, National Institutes of Health (2011), http://druginfo.nlm.nih.gov/drugportal/jsp/drugportal/DrugNameGenericStems.jsp, accessed December 7, 2011.

be able to find it listed in this or any other text that uses generic names. Trade names can be distinguished from generic names because the first letter is capitalized.

Strictly speaking, the trade name refers to more than just the active ingredient in the medicine; it refers to the drug's *formulation*. The active ingredient is marketed in the form of a pill, tablet, capsule, or liquid that may contain a number of other ingredients—fillers, coloring agents, binding agents, and coatings, collectively referred to as *excipients*. The excipients and the active ingredient are combined in a particular way, and this is known as the formulation. Different pharmaceutical companies may market the same drug but in different formulations that are given different trade names. It cannot be assumed that all formulations with the same active ingredient are equal. For example, different formulations may dissolve at different rates in different parts of the digestive system and, consequently, may not be equally effective.

Street Name

Drugs that are sold on the street for recreational purposes usually have a street name, which can change with time and differ geographically; however, a particular drug usually has one street name that is widely recognized. For example, the club drug MDMA (3,4-methylenedioxymethamphetamine) is widely known by most people by the street name *ecstasy*, even though it has had many other names at different times and in different places. A quick search of the Internet can turn up names such as X, E, XTC, Disco Biscuit, Go, Crystal, Adam, Hug Drug, Love Drug, Lover's Speed, Clarity, and Speed. Some street names for Valium include Downers, Tranks, Vs, Foofoo, Dead Flower Powers, and Sleep Away.

DESCRIBING DOSAGES

All of modern science uses the metric system, and drug doses are nearly always stated in *milligrams* (mg). A milligram is 1/1,000 of a gram (there are a little over 28 grams in an ounce).

It is generally true that the behavioral and physiological effects of a drug are related to its concentration in the body rather than the absolute amount of drug administered. If the same amount of a drug is given to individuals of different sizes, the drug will reach a different concentration in the body of each

individual. To ensure that the drug is present in the same concentration in the brains of all experimental participants or patients, different doses are frequently given according to body weight. For this reason, in research papers, doses are usually reported in terms of milligrams per kilogram (kg) of body weight—for example, 6.5 mg/kg (a kilogram is equal to 2.2 pounds).

Reporting doses in this manner also helps when comparing research on different species. If you account for such other factors as metabolic rate and body composition, a dose of 1 mg/kg in a monkey will be roughly comparable to a dose of 1 mg/kg in a human. Interspecies comparisons, however, can be tricky. Generally, smaller organisms have higher metabolic rates than larger animals. As we shall see later, many drugs are destroyed by the body's metabolism. What this means is that drugs are metabolized faster in smaller animals, and so it is often necessary to give them a higher dose if they are to reach an exposure equivalent to that of a human. Thus, a dose of 1.0 mg/kg in a human may be equivalent to a dose of 10.0 mg/kg in a mouse or a rat. For this reason, research done on rats and mice often uses doses that seem ridiculously high in human terms.

Dose–Response Curves

To establish a true picture of the physiological and behavioral effects of a drug, it is usually necessary to give a wide range of drug doses. The range should include a dose so low that there is no detectable effect, a dose so high that increases in dose have no further effect, and a number of doses in between. It is usual to plot the effect of this range of doses on a graph, with the dose indicated on the horizontal axis and the effect on the vertical axis. This type of figure is called a *dose–response curve* or a *dose–effect curve*. Some make a distinction between these terms, but such distinctions are not widely used and these terms are often used interchangeably. The term *dose–response curve* (DRC) will be used here.

Figure 1-1 shows a typical DRC. It indicates the effect of caffeine on a mouse's rate of pressing a lever on an FI (fixed interval) schedule (schedules will be explained in Chapter 2). Note that the scale on the horizontal axis is graduated logarithmically. It is generally found that a small change in low doses can have a big effect, but an equally small change in a large dose has no effect. Plotting doses on a log scale allows a wide range of doses

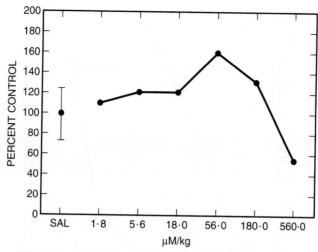

FIGURE 1-1 The dose–response curve for the effect of caffeine on the rate of responding of a mouse on an FI schedule with food reinforcement. Note that the dose is given in S.I. units. (Adapted from McKim, 1980)

to be reported and permits greater precision at the low end of the dosage range.

In the example just used, the drug effect was a measure of response rate, but there are other types of DRCs in which the effect is a discrete binary variable rather than a continuous one. For example, we could not use this type of curve if we wanted to report a DRC for the effectiveness of a drug as an anesthetic. Either subjects are anesthetized or they are not. If the vertical axis simply read *Yes* or *No*, we would not have any sort of a curve. When a binary variable is used, DRCs are constructed differently.

Binary drug effects are handled by working with groups of subjects. Each group is given a different dose of the drug, and the percentage of subjects in each group that shows the effect is then plotted. An example of this type of DRC is given in Figure 1-2. This hypothetical experiment is designed to establish the DRC for loss of consciousness and the lethal effects (another clearly binary variable) of a fictitious new drug Endital. In this experiment, there are 12 groups of rats. Each group is given a different dose of endital—from 0 mg/kg, a placebo, to 110 mg/kg. The vertical axis of the graph shows the percentage of rats in each group that showed the effect. The curve on the left shows how many rats lost consciousness, and the curve on the right shows the percentage of rats in each group that died.

ED_{50} AND LD_{50}. A common way of describing these curves and comparing the effectiveness of different drugs is by using the ED_{50}, *the median effective dose,* or the dose that is effective in 50% of the individuals tested. The ED_{50} for losing consciousness from endital in Figure 1-2 is 35 mg/kg. By checking the next curve, you can see that the dose of endital that killed 50% of the rats was 84 mg/kg. This is known as the *median lethal dose,* or the LD_{50}.

It is also common to use this shorthand to refer to lethal and effective doses that are not at the median. For example, the LD_{50} is the dose at which 50% of subjects die, the LD_1 is the dose that kills 1% of subjects, and the ED_{99} is the dose that is effective in 99% of all cases.

In DRCs constructed from continuous rather than binary measures, the ED_{50} is also used, but in this case, it refers to a dose that produces an effect that is 50% of the maximum effect that the drug causes at its most effective dose.

Drug Safety

When new drugs are being developed and tested, it is common to establish the LD_{50} and the ED_{50} to give an idea of the safety of a drug. Obviously, the farther the lethal dose is from the effective dose, the safer the drug. The *therapeutic index* (TI; also known as

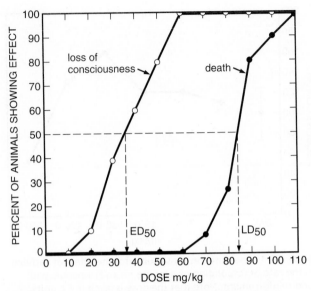

FIGURE 1-2 Results of a hypothetical experiment using 12 groups of rats. Each group was given a different dose of enditol, ranging from 0.0 (a placebo) to 110 mg/kg. One curve shows the percentage of animals in each group that lost consciousness; the other curve shows the percentage that died at each dose. The ED_{50} and the LD_{50} are also indicated.

the *therapeutic ratio*) is sometimes used to describe the safety of a drug. This is the ratio of the LD_{50} to the ED_{50}; TI = LD_{50}/ED_{50}. The higher the TI, the safer the drug. The TI of endital calculated from Figure 1-2 would be 84/35 = 2.4.

Drug safety may also be described as a ratio of the ED_{99} and the LD_1.

POTENCY AND EFFECTIVENESS

Potency and *effectiveness* (or *efficacy*) are terms that are sometimes used to describe the extent of a drug's effect. The two terms do not mean the same thing. When you are comparing two drugs that have the same effect, *potency* refers to differences in the ED_{50} of the two drugs. The drug with the lower ED_{50} is more potent. For example, if you constructed two DRCs for LSD and lysergic acid amide (a related hallucinogen found in morning glory seeds) for the ability to cause hallucinations, you would find that the ED_{50} of lysergic acid amide is 10 times higher than that of LSD. In other words, the nature and extent of the effect of lysergic acid amide

would be the same as that of LSD if you increased the dose of lysergic acid amide by a factor of 10—LSD is 10 times more potent than lysergic acid amide.

Effectiveness refers to differences in the maximum effect that drugs will produce at any dose. Both aspirin and morphine are analgesics or painkillers. When dealing with severe pain, aspirin at its most effective dose is not as effective as morphine. To compare these two drugs in terms of potency would not be appropriate. They both might produce analgesia at the same dose and, thus, be equally potent, but the extent of the analgesia would be vastly different. The difference between potency and effectiveness is shown in Figure 1-3.

PRIMARY EFFECTS AND SIDE EFFECTS

It is generally accepted that no drug has only one effect. In most cases, however, only one effect of a drug is wanted, and other effects are not wanted. It is common to call the effect for which a drug is taken the *primary* or *main effect* and any other effect a *side effect*. If a drug is taken to treat a disease symptom, that is its primary

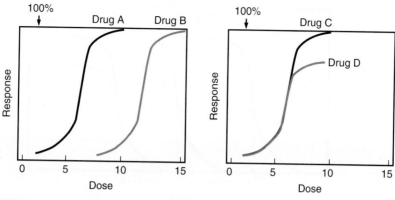

FIGURE 1-3 *Left*: Drugs A and B are equally effective, but the potency of Drug A is greater than that of Drug B. *Right*: Drugs C and D are equally potent, but the effectiveness of Drug C is greater than that of Drug D.

effect. Anything else it might do, harmful or otherwise, is a side effect.

Very often, the distinction between the two is arbitrary. Aspirin, for example, has several physiological effects: It brings down fever, it reduces swelling and inflammation, and it slows the blood's ability to clot. If you take aspirin because you have a high temperature, the temperature-reducing effect is the primary effect, and the other two are side effects. The inhibition of blood clotting is a potentially harmful effect because it can cause bleeding into the stomach, which can have serious consequences for some people. But this anticlotting effect can be useful. Strokes are caused by a clot of blood getting caught in the brain. It has been shown that taking low-dose aspirin every day can reduce the chances of stroke in people at risk. In this case, the anticlotting effect would be the primary effect, and any other effects that the aspirin might be having would be the side effects.

When new behaviorally active drugs are developed to treat diseases, the ability of a drug to be abused or to create an addiction is considered a dangerous side effect. To a drug user, however, this psychological effect of the drug is vitally important, and any other effects the drug may have on the body are considered unimportant or undesirable side effects.

DRUG INTERACTIONS

When two drugs are mixed together, their effects can interact in several ways. If one drug diminishes the effect of another, this interaction is called *antagonism*. Drug antagonism

is established by plotting two DRCs: one DRC for the drug alone and a second DRC for the drug in the presence of the other drug. If the DRC for the first drug is shifted to the right (i.e., the ED_{50} increases) by adding the new drug, this result indicates antagonism between the drugs.

If adding the new drug shifts the DRC to the left (i.e., the ED_{50} decreases), the drugs are said to have an *additive effect*. If drugs have an effect together that is greater than might be expected simply by combining their effects, a *superadditive effect*, or *potentiation*, exists. This can be particularly dangerous if the drugs' effects include respiratory depression, as is the case with alcohol and tranquilizing drugs (barbiturates). It is not always obvious whether a drug interaction is additive or superadditive, but in one situation the distinction is clear: If one drug has no effect alone but increases the effect of a second drug, potentiation is clearly occurring.

In these examples, drug interaction is defined in terms of shifts in the DRC indicated by changes in the ED_{50}, that is, changes in potency, but interactions may also change the effectiveness of drugs. That is, the ED_{50} may not change, but the maximum effect may increase or decrease (see Figure 1-4).

PHARMACOKINETICS

The study of how drugs move into, get around in, and are eliminated from the body is called *pharmacokinetics*. The pharmacokinetics of a drug can be described in three processes: *absorption*, how a drug gets into

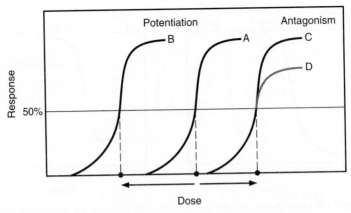

FIGURE 1-4 Drug interactions. The curve labeled A is the dose–response curve (DRC) for a drug, against which the effects of the addition of other drugs will be compared. The curve labeled B shows the DRC after the administration of a second drug. Note that the DRC has been shifted to the left and the ED_{50} has decreased. This indicates potentiation or an additive effect. Curve C is the DRC after another drug has been given. This drug has shifted the DRC to the right, increasing the ED_{50}. This indicates antagonism. Curve D shows the effect of another drug on the DRC. In this case the DRC has been shifted to the right, showing a decrease of potency, and the maximum effect has also been reduced showing a decrease in effectiveness.

the blood; *distribution*, where it goes in the body; and *elimination*, how the drug leaves the body.

Drugs do not have an effect on all body tissues. As a matter of fact, most drugs influence the operation of the body only at specific and limited places, called *sites of action*. A drug may get into the body, but it will have no effect unless it gets to its site of action where it will interact with the cell to change the cell's biochemical processes. It is, therefore, important to understand how drugs get from their place of administration to the place where they act (i.e., pharmacokinetics).

ROUTES OF ADMINISTRATION

Some foods and medications may contain large amounts of valuable nourishment and medicine, but simply swallowing them or otherwise putting them into the body is no guarantee that they will get to their site of action and have the desired effect. It is also true that the way a substance is administered can determine not only whether it gets to its site of action but also how fast it gets there and how much of it gets there.

A route of administration refers to the method used to get a drug from outside the body to some place under the skin. Some substances can be directly absorbed through the skin, but most are not. Getting drugs into the body can be accomplished by taking advantage of the body's natural mechanisms for taking substances inside itself (such as digestion, breathing, or absorption through mucous membranes), or the drug can be artificially placed under the skin by means of injection.

Parenteral Routes of Administration

Parenteral routes of administration involve injection through the skin into various parts of the body, using a hollow needle and syringe. Parenteral routes are further subdivided, depending on the specific point in the body where the drug is to be left by the needle.

VEHICLE. Before a drug can be injected, it must be in a form that can pass through a syringe and needle—that is, it must be liquid. Because most drugs are in a dry powder or crystalline form (the word *drug* is derived from the French *drogue*, meaning *dry powder*), it is necessary to dissolve or suspend a drug in some liquid before it can be injected. This liquid is called a *vehicle*. Most behaviorally active drugs tend to dissolve well in water and remain stable for long periods of time in water solution. Pure water is not totally inert with respect to the physiology of the body, so a weak salt solution is used instead. Because body fluids contain dissolved salts, the most common vehicle is *normal* or *physiological saline*, a solution of 0.9% sodium chloride (ordinary table salt), which matches body fluids in concentration and does not irritate the tissues when it is injected as pure water would.

In some cases, the drug to be injected does not dissolve in water. The primary active ingredient in marijuana, tetrahydrocannabinol (THC), is an example of such a drug; it requires a different vehicle, such as vegetable oil (see Chapter 14). Administering lipid-soluble drugs in an oil vehicle slows the rate of absorption, prolonging the drug's effects over several days.

When a drug is in liquid form and the syringe is filled, the needle can be inserted into various places in the body, and the drug and vehicle are then injected to form a small bubble, or *bolus*. There are four common parenteral routes, depending on the site where the bolus containing the drug is to be placed: (a) *subcutaneous*, (b) *intramuscular*, (c) *intraperitoneal*, and (d) *intravenous*.

SUBCUTANEOUS. In published material, the term *subcutaneous* is frequently abbreviated *s.c.* In jargon, it is called *sub-q*. As the name suggests, in this route of administration, the drug is injected to form a bolus just under the skin or cutaneous tissue. In most laboratory animals, the injection is usually made into the loose skin on the back, between the shoulders. For medical purposes in humans, s.c. injections are usually done under the skin of the arm or thigh, but the hand or wrist is sometimes used to self-administer recreational drugs such as heroin, a procedure referred to as *skin popping*. Some drugs, including contraceptives, may be manufactured as pellets for s.c. implantation, which prolongs absorption, sometimes for years.

INTRAMUSCULAR. In the *intramuscular* (*i.m.*) route, the needle is inserted into a muscle, and a bolus is left there. In humans, the most common muscle used for this purpose is the *deltoid* muscle of the upper arm or the *gluteus maximus* muscle of the buttock. To receive such an injection, the muscle must be fairly large, so i.m. injections are seldom given to rats and mice. They are more frequently given to monkeys. This route of administration is common for pigeons as well; the injection is given into the large breast muscle. Drugs administered i.m. are typically absorbed through the muscle's capillaries within about an hour.

INTRAPERITONEAL. The abbreviation for the *intraperitoneal* route is *i.p.*, and, as the name suggests, the needle is inserted directly into the peritoneal cavity. The *peritoneum* is the sack containing the visceral organs, such as the intestines, liver, and spleen. The aim of an i.p. injection is to insert the needle through the stomach muscle and inject the drug into the cavity that surrounds the viscera. It is not desirable to inject the drug directly into the stomach or any of the other organs. Doing so could be harmful and cause hemorrhaging and death. At the very least, injection into an organ is likely to alter the reaction to the drug.

Intraperitoneal injections are commonly used with rats and mice because they are easy and safe and cause the animals very little discomfort. They are much less convenient in larger animals and are almost never given to humans. At one time, rabies vaccine was commonly given to humans via this route, but this is no longer the case.

INTRAVENOUS. In an *intravenous* (i.v.) injection, the needle is inserted into a vein, and the drug is injected directly into the bloodstream. This procedure is more popularly known as *mainlining*. Before an i.v. injection can be given, it is necessary to find a vein that comes close enough to the surface of the skin that it can be pierced with a needle. In humans, this is usually the vein on the inside of the elbow. The most common procedure is to wrap a tourniquet around the upper arm between the injection site and the heart. Because veins carry blood toward the heart, the tourniquet will dilate or enlarge the vein at the injection site and make injection easier.

When the end of the needle is inserted into the vein, the tourniquet is removed, and the drug is injected when normal blood flow has resumed. This is essentially the reverse of the procedure used when blood is removed for a blood test. When a drug is administered i.v., it gets distributed throughout the body very quickly, reaching the brain in a matter of seconds and producing rapid effects. One difficulty with i.v. injections, however, is that a vein cannot be used too frequently or it will collapse and simply stop carrying blood. When veins have collapsed in the arms, other veins in the wrists, hands, and feet may be used, but they are more difficult to strike accurately with a needle. Another problem is that recreational drugs may contain contaminants that are insoluble (do not dissolve) and, once in the bloodstream, become lodged in and cause damage to small blood vessels in organs such as the lungs or eyes.

In laboratory animals, i.v. injections are not commonly used by behavioral pharmacologists because veins close to the surface of the skin are unusual in rats, mice, and pigeons, and the procedure is not easy in unrestrained animals. Fur and feathers also make the location of such veins difficult to find. When i.v. injections are necessary, they are usually accomplished by means of a permanently implanted catheter. A *catheter* is a tube that is surgically implanted into the body. One end of the tube is at a site inside the body, and the other end is outside. In rodents and monkeys, venous (in a vein) catheters are usually inserted in the jugular vein in the neck, and the free end of the tube emerges from the animal's back. When an intravenous injection is required, the syringe is attached to the end of the catheter outside the body, and the drug is injected. Researchers frequently use this type of preparation to study self-administration of drugs by animals (the catheter may be attached to a motor-driven pump that the animal can control by pressing a lever; see Chapter 5). Intravenous catheters are fairly permanent and may last for months before they have to be replaced.

OTHER PARENTERAL ROUTES. Experimental research with laboratory animals sometimes involves injections directly into the central nervous system (the brain and spinal cord; see Chapter 4). In *intrathecal* injections, for example, the needle is inserted into the nervous system between the base of the skull and the first vertebra. The drug is left in the *cerebrospinal fluid* (CSF; the fluid that bathes the nervous system) and quickly diffuses throughout the nervous system. A drug may also reach the CSF through an *intracerebroventricular* injection directly into one of the brain's *ventricles*, which are chambers filled with CSF. To more precisely determine drug effects on specific areas of the brain, *intracerebral* injections may be used in which a drug is administered directly into brain tissue. These forms of drug administration are often done through a

cannula. A cannula is like a catheter, except it is a rigid tube resembling a hypodermic needle. Cannulae are often attached to the animal's skull using dental cement and can remain permanently implanted.

ABSORPTION FROM PARENTERAL SITES

With intravenous injections, the drug is put directly into the blood, but when other sites are used, the drug must be absorbed into the circulatory system. The rate at which a drug gets into the blood from an injection site is determined by a number of factors associated with blood flow to the area. Generally, the volume of blood flow is greater to the peritoneal cavity than to the muscles, and it is greater to the muscles than under the skin. As a result, absorption is fastest from an i.p. injection and slowest from an s.c. injection.

Heat and exercise can speed absorption from i.m. and s.c. sites because such factors increase blood flow to muscles and skin. Thus, an i.m. injection will be absorbed faster if the muscle is exercised after the injection, and the drug from a subcutaneous site will get into the blood faster if heat is applied to the area and more slowly if the area is chilled.

To be absorbed into the bloodstream, a drug must pass through the walls of the capillaries. A *capillary* is a tiny vessel through which blood flows. Capillaries permeate most body tissues. They are so small in diameter that red blood cells can barely pass through. It is through the walls of capillaries that nutrients and oxygen pass out of the blood into body tissues, and it is also through these capillary walls that waste products and carbon dioxide pass into the blood and are removed. Blood leaves the heart and is distributed around the body in *arteries*. The arteries divide into smaller and smaller branches until they become capillaries. The blood in capillaries is eventually collected in *veins*, which carry the blood back to the heart and the lungs (see Figure 1-5).

The walls of the capillaries are made up of a single layer of cells. Between these cells are small openings, or *pores*, through which nutrients, waste products, and drugs may pass freely. The only substances in the blood that cannot move in and out of the capillaries through these pores are red blood cells and large protein molecules, which are trapped inside because they are larger than the pores.

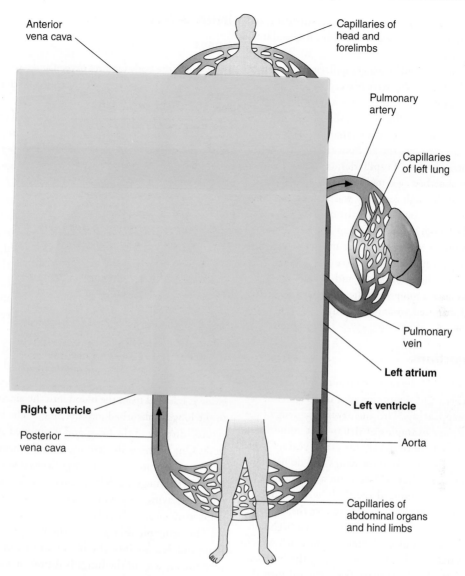

Anterior vena cava

Capillaries of head and forelimbs

Pulmonary artery

Capillaries of left lung

Pulmonary vein

Left atrium

Right ventricle

Left ventricle

Posterior vena cava

Aorta

Capillaries of abdominal organs and hind limbs

FIGURE 1-5 Circulatory system.

Injected drugs pass into capillaries and the blood-stream through these pores by simple *diffusion*. Diffusion is the process by which a substance tends to move from an area of high concentration to an area of low concentration until the concentrations are equal in both areas. If a drop of food coloring is placed in the corner of a tub of still water, it will remain as a highly colored drop for only a short period of time. The force of diffusion will soon distribute the coloring evenly throughout the tub of water. The same principle determines that a drug injected into a muscle or under the skin will move from the area of high concentration (the bolus at the site of the injection) into the blood, an area of low concentration, until the concentrations in the two places are equal. The drug from an injection site will move through the pores into the blood in the capillaries surrounding the injection site. Because this blood is constantly circulating and being replaced by new blood with a low concentration of drug, more will be absorbed as the blood circulates through the area.

Areas that are serviced by many capillaries will absorb drugs faster than areas that have few capillaries. Because muscles use more oxygen, they have a richer capillary supply than the skin; for this reason, absorption into the blood is faster from i.m. injections than from s.c. injections. Drugs injected into the peritoneum have access to an even greater number of capillaries; consequently, i.p. injections are absorbed even more rapidly.

Absorption through capillary walls is not a factor in intravenous injections because the drug is placed directly into the blood. Blood in the veins is transported to the heart and then redistributed around the body after a short detour through the lungs (see Figure 1-5). The body has about 6 liters of blood, and the heart pumps these 6 liters once a minute, so the drug in most i.v. injections is distributed around the body about a minute after injection.

Depot Injections

Some drugs need to be taken continuously or chronically to prevent the symptoms of a disease or disorder from reappearing. The antipsychotic drugs (see Chapter 12) are examples of drugs that sometimes need to be taken continuously for many years. Often people do not like to take these drugs and do not continue to use them after release from a hospital. As a result, they are readmitted regularly with recurring psychotic symptoms. It is possible to give these people *depot injections*—the drug is dissolved in a high concentration in a viscous oil (often sesame oil), which is then injected into a muscle, usually in the buttock. The drug then slowly diffuses from the oil into the body fluids over a long period of time. A single depot injection of an antipsychotic drug can be effective as long as 4 weeks. This technique usually works only with drugs that are highly lipid soluble (to be discussed shortly); otherwise, they would be released too quickly. Fortunately, antipsychotic drugs have this property (Lemberger, Schildcrout, & Cuff, 1987). Newer formulations use more advanced techniques to generate synthetic polymer beads that have no physiological effect, but degrade slowly in the body and release constant levels of a drug over an extended period of time (Fleischhacker, 2009).

INHALATION

Gases

Every cell in the body requires oxygen and gives off carbon dioxide as a waste product. The body has developed a very efficient system for absorbing gases from the air (that is, the lungs) and distributing them quickly and completely throughout the body (that is, the circulatory system). When drugs in the form of gases, vapors, or fine mists are breathed into the lungs, this system gets them into the blood very rapidly.

The lungs are an extremely efficient gas exchange system. Their inside surface is convoluted and contains many pockets of air so that the total surface area exposed to the air is very large. This entire area is richly supplied with blood by capillaries, which are close to the surface. When a gas or fumes of volatile substances (substances that evaporate rapidly, such as solvents) are inhaled, they are very quickly absorbed through the capillary walls and enter the circulating blood.

Figure 1-5 shows the circulation to and from the lungs. After blood returns to the heart through the veins, it is pumped directly to the lungs. Here the carbon dioxide is released from the blood into the air, and oxygen in the lungs is absorbed into the blood. The blood then returns directly to the heart and is pumped around the body. One of the main arteries from the heart goes directly to the brain. Consequently, drugs dissolved in the blood in the lungs are delivered very quickly to the brain without having to pass through the liver first, where some metabolism takes place.

The principle that governs the movement of gases from inhaled air into the blood and from the blood into the air within the lungs is diffusion. Gases move from areas of high concentration to areas of low concentration. If the concentration of drug in the inhaled air is higher than that in the blood, the drug will move from the air into the blood, but the reverse is also true; the drug passes out of the blood into the air and is exhaled so that the concentration of the gas in the blood reflects the concentration in the gas that is breathed. Thus, the inhalation of gases provides a means of controlling drug levels in the blood with considerable precision. This ability is one reason gases are used widely as general anesthetics, and inhalation is the favored route of administration for anesthesia. Volatile substances can also be exhaled from the lungs, although the rate is determined by how rapidly the substance evaporates.

Smoke and Solids

Gases and solvent vapors are not the only substances administered through the lungs. Drugs that occur naturally in some plants may be administered by burning the dried plant material and inhaling the smoke. Tobacco, opium, and marijuana are traditionally ingested in this manner. When the dried plant material is burned, the active ingredient remains either in the smoke as a vapor or in tiny particles of ash that are inhaled into the lungs. When contact is made with the moist surface of the lungs, the drug dissolves and diffuses into the blood. The major difference between smoke and gases is that the drug in the smoke particles will not revaporize after it is dissolved in the blood, and, consequently, it cannot be exhaled. These drugs must stay in the body until they are eliminated by other means.

The problem with administration of solids and smoke by inhalation is the susceptibility to damage of all the tissues in the respiratory system. Smoke from burning marijuana and tobacco contains many substances in addition to the active drug; there are tars, hydrocarbons, and other chemicals created by the burning process. In time, these substances may cause respiratory diseases such as emphysema, asthma, and lung cancer, and they may decrease the ability of the lungs to absorb oxygen and eliminate carbon dioxide from the blood. Other forms of the drug with unknown toxicity may also be created by the burning process. In addition, when most substances burn in air, carbon monoxide gas is given off. Carbon monoxide is a very toxic gas because it blocks the ability of the blood to carry oxygen.

Sometimes, refined drugs like cocaine, heroin, methamphetamine, and oxycodone are administered by heating them till they vaporize and inhaling the vapors. This works the same way as inhaling smoke, but has the advantage that there is no smoke involved and consequently no hydrocarbons or carbon monoxide.

In the experimental laboratory, drugs are seldom administered by inhalation to laboratory animals. This is unfortunate because inhalation is a common method used by humans to administer abused drugs. The major difficulty is that in order to make an animal inhale a gas or smoke, it is usually necessary to confine it in a closed environment filled with gas or smoke, or the experimenter must make it wear some kind of helmet or face mask. The uncertainty about total dose and the technical problems of administration make this a cumbersome and unpopular route of administration in behavioral pharmacology. However, some researchers have had some success in training monkeys to suck smoke or vaporized drugs from a spout inserted into their cage.

Powdered drugs such as cocaine, heroin, and tobacco snuff are sometimes sniffed into the nostrils. This practice is known as *intranasal administration* or *insufflation*. On the street it is called *snorting*. What happens to the drug when given in this manner is unclear. It appears that most of the drug sniffed in the nose is dissolved in the moist mucous membranes of the nasal cavities and is absorbed into the blood from there. Some drug enters the lungs, while more runs down the throat into the stomach and digestive system and may be absorbed there. Although the nasal cavity is not as richly supplied with blood as the lungs and although the area is not designed to transport substances into the blood, it is a reasonably efficient system for getting drugs into the blood.

ORAL ADMINISTRATION

Drugs absorbed into the body through the digestive system are taken into the mouth and swallowed—hence the term *per oral* or *per os* (*p.o.*). Sometimes substances can get into the digestive system by other means. As just explained, snuff from the nostrils can get down the throat and be swallowed.

A drug may be taken into the mouth and not swallowed, as with chewing tobacco. Although this is technically an oral administration, the absorption into the body is through the *buccal membranes*, or mucous membranes of the mouth, not the digestive system.

The digestive system may also be entered via its other end (*intrarectal* administration). Suppositories placed in the rectum also cause the drug to be absorbed into the blood. Such absorption is not as reliable as oral administration, but it can be a useful method of administering a medication when it is impossible to give it orally (e.g., when a patient or animal is unconscious or vomiting).

The Digestive System

After a drug is swallowed, it goes directly to the stomach. The stomach churns and secretes strong acids and digestive enzymes to break down food pieces and turn them into a liquid that is then released slowly into the intestines, where nutrients are absorbed. Drugs that are soluble in gastric fluids and resistant to destruction by digestive enzymes may be absorbed from the stomach, but absorption is most efficient in the intestines. The rate at which a swallowed drug will be absorbed may be determined by the speed with which it gets through the stomach to the intestines. Because solid food tends to be held in the stomach, taking a drug with a meal generally slows its absorption. When a drug is taken on an empty stomach, it passes quickly into the intestines and is absorbed rapidly.

The walls of the intestines are lined with capillaries to absorb nutrients from food, and these capillaries also absorb drugs. To get to the capillaries and be absorbed into the blood through the pores in the capillary walls, the drug must first pass through the membrane of the intestinal wall, which does not have any pores.

All body tissue is made of cells that form membranes. Figure 1-6 shows the cross section of a typical membrane in the body, made up primarily of what is called a *lipid bilayer*. *Lipid* is another name for fat, and the membrane consists of two layers of fat molecules held tightly together. Each lipid molecule has a clump of atoms at one end (the head region) and two chains of atoms at the other (the tail region). The lipid molecules in a membrane are organized so that, in each of the two layers, the heads point outward, toward the intracellular fluid for one layer and toward the extracellular fluid for the other, and the tails of each layer point inward, toward each other. The heads are *hydrophilic* (water loving) whereas the tails are *hydrophobic* (water repelling), thereby preventing the passage of water-soluble substances through the membrane. Therefore, the extent to which a drug can get through the lining of the intestine to the blood will depend on its ability to dissolve in lipids.

Large molecules of protein are embedded in the lipid bilayer, and they have specific functions that will be described in this chapter and in Chapter 4.

Lipid Solubility

Different drugs have different degrees of lipid solubility that are usually expressed in terms of the *olive oil partition coefficient*. To test lipid solubility, equal amounts of olive oil and water are placed in a beaker, and a fixed amount of drug is mixed in. Later the oil and water are separated, and the amount of drug dissolved in each one is measured. Drugs that are highly lipid soluble are more highly concentrated in the oil. Poorly lipid-soluble drugs mostly end up in the water. This test, although not perfectly accurate, predicts reasonably well the degree to which a drug will dissolve in fat tissue in the body.

All drug molecules vary in their degree of lipid solubility in their normal state, but when a molecule of a drug carries an electric charge, it loses its ability to dissolve in lipids. Such a charged molecule is called an *ion*. Ions are unable to pass through membranes. When a drug is dissolved in a liquid, some or all of its molecules become ionized. The percentage of ionized molecules in a solution is determined by (a) whether the drug is a weak acid or a weak base, (b) whether it is dissolved in

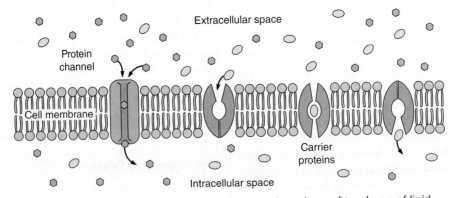

FIGURE 1-6 A cross section of a typical membrane. It is made up of two layers of lipid molecules with their hydrophilic heads pointing out and their lipophilic tails pointing inward. Embedded in this lipid bilayer are large molecules of protein that serve special functions such as protein channels, ion pumps, and transporters.

an acid or a base, and (c) its *pKa*. The pKa of a drug is the *pH* at which half its molecules are ionized.

The easiest way to understand pKa is to imagine the following experiment with a fictional drug called *damital*. A fixed amount of damital is dissolved in each of 15 bottles; each bottle contains a liquid with a different pH, ranging from 0 to 14. A solution's pH is a number that describes the degree to which it is either an acid or a base. On this scale, 7 is completely neutral. Numbers less than 7 indicate increasing acidity, and numbers greater than 7 indicate increasing alkalinity.

After we dissolve the damital in each bottle, we determine the percentage of damital molecules that are ionized and plot the results. As shown in Figure 1-7, the pH at which half the damital molecules are ionized is 5.

Most drugs are either weak acids or weak bases. Damital is a weak acid. If we do this experiment again with a drug that is a weak base, we see something different. One line in Figure 1-7 is a plot for an imaginary base, *endital*. The curve for the acid damital starts with 0% ionization at the acid end of the scale, and ionization increases as it moves toward the base end. Just the opposite is true for endital, the base. It starts with 100% ionization in the acids, but its percentage of ionization decreases as the solution gets more basic. The pKa for endital is calculated in the same way as that for damital. In this case, the pKa for endital is 8. By knowing whether a drug is an acid or a base and by knowing its pKa, it is possible to predict the degree to which it is likely to be ionized in a solution of known pH. The pH at the lining of the intestine is about 3.5. In Figure 1-7, we can see that damital is about 5% ionized at this pH, and endital is completely ionized. Because ionized molecules are not lipid soluble and do not pass through membranes, we can conclude that endital will not be very effective when taken orally, whereas damital will be readily absorbed.

Morphine is a base; its pKa is about 8. Bases are highly ionized in solutions with a low pH (acids), and the curve drops in solutions with higher pHs, so we can predict (correctly) that morphine will be poorly absorbed from the digestive system.

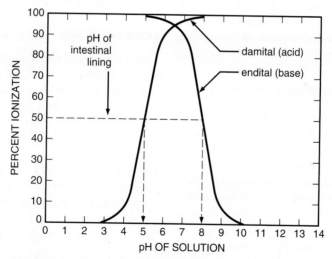

FIGURE 1-7   The percentage of ionized molecules in two fictional drugs dissolved in solutions with different pHs. Damital, a weak acid, becomes more highly ionized as the pH becomes more basic (higher numbers). Endital is a weak base, and it becomes more highly ionized at acid pHs. By drawing a horizontal line at the 50% ionization level, we can determine the pKa of each drug: damital, 5.0, and endital, 8.0. Caffeine is a weak base with a pKa of 0.5. Try to envision what its curve would look like on the graph. There is no significant ionization of caffeine at any of the physiological pHs in the body.

In general, most bases like morphine are poorly absorbed when taken orally, but their absorption depends on their pKa. For example, caffeine is a base, but it has a pKa of 0.5. Its ionization curve drops off quickly at very low pHs; consequently, it is almost entirely nonionized at pHs encountered in the digestive system. Caffeine, therefore, is readily absorbed when taken orally.

It should be pointed out that significant absorption will take place even if only a small percentage of molecules is not ionized. For example, if 97% of a drug is ionized at digestive system pHs, only 3% will be lipid soluble, but as soon as that percentage diffuses through the membrane and is removed by the blood, 3% of the remaining drug loses its charge, so the 97% ionization figure will stay constant for the drug remaining in the digestive system. The newly nonionized 3% now diffuses into the blood, and 3% more can lose its ionization. This process will continue until equilibrium is reached—that is, the concentration of nonionized molecules is the same on either side of the membrane. For this reason, it is not appropriate to think that the percentage of nonionized drug is all that is absorbed. Rather, the percentage of nonionized molecules determines the number of molecules available for absorption at any period of time and, therefore, determines the rate of absorption. If 50% of the molecules are not ionized, absorption will be rapid, but if 3% are not ionized, absorption will be much slower.

TRANSDERMAL ADMINISTRATION

Some drugs can be absorbed through the skin. This is called *transdermal administration*. The skin is composed of several layers, but the main barrier to absorption is the *epidermis*, the outer layer of skin. It is made up of a continuous sheet of flattened cells that are densely packed with *keratin*. This layer is virtually impermeable to water and can be penetrated only by lipid-soluble substances. Even then, absorption is very slow. The layer just under the epidermis, however, is made up of connective tissue and serviced by capillaries; therefore, drugs applied to areas where there is a break in the epidermis (as occurs when there is a cut or a wound) can be absorbed.

Considerable research has been aimed at developing ways to make transdermal administration more effective. Traditionally, a drug has been applied in ointments or salves. In this form, absorption of the drug is determined entirely by the lipid solubility of the drug. In some cases, an absorption enhancer may be added to increase the rate of absorption, or the drug may be fixed in a special substance that releases it slowly for absorption.

The technology of transdermal administration has greatly improved with the development of the patch technology where the drug is separated from the skin by a special membrane that limits the rate of absorption. Using systems such as this, it is possible to administer a drug at a constant rate and maintain a constant blood level for an extended period of time. Nicotine patches were first developed in the 1980s for the treatment of tobacco addiction (see Chapter 8), but now skin patches are used for the controlled delivery of many drugs including opioid analgesics such as fentanyl (see Chapter 11), methylphenidate for treating symptoms of Attention Deficit Hyperactivity Disorder (ADHD; see Chapter 10), and hormones including the contraceptive patch Ortho Evra.

DISTRIBUTION OF DRUGS

Even though most drugs get transported widely around the body by the blood, they tend to become concentrated in particular places and segregated from others. This process is called the *distribution* of a drug.

Lipid Solubility

It has been stressed that lipid-soluble substances can get through membranes easily, but as the olive oil partition coefficient experiment shows, this capacity also means that highly lipid-soluble drugs tend to stay in lipids wherever they encounter them. Consequently, highly lipid-soluble drugs tend to concentrate in body fat outside the central nervous system. Because few drugs have any effect in body fat, all of a drug dissolved in fat is, in effect, inactive. Very often, the body fat acts like a sponge, absorbing a lipid-soluble drug, preventing it from reaching its site of action, and diminishing its effect. Later, the drug is slowly released back into the blood from the fat over a long period of time.

Ion Trapping

The pKa of a drug can also influence where a drug ends up in the body. As pointed out earlier, drugs that are weak bases tend to ionize in acidic solutions, and drugs that are weak acids tend to ionize in basic solutions. Since ionized molecules are not lipid soluble, the pKa of a drug can hasten or retard its absorption and excretion. This process was described earlier in the discussion of lipid solubility and absorption of basic and acidic drugs from the digestive system.

The same process operates anywhere in the body where body fluids with different pHs are separated by a membrane; drugs can get *trapped* on one side of the membrane. Drugs that _____ weak bases will be concentrated in the fluid on the si_____ _____rane that is more basic, and weak bases w_____ _____ _____he fluids on the more acidic side of _____ _____ _____n be quite dramatic becau_____ _____ _____de of a membra_____ _____ _____ted or_____

_____ _____he bra_____ _____ dif-fusion of _____ _____came known as the *bloo_____* _____estab-lished that the blood–b_____ _____ special cells in the central nervous syste_____ _____emselves around the capillaries and block the _____s through which substances normally diffuse. These cells provide a solid lipid barrier so that non-lipid-soluble substances have great difficulty getting into the brain. If not for the blood–brain barrier, the delicate balance of chemicals inside and outside brain cells would be disrupted, even by the food we eat, altering the ability of the cells to communicate one with another.

The blood–brain barrier is incomplete or weak in some areas of the brain and will permit some non-lipid-soluble molecules to enter. For example, the *area postrema* of the *medulla oblongata* (see Chapter 4) contains specialized cells that play an important role in detecting impurities or toxins in the blood and elicits vomiting by stimulating the vomiting center in an attempt to rid the body of these substances. When opioid drugs such as heroin are first used, they activate the vomiting center this way. Also, the

subfornical organ in the brain plays an important role in detecting hormone levels in the blood, especially those hormones involved in regulating the balance of bodily fluids.

Active and Passive Transport Across Membranes

It is important for the body to get some non-lipid-soluble substances across membranes, so special *transport mechanisms* exist. This process is carried out by large protein molecules that span the cell membrane (visible in Figure 1-6) and may involve either active or passive mechanisms.

In the *passive transport mechanism*, the large protein _____ may create a channel that allows the non-_____luble molecule to pass through in response to _____on. In another variation it appears that the non-_____soluble molecule attaches itself to a *carrier protein* _____pecialized molecule that permits it to diffuse across _____e membrane and releases it on the other side. In this _____ay, a substance can move from areas of high to low concentration on either side of a membrane as though it were lipid soluble without the expenditure of energy. The protein molecules illustrated in Figure 1-6 are examples of passive transport mechanisms.

An *active transport mechanism* is similar to a passive mechanism except that it can work against normal diffusion by concentrating a substance on one side of a membrane. This is an active process that requires an expenditure of energy and takes place only in living membranes. Mechanisms such as ion pumps, which maintain electrical potentials of nerve cells, are examples of active transport systems. The sodium–potassium transporter protein, illustrated in Figure 4-2 of Chapter 4, is one example of an active transport system. The blood–brain barrier has a number of such systems, many of which actively remove undesirable substances, like toxic waste products, from the brain and some of which selectively concentrate substances, like glucose (blood sugar) and some amino acids, in the brain.

Protein Binding

The blood contains a number of large protein molecules that cannot diffuse out of the pores in the capillaries because of their size. Some drugs attach, or bind, themselves to these protein molecules so strongly that they remain attached until metabolized. Consequently, they never get to their site of action. Other times, protein-bound drug molecules may act like depot injections, becoming slowly released as the blood concentration of the drug declines so that they reach their sites of action and are eventually metabolized and excreted.

The Placental Barrier

The blood of the fetus and the blood of the mother are not continuous. Nutrients are transferred to (and waste products are transferred from) the blood of the unborn child through a membrane similar to the blood–brain barrier. This transfer takes place in the *placenta*, the intermediary organ between the fetus and the wall of the uterus. Most behaviorally active drugs can be transferred from the mother's blood through the placenta to the fetus. Highly lipid-soluble substances cross more easily than drugs with low lipid solubility. Drug concentration in the blood of the fetus usually reaches 75% to 100% of that of the mother within 5 minutes of administration. Thus, the fetus appears to have very little protection from any drug the mother takes.

ELIMINATION

Metabolism and Excretion

There are some substances—for example, heavy metals such as lead and mercury—that the body is not very good at getting rid of. Levels of these substances can build up over time and accumulate to high and toxic concentrations. However, the body has fairly efficient systems to rid itself of most unwanted substances, including drugs, which would continue to exert their effects if not metabolized and excreted. It has already been described how gases and volatile solvent vapors can be eliminated in exhaled breath. Small amounts of many drugs are eliminated in sweat, saliva, and feces, but the major job of elimination is done by the liver and the kidneys, the *dynamic duo* of excretion (the location of these organs can be seen in Figure 1-8).

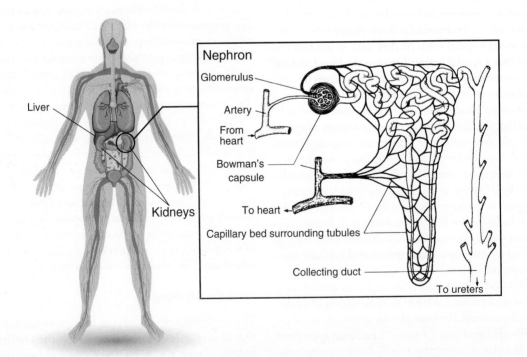

FIGURE 1-8 The location of the liver and kidneys within the body. The close-up is of a nephron, showing the capillaries of the glomerulus that filter fluid out of the blood into the nephron, and the capillary bed that reabsorbs water, nutrients, and lipid-soluble drugs into the blood. All material that is not reabsorbed is excreted in the urine.

The Liver

The *liver* is a large organ located high in the abdomen, under the diaphragm. Its function may best be compared to that of a chemical factory where molecules are modified to form new substances useful to the body, and where toxic molecules are changed into less harmful substances to be filtered out of the blood by the kidneys. These molecular changes are achieved by molecules called *enzymes*. An enzyme is a catalyst, a substance that controls a certain chemical reaction. The enzyme takes part in the reaction, but when the reaction is finished, the enzyme is released unchanged and is free to participate in another reaction in the same way. Without the presence of the enzyme, the reaction would proceed very slowly or would not take place at all. The body controls chemical reactions by controlling the amount of enzyme available to act as a catalyst. Not all enzymes that metabolize drugs are located in the liver. Some may be found in the blood and brain, or as we will see soon, in the digestive system.

An example of an enzyme is *alcohol dehydrogenase*. Someone with a background in chemistry can usually tell from its name what an enzyme does. Most enzymes end in the suffix *-ase*. The enzyme alcohol dehydrogenase removes hydrogen from a molecule of alcohol and makes it into acetaldehyde.

The process of restructuring molecules is referred to as *metabolism*, and the products of metabolism are called *metabolites*. In general, metabolites are either more useful to the body or less toxic than the original substance. Where drugs are concerned, the metabolic process is sometimes called *detoxification*. Although this term is appropriate some of the time, metabolites are not always less active or less toxic than the original drug. Chloral hydrate, psilocybin, and THC, are good examples of substances whose metabolites can be more active than the original drugs from which they are formed. Drugs with active metabolites typically show a prolonged action in the body, but these metabolites are eventually changed into inactive water-soluble substances and excreted from the body by the kidneys.

Another general rule is that metabolites are usually more likely to ionize. This tendency is very important for the functioning of the kidneys because ionized molecules cannot be reabsorbed into the blood through the nephron wall and, consequently, can be excreted more easily. In this way, the liver and kidneys work together to rid the body of unwanted substances (see the next section).

First-Pass Metabolism

Not all metabolism of drugs takes place after absorption and distribution have occurred. Drugs that are absorbed from the digestive system are absorbed into blood that goes to the liver before it returns to the heart. This means that any drug absorbed from the digestive system will pass through the liver before going anywhere else in the body and will be subjected to a certain amount of metabolism by liver enzymes. This is known as *first-pass metabolism*, and it may be responsible for a significant amount of the metabolism of some drugs. Drugs administered by other routes of administration, including drugs absorbed from the nasal cavities and the membranes of the mouth and rectum, are not subjected to first-pass metabolism by the liver and may reach higher levels in the body. For a drug such as alcohol, some metabolism takes place in the stomach and intestines even before it is absorbed. This is also referred to as first-pass metabolism.

The Kidneys

The *kidneys* are two organs, each about the size of a fist, located on either side of the spine. Their primary function is to maintain the correct balance between water and salt in body fluids. Along with the excretion of excess water in the form of urine, the kidneys can also excrete molecules of unwanted substances, the by-products of metabolism by liver enzymes. They function as a complex filtering system that physically removes certain substances from the blood. The close-up portion of Figure 1-8 shows the nephron, the functional unit of the kidney. Each kidney has millions of nephrons, all of which work in more or less the same way.

The *nephron* is essentially a long tube. At one end of the tube is a cuplike structure called *Bowman's capsule*, and inside Bowman's capsule is a clump of capillaries called the *glomerulus*. The other end of the nephron empties into collecting tubes, which, in turn, empty into the urinary bladder. The capillaries in the glomerulus have pores in their membranes, and most of the fluid in the blood that flows through these capillaries passes into Bowman's capsule and down the nephron. The remaining blood, which contains red and white cells and large protein molecules that are too large to pass out of the pores, continues out of the glomerulus and then moves through another bed of capillaries that surround the nephron along most of its length. At this point, most of the fluid and other substances are absorbed through the nephron wall back into the blood. Whatever is not reabsorbed passes through the length of the nephron and is excreted from the body in the urine.

The kidney works not by filtering impurities out of the blood but by filtering everything out of the blood and then selectively reabsorbing what is required. Reabsorption in the nephron is accomplished by the mechanisms just described: diffusion, lipid solubility, and active and passive transport. All lipid-soluble substances diffuse through the nephron wall into the blood, unless a selective transport mechanism is working against this diffusion. Desirable substances that are not lipid soluble, such as glucose, have a transport mechanism that successfully reclaims them into the blood. Unless they are reabsorbed by special transport systems, ionized or non-lipid-soluble substances will be excreted.

As with the digestive system, pH influences the degree of ionization and, as a consequence, can influence reabsorption. Urine tends to be acidic (pH = 6.0), and blood is basic (pH = 7.5), so, much like in the digestive system, acids tend to pass through and to concentrate on the blood side of the nephron wall, and bases tend to be retained in the urine and are excreted more easily.

Rate of Elimination

In most cases there are more than enough enzymes in the liver to handle a drug so that when the drug arrives in the liver in high concentrations, a lot of the drug will be metabolized at once. At low concentrations, the rate of metabolism will be lower. Thus, as drug levels fall, the rate of metabolism slows. The curve that plots the level of a drug in the blood over time is, therefore, not a straight line but tends to level off to an asymptote. Because of this trailing off, the rate of excretion for most drugs can be described in terms of a *half-life*. This is the time taken for the body to eliminate half of a given blood

level of a drug. In the example given in the top (A) panel of Figure 1-9, half of the original blood level is eliminated in 30 minutes. Thirty minutes later, the level has fallen to 25% of the original level, and 30 minutes after that, it is down to 12.5%. Every 30 minutes, the body gets rid of half of the drug circulating in the blood, so the half-life of the drug is 30 minutes. When the elimination of a drug changes with concentration in this manner, it is said to have *first order kinetics*.

The excretion of most drugs can be described in terms of half-life, but there is one important exception: alcohol. The excretion curve for alcohol is a straight line, as shown in the bottom (B) panel of Figure 1-9. It is not appropriate therefore to describe the excretion of alcohol in terms of half-life; an absolute rate of excretion is usually given, that is, about 15 mg of alcohol/100 ml blood/hour. When the rate of elimination of a drug is a straight line, it is said to have *zero order kinetics*.

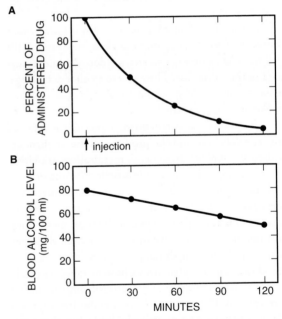

FIGURE 1-9 The top panel (A) shows a typical elimination curve for a drug like nicotine, which has a half-life of about 30 minutes. This is an example of first-order kinetics. The bottom panel (B) shows the elimination function for alcohol, which is metabolized at a constant rate (about 15 mg of alcohol/100 ml of blood/hour). Because the elimination function for alcohol is a straight line, the concept of half-life does not apply. This is an example of zero-order kinetics.

FACTORS THAT ALTER DRUG METABOLISM

A number of factors can influence the rate of metabolism of drugs in the liver and, consequently, the intensity and duration of a drug's effect. A great many individual differences in response to drugs can be explained in terms of variations in drug metabolism and enzyme systems that change according to such factors as age, gender, species, past experience with drugs, and genetics.

Stimulation of Enzyme Systems

To illustrate how enzymes work, we will use the metabolism of alcohol as an example. The steps in alcohol metabolism are shown in Figure 1-10. In the first two steps, alcohol is converted to *acetaldehyde* by the enzyme mentioned earlier: *alcohol dehydrogenase*. Then the acetaldehyde is converted to *acetyl coenzyme A* by another enzyme called *aldehyde dehydrogenase*.

Levels of a given enzyme can be increased by previous exposure to a specific drug that uses that enzyme or some other enzyme system. This process, known as *enzyme induction*, is responsible for the development of metabolic tolerance (discussed in Chapter 3). A good example of such a process is an increase in levels of alcohol dehydrogenase in the livers of heavy drinkers. Those who drink a great deal are able to metabolize alcohol slightly faster than nondrinkers, and this is one reason why they are more resistant to its effects. Box 1-1 gives another example of enzyme induction caused by the herbal antidepressant St. John's wort.

Depression of Enzyme Systems

When two drugs that use the same enzyme are introduced into the body at the same time, the metabolism of each will be depressed because both will be competing for the enzyme. In other cases, the activity of an enzyme can be blocked by another drug.

Again, we turn to the metabolism of alcohol as an example. Acetaldehyde is converted into acetyl coenzyme A by *aldehyde dehydrogenase*. *Disulfiram (Antabuse)* is a drug that blocks aldehyde dehydrogenase. Acetaldehyde levels then increase in the body because the enzyme is not readily available to metabolize it (refer back to Figure 1-10). Acetaldehyde is toxic and causes sickness and discomfort, so people who take disulfiram and then drink alcohol will get sick because of the buildup of high acetaldehyde levels. Disulfiram is sometimes used to discourage alcoholics from drinking; alcoholics will feel well and stay that way if they refrain from ingesting alcohol, but as soon as they take a drink, they will feel ill.

Even foods can alter drug metabolism. It was shown in the late 1990s that there are substances in grapefruit juice that can block *cytochrome P4503A4*, an enzyme located in the intestine. This important enzyme is responsible for the significant first-pass metabolism of many drugs. It has been shown that drinking grapefruit juice can significantly increase blood levels of many drugs. As a result, people should avoid drinking grapefruit juice if they are taking any of a number of drugs. These include the antianxiety drug *buspirone (Buspar)*, the cholesterol-lowering drugs *lovastatin (Mevacor)* and *simvastatin (Zocor)*, and the erectile dysfunction drug *sildenafil (Viagra)*.

Age

Enzyme systems are not fully functional at birth and may take time to develop completely. For this reason, immature members of a species may metabolize drugs differently from adults or may not metabolize them at all. For example, the liver of a newborn human first converts theophylline to caffeine and then metabolizes

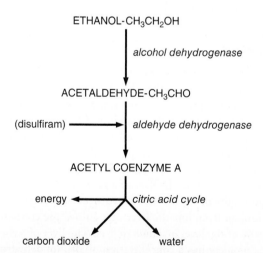

ETHANOL-CH$_3$CH$_2$OH

   alcohol dehydrogenase

ACETALDEHYDE-CH$_3$CHO

(disulfiram) ⟶ *aldehyde dehydrogenase*

ACETYL COENZYME A

energy ◀ *citric acid cycle*

carbon dioxide   water

FIGURE 1-10 Steps in the metabolism of alcohol. The enzyme that controls each step is shown to the right of each arrow. Note that disulfiram (Antabuse) blocks the enzyme aldehyde dehygenase. This stops the process at a point that causes a buildup of acetaldehyde.

BOX 1-1   Enzyme Induction Caused by St. John's Wort

St. John's wort is a plant that is widely used as an alternative medicine for treating depression (see Chapter 13). St. John's wort appears to be about as effective as standard antidepressant drugs. It is one of the top 10 natural products sold in the United States, used by about 12% of the population. Many believe that it has fewer unwanted sleep, sexual, and cognitive side effects compared to pharmaceutical antidepressant drugs, but it turns out that St. John's wort has some potentially serious side effects that may not be readily apparent. It can reduce the effectiveness of many other drugs because it induces production of the enzyme that destroys them.

St. John's wort has many potentially active ingredients, including *hyperfortin*, which is a potent activator of something called *PXR (pregnane X receptor)*. PXR is a protein that can be activated by a variety of chemicals and toxins, including hyperfortin. Its activation is the first step in an elaborate defense mechanism against being poisoned by an array of chemicals and toxins. PXR is a transcription factor that stimulates genes to produce a large number of enzymes responsible for the destruction of many drugs and toxins. One such enzyme stimulated by PXR is *cytochrome P4503A4*, which alone metabolizes about 60% of all clinically relevant drugs.

By taking St. John's wort in the recommended doses, you can stimulate the enzymes that destroy many important drugs that you may be taking concurrently. One such drug is the immunosuppressant *cyclosporine*, which is taken widely by organ transplant patients to prevent tissue rejection. Other drugs include *atorvastatin*, a cholesterol-lowering drug; *indinavir*, a drug used in the treatment of HIV; *amitriptyline*, an antidepressant; *theophylline*, a respiratory stimulant; and the tranquilizer *alprazolam*. St. John's wort can also increase the likelihood of unplanned pregnancy by reducing the effectiveness of oral contraceptives.

Thus, while it may appear that St. John's wort is an effective antidepressant with few side effects, the picture may not be that simple. This is an example of how use of a "natural" medicine can have significant unforeseen health consequences (Choudhri and Valerio (2005).

caffeine very slowly. In adults, theophylline is metabolized directly without this intermediate stage. Theophylline is similar to caffeine and is found in tea but is sometimes given to newborn babies to stimulate breathing. In infants, the effects of theophylline are greatly enhanced because of the intermediate stage of metabolism involving caffeine. For this reason, doses must be small and closely monitored to avoid overdose. A similar problem is encountered when drugs are given to a woman immediately before she gives birth. Drugs given at this time cross the placental barrier and circulate in the blood of the fetus. As long as the child's circulatory system is connected to the mother, the mother's liver can handle the drug, but if the baby is born and the umbilical cord is cut before all the drug is metabolized, the drug remains in the infant's body and is dependent solely on the baby's immature liver for metabolism, a process that may take many days.

There can also be impairments in metabolism at the other end of the life span. Liver functioning is less efficient in elderly people, so physicians prescribing for elderly patients often reduce drug doses accordingly.

Species

The vast majority of research in behavioral pharmacology uses species other than human beings. Studies are usually done on rats, mice, pigeons, or primates. It is important to understand how differences in drug metabolism can alter the intensity and duration of a similar dose in different species. As an example, the levels of alcohol dehydrogenase are quite different in different species. The liver of a rat or mouse contains about 60% of the alcohol dehydrogenase per gram in a human liver, but the liver of a guinea pig contains 160% of the level in a human liver. The liver of a rhesus monkey has a concentration of alcohol dehydrogenase similar to that of a human liver. As you can see, the same experiment, if performed on a guinea pig, a rat, or a human, might reach quite different conclusions.

COMBINING ABSORPTION AND EXCRETION FUNCTIONS

The effects of a drug change over time during a single administration. This change reflects increasing and decreasing drug levels after administration. When these varying effects are plotted on a graph, the result is usually called a *time course* (the drug effect is usually represented on the vertical axis, and time is on the horizontal axis). Figure 1-11 is a time course for the concentration of a drug in the blood after administration. Note that there are three curves. One shows the time course of absorption of a drug from the site of administration. This curve is hypothetical because it assumes that while the drug is being absorbed, the liver and kidneys are not working and no excretion is going on. The second curve is a hypothetical elimination curve; it shows the rate of elimination of a drug, but assumes instantaneous absorption. In reality, neither of these curves could exist. What is usually seen is a combination of the first two curves, shown here as a third curve that has both an ascending phase corresponding to the time when absorption is more rapid than elimination and a descending phase when elimination is more rapid than absorption.

The rate of excretion of any drug (i.e., its half-life) remains constant, but the absorption rate of any given drug can change, depending on the route of administration. Thus, the shape of this curve will vary depending on route of administration.

Figure 1-12 shows typical curves for various routes of administration. When drugs are given intravenously, the absorption phase is very steep; the drug achieves high levels and is metabolized and excreted quickly. When drugs are given orally, the absorption is slow, and blood levels do not reach the same high concentrations seen after i.v. administration, but the drug lasts much longer in the body. Intramuscular and subcutaneous routes are intermediate between i.v. and oral routes. The route of administration can determine whether a drug reaches high levels for a short period or lasts a long time at low levels. If the function of a drug depends on maintaining constant blood levels, as with antibiotics, oral administration is preferred. If it is necessary to achieve very high levels for brief periods, the drug is best given intravenously.

THE THERAPEUTIC WINDOW

When drugs are administered for therapeutic purposes, it is often important that the right level of the drug be maintained in the blood for an extended period of time. If the drug reaches too high a level, there will be an increase in unwanted side effects and no increase in the therapeutic effect. If the drug falls below a certain level, it will not have a therapeutic effect at all. This range, called the *therapeutic window*, is illustrated in Figure 1-13.

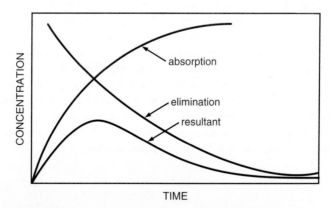

FIGURE 1-11 Shown is a theoretical absorption curve, assuming no elimination; a theoretical elimination curve, assuming instantaneous absorption and distribution; and a third line showing the resultant of these two theoretical processes. The resultant curve is typical of the time course for blood level of most drugs.

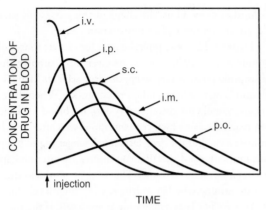

FIGURE 1-12 The time courses for blood levels of a drug typically seen after different routes of administration. After i.v administration, absorption is very rapid with a high peak and the drug leaves the body relatively quickly. When the drug is given orally, absorption is slow; the peak level is relatively low; and the drug stays in the body a longer time. The other routes have the same shape curve between these two. The faster the absorption, the higher the peak and the shorter the duration of action.

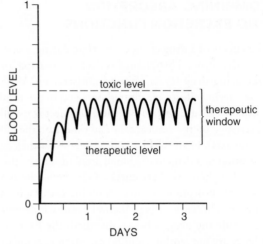

FIGURE 1-13 The therapeutic window is the range of blood concentrations of a medicine between a level that is ineffective (therapeutic level) and a level that has toxic side effects (toxic level). When drugs are taken chronically, it is important that the drug be given in the right dose and at the right frequency so that blood levels remain within the therapeutic window.

To keep its concentration within this range, a drug must be taken at the correct dose at regular intervals.

For drugs that are absorbed and excreted slowly, it is usually not difficult to achieve a dosing regimen that keeps the blood level within this window, but the task is more complicated for drugs that are absorbed and excreted rapidly. One such drug is *lithium carbonate*, which is given to people with bipolar disorder. Lithium has a rather narrow therapeutic window (the effective dose and a dose that causes side effects are very close). Lithium is also absorbed and excreted rapidly, so it must be given in small doses (as many as four times a day). To help solve this problem, pills have been developed in which the lithium is embedded in a material that dissolves slowly to delay the drug's absorption and,

hence, its peak blood level. Using this type of medication makes it easier to keep the blood level within the therapeutic window and reduce the number of doses to two a day.

With repeated use, individuals may build tolerance to some drugs (this will be discussed further in Chapter 3). Tolerance for some drug effects may build more quickly than tolerance for others. For example, tolerance to the analgesic effects of opioids like morphine builds rapidly, requiring a larger dose of the drug in order for it to be effective in relieving pain. Tolerance to the toxic effects of morphine builds more slowly, moving the curve for the effective dose closer to the curve for the toxic dose, increasing the risk of overdose and narrowing the therapeutic window.

2

Behavioral Analysis of Drug Effects

The term *behavioral pharmacology* was first used in the 1950s by Peter Dews of Harvard Medical School to refer to the investigation of drug effects using operant analysis of behavior (more on operant analysis later in this chapter). Before this time, the term *psychopharmacology* was common. This term was coined in the 1920s by David Macht of Johns Hopkins University and is still widely used outside of North America. It increasingly refers to research involving the study of drugs in the treatment of mental illness or psychological disorders. Nowadays, behavioral pharmacology more commonly refers to the study of the effects of drugs on behavior using any of the experimental techniques of modern behaviorally oriented psychology and, increasingly, behavioral neuroscience.

It is important to note that there may be several aims of research in behavioral pharmacology. As Travis Thompson and Charles Schuster (1964), the authors of the first text in the field, put it, "The behavioral pharmacologist is not only interested in observing behavioral changes produced by drugs, but analyzing the mechanisms of the drug's effect." We shall see many examples of this later in the text.

HISTORY OF BEHAVIORAL PHARMACOLOGY

It is clear that people have used mind-altering drugs for millennia, and scholars, including Aristotle and early Greek and Egyptian physicians, have shown a great interest in the effects of those drugs on behavior. Until the beginning of the twentieth century, investigations of these substances involved only verbal descriptions of the effects of the drug on the subjective experience, more often with literary rather than scientific intent. Such descriptions as De Quincey's *Confessions of an English Opium Eater* and Gautier's *Le Club des Hachichins* were fascinating illustrations of the drug experience, but were of limited value to science.

Scientific study of the effects of these substances first had to await the nineteenth-century development of modern chemical techniques that permitted the isolation of drugs from natural substances and the synthesis of substances that do not occur naturally. It also had to await the same sort of maturation of the study of behavior in the twentieth century. This development was inspired by the American scholar and philosopher John B. Watson who pointed out that, to be a science, psychology should study only behavior rather than thoughts and other subjective experiences that could not be observed. What psychology needed was a precise, systematic, and replicable means of describing, recording, and analyzing behavior. By the middle of the twentieth century, the technological, conceptual, and theoretical groundwork to study behavior of both humans and nonhumans had been developed by scientists such as Pavlov, Thorndike, and Skinner.

During the 1940s and 1950s, there was growing interest among pharmacologists with regard to how drugs that affected the central nervous system might alter behavior. Consequently, the behavioral research carried out by pharmacologists mostly involved unstructured observations of laboratory animals after they had been given a drug, and activity counts that estimated the degree of running, sleeping, convulsions, or other similar behaviors. If the drug increased locomotor activity (such as running), it was taken to indicate that the drug was a central nervous system *stimulant*; if activity decreased, the drug was a *depressant*. Similarly, psychologists had explored the effect of drugs on various behaviors in apparatuses such as the Skinner box, runways, and mazes.

Even though both psychologists and pharmacologists were doing behavioral research with drugs, up until the 1950s there was no separate discipline of behavioral pharmacology, per se. The impetus to develop such a field came in the early 1950s and arose largely from three events. The first was the tremendous therapeutic and commercial success of chlorpromazine and other antipsychotic drugs (see Chapter 12), and the resulting need to design tests for laboratory animals that were useful in screening drugs for potential therapeutic effects in humans. Second was the compelling demonstration by Peter Dews of the usefulness of Skinner's operant techniques to study drug effects. The third event was the application of physiology to the understanding of behavior, largely inspired by Joseph Brady, who you will learn more about later in this chapter.

Chlorpromazine and the Psychotherapeutic Revolution

Chlorpromazine was marketed in 1952 by the French pharmaceutical company Rhône-Poulenc as an antipsychotic drug. Until that time, there had been no effective treatment for psychoses, apart from institutionalization. After the development of chlorpromazine and other antipsychotic drugs, it became possible to close many psychiatric hospitals, and the development and marketing of antipsychotic drugs became immensely profitable. The success of chlorpromazine demonstrated the tremendous economic potential of behaviorally active drugs and sparked an intensive search by pharmaceutical and university laboratories for new drugs and new medical applications of older drugs.

The development of chlorpromazine hinged upon behavioral techniques that had been used to confirm its antipsychotic properties and that of other phenothiazine drugs as well. One such behavioral test, developed by David Macht, examined the effect of antipsychotic drugs on the ability of rats to avoid and escape electric shock by climbing up a pole (the *escape–avoidance test* is described later). There was a clear need for a better understanding of how drugs altered behavior; this could be accomplished only by a synthesis of pharmacology and the behavioral techniques developed by psychologists. Such a merger would not only be useful to pharmaceutical companies wanting to develop and test new compounds, but as a separate field of investigation that could lead to a better understanding of the interaction of drugs with behavioral processes.

Operant Analysis of Drug Effects

Peter Dews was trained as a physician, but was doing pharmacological and physiological research at Harvard Medical School when he became interested in the study of the effects of drugs on behavior. In his attempts at research, he was unsatisfied with the technology available to him for measuring the behavioral effects of drugs. But after an encounter with B. F. Skinner at Harvard University, he began studying the effects of drugs on pigeons' pecking for grain reinforcement in a Skinner box.

Dews soon demonstrated how useful operant methodology could be when he published a series of papers that are now considered to be the seminal works of the field that was to become behavioral pharmacology. Figure 2-1 is taken from a paper Dews published in 1955. It shows the effect of different doses of pentobarbital (a *sedative*) on the rate of key pecking of pigeons responding for food on two different schedules of reinforcement (schedules of reinforcement are described in more detail later in this chapter). The administration of pentobarbital produced varying results depending on the reinforcement schedule in effect. At doses of 1.0 to 2.0 mg/kg, the drug increased key pecking rates in pigeons responding on a fixed ratio 50 schedule, but decreased rates on a fixed interval 15-minute schedule.

Dews showed that the same dose of pentobarbital altered the behavior of the pigeon in a different manner depending on the schedule of reinforcement in effect at the time the drug was given. This showed convincingly that the drug's effects depend on the type of behavior that is occurring rather than simply depressing or

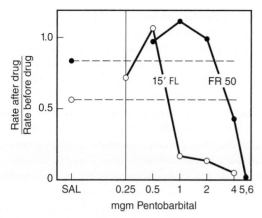

FIGURE 2-1 The log dose–effect curves for pentobarbital on the relative key pecking rate of pigeons responding on FI 15-minute (open circles) and FR 50 schedules (closed circles). The dotted lines indicate response levels after a control injection of saline. (From Dews, 1955.)

stimulating all behavior. This paper and several more like it were published in pharmacology journals. Operant techniques finally captured the attention of pharmacologists and became widely used for studying the effects of drugs on behavior.

Using Physiology to Understand Behavior

In the mid- and late-1950s, Joseph V. Brady established the first university-associated laboratory using behavioral technology to study drug–behavior interactions at Walter Reed Army Medical Center and later at the University of Maryland and Johns Hopkins School of Medicine. Like Dews, Brady, a pioneer in the field of *physiological psychology*, now commonly called *behavioral neuroscience*, was one of the first to use operant technology to study the effects of drugs. Unlike Skinner, he and his students believed that neuroscience could be useful in understanding the effects of drugs on behavior and that behavioral pharmacology research was a useful tool in understanding the nervous system. In addition to numerous publications, Brady stimulated the development of behavioral pharmacology by training many young researchers and urging the pharmaceutical industry and the federal government of the United States to support this new field. Among

others, Brady mentored Charles Schuster, a pioneer in the study of drugs as reinforcing stimuli (see Chapter 5), drugs as discriminative stimuli, and conditioned drug effects in addiction. Schuster also served as director of the National Institute on Drug Abuse (NIDA) in the United States from 1986 to 1992 (Schuster, 2004).

Founding of the Behavioral Pharmacology Society

In 1956, a conference was held on "The Techniques for the Study of the Behavioral Effects of Drugs," sponsored by the New York Academy of Sciences. It was chaired by Dews and Skinner and included Brady and many others from both pharmacology and psychology who were doing behavioral research with drugs. Also in 1956, Skinner made a formal call for the development of a new science of behavioral pharmacology. The new science got its formal start when the Behavioral Pharmacology Society was founded. In the mid-1950s, a group interested in pharmacology started having informal evening dinner meetings during the annual meeting of the Eastern Psychological Association. The Society evolved from this group in 1957.

Behavioral Pharmacology in Europe

Early interest in the behavioral analysis of drug effects was not confined to North America. In Britain, interest in the field was stimulated by a pioneering symposium held in London in 1963, sponsored by the Ciba Foundation. It was attended by many prominent European researchers of the time, as well as those from North America including Len Cook and Peter Dews. The proceedings were edited by Hannah Steinberg and published in 1964. Since that time, researchers including D. E. Blackman, David Sanger, Susan Iverson, Trevor Robbins, and Ian Stolerman and their students have had an extensive impact on the field. The continued expansion of behavioral pharmacology in Europe was marked by the founding of *The European Behavioral Pharmacology Society* in 1986.

RESEARCH DESIGN

All scientific experimentation can be thought of as a search for a relationship between events. In behavioral pharmacology, the researcher is usually trying to discover the relationship between the presence (or dose) of a drug in an organism and changes that occur in the behavior of that organism. In most true experiments, one of these events is created or manipulated by the experimenter, and the other event is measured. The manipulated event is called the *independent variable*, and the observed or measured event is called the *dependent variable*. The independent variable in behavioral pharmacology is usually the amount of drug put into the organism; that is what the researcher manipulates. The dependent variable is usually some change in the behavior of that organism, and this is what the researcher measures. Later in this chapter we will discuss some of the more commonly used measures of behavior, or dependent variables.

Experimental Research Design

EXPERIMENTAL CONTROL. It is not enough to give a drug and observe its effect. For an experiment to be meaningful, the experimenter must be able to compare what happened when the drug was given with what would have happened if the drug had not been given.

A controlled experiment is one in which it is possible to say with some degree of certainty what would have happened if the drug had not been given. This permits comparisons between drug and nondrug states. For example, a researcher could give each person in a group of participants a pill containing tetrahydrocannabinol (THC), an active ingredient in marijuana, and observe that everyone tended to laugh a great deal afterward. These observations would not be worth much unless the researcher could also demonstrate that the increased laughter was a result of the drug and not of the participants' expectations, their nervousness about being observed, or some factor other than the presence of the drug in their bodies. With most behavioral experiments, many factors could influence the results, so it is essential to be sure that the drug, and not something else in the procedure, caused the laughter.

The only truly reliable way to do this experiment and eliminate all other possible causes of the laughter would be to have a time machine so that, after the experiment, the researcher could go back and, under exactly the same circumstances, give the same participants pills identical in appearance but not containing any drug. Comparisons could then be made between the amount of laughter with and without the drug because all other factors (the participants, the situation, the time of day, and so on) would be the same. Only then could we be sure the laughter was caused by the drug and nothing else.

Unfortunately, time machines do not exist, so the behavioral pharmacologist must compare the behavior of a drugged participant with either (a) the drug-free behavior of that participant under similar conditions (i.e., use a *within-subjects design*) or (b) the behavior of other drug-free participants under similar conditions (i.e., use a *between-subjects design*). There are advantages and disadvantages to either strategy. For example, within-subjects designs use the same participant as his or her own control thereby eliminating random variations and the influence of genetic differences between participants. They typically use fewer participants, but take longer to run. Between-subjects experiments are typically faster and involve more participants, but must use group averages, and the behavior of individuals is seldom noted.

PLACEBO CONTROLS. It should be obvious that to be completely useful, a control condition must be as similar as possible to the experimental condition, except for one variable: the presence or absence of the drug. In our example in which the effect of THC on laughing was determined, the control procedure could have been improved. As you recall, we had two conditions: in one, the experimental participant was administered a pill containing THC, and, in the other, the participant was not given anything at all. It is quite possible that being given a pill might have caused the participants to become nervous and that could cause nervous laughter.

For this reason, behavioral pharmacologists always use a control condition that involves the administration of something to both groups. In this case, both groups could have been given an identical-looking pill, but the pill given in the control condition would have contained an inactive substance such as sugar. If injections had been involved, the control group would have been given only the vehicle with no drug dissolved in it (see Chapter 1).

PLACEBO EFFECTS. Such careful controls are especially important with human participants because of the placebo effect. As we have seen, a placebo is a totally inert substance that causes no physiological change but is administered as though it were a drug. If people believe they are getting a drug that will have a specific effect, they will frequently show that effect even though the drug does not cause it.

In an interesting experiment by Fillmore and Vogel-Sprott (1992), three groups of participants were given a cup of coffee before being tested on a psychomotor performance task. One group was told that caffeine would speed their performance, one group was told that caffeine would slow their responding, and the third group was not told anything. In actuality, all groups were given a placebo; the coffee was decaffeinated. The groups' performances matched what the participants had expected: Those who were told to expect improvement did better than those who were told nothing, and those who were told to expect impairment did worse than those who were told nothing.

The placebo effect makes careful control an absolute necessity when evaluating the clinical effectiveness of newly developed medicines because patients will frequently show an effect they expect the drug to produce. For example, let us suppose that we are testing a new pain reliever. We go to a hospital and give the drug to a group of patients who are in postoperative pain and tell them that this new drug should relieve their distress. The next day, we find that 68% of the patients report that their pain was relieved. By itself, this is not a useful experiment because we do not know how many patients would have reported the same thing simply because they had been told the drug was a pain reliever. To do this experiment the proper way, it would be necessary to have two groups of patients. Both groups would be told they were getting a pain reliever, but only one group would get the new drug; the other would be given an identical pill containing only inactive filler. The next day, pain ratings would be taken from all the patients, and comparisons could be made.

The balanced placebo design was developed in the mid-1970s by George Marlatt and his colleagues at Washington State University in Seattle (Marlatt & Rohsenow, 1980). It remains the gold standard for research with humans in which the participants' expectations could influence the results in a manner similar to the Fillmore and Vogel-Sprott experiment described previously. In the balanced placebo design, there are four groups. Two are the same as those in a standard placebo design where participants in both groups expect to get a drug, but one gets a drug whereas the other gets a placebo. In the two additional groups, none of the participants expect to get the drug, but participants in one group do, whereas participants in the other group get a placebo.

This design provides a powerful means of separating the drug effect from the expectancy or placebo effect because there is a group that does not expect the drug, but gets it. Any change in this group must be due entirely to the drug. There is also a group that expects the drug but gets a placebo. Any change seen in this group must be due entirely to the expectation effect and not the drug. In Chapter 3, there is an extended discussion of the nature of the placebo effect.

THREE-GROUPS DESIGN. When a new drug is undergoing clinical trials for use in the treatment of a disease (phase 3 in the long process described later in this chapter by which new medicines are approved), the standard design is what is known as a *three-groups design*. One group is given the experimental drug to be tested, a second group is given a placebo, and a third group is given an established drug with known therapeutic effect. By having three groups, the researchers can answer a number of important questions. Comparisons between the experimental drug group and the placebo group show whether the drug caused any improvement; comparisons between the placebo group and the established drug group indicate whether the research measures were sensitive enough to detect an improvement; and comparisons between the experimental and established drug groups tell whether the new drug has any advantage over established treatment (Overall, 1987). There are some circumstances where the placebo group may be left out. If the drug is being used to treat a life-threatening or serious disease, it would not be ethical to give anyone a placebo. In this case, the new drug would be compared only with the established treatment.

EXPERIMENTER BIAS. Further precautions must be taken in experiments investigating drug effects. It has been known for some time that an experimenter can influence the outcome of research without knowing it. For example, if the researcher knows which patients have been given a placebo, the researcher might unconsciously change the manner in which the patients are interviewed or even make systematic mistakes in recording data. To eliminate experimenter bias, it is usually necessary to conduct the experiment so that neither the patients nor the researchers giving the drug and interviewing the patients know who has been given the drug and who has been given the placebo. This procedure is called a *double-blind procedure*, and it is essential because it eliminates the possibility of placebo effects and experimenter-bias effects. Experimenter bias can also be a factor in research on laboratory animals, especially in tests where the researcher must make judgments or score some aspect of the animal's behavior.

Nonexperimental Research

A good deal of what we know about drugs is a result of research that does not involve experiments. As explained earlier, experiments attempt to find relationships between two events: a manipulated event and a measured event. *Nonexperimental research* looks for a relationship between two measured events. A good example is the discovery of a relationship between smoking during pregnancy and infant mortality. It was shown some time ago that there was a higher rate of infant death among babies born to women who smoked during pregnancy than among babies born to nonsmoking mothers (see Chapter 8). In this research, nothing was manipulated; there was no independent variable. The two events, smoking and infant mortality, were measured and found to be correlated.

One major difficulty with this type of finding is that it can only show that two variables are correlated. It cannot tell us that one event caused the other. We know that children born to smoking mothers are more likely to die, but we cannot conclude that smoking causes the infants' deaths. The relationship might be due to some third factor that causes both events. For example, it may be that women smoke because they have a biochemical imbalance that causes their bodies to need the nicotine in cigarettes. This imbalance might also be responsible for the higher infant mortality rates. The only way we could be sure that the smoking caused the infant mortality would be to do a true experiment by randomly assigning pregnant women to either one of two groups: forcing the women in one group to smoke and preventing women in the other from smoking. If there were a difference in infant mortality between the two groups, we would be in a good position to argue that smoking caused the infant deaths. Of course, such an experiment is out of the question on ethical grounds and could never be done with humans. For this reason, we must be satisfied with correlation rather than causal data on many issues of drug effects in humans.

MEASURING UNCONDITIONED BEHAVIOR OF NONHUMANS

It is often interesting to know the effect of a drug on the unlearned behavior of laboratory animals, that is, the effect of a drug on coordination, movement, anxiety, or the effect of a painful stimulus. Described next are several standard tests that are often used to evaluate the effects of a drug on such behaviors.

Unconditioned Behavior

The simplest measure of behavior in nonhumans is how much of it there is. Such measures are usually referred to as *spontaneous motor activity* (SMA), which may be quantified in a number of ways. Usually, the animal is placed in an *open field* (a large open box), and its movements are measured either electronically or by drawing a grid on the floor of the open field and counting the number of times the animal crosses a line.

Much can also be learned simply by observing the behavior of animals after they have been given drugs. Some classes of drugs cause animals to exhibit *stereotyped behavior*—the continuous repetition of simple, purposeless acts such as rearing or head bobbing. Other drugs may cause sleep or convulsions.

It is also possible to measure other unconditioned behavior using very simple techniques. For example, muscle tone in rats can be measured using an *inclined plane test* where the animal is placed on a board that can be tilted to various degrees. The degree of tilt where the animal is unable to hold on to the surface and slides off is a measure of muscle tone.

A test used to measure anxiety is the *elevated plus maze*, which consists of narrow boards in the shape of a *plus* raised a foot or more off the ground. Two opposite arms of the plus have walls, and the other two do not. Normally, rats spend most of their time on the arms that have walls and only occasionally venture out on the unprotected arms. Drugs that are known to relieve anxiety cause rats to spend more time than they normally would on the unprotected arms.

There are several tests for *analgesia*, or the ability of a drug to block pain. The most common is the *paw lick latency test*. Rats are placed on a metal surface that is heated to about 50 degrees Celsius. This is about the temperature of a hot cup of coffee. When you first pick it up it feels warm, but the longer you hold it the hotter it becomes until you have to put it down. When rats are first placed on the hot surface, they do not react. But within a few seconds, they raise one of their hind paws to their mouth as though they were licking it. The length of time it takes for this to happen is called the *paw lick latency*. Analgesic drugs like morphine lengthen this latency, which is often used as a measure of a drug's analgesic effect. Even if the rat does not show this response, it is removed after a fixed number of seconds to prevent the heat from burning the skin.

MEASURING CONDITIONED BEHAVIOR OF NONHUMANS

Learned or *conditioned* behavior is frequently classified by whether it is a result of *classical* or *operant* conditioning.

Classical Conditioning

When a dog salivates at the sight and smell of food, the salivation is a reflexive behavior under the control of the stimulus of food. Such a reflex or response is considered to be unconditioned. Thus, the stimulus, that is, the food, is the *unconditioned stimulus* (UCS), and the salivation is the *unconditioned response* (UCR). Pavlov (1927) found that if the sight of food is paired with a neutral stimulus, such as a ringing bell, the bell alone eventually elicits the salivation in the absence of food. Thus, the bell becomes a *conditioned stimulus* (CS), and the salivation to the bell in the absence of food is the *conditioned response* (CR).

In Pavlov's laboratory in St. Petersburg, one of his students observed the effect of caffeine, cocaine, morphine, and alcohol on conditioned reflexes. These studies were some of the very first experiments in behavioral pharmacology, but such studies are rare in behavioral pharmacology today. It was another experiment from Pavlov's laboratory that had a far greater influence on the field. In that experiment, it was demonstrated that a stimulus that preceded the delivery of a drug could be a CS, which could elicit conditioned drug-like effects (CR; see page 47 in Chapter 3 for a description of this experiment). Pavlov did not pursue this line of research, but, later, other scientists did. Chapter 3 describes the many applications of classical (Pavlovian) conditioning for understanding the effects of drugs on the development of tolerance and addiction.

Operant Conditioning

A dog that learns to beg for food at the table is demonstrating operant conditioning. The begging is the operant, and it is maintained by the occasional delivery of food. If begging no longer results in the delivery of food, the begging stops.

The principles of operant conditioning are thought to apply to nearly all behavior of all animals. Operant behavior is usually studied in the laboratory using a *Skinner box*—a small cage attached to an apparatus that will deliver small quantities of food, water, or some other reinforcing stimulus. It also contains a *manipulandum*, something that the animal can manipulate or move (e.g., a bar, lever, or knob). Figure 2-2 shows a Skinner box for a rat. In this box, a food delivery system delivers one small pellet of rat food at a time. The manipulandum is a lever on the wall near the food dish.

To study operant conditioning, it is usual to first deprive the subject of food or water so that it can act as a reward for performing the desired operant (in this case, pressing the lever). Each lever press is detected electronically and causes food to be delivered. In this way, the rat is rewarded, or *reinforced*, each time it makes the desired response. When the rat has learned this response, it makes it frequently and reliably.

Reinforcement

Many different stimuli can act as a reinforcer depending on the state of the animal and its past experience. Skinner defined a reinforcer as any event that increases the frequency of a response that it is contingent upon. Notice that a reinforcer is defined in terms

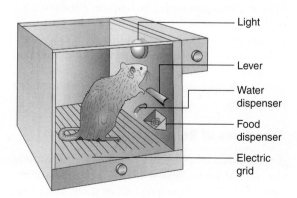

FIGURE 2-2 A typical Skinner box.

of its effect on behavior, not on whether it satisfies a particular need or motivation or causes pleasure. Reinforcers can be either positive or negative. *Positive reinforcers* will increase behavior when they are given or applied following the behavior's occurrence, like food tends to do. *Negative reinforcers* will increase behavior when they are removed or prevented following the behavior's occurrence, as is often seen with electric shock.

Reinforcers can also be primary or secondary. A *primary reinforcer* is a stimulus that acts as a reinforcer without prior experience (i.e., it is rewarding in and of itself). A *secondary reinforcer* is also known as a *conditioned reinforcer* because it acquires its reinforcing properties through classical conditioning when it is paired with a primary reinforcer. As we shall see later in this chapter and in Chapter 5, drug administration can act as a primary reinforcer, and the stimuli associated with its delivery can become secondary or conditioned reinforcers.

Punishment

Responding that is maintained by positive reinforcement may be suppressed if it is also followed by a stimulus such as an electric shock. The effect of punishment on behavior is usually measured by having the animal respond for a positive reinforcer delivered in a manner that produces a steady rate of responding (see schedules of reinforcement next). At various times during a session, a light is turned on and lasts for a minute or two. During this stimulus, each response is followed not only by the positive reinforcer but also by a shock. Responding during the presence of the light will be suppressed. The frequency and intensity of the shock can be manipulated to produce a specific amount of suppression. Some varieties of drugs, such as barbiturates, increase the frequency of behavior that has been suppressed by punishment. Other drugs, such as amphetamine, lack the ability to suppress responding.

Schedules of Reinforcement

To maintain a behavior, it is not necessary to reinforce the animal every time it responds appropriately. Animals will usually respond many times for one reinforcement, and in most operant research, this is the case. Reinforcement may be given after a specific number of responses or on the basis of time. The term *schedule of reinforcement* refers to the pattern that determines when reinforcements are to be given.

Each schedule of reinforcement engenders a characteristic pattern of responding that will be seen no matter what the species or type of reinforcer. These patterns are reliable and predictable, and they are sensitive to the effects of many drugs. Behavioral pharmacologists have found them a useful means of analyzing the behavioral effects of drugs because, as Peter Dews showed, specific schedules are more sensitive to some drugs than others, and similar drugs affect schedule-controlled behavior in a similar manner (refer back to Figure 2-1).

RATIO SCHEDULES OF REINFORCEMENT. When reinforcement is given based on the number of responses an animal makes, the schedule is known as a *ratio schedule*. On a *fixed ratio* (FR) schedule, the animal is required to make a fixed number of responses in order to be reinforced. For example, on an FR 30 schedule, every 30th response produces reinforcement. If only 29 responses are made, the reinforcer is not given. A *variable ratio* (VR) schedule is similar except that the number of required responses varies from reinforcer to reinforcer, so that at any given time the occurrence of a reinforced response cannot be predicted. A VR 30 schedule will produce reinforcement after every 30 responses, on average.

INTERVAL SCHEDULES OF REINFORCEMENT. On an *interval schedule*, an animal's responding is reinforced only if a period of time has elapsed since the previous reinforcer was applied. Responses that the animal makes during (but before completion of) the time interval are recorded, but do not influence the delivery of reinforcement. On a *fixed interval* (FI) schedule, a response is reinforced only after a fixed time has elapsed. A typical example might be an FI 3 schedule; the animal must wait 3 minutes after the delivery of reinforcement for a response to be reinforced again. On a *variable interval* (VI) schedule, the interval during which the animal is required to wait before a behavior is reinforced varies. When a value is specified for a VI, such as VI 2, this indicates that the interval is an average of 2 minutes long.

AVOIDANCE–ESCAPE TASK.   Not only will animals learn to press a lever to obtain a positive reinforcer like food, but they will also learn to avoid and escape aversive stimuli such as electric shocks. On a typical avoidance–escape schedule, the animal is presented with a stimulus, such as a buzzer or a light, as a warning that a shock is coming. The warning comes several seconds before the shock. If the animal makes a response during that time, the warning stimulus is turned off and the shock never comes; that is, this is the *avoidance* of shock. If the animal does not respond to the warning stimulus, the shock turns on, and the animal can then *escape* the shock by responding.

As mentioned earlier, the avoidance–escape task has proved to be a valuable tool in identifying drugs that treat psychotic behavior in humans. These drugs interfere with an animal's ability to avoid shock, but do not have any effect on the animal's ability to turn off or escape from the shock when it does come. This finding shows that the drug has not interfered with the motor ability of the animal to respond but has selectively blocked the motivation to avoid the shock.

The avoidance–escape procedure is used in a number of different apparatuses in addition to the Skinner box. It can be used in a *shuttle box*, which is a long narrow box with a grid floor that can be electrified. When the warning signal is sounded, the animal must run across the midline and to the other end of the box to avoid getting the shock. If it does not avoid the shock, it can escape the shock by crossing the midline to the safe end of the box. When the warning stimulus sounds again, the animal must run back to the other side of the box. The *pole climbing task* used by David Macht in the development of chlorpromazine was also an avoidance–escape task.

STIMULUS PROPERTIES OF DRUGS

Drugs as Discriminative Stimuli

A large and productive branch of contemporary behavioral pharmacology deals with drugs as discriminative stimuli. Investigations into the discriminative properties of drugs originated with research in the early neurophysiological theories of Donald Hebb at McGill University.

For years, there had been anecdotal accounts suggesting that events experienced in a drugged state might not have the ability to control behavior when the organism was not in a drugged state, and vice versa. This phenomenon is called *dissociation* or *state-dependent learning*.

While investigating dissociation, Donald Overton, then a graduate student in McGill University's Psychology Department, performed a series of shock escape–avoidance experiments using rats in a *T-maze* (literally, a maze shaped like a "T" in which animals are placed at the bottom of the T and choose to enter the left or right arm at the top of the T). Overton was easily able to demonstrate that rats that learned to avoid the shock in the maze when drugged with pentobarbital were unable to avoid the shock later when given a placebo, and vice versa.

To explore the extent of dissociation, Overton wanted to determine whether information learned on drug days (e.g., turn into the right arm of the T to avoid shock) would interfere with information acquired on saline days (e.g., turn into the left arm of the T to avoid shock), and vice versa. On alternate days, the rats were administered pentobarbital, and one arm of the T-maze led directly to safety. On other days, they were given a saline placebo, and the other arm was safe. Overton discovered that the rats very quickly learned to make the appropriate response depending on whether they were drugged or not. In other words, he showed that the drug administration was acting as a discriminative stimulus, which controlled the direction in which the rat would turn at the choice point of the maze on the first trial of each day. He also found that rats would learn to make the appropriate response at doses much lower than those required to cause complete dissociation.

Since Overton's early experiments, research on the discriminative stimulus properties of drugs has expanded rapidly, and the electrified T-maze has been replaced with the Skinner box. Herbert Barry III, then at Yale, is generally credited with applying operant techniques to the field. In this type of task, a hungry animal, usually a rat, is given a choice of two levers to press for food reinforcement. In some sessions, lever A will be reinforced, and, in other sessions, lever B will be reinforced. The reinforcement is on an FR 20 schedule so that without a cue to guide it, the rat will not know which lever will produce the food until it has made 20 responses on one lever. In this situation, the only cue is the presence of a drug—on days when lever A is reinforced, the rat is injected with a drug, but on days when lever B is reinforced, it is injected with saline. After a short period of training, the rat will learn to discriminate between the drug and saline so that, on drug days, it will start off responding on lever A, and on saline days, it will start off on lever B. Thus, the first 20 responses on any given day will show whether the rat thinks it has been injected with the drug or with saline.

Using these techniques, it has been demonstrated that most drugs that act on the central nervous system have discriminative stimulus properties, although some classes of drugs, such as the barbiturates, appear to be more easily discriminable than other classes. Such drugs can acquire discriminative control at least as rapidly, and in some cases more rapidly, than more conventional stimuli like noises and lights. It has also been shown that, as well as discriminating between a drug and saline, laboratory animals can discriminate between different doses of the same drug and between different drugs.

The drug discrimination paradigm has been successfully used to investigate many aspects of drug action. For example, you can use this technique to detect how soon the subjective effect of a drug begins after administration, and how long it lasts. Also, by administering drugs that block specific receptor sites (see Chapter 4), it is possible to determine which type of receptor site is targeted by the drug to produce its subjective effects.

A database of all drug state discrimination experiments is available online at www.drugrefs.org (Drug Self-Administration and Discrimination Database, 2011). This database is combined with a similar database for drug self-administration studies.

In addition to determining whether a drug can act as a discriminative stimulus, behavioral pharmacologists can test for generalization between drugs. Such a test is called a *substitution test*. First, an animal is trained to discriminate between saline and a drug. Then, the animal is given a substitute drug. The animal's response will indicate how the new substitute drug makes it feel. If the animal presses the same lever as it learned to do after the training drug, this indicates that the substitute drug made the animal feel the same as the training drug. Otherwise, the animal will press the saline lever. Thus, a rat might learn to press lever A after an administration of cocaine and then be tested with caffeine. If it presses

the cocaine lever, this indicates that its subjective state following caffeine administration was similar to that following cocaine. Animals will usually generalize responses across drugs of the same pharmacological class, thus making the substitution test a valuable tool in drug screening and drug development.

REINFORCING PROPERTIES OF DRUGS—ABUSE LIABILITY

As noted previously, Skinner defined a reinforcer as any stimulus that would increase the frequency of a behavior on which it was contingent. As an example, if food follows a lever press and the frequency of that lever press increases, then food is a reinforcer. As you will see in Chapter 5, it is well established that some drugs act as reinforcers. Laboratory animals and people will learn to make some response if it is reliably followed by the administration of these drugs. The reinforcing property of a drug is an indication of its potential for abuse, that is, its *abuse liability*.

It is useful to have a measure of the abuse potential of a drug and a means of determining factors that can alter abuse potential. Several techniques have been developed to measure abuse potential, and they do so by measuring the ability of a drug to act as a reinforcer (Sanchis-Segura & Spanagel, 2006). These techniques were first used with nonhumans and later applied to humans.

Rate of Responding

With traditional reinforcers, we know that the greater the reinforcement, the faster an animal will respond. For example, rats will respond faster for three food pellets than they will for one. We might expect that animals will respond faster for drugs that are more reinforcing, but rate of responding has some problems. One problem is that drugs have different durations of action, and a long-acting drug might well be self-administered at a slower rate than a short-acting drug, merely because the effect of each dose lasts longer. In addition, rate of responding depends on the animal's ability to make a response. Many drugs have effects that interfere with self-administration. For example, monkeys will give themselves infusions of anesthetic doses of pentobarbital that immediately cause them to go to sleep. Such a drug may be highly reinforcing, but it could not be self-administered at a high rate. Conversely, many drugs, such as cocaine, could stimulate their own self-administration.

Progressive Ratio Schedule of Reinforcement

In a progressive ratio (PR) schedule, the subject is required to work for a drug infusion on an FR schedule that consistently becomes more demanding. For example, the schedule may start at FR 5. After the first drug reinforcement is received, it might change to FR 10, then to FR 20, and so on. At some point, known as the *breaking point* or *break point*, the demand of the schedule will be too high, and the animal will stop responding. Compared to drugs that are not so reinforcing, highly reinforcing drugs will motivate the animal to work harder and will, consequently, produce a higher breaking point and greater potential for abuse. Nevertheless, there is evidence that measures of the reinforcing value of drugs, using the PR schedule, may also be affected by a drug's effect on the ability of an organism to respond (Rowlett, Massey, Kleven, & Woolverton, 1996). Box 10-2 in Chapter 10 provides an excellent example of the use of a PR schedule in rats to model the addictive behavior of humans.

Choice

The choice procedure is fairly simple. With laboratory animals, two levers are presented. In the first session, one lever will cause an infusion of drug A, and the other lever has no consequences. This is followed by a session in which the second lever will cause an infusion of drug B, and the first lever has no consequences. This procedure ensures that the animal has an equal exposure to both drugs A and B. Following this phase of the experiment, both levers will dispense their respective drugs, and the animal has the opportunity to respond on either lever. Presumably, the animal will respond more frequently on the lever that delivers the more reinforcing drug.

Conditioned Place Preference

The *conditioned place preference* (CPP) technique uses a long box that has two distinctive halves separated by a partition. One half of the box may have striped walls and a metal rod floor, whereas the other half may have solid white walls and a mesh floor. Rats are confined to one half of the box after being given an injection of a drug, and they experience the effect of the drug there. On an equal number of occasions, rats are injected with a placebo and confined to the other half of the box. Later, the partition is removed and rats are placed in the center of the box, free to wander between the chambers. The amount of time spent in each half of the box is recorded. Usually, rats will spend more time in the half of the box that has been associated with the reinforcing effects of the drug. The strength of their preference for that end of the box is a good indication of the reinforcing value of the drug (van der Kooy, 1987). A CPP is thought to develop because the location where the drug was experienced has become a conditioned stimulus that evokes the reinforcing effects of the drug. Therefore, the animal is reinforced for approaching that location and spending time there.

MEASURING BEHAVIOR OF HUMANS

Subjective Effects

It is often of interest to determine what effects a drug might have on how people feel; that is, does the drug make them feel happy, sad, or energized? In the early days of drug investigation, determining subjective effect was often done by giving the drug to someone and asking him or her to report his or her experiences, a process called *introspection*. In fact, it was not at all uncommon for investigators to take the drug themselves; because the drug experience is private, it can be observed only by the person who takes it. An essential requirement of scientific data is that they be observable to anyone; therefore verbal self-reports are not particularly helpful as a tool in behavioral pharmacology. This is not to say that unstructured verbal descriptions of drug-elicited internal states are not useful to a researcher. On the contrary, they guide and inspire more systematic study. But the accounts themselves are not adequate scientific data unless they are collected in a systematic or structured fashion.

Rating Scales

Introspection by itself is of no value to the scientist, but it is possible to collect subjective data in a systematic, quantitative manner that is useful. Psychologists have been doing this for many years by creating scales.

They might ask a person to rate how happy they are on a seven-point scale ranging from extremely sad to extremely happy. Sometimes a *visual analog scale* (VAS) is used where the participant makes a mark on a line between the two extreme alternatives to indicate how the variable applies to them. Many scales have been developed over the years and have been tested for their reliability (the stability of results at different time points) and validity (that the scales are measuring what they were designed to measure). Such rating scales have been adopted for use in drug research, and some have been specifically developed to study drug effects.

One scale that has been widely used in drug research is the *Profile of Mood States* (POMS), a paper-and-pencil test that asks participants to indicate on a five-point scale how each of 72 adjectives applies to them at a particular moment. These 72 items yield a score on eight independent subscales: anxiety, depression, anger, vigor, fatigue, confusion, friendliness, and elation. These scales give a reliable and quantifiable measure of a participant's internal state.

Another much more elaborate test is the *Addiction Research Center Inventory* (ARCI). It was developed so that each class of drugs creates a unique profile of mood and physical changes. This makes it possible to classify a new drug and assess its abuse potential by examining its profile and comparing it to the profiles of existing drugs.

Perhaps the simplest scale used to test drug effects is the *liking scale* where the participant indicates how much the drug is *liked*. Other scale items ask the participants to indicate how much they would *want* to use the drug again or whether the drug makes them feel *high* or *sedated*.

Drug State Discrimination

Although human drug state discrimination studies are not as common as those using laboratory animals, the procedure is similar. The big difference is that humans are often given instructions, which speeds up the process. Typically, the person is given a series of separate exposures to a drug and a placebo, either by pill or injection. In each trial, they are told they are getting either condition A or B. Then they are given a series of unidentified exposures to each condition and asked to identify whether it is condition A or B, oftentimes with the promise of a monetary reward for a correct identification. There does not seem to be any significant difference between humans and nonhumans in the ability to discriminate drugs, and the patterns of generalization between drugs are also similar.

Perception

A number of tests and techniques have been developed to measure the acuity of the senses, particularly sight and hearing. Sensitivity changes are reported as changes in thresholds. The term *absolute threshold* refers to the lowest value of a stimulus that can be detected by a sense organ. It is a measure of the absolute sensitivity of the sense organ. *Difference thresholds* are measures of the ability of a sense organ to detect a change in level or locus of stimulation. If a threshold increases, it means that the intensity of the stimulus must be increased in order for it to be detected. In other words, the sense has become less keen. A lowering in threshold means that a sense has become more sensitive.

An example of how threshold is measured is *critical frequency at fusion*. If the speed with which a light flickers is increased, eventually a speed will be reached where the light appears to be steady. This is the critical frequency at fusion, and it is sensitive to many drugs. The ability to detect flicker is a reliable measure of how well the visual system is functioning. To measure the functioning of hearing, an auditory flicker fusion test has also been developed.

Motor Performance

Motor performance is a major concern in assessing the effects of drugs on humans. One of the simplest measures of performance is *simple reaction time* (RT) test where the participant must make a response, like pressing a button as fast as possible, after a noise or a light is turned on. In a *complex reaction time* (CRT) test, there are several possible responses and several different signals associated with each one.

Hand–eye coordination is often measured by a device called a *pursuit rotor*. With this device, the participant is instructed to hold the end of a stylus on a spot contained on a rotating disk. The total time the participant is able to hold the stylus on the moving spot is a measure of hand–eye coordination.

Other commonly used tests of motor ability are finger tapping rate and hand steadiness.

Attention and Vigilance

Attention and vigilance can be affected by many drugs. One widely used test of attention and vigilance is the *Mackworth clock test*. It was developed during the World War II to test the performance of radar operators. In this test, the participant looks at a large circular dial like a radar screen. A clock hand moves around this dial in a step-by-step fashion at regular intervals. Occasionally, the hand will move two steps at once rather than one step. The participant must detect when this happens and push a button. The test may continue for several hours. This test was originally presented on a real panel, but is now administered on a computer, as are most of these tests.

Memory

There are several types of memory that can be affected differently by different drugs. One distinction that is often made is between *short-term memory* (also called *working memory*) and *long-term memory*.

Short term memory can hold a limited amount of information while it is being used for some purpose. We can remember a telephone number for a brief time between looking it up and dialing it. Information can be displaced from this short-term storage easily and is quickly lost unless actively rehearsed. Long-term memory is more or less permanent and can last for years. Memories are transferred from short term to long term by a consolidation process. We are sometimes not able to recall long-term memories without the aid of cues and prompts. Drugs are able to alter both the consolidation and the recall of long-term memories.

One test of short-term memory is the *N-back test*. This test is often used in conjunction with brain imaging. In this test, a series of letters or pictures is shown one at a time on a screen. When a target stimulus, such as an "X", appears on the screen, the participant must recall the stimulus that was shown previously (1-back); two stimuli back (2-back); or three, four, or more stimuli back. In a variation of the procedure, the participant must indicate when the stimulus on the screen is identical to the one that was one, two, three, or more back.

Long-term memory is further classified into two types: *implicit* and *explicit*. Implicit memory is sometimes called *procedural memory*; it is the memory of how to do things. Often, implicit memory is used without conscious awareness. Explicit memory, sometimes called *declarative memory*, is the ability to recall pieces of information—names, facts, dates, etc. There is a special type of explicit memory called *episodic memory* where we remember events that have happened to us. Thus, remembering how to ride a bicycle, even without much conscious effort, is implicit memory, but remembering that it is called a bicycle and recalling the experience of first learning to ride it is explicit memory. Explicit and implicit forms of memory seem to use different brain mechanisms because in some cases of amnesia, explicit memory can be lost, but implicit memory is unaffected. It is also possible for people to lose episodic memory, but not other types of declarative memory. This happens with Alzheimer's disease.

There are many tests of long-term memory, but in the traditional method, the participant is asked to remember a list of words or objects and then, after a period of time, to recall them. The participant may be asked to reproduce the items in the list (*free recall*) or may be shown an array of items and asked to identify the ones that were on the list (*cued recall*). Cued recall is much less demanding than free recall, which is why students typically prefer a multiple-choice exam over an essay exam! Sometimes, drugs can interfere with free recall of memories but have little effect on cued recall, indicating that the memories are there but the drug made them more difficult to retrieve.

Tests of Response Inhibition

It is sometimes noted that drugs can interfere with one's ability to withhold or inhibit actions; this is sometimes called *disinhibition*. Two tests of inhibition or impulse control are the go–no go task and the go–stop task. Both tests are very much like the simple reaction time test described earlier. In the go–no go task, the participant must respond as quickly as possible to one stimulus, but must not respond to a different stimulus. The percent of no go trials may vary in any session and may be very infrequent. The participant must withhold responding until the nature of the signal, go or stop, is determined. Drugs that interfere with inhibitory control are likely to cause an increase in responding to the no go signal.

The go–stop task is more difficult. There is a go signal, and the participant is instructed to respond to it as quickly as possible, but on some trials, the go signal is rapidly followed by a stop signal. The participant is instructed to withhold the response if there is a stop signal. The time between the go signal and the stop signal may vary. If the delay is very short, the response to the go signal is easily inhibited, but as the interval is lengthened, it becomes more and more difficult to stop the response. For each participant, the delay at which he or she is able to inhibit the response 50% of the time is determined. Some drugs, like alcohol, lengthen this delay.

Driving

Because driving is such a necessary and common activity, it is important to know the effect many drugs have on the ability of a person to operate an automobile. Determining the effect of a drug on driving ability, however, is not as easy as it might seem. To begin with, driving is a complex activity requiring many skills of perception, motor control, and judgment. There is much more involved than simply moving a car from one place to another. Researchers have tried to assess driving skill using many different strategies. Some simply have participants drive a car through city traffic and have professional driving instructors rate participants' performance on a number of factors. One difficulty with this approach is that the demands of the task will be different for each person tested because traffic conditions are constantly changing. However, the bigger problem is that it is unethical to permit participants to drive in real traffic and endanger their lives and the lives of others if there is any possibility that their skills might be impaired by drugs.

To get around these issues, researchers sometimes have participants operate a vehicle around a closed course where various demands are made on the skill of the driver. This approach is more artificial but safer, and because the task is the same for each participant, comparisons are more easily made between and within participants.

One difficulty with using a real car is that it is sometimes difficult to accurately measure a participant's performance. You can tell if the participant knocks over a pylon, but you will not be able to determine whether the error resulted because the object was not seen, the participant could not estimate the speed of the car, the participant was unfamiliar with the car, or the reaction time was too slow. To answer such questions, many researchers use computerized driving simulators that are capable of measuring a participant's response time, steering ability, and capacity to react to specific crises. With some simulators, it is even possible to measure the participant's eye movements while driving. As you will see in Chapter 6, some laboratories use brain imaging technology to assess participants' processing while in a driving simulator.

DEVELOPMENT AND TESTING OF PSYCHOTHERAPEUTIC DRUGS

From time to time in the news we hear that some laboratory or hospital has made a breakthrough discovery of a new drug that promises to be a great improvement on current treatments for a particular disease. Often these stories end with the warning that it may be years before the new drug will be approved for use. The reason for this delay is that all drugs must undergo rigorous development and testing to demonstrate that they are effective and safe. Only then will they be approved by governmental agencies for sale as a medicine. In the United States, approval is granted by the federal Food and Drug Administration (FDA). Other countries have similar agencies.

Initial Screening and Therapeutic Testing

Scientists do not understand the biochemical basis of mental illness well enough to specifically design drugs with any certainty that they will have a desired effect on psychiatric symptoms and will produce a minimum of side effects. Instead, the laboratories of pharmaceutical companies synthesize many new chemicals they think might be effective. These drugs are then screened using nonhumans to determine whether they have effects similar to those of known therapeutically useful drugs and whether they are safe.

Screening tests, using laboratory animals, can help determine whether a drug might have therapeutic properties. Screening tests can also determine the safety of various drugs by determining the ED_{50} of the drug's behavioral effect and comparing it to the LD_{50} of that drug. When a new drug appears to be reasonably safe and shows interesting behavioral properties in nonhumans, it goes to phase 1 of human testing, which assesses the toxicity and side effects of the drug on healthy human volunteers. These studies are usually carried out using paid volunteers in an inpatient setting.

In phase 2, the drug is tested on patients under very carefully supervised conditions. In addition to recording adverse effects, changes in the medical condition are noted. If phases 1 and 2 show that the drug has minimal toxic effects and also has a potential therapeutic effect, it then goes to phase 3, expanded clinical trials. These are usually carried out in university-teaching hospitals and other institutions and often use the three-groups design discussed earlier.

If phase 3 investigations are successful, the drug is licensed and marketed. The research, however, does not stop here. Phase 4 involves the accumulation of data on the success of the drug as used in the clinic. Attempts are made to identify adverse effects that were not apparent in the short-term testing during the early stages. In phase 4, improved dosing schedules may be developed, and individuals who are at risk of having adverse reactions to the drug can be identified.

Off-Label Use

When drugs are approved for use by a government agency, it usually specifies the medical condition it was designed to treat and on which it was tested, but the drug may be used by physicians to treat other disorders. This is called *off-label* use. It sometimes happens that the drug works surprisingly well for its off-label prescriptions. An example of this is the drug bupropion. It was developed originally as an antidepressant and given the trade name Wellbutrin. Later, it was coincidently discovered that it reduced smoking in people who took it. Clinical trials were done, and it was found to be an effective aid to smoking cessation. Now, in addition to being marketed as an antidepressant, it is sold as Zyban, a smoking cessation aid.

3

How We Adapt to Drugs— Tolerance, Sensitization, and Expectation

TOLERANCE

In the year 63 BCE, Mithridates VI, king of Pontus, tried to commit suicide by poisoning himself. Mithridates was a great leader and great warrior; he had defeated the Roman legions and spread his influence over Asia Minor. But in 63 BCE, he had been defeated by the Roman general Pompey, and his son had just led a successful revolt against him. To end it all, the king took a large dose of poison, but it had no effect on him. He was finally forced to have one of his Gallic mercenaries dispatch him.

What was the source of the king's resistance to poison? King Mithridates was also a good pharmacologist. Throughout his life, he lived in great fear of being poisoned, so, to protect himself, he repeatedly took increasing doses of poison until he could tolerate large amounts without ill effects. This effect has been called *mithridatism* (Lankester, 1889) after the king; today, we know it as *tolerance*. Mithridatism was also practiced by other historical figures, including Vespasia, the mother of the Roman emperor Nero, and the infamous Lucretia Borgia.

Drug tolerance is defined either as the decreased effectiveness (or potency) of a drug that results from repeated administrations, or as the necessity of increasing

the dose of a drug in order to maintain its effectiveness after repeated administrations. The term *tolerance* is frequently used in a way that suggests that all of the effects of a drug diminish at the same rate, but this is usually not the case. Some effects of a drug may develop tolerance very quickly, some others may show tolerance slowly, and some effects may never show tolerance, no matter how often the drug is given. Among the effects of morphine, for example, are nausea and vomiting. These effects show rapid tolerance, but the ability of morphine to constrict the pupils of the eyes shows no tolerance at all, no matter how long the drug has been taken. Because tolerance to different effects of a drug develops at different rates, it is apparent that many mechanisms must be responsible for tolerance (Young & Goudie, 1995). For this reason, it is more appropriate to think of tolerance developing to the effect of a drug rather than to the drug itself (Stewart & Badiani, 1993).

The term *tachyphylaxis* is sometimes used as a synonym for tolerance, particularly in medical literature. It is derived from the Latin *tachy* meaning *accelerated* and *phylaxis* meaning *protection*, and is sometimes used to designate a rapidly developing tolerance, that is, what is called "acute tolerance" in the next section. In other cases,

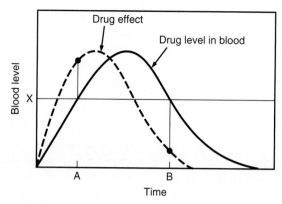

FIGURE 3-1 This shows the time course for the level of drug in the blood (solid line) and an effect of the drug (dashed line). Point A indicates a particular blood level on the ascending limb of the curve, and point B indicates exactly the same blood level on the descending limb of the curve. You can see that the drug effect at time A is greater than it is at time B even though there is the same drug blood level. When this happens, it indicates acute tolerance.

the term is used to refer specifically to a diminished effect of a drug that results from a loss of sensitivity or some adaptation at the drug's site of action, as opposed to other mechanisms of tolerance (Katz, 2011). Because of confusion surrounding the use of the term, tachyphylaxis will be avoided in this text.

Acute Tolerance

It is usually assumed that a drug must be given repeatedly before tolerance can occur, but it is also possible for tolerance to develop during a single administration of a drug. As we have seen in Chapter 1, after a drug is taken into the body, the level of the drug in the blood rises during the absorption phase and then falls during the elimination phase. With some drugs and depending on the effect being measured, the drug effect can be greater at a specific blood level during absorption than it is at that same blood level during elimination, showing that tolerance has developed during a single administration. This is called *acute tolerance*. A good example of acute tolerance is given in Chapter 6.

Figure 3-1 illustrates acute tolerance. The solid line shows the time course of the blood level of a drug after administration. The dotted line shows the time course for

an effect of the drug if acute tolerance is developing. The effect will peak before the blood level peaks, and the effect will be gone before all of the drug is eliminated from the body. Thus, if you measure the effect of the drug at time A as the blood level is rising and again at time B when the blood level is exactly the same but falling, you will see that the effect at time B is much less. A good example of acute tolerance is the subjective effect of alcohol; as blood alcohol level rises, you feel increasingly intoxicated, but the subjective effect peaks before blood level and the subjective effect disappears before the alcohol does. This makes it very difficult for a person to estimate his or her own blood alcohol level or the effects alcohol may be having on him or her (Cromer, Cromer, Maruff, & Snyder, 2010).

When tolerance develops, it does not last indefinitely. Tolerance may disappear with time after the use of a drug has been discontinued. During the development of tolerance, the disappearance of different drug effects may take place at different rates and may depend on the circumstances or environmental setting in which the drug is administered.

Tolerance to one drug may well diminish the effect of another drug. This phenomenon, called *cross-tolerance*, is usually seen between members of the same class of drugs. For example, all opioid drugs, which include morphine, heroin, and oxycodone (see Chapter 11), will show cross-tolerance. Cross-tolerance is sometimes taken as evidence that the drugs may be producing their effect by common mechanisms.

MECHANISMS OF TOLERANCE

Pharmacokinetic Tolerance

Pharmacokinetic tolerance (also called *metabolic tolerance* or *dispositional tolerance*) arises from an increase in the rate or ability of the body to metabolize a drug, resulting in fewer drug molecules reaching their sites of action. For the most part, this is a result of enzyme induction, an increase in the level of the enzyme the body uses to destroy the drug (see Chapter 1). When a drug is given repeatedly, it may induce or increase the action of the enzyme the body uses to destroy it. With increases in the rate of metabolism, a given amount of a drug will not reach the same peak levels at its site of action and will not last as long, so that more and more of the drug will be needed to produce the same effect. When pharmacokinetic tolerance takes place, all effects of the drug will be diminished because of the diminished concentration of the drug at the site of action. This will also create cross-tolerance with drugs that may be metabolized by the same enzyme.

Pharmacodynamic Tolerance

Pharmacodynamic tolerance is also known as *physiological* or *cellular tolerance*. These terms generally describe a type of tolerance that arises from adjustments made by the body to compensate for an effect of the continued presence of a drug. It is generally believed that such adjustments are a result of a process called *homeostasis*. Many of the body's physiological processes are controlled by feedback loops, in much the same way a thermostat controls the temperature in a room. The thermostat is set to a specific temperature, called a *set point*. It detects the temperature, and when the temperature falls below the set point, it turns the heat on. When the room temperature rises to the set point, it turns the heat off again, thus maintaining an even temperature at the set point. Homeostasis provides a flexible system for maintaining a set point in circumstances in which environmental conditions change. For example, if someone were to leave a window open on a cold day, the thermostat would keep the heat on longer in an attempt to maintain the temperature at the set point.

Homeostatic processes work inside the body. They control nearly all of the body's operations so that when a drug is taken and it alters some aspect of the body's functioning, the body's response is controlled by a homeostatic mechanism. The disruption or disturbance created by the drug is detected, and this information is sent to the mechanism that controls the disrupted function. The control center responds by compensating for the effect of the drug thus restoring normal functioning; that is, it returns the function to its set point. If the drug is repeatedly administered, the body gets better and better at restoring normal function and diminishing the disruptive effect of the drug. This means that the drug will have a smaller and smaller effect the more it is administered. Some of these compensatory processes kick in quickly, but others take longer to develop or do not develop at all. Thus, tolerance may appear rapidly to some drug effects and very slowly to others.

When drug administration is stopped and the drug's disruptive effect is removed, the compensatory process weakens because it is no longer being used. Again, some compensatory effects may disappear rapidly, but others may go away slowly. Weeks or months may be required for normal functioning to return.

One example of pharmacodynamic tolerance is upregulation and downregulation of neurotransmitter receptors. As described in detail in Chapter 4, nerve cells communicate with each other by releasing a substance called a *neurotransmitter*, which interacts with specialized molecules called receptor sites on the membrane of a neighboring nerve cell. Some drugs work by blocking these receptor sites and reducing the effect of the neurotransmitter. There is a homeostatic mechanism that detects when this happens, and the cell can respond in a number of ways, such as by manufacturing more and more receptor sites, increasing synthesis and release of the transmitter, or changing its sensitivity to the transmitter. This is called *upregulation*. If the drug stimulates the receptor sites rather than blocking them, an opposite compensatory effect called *downregulation* occurs. Upregulation and downregulation may take a week or longer to occur. Such a process is at least partially responsible for the delay in therapeutic effects of antidepressants, which often need to be taken for a number of weeks before their antidepressant effects are seen (see Chapter 13).

Functional Disturbances

Constantine Poulos and Howard Cappell (1991) have pointed out that disruptions of physiology alone are not always sufficient to cause tolerance. The drug-induced change usually needs to be of some significance to the animal. For example, we know (a) that amphetamine causes *anorexia* (loss of appetite) in rats, and (b) that this effect will show tolerance when the drug is repeatedly administered to hungry rats in the presence of food. This is not surprising because food intake is controlled by complex homeostatic mechanisms that will attempt to overcome the anorexia so that the rat will consume a sufficient amount of food to stay healthy. But what happens if you give rats repeated doses of amphetamine when no food is present? Anorexia will still occur, but it will have no significance to the rat since the animal cannot eat. It turns out that rats do not develop tolerance to the anorectic effects of amphetamine if the drug is not given in the presence of food so that the amphetamine does not have an opportunity to interfere with eating. As Poulos and Cappell point out, the anorectic effect of the drug does not have a chance to interfere with the functioning of the organism. Consequently, there is no feedback to the feeding control mechanism. Similarly, tolerance to the *hypothermic* (body-cooling) effect of alcohol does not develop in rats in a very warm environment where alcohol does not have a hypothermic effect, and tolerance to the *analgesic* (pain-relieving) effect of morphine develops faster in rats that are subjected to painful stimuli after being given the drug (Poulos & Cappell, 1991). In other words, tolerance will develop (or will develop much faster) only in a circumstance where a drug places a demand on an organism's homeostatic mechanisms. Tolerance to drug effects that are not detected or that do not disrupt functioning does not develop.

Behavioral Tolerance

It has often been demonstrated that tolerance can be influenced by learning and conditioning processes. In other words, through experience with a drug, an organism can learn to decrease the effect that the drug is having. This is called *behavioral tolerance*. This learning, which can involve both operant and classical conditioning processes, is extensively discussed later in this chapter.

WITHDRAWAL

Withdrawal symptoms are physiological changes that occur when the use of a drug is stopped or the dosage is decreased. Different drugs produce different withdrawal symptoms, but drugs of the same family generally produce similar withdrawal. Withdrawal can be stopped almost instantly by giving the drug that has been discontinued. Often, another drug of the same family will also stop withdrawal. This phenomenon is known as *cross dependence*.

Withdrawal symptoms may vary in intensity from one drug to another. With some drugs, withdrawal symptoms may be so slight that they can be detected only using sensitive instruments, and the individual might not notice them. With other drugs, withdrawal can be so severe as to cause death. The extent of withdrawal may also depend on the dose and administration schedule of the drug.

Withdrawal symptoms usually begin some hours after the use of a drug has been stopped, but it can be produced much more quickly by giving an antagonist drug. Naloxone, a powerful antagonist to morphine, rapidly blocks all morphine effects soon after it is given by blocking the receptor used by morphine. When naloxone is given to morphine-dependent humans or nonhumans, severe withdrawal can be seen within minutes.

Dependence

The word *dependence* can be confusing because over time it has come to mean different things. For many years, the word was used in two ways: (a) to describe a state in which discontinuation of a drug causes withdrawal symptoms, and (b) to describe a state in which a person compulsively takes a drug—this state is often described as addiction. Thus, when you said that a person was dependent, you meant that he or she would experience withdrawal when a drug was discontinued and that he or she used the drug in a compulsive, addicted manner. This is because at one point, it was believed that the two states (dependence and addiction) were exactly the same. It was assumed that if you took a drug to the point that withdrawal symptoms would occur when you stopped, you were *dependent*, and you would then be driven to seek out and consume the drug in a compulsive manner in order to avoid those withdrawal symptoms. We now know that this is not the case; people who have withdrawal symptoms when a drug is discontinued do not necessarily take that drug compulsively, and people may take a drug compulsively even though they will not experience withdrawal symptoms when they stop. The relationship between withdrawal symptoms and addiction or compulsive use and drug craving will be discussed in great detail in Chapter 5. In this text, we will use the terms *dependence, physical dependence,* and *physiological dependence* interchangeably to indicate a state in which withdrawal symptoms will occur when the drug use stops. These terms will not imply anything about compulsive drug use, abuse, or addiction.

Opponent Process Theory

Tolerance and dependence are believed to be closely related. Withdrawal symptoms are usually thought of as expressions of the compensatory adjustment that homeostatic mechanisms have made to the effects of a drug after repeated administrations. As described earlier, with repeated administration of a drug, the body changes its functioning, and, through homeostatic feedback, it compensates for the physiological changes the drug produces. Later, when the drug is discontinued and its effects disappear, it takes some time for the body to readjust to the drug's absence. During this readjustment, the compensatory responses are what cause withdrawal symptoms.

The dynamics of this process were first formulated by Solomon and Corbit (1974) who were proposing a theory of acquired motivations, a theory that also applies to drug use. They proposed that abused drugs stimulate an A process that creates a euphoric (pleasant) state, but soon after, a compensatory B process is evoked that creates a dysphoric (unpleasant) state. This is shown in the top panel of Figure 3-2. During a single administration of a drug, at first the A process dominates, but once the B process kicks, it very quickly cancels out some of the euphoria. As the drug wears off, so too does the A process, but the B process endures for a while. This net experience (the overall affective state) is shown in the middle panel of Figure 3-2. When the drug is first administered, the person experiences pleasure, but this decreases as the B process becomes active. When the drug

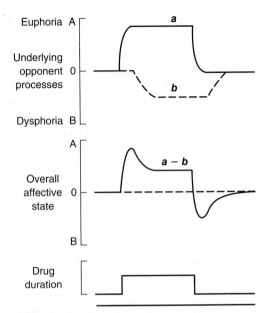

FIGURE 3-2   The upper panel shows the effect of a single drug administration on both the A process and the opposing B process. When a drug is given, the A process increases, but shortly thereafter, the opposite B process begins. When the drug wears off, the A process diminishes, but the B process continues for a while before disappearing. The middle panel shows the result of combining the A and B effects. It shows that the A effect will be strongest right after the drug is taken and then diminish. This decreased effect is what would be called acute tolerance. The B effect dominates for a time after the drug has worn off. The B effect would be experienced as withdrawal effect. Solomon and Corbit originally proposed this mechanism to explain changes in pleasure (hedonic state) caused by a drug, but the idea can be used to explain many drug effects. (Adapted from Solomon & Corbit, 1974.)

activity terminates, the A process stops and so does the pleasure, but the continuation of the B process for a brief time causes the person to experience dysphoria.

When you think of withdrawal symptoms, you normally think of what happens when a person takes a drug repeatedly for an extended period, but as you can see from the opponent process theory, we can expect withdrawal after each administration. Often when this happens, we might use the word *hangover* to describe this, but we must be careful because hangover implies something more than a compensatory response. *Hangover* is a term that usually refers to the aftermath of the acute effects of a drug, such as when you go out drinking at night and then feel sick the next day. Many of the symptoms of an alcohol hangover are a direct result of toxic effects of alcohol, such as dehydration or stomach irritation (see Chapter 6), which remain after the intoxication. But some effects, like sensitivity to lights and noise, can be thought of as brief withdrawal symptoms that are compensatory responses to the effects of alcohol. An example of a hangover that is mostly a compensatory response occurs after taking cocaine. After the euphoric effects of a dose of cocaine wear off, users often experience a letdown or a period of depression that can be thought of as a compensatory response to the euphoric high caused by the drug (see Chapter 10), although it is not usually referred to as a hangover.

An example of the opponent process effect within a single administration of the tranquilizer chlordiazepoxide is shown in Box 3-1, where the A state is the tranquilizing (*anxiolytic* or *anxiety-relieving*) effect of chlordiazepoxide, and the compensatory B state is the opposite: anxiety.

Acute tolerance can also be explained by opponent process theory. When you take a drug, its effect will be greatest before the B processes build up. As the B processes get stronger, the strength of the A process will diminish. This would explain why a drug effect could be greater at a particular blood level as the drug levels are rising than at the same point as the blood levels of a drug are falling.

If you take a drug continuously for weeks or months and maintain a certain level of the drug in the body so that withdrawal symptoms never occur, the compensatory response builds up. When you stop taking the drug, this compensatory response is expressed as withdrawal symptoms. These can be very unpleasant and, depending on the nature of the drug, intense and severe. Withdrawal symptoms are often exaggerated effects opposite those of the drug, indicating that they are compensatory responses. Figure 3-3, on page 47, is an extension of Figure 3-2. It shows that, as a drug is administered repeatedly, the compensatory B process gets stronger and kicks in sooner so that the A process almost disappears entirely (i.e., this is increased tolerance) and the B process (i.e., the withdrawal effect) is more intense and longer lasting. This change, along with other adaptations in the nervous system, has important implications for the development of addiction, described in Chapter 5.

BOX 3-1   Anxiety As a Conditioned Compensatory Response to a Tranquilizer

Using a two-lever, drug discrimination procedure, Barrett and Smith (2005) of Vanderbilt University in Nashville, Tennessee, trained rats to discriminate between a dose of chlordiazepoxide (CDP) and a dose of pentylenetetrazol (PTZ). Chlordiazepoxide is a benzodiazepine tranquilizer that relieves anxiety and has a calming effect (it is an anxiolytic). It works by enhancing the effect of the inhibitory transmitter GABA. Pentylenetetrazol has exactly the opposite effect; it reduces the effects of GABA and causes tension and anxiety (it is an anxiogenic) (see Chapter 7). Barrett and Smith trained rats to press one lever after being injected with CDP, that is, when they were calm and relaxed, and the second lever after being injected with PTZ, that is, when they were tense and anxious. After being given saline, the rats distributed their responding equally between the two levers.

They then gave the rats an injection of chlordiazepoxide and tested them in the two-lever apparatus at various times after the injection. As can be seen in the following diagram, 8 hours after the CDP injection, rats made 90% of their responses in the CDP lever, but by 16 hours after the injection, they made most of their responses on the PTZ lever. Responding slowly approached the 50% level over a number of days.

What appeared to be happening was that 8 hours after the CDP injection, the rats still felt calm and relaxed and responded on the CDP lever, but all this time, a compensatory response had been developing that was opposite to the CDP effect. After the drug had left the system, the compensatory response remained. This made the rats anxious and tense, a feeling like that produced by PTZ, so they pressed the PTZ lever at the 16-hour test. Eventually, this compensatory response diminished, and by 48 hours the rats were closer to drug-free response levels of 50% on each lever.

It is this sort of process that seems to be responsible for hangovers to many drugs and makes it so that drugs, after they have worn off, sometimes have an effect opposite to their normal effect.

This experiment illustrates the Solomon and Corbit theory described in the text. The A process is the tranquilizing effect of the CDP, and the B process is compensatory anxiety. Compare the lower panel of Figure 3-1 with this figure.

(Continued)

BOX 3-1   *(Continued)*

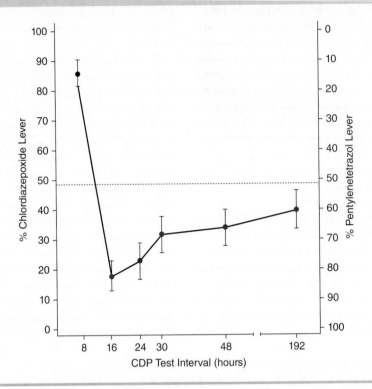

If withdrawal is an expression of compensatory effects that cause tolerance to drugs, you might expect there to be a strong correlation between tolerance and withdrawal symptoms. This does not seem to be the case; it is not unusual for a person to show considerable tolerance to the effects of a drug but to have no withdrawal symptoms when the drug is discontinued. Alcohol is a good example. Many long-time casual drinkers have a considerable tolerance for some of the effects of alcohol, but do not show any signs of withdrawal when they stop drinking. There are a number of reasons why this could be so. To begin with, there may be some tolerance, like behavioral tolerance (described in the next section), that is not created by a physiological compensatory effect, and so there would be no physiological withdrawal. In addition, withdrawal symptoms may not be experienced if the rate of elimination of the drug from the body is very slow, as is the case with THC, an active ingredient in marijuana (see

Chapter 14). With slow elimination, the body may be able to readjust at the pace of the drug's elimination, and withdrawal symptoms may not be expressed.

CONDITIONING OF DRUG EFFECTS

In Chapter 2, we looked at conditioned behaviors as dependent variables in drug research; that is, we asked how drugs affect conditioned behavior. In this section, we will look at some ways in which conditioning, both operant and classical, can alter the effects of drugs and how such effects can explain phenomena such as tolerance and withdrawal.

Classical Conditioning of Drug Effects

CLASSICAL CONDITIONING OF DRUG STIMULI AND RESPONSES.   At the end of the nineteenth century, Ivan Pavlov and his colleagues in St. Petersburg,

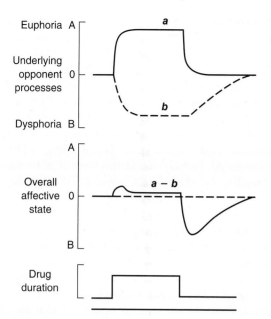

FIGURE 3-3 The upper panel shows the drug effect on both the A process and the opposing B process after chronic administration of the drug. When the drug is taken repeatedly, the A process remains unchanged, but the compensatory B process gets stronger and kicks in sooner. The overall affective state (illustrated in the middle panel) is such that the A process almost disappears entirely (i.e., this is increased tolerance) and the B process (i.e., the withdrawal effect) is more intense and longer lasting. (Adapted from Solomon & Corbit, 1974.)

Russia, first demonstrated the principles of classical conditioning that were outlined in Chapter 2. Researchers in Pavlov's laboratory were also the first to show that the effects of a drug could be conditioned to neutral stimuli present at the time the drug was having its effect. One of these experiments was conducted in the following manner:

> A dog was given a small dose of apomorphine subcutaneously and after one to two minutes a note of definite pitch was sounded during a considerable time. While the note was still sounding the drug began to take effect upon the dog: the animal grew restless, began to moisten its lips with its tongue, secreted saliva and showed some disposition to vomit. After the experimenter had reinforced the tone

with apomorphine several times it was found that the sound of the note alone sufficed to produce all the active symptoms of the drug, only in a less degree [experiments by Podkopaev]. (Pavlov, 1927, p. 35)

Later, the researchers were able to show that after a number of injections, the preliminaries to the injection and the administration procedure itself were sufficient to produce salivation and other drug effects, even though no drug was given. In Pavlov's terminology, the drug was the *unconditioned stimulus* (UCS); the effects of the drug—the salivation and vomiting—were the *unconditioned response* (UCR); the stimulus preceding the drug was the *conditioned stimulus* (CS); and the salivation and nausea produced by these stimuli presented in the absence of the drug was the *conditioned response* (CR).

CLASSICAL CONDITIONING OF COMPENSATORY RESPONSES. The conditioning of drug effects is more complicated than it would first appear because the unconditioned response and the conditioned response to the drug are not always the same. Sometimes the stimuli paired with a drug (the conditioned stimuli), when presented in the absence of the drug, produce a physiological response (the conditioned response) opposite to that produced by the drug (the unconditioned response). For example, it has been shown in rats that an unconditioned response to morphine is analgesia (a decreased responsiveness to painful stimuli), whereas the conditioned response to stimuli repeatedly paired with morphine injections is *hyperalgesia* (an increased sensitivity to pain). The reasons for this can be understood if you realize that often what is being conditioned is not the effect of the drug itself, but the body's attempt to resist the effect of the drug—the compensatory effect (Eikelboom & Stewart, 1982).

Earlier, you read that the body resists drug-induced changes by making adjustments or compensatory changes in its physiology in an attempt to restore normal functioning. As we have seen, these compensations make the body less susceptible to the drug when it is given later, and they are responsible for tolerance. It appears that, in many cases, these compensatory responses, not the initial effects of the drug, become conditioned to stimuli that are repeatedly paired with the administration of the drug. In other words, the UCR is the compensatory response, which becomes the CR. Because the compensatory response is opposite to that of the drug effect, the conditioned drug effect will also be opposite to the initial drug effect, that is, a conditioned compensatory effect.

It is important to understand the nature of conditioned drug effects because they play an important role in how the effects of a drug are expressed when the drug is administered later. An example is conditioned drug tolerance.

CLASSICAL CONDITIONING OF DRUG TOLERANCE.
Early research into tolerance and the development of conditioned compensatory responses to drugs was conducted at McMaster University by Shepard Siegel and his colleagues. Siegel investigated the development of tolerance to the analgesic effect of morphine. To test analgesia, Siegel used the *paw lick test* (described in Chapter 2). After an injection of morphine, the paw lick latency increases, indicating that the morphine has reduced the animal's sensitivity to pain. With repeated morphine trials, the latency tends to get shorter and shorter as tolerance to the morphine develops (Siegel, 1975).

In Siegel's experiment, there were two main experimental groups of rats: the M-HP group and the M-CAGE group. The training phase consisted of three trials, 2 days apart. Rats in the M-HP group were taken from their home cage, injected with morphine (M), and tested for analgesia using a paw lick latency test on a hot plate (HP) in a testing room. These rats showed an analgesic effect of morphine on the first day, but by day 3, their responding was the same as that of the control rats given saline; that is, complete tolerance had developed. Rats in the M-CAGE group were injected with morphine in the colony room and returned directly to their home cage without being tested.

Two days later, rats in both groups were injected with morphine and tested on the hot plate in the testing room (Test 1). Just as in day 3 of training, the M-HP group showed complete tolerance to morphine, but the rats in the M-CAGE group showed a large analgesic effect, indicating no tolerance to morphine. On a later day (Test 2), the rats in the M-HP group were tested in the testing room, but were given saline rather than morphine. They showed faster paw lick latencies (i.e., they licked their paws sooner) than control rats that had never been exposed to morphine. This finding indicated that the M-HP group experienced hyperalgesia, demonstrating that the tolerance to morphine exhibited across trials was due to a compensatory response to the analgesic effect of the morphine (Siegel, 1975).

In his experiment, Siegel was able to demonstrate that rats would show tolerance to the analgesic effects of morphine only if they were given the paw lick test in the same room where repeated morphine injections had been experienced earlier. If they were given morphine in the colony room where they were normally housed, but were tested in a different room, the animals did not show any tolerance. The tolerance to morphine was evident only in the environment where the drug had been experienced. For this reason, this form of tolerance is sometimes called *conditional tolerance*. Table 3-1 shows the design and results of Siegel's experiment.

To explain this effect, Siegel proposed that the environment repeatedly associated with the drug acts like a conditioned stimulus, but rather than becoming a conditioned stimulus for the effect the drug is having, it becomes a conditioned stimulus for the physiological changes the body is making to compensate for the drug's effect. Thus, the environment associated with the administration of the drug elicits physiological responses opposite to the effect of the drug. These changes help prepare the rat for the drug and diminish its effect.

In support of his theory, Siegel was able to show that if he injected a rat with saline and gave it the paw lick test in an environment that had previously been associated with repeated injections of morphine, the rat's latencies would be even shorter than normal; that is, the animal would show hyperalgesia. This was the compensatory response that had been produced by the morphine environment through conditioning.

Box 3-2 gives an example of how conditional tolerance can protect humans and nonhumans from a heroin overdose.

CLASSICAL CONDITIONING OF WITHDRAWAL. Besides explaining some tolerance, learning processes may be responsible for some withdrawal symptoms. We have seen how compensatory responses may be conditioned to a particular environment where the drug is repeatedly given. Later, if an animal is placed in that environment without the drug, it will show conditioned compensatory responses—physiological changes opposite to the drug's effect. When they occur in the absence of the drug, they are withdrawal symptoms, as described earlier in this chapter. Therefore, some aspects of withdrawal can be conditioned and may be evoked by specific stimuli previously associated with the use of the drug (Siegel, 1983). For example, former heroin addicts who have gone through withdrawal

TABLE 3-1   Experiment by Shepard Siegel Showing Conditioned Tolerance to Morphine

Group	Training Phase	Test 1	Test 2
	Training Condition	morphine→Hot Plate	saline→Hot Plate
M-HP	Rats were tested on the Hot Plate after morphine in the Test Room	No Analgesia indicating Tolerance	Hyperanalgesia (Compensatory Response)
M-CAGE	Rats were given morphine in the Colony Room but not tested on the Hot Plate	Analgesia indicating No Tolerance	

after they stop using a drug will frequently experience withdrawal symptoms again when they return to places where they have experienced the effects of the drug even though they are no longer physically dependent. As the following example illustrates, there can be little doubt that these conditioned withdrawal symptoms play an important role in relapse to drug use in previously dependent addicts and are probably responsible for drug cravings:

> The patient was a 28-year-old man with a ten-year history of narcotic addiction. He was married and the father of two children. He reported that, while he

BOX 3-2   The Mystery of Heroin Overdose

One of the greatest risks of being a heroin addict is death from heroin overdose. Each year, about 1% of all heroin addicts in the United States die from an overdose of heroin despite having developed a fantastic tolerance to the effects of the drug. In a nontolerant person, the estimated lethal dose of heroin may range from 200 to 500 mg, but addicts have tolerated doses as high as 1,800 mg without even being sick (Brecher & the Editors of Consumer Reports, 1972). No doubt, some overdoses are a result of mixing heroin with other drugs, but many appear to result from a sudden loss of tolerance. Addicts have been killed by a dose that was readily tolerated the day before. An explanation for this sudden loss of tolerance has been suggested by Shepard Siegel of McMaster University and his associates Riley Hinson, Marvin Krank, and Jane McCully.

Siegel reasoned that tolerance to heroin was partly conditioned to the environment where the drug was normally administered. If the drug is consumed in a new setting, much of the conditioned tolerance disappears, and the addict is more likely to overdose. To test this theory, Siegel, Hinson, Krank, and McCully (1982) ran the following experiment. Rats were given daily intravenous injections for 30 days. The injections, either a dextrose placebo or heroin, were given in either the animal colony room or a different room where there was constant white noise. The drug and the placebo were given on alternate days, and the drug condition always corresponded with a particular environment so that some rats always received the heroin in the white-noise room and the placebo in the colony. For other rats, the heroin was always given in the colony, and the placebo was always given in the white-noise room. Another group of rats served as a control. They were injected in different rooms on alternate days but were injected only with dextrose and had no experience with heroin.

All rats were then injected with a large dose of heroin: 15 mg/kg. The rats in one group, labeled the ST group, were given the heroin in the same room where they had previously been given the heroin. The other rats, the DT group, were given the heroin in the room where they had previously been given the placebo.

Siegel found that 96% of the control group died, showing the lethal effect of heroin on nontolerant animals. Rats in the DT group that received heroin were partly tolerant; 64% died. Only 32% of the ST rats died, showing that their tolerance was greater when the overdose test was done in the same environment where the drug had previously been administered.

Siegel suggested one reason for addicts' sudden loss of tolerance: They take the drug in a different or an unusual environment, like the rats in the DT group. Surveys of heroin addicts admitted to hospitals and diagnosed as suffering from heroin overdose tend to support this conclusion. Many addicts reported that they had taken the near-fatal dose in an unusual circumstance or that their normal pattern was different on that day (Siegel et al., 1982).

was addicted, he was arrested and incarcerated for six months. He reported experiencing severe withdrawal during the first four or five days in custody, but later he began to feel well. He gained weight, felt like a new man, and decided that he was finished with drugs. He thought about his children and looked forward to returning to his former job. On the way home after his release from prison, he began thinking of drugs and feeling nauseated. As the subway approached his stop, he began sweating, tearing from his eyes, and gagging. This was an area where he had frequently experienced narcotic withdrawal symptoms while trying to acquire drugs. As he got off the subway he vomited onto the tracks. He soon bought drugs and was relieved.

The following day he again experienced craving and withdrawal symptoms in his neighborhood, and he again relieved the symptoms by injecting heroin. The cycle repeated itself over the next few days and soon he became readdicted. (O'Brien, 1976, p. 533)

The addict's eyes teared and he began sweating when he came into the subway station where he had previously acquired drugs. It is likely that his body was preparing itself for an injection of heroin, which it had become conditioned to expect in that environment.

This example shows that conditioned withdrawal symptoms do not disappear when the body makes its initial readjustment to the absence of a drug. Because it is learned, conditioned withdrawal symptoms will go away only through the process of extinction—that is, the presentation of conditioned stimuli in the absence of drug administration.

Operant Conditioning of Drug Effects

OPERANT CONDITIONING OF DRUG TOLERANCE.
An early experiment in this area was done by Judith Campbell and Lewis Seiden (1973) at the University of Chicago. They trained rats to respond for food reinforcement in a Skinner box on a *differential reinforcement of low rates* (DRL) schedule. On a DRL schedule, the animal is reinforced only if it waits for a fixed period of time between responses. In other words, it is reinforced for responding at a low rate. When amphetamine is given, it stimulates responding, and the rat loses reinforcements because it cannot wait long enough between responses.

For 28 sessions, Campbell and Seiden gave amphetamine to one group of rats immediately before placing them in a Skinner box where they were reinforced on a DRL schedule. Another group of rats was given the same number of injections and the same number of sessions on the DRL schedule, but the amphetamine was given after the DRL trials. Over the period of the experiment, the amphetamine-pretreated rats developed tolerance and were able to obtain more and more reinforcements, but when the other rats were tested on the DRL with amphetamine, they performed as though they had never received the drug—they had no tolerance. If the tolerance shown by the first group had been the result of metabolic or physiological changes that develop in response to the presentation of the drug alone, it should have shown up in both groups because both groups received the same number of exposures to the amphetamine.

Campbell and Seiden concluded that the difference had only one explanation: The rats had learned to alter their behavior to compensate for the change that the amphetamine caused. This interpretation was supported by the observation that no tolerance develops to the rate-increasing effect of amphetamine on fixed interval (FI) responding (Schuster, Dockens, & Woods, 1966). Increased responding on the FI does not cause the rat to lose reinforcements, whereas it does on the DRL schedule. Thus, it appeared that the rats had developed a particular strategy for overcoming the effect of the amphetamine on DRL. This strategy was learned because it was reinforced by an increase in food presentations.

A similar hypothesis was tested by Muriel Vogel-Sprott (1992) and her colleagues at the University of Waterloo, who have done considerable research on the development of behavioral tolerance to the effects of alcohol in humans. They used a different technique. They reasoned that if tolerance was a result of learning strategies to compensate for the effect of a drug, then the development of tolerance should depend on the occurrence of reinforcement when a compensatory response is made.

In her experiments, human participants are trained on a cognitive or motor task such as the pursuit rotor (see Chapter 2) until their performance is stable. Then they are given alcohol for a number of sessions, and this interferes with their performance. Typically, Vogel-Sprott has one group of participants who are told that they will be given a 25-cent reward immediately after each trial in which they are able to resist the disruptive effects of alcohol and perform in their normal, drug-free range. A second group of participants is also given a 25-cent reward for each such trial, but the money is saved up and given at the end of the session, and no information is given about which trials were in the drug-free range. A third group is not given any information or money.

Vogel-Sprott has repeated this experiment many times and always finds that participants given information or feedback about their performance, whether they are given money or not, develop tolerance rapidly, and the other groups develop tolerance slowly, if at all (Vogel-Sprott, 1992). It seems that, in her experiments, the participants' knowledge that they are resisting the effects of alcohol is sufficient reinforcement for learning to resist the effects of alcohol.

The Campbell and Seiden and the Vogel-Sprott studies can be understood in terms of homeostatic theory. In the Campbell and Seiden study, the disruptive effects of the amphetamine caused a loss of reinforcements; consequently, the drug effect had functional significance for the

rat. As a result, a homeostatic mechanism kicked in, and a compensatory response was acquired that permitted the animal to respond more slowly and receive more food. No compensatory response developed to the FI responding because the effect of the drug (an increased response rate) did not cause the animal to lose reinforcements and had no biological significance. Similarly, in the Vogel-Sprott experiment, the effect of the alcohol on the pursuit rotor task had no significance for the participants in the control group, who were not informed that the alcohol was having an effect. The participants in the experimental group who were paid for good performance, however, found that the disruptive effect of the alcohol had significance for them, and so tolerance developed. Box 3-3 gives an example of how tolerance to alcohol could have played a role in the crash that killed Princess Diana in 1997.

BOX 3-3   Did Alcohol Kill Princess Diana?

On August 31, 1997, the world was shocked to learn that Britain's Princess Diana was killed in a car crash in a tunnel in Paris. The reasons for the deadly crash have never been clearly established, but a contributing factor could have been that Henri Paul, the driver of the princess's car, had a blood alcohol level of 175 mg/100 ml of blood—three times the legal limit. Under other circumstances, an accident like this might have been clearly blamed on the intoxicated state of the driver, but the blame is not so readily placed in this case. Diana's car was speeding in an attempt to avoid photographers who were chasing it in other cars and on motorcycles. Reports of witnesses say that Henri Paul "seemed fine" when he took the wheel that night. In fact, videotapes from security cameras in Diana's hotel show Henri Paul walking quite normally, carrying on conversations, and showing no signs of intoxication.

What we know about the development of tolerance to drugs might explain why Henri Paul could "seem fine" and still have such a high level of alcohol in his blood.

Given the reports that Henri Paul had a history of heavy drinking, it is likely that he had developed a considerable tolerance to many of the direct effects that alcohol had on his nervous system (physiological tolerance). In addition, on that day, he had not expected to be called back to work, and he seems to have started drinking early in the morning. He probably had been drinking continuously for an extended period of time. Under these circumstances, extensive acute tolerance has a chance to develop. It may not be surprising, then, that Henri was able to show normal behavior even though his blood alcohol level was excessive.

If Henri Paul was that tolerant, could alcohol have played a role in the accident? It seems so. To begin with, we know that tolerance does not develop to all the effects of a drug at the same time, and it is possible to be tolerant to some effects of a drug and not others. All we know is that Henri Paul was able to walk and talk normally. On the basis of the work of Vogel-Sprott, we know that tolerance to an effect of alcohol develops if the individual is provided with feedback on the effect of alcohol and is reinforced for making a compensatory response to overcome alcohol's effect. Walking and talking are behaviors that most people who drink regularly are able to practice under the influence of alcohol; very often those behaviors are rewarded with social approval. Because Henri Paul was a professional driver, it would have been disastrous for him to exhibit any effects of alcohol intoxication before driving. Therefore, walking and talking were likely to be the first behaviors restored by both acute and chronic tolerance.

The effects of alcohol on driving might also be subject to learning compensatory strategies that cause tolerance. Indeed, in Vogel-Sprott's laboratory, research on a driving simulator shows such an effect. Diana's driver might possibly have been able to drive safely under normal driving conditions. In fact, he may have done so many times. But it is unlikely that Henri Paul had had a chance, while intoxicated, to practice the skills required to race through a tunnel at high speed in an effort to elude photographers. Such skills may not have had a chance to develop, regardless of his tolerance to all other effects of alcohol.

(Continued)

BOX 3-3   (Continued)

That fateful night, alcohol may have had a big effect on Henri Paul, but because of his tolerance to some effects, no one, not even Henri Paul himself, was able to detect the debilitating effect. In fact, under most circumstances, it would have gone undetected.

Driving is a complex task requiring many different cognitive and motor skills. In addition, the demands that will be made on a driver on any particular trip cannot be predicted. A person may be able to drive a car safely at a given blood alcohol level, provided that nothing unusual happens. But a driver can never know what demands will be made and whether alcohol, even at a low dose, will be responsible for an accident.

SENSITIZATION

Most of the time, when a drug is repeatedly administered, tolerance develops to the many effects of the drug. In some circumstances, however, an effect of a drug can increase with repeated administrations. This is known as *sensitization* or *reverse tolerance*.

Sensitization is much less common than tolerance, and much less is known about it. Most of what we know about sensitization comes from studies of the activating effects of a variety of drugs, including cocaine, amphetamine, nicotine, alcohol, phencyclidine, and opioids such as morphine. At low doses, all these drugs produce an activating effect when first given to laboratory animals. This effect is characterized by increased motor activity and rearing behavior in rats. At high doses, *stereotyped behaviors* are seen. Stereotyped behaviors are invariable, repetitive movements, such as head bobbing and sniffing, which are engaged in for extended periods of time and appear to have no purpose. When repeated low doses of a drug are given, there is a progressive increase in behavioral activation with each administration. Repeated administration of higher doses will eventually cause stereotyped behavior where only activation was caused by the initial dose (Robinson & Berridge, 1993).

Like tolerance, sensitization may also be conditioned to a particular environment (Stewart & Badiani, 1993). This has been demonstrated in two different ways. First, it has been shown that, as with tolerance, if sensitization is created by repeatedly administering the drug in a specific environment, then sensitization will be greatly diminished or will not appear at all when the drug is given in a different environment. Second, if sensitization results from repeated injections in a specific environment, then that environment will act as a conditioned stimulus for a drug-like conditioned response. In other words, if you place an animal in the environment after a placebo injection, it will show increased activity—the same response that the drug

causes (Robinson & Berridge, 1993; Silverman & Bonate, 1997). In this regard, sensitization appears to be a mirror image of tolerance, except that the conditioned response is a drug-like response rather than a drug-opposite response. When the drug-like conditioned response (activation) is elicited in conjunction with the drug effect (also activation), there is an enhanced drug effect.

In some circumstances, sensitization may also be produced by operant conditioning processes. We saw that Vogel-Sprott was able to create tolerance to the disruptive effect of alcohol by paying participants to resist the effects of alcohol on a motor task. She was also able to increase the effects of alcohol by giving participants money when their performance was further disrupted by alcohol (Zack & Vogel-Sprott, 1995).

Cross sensitization of drug effects can also be demonstrated. Laboratory animals with a sensitization to morphine will also show increased activation to cocaine and amphetamine, and vice versa. In fact, even stress will sensitize a rat to the activating effect of many of these drugs (Piazza & Le Moal, 1998).

Sensitization may differ from tolerance in the fact that it seems to be very persistent. Both conditioned and nonconditioned sensitization can last as long as a year after drug exposure in rats (that is one-third of their lifetime), and there are no reports of it dissipating over time. In fact, there is evidence that sensitization might *increase* with time (Robinson & Berridge, 1993; Silverman & Bonate, 1997).

From the considerable work directed at discovering the brain mechanisms responsible for the sensitization of behavioral arousal, it has become evident that no single neuronal effect can be responsible (Pierce & Kalivas, 1997). Sensitization clearly involves the brain's general motivation control system. It is responsible for arousal and approach to both conditioned and natural incentives such as food and receptive sexual partners. The part of this system that becomes sensitized is the *mesolimbic dopamine system*. As we shall see in Chapters 4 and 5, this mechanism also appears to be responsible for the reinforcing effects of drugs. Sensitization of this system has been proposed as an explanation for drug abuse (Robinson & Berridge, 2000). This process is described in more detail in Chapter 5.

Sensitization of drug-induced activation has not been demonstrated in humans, but it is commonly observed that drugs like cocaine and amphetamine at low doses are able to produce symptoms of psychosis and even convulsions in heavy users, even though they do not cause these effects in beginning users (see Chapter 10).

EXPECTANCY AND CONTEXT

The Placebo Effect

It is becoming clear that the context in which a drug is administered is capable of having a significant influence on the effect of that drug. One of the most powerful contextual effects is whether you know a drug is being administered at all, that is, whether you are expecting a drug effect and what you think that effect will be like. This is the *placebo effect*, which was discussed in Chapter 2 in reference to research design. The placebo effect has been shown to be responsible for a considerable part of the therapeutic effect of many medications. For example, it appears that the placebo effect may be responsible for up to 70% of the effectiveness of antidepressant drugs and 50% of the effectiveness of pain relievers (Mora, Nestoriuc, & Rief, 2011). It is of little wonder then that the placebo effect has become the subject of considerable research. As described in Chapter 2, understanding the properties and mechanisms of the placebo effect is of particular interest not only to researchers evaluating the effects of medicines, but it is also clear that such knowledge could be used to enhance and optimize treatments through suggestion and enhanced caregiver–patient interactions.

One of the more interesting studies of the mechanisms of the placebo effect was published in 1995 by Benedetti, Amanzio, and Maggi, researchers at the University of Turin Medical School in Italy. They were investigating the effect of the drug proglumide on pain in human subjects. The experimental design and results are summarized in Table 3-2. Their results showed that proglumide was better at relieving pain than a placebo, and that a placebo was better than no treatment at all. This is not surprising, and these results would normally be interpreted as indicating that

proglumide was an effective painkiller above and beyond the placebo effect, but these researchers included an additional treatment group in their research. They had a group of participants that received an injection of proglumide through an automated infusion pump without knowing that they had received any drug at all, that is, a "hidden drug" treatment group. Interestingly, in this group, proglumide had no effect on pain. The entire effect of the drug depended on the participants knowing that they were getting it.

But if all the pain relief was placebo effect, why did the drug have a stronger effect than the placebo alone? Colloca and Benedetti (2005) explained the effect by proposing the existence of an *expectation mechanism*—a top-down pain-relieving pathway from the cortex to a pain control center in the lower brain that is capable of blocking pain. This system is not the same one affected directly by pain-relieving drugs; rather, it is activated by the expectation of such drugs. When a person believes that a drug is being administered, this pathway is activated, and pain is diminished. It is this pathway that is responsible for the placebo effects of pain-relieving drugs. Colloca and Benedetti proposed that the proglumide in their experiment had no direct effect on pain. Rather, it directly stimulated this expectation mechanism, and placebo response was enhanced. This is why the proglumide group showed a greater response than the placebo alone and why the hidden proglumide injection had no effect at all on pain.

Brain imaging studies using fMRI (see Chapter 4) have identified areas of the brain known to be involved in placebo-induced analgesia and which could be part of this expectation mechanism. These include areas such as the dorsolateral prefrontal cortex (DLPFC) and the anterior cingulate cortex (ACC) known to be involved in planning and evaluation of expected events. Activity changes in other areas associated with aversion, reward and emotions, and pain control have also been identified in fMRI studies of placebo analgesia (Price, Finniss, & Benedetti, 2008).

Many studies have explored the role of endogenous opioid systems in placebo analgesia. Most have shown that the placebo response can be blocked by naloxone, a drug that blocks the receptor for the endorphins, indicating that the placebo effect involves the same pain control mechanisms as morphine and the opioids. Other studies, however, have shown that placebo effects that depend on past experience with analgesics and thereby do not work on the endogenous opioid systems are not blocked by naloxone, demonstrating that placebo analgesia can be mediated by more than one system.

TABLE 3-2 Experimental Design and Findings of Beneditti, Amanzio, and Maggi (1995)		
Group	**Treatment**	**Pain Reduction Score**
1. Natural History	Hidden saline injection	Less than 1.0
2. Hidden Drug	Hidden proglumide injection	Less than 1.0
3. Placebo	Open saline injection	About 2.0
4. Open Drug	Open proglumide injection	Between 3.0 and 4.0

There were four groups in this experiment; all were patients recovering from a surgical procedure. Patients rated their pain on a 10-point scale where 0 indicated no pain and 10 indicated unbearable pain. The table illustrates the reduction in pain scores of patients in various treatment groups. The Natural History group received a hidden injection of saline and showed very little analgesia. The same was true of the Hidden Drug group who, unbeknownst to them, received injections of proglumide; these results show that the proglumide was not a natural pain reliever. The Placebo group reported a pain reduction of about 2.0, showing a moderate placebo effect. Finally, the Open Drug group who knowingly received the injection of proglumide reported a large amount of analgesia.

While much of the research on the placebo effect has been done studying placebo analgesia, there are many other examples of how the expectation of a drug effect can alter the actual effect of a drug on the brain. For example, Volkow and colleagues (2003) used PET scans (see Chapter 4) to measure glucose metabolism in the brain and showed that an injection of methylphenidate (Ritalin; a drug similar in effect to cocaine) increased glucose metabolism in some brain regions of cocaine abusers. Interestingly, the effect was twice as great if the participants were expecting the drug than if they were not. In addition, Volkow and her associates showed that self-reports of being *high* were also about 50% greater when the drug was expected.

Factors That Modify the Placebo Effect in Medical Treatment

Numerous studies have investigated the placebo effect in medical treatment. The factor that seems to be most effective in enhancing the placebo effect is the strength of the expectation of a particular drug effect. Expectation can be created and modified by subtle verbal suggestion by the experimenter or physician or by past experience with other medications and treatments. In addition, participants in experiments are more likely to show a placebo effect if they believe that they are in a treatment group rather than a placebo group. This belief can be enhanced by cues that signal that they have been given an active substance. In addition to expectation, the patient's desire for an effective treatment and motivation

to avoid pain and other symptoms can also be important in generating the placebo effect (Price et al., 2008). For these reasons, it is extremely important to use a double-blind procedure when testing drugs to be sure that participants receiving the drug and the placebo have exactly the same expectations and experiences.

The Nocebo Effect

One interesting finding in placebo-controlled studies is that a placebo can often generate side effects. This is called the *nocebo effect*. Like placebo effects, nocebo effects are caused by expectations that can arise from patient instructions and from other sources like package inserts or ads on television where endless lists of possible side effects are recited (Mora et al., 2011).

Self-Administration

It has also been shown that drugs may have different effects when they are self-administered than when the person or laboratory animal has no control over the drug administration. Hemby, Koves, Smith, and Dworkin (1997) showed that levels of dopamine in the nucleus accumbens (a part of the mesolimbic dopamine system) were higher in rats that were allowed to press a lever to give themselves injections of cocaine than in rats that passively received an injection every time the rats in the self-administration group gave themselves an injection. As we shall see later, dopamine levels in this part of the brain are important in forming addiction to a drug.

Novel Environments

It is also clear from research on nonhumans that many drug effects are different when the drug is administered in a novel environment. As discussed in the previous section, stimulant drugs like cocaine and amphetamine tend to cause increases in motor behavior after they are administered, and with repeated administrations, this effect shows sensitization. The influence of the environment in modifying a drug's effect is illustrated in research showing that if the drug is administered in a novel environment, the amount of locomotor stimulation is considerably more than would be seen if the drug had been administered in a familiar setting (reviewed by Badaiani & Robinson, 2004). In addition, sensitization of this effect is much more rapid and can be induced at a lower dose if the drug is given in a novel setting. Investigations of this effect have shown that when these drugs are administered in a novel setting, they actually have different effects on the nervous system, effects that are likely to make them more addictive (Badaiani & Robinson, 2004).

4

Neurophysiology, Neurotransmitters, and the Nervous System

All behavior is under the control of the nervous system, and the effect of behaviorally active drugs can ultimately be traced to a direct or an indirect action on some aspect of the functioning of the nervous system. It is therefore necessary to have at least a rudimentary grasp of the normal functioning of the nervous system to understand the behavioral effects of drugs.

THE NEURON

Like all other tissues in the body, the nervous system is made up of cells. The two main types of cells are *neurons* and *glial cells* (or *glia*), which exist in the brain in roughly equal proportions of about 100 billion each. Neurons are excitable cells that analyze and transmit information. They are responsible for receiving sensory information from outside the body, for integrating and storing information, and for controlling the action of the muscles and glands—in other words, for everything that we see and understand as behavior. Glia support neurons. For much of the past century, it was thought that glia simply fulfilled a structural role, gluing neurons in place (*glia* is Latin for glue). But we now know that glia also play a protective role, helping to maintain efficient cell communication by

shielding neurons from microorganisms and chemicals in the blood as well as from other neurons with which messages may become scrambled. They fulfill a metabolic role, supplying neurons with oxygen and nutrients and removing waste. And they play a maintenance role, destroying dead neurons. Glia are also active, reciprocal communicators within the nervous system. They form circuits; contain special receptor sites that are sensitive to chemicals released by neurons; and, in turn, influence communication between neurons by supplying chemical transmitters, limiting the dispersion of these chemicals, and getting rid of these chemicals when they are no longer needed. With these remarkable discoveries, glia have become the focus of intense investigation.

Nerve cells come in many shapes and sizes and contain a number of identifiable parts. A typical nerve cell is shown in Figure 4-1. The cell is covered by a *membrane* and is filled with a fluid called *cytoplasm*. All nerve cells have a *cell body* or *soma*, which is the largest part of the cell and contains structures vital to the cell's life processes, as well as the cell's *nucleus*. The nucleus contains *chromosomes*, long strands of *deoxyribonucleic acid* (*DNA*) in which distinct segments, called *genes*, code for the production of specific *proteins*. A protein is a chain

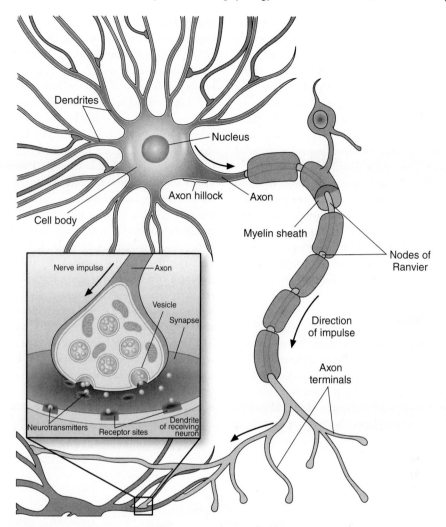

FIGURE 4-1 A prototypical nerve cell. Note that the neuron receives input at its dendrites and cell body through synapses from several other nerve cells. In turn, it synapses onto other nerve cells. The molecules of transmitter normally stored in vesicles in the axon terminals are released into the synaptic cleft in response to the arrival of an action potential. The transmitter molecules diffuse across the synapse and occupy receptor sites on the dendrites and/or cell body of the postsynaptic neuron. These events cause changes in the excitability of the postsynaptic cell membrane, making it either easier (excitation) or more difficult (inhibition) to fire. (Adapted from *Society for Neuroscience Brain Facts,* 2008, p. 7, reprinted with permission.)

of fairly simple building-block molecules called *amino acids*. There are only 22 standard amino acids that link together in varying sequences to create all of the proteins in our body. Eight of these are not produced by the body in sufficient quantities and must be ingested in food. Proteins can be hundreds of amino acids long, but these chains do not form in a straight line. Rather, they fold up into very complex three-dimensional shapes, which allows them to have the sophisticated mechanical properties they need to perform functions such as cell communication, growth, and repair; biochemical reactions; immune system functions; and many more.

Arising from the cell body are several structures. At one end are projections called *dendrites*, which divide into smaller and smaller fibers, reaching out like the roots of a tree to receive messages from up to thousands of other neurons. The *axon* is a long process attached to the cell body at the *axon hillock*, which is located at the opposite end of the cell body from the dendrites. The axon transmits an electrical message (called an *action potential*, to be discussed later in this chapter) to the many other neurons with which it communicates. Sections of the axon may be covered by a layer of fatty material called the *myelin sheath*. The myelin sheath is an extension of a special type of glial cell that wraps and insulates the axon in sections. Uninsulated sections of the axon are called *Nodes of Ranvier*, which play an important role in the conduction of an action potential, as you will see. At the end of the axon are branches containing small bulbous structures called *terminal buttons* or *axon terminals*, the importance of which will also soon become clear.

Resting Potential

If we take two very fine wires called *microelectrodes*, insert one into the intracellular fluid (the cytoplasm inside a neuron) and the other into the extracellular fluid (outside the membrane), and then attach the wires to a *voltmeter* (a device that measures differences in electrical potential energy between two places), we will see that there

is a difference in electrical charge; the inside is slightly negative relative to the outside. This potential difference across the membrane is called the *resting potential* or *membrane potential*, which varies slightly from cell to cell but is usually around −70 millivolts (mV; one millivolt is 1/1,000 volt). This potential difference results from an uneven distribution of ions between the inside and outside of a cell. As discussed in Chapter 1, *ions* are particles that possess an electrical charge, either positive or negative. The ions described in Chapter 1 were usually large drug molecules; those responsible for the resting potential of a cell are ionized molecules of the elements potassium (K^+), sodium (Na^+), and chlorine (which, as an ion, is called chloride, Cl^-), although some larger molecules of negatively charged amino acids (A^-) are also involved.

To understand the resting potential, we need to understand two things: (a) The membrane potential is a relative potential—that is, we are always comparing the inside to the outside of the membrane; and (b) the outside of the membrane is always considered equal to zero. The resting potential exists because the ratio of negative to positive ions is higher inside the cell. Both passive and active processes create this uneven distribution of ions whereby higher concentrations of Na^+ and Cl^- ions exist outside the cell and higher concentrations of K^+ and A^- ions exist inside the cell (see Figure 4-2).

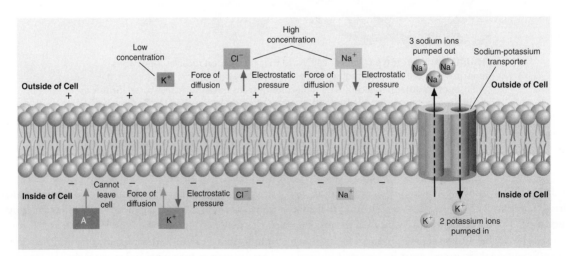

FIGURE 4-2 Passive and active forces produce differential ion distribution across the cell membrane to create the cell's resting potential. The relative size of each box represents the abundance of that ion inside versus outside the cell. An ion pump actively moves potassium ions (K^+) into the cell and sodium ions (Na^+) out of the cell. (Adapted from Carlson, 2011, figs. 2.15 & 2.16, pp. 40, 41, reprinted with permission.)

The first passive process is simple *diffusion*, the tendency for a substance to move down its *concentration gradient*, from an area of higher concentration to an area of lower concentration. Diffusion would force Na^+ and Cl^- ions into the cell and K^+ and A^- ions out of the cell.

The second passive process is *electrostatic charge*, the tendency for similar electrical charges to repel each other and for opposite electrical charges to attract each other. Positive ions (K^+ and Na^+) are repelled by the net positive charge outside the membrane and attracted to the negative charge inside. The reverse is true for negative ions (Cl^- and A^-).

The third passive process involves the *differential permeability* of the cell membrane to particular ions. As we saw in Chapter 1, the cell membrane consists of a lipid bilayer with large proteins embedded in it (see Figure 1-6). In neurons, these large protein molecules serve special functions that make the cells excitable and capable of conveying, storing, and integrating information. These actions are accomplished by the flow of ions across the membrane. The only way ions can move into and out of the cell is through thousands of these specialized protein channels called *ionophores* or *ion channels*. These proteins are often a target of behaviorally active drugs.

Nongated ion channels are always open but are specialized so that only certain ions are permitted to pass through, and then only at a particular rate and with varying ease. K^+ and Cl^- ions cross the cell membrane by easily passing through these channels, but tend to maintain their relative concentrations inside and outside the cell (respectively) because the forces of diffusion and electrostatic charge offset each other, either fully (in the case of Cl^-) or partly (in the case of K^+; there is a slightly greater tendency for K^+ ions to leave the cell). A^- ions are too large to cross the cell membrane and therefore remain trapped inside the cell. Na^+ is forced into the cell, both by diffusion and by electrostatic charge. Why, then, are Na^+ ions more highly concentrated outside the cell? The answer lies in the fourth process at play.

The fourth process is an active one, involving *transporters* or *ion pumps* spanning the cell membrane. These specialized protein molecules selectively move ions from one side of a membrane to another. *Sodium–potassium pumps* transport three Na^+ ions out of the cell for every two K^+ ions they move in, thereby creating an excess of positive ions outside the membrane. Importantly, Na^+ cannot pass easily through ionophores in the cell's membrane, thereby preventing complete reversal of the work carried out by sodium–potassium pumps. However, it should be clear that anything that speeds or slows the passage of ions through the membrane can increase or decrease the resting potential.

There are also channels for Ca^{2+} ions as well as *gated* ion channels, which open and close in response to specific stimuli, but these are not involved in the resting potential and have special functions, described next.

Stimulation of the Axon

GENERATING AN ACTION POTENTIAL. The resting potential of a neuron describes the distribution of ions in the absence of stimulation, but this membrane potential can vary substantially in response to a variety of stimuli. When the membrane potential becomes less negative (i.e., moves toward zero and positive numbers), it is called *depolarization*. When the membrane potential becomes more negative (i.e., moves further away from zero), it is called *hyperpolarization*. Normally, changes in ion distribution are responsible for deviation from the resting potential, but to illustrate the process, we can change the resting potential artificially. We can hyperpolarize a cell by inserting a stimulating microelectrode into a neuron and applying electricity to make the inside even more negative than the outside. The more current we apply, the greater the hyperpolarization. When the current is turned off, the cell returns to its normal resting potential of about -70 mV. We can depolarize the cell by reversing the polarity of the microelectrode and making the inside of the cell less negative with respect to the outside, but depolarizing a neuron can lead to some startling changes. Small amounts of depolarization simply cause the resting potential to decrease. When the electricity is turned off, the normal resting potential returns. But if the neuron is depolarized to about -55 mV, called the *threshold*, the entire resting potential and the processes that maintain it break down. Follow along in Figure 4-3 as this process is explained.

This breakdown occurs because of special gated ion channels that are sensitive to the number of positive charges inside the cell. When the potential difference is reduced beyond the threshold, these *voltage-gated ion channels* open, allowing the free flow of ions across the membrane. First, sodium channels open, and Na^+ ions, which have great difficulty crossing the cell membrane during the resting potential, rush into the cell driven by their concentration gradient and their electrostatic charge. Also embedded in the cell membrane are voltage-gated potassium channels. In comparison to Na^+ channels, the

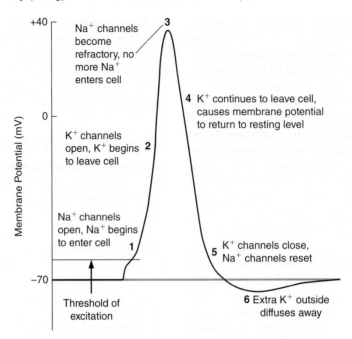

FIGURE 4-3   The flow of ions during an action potential. (Adapted from Carlson, 2011, fig. 2.18, p. 42, reprinted with permission.)

opening of K+ channels requires a greater degree of depolarization. Triggered by the *influx* (inflow) of Na+ ions, K+ channels open and K+ ions rush out of the neuron, driven by their concentration gradient and the transient positive charge created by the influx of Na+ ions. As a result, the resting potential of the membrane is neutralized, and, in fact, the polarity is actually reversed so that the inside of the neuron reaches approximately +40 mV. At this point, Na+ channels close, marking the end of the *rising phase* of the action potential. K+ channels remain open, and the *efflux* (outflow) of K+ continues; this is called the *repolarization phase* of the action potential. K+ channels close gradually, allowing slightly too many K+ ions to leave the cell, resulting in hyperpolarization of the cell membrane. Over time, sodium–potassium pumps restore the cell's resting potential.

This breakdown and restoration of the resting potential is known as an *action potential*, and it occurs very quickly. Some cells are capable of producing and recovering from up to a thousand action potentials each second. The term *firing* is often used to indicate an action potential. It is by means of action potentials that the cells in the nervous system integrate and convey information.

CONDUCTION OF ACTION POTENTIALS ALONG THE MEMBRANE.   An action potential is generated at the section of the neuron's axon that lies adjacent to the axon hillock. But it does not stay there. The Na+ ions that move into the cell through ion channels also move sideways along the inside surface of the membrane. This passive movement, due to diffusion and electric charge, reduces the resting potential of the surrounding membrane—that is, it depolarizes it. This depolarization causes voltage-gated ion channels to open, which, in turn, depolarizes the adjacent section of membrane. Myelinated areas of the axon have no direct contact with extracellular fluid, and, for this reason, Na+ cannot flow into the cell at these sections. However, recall that myelinated axons contain small, uninsulated Nodes of Ranvier. As the axon potential sweeps down the axon, away from the stimulus that produced it, it does so passively underneath sections of myelin sheath and is retriggered or regenerated by the opening of Na+ channels at each Node of Ranvier. We say that action potentials are *nondecremental* because they reach the axon terminal with the same strength as which they were initiated near the axon hillock.

Action potentials are conducted much more quickly along myelinated, compared to unmyelinated, axons as they jump from node to node; this is called *saltatory conduction*. Depending on the type of axon, an action potential can move as fast as 120 meters per second (431 km/hour or 268 miles/hour).

THE ALL-OR-NONE LAW. Action potentials are always the same. As long as a stimulus is strong enough to depolarize a cell to its threshold, an action potential will occur. Increases in the magnitude of the depolarizing stimulus beyond this point will not change the size of the action potential. This principle is known as the *all-or-none law*.

If all action potentials are the same, how does a neuron convey information about the strength of the stimulus depolarizing it? This information is reflected in the rate at which action potentials are generated. If a depolarizing stimulus is applied continuously to a cell, it will cause the cell to produce repeated action potentials. Weaker stimuli will permit the membrane a bit of recovery time, perhaps producing fewer than 100 action potentials per second, whereas stronger stimuli permit less recovery time, perhaps producing 1,000 action potentials per second. Therefore, the stronger the depolarizing stimulus, the faster the membrane will fire. This process, known as the *rate law*, is illustrated in Figure 4-4.

Stimulation of the Dendrites and Cell Body

POSTSYNAPTIC POTENTIALS. What has just been described is what happens if one depolarizes the membrane of an axon. The action potential is invariable in axons because axons have only voltage-gated ion channels and nothing else that can modulate the effect of depolarization. In contrast, the dendrites and cell body contain a great many proteins and enzymes that influence the behavior of ion channels and cell excitability. If you were to insert a microelectrode into the membrane of a dendrite or cell body and disturb the cell's resting potential, the same depolarizing stimulus that caused an action potential in an axon might give rise to very different events, depending on which modulating influences are active. Because the consequence of this disturbance is variable, we refer to depolarization in the cell body and dendrites as *graded* or *postsynaptic potentials* (PSPs), rather than action potentials (PSPs are normally created in membranes located at synapses, which will be discussed later). Postsynaptic potentials arise from the same type of ion flows as action potentials, and they spread across the membrane of a dendrite or cell body in a similar manner. The intensity of PSPs is proportional to the magnitude of the disturbance; however, this intensity decreases as the distance from the site of stimulation lengthens. The region of the axon adjacent to the axon hillock is the place where variable PSPs have the potential to be converted to unvarying action potentials.

EXCITATION. If stimulation of dendrites or the cell body results in the opening of voltage-gated Na^+ channels, Na^+ ions will rush into the cell and the resting potential will move closer to the action potential threshold. In other words, the neuron will be depolarized. This depolarization has a special name: *excitatory postsynaptic potential* (EPSP). With enough EPSPs, the cell may be depolarized past its threshold and create action potentials in its axon. As described earlier, the more the cell is depolarized past its threshold, the faster it will fire.

INHIBITION. If stimulation of dendrites or the cell body results in the opening of voltage-gated K^+ channels, K^+ ions will rush out of the cell and the resting potential will increase; that is, the neuron will be hyperpolarized. As a result, it is harder for the cell to produce action potentials.

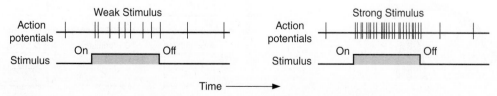

FIGURE 4-4 The rate law. The magnitude of an action potential is always the same. The strength of a stimulus producing an action potential is encoded by the rate at which a neuron fires. (Adapted from Carlson, 2011, fig. 2.20, p. 43, reprinted with permission.)

This type of stimulation is called an *inhibitory postsynaptic potential* (IPSP). IPSPs may also result from the opening of voltage-gated Cl⁻ channels. Recall that, at resting potential, the forces of diffusion and electrostatic charge perfectly offset each other so that Cl⁻ ions maintain their concentration across the membrane. However, if the cell has been depolarized somewhat by EPSPs, the opening of Cl⁻ channels will result in an influx of Cl⁻ ions, thereby offsetting the depolarization caused by the EPSPs.

SUMMATION OF EXCITATION AND INHIBITION. Each PSP, in and of itself, is of very little consequence to a cell. However, neurons integrate the often thousands of concurrent excitatory and inhibitory signals they receive at their many synapses, and this determines the rate at which action potentials will be generated or whether any will be generated at all. There are two major types of integration: (a) *temporal summation* and (b) *spatial summation*.

Temporal summation occurs when a neuron experiences several PSPs closely in time (see Figure 4-5, top panel). In the case of EPSPs, although each one may be too small to initiate an action potential, they may summate and reach threshold. Spatial summation occurs when two or more PSPs occur in close proximity on a neuron. The neuron may have Na⁺ ions entering in some regions (excitation) and Cl⁻ ions entering or K⁺ ions leaving in other regions (inhibition). These local changes in ion distribution may cancel each other out if they are different or add together if they are the same (see Figure 4-5, bottom panel). The net sum of these effects must be able to depolarize

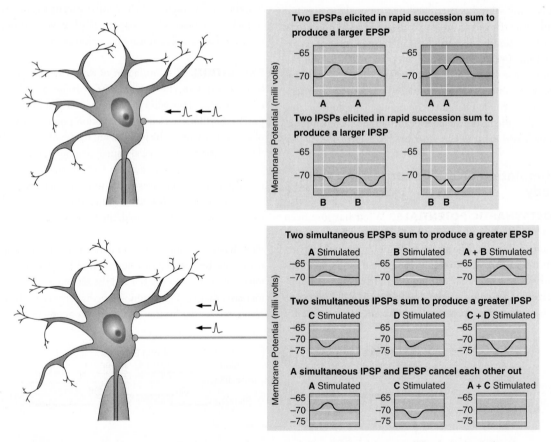

FIGURE 4-5 Temporal and spatial summation of PSPs on a neuronal dendrite or cell body. Temporal summation occurs when a neuron experiences several PSPs closely in time (*top panel*). Spatial summation occurs when two or more PSPs occur in close proximity on a neuron (*bottom panel*).

the cell beyond the threshold if an action potential is to occur.

You may be wondering what determines whether voltage-gated Na^+, K^+, or Cl^- channels will open when the dendrites or cell body of a neuron receive stimulation. Opening of these ion channels is controlled by activation of various receptor subtypes by neurotransmitter chemicals. This complex process will be explained later.

Action Potentials from Sensory Neurons

We have seen how postsynaptic potentials and action potentials are created when a section of a neuron's membrane is depolarized and how, if depolarized past its threshold, an action potential is triggered that moves along an axon. But our discussion thus far has focused on artificially producing disturbances in the cell's membrane by inserting a stimulating microelectrode into the cell. Where do natural action potentials come from?

Action potentials arise in neurons from several sources. One of these is the outside world. Sensory neurons are specialized nerve cells that are depolarized or hyperpolarized by events in the environment. In the skin are neurons whose cell bodies are depolarized by pressure, sending action potentials along their axons into the brain and causing us to experience the sensation of touch. The stronger the stimulation, the greater the depolarization and the faster sensory neurons generate action potentials. The skin also has nerve cells that are specialized to detect heat, cold, and pain. Cells in the ear are depolarized by vibration, and cells in the muscles are depolarized by movement. In fact, all that we know about the outside world comes to our brains in the form of action potentials generated by these specialized receptor neurons.

THE SYNAPSE

We still have not come to the most interesting part: how neurons communicate with one another. A nerve cell is like any other cell in the body; it is completely surrounded by a membrane. In order for the information received from the outside world to get from the sensory receptor neuron to other neurons in the brain, there must be a mechanism by which one cell is able to communicate with another. Electron microscopes reveal that although the membranes of adjacent neurons come

extremely close to each other, their membranes never touch, and there is no way that an action potential on one cell can directly depolarize the membrane of another cell (although this type of conduction does occur in other tissues, such as the heart). The way in which neurons communicate across this gap is of vital interest to behavioral pharmacologists because this process is altered, in one way or another, by many drugs that affect behavior.

Information is transferred between neurons at *synapses*. A synapse, which can be seen in Figure 4-1, occurs where the terminal buttons of one cell (the *presynaptic cell*) intertwine with structures of another cell (the *postsynaptic cell*). Between the presynaptic terminal buttons and the postsynaptic cell is a small gap called the *synaptic cleft*. Synapses are most frequently located between terminal buttons and dendrites (*axodendritic synapses*) or between terminal buttons and cell bodies (*axosomatic synapses*). They may also be located on or near another neuron's axon or terminal buttons (*axoaxonic synapses*), thereby allowing one neuron to modulate another neuron's influence on the postsynaptic cell.

Action at a Synapse

NEUROTRANSMITTERS. Another very important feature of the synapse is the presence of *synaptic vesicles* within terminal buttons. These are spherical structures, of which there may be a few hundred or nearly a million, each containing chemicals called *neurotransmitters* that undergo *exocytosis* (i.e., release from the vesicles into the synaptic cleft) in response to an action potential. Synaptic vesicles are more densely packed in the *release zone* of the terminal button where there also exist many voltage-gated calcium (Ca^{2+}) channels. Upon arrival of an action potential, these channels open, permitting an influx of Ca^{2+} ions into the terminal button. Ca^{2+} influx triggers the movement and fusion of synaptic vesicles with the presynaptic membrane and the exocytosis of neurotransmitter. Neurotransmitter molecules diffuse across the cleft where they come in contact with the membrane of the postsynaptic cell.

There are places in the brain where neurotransmitters are not released directly at synapses, but rather are secreted from regions along the axon in the general vicinity of a number of cells and diffuse to their synapses where they influence the activity of many cells at the same time. Such release is usually long lasting compared to the brief impulses of activity at synapses. Thus, the excitability of entire brain systems can be modulated.

NEUROMODULATORS. A *neuromodulator* is a chemical that is synthesized and released by neurons and that modulates the effects of neurotransmitters. It may have short- or long-term effects. Neuromodulators may act within the postsynaptic cell, or they may also have an effect on the presynaptic cell to modify the release of a neurotransmitter. Neuromodulators are typically released in greater amounts and travel further distances, compared to neurotransmitters. Substances that act as neurotransmitters in one synapse may also act as neuromodulators of transmission at a different synapse.

RECEPTORS. Recall that much of the machinery needed for cell communication is molecules of protein. A *receptor* or *receptor complex* is a specialized protein that spans the membrane of the postsynaptic cell and contains a binding site to which a specific neurotransmitter molecule can briefly attach, much like a key fitting into a lock. When a neurotransmitter with the correct configuration (the key) attaches to a receptor (the lock), the receptor changes its shape (we sometimes say the receptor has been activated). This reconfiguration alters the functioning of the cell, causing certain events to occur such as a shift in its resting potential or a change in its biochemistry.

Given that the lock-and-key analogy has become the standard way of illustrating neurotransmitter–receptor binding, one would think that each neurotransmitter molecule must have only one receptor to which it can bind. This is not the case. As you will see in the Neurotransmitters section later in this chapter, there are often many different receptor *subtypes* to which a particular neurotransmitter molecule can bind. These subtypes often exist in different regions of the brain, and their activation can produce varying effects in the cell. In this way, a single neurotransmitter can produce a variety of results. Such changes can be brought on directly or indirectly.

IONOTROPIC RECEPTORS. In some synapses, postsynaptic receptor proteins contain binding sites directly connected to a gated ion channel; these are called *ionotropic receptors* (see Figure 4-6, top panel). Neurotransmitter binding activates the receptor, leading to a reconfiguration of the protein so that the ion channel opens or closes and there is an influx or efflux of particular ions. Depending on the ion channel, this could either increase or decrease the resting potential of the membrane. This effect occurs very rapidly, in the order of milliseconds, and lasts only briefly.

METABOTROPIC RECEPTORS. In other cases, the effects of receptor activation are indirect, initiating a cascade of events that occur more slowly and are longer lasting. The binding sites on *metabotropic receptors* are not directly connected to an ion channel. Instead, receptor sites are situated on the extracellular portion of a long protein that weaves its way back and forth seven times across the cell membrane, like a snake (this is called a seven-helix structure; see Figure 4-6, bottom panel). The intracellular portion of the signal protein is linked to another specialized structure called a G protein (short for *guanine nucleotide-binding protein*). When a neurotransmitter molecule binds to its receptor, a subunit (portion) of the G protein breaks away. The subunit may travel a short distance inside the cell's membrane to activate a nearby ion channel, thus stimulating an EPSP or IPSP. Or, the subunit may initiate a biochemical (enzymatic) reaction that leads to the synthesis of another molecule called a *second messenger* (neurotransmitters are considered first messengers).

SECOND MESSENGERS. Second messengers can do a number of things inside the postsynaptic cell (follow along in Figure 4-7). The best known second messenger is *cyclic adenosine monophosphate* or *cyclic AMP* (cAMP). Another common second messenger is *cyclic guanosine monophosphate* or *cyclic GMP* (cGMP). Often, a second messenger interacts with gated ion channels from inside the cell, with similar but more long-lasting effects to those of directly gated ion channels. Or, the second messenger can alter the operation of nongated ion channels in a way that changes the resting potential or the cell's sensitivity to other stimuli.

An Ionotropic Receptor

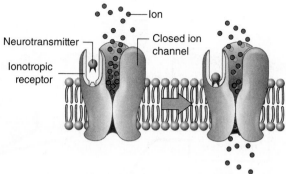

Some neurotransmitter molecules bind to receptors on ion channels. When a neurotransmitter molecule binds to an ionotropic receptor, the channel opens (as in this case) or closes, thereby altering the flow of ions into or out of the neuron.

A Metabotropic Receptor

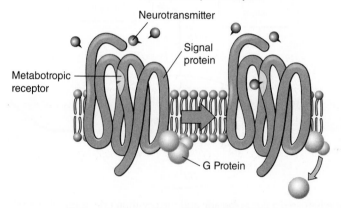

Some neurotransmitter molecules bind to receptors on membrane signal proteins, which are linked to G proteins. When a neurotransmitter molecule binds to a metabotropic receptor, a subunit of the G protein breaks off into the neuron and either binds to an ion channel or stimulates the synthesis of a second messenger.

FIGURE 4-6 Ionotropic and metabotropic receptors (Adapted from Pinel, 2011, fig. 4.12, p. 89, reprinted with permission.)

Second messengers may also have even longer-term or permanent effects because they activate a type of protein called a *kinase*. For example, cAMP activates *protein kinase A*, whereas cGMP activates *protein kinase G*. A kinase is much more persistent than a second messenger and can remain active for many minutes or even for hours. Kinases alter the functioning of both ion channels and receptors, but they do so for a much longer time than second messengers. Kinases also influence many other regulatory processes in the cell, including the release of second messengers from other receptors and the efficiency of ion pumps.

Kinases may also activate (phosphorylate) transcription factors such as *CREB* and *c-fos*. Genes in the cell nucleus have switches that can turn them on or off. These switches are turned on and off by chemicals called *transcription factors*. Whether a particular gene is active at any given time is determined by the

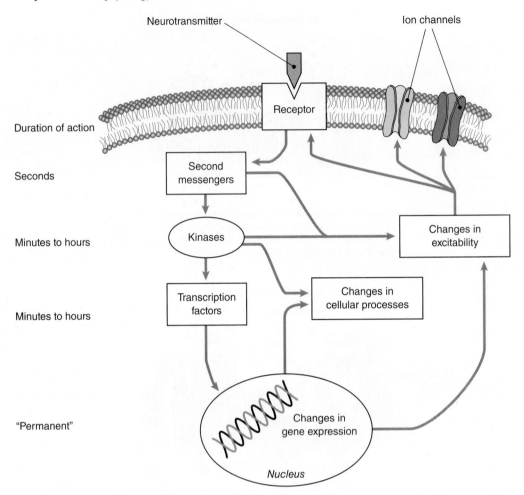

FIGURE 4-7   The relation between a signal cascade and the resulting effects on cell excitability. As the cascade progresses, the duration of the effect increases. No matter how many steps there are in the cascade and how long those steps are active, all the alterations have common end points. Every change in excitability is the result of alterations to ion channels or receptors or of a change in the biochemical processes of the cell.

presence or absence of particular transcription factors. Thus, when kinases activate transcription factors, they are controlling the expression of particular genes in the cell. Genes contain the code for the order in which amino acids need to be strung together to create a particular protein, and the process of creating these proteins from the genetic code is called *transcription*. The proteins created by the DNA could be receptor sites, ion channels, ion pumps, or any of the other molecules used by the cell in receiving and transmitting information, or they could be transcription factors for other

genes. Thus, a transcription factor may turn on the gene that makes receptor sites for a given transmitter. With more receptor sites, the cell will become more sensitive to that neurotransmitter. In the same way, some ion channels may become more numerous, and others may become less numerous. Second messengers (via kinases and transcription factors) can even cause a synapse to be made or removed, thus permanently altering the connections of a cell. Changes in neuron excitation or sensitivity that arise from changes in gene expression can be very long lasting and are thought to be responsible for the formation and storage of memories in the brain.

Presynaptic Effects of Neurotransmitters

AUTORECEPTORS. Receptor sites for neurotransmitters are located not only on the postsynaptic neuron but also on the presynaptic neuron. Some of these are called *autoreceptors*. These metabotropic receptors provide feedback on the amount of neurotransmitter released in the synaptic cleft in order to regulate its levels through the activity of G proteins and second messengers. If levels of the neurotransmitter get too high, the autoreceptors will cause a reduction in the synthesis and release of the transmitter. It is believed that a mechanism such as this causes a delay in the effectiveness of some psychotherapeutic drugs, such as antidepressant medications (see Chapter 13). Antidepressants produce a buildup of crucial neurotransmitters, but autoreceptors detect this excess and reduce production and release of the neurotransmitter molecules, thus blocking the effectiveness of the drug. It sometimes takes a few weeks to exhaust the autoreceptors before the drug can make changes in the functioning of the synapse.

HETERORECEPTORS. The release of neurotransmitters from the presynaptic cell to alter the excitability of a postsynaptic cell is the most common and best-understood mechanism by which cells communicate, but it is not the only mechanism. In addition to autoreceptors, the presynaptic cell contains *heteroreceptors*. These are metabotropic receptor sites that function very similarly to autoreceptors except that they respond not to the release of neurotransmitter by the cell upon which they reside, but to chemicals released by the postsynaptic cell or other nearby cells when they become depolarized. This transmission of chemical information from a postsynaptic to presynaptic cell is termed *retrograde signaling* and is thought to be a mechanism through which the postsynaptic neuron can modulate its level of stimulation by altering neurotransmitter synthesis and release by the presynaptic neuron. This is called *depolarization-induced suppression of excitation* (DSE) or *depolarization-induced suppression of inhibition* (DSI), depending on whether activity of the synapse was excitatory or inhibitory. In fact, receptors for THC

are located presynaptically and respond to a chemical released by the postsynaptic neuron (see Chapter 14).

Terminating Synaptic Action

After the arrival of an action potential at the terminal button initiates the release of a transmitter into the synaptic cleft, it is important to have some mechanism by which to rid the transmitter from the cleft. Otherwise, the transmitter would stay in the cleft and continue to influence the postsynaptic cell. Every synapse has a system to accomplish this purpose and does so in one of two ways: (a) The presynaptic cell may quickly reabsorb the intact neurotransmitter molecule, taking it back into the cytoplasm of the terminal button where it gets repackaged into vesicles (which also get recycled) for future use. This is the most common process. It is called *reuptake* and is accomplished by a specialized mechanism that actively employs *transporter protein* molecules embedded in the membrane of the presynaptic cell. New research suggests that glial cells are also actively involved in the reuptake of neurotransmitter (specifically, glutamate, described later in this chapter); (b) The synapse may contain an enzyme, produced in and released from the same neuron as the neurotransmitter. This process, called *enzymatic degradation* or *deactivation*, breaks the neurotransmitter into its precursors (constituent parts), which may also be taken back into the presynaptic cell to be remanufactured for future release.

THE NERVOUS SYSTEM

The nervous system can be divided into various parts, but the most basic distinction is between the *central nervous system* (CNS) and the *peripheral nervous system* (PNS). The CNS is made up of the brain and spinal cord, and the PNS is everything outside the brain and spinal cord. In both systems, neurons are organized in a similar manner; cell bodies tend to be located together in clusters, and the axons from these cells also tend to bundle together to form a pathway connecting to other clusters of cell bodies. We find, therefore, that the nervous system is made up of groups of cell bodies with bundles of axons running between them. In the PNS, these groups of cell bodies are called *ganglia* (singular is *ganglion*), and the bundles of axons are called *nerves*. In the CNS, the cell body groups are called *nuclei* (singular is *nucleus*) or *centers*, and the bundles of axons are called *tracts*. Because axons are generally covered with myelin, which is white, the nerves and tracts are called *white matter*. The unmyelinated cell bodies are called *gray matter*.

The PNS

The PNS may be further divided into two functional units: (a) the *somatic nervous system* and (b) the *autonomic nervous system*.

SOMATIC NERVOUS SYSTEM. The somatic nervous system is the means by which the brain and spinal cord receive information from, and allow us to interact with, our environment. It is made up of sensory nerves that convey information from the senses to the CNS, such as the nerves running from the sensory receptors in the eyes, ears, and skin. The somatic nervous system also contains the motor nerves, which have their cell bodies in the spinal cord and send axons directly to glands or *striated muscles* (muscles over which we normally have voluntary control). The motor nerves control these muscles at neuromuscular junctions, which are very much like synapses. Acetylcholine (ACh) is the transmitter at most neuromuscular junctions, and the receptor sites are of the nicotinic cholinergic type. You will learn more about acetylcholine and many other chemical transmitters and their receptor subtypes in the upcoming section on Neurotransmitters. The somatic nervous system also includes the *cranial nerves*, which are attached to the undersurface of the brain. Mostly, these nerves convey motor commands and/or sensory information to and from areas of the face and neck.

AUTONOMIC NERVOUS SYSTEM. Whereas the somatic nervous system usually carries information into the CNS from our conscious senses, the autonomic nervous system is concerned with sensory information that we are usually unaware of: information about blood pressure and blood gases, the functioning of organs, and levels of hormones. Whereas the somatic system usually commands muscles over which we have voluntary control, the autonomic nervous system commands the muscles of the heart and intestines, the secretions of glands, and other regulatory systems over which we normally have no conscious control.

The autonomic nervous system is actually divided into two distinct divisions that control the body's organs and glands in a highly coordinated balancing act (these divisions can be seen in Figure 4-8). The division that is dominant and in control most of the time is called the *parasympathetic division*. It generally keeps the internal functioning of the body running smoothly, in a *rest-and-digest* mode of operation. The other autonomic nervous system division, called the *sympathetic division*, is connected to the same internal organs as the parasympathetic division. In times of stress and danger, it takes over from the parasympathetic division to prepare the body for a sudden expenditure of energy, as is required for fighting or running. Blood is directed away from the digestive system to the arms and legs, the pupils dilate, and heart and breathing rates increase. This series of changes is called the *fight-or-flight response*, which is energetically expensive and taxing on the body. Therefore, once danger has passed, control of the body's organs and glands is once again taken over by the parasympathetic division to restore a relaxed, balanced state.

The parasympathetic and sympathetic divisions of the autonomic nervous system are anatomically, functionally, and neurochemically distinct. Cell bodies of parasympathetic neurons originate in the sacral region of the spinal cord and in nuclei of the cranial nerves (especially the vagus nerve, which, unlike the other cranial nerves, controls the visceral organs); cell bodies of the sympathetic division originate in the thoracic and lumbar regions of the spinal cord. The parasympathetic system uses ACh as a transmitter to control glands and muscles. Consequently, drugs that alter transmission at cholinergic synapses interfere with parasympathetic functioning. Perhaps the best example of such drugs is atropine, which is a cholinergic muscarinic blocker, otherwise called an *anticholinergic*. Atropine has been used by optometrists to dilate the pupils in the eye so that the retina at the back of the eye can be examined. When atropine is placed in the eye, it blocks the receptor sites at parasympathetic neuromuscular junctions. Because the parasympathetic division can no longer control the size of the pupil, it dilates. The muscles that control the eye's lens are also under parasympathetic control, so the atropine also makes vision blurry. Some drugs, such as the tricyclic antidepressants

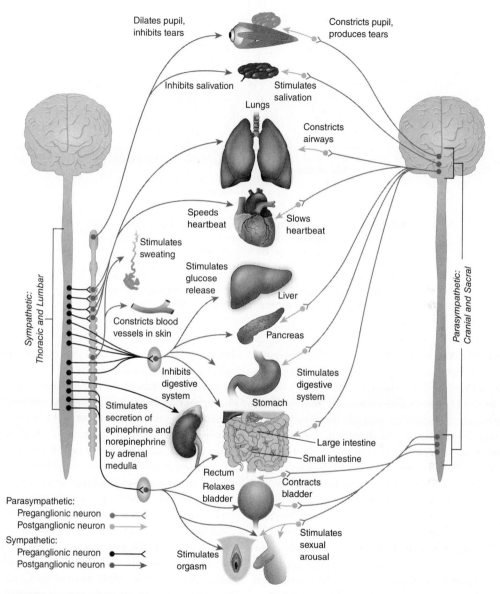

Dilates pupil, inhibits tears

Constricts pupil, produces tears

Inhibits salivation

Stimulates salivation

Lungs

Constricts airways

Speeds heartbeat

Slows heartbeat

Stimulates sweating

Stimulates glucose release

Liver

Constricts blood vessels in skin

Pancreas

Inhibits digestive system

Stimulates digestive system

Stomach

Stimulates secretion of epinephrine and norepinephrine by adrenal medulla

Large intestine

Small intestine

Rectum

Relaxes bladder

Contracts bladder

Sympathetic: Thoracic and Lumbar

Parasympathetic: Cranial and Sacral

Parasympathetic:
Preganglionic neuron
Postganglionic neuron
Sympathetic:
Preganglionic neuron
Postganglionic neuron

Stimulates orgasm

Stimulates sexual arousal

FIGURE 4-8 Roles of the sympathetic (*left*) and parasympathetic (*right*) divisions of the autonomic nervous system. (Adapted from Carlson, 2011, fig. 3.23, p. 84, reprinted with permission.)

and antipsychotics (see Chapters 12 and 13), have anticholinergic side effects that include blurred vision and dry mouth.

The primary transmitter in the sympathetic system is epinephrine (adrenaline). In times of stress, the adrenal glands secrete epinephrine into the blood, directly stimulating receptors in the sympathetic division and causing the fight-or-flight response. Drugs such as amphetamine

and cocaine that stimulate adrenergic synapses will also cause sympathetic arousal, such as increased heart rate and blood sugar.

The CNS

SPINAL CORD. The CNS has two basic parts: the *brain* and the *spinal cord*. Some integration of

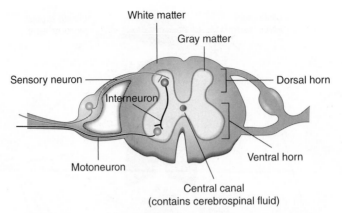

FIGURE 4-9   A cross section of the spinal cord, showing the white matter and gray matter. Axons of sensory nerves come in through the dorsal horn (toward the back) and form synapses in the gray matter. Cell bodies in the ventral horn (toward the front) send axons to the muscles out the ventral side of the cord. The white matter consists of bundles or tracts of myelinated axons running between the brain and different parts of the body.

information and reflex activity goes on within the spinal cord, but it functions primarily as a relay station. The spinal cord transmits information from sensory nerves to the brain and carries motor commands from the brain to the muscles. The central part of the spinal cord is composed of gray matter and shaped, in cross section, somewhat like a butterfly, as seen in Figure 4-9. It is made up of cell bodies and synapses with *interneurons*, which help coordinate sensory and motor behavior. Axons from sensory nerves enter the gray matter of the spinal cord from the side nearest the back (the *dorsal* side), and motor axons leaving the spinal cord do so from the side nearest the front (the *ventral* side). The *ventral horn* of the gray matter of the spinal cord contains the cell bodies of the *motoneurons*, the neurons that directly control the action of muscles. This area also mediates many reflexes. The *dorsal horn* contains cells that convey sensory information. Surrounding the gray matter are a number of tracts of axons running both up and down the spinal cord, connecting the brain to various parts of the body.

BRAIN.   It has been estimated that the human brain contains 10^{11} (i.e., 100 billion) neurons. On average, each neuron has synapses on 1,000 other neurons and receives an average of 10,000 synapses (Costa, 1985).

For many years, it was thought that the number of brain cells was fixed at birth and that cells were lost as aging progressed. We now know that new nerve cells can form throughout life in species as diverse as canaries, rats, and humans. However, not all areas of the brain experience *neurogenesis*, the birth of new neurons. In adult humans, neurogenesis occurs only in a couple of distinct areas: (a) a region of the *hippocampus* involved in the formation of new memories (Eriksson et al., 1998; you will learn more about the hippocampus later in this chapter); and (b) the *subventricular zone* (which lines the walls of the brain's lateral ventricles, cerebrospinal-filled cavities) from which new neurons migrate to the *olfactory bulbs*, involved in the sense of smell (Curtis et al., 2007; Doetsch et al., 1999). Most of the CNS is able to restructure and reorganize its connections during learning and development, and repair itself to some degree following injury—we call this *neuroplasticity*—but neurogenesis is a special case indeed.

The brain is a complicated structure made up of numerous nuclei and complex fiber tracts connecting those nuclei. For this reason, the brain has been called a "great raveled knot." In recent years, neuroscientists have made great strides in unraveling the knot, but it still contains many mysteries and is the subject of intensive study. The brain is too complex a structure to be explained in a simple fashion, but we will introduce some of the features that appear to be important in an understanding of many drug effects. Figure 4-10 illustrates the brain and identifies some of its structures.

Hindbrain Structures

MEDULLA OBLONGATA. The area at the base of the brain, where the spinal cord arises, is called the *medulla oblongata* (or just the *medulla*). It is, in part, made up of fiber tracts running to and from the spinal cord and connecting to higher centers in the brain, such as the motor cortex (an area involved in commanding motor activity; you will learn more about this later in this chapter). In addition, the medulla contains part of the *descending reticular formation* (to be discussed shortly), which consists of numerous nuclei that act as control centers for the autonomic nervous system. Therefore, proper functioning of the autonomic nervous system depends on the general level of arousal in the medulla. These control centers regulate consciousness as well as heart rate, blood pressure, breathing, muscle tone, and even reflexes such as coughing, swallowing, sneezing, and vomiting. The respiratory center, which controls breathing, is very sensitive to many drugs. Barbiturates,

opioids, and alcohol depress this center and, consequently, depress breathing. Death from a drug overdose is usually a result of suffocation because the respiratory center becomes depressed to the point where breathing stops. Quite often people who survive drug overdoses have brain damage because low oxygen levels in their blood resulted from extended depression of their respiratory center.

The vomiting center, which is named the *area postrema*, is also sensitive to drugs. This center is one of very few areas in the brain that is not shielded by the blood–brain barrier. It is therefore able to monitor the blood for toxins and can initiate vomiting, presumably to rid the digestive system of a poison that has just been ingested. Some drugs, such as opiates and nicotine, stimulate this center and cause nausea and vomiting even though the drug was inhaled or injected.

PONS. The pons (Latin for *bridge*) is a large bulbous structure located in the hindbrain, above the medulla. It too contains nuclei of the reticular formation that play a role in sleep and arousal. The pons also bridges and refines motor commands conveyed between parts of the cortex (including the motor cortex) and the cerebellum (see next). The pathway between the cortex, pons, and

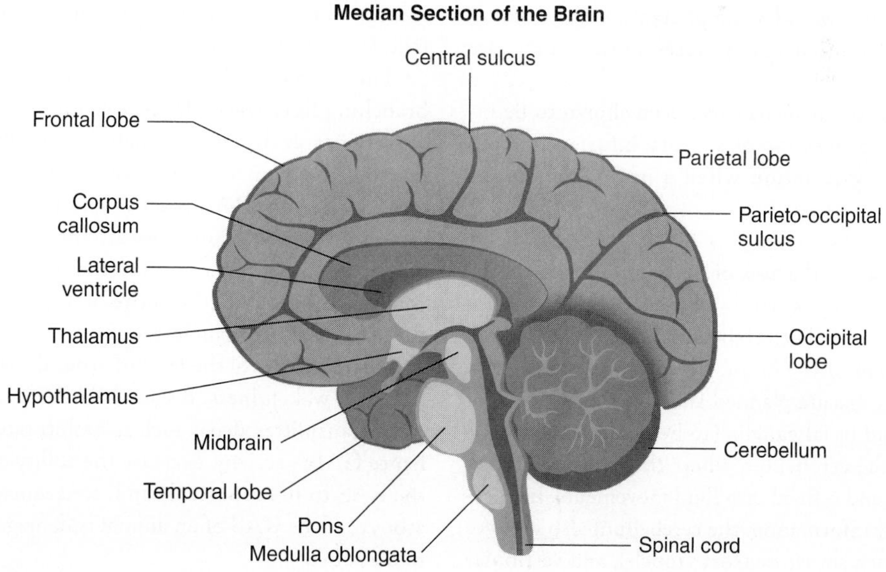

Median Section of the Brain

Central sulcus

Frontal lobe

Corpus callosum

Lateral ventricle

Thalamus

Hypothalamus

Midbrain

Temporal lobe

Pons

Medulla oblongata

Parietal lobe

Parieto-occipital sulcus

Occipital lobe

Cerebellum

Spinal cord

FIGURE 4-10 A cross section of a human brain. Note the locations of some of the structures mentioned in the text.

cerebellum is a superhighway of motor information, containing about 20 million axons.

The *locus coeruleus* is a group of cell bodies residing in the pons. It receives input from many sources, both inside and outside the CNS, and projects its axons diffusely to areas you will soon become more familiar with, such as other hindbrain regions, the thalamus, limbic system, cortex, and other higher-brain centers, as well as to the cerebellum and spinal cord. Its synapses use norepinephrine as a transmitter (more about this in the Neurotransmitters section). It is believed that the locus coeruleus contains about 50% to 70% of the norepinephrine-containing neurons in the brain. This system, along with several other similar systems (such as the serotonin-containing raphe nuclei, described later in this chapter), projects to higher-brain centers through a pathway called the *medial forebrain bundle*. Depression is associated with abnormal functioning of these systems.

Activity of the locus coeruleus is controlled by a large inhibitory input of synapses that release the neurotransmitter GABA. Activity in the locus coeruleus is associated with arousal, fear, panic, and anger. *Positron emission tomography* (PET), a brain imaging technique, shows that the locus coeruleus and brain areas to which it projects become highly active during a panic attack. Drugs like the benzodiazepines (e.g., Valium), which increase the inhibitory effects of GABA, relieve anxiety (see Chapter 7), and drugs like amphetamine and cocaine, which stimulate adrenergic synapses, cause anxiety (see Chapter 10).

The locus coeruleus has also been shown to be involved in the processing of sensory information and has an alerting function when a novel stimulus is experienced.

CEREBELLUM. At the back of the brain, attached to the dorsal side of the pons, sits a structure called the *cerebellum* ("little brain"). The cerebellum functions primarily as a component of the brain's extensive motor system. Voluntary actions are planned and initiated by parts of the cortex and basal ganglia (to be discussed shortly) and sent to the cerebellum where they are integrated, coordinated, and refined into fluid movements. In addition to motor information, the cerebellum also receives visual, auditory, somatosensory (touch), and vestibular (balance) information from the cortex, as well as information regarding movement of the muscles sent through the spinal cord. It integrates all of this information and sends signals back to the motor cortex, via a structure called the thalamus, to modify motor commands. These feedback loops make smooth and accurate muscle movements possible. The cerebellum also helps maintain posture, fine-tunes the timing of movements, smoothes eye movement as focus shifts from one fixation point to another, and is important for procedural memory; that is, the learning and memory of movements, such as how to ride a bike. People with damage to the cerebellum are slow and clumsy and often appear to be intoxicated with alcohol. It is quite likely that many of the motor effects of alcohol are due to a specific effect on the cerebellum.

Midbrain Structures

RETICULAR FORMATION. The reticular formation is a diffuse system consisting of more than 110 individual nuclei located in the core of the brainstem. As mentioned earlier, some of these nuclei project axons downward, into the spinal cord; this is referred to as the *descending reticular formation*. These projections are involved in autonomic nervous system activity (e.g., breathing and heart rate), reflexes (e.g., coughing and swallowing), as well as posture, balance, and motor movement. In addition, some nuclei of the reticular formation project axons upward, through the thalamus and into the cortex; this is referred to as the *ascending reticular formation* or the *reticular activating system* (RAS).

The RAS contains numerous centers with widely branching fiber tracts. It receives input from axons of sensory nerves that run through the reticular formation on their way from a sense organ to sensory areas of the cortex. Thus, the RAS is activated by incoming stimulation and projects axons forward into the entire cortex and higher parts of the brain so that when the RAS becomes active, so does the entire brain. One function of the RAS is to maintain levels of activation in the cortex and thereby control the level of arousal, selective attention, and wakefulness. Because GABA is an inhibitory neurotransmitter, drugs such as barbiturates, which enhance GABA activity, decrease the ability of neurons in the RAS to fire repeatedly and, consequently, decrease arousal. If the RAS of an animal is damaged, it will fall into a coma.

One subset of nuclei located within the reticular formation is referred to as the *raphe nuclei* or *raphe system*, some of which project downward, to the lower hindbrain and spinal cord, and some upward, to the thalamus, limbic system, and cortex. Unlike the RAS, artificial stimulation of some raphe nuclei causes sleep and damage to them produces an animal that seldom sleeps. This finding shows that sleep is not just a lack of stimulation in the RAS but an active process as well. Most raphe nuclei use serotonin as a neurotransmitter, and drugs that alter serotonin activity also seem to interfere with sleep.

PERIAQUEDUCTAL GRAY (PAG). The PAG is involved in pain sensation and in defensive behavior. The PAG serves as one of several relays for axons that carry pain signals from the dorsal horn of the spinal cord to the cortex. Stimulation of the PAG causes an immediate loss of pain sensation (analgesia). This is because the PAG is rich in receptor sites for opioid drugs (e.g., morphine) and their endogenous counterparts, endorphins and enkephalins (you will learn more about these in the Neurotransmitters section of this chapter and in Chapter 11 on Opioids). These neurons send axons to the raphe nuclei of the hindbrain, which, in turn, project downward to release serotonin in the spinal cord, indirectly stimulating further release of endorphins in the spinal cord, inhibiting pain. Thus, opioid drugs can block pain by stimulating cells in the PAG and the spinal cord.

Also located in the PAG is a system that has been described as a "punishment" system. These are sites where electrical stimulation appears to have a punishing effect on experimental animals. Animals will learn to perform a task in order to avoid stimulation in this area. It has not been determined whether the pain perception and the punishment functions of these systems are related, but it is certainly tempting to speculate that they are. The PAG also receives input from a limbic structure called the *amygdala*, a center that mediates fear and fear conditioning.

SUBSTANTIA NIGRA. The substantia nigra is a motor area of the brain, which is highly interconnected with another motor region, the basal ganglia (to be described shortly). Cell bodies that reside in the substantia nigra produce the neurotransmitter dopamine (DA); degeneration of these cells is associated with Parkinson's disease. You will learn more about this structure and dopamine in the upcoming Neurotransmitter section.

VENTRAL TEGMENTAL AREA (VTA). The VTA is a vital component of the brain's reward circuit, for both natural and drug reinforcers. It is the site of origin for a projection pathway called the *medial forebrain bundle*. The VTA contains cell bodies of dopamine-producing neurons that project to and release dopamine in multiple regions of the brain, including the thalamus; hypothalamus; substantia nigra; nucleus accumbens; areas of the limbic system including the hippocampus, septal nuclei, and amygdala; and the prefrontal cortex (information on unfamiliar brain areas is upcoming in this chapter). Stimulation of the medial forebrain bundle projection that runs between the VTA and the nucleus accumbens is associated with pleasure and has been implicated in drug euphoria and addiction, as well as in schizophrenia (see Chapter 12). In addition to dopamine, the VTA also contains neurons that produce GABA (Olson & Nestler, 2007) and glutamate (Yamaguchi, Sheen, & Morales, 2007), which regulate dopamine neuron activity and send projections to other brain regions.

Forebrain Structures

BASAL GANGLIA. The basal ganglia (*basal* means "at the base of"; *ganglia* refers to a group of cell bodies) are located just under the cortex and are important in controlling voluntary movement, action selection and switching between motor behaviors, motor habits, and eye movement. In addition to motor actions, the basal ganglia control some cognitive processes such as memory for locations in space and classical conditioning of behaviors. Given the wide variety of functions they control, it is not surprising that the basal ganglia contain several interconnected nuclei. The *striatum* (also called the *neostriatum*) is the largest component of the basal ganglia and is the major input center for information from the cortex and thalamus. The striatum can be subdivided as follows: the *dorsal striatum* includes the *caudate nucleus*, the *putamen*, and the *fundus*, which links them; the *ventral striatum* includes the *olfactory tubercule* and the *nucleus accumbens*, which you recall is part of the medial forebrain bundle—the brain's pleasure pathway. Projections from the striatum are sent to the *globus pallidus* (or *pallidum*), which is the output side of the basal ganglia. The globus pallidus projects to an additional component of the basal ganglia, called the *subthalamic nucleus*, and also sends projections back, via the thalamus, to a motor area of the cortex. Together, the basal ganglia, the thalamus, and the cortex make up the "motor loop" and control all voluntary movement. You may read other texts or papers that consider the substantia nigra to be part of the basal ganglia. It is, as you have learned, located in the midbrain but is highly interconnected with the basal ganglia and is therefore sometimes considered a substructure.

Parkinson's disease is the result of a malfunction of the basal ganglia, specifically a depletion of dopamine release in the dorsal striatum due to the death of dopamine cells originating in the substantia nigra. This pathway is known as the *nigrostriatal system*; you will learn more about it in the Neurotransmitters section on dopamine. People suffering from Parkinson's disease have tremors, rigidity in the limbs, and difficulty initiating movement. In many people, the symptoms of Parkinson's disease can be alleviated if the patient is given DOPA (or *L-dopa*), the metabolic precursor of dopamine. Unlike dopamine, which cannot pass through the blood–brain barrier, DOPA is taken into the brain and transformed into dopamine, which then increases activity at these synapses in the basal ganglia. We also know that drugs like the antipsychotics, which block DA receptors, have side effects that resemble Parkinson's disease (see Chapter 12).

By now, you have read about quite a number of brain structures that participate in the planning, execution, and refinement of motor movements. In the section on the cortex, you will encounter what might be considered the most important of these structures—the motor cortex. The system that connects the motor cortex to the muscles is called the *pyramidal motor system*; consequently, the system involving the basal ganglia and substantia nigra is called the *extrapyramidal motor system*.

LIMBIC SYSTEM. The limbic system is quite possibly the most difficult brain system to describe, mainly because of varying opinions as to which of the hundreds of complexly interconnected nuclei truly belong in this category. The many structures that form the limbic system integrate such vast processes as learning, memory, emotion, motivation, and executive functions including decision making and planning. They are a target for a variety of drugs.

Early neuroanatomists defined the limbic system as a looped circuit that included the *hippocampus, mammillary bodies* (located in the *hypothalamus*), *thalamus,* and *cingulate gyrus*. In the past 50 or so years, many more structures have been included in this seemingly ever-expanding megasystem. Many of these are areas of the

cortex, including, but not limited to, the *insular cortex, orbitofrontal cortex, dorsolateral prefrontal cortex, subcallosal gyrus,* and *parahippocampal gyrus.* Others are areas below the cortex, including, but not limited to, the *olfactory bulb, amygdala, septal nuclei,* and *fornix.* The nucleus accumbens, which you recall forms part of the ventral striatum of the basal ganglia, and the ventral tegmental area, which is a midbrain structure, may also be considered part of the limbic system due to their intricate connections and extensive communication with other limbic structures. In addition, the hypothalamus is considered by many to be part of the limbic system. All of these structures communicate extensively with each other and with other structures outside of limbic system circuitry. As you can see, this megasystem can be quite confusing. But if we try to imagine separating memory from emotion or motivation from learning, the intertwined circuitry of the limbic system makes sense.

We will not discuss all areas of the limbic system (some of its structures can be seen in Figure 4-11). The nucleus accumbens and ventral tegmental area have been discussed already, and some important areas of the cortex will be discussed in the next section. In this section, we will review the functions of only two limbic system structures: the hippocampus and the amygdala. The thalamus and hypothalamus will be discussed next as additional forebrain structures; keep in mind, however, that they communicate extensively with the limbic system.

The *hippocampus* is a large limbic structure, located beneath the cortex in the temporal lobe (see Cortex section that follows shortly). It plays important roles in learning and memory. Removal of the hippocampus in humans (as was done years ago to treat epilepsy) causes amnesia, particularly for the more recent events of one's past, and an inability to form new declarative memories. The hippocampus is also important for spatial memory. In rats, destruction of the hippocampus prevents learning of even a very simple maze, such as an open field with no walls. In individuals who have experienced stress for prolonged periods (or have posttraumatic stress disorder), the size of the hippocampus is reduced, likely due to the detrimental effects caused by stress hormones, which bind to receptors there. The hippocampus is highly interconnected with another limbic region, the amygdala.

Most drugs have effects on the hippocampus, although they can be difficult to spot in traditional behavioral tests. Drug effects on the hippocampus may be related to

Limbic System

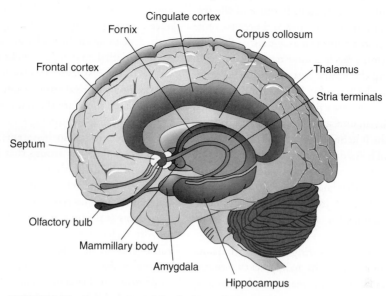

FIGURE 4-11 Components of the limbic system.

state-dependent learning. Place preference, created by associating a place with a drug (discussed in Chapter 2), is also mediated, at least in part, by the hippocampus.

Like the hippocampus, the *amygdala* sits below the cortex in the temporal lobe. It is implicated in the processing of emotions, especially negative emotions such as fear and rage; in the formation of emotional memory; and in behavioral reactivity, especially aggression. Like other limbic structures, the amygdala is highly interconnected with many brain regions. It receives sensory information from the cortex as well as information about pain and stress levels. Many studies have found hyperactivity of the amygdala in individuals with posttraumatic stress disorder (Hughes & Shin, 2011). Destruction of the amygdala causes a normally aggressive animal to become calm and placid. In humans, amygdala damage reduces stress responsivity and prevents emotional reaction to memories. Amygdalectomy (removal of the amygdala) was once a court-ordered procedure in the United States for particularly violent prison inmates; they became much more docile following surgery. Stimulation of an animal's amygdala elicits aggression and attack against other animals or even objects in the vicinity. In patients remaining conscious during brain surgery, stimulation of the amygdala elicits a sense of fear and anxiety.

THALAMUS. The thalamus is located in the center of the brain, above the hypothalamus. It acts as a sort of relay center, transmitting information from sensory organs, such as the inner ear and retina of the eye, to the areas of the cerebral cortex where the information can be further processed. The thalamus also relays nonsensory information, including motor messages from the cerebellum to the cortex. Further, in communication with the reticular formation, the thalamus regulates general arousal and excitability of the cortex.

HYPOTHALAMUS. The hypothalamus is the primary recipient of information flowing from the limbic system. It is a tiny structure, only about the size of a pearl, but it contains more than a dozen individual nuclei that serve a wide variety of functions. In a way, these functions are all related in that they are all concerned with maintaining homeostasis, or functional balance, in the body. For example, the hypothalamus regulates body temperature, blood pressure, fluid balance, and concentrations of glucose and sodium. It controls metabolism and motivates us to eat or drink when our body needs energy or fluid and to stop when balance has been restored. It mediates circadian rhythm, sexual motivations, and hormonal balance. It governs instinctual behavior and emotions. The hypothalamus can perform all of these functions because of the tremendous amount of input it receives and because of its ability to output instructions just as widely.

The hypothalamus receives information from CNS regions, including the limbic system and other forebrain structures, the reticular formation, hindbrain structures such as the area postrema, and the spinal cord. The hypothalamus also receives information from the PNS about the functioning of organs (via the vagus cranial nerve) and light/dark cycles (via the retina), and contains specialized receptors, such as thermoreceptors and osmoreceptors, that monitor body temperature and the balance of bodily ions, respectively. In addition, the hypothalamus contains receptors for various hormones.

When balance needs restoring, the hypothalamus sends instructions to the body, mainly via two routes. First, information is sent to the medulla, which you recall contains part of the descending reticular formation wherein control centers for the autonomic nervous system are located. Through this route, the hypothalamus can control heart and breathing rates, digestion, perspiration, vasoconstriction, and other autonomic functions. Second, the hypothalamus acts as a link between the nervous system and the endocrine (hormone) system. It does so by controlling the *pituitary gland*. In some cases, hormones synthesized in the hypothalamus, such as vasopressin or oxytocin, are released directly into the posterior (rear) portion of the pituitary gland by the axon terminals of hypothalamic cells. This pathway is called the *tuberoinfundibular tract* or the *hypothalamo-hypophysial tract* (*hypothalamo* referring to the hypothalamus; *hypophysial* referring to the pituitary, which is sometimes called the *hypophysis*). Alternatively, some cells originating in the hypothalamus control the pituitary gland in a more indirect way, secreting hormones (called *releasing factors* or *releasing hormones*) into the blood of a circulatory system that runs between the hypothalamus and the anterior (front) portion of the pituitary. This system is called the *hypophyseal portal system*. Release of factors, such as corticotropin-releasing hormone or gonadotropin-releasing hormone, stimulates the anterior pituitary to secrete its own hormones, such as ACTH or luteinizing hormone, into the bloodstream. These hormones then travel throughout the body, affecting various target organs or glands.

Lesioning various hypothalamic nuclei disrupts its many functions. For example, lesions can abolish or induce excessive eating or drinking in experimental animals, depending on the nuclei affected. Stimulating parts of the hypothalamus appears to be rewarding as animals will learn to press levers or engage in activities that are followed by electrical stimulation of certain areas. It is thought that these are the reinforcement centers activated by natural reinforcing stimuli like food and water. The function of such systems is to ensure that the organism will repeat actions that have led to the satisfaction of the drive; that is, they are motivational centers. They have also been called *pleasure centers* because humans sometimes report experiencing pleasure when these areas of the brain are stimulated electrically.

Although it is not entirely clear how drugs affect neurotransmitters in various regions of the limbic system, it appears that many benzodiazepine receptors are located here. The benzodiazepines enhance the inhibitory effects of GABA, and this increased inhibition in the limbic system may be one mechanism by which the benzodiazepines, such as chlordiazepoxide (Librium) and diazepam (Valium), reduce aggression in nonhumans and produce a calming effect (see Chapter 7).

CORTEX. The *cortex* (or *neocortex*) makes up the uppermost surface of the brain. It is, on average, about 3 mm thick and is highly convoluted, giving the brain the appearance of a walnut. Because of its convolutions, about two-thirds of the cortex cannot be seen. If it were flattened out, it would cover an area of 2.5 square feet. The cortex contains mostly glial cells and neuronal cell bodies and dendrites.

The cortex is undoubtedly the most complex and advanced part of the brain. Its neurochemistry is not well understood, but glutamate and GABA are known to be its predominant excitatory and inhibitory transmitters. Dissociative anesthetics like PCP and ketamine (see Chapter 15) act at NDMA receptors for glutamate, and these drugs probably exert their effects directly on the cortex.

One of the functions of the cortex is to handle the integration of sensory information. Information from sense organs is projected to different parts of the cortex. Visual information is projected to the *primary visual cortex* at the back of the brain, in what are called the *occipital lobes*; sound is projected to the *primary auditory cortex*, located in the *temporal lobes*. The *primary somatosensory cortex*, located in the *parietal lobes*, handles sensory input from the body, as well as the sense of taste. You may have noticed that all of these cortices have *primary* in their name. This is because there are additional areas of the cortex, called *secondary* and *association* cortices, where sensory information is further processed, integrated with other sensory perceptions, and stored as memories. For example, memory of a loved one does not consist solely of information about his or her appearance, but about the sound of his or her voice, the feelings you have when you are with him or her, and much, much more.

The *primary motor cortex* is the principal area responsible for commanding voluntary motor actions; it is located close to the somatosensory cortex, in the *frontal lobes*. Cell bodies residing in the primary motor cortex send their axons down through the midbrain and pons, into the lower portion of the medulla where they cross over to the contralateral (opposite) side of the body and enter the spinal cord. There, they form connections with motoneuron cell bodies, which connect with striated muscles. Because of this crossover in the lower medulla,

neurons originating in the left side of the motor cortex initiate movement on the right side of body and vice versa. Other axons from the motor cortex go to the basal ganglia and the cerebellum, which modify the direct output of the motor cortex and coordinate bodily movement. Motor commands are anticipated and planned outside of the primary motor cortex, in association motor areas. Many of these areas of the cortex are shown in Figure 4-12.

While sensory and motor functions are handled mainly by central and posterior parts of the cortex, higher mental processes of thought and cognition are governed mostly in *rostral* areas of the brain (*rostral* means toward the front; it is easy to remember if you think "rostral is toward the nostril"). All of the cortex that sits rostral to the primary motor cortex and its adjacent association motor areas in the frontal lobe is referred to as the *prefrontal cortex*. The prefrontal cortex sends and receives information from areas of the limbic system, such as the amygdala and septal nuclei. It too can be subdivided into various regions, such as the *orbitofrontal cortex* (just behind the eye sockets) and the *dorsolateral prefrontal cortex*

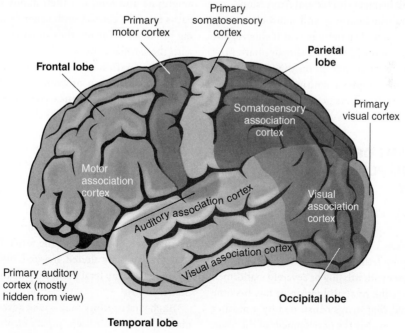

FIGURE 4-12 The cortex showing some of its major areas. (Adapted from Carlson, 2011, fig. 3.11, p. 70, reprinted with permission.)

(sitting toward the back [*dorsal*] of the orbitofrontal cortex, toward the top of the skull).

Areas of the prefrontal cortex govern an astonishing array of high-level cognitive functions: abstract reasoning; insight; planning; motivation; judgment; decision making; attention; task switching; impulse inhibition; memorization; expression of situationally appropriate emotions; monitoring and acting in accord with consequential relationships between stimuli, actions, and reinforcers (including predicting the availability of drugs); and the ability to prioritize behaviors and adapt to change. Perhaps not surprisingly, the prefrontal cortex is strongly affected by alcohol. In addition, individuals with schizophrenia have diminished dopamine activity in the prefrontal cortex, which might explain some symptoms, such as social withdrawal and blunted emotional responsiveness (see Chapter 12).

Two additional cortical structures deserve mentioning, as these are part of the limbic system and very important to its functioning. The *cingulate cortex* and *entorhinal cortex* mediate attention; response competition and selection; suppression of prepotent response tendencies; conditioned drug seeking; and craving, learning, and memory. Degeneration or dysfunction in these areas is implicated in Alzheimer's disease and depression.

Understanding the anatomy and neurochemistry of these complex cortical structures is still elusive, but modern imaging studies (discussed shortly) have provided a great deal of information on their role in the expression of many complex cognitive and behavioral functions, including the effects of drugs and the process of addiction.

DEVELOPMENT OF THE NERVOUS SYSTEM AND POTENTIAL FOR DISRUPTION

In the early 1960s, a drug called *thalidomide* was prescribed to many pregnant women to treat the nausea of morning sickness. Unfortunately, the drug interfered with the developing fetus, and many of these mothers gave birth to babies with missing or severely malformed limbs. Since the time of thalidomide, it has become widely recognized that drugs consumed by a mother during pregnancy can alter the development of the fetus. Drugs that cause such malformations are called *teratogens* (literally, "monster makers").

The developing nervous system is particularly vulnerable to disruption by drugs, and there are two reasons to believe that behaviorally active drugs are especially potent teratogens. First, in order to be behaviorally active, drugs must readily penetrate the brain, and this property also gives these drugs easy access across the placenta to the body of the developing fetus. Second, drugs that act to alter the functioning of neurotransmitters are particularly dangerous because of the way the nervous system develops.

The growth of the nervous system is a complex and delicate process involving the formation, migration, and interconnection of billions of nerve cells. All these cells form during the first 12 weeks after conception. During this time, therefore, brain cells are forming at a rate of 150,000 cells per minute. These cells do not develop in the part of the brain they are destined to occupy during adulthood. Many neurons have to migrate from one place in the brain to another. This journey must take place only at particular times in the development of the brain and in the appropriate order, or the brain will develop incorrectly. When these cells reach their target area, their growth is still not completed. They must attach themselves to their neighbors and send out their axons along prescribed paths to make contact with other cells in the developing brain. In addition, they must then form synapses with these other cells.

The formation, differentiation, and migration of cells; the projection of axons; and the formation of synapses are under chemical control. Chemicals are released by different parts of the developing brain, and the migrating cells and axons move either toward or away from these sources of chemicals. It is now believed that these control chemicals are similar to substances used as neurotransmitters in the adult brain. Consequently, if a mother consumes a psychoactive drug at crucial times during the development of the fetal brain, it could interfere with the delicate chemical signaling taking place in the developing brain of the fetus. If these chemical control signals are altered, masked, or inhibited, the development of the fetal brain may be disrupted (Abel & Sokol, 1989).

Such disruptions may cause severe brain malformation of the sort seen in *fetal alcohol syndrome* (described in Chapter 6), or they may cause much less apparent disruptions in the functioning of the brain that can be detected only after careful systematic study of the organism's behavior. This kind of damage is called *functional teratology* or *behavioral teratology*. Functional teratology is an exciting and comparatively new field of research. Early functional teratology research has been done on laboratory animals, but more recently this research has been extended to studies on humans (Bushnell, Kavlock, Crofton, Weiss, & Rice, 2010). What is clear is that exposure to low levels of behaviorally active drugs during certain stages of fetal development can cause alterations in the functioning of the nervous system, which can be apparent at many stages throughout the organism's life span (Boer et al., 1988; Spear, 1997).

NEUROTRANSMITTERS

In recent years, more than 50 different substances have been identified that meet all criteria required for a chemical to be considered a neurotransmitter, and another 50 have been found that meet most criteria. These criteria are (a) the substance is synthesized within the neuron by coexisting enzymes, (b) the substance is released in response to cell depolarization, (c) the substance binds to receptors to alter the postsynaptic cell, and (d) the substance is removed or deactivated by some mechanism within the synaptic cleft. Figure 4-13 illustrates the steps involved in the synthesis, release, action, and deactivation of most neurotransmitters. You will notice some of the above-mentioned criteria within these steps.

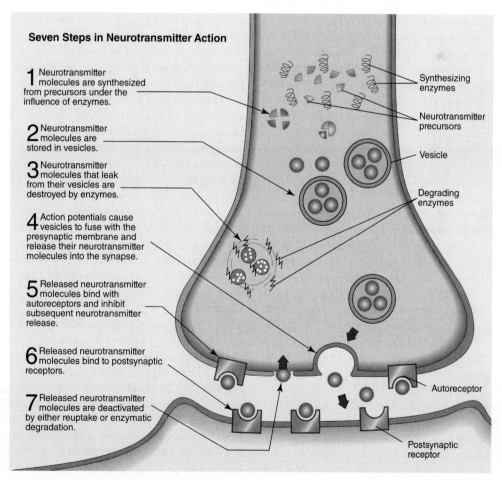

Seven Steps in Neurotransmitter Action

1 Neurotransmitter molecules are synthesized from precursors under the influence of enzymes.

2 Neurotransmitter molecules are stored in vesicles.

3 Neurotransmitter molecules that leak from their vesicles are destroyed by enzymes.

4 Action potentials cause vesicles to fuse with the presynaptic membrane and release their neurotransmitter molecules into the synapse.

5 Released neurotransmitter molecules bind with autoreceptors and inhibit subsequent neurotransmitter release.

6 Released neurotransmitter molecules bind to postsynaptic receptors.

7 Released neurotransmitter molecules are deactivated by either reuptake or enzymatic degradation.

Synthesizing enzymes

Neurotransmitter precursors

Vesicle

Degrading enzymes

Autoreceptor

Postsynaptic receptor

FIGURE 4-13 Steps involved in the synthesis, release, action, and deactivation of most neurotransmitters. (Adapted from Pinel, 2011, fig. 4.18, p. 96, reprinted with permission.)

Most neurotransmitter substances are *small molecule* neurotransmitters, which are stored in synaptic vesicles and released from the terminal button in response to an action potential. These neurotransmitters are synthesized from precursors under the guidance of enzymes created in the neuron's cell body and then transported to the axon terminal. Small molecule neurotransmitters act principally in their release zone to stimulate ionotropic or metabotropic receptors in a rapid, brief manner.

Neuroactive *peptides*, which are comprised of short chains of amino acids, are *large molecule* neurotransmitters. Neuropeptides are synthesized and packaged into vesicles within the neuron's cell body as amino acid chains that are much larger than their active end products. During transport from the cell body to the axon terminal, enzymes *cleave* (chop) the larger amino acid chain into its smaller neuropeptide forms. When released, many neuropeptides act as neuromodulators, diffusing away from their release zone and almost always binding to metabotropic receptors to produce slow, long-lasting effects. An additional feature distinguishing small and large molecule neurotransmitters is their deactivation following exocytosis. Neuropeptides are degraded in the synaptic cleft by enzymes and do not undergo reuptake into the terminal button, as do small molecule neurotransmitters.

For years, many of the neuroactive peptides have been known as *hormones*. A hormone is a chemical messenger released into the bloodstream by a gland or by endocrine cells of some organs. Many peptides were first identified as hormones and given appropriate names, such as growth hormone. It is now clear that the body uses many of these substances as both hormones and neurotransmitters. Whereas neurotransmitters carry messages over very short distances, a hormone circulates throughout the body and has an effect on some biological process distant from the place where it is released. The distinction between a hormone and a neurotransmitter may not always be clear. Early in the chapter, there was a discussion of how a neurotransmitter may be secreted near a brain structure and may exert effects on many synapses simultaneously. These substances are acting more as a hormone than a transmitter and are sometimes called *neurohormones* when they act in this capacity.

Table 4-1 lists examples of the most common neurotransmitter and neuromodulator substances. The earliest discovered and best understood neurotransmitter is *acetylcholine* (ACh), which is a small molecule neurotransmitter. Another family of small molecule neurotransmitters, called *biogenic amines* or *monoamines*, is composed of the *catecholamines*, which include *dopamine* (DA), *norepinephrine* (NE), and *epinephrine* (E), and the *indoleamines*, serotonin, which is often called *5-hydroxytryptamine* (5-HT), and *histamine*. Some transmitters are amino acids. Four of the most common are the excitatory amino acids *glutamate* and *aspartate* and the inhibitory amino acids *gamma-aminobutyric acid* (GABA) and *glycine*. Many of these amino acids are found normally in all cells in the body where they serve metabolic and other biochemical functions. In some neurons, they can be transmitters as well. Other small molecule neurotransmitters include *adenosine* and the *endocannabinoids*, which include *anandamide* and *arachidonylglycerol* (2-AG). Recently, *nitric oxide* (NO; not to be confused with nitrous oxide, NO_2, known as laughing gas) and *carbon monoxide* (CO) have been identified as unconventional neurotransmitters. Our understanding of CO as a neurotransmitter is somewhat vague, but continues to grow.

The large molecule neuropeptides include the *opioid peptides*, which are morphine-like molecules such as *beta-endorphin, enkephalins, dynorphins, endomorphins, and nociceptin*. A number of other peptides known to be neurotransmitters, neuromodulators, or neurohormones are released from the hypothalamus, the pituitary gland, or various organs. Some of these peptides are also listed in Table 4-1.

For a very long time it was believed that a neuron always produced the same neurotransmitter at every one of its synapses. This principle, known as *Dale's law*, is named after Sir Henry Dale, its proposer. The law needed to be modified when it was discovered that some neurons may produce and release more than one substance, usually a small molecule neurotransmitter and a neuropeptide, from their synapses. Although it is not common, we now know that some cells in some circumstances can release different substances at different synapses.

TABLE 4-1 Examples of Neurotransmitters and Neuromodulators in the Central Nervous System

Small Molecule Neurotransmitters	Large Molecule Neurotransmitters
Acetylcholine (ACh)	**Opioid peptides**
	Enkephalins
Biogenic amines (monoamines)	Endorphins
Catecholamines	Dynorphins
Dopamine (DA)	Endomorphins
Norepinephrine (NE)	Nociceptin
Epinephrine (E)	**Hypothalamic peptides**
Indoleamines	Oxytocin
Serotonin (5-HT)	Vasopressin
Histamine	Somatostatin
	Gonadotropin-releasing hormone (TRH)
Amino acids	Corticotropin-releasing hormone (CRH)
Excitatory amino acids	**Pituitary peptides**
Glutamate	Growth hormone
Aspartate	Thyroid-stimulating hormone (TSH)
Inhibitory amino acids	Prolactin
Gamma-aminobutyric acid (GABA)	Luteinizing hormone (LH)
Glycine	Adrenocorticotrophic hormone (ACTH)
Others	**Brain-gut peptides**
Adenosine	Cholecystokinin (CCK)
Endocannabinoids	Neuropeptide Y
Anandamide	Galanin
2-AG	Substance P
Gaseous neurotransmitters	**Miscellaneous peptides**
Nitric oxide (NO)	Insulin
Carbon monoxide (CO)	

Neurons are classified according to the primary neurotransmitter they release. Those that release acetylcholine are called *cholinergic* neurons. Epinephrine is also known as adrenaline (the name used primarily in Europe), so synapses that use epinephrine and norepinephrine are called *adrenergic* and *noradrenergic*, respectively (which is a good thing—try saying "epinephrinergic" or "norepinephrinergic"!). Those that use dopamine are *dopaminergic*, those that use serotonin are *serotonergic*, and so on.

Even though each neuron almost always releases the same transmitter(s), its effect on various cells can be quite different. The effect of a transmitter depends on the nature of the receptor site to which it binds. Because any transmitter may have a number of different receptor sites, activity at its synapses may produce many different effects. These receptor sites may cause IPSPs or EPSPs;

they may be directly connected to an ion channel, or they might use a second messenger. Thus, a substance released from a neuron into the cleft can be either an excitatory or inhibitory neurotransmitter or a neuromodulator. Using the lock-and-key analogy, whatever lurks behind a locked door does not depend on the size or shape of the key.

Drugs and Neurotransmission

Communication between neurons is a chemical process, and it is primarily at synapses that drugs have the opportunity to interfere with neurotransmitter synthesis, release, action, and deactivation. Figure 4-14 illustrates some of the ways in which drugs can alter neurotransmission. The mechanisms of drug action illustrated on the left of Figure 4-14 are *agonistic*—they are drug

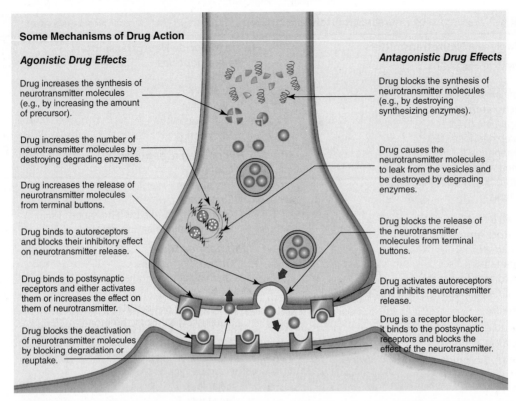

FIGURE 4-14 Mechanisms of agonistic and antagonistic drug effects. (Adapted from Pinel, 2011, fig. 4.19, p. 97, reprinted with permission.)

actions that facilitate either excitatory or inhibitory cell communication of a particular neurotransmitter. The mechanisms of drug action illustrated on the right of Figure 4-14 are *antagonistic*—they are drug actions that impede either excitatory or inhibitory cell communication by a particular neurotransmitter.

When an externally administered drug binds to and activates a receptor, mimicking the effects of a neurotransmitter, it is referred to as a *direct agonist*. A drug that has a high binding affinity (attraction) for a particular receptor but that activates that receptor only weakly, to a lesser degree than would its natural ligand (neurotransmitter), is referred to as a *partial agonist*. The term *partial agonist* is sometimes used interchangeably with the term *mixed agonist–antagonist*; however, they do mean different things. Mixed agonist–antagonist drugs were so-named before researchers discovered the existence of multiple subtypes of receptors in the brain for various neurotransmitter molecules. A mixed

agonist–antagonist is a drug that acts as an agonist at one receptor subtype while also acting as an antagonist at another receptor subtype. Drugs sometimes bind to receptor sites but do not activate them at all, instead preventing the neurotransmitter from binding and exerting its effect. These drugs are *receptor blockers* or *direct antagonists*.

Keep in mind that drug molecules can bind to both postsynaptic receptors and autoreceptors. When drugs act as receptor blockers, binding will decrease neurotransmission to the postsynaptic cell as well as activity in the autoreceptor. This decrease in autoreceptor activity stimulates the cell to produce more neurotransmitter to compensate for the decreased activity at the postsynaptic site, thus canceling the effect of the receptor blocker on the postsynaptic cell. Such a drug would have no net effect on neurotransmission. If the blocker has a greater effect on the autoreceptor than on the postsynaptic receptor, then the longer-term result might be an increase in transmission across the synapse because the presynaptic cell will overcompensate by releasing too much transmitter.

Other agonistic and antagonistic actions illustrated in Figure 4-14 are considered *indirect* because the drug molecule does not exert its effects by mimicking the neurotransmitter. Some neurotransmitter receptor complexes have more than one binding site. For example, the $GABA_A$ receptor protein contains a binding site for the neurotransmitter GABA and additional sites to which drug molecules, such as ethanol (alcohol) and benzodiazepines (anxiety-reducing drugs), can bind to enhance GABA's effects. Because GABA's binding site can be occupied only by GABA, binding by alcohol or benzodiazepines to other receptor sites is referred to as *noncompetitive binding*. An illustration of the GABA receptor complex and its binding sites can be seen in Figure 7-1 of Chapter 7.

Table 4-2 lists some of the major neurotransmitters and neuromodulators that you will encounter throughout the remainder of this text, as well as examples of some drugs that affect their neurotransmission. Also included in the table are the main receptor subtypes for each of the transmitters. This book indicates receptor subtypes using a subscript (e.g., D_1 or D_2), but in other books and papers, you may sometimes see receptor subtypes designated without subscripts (e.g., D1 or D2). Do not be confused—these refer to the same thing.

Acetylcholine

Acetylcholine (ACh) was the first neurotransmitter to be discovered. It is synthesized in cholinergic cells by combining *acetate* and *choline* with the help of the enzyme *choline acetyltransferase*. ACh molecules that leak from presynaptic storage vesicles and those released into the synaptic cleft in response to an action potential are quickly degraded by the enzyme *acetylcholinesterase* (AChE). The choline molecule is taken back into the presynaptic cell by choline receptor transporter proteins located in the membrane of the axon terminal. Several drugs interfere with the activity of AChE—consequently, they interfere with transmission across cholinergic synapses. This is the mechanism of action of many commonly used insecticides and even some older nerve gases, such as sarin.

There are two major systems of cholinergic neurons that project through the brain (refer to the top-left panel of Color Plate A). Within the *basal forebrain* sit two structures called the *basal nucleus of Meynert* and the *medial septal nuclei* (recall that the septal nuclei form part of the limbic system). These two structures project their axons throughout the neocortex as well as to the thalamus, hippocampus, and amygdala where they release ACh from axon terminals. This cholinergic system plays an important role in cortical activation and in learning and memory. Alzheimer's disease, which is a form of dementia characterized by severe deficits in learning and memory, is marked by a profound loss of ACh neurotransmission. The second major ACh system originates in a part of the pons called the *mesopontine tegmentum area* (also referred to as the *pontomesencephalotegmental complex*). This system also projects to the thalamus as well as to the hypothalamus, reticular formation, cerebellum, and the basal ganglia, and plays a role in REM sleep (deep, dreaming sleep). In addition, it is worth noting that receptors for ACh are also found in the ventral tegmental area, which you recall is a vital component of the brain's reward system. ACh neurotransmission is important for the rewarding and addictive effects of drugs such as morphine and heroin.

Some drugs alter the functioning of cholinergic synapses by acting as direct agonists at ACh receptors. Although all ACh receptor sites are stimulated by ACh, they can be classified according to other substances that also affect them. *Nicotinic* cholinergic receptors are ionotropic. When stimulated, the ion channel opens to allow influx of Na^+ ions and efflux of K^+ ions, producing EPSPs. They are stimulated by nicotine (a direct agonist) and inhibited by a drug called *curare* (a receptor blocker). Curare is a poison that some South American tribes place on the point of their spears and arrows. If struck with one of these weapons, an animal's muscles (including the diaphragm, which allows for breathing) will become paralyzed, and the animal will suffocate and die. This happens because nicotinic receptors are also present at neuromuscular junctions, where terminal buttons of motor neurons synapse with muscle fibers in the PNS. When injected into the muscles of the face, the cosmetic drug Botox (botulinum toxin) blocks the release of ACh at neuromuscular junctions, preventing muscles from contracting and lessening the appearance of wrinkles. *Muscarinic* cholinergic receptors are metabotropic. ACh binding activates second messenger systems to open K^+ and Cl^- ion channels

TABLE 4-2 Receptor Subtypes and Examples of Drug Actions for Major Neurotransmitters and Neuromodulators in the Central Nervous System

Small Molecule Neurotransmitters

Acetylcholine (ACh)	(I): nicotinic (M): muscarinic (A): muscarinic	Nicotine—stimulates nicotinic receptors (agonist) Muscarine—stimulates muscarinic receptors (agonist) Curare—blocks nicotinic receptors (antagonist) Atropine—blocks muscarinic receptors (antagonist)

Biogenic amines (monoamines)

Dopamine (DA)	(M): "D_1-like" (D_1, D_5) and "D_2-like" (D_2, D_3, D_4) (A): D_2	Cocaine—blocks DA reuptake transporter proteins (agonist) Amphetamine—causes reversal of reuptake transporter proteins (agonist) Chlorpromazine—blocks D_2 receptors (antagonist) AMPT—inactivates tyrosine hydroxylase (antagonist)
Norepinephrine (NE)	(M): $alpha_1$, $alpha_2$, $beta_1$, $beta_2$ (A): $alpha_2$	Amphetamine—stimulates NE release (agonist) Idazoxan—blocks $alpha_2$ autoreceptors (agonist) Reserpine—inhibits transport of NE into synaptic vesicles (antagonist)
Serotonin (5-HT)	(I): $5\text{-}HT_3$ (M): $5\text{-}HT_1$, $5\text{-}HT_2$, $5\text{-}HT_4$, $5\text{-}HT_5$, $5\text{-}HT_6$, $5\text{-}HT_7$ (A): $5\text{-}HT_1$	Fluoxetine—blocks serotonin reuptake transport proteins (agonist) LSD—stimulates $5\text{-}HT_2$ receptors (agonist) Agomelatine—blocks $5\text{-}HT_2$ receptors (antagonist)

Amino acids

Glutamate	(I): NMDA, AMPA, Kainite (M): $mGlu_1$–$mGlu_8$ (A): mGlu	AMPA—stimulates AMPA receptors (agonist) PCP—blocks a binding site inside the NMDA receptor ion channel (antagonist) AP5—blocks glutamate binding site on NMDA receptor (antagonist)
GABA	(I): $GABA_A$ (M): $GABA_B$ (A): $GABA_B$	Alcohol—stimulates $GABA_A$ receptors (agonist) GHB —stimulates $GABA_B$ receptors (agonist) Picrotoxin—blocks $GABA_A$ receptor complex ion channel (antagonist) Allylglycine—inactivates GAD enzyme preventing GABA synthesis (antagonist)

Others

Adenosine	(M): A_1, A_{2A}, A_{2B}, A_3	Caffeine—blocks A_{2A} receptors (antagonist) Theophylline—blocks adenosine receptors (antagonist)
Anandamide	(M): CB_1, CB_2	THC—stimulates CB_1 receptors (agonist) Rimonabant—blocks CB_1 receptors (antagonist)

Large Molecule Neurotransmitters

Opioid peptides

beta-Endorphin	(M): mu_1, mu_2, mu_3, $delta_1$,	Morphine—stimulates mu receptors (agonist)
Enkephalins	$delta_2$, $kappa_1$, $kappa_2$,	Methadone—stimulates mu receptors (agonist)
Dynorphins	$kappa_3$, ORL_1	Naltrexone—blocks mu receptors (antagonist)
Endomorphins		Naloxone—blocks mu receptors (antagonist)
Nociceptin		

(I) = ionotropic; (M) = metabotropic; (A) = autoreceptor.

and hyperpolarize the cell. Muscarinic receptors are also stimulated by muscarine, found in poisonous mushrooms, and blocked by drugs like scopolamine and atropine from the deadly nightshade plant. In the PNS, muscarinic receptors are involved in the functioning of the autonomic nervous system.

Biogenic Amines (Monoamines)

The catecholamines—DA, NE, and E—and the indoleamine 5-HT are all monoamines, meaning they are synthesized from a single amino acid.

In the case of the catecholamines, the amino acid precursor is tyrosine, which is produced by the body but also consumed in foods. The biosynthetic pathway of the catecholamines is illustrated in Figure 4-15. In the cytoplasm of catecholaminergic axon terminals, tyrosine is converted into *dihydroxyphenylalanine* (DOPA) with the help of the enzyme *tyrosine hydroxylase*. Tyrosine hydroxylase is referred to as a *rate-limiting enzyme*, meaning that the amount of catecholamine synthesized depends on the availability of that enzyme. When axon terminal neurotransmitter levels rise to high levels, tyrosine hydroxylase is inhibited; when the neuron is firing at a high rate and neurotransmitter is being released quickly, tyrosine hydroxylase is facilitated. DOPA is converted to DA via the enzyme *DOPA decarboxylase*. At this point, DA is transferred into synaptic vesicles, and, in dopaminergic neurons, the biosynthetic pathway stops there. In neurons that use NE as their neurotransmitter, however, there is an additional step. The synaptic vesicles of noradrenergic neurons contain an enzyme that dopaminergic neurons do not; this enzyme is called *dopamine beta-hydroxylase* and converts DA into NE. In adrenergic neurons, NE leaks from its vesicles into the cytoplasm

of the axon terminal where an additional enzyme, *phenylethanolamine-N-methyl-transferase* (PNMT), converts NE into E. Epinephrine molecules are then transported into their own storage vesicles within the axon terminal.

For the indoleamine 5-HT, the amino acid precursor is *tryptophan*, which is actively transported into the brain from the foods we eat; it is not produced by the body. In serotonergic neurons, tryptophan is converted into *5-hydroxytryptophan* by the enzyme *tryptophan hydroxylase* (the rate-limiting enzyme) and finally into 5-HT by the enzyme *aromatic amino acid decarboxylase*.

When released from their vesicles into the synaptic cleft by an action potential, the monoamines are taken back into the presynaptic cell by specialized dopamine, norepinephrine, and serotonin reuptake transporter proteins embedded in the cell membrane. Most get repackaged in synaptic vesicles for future exocytosis. Neurotransmitter molecules that remain unpackaged get broken down by two enzymes: *monoamine oxidase* (MAO) and *catechol-O-methyltransferase* (COMT). Drugs used to treat major depression (described in Chapter 13) often target the reuptake and enzymatic degradation of the catecholamines so that more neurotransmitter is available. For example, phenelzine (Nardil) is a monoamine oxidase inhibitor (MAOI) and fluoxetine (Prozac) is a selective serotonin reuptake inhibitor (SSRI). Drugs such as cocaine and methylphenidate (Ritalin) also block reuptake transporter proteins so that the monoamines stay longer in the synaptic cleft.

DOPAMINE. Dopaminergic neurons form four major systems in the brain. In one of these systems, called the *tuberoinfundibular pathway*, dopamine acts as a

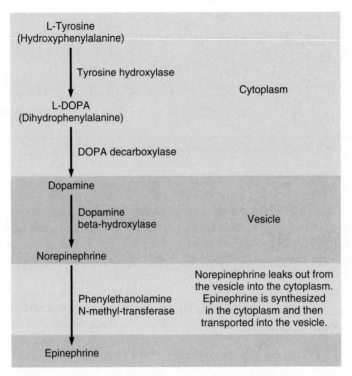

FIGURE 4-15 Biosynthetic pathway of the catecholamines.

neurohormone. Cells in part of the hypothalamus release dopamine directly into the *hypophyseal portal system* (the circulatory system that connects the hypothalamus and pituitary gland) to inhibit the release of prolactin. In the three other major systems, dopamine acts as a neurotransmitter. The location of dopamine cell bodies is indicated by the first part of the pathway's name, and the location of axon terminals is indicated by the second part. In the *nigrostriatal pathway*, dopamine cell bodies in the substantia nigra of the midbrain project their axons to two regions of the striatum called the caudate nucleus and putamen (refer to the top-right panel of Color Plate A). This pathway plays an important role in the control of motor movement, and dopamine cell degeneration in this pathway is linked with Parkinson's disease. In the final two major pathways, dopamine cell bodies reside in the ventral tegmental area. *Meso* is Greek for *middle* (referring to the midbrain), and these pathways are called the *mesocortical pathway* (from the ventral tegmental area to the *cortex*) and *mesolimbic pathway* (from the ventral tegmental area to the nucleus accumbens and parts of

the limbic system, such as the hippocampus and amygdala). These latter two pathways receive a lot of attention from researchers because they are important in the motivational aspects of drug use and are also implicated in schizophrenia (see Chapter 12).

The D_1 and D_2 families of receptors are distributed throughout the caudate nucleus and putamen and the mesolimbic system, where they serve opposite functions. D_2 receptor activation leads to the inhibition of the cAMP second messenger system pathway, whereas D_1 receptor activation facilitates this system. D_2 receptors also act as autoreceptors. Drugs used to treat psychotic disorders selectively block D_2 receptors, but some of the newer antipsychotic drugs also have effects on other dopamine receptors (see Chapter 12).

NOREPINEPHRINE. The major noradrenergic system in the brain consists of cell bodies that reside in an area of the pons called the locus coeruleus and project axons widely throughout the cortex, thalamus, hypothalamus, hippocampus, amygdala, cerebellum, and spinal cord (refer to the bottom-right panel of Color Plate A). Norepinephrine plays a role in attention, sleep and wakefulness, feeding behaviors, and emotion. Dysfunction of the NE system is linked with depression and attention-deficit disorders. All four noradrenergic receptor subtypes are metabotropic; alpha$_1$, beta$_1$, and beta$_2$ are excitatory whereas alpha$_2$ is inhibitory and acts as an autoreceptor. NE receptors are also found in the PNS where they mediate hormonal control of various organs by catecholamines and activation of the autonomic nervous system.

SEROTONIN. The major collections of cell bodies for serotonin sit within brainstem *raphe nuclei* of the pons, medulla oblongata, and reticular formation (refer to the bottom-left panel of Color Plate A). These are called the *dorsal raphe nucleus* and *median raphe nucleus*. The raphe nuclei project their axons to the cortex, thalamus, basal ganglia, hippocampus, and amygdala, as well as areas of the lower brainstem and spinal cord where they control the release of enkephalins to decrease pain sensitivity. Serotoninergic receptor subtypes (5-HT$_1$ through 5-HT$_7$) are all metabotropic, with the exception of the 5-HT$_3$ receptor, which controls Na$^+$ and K$^+$ ion channels to produce EPSPs. The remaining subtypes regulate second messengers, such as cAMP; some are inhibitory, and some excitatory. 5-HT regulates a wide variety of functions, including sleep–wake cycle, dreaming, mood, aggression, and appetite.

Amino Acid Neurotransmitters

Of the 22 amino acids that are used in cellular functions and that form the building blocks for proteins in the body, approximately eight are thought to also act as neurotransmitters. Two of the most widespread and abundant of these are the excitatory neurotransmitter *glutamate* and the inhibitory neurotransmitter *GABA*. The actions of an additional inhibitory amino acid neurotransmitter, *glycine*, are less understood and will be discussed in minor detail.

GLUTAMATE. Glutamate is the major excitatory neurotransmitter in the brain. It is synthesized inside terminal buttons from the amino acid *glutamine*, via the enzyme *glutaminase*, and packaged in synaptic vesicles. Following exocytosis, it is removed from the synaptic cleft by glutamate reuptake transporter proteins embedded in presynaptic terminal buttons and also on surrounding glial cells. When taken up by glial cells, glutamate is converted into its precursor, glutamine, by the enzyme *glutamine synthetase*. Glial cells release glutamine back to the glutamatergic neuron where, once inside terminal button, it is converted to glutamate and stored in synaptic vesicles as previously described.

Unlike the ACh or monoamine systems, glutamatergic axon terminals exist almost throughout the entire brain with widespread projections within the cortex and between the cortex, thalamus, striatum, substantia nigra, and many other structures. Glutamate binds to a number of metabotropic and ionotropic receptor subtypes. There are at least eight metabotropic receptors (mGlu$_1$–mGlu$_8$) expressed throughout the brain that stimulate or inhibit second messenger systems and control functions such as learning, motor activity, and pain sensitivity. Three ionotropic receptors, called *kainate*, *AMPA*, and *NMDA* receptors, open to allow an influx of Na$^+$ ions and efflux of K$^+$ ions when stimulated, producing EPSPs. The most complex of these is the NMDA receptor, which is dependent on the presence of several other substances (see Figure 4-16). The NMDA receptor contains four externally located binding sites: one for glutamate and additional sites for zinc (Zn^{2+}), polyamines, and glycine. Inside the NMDA receptor ion channel, there is also a binding site for magnesium (Mg^{2+}) and an additional site to which various substances, including the dissociative drugs ketamine and PCP (see Chapter 15) and alcohol (see Chapter 6), can all bind.

At resting potential, the NMDA receptor ion channel is blocked by Mg^{2+} sitting in its binding site, preventing the movement of ions through the channel. As the postsynaptic cell depolarizes (often from the activation of coexisting AMPA receptors), the Mg^{2+} ion becomes dislodged from its binding site, thereby freeing up the ion channel. Thus, NMDA receptor activation is voltage dependent. In addition, NMDA receptor activation is neurotransmitter dependent, meaning that glutamate released from the presynaptic cell must bind to its receptor site. Still, this is not enough to fully activate the NMDA receptor. In addition to glutamate binding, glycine must also bind to its site on the NMDA receptor. When these conditions are met, the NMDA ion channel opens and Na$^+$ rushes through the channel. In addition, NMDA receptor ion channels admit Ca^{2+} ions into the cell. This is extremely important, not only

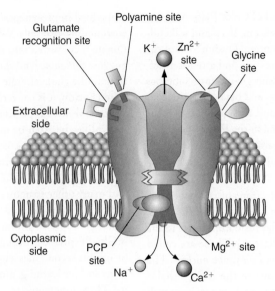

FIGURE 4-16   Glutamate NMDA receptor.

because the presence of additional positive ions further depolarizes the cell, but also because Ca^{2+} serves an important, additional purpose—it acts as a second messenger to active enzymes, protein kinases, and transcription factors to produce long-lasting effects on the cell's excitability.

It is this kind of NMDA-mediated change in the function of glutamate neurons that is thought to underlie learning and memory. Drugs that inhibit NMDA receptor activation also impede learning and memory. Modification of this system, brought about by chronic drug use, has also been linked with craving and addiction (Volkow et al., 2010). Overstimulation of glutamate receptors can be toxic, causing cell death. This is referred to as *excitotoxicity*, which has been linked to NMDA receptor loss in Alzheimer's disease.

GAMMA-AMINOBUTYRIC ACID (GABA). GABA is the most widespread inhibitory neurotransmitter in the brain—an estimated 20–30% of CNS neurons are GABAergic. GABA is synthesized in GABAergic cells from the amino acid glutamine, which you recall is converted to glutamate by the enzyme *glutaminase*. In GABAergic neurons, there is an additional enzyme not present in glutamatergic neurons or in glia; it is called *glutamic acid*

decarboxylase (GAD). GAD is the rate-limiting enzyme that converts glutamate to GABA. Interestingly, GAD requires a coenzyme, vitamin B6, to complete this conversion; a diet deficient in vitamin B6 can lead to a decrease in GABA synthesis, resulting in convulsions and possibly death. Following exocytosis, GABA is taken back into the presynaptic cell, via reuptake transporters, and into glial cells where it is converted into glutamate and then glutamine. Glial cells release glutamine back to the axon terminals of GABAergic neurons for resynthesis and packaging into synaptic vesicles. GABA in also broken down into its precursor, glutamate, by the enzyme *GABA aminotransferase*.

Like glutamate, GABA neurons project widely throughout the brain, including the cortex, basal ganglia, hippocampus, hypothalamus, brainstem, and cerebellum.

There are two classes of GABA receptors: $GABA_A$ receptors are ionotropic and control a Cl^- ion channel to permit an influx of negative ions when stimulated; $GABA_B$ receptors are metabotropic; they inhibit Ca^{2+} channels and, through the actions of a second messenger, indirectly control the opening of a K^+ channel to hyperpolarize the neuron. $GABA_B$ receptors also decrease cAMP second messenger activity and act as autoreceptors. The structure of $GABA_A$ receptors, which has

19 known subunit genes, is much more diverse than that of GABA$_B$, which has only three known subunit genes (more about this in Chapters 6 and 7).

Most drugs affect GABA$_A$ receptors, which, like NMDA receptors, are rather complex in that they contain more than one externally located binding site. In addition to the binding site for GABA, the receptor complex contains additional sites to which the tranquilizing drugs barbiturates and benzodiazepines (e.g., Valium; see Chapter 7), steroids (e.g., progesterone), picrotoxin (a poisonous plant compound), anaesthetic gases (e.g., nitrous oxide), and alcohol (see Chapter 6) can all bind. These drugs enhance the inhibitory properties of GABA by prolonging or increasing its ability to open the chloride ion channel. Drugs like bicuculline, which blocks the GABA$_A$ receptor binding site, or allylglycine, which prevents GABA synthesis, lead to neural excitation and convulsions. Drugs that increase GABA neurotransmission are used to treat seizures and other disorders such as anxiety and insomnia.

The GABA$_A$ receptor is made up of five subunits that show considerable variation in configuration in different brain systems. This makes them deferentially sensitive to different benzodiazepines and other drugs. Different benzodiazepines may have different affinities for some of these variations, which makes it possible for different benzodiazepines to have different effects on behavior. Some are more potent tranquilizers, some are better sedatives, and so on. By identifying the variations in the GABA receptor molecule and designing drugs that activate only those receptors, it might be possible to create benzodiazepines with very specific effects (Möhler, Fritschy, Crestani, Hensch, & Rudolph, 2004).

GLYCINE. Glycine is formed in the axon terminal from the amino acid *serine*. Following release, it is taken back into the cell by reuptake transporters. Receptors for glycine exist in the lower brainstem and spinal cord and are always ionotropic, controlling a Cl$^-$ ion channel to produce IPSPs when stimulated. Glycine receptors are antagonized by the drug *strychnine*, which occurs in the seeds of a tree found in India, called the Poison Nut tree. When consumed in even very small doses, strychnine can cause convulsions and death. Glycine receptors are also blocked by caffeine.

Other Small Molecule Neurotransmitters and Neuromodulators

ADENOSINE. Adenosine molecules consist of *adenine* and the sugar *ribose*. All cells contain adenosine, as it is required for some very basic life processes; therefore, there are no major adenosine pathways that have been identified in the brain. When neurons are running low on oxygen or energy, they release adenosine (glia do so also), which causes dilation of blood vessels in the cells' proximity and a consequent increase in blood flow and in fuel and oxygen supply to the neurons. Adenosine binds to four receptor subtypes (A$_1$, A$_{2A}$, A$_{2B}$, and A$_3$), all of which are metabotropic and coupled to G proteins that influence cAMP activity. In the brain, adenosine receptor binding exerts inhibitory effects via the opening of K$^+$ ion channels. Adenosine plays a major role in sleep and wakefulness, in large part through its neuromodulatory actions on ACh, NE, 5-HT, DA, and glutamate neurons. Low levels of adenosine correspond with alertness and wakefulness, whereas high levels correspond with sleepiness and fatigue. During wakefulness and heightened neural activity, adenosine levels slowly rise; during sleep and lowered neural activity, they slowly fall. The inhibitory effects of adenosine receptor binding can be antagonized by the A$_{2A}$ and A$_1$ receptor blockers caffeine and theophylline, found in coffee and tea (see Chapter 9).

ENDOCANNABINOIDS. The endocannabinoids are a group of small lipid molecules that act as neuromodulators within the CNS in a manner similar to THC, the active ingredient in marijuana (see Chapter 14). Two of the well-researched endocannabinoids are called *anandamide* (meaning "internal bliss") and *arachidonylglycerol* (2-AG). These molecules bind to two types of cannabinoid receptors, both of which are metabotropic and coupled to G proteins. CB$_2$ receptors are found in the PNS and control immune system functions. CB$_1$ receptors are the most abundant metabotropic receptor subtype in the entire brain and are found in the frontal cortex, anterior cingulate cortex, hypothalamus, hippocampus, basal ganglia, and cerebellum. Endocannabinoids act at CB$_1$ receptors as *retrograde messengers*. That is, they are released from the dendrites and cell body of the postsynaptic cell in response to the firing of action potentials and bind to heteroreceptors on the terminal button of the presynaptic cell membrane. CB_1 receptors can be found on axon terminals of neurons releasing ACh, DA, NE, 5-HT, glutamate, and GABA. Endocannabinoids are unconventional neurotransmitters in that they are not synthesized and stored in synaptic vesicles, but are produced from lipid compounds in the cell membrane. Once synthesized, they immediately diffuse across the postsynaptic cell membrane and bind to CB_1 receptors on the presynaptic cell. Here, they stimulate G proteins, which inhibit neurotransmission by inhibiting Ca^{2+} channel opening (recall that the entry of Ca^{2+} into the presynaptic terminal button initiates the movement of synaptic vesicles to the cell membrane and the exocytosis of neurotransmitter molecules into the synaptic cleft). A high rate of action potential firing in the postsynaptic neuron leads to increased release of endocannabinoids and, thereby, greater inhibition of the presynaptic cell. CB_1 receptor activation by endogenous cannabinoids or THC causes sedation, analgesia, stimulates appetite, and impairs concentration and memory. CB_1 receptor activation is also pivotal in the euphoric and addictive properties of opioid drugs, such as heroin, morphine, and oxycodone (see Chapter 11).

NITRIC OXIDE. *Nitric oxide* (NO) is a soluble gas produced in many cells throughout the body where it plays an important role in vasodilation and blood flow. In neurons, NO is synthesized in the cytoplasm from the amino acid *arginine* with the help of the enzyme *nitric oxide synthase* (NOS). Like the endocannabinoids, NO is not stored in vesicles or released by exocytosis in response to an action potential. Instead, it is created on demand and diffuses instantaneously and passively through the cell membrane (it is an uncharged molecule, not an ion), into the extracellular fluid, and penetrates nearby cells—both postsynaptic and presynaptic (i.e., it is a retrograde messenger). NO does not bind to a receptor but instead activates *guanylate cyclase*, the enzyme responsible for the production of the second messenger cGMP, to enhance neurotransmission of the presynaptic neuron. In just a few seconds following its synthesis, NO spontaneously decays into biologically inactive compounds. cGMP activity is much more prolonged, although it too is eventually halted by enzymatic degradation. The drug sildenafil (Viagra), sold primarily as a treatment for erectile dysfunction, works by inhibiting the enzymatic degradation of cGMP, thereby enhancing its vasodilatory effects.

Large Molecule Neurotransmitters: Peptides

More than 100 different neuropeptides have been identified that act as neurotransmitters, neuromodulators, and neurohormones. Neuroactive peptides can be grouped into one of five categories, including a *miscellaneous peptides* category for those (such as insulin) that do not fit neatly into one of the other four. The *brain–gut peptides* (such as substance P) were first discovered in the gut. The *pituitary peptides* and *hypothalamic peptides* were first identified as hormones released from the pituitary (such as vasopressin and ACTH) and hypothalamus (such as somatostatin and CRH), respectively. Finally, the *opioid peptides* are a family of more than 20 endogenous morphine-like molecules that bind to opioid receptors in the brain and spinal cord and throughout the body. Opioid peptides play important roles in regulating blood pressure and temperature, food and fluid intake, stress responsiveness, sensitivity to pain, aggression, emotion, sexual behavior, and the euphoric and reinforcing value of natural and drug rewards.

Opioid peptides are synthesized within the neuron's cell body as much larger protein chains (*polypeptides*) that are hundreds of amino acids in length. Polypeptides serve as precursor molecules that get packaged, along with enzymes, into vesicles where they are cleaved (chopped) into their smaller, active form during transport from the cell body to the axon terminal. Peptides often coexist in the axon terminal with small molecule neurotransmitters (such as 5-HT, glutamate, or GABA), and both are released in response to an action potential.

One kind of endogenous opioid peptide is called *beta-endorphin*. It is synthesized in the hypothalamus and pituitary from the precursor polypeptide *proopiomelanocortin*. An additional active peptide produced from proopiomelanocortin is *adrenocorticotropic hormone* (ACTH), which is an important stress hormone. Additional endogenous opioid peptides are called the *enkephalins* (*met-enkephalin* and *leu-enkephalin*; *enkephalin* means "in the head"), which are five amino acids long, cleaved from the polypeptide *proenkephalin A*. *Dynorphin* is the product of the polypeptide *prodynorphin*, synthesized in the pituitary. Less is known about the more recently discovered opioid peptides *nociceptin* and the *endomorphins*. Nociceptin is the product of the polypeptide *prononiceptin*; the precursor for the endomorphins is unknown.

Opioid peptides have several types of receptors that are widely distributed throughout the brain, including the cortex, thalamus, hypothalamus, amygdala, hippocampus, ventral tegmental area, nucleus accumbens, and periaqueductal gray, and in the spinal cord. All receptor subtypes are metabotropic. Receptor activation stimulates G proteins that regulate ion channels for K^+ or Ca^{2+} or second messenger systems to inhibit cell excitability. Beta-endorphin acts on all three main receptor types: *mu* (μ), *delta* (δ), and *kappa* (κ). The enkephalins act mainly on delta receptors, the endomorphins on mu receptors, the dynorphins on kappa receptors, and nociceptin binds to its own ORL_1 receptor. Most of the analgesic and reinforcing effects of morphine and other opiate drugs are mediated by the mu receptor, although some analgesia is associated with all of the opioid receptor types.

Following release from the cell, neurotransmitter peptides are broken down by enzymes called *peptidases*; they are not taken back into the presynaptic cell for recycling. Hormone peptides released into the circulatory system are too large to pass through the blood–brain barrier and remain outside the CNS. For this reason, the same peptide can produce different effects when released as a neurotransmitter or neuromodulator compared to when it is released as a neurohormone.

BRAIN IMAGING OF DRUG EFFECTS

In the next chapter, you will learn that addiction is a brain disease; chronic drug use changes the structure and function of the brain. We know this thanks to technology that allows researchers to image the brains of addicts. Some of the most common brain imaging techniques used in addictions research are outlined next.

Positron Emission Techniques

POSITRON EMISSION TOMOGRAPHY (PET). PET makes use of the unstable, chemical properties of *radioactive tracer isotopes (radiotracers)* to produce three-dimensional images of the brain. Radioisotopes most commonly used in PET imaging of the brain include ^{15}oxygen (^{15}O), ^{13}nitrogen (^{13}N), ^{11}carbon (^{11}C), and ^{18}fluorine (^{18}F). Participants ingest a radiotracer made up of a metabolically active agent, such as glucose, water, or a drug of abuse, that has been made radioactive by being combined with a radioactive isotope. For example, when a stable carbon atom

in a molecule of cocaine is replaced by the unstable isotope of carbon, ^{11}C, the result is the radiotracer $[^{11}$C]-cocaine, which can be detected in the brain. A machine called a *cyclotron* is needed to create these radiotracers.

Radiotracers can be given by injection, inhalation, or orally, depending on the agent being administered. Participants must wait for a short period while the radiotracer becomes concentrated in brain areas where the metabolically active agent or drug is distributed. They are then placed in the PET imaging scanner, which is shaped like a cylinder and contains a series of connected radiation detector cameras. Radioisotopes are short-lived, with half-lives ranging from 2 to 110 minutes, and decay by emitting positrons. An emitted positron travels less than 1 mm before colliding with an electron. The collision produces high-energy *gamma rays* that pass out of the brain and are detected by radiation detector cameras comprised of a ring of *scintillator crystals* that fluoresce momentarily when struck by high-energy gamma rays. This information is then transmitted to a computer. By measuring where gamma rays hit the scintillator crystals, researchers can plot the origin of positron emission to create an image of exactly where the radiotracer activity is within the brain.

PET scans can be used for a wide range of purposes. First, they allow researchers to directly measure the brain distribution and activity of stimulant drugs such as cocaine, methamphetamine, and amphetamine; opioids such as heroin and morphine; hallucinogens such as PCP and ketamine; and other commonly used drugs, such as nicotine, alcohol, and marijuana.

Second, local concentrations of drug receptor sites can be determined by administering tiny doses of radiotracers that contain pharmacologically inactive amounts of a drug and occupy only a small fraction of available receptor sites. This allows researchers to estimate drug receptor density in specific brain areas and to keep track of changes in the number of receptors that might occur over time, for example, because of tolerance.

Third, PET scanning can be used to assess competition for receptor binding sites, as when molecules of a drug or radiotracer compete with a neurotransmitter for binding on the same receptor site. Competition between a drug and a radiotracer that occupies the same receptor site but produces no changes in mood can provide an index of the degree of drug binding required to produce subjective feelings of drug-induced euphoria. This method can also be used to measure the actions of naturally occurring chemicals, such as neurotransmitters, or to assess potential treatments (antagonists) that might block or reverse the effects of an abused drug.

Fourth, PET scanning can be used to isolate areas of the brain that are active during a mental activity, such as drug craving. Changes in brain glucose metabolism that occur as neurons are activated and deactivated can be pinpointed using a glucose-mimicking radiotracer, and regional cerebral blood flow (which is correlated with glucose metabolism) can be assessed using $[^{15}O]$-water.

Finally, PET scanners for laboratory animals, such as rats and apes, aid in the preclinical assessment of newly developed drug treatments. Animal researchers use this technology to radiolabel and monitor drug absorption, distribution, and excretion more efficiently compared to the time and cost involved in sacrificing multiple animals and analyzing brain tissue.

PET scanning of the human brain was developed in 1973 by researchers at Washington University in St. Louis, Missouri. It was superior to other techniques used at that time because PET could isolate areas of drug activity and glucose and oxygen use deep within the brain and could be completed in as little as 30 seconds. Currently, radiolabeling allows researchers to locate the sites of action of a virtually unlimited number of biologically active compounds.

PROBLEMS WITH PET. PET imaging does have its limitations. Compared to newer technologies, such as *magnetic resonance imaging*, PET offers a low degree of spatial resolution, and it is sometimes difficult to distinguish between two structures very close together in the brain. Because of the necessary size of scintillator crystals, which measure approximately 3 to 4 mm in width, PET scanners achieve a reconstructed image resolution of 4 to 4.5 mm, which makes it difficult to distinguish between small structures in the brain. PET scanning also poses some health risk in that radioactive agents are administered into a patient's body. The health costs and benefits of radiation exposure associated with PET scans must be weighed carefully, especially if multiple scans are to be performed on a single patient.

Finally, the expense of PET scanning, in terms of medical personnel and equipment required, limits its use. Because the radioisotopes used to create radiotracers

decay so quickly, they must be produced on-site. This means that a cyclotron, which produces the radioisotopes, must be bought or located very nearby.

SPECT. As an alternative to PET, brain imaging can be completed using its sister technique, *single photon emission computed tomography* (SPECT). SPECT uses a *collimator*, consisting of lead blocks containing many tiny holes that allow gamma rays to pass through and hit scintillator crystals. This information is then transmitted to a computer. Compared to PET scanning, SPECT uses radioisotopes such as ^{99m}technetuim (^{99m}Tc), ^{123}iodine (^{123}I), and ^{133}xenon (^{133}Xe) with half-lives ranging from 6 hours to 5 days. This allows for more long-lasting brain functions to be measured and also eliminates the need for having a cyclotron on-site, greatly reducing the cost of scanning. However, compared to PET, SPECT can be technically challenging and more susceptible to error. Furthermore, the spatial resolution of SPECT is even less than that of PET, generating an even less precise image of active brain regions.

Magnetic Resonance Techniques

MAGNETIC RESONANCE IMAGING (MRI). MRI is a technique that takes advantage of the magnetic charge of billions of hydrogen atoms that exist in the body. The nucleus of the hydrogen atom has a single proton (which has a positive electrical charge) and a large *magnetic moment*, making it ideal for the purposes of MRI. Having a large magnetic moment means that when hydrogen atoms are placed within a magnetic field, they will align with the field, similar to the way in which iron filings scattered randomly on a sheet of paper will align parallel to a bar magnet placed beneath the paper. Just because hydrogen nuclei are aligned with the magnetic field does not mean they stand still. In fact, the atoms are in constant movement, each spinning on its axis like a child's toy top. It is this spinning of positively charged protons that produces the magnetic property of hydrogen nuclei.

The most fundamental component of an MRI machine is the very powerful magnet that creates an external magnetic field, forcing the alignment of hydrogen nuclei within the body. The MRI machine looks like a giant cube, typically measuring 2 meters tall by 2 meters wide and 3 meters long. It contains a horizontal tube, called the *bore* of the magnet, in which a participant is placed. The magnetic field that runs through the bore of the MRI machine is up to 40,000 times more intense than the magnetic field of the earth. The type of magnet most commonly used to create this amazingly powerful field is called a *superconducting magnet.*

Once the participant is placed within the center of the bore and the magnetic field is turned on, the spinning hydrogen protons within the participant's body align in the direction of the field, which, running from head to toe, is called the *z-axis.* Because of the complex laws of quantum mechanics, approximately half the protons will line up in the direction of the participant's feet and half in the direction of the participant's head. However, they largely cancel each other out and produce a net magnetization *angle of alignment* (a) of 0 degrees. While they are aligned, spinning hydrogen protons also rotate, or *precess,* around the axis of the externally created magnetic field, somewhat similar to how the earth revolves around the sun. The precession frequency of an atom (how quickly the protons precess) is specific to the type of atom and is known as the *Larmor frequency.* Although all hydrogen nuclei precess at this frequency, at any given time the protons may be at any *phase* of their precession around the axis of the externally created magnetic field. It helps to think of phase in terms of an analog clock. Imagine that multiple clocks are purchased in an airport shop and taken by the purchasers to various parts of the world. Once they arrive in their particular time zone, each purchaser sets the clock to the proper time of day. The second hand, minute hand, and hour hand on each of the clocks should move (precess) around the center (axis) of the clock at the same speed. However, each of the clocks would be at a different phase of its precession since each time zone is different. So while the frequency of precession for each clock is identical, each clock would be at a different phase of its precession around the axis of the clock at any given time. Phase is an important component in obtaining an MRI image, which we will review shortly.

So far we have discussed the *magnetic* component of MRI, but what about *resonance?* Resonance is defined as the transfer of energy, at a particular frequency, between two systems. Every material has a natural frequency at which it resonates. If you have ever rubbed a moist fingertip around the rim of a crystal wine glass, you will have noticed that the glass seems to "sing." This phenomenon is produced by the transfer of energy from the friction generated by the contact of your moving fingertip with the glass, causing the molecules of the crystal to vibrate at their natural resonant frequency. If a singer could produce a tone of the exact resonant frequency of crystal and of great enough amplitude (volume), the glass would absorb enough energy from the sound waves produced by the singer that it would shatter under the strain. In MRI, electromagnetic energy in the form of *radiofrequency* (RF) *waves* is directed into the body. Electromagnetic energy is a combination of electric and magnetic fields that travel at the speed of light. In addition to RF waves, other forms of electromagnetic energy include X-rays, microwaves, gamma rays, and all forms of light, including ultraviolet and infrared. When directed into the body, pulses of RF energy that are at the precise Larmor frequency of hydrogen protons cause the protons to absorb the energy and resonate. As the protons resonate, their net magnetization, or angle of alignment (a) with the z-axis (the external magnetic field), diverges from 0 degrees and, if enough energy is applied, approaches 90 or even 180 degrees. When a = 90 degrees, the RF pulse is referred to as a 90-degree pulse; at 180 degrees, it is referred to as a 180-degree pulse. As RF waves are applied through the MRI machine, hydrogen protons not only increase their angle of alignment from the z-axis but also acquire the same phase of precession around the axis of the external magnetic field. Thinking back to our clock analogy, it is as if all clocks all over the world suddenly began to display the same time of day and rotate in step with each other. When the RF pulse is turned off, the protons begin to return to their 0-degree alignment with the z-axis and also begin the process of *dephasing,* or rotating out of step. As they do so, the protons release the excess of energy (in the form of RF waves) that was stored during resonation, creating a signal that is picked up by the MRI machine and sent to a computer.

It is these two components of relaxation—proton realignment with the z-axis and proton dephasing—that are used to create an MRI image of the body. These two components of proton relaxation are characterized by *relaxation times* that will be used to describe MRI data. The first is called *spin–lattice relaxation time* (T1) and is the amount of time in milliseconds for the strength of the net magnetization (e.g., a = 90 or 180 degrees) to return to 63% of its value before RF waves were applied. This measure will vary according to the type of tissue being resonated. The second component of proton relaxation is called *spin–spin relaxation time* (T2) and is the amount of time required for protons to complete their dephasing (or to stop rotating in step) once the RF waves have been stopped. A T1-weighted image (where spin–lattice relaxation is the dominant source of the MR signal) produces a clear image of neuroanatomy in which gray matter appears gray, white matter appears white, and cerebrospinal fluid is dark. A T2-weighted image (where spin–spin relaxation is the dominant source of the MR signal) highlights areas of pathology in which gray matter appears dark, white matter appears bright, and cerebrospinal fluid is even brighter.

When an MRI exam is being administered, the most widely used methodology is called the *spin echo sequence*, which allows researchers to construct three-dimensional images of the body. A series of 90-degree RF pulses are repeatedly applied to the participant at a constant repetition time. As protons relax following the cessation of the 90-degree RF pulse, a 180-degree RF pulse is applied that reverses proton relaxation, causing an increase in the angle of alignment and a rephasing of protons, thereby increasing the emitted signal. The images created have a high spatial resolution in the order of 0.5 to 2.0 mm, making the produced image visually superior to that produced in PET imaging.

The MRI room must be specially constructed with a reinforced floor and a magnetic shield not only to block the effects of the superconducting magnet but also to prevent interference from other sources of radiofrequency waves (such as FM radio) that can be picked up and sent by the machine and interfere with data acquisition.

FUNCTIONAL MAGNETIC RESONANCE IMAGING (FMRI).

Like PET scanning, magnetic resonance can also be used to link changes in cerebral blood flow with activity in specific areas of the brain using a technique called *functional magnetic resonance imaging* (fMRI). Rather than injecting radioactive tracers, however, fMRI relies on the intravenous injection of a magnetic agent (the *contrast technique*) or the magnetic properties of iron-rich deoxygenated hemoglobin (the *noncontrast technique*). A commonly used contrast technique requires the injection of gadolinium, a silvery-white metal that is highly magnetic. Injection of gadolinium increases the strength of the magnetic field only in those regions of the brain that are activated by a particular stimulus (such as a word, picture, or sound broadcast to the participant in the MRI machine) or a particular emotional state. The change in magnetic field strength alters spin–spin (T2) relaxation time, thereby producing a visually contrasting image in active versus inactive areas of the brain.

The most commonly used noncontrast fMRI technique is referred to as *blood oxygen level-dependent* (BOLD) *imaging*, which uses T2-weighted images to assess changes in local concentrations of deoxygenated hemoglobin. During brain activation, changes in blood flow and volume exceed the speed at which oxygen is consumed from the blood. This leads to increased quantities of oxygenated hemoglobin (and a reduction in the ratio of deoxygenated to oxygenated hemoglobin) in the brain, thereby producing changes in fMRI signal intensity.

fMRI frequently uses a methodology called *gradient echo sequence*, which is very similar to spin echo sequence used in MRI. In fact, both spin echo and gradient echo sequences can be used in both MRI and fMRI. In gradient echo sequence, series of RF pulses are applied at the Larmor frequency of hydrogen, and T1 and T2 relaxation times are used to produce an image, as in spin echo sequence. In gradient echo sequence, however, as RF pulses are applied to the brain, a *gradient magnet*, much weaker in intensity compared to the superconducting magnet, produces an additional magnetic field that is superimposed on the main magnetic field. Brief application of this gradient field accelerates the dephasing of hydrogen protons (i.e., spin–spin relaxation). A second gradient is then applied to reverse the process of dephasing, causing rephasing of protons. The purpose of using gradient magnets is to cause brief disturbances in the external magnetic field rather than administering additional RF pulses, as is the case in spin echo imaging. The gradient magnets excite only a small slice of tissue rather than the entire volume and are thereby used to alter the resonance of hydrogen protons at very precise areas of the brain that researchers are interested in imaging. As such, multiple gradients can be applied to different regions of the brain in succession, thereby significantly reducing the amount of time required for scanning.

ADVANTAGES AND PROBLEMS WITH MRI.

Magnetic resonance techniques are superior to many other forms of brain imaging because they produce images with very high contrast resolution (the ability to distinguish two similar but not identical tissues in a very small area) and spatial resolution in relatively little time. They are also quite safe in that they do not require the injection of radioactive materials, as does PET

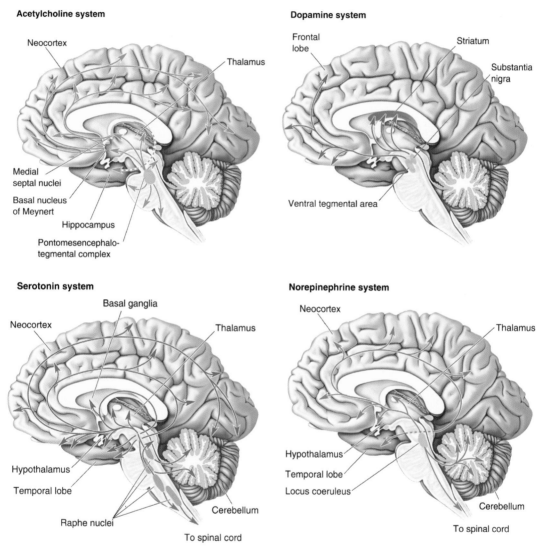

Acetylcholine system

Neocortex

Thalamus

Medial
septal nuclei

Basal nucleus
of Meynert

Hippocampus

Pontomesencephalo-
tegmental complex

Dopamine system

Frontal
lobe

Striatum

Substantia
nigra

Ventral tegmental area

Serotonin system

Basal ganglia

Neocortex

Thalamus

Hypothalamus

Temporal lobe

Raphe nuclei

Cerebellum

To spinal cord

Norepinephrine system

Neocortex

Thalamus

Hypothalamus

Temporal lobe

Locus coeruleus

Cerebellum

To spinal cord

COLOR PLATE A Four major neurotransmitter systems (Adapted from Bear, Connors, & Paradiso, 2007; figures 15-12 [p. 500], 15-13 [p. 501], 15.14 [p. 503], 15.15 [p. 504]; reprinted with permission).

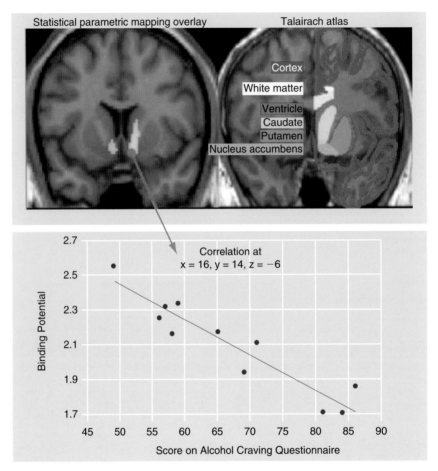

COLOR PLATE B This figure shows the relationship between activity in the ventral striatum (the location of the nucleus accumbens) and craving for alcohol caused by exposure to alcohol-related cues in long-term alcoholics. The yellow brain image at the right shows the area of the brain that was activated when the participants were exposed to the alcohol cues. As you can see, this corresponds to the area of the nucleus accumbens, as shown in the brain image on the left. The lower panel shows the negative correlation between craving and the binding potential for dopamine D_2 receptors in the nucleus accumbens. As you can see, the lower the binding potential at D_2 receptors, the higher the craving induced by the alcohol-related cues. (Heinz et al., 2004; reprinted with permission)

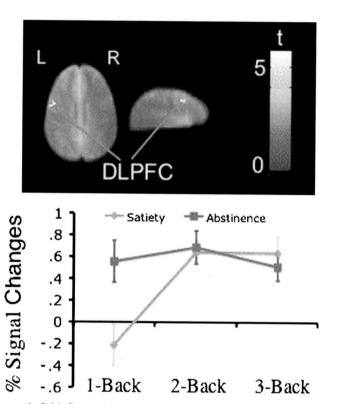

COLOR PLATE C The top panel of this figure shows the BOLD image of the brain. The location of the dorsal lateral prefrontal cortex (DLPC) is indicated. The color bar at the right indicates the level of activity in the DLPC during the task. The lower panel shows the amount of activity in the DLPFC during the 1-, 2-, and 3-back tests when subjects had smoked within the previous 1.5 hours (Satiety) and when they were deprived of nicotine for 14 hours (Abstinence). (Adapted from Xu et al., 2005, fig. 3, p. 147; reprinted with permission)

[¹¹C] -WIN 35,428 Labeled DAT

pre-METH post-METH

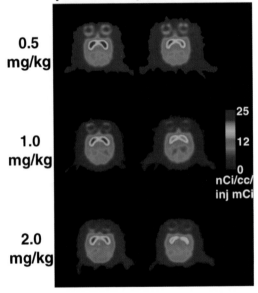

COLOR PLATE D This figure shows the effect of giving various doses of methamphetamine to baboons four times at 2-hour intervals. These PET images were taken 2 to 3 weeks after the drug treatment. The color bar in the left panel shows the color associated with the amount of binding to the dopamine transporter (DAT), with red showing many transporter molecules and blue showing fewer. The images show the pre- and postmethamphetamine activity in the brain. The yellow and red areas are in the caudate nucleus. You can see a dose-related decrease in DAT binding, indicating that there has been death of some dopamine cells in the area. (Adapted from Villemagne et al., 1998, fig. 1, p. 421; reprinted with permission)

TABLE 4-3   Summary of the Advantages and Disadvantages of Different Brain Imaging Techniques

PET and SPECT	MRI and fMRI
Advantages	*Advantages*
• Ability to radiolabel an almost infinite number of naturally occurring and synthetic chemicals	• Superior spatial resolution
• Can be completed very quickly	• Can be completed very quickly
• Good spatial resolution	• Can image any region of the brain
• Can image any region of the brain	• Thought to be noninvasive
Disadvantages	*Disadvantages*
• Uses radioactive chemicals	• Cannot accommodate individuals with metallic implants
• High cost of cyclotron, scanner, and numerous medical personnel	• Increases in regional blood flow may be altered by mood or even daydreaming
• Provides an indirect measure of brain function, thereby reducing temporal resolution	• Only a moderate level of temporal resolution in fMRI

scanning. However, MRI and fMRI are not without shortcomings. Like PET scanning equipment, MRI equipment is very expensive to purchase and use. In addition, the physical setup of the MRI machine can be problematic for heavier individuals. Furthermore, a significant number of people feel highly anxious, uncomfortable, and claustrophobic within the small confines of the MRI machine. The loud clanking noise created by the scanner and scanning sessions ranging from 20 to 90 minutes only exacerbate this problem. An additional problem is the need for participants to remain entirely motionless throughout the session, which is especially difficult if they are feeling anxious or uncomfortable. Even very slight head movements can create significant loss of spatial resolution and distortion in the created image.

Because of the extreme intensity of the superconducting magnet, participants and medical personnel are checked carefully for any metal objects they may be carrying before they enter the MRI room. Paper clips, keys, hemostats, stethoscopes, hair clips, and any other small magnetic objects can be pulled off the body and become dangerous flying projectiles, getting sucked into the bore of the MRI where the participant is lying. In addition to external objects, metallic objects inside the body, such as

aneurysm clips in the brain, some dental implants, heart pacemakers, and metal objects not secured in place by the growth of scar tissue can be dislodged or heated to scalding temperatures by the magnet, causing severe internal damage. Pacemakers are particularly sensitive and can malfunction even if the wearer goes near the scanning room. In addition, heart monitors, oxygen tanks, IV poles, and many other forms of lifesaving and monitoring equipment that contain metal cannot enter the MRI room.

Additional caveats apply to fMRI. Changes in blood flow and volume measured by fMRI BOLD imaging that are thought to result from experimental stimuli or manipulation may be the result of boredom, anxiety, or simply thinking about something outside the experimental context. Standard lag times of 4 to 8 seconds between stimulus onset and signal acquisition, dictated by the relationship between neuronal activation and changes in blood flow and volume, make it all the more difficult to correlate the presentation of stimuli with changes in regional blood flow.

Table 4-3 provides a comparison of the advantages and disadvantages of these brain imaging techniques, and Color Plates B to D give examples of the images they can produce.

5

Substance Use and Addictive Disorders

Why do people use drugs? On the surface it may seem like an easy question to answer, but like most "easy" questions, the more you think about it, the more difficult it becomes. To people who use drugs, the reasons may seem obvious, at least to them, but can we depend on these insights to formulate a scientific theory of drug taking? When we drink a beer, smoke a cigarette, or drink a cup of coffee, we are using a drug. If we are asked why we do this, most of us can come up with an answer that sounds reasonable: "Because I like it," "It wakes me up," or "I need to unwind after a long, hard day." These are reasonable statements, but even though they may satisfy us and those around us, the history of research into drug use shows that self-analysis and "obvious" explanations have led researchers down many dead-end paths and should be approached with caution.

A more difficult question to answer is why people abuse drugs; why do some people insist on using a drug to the point where it jeopardizes their health, finances, family life, and comfort? There may be equally obvious reasons for the overuse or abuse of drugs: "Losing his wife drove him to drink" or "She started smoking pot because of peer pressure but soon became hooked." Once again, such explanations seem reasonable, but is there any scientific basis for them?

Even though drug use and abuse have been the subject of scientific investigation since the middle of the

nineteenth century, it is only in the past half-century or so that real progress has been made. In this chapter we will look at some of the attempts to answer these questions and examine some of the more widely held ideas about drug use and addiction.

Early attempts to understand drug use were directed strictly at addiction. No one thought of studying the normal use of drugs. People were content to assume that drug use that did not create problems for the user could be explained in the same way one might explain any activity. Whether the drug was alcohol, tobacco, or cocaine, drug use was just another pleasurable activity that people might choose to pursue, like eating a good meal or having sex. Because it is considered *normal* to seek pleasure and avoid pain, the reason for using drugs was obvious and did not require further explanation. For this reason, *normal* drug use was never studied systematically until the middle of the twentieth century.

Addiction, on the other hand, did not seem normal. Addicted people often caused themselves great personal, financial, and social harm, which they acknowledged. Yet, in spite of knowing the damage they were doing, they continued to use their drug. Because addiction did not appear to follow normal rules, there did not seem to be any point to studying *normal* drug use as it was unlikely to provide any understanding of addiction.

DEFINING ADDICTION

This chapter is not just about addiction; it is about why people use drugs. This includes all sorts of drug use, from the grandmother who takes a casual and occasional cup of tea, to the person whose only thought is of getting the next hit of heroin and who is willing to sacrifice his or her health, money, and family to do so. People have believed for a long time that there is a natural progression from *normal* drug use to addiction. Later on, we will trace this progression in great detail. But we should start by defining the sort of behavior at the extreme end of the process often called drug abuse, dependence, or, more commonly, *addiction*.

Over the years, there have been many attempts to describe addiction precisely. In this book we will be guided by the revised fourth edition of *The Diagnostic and Statistical Manual of Mental Disorders* (the *DSM-IV-TR*, colloquially referred to as the *DSM*) published by the American Psychiatric Association (*APA*). The *DSM* provides criteria for diagnosing all sorts of psychiatric disorders including disorders that involve addictive behaviors. The first version of the *DSM* was published in 1952; a number of major revisions have since taken place. The *DSM* currently in effect is the *DSM-IV-TR* (TR means "Text Revision") published in 2000. It is an updated version of the *DSM-IV* (published in 1994). The APA is planning a new edition, the *DSM-5*, which is scheduled for publication in May 2013. As part of the planning and consultation process, the APA has created a website outlining the recommendations of the *DSM-5* Substance-Related Disorders Work Group and has invited comments from professionals and the public. Details of those proposed revisions can, at the time of writing this text, be found at: http://www.dsm5.org/ProposedRevision/Pages/proposedrevision.aspx?rid=431, although this site may cease to exist following the actual publication of the new manual. Additionally, there is yet to be another round of consultation and revision, so the final recommendations may result in further changes to *DSM* criteria. Even though the most recent recommendations may not be adopted in the *DSM-5*, their rationale will be discussed in this chapter because it demonstrates how thinking about addiction has changed since 2000.

The *DSM* does not discuss normal or recreational drug use, but does provide criteria for diagnosing two succeeding stages of drug use that cause problems for the user. The *DSM-IV-TR* does not use the term *addiction*. Instead, it uses the terms *substance dependence* and *substance abuse* and provides very specific criteria by which these conditions can be diagnosed, as shown in Box 5-1.

Substance dependence includes symptoms such as the need to use increased doses of the drug, withdrawal symptoms, unsuccessful attempts to cut down on drug use, and continued use in spite of the drug's harmful effects. If a person meets three or more of these criteria concurrently within a 12-month period, he or she is diagnosed with substance dependence. The criteria for *substance abuse* are more extreme and include failure to fulfill major obligations at one's job, at school, or to one's family; recurrent problems with the legal issues; and persistent social or personal problems. The presence of any one of these criteria leads to a diagnosis of substance abuse.

There are a number of significant changes proposed for the *DSM-5*. In the first place, it is recommended that the name of this category *Substance-Related Disorders*, as it exists in the *DSM-IV-TR*, be changed to *Substance Use and Addictive Disorders* (O'Brien, 2010). Also proposed for the *DSM-5* is the removal of the terms *substance abuse* and *substance dependence*. Rather than describe two different diagnostic categories, it is recommended that there be only one diagnosis: *Substance Use Disorder*, which can be described as either *moderate* or *severe*. This change was suggested in order to clarify the view that there is one disorder with varying degrees of severity rather than two separate disorders as the *DSM-IV* seems to imply.

It is recommended for the *DSM-5* that the diagnosis of substance use disorder involve 11 criteria, similar to those of the *DSM-IV*. If the person exhibits two to three of these symptoms, this would indicate a diagnosis of *moderate severity*; if the person shows four or more symptoms, the disorder is considered *severe*. To complete the diagnosis, the specific substance needs to be identified according to the following list: Alcohol Use Disorder, Amphetamine Use Disorder, Cannabis Use Disorder, Cocaine Use Disorder, Hallucinogen Use Disorder, Inhalant Use Disorder, Opioid Use Disorder, Phencyclidine Use Disorder, Sedative–Hypnotic or Anxiolytic Use Disorder, Tobacco Use Disorder, and Other (or Unknown) Substance Use Disorder. Although not included in the category of Substance Use Disorder, the *DSM-5* may include gambling as an addictive disorder (O'Brien, 2010). As we shall see later in this chapter,

BOX 5-1   Substance Dependence and Substance Abuse Criteria

Substance Dependence

A maladaptive pattern of substance use, leading to clinically significant impairment or distress, as manifested by three (or more) of the following, occurring at any time in the same 12-month period:

1. tolerance, as defined by either of the following:
   (a) a need for markedly increased amounts of the substance to achieve intoxication or desired effect
   (b) markedly diminished effect with continued use of the same amount of the substance

2. withdrawal, as manifested by either of the following:
   (a) the characteristic withdrawal syndrome of the substance
   (b) the same (or a closely related) substance is taken to relieve or avoid withdrawal symptoms

3. substance is often taken in larger amounts or over a longer period than was intended

4. there is a persistent desire or unsuccessful efforts to cut down or control substance use

5. a great deal of time is spent in activities necessary to obtain the substance (e.g., visiting multiple doctors or driving long distances), use of the substance (e.g., chain smoking), or recovering from its effects

6. important social, occupational, or recreational activities are given up or reduced because of substance use

7. the substance use is continued despite knowledge of having a persistent or recurrent physical or psychological problem that is likely to have been caused or exacerbated by the substance (e.g., current cocaine use despite recognition of cocaine-induced depression, or continued drinking despite recognition that an ulcer was made worse by alcohol consumption)

Specify if:

With Physiological Dependence: evidence of tolerance or withdrawal (i.e., either item 1 or 2 is present)
Without Physiological Dependence: no evidence of tolerance or withdrawal (e.g., neither item 1 nor 2 is present)

Substance Abuse

A. A maladaptive pattern of substance use leading to clinically significant impairment or distress, as manifested by one (or more) of the following, occurring within a 12-month period:
   (1) recurrent substance use resulting in a failure to fulfill major role obligations at work, school, or home (e.g., repeated absences or poor work performance related to substance use; substance-related absences, suspensions, or expulsions from school; neglect of children or household)
   (2) recurrent substance use in situations in which it is physically hazardous (e.g., driving an automobile or operating a machine when impaired by substance use)
   (3) recurrent substance-related legal problems (e.g., arrests for substance-related disorderly conduct)
   (4) continued substance use despite having persistent or recurrent social or interpersonal problems caused or exacerbated by the effects of the substance (e.g., arguments with spouse about consequences of intoxication, physical fights)

B. The symptoms have never met the criteria for Substance Dependence for this class of substance.

Source: Reprinted with permission from the American Psychiatric Association. © 2000, *DSM-IV-TR.*

---

this move acknowledges that the same brain and behavior mechanisms responsible for drug addiction appear also to be involved in non-drug-related addictions.

The 10th revision of the *International Statistical Classification of Diseases and Related Health* *Problems (ICD-10)* is a similar catalog of diseases issued by the World Health Organization (*WHO*, 1993). The *ICD-10* distinguishes between *harmful use* and a *dependence syndrome.* The criteria it uses are similar to those of substance dependence and substance abuse in the *DSM-IV-TR* (these can be viewed online at: http://www.who.int/substance_abuse/terminology/ICD10ClinicalDiagnosis.pdf). This distinction makes it clear that the *ICD-10* also recognizes addiction as one disorder with varying degrees of severity; that is, harmful use progresses to dependence syndrome. The APA and the developers of the *ICD-10* work closely together to ensure that the two publications maintain a similar approach to these diagnoses.

No doubt you will find many other definitions of addiction in other sources. Most definitions, like those of the *DSM-IV-TR*, have several elements in common. They usually state that (a) the addicted individual has impaired control over the use of the drug, and (b) the drug use has harmful consequences (West, 2001). It should be noted, however, that loss of control and drug-related harm are really different aspects of the same thing. Symptoms that involve a loss or impairment of control present a real conceptual problem for scientific investigations of addiction. The problem with this criterion is that there is no way to tell the difference between behavior that is controlled and behavior that is not controlled by the individual. If you watch a person drinking beer in a bar, is there any way to detect whether it is that person, or something else, that is controlling the beer drinking? The crucial question is whether that person could stop drinking beer if he or she wanted to. By simply studying the person's behavior, there is no way to tell. Of course you could ask the individual, but then you have to depend on self-report, which is often self-serving, inaccurate, and, in this case, unverifiable. The question of control also presents problems when using nonhumans to study addiction since lab animals cannot tell you if they have lost control of their behavior or what they really intended to do.

To get around this problem, definitions of addiction invoke the second element: harm. The reasoning here is that self-injurious behavior must be *out of control* because no person or animal who has control of their behavior would deliberately injure themselves. This reduces the definition of addiction to one criterion, that is, the harm the drug use does to the user. If you examine the *DSM-IV-TR* criteria for substance dependence outlined in Box 5-1, you will notice that most of the symptoms involve doing some sort of harm to oneself. There are two, criteria 3 and 4, that involve the element of self-control. Criterion 3 states that the person used the drug for longer and in higher doses than intended,

and criterion 4 states that the person desires to quit, but is unable. Assessing an individual for both of these criteria requires self-report; they are not independently verifiable.

Another term often encountered in discussions of addiction is *craving*. It does not appear in *DSM-IV-TR* criteria, but has been recommended as a new criterion for diagnosing substance use disorder in the *DSM-5* (O'Brien, 2010). Craving can have a number of definitions, which include concepts such as "intense preoccupation," "strong desire," or "urge" to use the drug. Once again, craving, like control, is a subjective state and ultimately depends on self-report of the user; consequently, it presents the same problems as *control*. As with control, the only behavioral evidence for craving is usually the sort of extreme behavior addicts will engage in and the harm they will tolerate to obtain the drug. Modern neuroscience is working to gain an understanding of the changes that take place in the brains of addicts that can explain both loss of control and craving, and thus has offered neurological definitions of these terms, which will be discussed later in this chapter.

It should be noted that the *DSM-IV-TR* has two additional criteria not related to loss of control, harm, or craving. They are criterion 1, the development of tolerance, and criterion 2, the presence of withdrawal symptoms. The role of withdrawal and tolerance in addiction will be discussed in greater detail in the next section of this chapter. At one time, physical dependence was considered to be not only the definition of addiction, but its cause. In fact the terms *dependence* and *addiction* were often used interchangeably. This is no longer the case and is in fact why it has been recommended that the *DSM-5* no longer use the term *dependence*, but *addiction* instead (O'Brien, 2010).

A final concept often included in definitions of addiction is that addiction is a chronic, relapsing disorder. This means that an addict may be free of his or her symptoms of addiction and remain free for extended periods, but the symptoms can and often do reappear at any time. This aspect of addiction is acknowledged in the *DSM-IV-TR* and has been recommended for inclusion in the *DSM-5*. Along with diagnosis, specifications are made as to the course of the disorder—whether the patient is in early or late (sustained) remission and whether the remission is full or partial. Thus, once diagnosed with an addictive disorder, the person is never "cured," but in remission of symptoms, which could reappear at any time.

HISTORY OF RESEARCH ON DRUG USE AND ADDICTION

Addiction as a Disease

BACKGROUND. Until the middle of the nineteenth century, people who had problems with drugs were considered to be deficient in character, moral fiber, willpower, and/or self-control; in other words, they were sinners or criminals. Consequently, addiction to drugs was a problem for priests and clerics to understand and for the legal system to deal with. Excessive or destructive use of drugs was not considered a medical problem and received no scientific attention. In the mid-nineteenth century, these ideas were challenged on two fronts.

A powerful social reform movement under way in England and North America advocated reform for a variety of social problems of the time: child labor, slavery, poverty, and the treatment of criminals, including *inebriates* (alcoholics). The American Association for the Cure of Inebriates was established in 1870 and became the forerunner of the temperance movement. Its first principle was, "Inebriety is a disease." The idea that alcoholism was a disease was not based on any medical research at the time but was motivated strictly by humanitarian concerns. The Social Reformers were concerned with the welfare of inebriates. By describing excessive drinking as a disease rather than a sin, they were able to convince governments and the rest of society to offer treatment rather than punishment.

In addition to the social reform movement and its zeal to help inebriates, the medical profession at that time was already involved in other drugs of abuse: morphine and opium. Opium, the raw extract of the opium poppy, was usually consumed in the form of laudanum, a mixture of opium and alcohol. Morphine, the principal active ingredient in opium, was usually injected. Laudanum was sold as a patent medicine (you could even order it from the Sears Roebuck catalogue), and morphine was widely used by physicians to treat a number of ailments (see Chapter 11). It was logical, then, to think of abuse of these drugs as a problem that physicians should solve, that is, as a medical problem (Berridge & Edwards, 1981).

This reconceptualization of drug abuse as a disease rather than a sin led to the adoption of new terminology. Toward the end of the nineteenth century, the temperance and antiopium social movements started using the term *addiction* to refer exclusively to the excessive use of drugs and to replace terms such as *intemperance* and *inebriety* (Alexander & Schweighofer, 1988). The medical profession also adopted the term *addiction* and started using it as a diagnosis of, and an explanation for, excessive drug use, thereby giving addiction the implication of a disease.

Popularity of the *disease model*, as we shall call it, seemed to fade until the middle of the twentieth century when the Alcoholics Anonymous movement gained prominence and influence. One of its most articulate theorists, E. M. Jellinek, focused attention on the issue and eventually wrote a book called *The Disease Concept of Alcoholism* (Jellinek, 1960). Thanks to Jellinek, the idea of addiction as a disease became formalized first with alcoholism, which was declared a disease by the World Health Organization in 1951 and the American Medical Association in 1953 (Room, 1983). By implication, then, all forms of drug addiction became a disease.

This new status of addictions was also acknowledged in the revised third edition of the *DSM* (*DSM-III*) published by the American Psychiatric Association in 1987, although the *DSM* uses the term *disorder*, not *disease*, which makes the issue a bit less clear. The *DSM* has traditionally defined *disorder* as "a clinically significant behavioral or psychological syndrome or pattern that occurs in an individual and that is associated with present distress (e.g., a painful symptom) or disability (impairment in one or more important areas of functioning), or with a significantly increased risk of suffering death, pain, disability, or an important loss of freedom" (American Psychiatric Association, 1987). The definition of disorder sounds very much like a disease, but falls somewhat short of what the social reformers had in mind. In its discussion of possible revisions of this definition for the *DSM-5*, the APA points out in a "cautionary statement" that the designation of *mental disorder* does not necessarily imply that the condition meets all definitions of *mental disease* and may not be relevant to legal or moral issues such as whether a person is competent or responsible for his or her actions. Thus, the term *disorder* does not necessarily absolve the disordered individual from criminal or moral sanction as hoped by the early social reformers.

WHAT IS THE DISEASE LIKE? In spite of this insistence that addiction (or dependence or abuse) is a disease, there have been few attempts to describe exactly what sort of a disease it is. This is unfortunate because simply declaring that something is a disease does little to help us understand it and even less to help us treat it. There are two sorts of suggestions: (a) *predisposition theories*, which say that people either are born with the disease or acquire it at some time before they begin abusing the drug. This disease predisposes certain people to become addicts whenever they start using the drug, and (b) *exposure theories*, which suggest that addiction is a disease that is caused by repeated exposure to the drug.

PREEXISTING DISEASES AND VULNERABILITIES. In a series of papers published in the 1950s and in his book *The Disease Concept of Alcoholism*, Jellinek was the first to formulate a disease theory. His theory explained only addiction to alcohol, not all addictions, but some of his ideas have been widely applied to other drugs. As we shall see in greater detail in Chapter 6, Jellinek proposed that alcoholism is not caused by alcohol. It is a disease that is inherited; people are born with it. Jellinek suggested that it works like an allergy. People with an allergy to cats will have no allergic reaction if they do not go near cats. Similarly, if alcoholics do not drink alcohol, they will never develop alcoholism, but if they do drink it, the disease will make them lose control of their drinking and they will be unable to stop. The exact mechanism responsible for this behavior was never made clear. One can understand how an allergy to cats can make you sneeze, but Jellinek never explained how a disease can make a person crave alcohol.

Jellinek also believed that there was no cure for the disease of addiction—you had it for life. This means that if a person with the disease takes a single drink, he or she will experience complete loss of control over drinking; that is, "One Drink = One Drunk." Jellinek's ideas have been widely adopted by the Alcoholics Anonymous movement and are believed by millions of people. This view is the basis of all 12-step treatment programs (see the section on treatments later in this chapter, and in Chapter 6 on Alcohol). Perhaps surprisingly, these treatment programs are not widely supported by research.

Since Jellinek, there have been other attempts to explain addictions in terms of individual predispositions. These can arise from either natural genetic variations or genetic damage, or exposure to certain environmental conditions in childhood or later in life. Proposed vulnerabilities include metabolic and neurological variations that alter a person's physiological response to a drug and, consequently, their motivation to consume it, and experiences such as abuse during childhood. Whether these vulnerabilities are diseases depends largely on the point of view of the theorist.

DRUG EXPOSURE DISEASES. There are some disease theories that claim that people are not born with the disease of addiction, nor do they acquire it somehow before using the drug. These theories propose that addiction is caused by exposure to the drug alone. Alan Leshner, a past director of the U.S. National Institute of Drug Abuse (NIDA), has expressed this idea as follows:

> This unexpected consequence of drug use [addiction] is what I have come to call the oops phenomenon. Why oops? Because the harmful outcome is in no way intentional. Just as no one starts out to have lung cancer when they smoke, or no one starts out to have clogged arteries when they eat fried foods, which in turn usually cause heart attacks, no one starts out to become a drug addict when they use drugs. But in each case, though no one meant to behave in a way that would lead to tragic health consequences, that is what happened just the same, because of the inexorable, and undetected, destructive biochemical processes at work.
>
> While we haven't yet pinpointed precisely all the triggers for the changes in the brain's structure and function that culminate in the "oops" phenomenon, a vast body of hard evidence shows that it is virtually inevitable that prolonged drug use will lead to addiction. From this we can soundly conclude that drug addiction is indeed a brain disease. (http://archives.drugabuse.gov/Published_Articles/Oops.html)

Modern theories of addiction appear to follow Leshner's description of a process that starts off as casual or recreational use of a substance and eventually develops into the harmful and self-destructive use we call addiction. This change takes place in the brain and is caused by exposure to the substance. Later, we will review what these changes might be and what specifically causes them.

IS ADDICTION A DISEASE? When the disease idea was first proposed by the social reformers in the mid-nineteenth century, the suggestion was not based on any scientific or medical evidence. In fact, their motivations were political. They wanted to remove the stigma of sinner and criminal from inebriates so that they could be treated rather than punished. Over the years, this idea has been widely adopted, and it is now quite clear that addictive behavior can be understood in terms of anatomy, physiology, biochemistry, genetics, and behavioral science rather than morality. It is now widely accepted that addicts need help and treatment rather than punishment and rejection. It may have taken more than a century, but the political and social goals of these Victorian reformers have largely been realized. But does this mean they were right? Is addiction a *disease*? Well, for the purpose of understanding addiction, it does not really matter anymore whether it is a disease or not. However, for some like Leshner, it may still be important, for political reasons, to remind people that addiction is a process that can be understood in terms of physiology rather than lifestyle. At the time he declared addiction to be a brain disease, Leshner was head of the NIDA, an agency of the U.S. government that funds and oversees a vast amount of addiction research and that requires the continuing support of politicians and the public.

There has been a great deal of ink spilled in the debate over whether addiction is a disease, but what all these arguments boil down to is how the term *disease* is defined. There are several ways you can define disease, but in many cases, a distinction is made between a disease and an injury. A disease is usually caused by a pathogen—bacteria causing tuberculosis or a virus causing the measles—or some genetic malfunction such as in Lou Gehrig's disease. An injury is like a broken leg. Both are medical conditions and treated by physicians, but a broken leg is seldom thought of as a disease. It may, therefore, be more appropriate to think of addiction as an injury rather than a disease. The distinction, however, is not always so clear. To use Leshner's example, if we eat too much fried or fatty food, we can injure our arteries with the buildup of fatty plaques on the artery wall. This restricts the flow of blood to vital organs like the heart, and that can make us very sick indeed. We could think of plaques as injuries created by eating too much fat, but we nonetheless call the result heart *disease* or atherosclerosis. As pointed out earlier, the fact that the *DSM* uses

the term *disorder* rather than *disease* acknowledges this distinction because the term *disorder* can include disabilities caused by both diseases and injuries.

Whether you think addiction is a disease or an injury will depend on your definition of disease, not on the mechanisms that cause addiction. We shall spend part of this chapter exploring why people use and abuse drugs. At the end of this process, you can decide for yourself if you think addiction is a disease.

ADDICTION AS PHYSICAL DEPENDENCE

Background

Early in the twentieth century, addiction researchers drew attention to the sickness that develops when a user of opium or morphine tries to stop. They proposed a hypothetical substance called an *autotoxin*—a metabolite of opium that stayed in the body after the drug was gone. This autotoxin had effects opposite to opium, and, when left in the body, it made the person very sick. Only opium or a related drug could antagonize the extremely unpleasant effects of the autotoxin and relieve the sickness. It was believed that the sickness was so unpleasant that the relief provided by opium was responsible for the continuous craving seen in addicts for more opium (Tatum & Seevers, 1931). In other words, to use the language of Skinner, addiction is a result of negative reinforcement (see Chapter 2); that is, the addicts use the drug to avoid withdrawal, like a rat learns to press a lever to avoid foot shock in a Skinner box. Later, the existence of the autotoxin was disproved. The sickness that remained after the drug was gone became known as *withdrawal* or *abstinence syndrome*, and more accurate explanations were developed to account for it (see Chapter 3). Avoidance of painful withdrawal symptoms, however, was still regarded as the explanation for opium use and the compulsive craving for the drug.

Because alcohol was the other major addicting drug at the time and because alcohol also causes severe withdrawal symptoms, it was logical for scientists to consider avoidance of withdrawal as a general explanation for the excessive use of all drugs. The ability of a drug to cause dependence (and, consequently, withdrawal) became accepted as the universal indication of an addicting drug, and the presence of physical dependence became the defining feature of an addict and an addiction.

This assumption became crystallized in the language developed to talk about drug use. The term *dependence* came to describe two separate effects that were synonymous in the minds of scientists at the time. Dependence meant both (a) the state in which a drug produces physical dependence (withdrawal symptoms occur when the drug is stopped) and (b) the compulsive self-administration of a drug (addiction). This model of drug abuse, which we shall call the *dependence model*, is still widely accepted.

At the core of the dependence model is the belief that withdrawal symptoms are so painful and distressing that dependent individuals are willing to sacrifice almost anything to avoid having to go through withdrawal (Wikler, 1980), and that addicts crave the drug because it will prevent the withdrawal. This view of the addict is still commonly presented in movies and on television.

The dependence model, however, has a big problem: The correspondence between dependence and addiction is less than perfect; that is, it is possible to have an addiction in the absence of dependence and to have dependence without addiction. Powerful addictions can develop from intake of substances such as cocaine and marijuana, which cause only mild (if any) withdrawal symptoms, and people can be physiologically dependent on medicines such as pain relievers and yet show no addictive behaviors such as craving and loss of control.

DEPENDENCE WITHOUT ADDICTION. During the planning of the *DSM-5*, it was recognized that the term *dependence*, as used to indicate addiction, was creating problems for many people taking dependence-producing drugs as part of medical treatment. These people often became physically dependent on their medication. This caused concern among physicians who were reluctant to turn their patients into out-of-control addicts and may have needlessly reduced or denied their patients adequate pain medication. For this reason, it has been recommended that the *DSM-5* restrict the use of the word *dependence* to indicate only physical dependence rather than addiction (O'Brien, 2010).

ADDICTION WITHOUT DEPENDENCE. The fact that people could become addicted to substances that did not cause severe physiological withdrawal was noted very early and created a much bigger problem for the dependence model. In 1931, Tatum and Seevers suggested the adoption of "some non-committal term such as psychic addiction" (p. 119) to explain the addictive use of drugs like marijuana. This alternative was later developed into the concept of *psychological dependence* and soon became widely used. It expanded the dependence model by assuming that drugs such as marijuana caused unobservable psychological withdrawal symptoms, that is, psychological, or psychic, dependence. In other words, the concept of psychological dependence presumed that there was some sort of psychological, as opposed to physical, withdrawal symptoms that were so distressing that people were highly motivated to avoid them. This psychological withdrawal was not observable; it took place in the mind and did not have any outward manifestations apart from the fact that the user became highly motivated to take the drug to avoid these psychological symptoms. Behaviorally, psychological dependence created an "impaired control of psychoactive substance use" as described in the *DSM-III* (American Psychiatric Association, 1987, p. 166).

PROBLEMS WITH PSYCHOLOGICAL DEPENDENCE. The way it has been traditionally used, the concept of psychological dependence presents a serious conceptual problem. It cannot be used by itself as an explanation because it is circular. For example, if we say that we know that John is psychologically dependent because he uses a drug excessively, we cannot say that John uses a drug excessively because he is psychologically dependent. The term may be used to describe a state of affairs, but it cannot be used as an explanation. This problem does not arise with physical dependence because there is independent evidence—withdrawal symptoms—that physical dependence exists. However, it now looks as though this circularity problem with psychological dependence may be soon resolved. Modern research in neuroscience has been able to look inside the brain and has found many neurological changes caused by repeated drug use that appear to be the physiological basis of this psychological withdrawal effect. These neurological processes are much more complex than simple withdrawal symptoms. They involve long-lasting changes in neural circuitry and are able to explain how addictive behavior can be created by drugs that do not cause overt physiological withdrawal.

MODERN BEHAVIORAL EXPLANATIONS OF DRUG USE

Background

We have seen that people start using drugs in a casual, recreational manner, and most are able to continue to do so. But for some people, the use escalates until it starts to create the sorts of problems described in the *DSM*; that is, they become addicted. Both the disease model and the physical dependence model are primarily attempts to explain addiction, but the processes they describe also apply to the beginning stages of casual use. The disease model suggests that casual use is a result of the initial stages of the disease. The dependence model implies a rapidly forming physical or psychological dependence that results from occasional drug use motivated by curiosity, experimentation, peer pressure, and other factors.

One of the mysteries of casual use was that it did not seem to be associated with any known motivation. People are motivated by food if they are hungry and water if they are thirsty, but what drive does drug use satisfy? Sex clearly serves the purpose of reproduction, and social motivations are important for survival, but why would we be designed to be motivated to take a mind-altering substance? Some theorists went so far as to suggest that there is a natural *drive* to use drugs; that is, humans have a need to alter their state of consciousness.

One reason for the delay in studying the nonharmful use of drugs was the fact that addictive behavior was considered uniquely human. Attempts to create addictions in other species had generally been unsuccessful, largely because nearly all these studies provided drugs via the oral route, which creates several problems. Most drugs have a bitter taste that laboratory animals dislike, and animals have a built-in protective mechanism, called *conditioned taste aversion* that causes them to reject any taste that is followed by sickness or an alteration in nervous system functioning. Slow absorption from the digestive system after oral administration also causes a delay between consumption and the effect of the drug on the brain, which can interfere with the development of addiction. The assumption that only humans could become addicted held back the development of new ideas and properly controlled scientific research.

It had been shown, as early as the 1920s, that laboratory animals could be made physically dependent if they were forced to consume a drug such as morphine or alcohol. However, it could never be shown that they would make themselves physically dependent (which, during that time, was considered the defining feature of addiction) if a drug were made freely available to them. Even animals made physically dependent by forced consumption seldom continued to consume a drug when alternatives were made available. In 1937, A. R. Lindesmith, a sociologist, wrote, "Certainly from the point of view of social science it would be ridiculous to include animals and humans together in the concept of addiction" (quoted in Laties, 1986, p. 33).

The failure of laboratory animals to show the compulsive and self-destructive drug taking that humans so often exhibit, or even to show low levels of drug consumption, also led people to believe that addiction must be caused by some trait that distinguishes humans from animals. This line of reasoning supported an older, moralistic view that because humans had *free will* and nonhumans did not, humans could "sin" by choosing to take drugs and that this sinning was punished by the misery of addiction.

Another more scientific explanation originated in the physical dependence model: Nonhuman animals could never become addicted to a drug because they were not capable of learning the association between an injection and relief from withdrawal sickness, which might occur 15 or 20 minutes later (Goldberg, 1976). Whatever the explanation, it was widely accepted for many years that there was no point in using laboratory animals to study the addictive behavior of humans.

In the absence of laboratory techniques to adequately test it, the dependence model seemed to account nicely for addiction and was virtually unchallenged until a few simple technological breakthroughs were made in the 1950s. At that time, a number of researchers began to show that laboratory animals would learn to perform a behavior that resulted in a drug injection. This line of research expanded quickly when the technology was developed that allowed intravenous drug infusions to be delivered to freely moving animals by means of a permanently implanted catheter (see Figure 5-1). With this one development, our whole view of drug self-administration and addiction changed.

Self-Administration in Humans and Nonhumans

Thousands of studies have explored the drug-taking behavior of laboratory animals. In fact, we now probably know more about nonhuman drug taking than we do about human drug taking. The success achieved by studying laboratory animals using operant techniques has prompted some scientists to adopt these research strategies to study human behavior (Spiga & Roache, 1997). These techniques were pioneered by Nancy Mello and Jack Mendelson at the McLean Hospital in Belmont, Massachusetts.

In this research, paid volunteers live in a hospital ward so that they may be kept under constant medical supervision. Only people who have a history of drug use or previous exposure to a specific drug are generally permitted to participate in these experiments. Their health and their behavior are carefully monitored. They are given the opportunity to perform some operant task, such as pushing a button or riding an exercise bicycle, to earn tokens or points that they are able to exchange for doses of a drug. This arrangement is analogous to the operant task with laboratory animals and can probably tell us a great deal more about drug self-administration

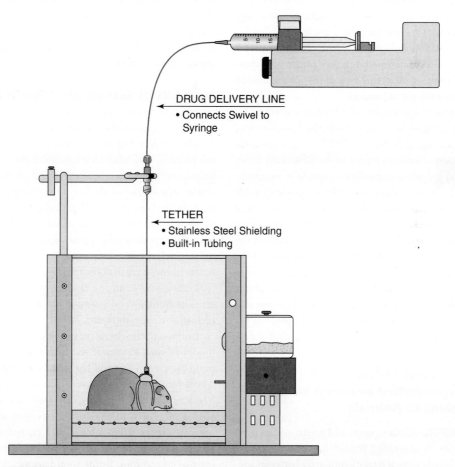

DRUG DELIVERY LINE
• Connects Swivel to Syringe

TETHER
• Stainless Steel Shielding
• Built-in Tubing

FIGURE 5-1 A schematic drawing of the drug self-administration preparation for the rat. The rat presses the lever, which causes the activation of the pump by the programming equipment. The pump injects a specific amount of a drug solution through a catheter that has been implanted into the jugular vein near the rat's heart.

than simply observing the behavior of addicts in their natural environment. For example, researchers are able to test and compare the effects of different doses and types of drugs and to contrast drugs with placebos. They can also manipulate other variables, such as availability, route of administration, and work required; check the effects of other drugs administered at the same time; and carefully measure and observe changes in behavior that might be caused by the test drug. The situation is artificial, but it permits researchers to exercise considerable precision and control, which is not possible in any other circumstance (Mello & Mendelson, 1987).

One disadvantage of this method is that it can present an ethical dilemma. It would be unethical to use inexperienced or nonaddicted participants in research of this type if it involved unrestricted exposure to drugs, like heroin, which are known to be habit forming. Such a procedure would introduce participants to the reinforcing effects of a drug, an experience they might not otherwise have. For this reason, this type of research is usually done only on addicted volunteers.

Operant techniques have been further refined to allow some testing of humans outside the laboratory or research ward (Spiga & Roache, 1997). In this research, normal human volunteers report to the laboratory every morning and are asked to swallow a capsule of a particular color. On alternate days, they take a capsule of a different color. Usually, one color is a drug and the other a placebo. When they have been exposed to both, they are asked to choose which one they want to take. If the drug is a reinforcer, it will be chosen more often than the placebo. This procedure has the advantage of not being carried out in an artificial laboratory environment, but a considerable amount of precision is lost. There are also some ethical restrictions on the types and doses of drugs that can be given.

Similarities and Differences in Self-Administration between Humans and Nonhuman Animals

TYPE OF DRUG. Comparisons of human and nonhuman behavior in controlled studies have made it quite clear that there is a great deal of similarity between species (Griffiths, Bigelow, & Henningfield, 1980). Laboratory animals, including dogs, monkeys, baboons, rats, cats, and mice, will take most of the drugs that humans

use. Only recently have there been demonstrations that nonhumans do self-administer THC, the active ingredient in cannabis (Tanda, Manzar, & Goldberg, 2000; see Chapter 14). It has also been shown that both humans and nonhumans will self-administer anabolic steroids (Wood, 2004).

Some drugs appear to have aversive properties; that is, laboratory animals will work to shut off infusions of these drugs or will learn to perform tasks to avoid receiving such infusions. In the avoidance training task described in Chapter 2, laboratory animals are taught to make a response that turns off a stimulus that always precedes an electric shock. To demonstrate that some drugs have aversive properties, a similar procedure is used, except that a drug infusion replaces the shock. Drugs that have been demonstrated to have aversive properties include the hallucinogenic drug LSD, antipsychotic drugs such as chlorpromazine, and the antidepressant imipramine.

PATTERNS OF SELF-ADMINISTRATION. Not only do humans and nonhumans appear to self-administer similar drugs, but the patterns of self-administration are also similar. Figure 5-2 shows the records of a rhesus monkey self-administering alcohol (ethanol) and a human volunteer in a research ward of a hospital who could earn drinks of alcohol by pressing a button. The records are very similar. Both subjects worked for the alcohol in an erratic pattern, and both subjects voluntarily experienced periods of withdrawal, a pattern quite similar to alcohol consumption patterns of alcoholics in more natural settings. As we proceed through this book and examine the self-administration patterns of humans and nonhumans, many more similarities will become apparent.

Because of the pervasive influence of the dependence model, in early studies it was assumed that physical dependence was essential for drug self-administration. Thus, rats and monkeys were first made physically dependent on morphine by repeated injections. Then they were placed in an operant chamber and given the opportunity to press a lever that caused a delivery of morphine through a catheter. The animals quickly learned to respond. But it soon became obvious that it was not necessary to create a physical dependence; the drug infusion was acting like a more traditional positive reinforcer, such as food or water, rather than a negative

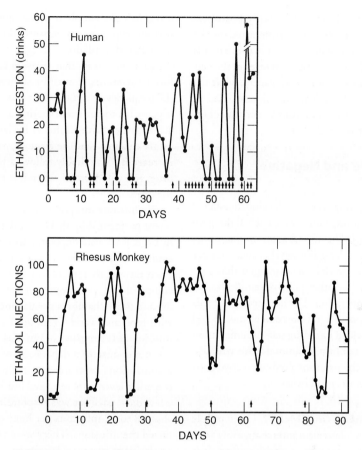

FIGURE 5-2 The similarity between the patterns of self-administration of ethanol in a human and a rhesus monkey under continuous drug availability. The arrows indicate the occurrence of withdrawal symptoms. *Top:* Data from an experiment in which a volunteer earned tokens by pressing a button. The tokens could be exchanged for drinks. *Bottom:* Intake of ethanol by a rhesus monkey pressing a lever for intravenous infusions. (Adapted from Griffiths et al., 1980, p. 19.)

reinforcer in which the animal was escaping withdrawal (Thompson & Schuster, 1964).

The role of physical dependence in the positive reinforcing effects of drugs was further explored by Charles Schuster and his colleagues, who showed that animals that were not physically dependent would self-administer doses of morphine so low that no physical dependence ever developed (Schuster, 1970). It was also demonstrated that rats would press a lever to give themselves infusions of cocaine and other stimulants that do

not cause marked withdrawal symptoms (Pickens & Thompson, 1968).

These and other studies clearly demonstrated that many of the assumptions of the dependence model are not correct. As we will see, the presence of overt withdrawal symptoms can be an important factor controlling the intake of some drugs, but it is not essential for drug self-administration and cannot serve as the sole explanation for either drug use or drug addiction. It should be pointed out that one of the modern theories of addiction we will discuss later in this chapter, called the *hedonic dysregulation theory*, postulates that addictive behavior arises in part from avoidance of drug withdrawal symptoms. This theory, however, extends the definition of withdrawal to include changes in the nervous system, which are more or less permanent, while the assumptions of the early dependence model were based on the short-term compensatory readjustments in physiology traditionally thought of as withdrawal.

Drugs as Positive and Negative Reinforcers

The model of drug taking that has developed as a result of self-administration studies we shall call the *positive reinforcement model*. This model assumes that drugs are self-administered, at least initially, because they act as positive reinforcers and that the principles that govern behavior controlled by other positive reinforcers apply to drug self-administration. The next section of this chapter will discuss positive reinforcement model and the insights it has provided into drug self-administration in both humans and nonhuman animals. We will also examine the brain mechanisms involved in positive reinforcement and how they control behavior.

WHAT IS POSITIVE REINFORCEMENT? Often people use the term *positive reinforcement* interchangeably with pleasure, euphoria, or some sort of positive affect. It is true that stimuli that act as positive reinforcers are often reported to give pleasure, which is then assumed to be a cause of the behavior (e.g., "I do it because it makes me feel good"), but there are plenty of examples of stimuli that can act as positive reinforcers but do not cause pleasure. In fact, there are circumstances in which an electric shock can be a positive reinforcer (Kelleher & Morse, 1964). Traditionally, a positive reinforcer has been defined only in terms of its effect on behavior; that is, *a positive reinforcer is any stimulus that increases the frequency of a behavior it is contingent upon* (see Chapter 2). Over the years, there has been much speculation about the nature of positive reinforcement. For example, it has been suggested that it is a result of such things as drive reduction, drive induction, and consummatory behavior (Domjan, 2010). Later in this chapter, we will present information linking positive reinforcement to activity in certain parts of the brain. The neurophysiology of reinforcement is complex and not well understood; however,

it is a mistake simply to equate positive reinforcement with the experience of pleasure, although, as we shall see, some theories still do.

To demonstrate that an event can be a positive reinforcing stimulus, it must be shown that it will increase the frequency of a response it is contingent upon. Thus, if you wish to demonstrate that an infusion of a drug is acting as a positive reinforcer for lever pressing, it is necessary to show that the frequency of lever pressing will increase if it is reliably followed by an infusion of the drug, and will decrease when it is no longer followed by the drug.

To illustrate this point, we will look at a classic experiment performed by Pickens and Thompson, published in 1968. Rats were implanted with catheters so that they could receive infusions of cocaine into the jugular vein. Each rat was then placed in a small chamber that was equipped with two levers and a stimulus light. The rats lived in these chambers permanently and were provided with food and water. From 9:00 A.M. to 11:00 P.M., an infusion of 0.5 mg/kg cocaine was administered to each rat in response to a depression of one of the levers on a continuous reinforcement schedule. Responses on the other lever were recorded but had no effect. Within a few days, each rat was responding at a steady rate of about 8 to 12 infusions per hour on the lever that produced the infusions. There were virtually no responses on the other lever.

Because many people were skeptical about these findings, Thompson and Pickens were careful to design the experiment to show that the drug was acting as a positive reinforcer and that there could be no other explanation. For example, the increases in responding to the drug lever could be due to a general stimulating effect of cocaine on the behavior of the rats. In other words, the rats might hit the lever accidentally, and the resulting infusion of the stimulant cocaine would cause the animal to be more active. This increased activity in turn might cause more accidental lever presses and, consequently, more activation caused by more of the drug. However, in this experiment, there was no increase in responding on the second lever, which might be expected if bar pressing was the result of increases in general activity. In addition, the experimenters demonstrated that responding on the drug lever stopped when they discontinued reinforcing it with cocaine, and the rats were given noncontingent or unearned infusions of cocaine. Thompson and Pickens also showed that when the contingency was switched from one lever to the other, the rats' choice of levers also switched. This made it clear that behavior was being controlled by the contingency between the lever press and the drug infusion rather than any other property of the drug or the situation.

Thompson and Pickens found that extinction of responding occurred if saline placebo infusions were substituted for the cocaine infusions after each lever press. When the cocaine infusions were stopped, there was a short burst of lever pressing before the rat stopped responding. This pattern is typically observed at the beginning of extinction with other reinforcers. They were also able to show that rats would respond on fixed ratio (FR) schedules for cocaine reinforcement and that the pattern of lever pressing generated by the schedule was similar to the pattern FR schedules generated with other positive reinforcers.

Since these early studies, it has been demonstrated that a variety of laboratory animals will self-administer nearly all drugs that humans consume (with some exceptions, as described previously). Animals will self-administer these drugs through a variety of different routes of administration, which include *intragastric* (direct injection through a cannula into the stomach), *intracranial* (direct injection of tiny amounts of drug through a cannula into specific parts of the brain), *intraventricular* (injection through a cannula into the ventricles in the brain), and *inhalation*. Laboratory animals will also consume drugs orally (techniques have been developed to overcome the delay in effect and the natural protective mechanisms described earlier).

As a result of the vast number of studies using these and similar techniques, the defining characteristics of drug use and abuse have been thoroughly explored. Indeed, much of what we know today about drug use has come from self-administration experiments using both laboratory animals and humans.

Problems with the Positive Reinforcement Model

POSITIVE REINFORCEMENT PARADOX. The positive reinforcement model seems to account nicely for the normal or nonaddictive aspect of drug use, but can we explain addiction using positive reinforcement? The consequences of using some drugs can, indeed, be painful and unhealthy and ought to be punishing enough to

make an organism stop using them. For example, when cocaine and amphetamine are made freely available to a monkey for a period of time, very often it will refuse to eat or sleep for extended periods. The drug will cause it to mutilate parts of its body, and ultimately the monkey will die of an overdose or bleed to death from its self-inflicted wounds. This is not unlike the economically and physically destructive behavior motivated by cocaine in some humans. It may seem paradoxical that behavior motivated by positive reinforcement should persist in the face of such punishing consequences. Addicts themselves often acknowledge that continued drug use creates an aversive state they generally would like to avoid or terminate. For this reason, drug users often seek treatment for their addiction. How can an event like the administration of a drug be both positively reinforcing enough to make people continue to use it and at the same time aversive enough to motivate people to stop? As Gene Heyman of Harvard University asks, "If addictive drug use is on balance positively reinforcing, then why would a user ever want to stop?" (Heyman, 1996, p. 16).

Such a paradox is not unique to drugs and cannot be used to disqualify drugs as positive reinforcers. More traditional reinforcers such as food can be destructive and cause pain. People often overeat, become obese, and experience physical discomfort, health risks, and social censure and yet continue to overeat. Sexual activity also acts as a reinforcing stimulus. It has positive reinforcing effects, but it also has the potential to cause unpleasant and undesirable consequences, such as sexually transmitted diseases and unwanted pregnancy. In fact, most positive reinforcers, including drugs, can have negative and destructive effects that can motivate people to seek treatment to help them quit. The question is can this seemingly excessive and self-destructive behavior be explained by what we know about positive reinforcement? In fact, it can.

One of the reasons that positive reinforcing stimuli continue to control behavior, in spite of punishing effects, is that they are immediately experienced after behavior, whereas the punishing and painful effects are often delayed. One well-understood principle of operant conditioning is that if a reinforcer is delayed, its ability to control behavior is diminished. Thus, if an intake of alcohol causes pleasure within minutes and a hangover a number of hours later, the pleasure, rather than the hangover, will be more likely to determine whether the person will drink alcohol again. When punishing consequences occur infrequently and after a considerable delay, no matter how severe they might be, they are less likely to exert as much control over behavior as will immediate gratification. Later, we will discuss a theory called *incentive sensitization theory*, which shows that drugs can sensitize certain parts of the brain that control positive reinforcement, and this too can explain addiction.

CIRCULARITY. Another problem with the positive reinforcement model is that, by itself, it provides a circular explanation of drug use. If we say that a drug is a positive reinforcer because it will increase a behavior upon which it is contingent, then we cannot explain drug use by saying that a drug is a positive reinforcer (Robinson & Berridge, 1993). One way out of this dilemma would be to define positive reinforcement in terms of something other than behavior. For example, many have defined it as a stimulus that causes pleasure (or a positive hedonic state, if we want to sound scientific), but this is not a satisfactory solution because, as we have already shown, positive reinforcers need not always be pleasurable. In addition, pleasure is a subjective state, and it is difficult to define the concept scientifically. Fortunately, there are more acceptable explanations of reinforcement.

We can escape this dilemma in two ways. First, decades of research have told us a great deal about positive reinforcement. By saying that a drug is a positive reinforcer, we know a lot more than just the fact that it increases behavior. This means that we can use the principles already established for positive reinforcers to understand and predict the way drugs will control behavior. To the extent that drugs conform to these predictions, it is useful to think of them as positive reinforcers. As we proceed through this chapter it should become apparent that drug use and addiction become more understandable if we think of them in terms of positive reinforcement.

Second, advances in neuroscience have provided considerable insight into the neurological mechanisms of reinforcement. As discussed in Chapter 4 and in the next section of this chapter, there are specific brain systems that are the mechanisms for positive reinforcement and for the motivational effects of stimuli that act as positive reinforcers. Using this neural circuitry, we can now define reinforcement in terms other than the behavior it generates.

Factors That Alter the Reinforcing Value of a Drug

In Chapter 2, we discussed techniques used to determine the reinforcing value of different drugs and the effect of various manipulations on the reinforcing value of drugs in general. With laboratory animals, these techniques include the progressive ratio schedule, choice, and conditioned place preference. In research with humans, choice between a drug and a placebo is widely used, and in studies with human volunteers in hospital research wards, rate of responding or amount consumed and progressive ratio schedules have been used as measures of reinforcement.

DIFFERENT DRUGS. Various drugs differ in their capacity to act as positive reinforcers. This property of a certain drug is sometimes referred to as its *abuse potential* or *abuse liability*. It is important to be able to assess the abuse potential of new drugs as they are developed, and abuse potential is becoming an important consideration in the legal classification of drugs. Assessments have shown that psychomotor stimulants in general, and cocaine in particular, are the most robust reinforcers yet encountered. Cocaine is extensively used to train laboratory animals to self-administer drugs, and it has become a standard against which other drugs are often compared. In the following chapters, the reinforcing value of many drugs will be described.

DOSE OF DRUG. Assessment techniques have also demonstrated that larger doses of any drug are generally more reinforcing than smaller doses, although some studies suggest that there may not be much difference between very large doses. In fact, reinforcing ability may decline with some drugs when very large doses are used (Brady et al., 1987; Depoortere, Li, Lane, & Emmett-Oglesby, 1993).

BREEDING AND STRAIN DIFFERENCES. Genetic differences between individuals may be responsible for variations in drug use. Self-administration techniques have been used to test the reinforcing properties of drugs in different strains of laboratory animals (George, Ritz, & Elmer, 1991). It has been known for some time that different strains of laboratory rats and mice differ in alcohol consumption. In fact, both alcohol-preferring and alcohol-avoiding strains of rats have been selectively bred in the laboratory. It seems that this genetic predisposition is not unique to alcohol. Frank George at the University of New Mexico and Stephen Goldberg at the National Institute on Drug Abuse in Baltimore have shown that different strains of rats and mice have different preferences for cocaine. Similar strain differences have been shown in the consumption of opiates (George, 1997; George & Goldberg, 1989).

RELIEF OF UNPLEASANT SYMPTOMS. It would be reasonable to assume that drugs that have therapeutic effects (they relieve unpleasant symptoms of a disorder) might have enhanced reinforcing value in people who have that disorder. In fact, it has often been suggested that alcohol is used by some people to relieve the symptoms of stress or depression, and that people with attention deficit hyperactivity disorder (ADHD) smoke because nicotine has been shown to improve attention. In fact, there is a correlation between certain disorders and the use of drugs that are known to mitigate those disorders, but the idea is not widely supported in experimental research with humans.

It has been speculated that the motivation for abuse of diazepam (Valium) might be to gain protection against the distress of anxiety. Thus, people experiencing high levels of stress and anxiety might be particularly susceptible to the overuse of diazepam. At the University of Chicago, a research team that includes Harriet de Wit and Chris Johanson has tested some of these assumptions, using a variation on the choice procedure with human participants. In this procedure, volunteers report to the lab every morning for a number of days. Each day, they are given a capsule to consume at that time. On days 1 and 3 they get a capsule of one color, and on days 2 and 4 they get a capsule of a different color. Over the next 5 days, they are given their choice of capsule color. By definition, the more reinforcing pill will be chosen more frequently. Using this technique with normal (nondisordered) volunteers as participants, de Wit and Johanson (1987) found that there is generally no preference for diazepam over a placebo. This result is somewhat surprising because diazepam is an extensively prescribed drug that is suspected of being overused.

The researchers reasoned that diazepam might be preferred and excessively used only by very anxious people, so they screened their participants by administering a diagnostic test for anxiety. Surprisingly, highly anxious people did not consistently choose diazepam over the placebo, even though the anxious participants rated the drug more highly than the placebo and reported that the drug reduced their anxiety.

In addition to testing diazepam in various populations, these researchers found that amphetamine, which improves mood and decreases appetite (see Chapter 10), was not preferentially chosen by people who were depressed or overweight (de Wit & Johanson, 1987; de Wit, Uhlenhuth, & Johanson, 1987).

In one circumstance, however, anticipated relief of unpleasant symptoms is reinforcing. Opioids will be self-administered to a greater extent by humans if they know that they are about to experience a painful stimulus (Pirec et al., 1995; Zacny et al., 1996; see the next section on task demands).

Understanding drug use as a form of self-medication to relieve unpleasant psychological states has considerable intuitive appeal, but as yet there are few experimental studies to support the idea.

TASK DEMANDS. It seems clear from human experience that the decision to use or not to use a drug depends on the expected demands of a situation. For example, people may choose not to drink alcohol if they know that they will be driving, or they may take a stimulant if they know that they will be driving long distances at night. Task demand has been systematically examined by Kenneth Silverman and his colleagues at Johns Hopkins Medical School. They have shown that this variable can affect drug choice in human participants.

Silverman had volunteers ingest color-coded capsules containing triazolam, a short-acting benzodiazepine tranquilizer (see Chapter 7); d-amphetamine, a stimulant (see Chapter 10); or a placebo. Then they were required to engage in one of two activities, either (a) a vigilance task in which participants stared at a computer screen for 50 minutes and were required to respond when a star appeared, or (b) a relaxation task in which they were required to lie on a bed for 50 minutes without moving. Seven of eight participants reliably chose the amphetamine capsules when they knew that the vigilance task was to follow, and all eight always chose the triazolam when they knew they would be in the relaxation situation (Silverman, Kirby, & Griffiths, 1994).

In a later experiment, Silverman, Mumford, and Griffiths (1994) showed that participants reliably chose a capsule containing 100 mg of caffeine rather than a placebo before the vigilance activity. Participants will choose an analgesic (nitrous oxide or fentanyl) more often if they are required to undergo the painful experience of immersing their forearms in icy water (Pirec et al., 1995; Zacny et al., 1996). Thus, it appears that task demands can either enhance or diminish the reinforcing value of a particular drug.

STRESS. Stress has often been given as an excuse for the use of drugs by humans, but there have been extensive studies of stress and the self-administration of drugs by laboratory animals. From these studies, we know that stress not only enhances the acquisition of the self-administration of a number of drugs, including cocaine, opiates, and alcohol, but also has been shown to increase the reinforcing value of these drugs as determined by rate of responding and progressive ratio breakpoint (Piazza & Le Moal, 1998). The stressors that produce this effect are of various kinds: tail pinch, social isolation, exposure to aggression by members of the same species, and unpredictable foot shock.

As we shall see later in this chapter, the neurophysiological mechanisms that seem to be involved in stress-induced increases in drug intake do not involve relief from stress; rather stress directly activates and sensitizes brain mechanisms responsible for the reinforcing value of a drug. It is clear that stress not only increases drug use when it is experienced during drug self-administration, but a history of stressful experiences is also able to sensitize brain reinforcement mechanisms.

OTHER DEPRIVATIONS AND MOTIVATIONS. Hungry animals will drink more alcohol compared to satiated animals. It was always assumed that they did so because alcohol has calories that supply the hungry animals with energy. It turns out, however, that hunger also stimulates the self-administration of many other drugs that contain no calories, including cocaine and phencyclidine (PCP, a dissociative anesthetic; see Chapter 15), and thirst seems to have the same effect as hunger (Carroll & Meisch, 1984). This may be an expression of the stress effect, discussed in the previous section, because hunger can be thought of as a form of stress. As yet, there have been no studies of deprivation effects on drug self-administration in humans.

PREVIOUS EXPERIENCE WITH OTHER DRUGS. In general, most research shows that slower-acting drugs in the benzodiazepine family, such as diazepam (Valium), are not self-administered by humans and nonhumans. It turns out that an important determinant of whether diazepam is self-administered is past experience with sedative-hypnotic or depressant drugs such as barbiturates. Bergman and Johanson (1985) found that baboons did not self-administer diazepam when they were switched to it from cocaine, but they did self-administer diazepam to some degree when switched to it from pentobarbital.

This difference does not appear to be unique to baboons. Other research using the choice procedure has consistently found no preference for diazepam over a placebo in normal populations of volunteers. In similar experiments conducted with moderate alcohol users, however, people who consumed an average of one drink per day showed a marked preference for the diazepam. In a different experiment, participants living on a hospital research ward did work for a benzodiazepine reward when given the opportunity, but they were all former sedative abusers (de Wit & Johanson, 1987). Similarly, nitrous oxide, a volatile anesthetic sometimes known as laughing gas, is more reinforcing to moderate drinkers than to light drinkers (Cho et al., 1997).

PREVIOUS EXPERIENCE WITH THE SAME DRUG. In naive laboratory animals, caffeine does not appear to be a robust reinforcer. In one experiment, only two out of six monkeys self-administered caffeine spontaneously. The four monkeys that did not give themselves caffeine were then given automatic infusions of caffeine for a period of time. Caffeine then acted as a reinforcer in three of these four monkeys (Deneau, Yanagita, & Seevers, 1969). In another example, previous exposure to amphetamine increased the breaking point for self-administered amphetamine on a progressive ratio schedule (Lorrain, Arnold, & Vezina, 2000).

It has been demonstrated repeatedly that a history of either self-administration or passive exposure to a drug can enhance that drug's reinforcing ability (Goldberg, 1976; Samson, 1987). It is likely that the effect of previous exposure to the same or a similar drug is mediated by a general sensitization to the reinforcing effects of drugs (see Chapter 3 and the section on incentive sensitization later in this chapter). The increased reinforcement may also be due to the presence of withdrawal effects caused by previous exposure to the drug; the animal may increase responding for the drug to alleviate the unpleasant symptoms of withdrawal, as described in the next section. Such an effect has been demonstrated with alcohol, cocaine, methamphetamine, and heroin. These increases in responding for drugs, brought about by repeated exposure to withdrawal, can last for extended periods of time. They seem to last longer than the presence of acute withdrawal symptoms, thus suggesting that the withdrawal exposure created more or less permanent changes on the brain (Koob & Le Moal, 2008).

WITHDRAWAL SYMPTOMS. Although physical dependence is not necessary for drug self-administration, it appears that the presence of withdrawal symptoms can influence the reinforcing effect of many drugs. For example, early research on the self-administration of morphine showed that the rate of self-administration will increase if the animal is denied the opportunity to self-administer for a period of time and is experiencing withdrawal symptoms during testing (Thompson & Schuster, 1964).

In another early study, Tomoji Yanagita (1987) compared physically dependent and nondependent animals for their breaking points on a progressive ratio schedule. Physical dependence was established in some animals by giving them pretreatments with a drug; control animals were pretreated with a placebo. Yanagita showed that animals made physically dependent on morphine and codeine had higher breaking points compared to nondependent controls. Physical dependence on ethanol caused only a slight increase in the breaking point for ethanol, but the same effect was not seen with diazepam (Valium). With alcohol at least, the presence of withdrawal symptoms can reliably increase drug intake, but it is necessary for the animal to have had the opportunity to learn that obtaining the drug relieves the withdrawal (Becker, 2008).

EXTENDED ACCESS. Early research into the self-administration of cocaine by both rats and monkeys showed that if the animals were given short, daily sessions, their responding would quickly become stable. But if they were allowed continuous access to the drug, the animal's intake would exceed that of the daily dose and the animal would, within a few days, often die from overdose or other side effects.

This effect was systematically investigated in an experiment by Ahmed and Koob (1998). In their experiment, one group of rats was given daily access to cocaine for only 1 hour. Another group was given access to cocaine for 6 hours per day. Rats in the short exposure group (1 hour per day) quickly developed a slow, stable rate of responding for cocaine—their daily intake leveled off and remained stable during the 12 days of testing. Not surprisingly, rats in the long exposure group (6 hours per day) consumed more cocaine, compared to rats in the short exposure group, but their consumption did not stabilize. Instead, their daily consumption increased over the 12 days. Later, after 1 month of abstinence, the rats were returned to their initial treatment condition. The short exposure rats continued to administer cocaine at the same slow rate as before, but the long exposure rats continued to escalate their consumption to an even greater level. This effect of extended exposure has also been seen with heroin.

PRIMING OR REINSTATEMENT. The priming effect, also called reinstatement, has been studied for many years and appears to occur with many reinforcing stimuli. It has been shown that extinguished responding for a reinforcer can be reinstated by a noncontingent presentation of that reinforcer (Reid, 1957). This is also true for drugs (de Wit, 1996).

The priming effect for drugs was demonstrated by Stewart and de Wit (1987). They trained monkeys to bar press for an infusion of cocaine or heroin and then extinguished the response by withholding the drug. They then found that a noncontingent infusion of the drug would start the animal bar pressing again. Reinstatement has since been demonstrated with many other drugs.

In addition to the original training drug, reinstatement can be caused by injections of a different reinforcing drug and by injections of drugs directly into the ventral tegmental area of the mesolimbic dopamine system. Priming can also be caused by a stressful stimulus (de Wit, 1996) and stimuli previously associated with drug delivery. This reinstatement of drug self-administration, even after a lengthy period without the drug, is very similar to the relapse of addicted individuals following long periods of abstinence. It is known that such relapses are sometimes triggered by the drug itself, stress, or even people and situations that have been associated with previous drug use (i.e., conditioned stimuli). Stimuli associated with withdrawal can also stimulate self-administration and relapse (Kenny, Chen, Kitamura, Markou, & Koob, 2006). This was demonstrated by the example in Chapter 3 where a former heroin addict relapsed after his subway car entered a station where he had often experienced withdrawal.

CONDITIONED REINFORCEMENT. It has long been known that if a neutral stimulus is paired with a reinforcing stimulus, it will acquire reinforcing properties through classical conditioning. In Chapter 3, you learned how many of the effects of a drug could be conditioned to environmental stimuli. The same is true of the reinforcing effects of drugs. Conditioned reinforcement or conditioned incentive has been demonstrated in a number of different ways, including through conditioned place preference (described in Chapter 2) and second-order schedules of reinforcement (described next).

SECOND-ORDER SCHEDULES. This is a modification of the standard drug self-administration technique, described previously. When a drug is administered, it is preceded or accompanied by a distinctive stimulus, such as a light. Eventually, the animal will learn to emit a response (such as bar press) just to make the light come on; that is, the light acquires reinforcing properties because of its association with the drug. These reinforcing properties can be demonstrated using a *second-order schedule* (Katz & Goldberg, 1987). The light is presented on a schedule of reinforcement such as an FR 10. The FR 10 itself is considered to be a single response in another schedule that is reinforced by a drug infusion—perhaps an FR 20. Thus, the light comes on after every 10 responses, and after 20 of these FR 10s are completed, the light and the drug are presented together. Thus, the animal gets the drug after making 200 responses.

Intermittently reinforcing behavior by presenting a stimulus associated with the drug and only occasionally presenting the drug and the stimulus together makes it possible to maintain much more behavior than if the drug were administered alone and no stimulus was used (Goldberg, Spealman, & Goldberg, 1981).

In Chapter 3, it was shown that many of the conditioned effects of a drug are compensatory, or opposite, from the unconditioned effects of the drug. If drug-related stimuli cause a compensatory response,

they will reduce the effect of the drug when they are presented along with the drug. This is called *conditioned tolerance*. It does not occur with the conditioned reinforcing effects of drugs. As place preference and second-order schedules show, stimuli paired with a reinforcing drug also acquire reinforcing properties. This means that if the conditioned stimulus and the drug produce the same effect, presenting the drug and the stimulus together will enhance the effect of the drug and cause sensitization (see Chapter 3).

The role of conditioned reinforcers in maintaining drug self-administration and relapse has long been recognized. As described in the section on priming, stimuli associated with drug consumption—the sight and smell of cigarettes, the sight of drug injection apparatus, or the environment of a bar—are all factors that are known to stimulate drug use and precipitate relapse in those who are trying to quit or remain abstinent. Some drug therapies deliberately attempt to extinguish the reinforcing effect of these cues by presenting them without the subsequent delivery of a drug (Silverman & Bonate, 1997).

THE NEUROANATOMY OF MOTIVATION AND REINFORCEMENT

Any system that controls motivation must have at least two components. It must be able to energize or activate behavior, and it must be able to direct that behavior toward a particular goal and make sure the organism acts appropriately to obtain that goal. Think of it like a guided missile; it needs a rocket motor to make it go, and it also must have a guidance system that directs it to the right place. In the case of motivation, the organism has a need, drive, or motivation (e.g., hunger or thirst), which is the rocket motor that gets the animal moving. The guidance system is a bit more complicated. There can be two types of guidance systems for a missile. In one, the coordinates of the target can be programmed and that is where the guidance system takes the missile. It is also possible that the missile can be programmed to recognize a particular configuration of buildings on the ground and select that as a target, or it can be programmed to seek a signal from a homing device that has been left at the target. This second possibility is clearly the better one because this would give the missile considerable flexibility and even permit it to find a moving target. In motivational terms, animals seem to be equipped with this second type of guidance system. We are attracted to specific targets: the taste of sugar (candy) or an attractive member of the opposite sex. This attraction to a specific stimulus is called *incentive*.

One feature that a motivational system has that a guided missile does not have is the ability to program itself on the basis of past experience. Animals are able to learn how to satisfy their drives and motivations in a particular environment and to change their behavior when the environment changes. How it is able to do this has been the subject of considerable study and is still not entirely understood, but we have a pretty good idea of what goes on in the nervous system that makes it happen. Operant behavior provides a good model for studying how this happens—animals learn to make a response to obtain food or some other reinforcer and change their behavior in response to changes in the environment or the delivery of the reinforcer.

In the 1950s, James Olds and Peter Milner at McGill University discovered that electrical stimulation of certain areas of the brain would act as reinforcement; that is, rats would learn to perform a task in order to cause the stimulation (Olds & Milner, 1954). In addition, it appeared that these reinforcement centers were associated with the limbic system, which normally controls the expression of motivational behavior, such as eating, drinking, and sexual activity. These early experiments led people to believe that there was a single site in the brain that, when activated, would function as reinforcement, a so-called *reinforcement center*. It has turned out that things are not really that simple. It is now clear that a number of brain regions form an integrated circuitry responsible for learning, motivation, and the control and direction of behavior—that is, a *motivation control system*. Stimuli that act as reinforcers interact with this motivation control system in complex ways, and the motivation control system handles a number of different functions. Figure 5-3 summarizes its neurophysiology and how it is believed to work.

ACTIVATION. As described in Chapter 4, when there is an imbalance or deficiency in some internal system, such as when the organism is hungry, this input stimulates the *ventral tegmental area* in the midbrain. Axons from the ventral tegmental area are connected to the *nucleus accumbens*, and the ventral tegmental area stimulates the

nucleus accumbens by releasing dopamine at its synapses. Recall that the connection between the ventral tegmental area and the nucleus accumbens is known as the *mesolimbic dopamine system*, and it plays important roles in reinforcement, motivation, and reward seeking. Cells in the nucleus accumbens send axons back to the ventral tegmental area where they release an opioid-like peptide neurotransmitter, forming a circuit. The nucleus accumbens also sends axons to the *basal ganglia*, which, together with parts of the cortex, belong to the *motor loop*. In the absence of any other sensory input, activation of the mesolimbic dopamine system by a homeostatic imbalance, such as hunger, will stimulate the motor system and cause a general increase in the activity of the organism. The discovery that dopamine mediates general arousal, physical effort, and motor activity formed the basis of *activation–sensorimotor hypotheses* of dopamine function, for which there is a wealth of empirical support (Salamone, Correa, Mingote, & Weber, 2005). In fact, the output of the nucleus accumbens normally provides continuous inhibition of the motor system. When dopamine is released in the nucleus accumbens, it actually inhibits the inhibitory output to the motor system, and this has the same effect as stimulating the motor system. This aspect of the motivation system is equivalent to the rocket motor and provides no guidance, so the activation–sensorimotor hypotheses cannot explain other properties of reinforced behavior. These properties are better accounted for by other features of dopamine function.

GUIDANCE. In addition to receiving information about the internal state of the organism, the motivation control system also receives sensory information about the environment. This information is processed by the *thalamus* and *cortex* and then sent to the *amygdala* and the *hippocampus*, which are part of a *learning and memory system*. This system holds information about previously experienced stimuli, past actions, and their outcomes. With the aid of these memories, it is determined whether these external stimuli are biologically significant (e.g., food, or a lever that, when pressed, leads to the presentation of food). Behavior is activated and directed so that the organism approaches objects in the environment and performs acts that have resulted in the restoration of homeostatic balance in the past. In this way, the motivational control system enhances

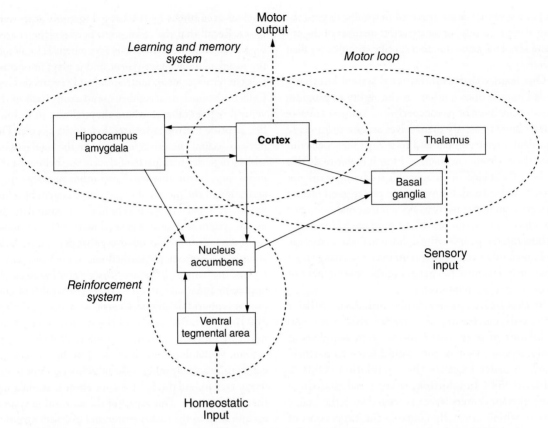

FIGURE 5-3 The motivation control system of the brain. The reinforcement system stimulates behavior by stimulating the motor loop in response to internal homeostatic input (such as hunger or thirst). Behavior will be directed by sensory input and by memory of the outcome of past behaviors stored in the learning and memory system. Motor behavior can also be stimulated and directed by sensory input to the thalamus, which is compared to past experiences in the learning and memory system. This then activates the reinforcement system. See the text for details.

survival. Learning and memory circuitry provides the basis for *reward learning hypotheses* of dopamine function, which implicate dopamine in the acquisition of operantly conditioned response–reward actions, classically conditioned stimulus–reward associations, and the coding of predictions about reward availability based on the presence of conditioned stimuli, that is, the guidance system.

The motivation control system has evolved so that an organism will be able to show maximum flexibility in a very wide variety of environmental conditions, thus ensuring its survival and increasing the chances that it will pass its genes (including the genes that create this neural circuitry) along to another generation. In general, it works in the following manner.

When a need state occurs (e.g., hunger), it is detected by the motivation control system and the mesolimbic system is activated. This causes an increase in general activity. In the absence of any previous learning or relevant salient stimuli, this activity ensures that the organism will move around its environment and maybe find food accidentally. For illustrative purposes, think of an animal living in the woods. This animal normally eats insects, but all the insects have flown away and it is hungry. This hunger activates the animal, and it rummages around its environment. Finally it finds grubs after turning over a rock in a streambed. This outcome (the accidental discovery of food) causes the release of mesolimbic dopamine, and neurons in the nucleus accumbens will become active. Information associated with the discovery is stored in the cortex and hippocampus. As a consequence, grubs and the streambed acquire *incentive salience*. The *salience* part means that these stimuli will be able to grab the animal's attention in the future. The *incentive* part means that the animal will be attracted to them. In the future, when the organism gets hungry and the nucleus accumbens is stimulated by the ventral tegmental area, general activity will increase, but now the stones in the streambed will draw the animal's attention, it will be attracted to them and consequently it will find food. The stones, the streambed, and the act of turning over the stones then acquire more incentive salience. In addition, the rocks and the streambed, because they have acquired incentive salience, will also have the power to activate the nucleus accumbens, so the organism will tend to approach and spend time there, even if it is not hungry. In fact, once an animal learns the incentive value of once-neutral stimuli that have come to reliably predict reward, its dopamine neurons respond, not to the reward itself (eating grubs), but to those predictive stimuli (stones in the streambed; Schultz, Dayan, & Montague, 1997).

This system of controlling behavior applies to other motivations, including thirst and reproduction, and it provides considerable adaptability in a changing ecology. Suppose there is a drought, the streambed dries up, and no more grubs are to be found there. After turning over a number of rocks and not finding any food, the behavior will extinguish, the streambed will lose its reinforcing and incentive value, and the activation caused by the hunger would drive the animal to seek food in other places. This newly learned association, that rocks and the streambed now erroneously predict the presence of food, is also coded by the mesolimbic dopamine system. Dopamine activity elicited by the presence of the predictive (conditioned) stimuli is quickly followed by a sudden lack of activity at the point in time during which the grubs would have been consumed. Thus, inactivity of dopamine neurons codes a prediction error; rocks and the streambed no longer signify the availability of food (Schultz et al., 1997), and so those stimuli lose their incentive salience. The animal no longer wants to hang around the streambed and is free to look elsewhere for food. Such a system clearly contributes to the fitness and survival of organisms and appears to have done so for a very long time. Even nonmammalian and invertebrate

nervous systems have circuitry similar to the mesolimbic dopamine system that runs from the midbrain to subcortical structures. In addition, dopamine is known to mediate feeding in a range of organisms, from slugs to humans (Nesse & Berridge, 1997).

THE ROLE OF DOPAMINE. The surge of dopamine in the nucleus accumbens is clearly correlated with changes in the animal's behavior caused by reinforcement, but how exactly does it guide behavior? Does dopamine cause the animal to remember what happened the last time it turned over a rock, or is it that the rock-turning attracts the animal, as we have described? An answer to this question has been provided by advances in research made possible by genetic manipulations. One such discovery is that dopamine-deficient mice (those with a genetic mutation that leads to a lack of the enzyme tyrosine hydroxylase and, thereby, an inability to synthesize dopamine from DOPA) are still able to learn stimulus–reward associations (Cannon & Palmiter, 2003; Robinson, Sandstrom, Denenberg, & Palmiter, 2005). Another is that hyperdopaminergic mice (those engineered to possess only a small fraction of dopamine transporter proteins, thereby prolonging dopamine activity in the synapse) do not learn any faster than normal mice (Yin, Zhuang, & Balleine, 2006). It appears, then, that the dopamine surge is not responsible for actually acquiring the stimulus–reward association. What then is its role in guiding behavior? It may be that dopamine contributes to learning indirectly, through the enhancement of attention, motivation, rehearsal, and memory consolidation (Berridge, 2007) rather than directly, through a "teaching" role. The dopamine surge may be a consequence, rather than a cause, of associative learning and reward prediction (Berridge, 2007).

Supposing this is the case, why would dopamine activity result from learning, and how does this play into reinforcement? The answer appears to lie in incentive motivation (Berridge, 2007). As mentioned earlier, stimuli associated with reinforcement are said to have acquired *incentive salience*; they are easily noticed, they capture the attention of the organism, elicit wanting, and motivate approach. In the presence of these salient stimuli, the hippocampus, amygdala, and prefrontal cortex stimulate the mesolimbic dopamine system via the nucleus accumbens. The nucleus accumbens then activates the motor loop via the basal ganglia. The motor output that results will be directed toward the significant stimulus (the food or lever), guided by sensory input received via the thalamus. Because behavior is directed toward the significant stimulus, in a Skinner box, the lever will be pressed and the food will be eaten; in the natural environment, the rocks will be turned over and the grubs will be eaten. This outcome will then be stored in the learning and memory system and used to modify behavior in the future, either when the need arises or the appropriate environmental stimuli are present.

Liking In Reinforcement

When Olds and Milner first demonstrated the reinforcing properties of stimulation of certain brain centers, people started to call these centers *pleasure centers*, partly because when these centers were stimulated in individuals, they reported experiencing extreme pleasure. They said that they liked it. It was, therefore, reasonable to think that the rewarding value of brain stimulation (and any other reinforcing stimulus) was derived from the pleasure it produced. This premise formed the foundation of the *hedonia hypothesis* of dopamine function (*hedonia* means *pleasure*), which was highly influential (Wise, 1980). Proponents explained the concept of reinforcement by saying that food, for example, stimulates the mesolimbic dopamine system, and this means that the organism experiences the sensation of pleasure. The pleasure reinforces the behavior of seeking food, and this behavior is, therefore, repeated. In fact, many theorists still refer to pleasure seeking (*hedonism* means the same thing, but sounds more technical) to explain many of these concepts (Koob, Sanna, & Bloom, 1998).

The hedonia hypothesis of dopamine function seems to make intuitive sense, but it is not necessary for an explanation of reinforcement in behavioral or neurological terms. Pleasure is a subjective state that often accompanies activation of the mesolimbic dopamine system, but this does not make dopamine the *pleasure* neurotransmitter it was traditionally thought to be. It may even be misleading because, even though there is a high correlation between reinforcement and reports of pleasure, stimuli can act as reinforcers even without the sensation of pleasure. Recall that, after repeated presentations, activation of the mesolimbic dopamine system occurs in response to the stimuli that precede or anticipate a biologically significant stimulus, like food, rather than

to consumption of that reinforcer itself, which subjectively would seem to be the source of pleasure (Schultz et al., 1997; Wickelgren, 1997). People with Parkinson's disease have a deficiency in dopamine. If dopamine were responsible for pleasure, you might expect that they would not be able to experience pleasure associated with a reinforcer. Yet, despite a lack of dopamine, Parkinson's patients do not report feeling less pleasure than do others when eating sweet foods (Sienkiewicz-Jarosz et al., 2005). Similarly, increasing levels of dopamine in the nucleus accumbens of Parkinson's patients through administration of DOPA does not increase feelings of pleasure or liking (Evans et al., 2006).

Rather than rely on self-report measures of pleasure related to reinforcement, Kent Berridge and colleagues from the University of Michigan have developed objective measures of "liking" and "disliking" that can be used with laboratory animals. "Liking" of sweet tastes elicits cross-species patterns of facial reactions, such as rhythmic tongue protrusions, whereas "disliking" of bitter tastes elicits reactions such as gaping (Berridge, 2000; you can view video of these reactions on Dr. Berridge's laboratory Web site at http://www.lsa.umich.edu/psych/research&labs/berridge/VideoIndex.htm).

Using these objective measures, Berridge and colleagues have pinpointed tiny *hedonic hotspots* in the nucleus accumbens and ventral portion of the pallidum (recall from Chapter 4, this is the output side of the basal ganglia) that mediate pleasure. Increases in "liking" reactions result from the activation of these hotspots, whereas damage to these hotspots corresponds with "disliking" reactions, even to sweet tastes (Peciña, 2008; Peciña & Berridge, 2005). But stimulation of these hotspots and "liking" reactions are not dependent on dopamine. Destroying medial forebrain bundle dopamine projections or administering dopamine antagonist drugs do not decrease "liking" reactions—animals demonstrate pleasure, despite a lack of dopamine function (Berridge & Robinson, 1998; Peciña, Berridge, & Parker, 1997). In addition, hyperdopaminergic mice do not "like" sucrose more than any other mice (Peciña, Cagniard, Berridge, Aldridge, & Zhuang, 2003), and injections of dopamine-enhancing drugs, such as amphetamine, either systemically (i.p.) or via microinjection directly into the nucleus accumbens, fail to increase rats' "liking" reactions to sucrose (Tindell, Berridge, Zhang, Peciña, & Aldridge, 2005; Wyvell & Berridge, 2000).

If dopamine is not responsible for "liking" or for the subjective feelings of euphoria and drug-related high, what is? "Liking" reactions to sweet rewards are potentiated by stimulation of *hedonic hotspots* by opioids (Peciña, 2008), endocannabinoids (Mahler, Smith, & Berridge, 2007), and GABA (Faure, Richard, & Berridge, 2010).

Wanting in Reinforcement

If the nucleus accumbens and the mesolimbic dopamine system do not make up a pleasure or *liking* system, what are their roles in reinforcement? As we have seen, the mesolimbic dopamine system has two roles in motivating behavior. The first role is general activation. This can be thought of as a *pushing* behavior without any general direction. When we do not eat for a while, we get *hungry*—we get up and do something. What we do is controlled by the second function. The second function of the mesolimbic dopamine system is to direct that behavior toward a particular goal. This is done by the process of incentive salience; that is, various stimuli in the environment have or acquire special motivational properties that cause us to notice them, be attracted to them, and do something to them.

There appear to be some stimuli that have natural incentive salience. Such a stimulus might be an attractive person; our attention is immediately drawn to such a person, we are attracted to him or her, and we enjoy his or her company. Sweet tastes are also naturally attractive and can act as incentives. Neutral stimuli can also acquire incentive salience when they are associated with basic motivations like hunger and sex. The act of pressing a lever in the Skinner box acquires incentive salience when it is repeatedly associated with the delivery of food; rats will approach the lever and begin pressing it when they get the chance. Thus, stimuli and actions associated with these natural incentives acquire incentive value of their own and come to control behavior. This is how reinforcement operates. It is not a matter of the rat remembering that pressing the lever causes food to appear. That may well happen, but the behavior of the rat appears to depend on the attractive motivational properties of the lever and the act of pressing it; that is, the lever becomes *wanted*.

The crucial role of the nucleus accumbens in reinforcement is in the formation of incentive salience. It is the nucleus accumbens that is responsible for turning a previously neutral stimulus into a stimulus that we *want*, and dopamine appears to be a crucial element in this process. As mentioned previously, natural reinforcers cause the release of dopamine in the nucleus accumbens. Blocking dopamine receptor activity or destroying dopamine axon terminals does not stop an animal from consuming a sweet food reward, but it does reduce motivation and goal-directed actions aimed at obtaining that reward (Palmiter, 2008). Despite normal levels of "liking" for sucrose, hyperdopaminergic mice are more motivated to obtain it (they pause less and run faster to reach the goal box in a runway task; Peciña et al., 2003). And although injections of amphetamine fail to increase rats'"liking" of sucrose, they do show increased "wanting" (they lever press more in the presence of a conditioned stimulus associated with sucrose availability; Wyvell & Berridge, 2000). Finally, Parkinson's patients receiving dopamine agonist treatments are at increased risk of developing compulsive behaviors, such as excessive gambling (Ambermoon, Carter, Hall, Dissanayaka, & O'Sullivan, 2011).

Thus, the mesolimbic dopamine system, and the nucleus accumbens in particular, constitutes a "wanting" system rather than a pleasure system. In other words, the brain system is there to make you repeat certain actions, not to make you feel good; it is a do-it-again system, not a pleasure system.

Drugs as Reinforcers

Imaging studies and studies of brain chemistry have shown that administration of reinforcing drugs, including cocaine, amphetamine, nicotine, alcohol, morphine, and methadone, all transiently increase extracellular dopamine levels in the nucleus accumbens in the same way that the consumption or availability of natural reinforcers, such as sweet foods or sexual activity, do (Di Chiara & Imperato, 1988; Di Chiara et al., 2004; Fiorino & Phillips, 1999). Even though they are not natural reinforcers, drugs control behavior by using the same brain mechanisms as other *natural* positive reinforcers (like food). Drugs stimulate the mesolimbic dopamine system, either by direct stimulation of the nucleus accumbens or by indirect stimulation through facilitation of excitatory input or blocking of inhibitory input to motivation circuitry (Wise, 1998). Knowing this can help us understand and predict the effects of drugs and provide clues as to how their ability to control behavior might be diminished. In addition, when natural reinforcers, such as food or sex, produce addictive-like behaviors, there are corresponding changes in the motivation system that resemble those associated with drug addiction (Frascella, Potenza, Brown, & Childress, 2010; Volkow, Wang, & Baler, 2011). Drug-associated cues also have the capacity to elicit dopamine surge. In fact, fast bursts of dopamine release that occur in response to drug use are a necessary occurrence for the development of conditioned responses to drug-associated cues.

There are, however, some important differences between drug reinforcement and reinforcement by more natural stimuli. One of the most important differences is that, under normal conditions, natural reinforcers have a satiation mechanism that terminates their reinforcing effect. Food, for example, is a reinforcer only if we are hungry. After we have eaten a certain amount, food loses its reinforcing value, and we stop eating. The same is true for water, and there are physiological limits on sexual activity as well. Most drugs, on the other hand, do not appear to have any natural limits to their reinforcing ability.

Another difference between drug and natural reinforcers is the immediacy and intensity of the latter's effect. Drugs are capable of getting to the brain in high concentrations very soon after they are administered, making drug reinforcement more immediate than natural reinforcers. The reinforcing effect is also more intense. For drugs of abuse, dopamine levels can surge well above those produced by natural rewards, to many hundreds of times baseline levels (Di Chiara & Imperato, 1988; Di Chiara et al., 2004; Fiorino & Phillips, 1999).

Positron emission tomography (PET) studies indicate that both the magnitude and the rate of dopamine surge in the nucleus accumbens correspond with individuals' reports of drug-related euphoria and pleasure. Therefore, the greatest subjective drug *high* comes from drug classes and routes of administration that result in the fastest and highest peaks in dopamine activity (Volkow et al., 2000, 2010). When drug absorption in the brain is slowed, the pleasurable effects are greatly blunted (Parasrampuria et al., 2007). Remember, though, that the fast, high surges in dopamine that correspond with drug taking are not what *cause* the feelings of euphoria—correlation, however strong, does not imply causation. Instead, these surges ensure that any stimulus that elicits extreme pleasure also gain incentive

salience and be emblazoned in the motivational system. Increases in the activity of other neurotransmitter systems, such as opioids and endocannabinoids, which are highly implicated in *liking*, may in fact be causing the pleasure. The heightened surge in dopamine related to these highly pleasurable stimuli ensures that we are motivated to seek and use them again.

STRESS AND REINFORCEMENT. Other significant events, even aversive ones, will cause the release of dopamine as well. Earlier we saw that stress, both present and in the past, increases the strength of a reinforcing stimulus. This effect of stress is thought to be a result of increased levels of glucocorticoid hormones. These stress hormones cause the release of dopamine in the nucleus accumbens and are known to act as reinforcers. Animals will work for intravenous infusions of them. Because of this connection between stress hormones and dopamine, stress stimulates the mesolimbic dopamine system and intensifies the reinforcing value of drug reinforcers and related stimuli.

Research into sensitization has demonstrated that, like repeated exposure to reinforcing drugs, repeated exposure to stressful stimuli sensitizes the mesolimbic dopamine system. Long-term exposure to stress can increase the incentive value of drugs well after the stressful stimulus has been removed. In fact, it has been shown that there is increased self-administration of amphetamine in rats whose mothers were stressed while they were pregnant (Deminiére et al., 1992; Meaney, 2001).

What Happens During Addiction?

By considering that drugs act in similar ways to natural reinforcers, we are able to understand the casual use of drugs that does little harm. But in some individuals this "normal" process escalates to a pathological level where the motivation to obtain and use a drug is all-consuming. Compulsive drug use disrupts all other aspects of thought and behavior and can create serious adversity. Attempts at reverting to abstinence or casual drug use are frequently in vain, and individuals are vulnerable to relapse, even in the absence of withdrawal symptoms and after long drug-free periods. This is addiction.

The motivational system in the brain evolved because it increased the survival fitness of organisms in a wide variety of environments, but none of these environments included the availability of refined, high-strength drugs available today or the efficient drug delivery mechanisms we now use. It is not surprising, therefore, that drug addiction is marked by neural adaptations not precipitated by consumption of natural reinforcers. How drugs alter the functioning of the motivation system and the behavior it controls is not entirely clear, but there are many interesting theories. We will examine the most influential of these theories that make use of the behavioral and neural mechanisms described earlier.

INCENTIVE SENSITIZATION THEORY

In the discussion of sensitization in Chapter 3 we saw that when reinforcing drugs are repeatedly administered, the animal becomes more sensitive, rather than less sensitive, to some of the drug's behavioral effects. There is an increase in activation, usually measured by the amount of locomotor activity or the severity of stereotyped behaviors such as head bobbing or gnawing. It is now known that the cause of the animal's heightened activity is an increase in sensitivity of the mesolimbic dopamine system to the drug. Sensitization of a drug's behavioral effects, however, is not the defining feature of addiction. In addition to behavioral sensitization, there is also sensitization of motivation circuitry—the animal or individual develops an attentional bias toward, and a compulsive wanting or craving for, the drug. Intrinsically neutral cues associated with drug use also gain incentive salience; they too become more noticeable, attractive, and desirable. Their representation in the brain is transformed into more than a simple perception or memory; they become *motivational magnets* (Robinson & Berridge, 2008). In other words, there is a sensitization of *incentive motivation*. The *incentive sensitization theory* uses this change in motivational sensitivity to explain addictive behavior.

Incentive Sensitization and Craving

The incentive sensitization theory of addiction was proposed by Terry Robinson and Kent Berridge (1993, 2003) at the University of Michigan. It was designed to explain the phenomenon of drug craving: "a strong desire or urge to use a specific substance" (*DSM-5*; newly proposed criterion for Substance Use Disorder). This desire has long been recognized as a common characteristic of addiction and is excessive in people with substance addictions. The concept of craving refers to

a subjective state, making it difficult for researchers to agree on a definition of craving in behavioral terms (Markou et al., 1993). Therefore, the concept has traditionally been of little use to the scientific investigation of drug abuse. Robinson and Berridge changed that, however, by suggesting that craving could be thought of as the manifestation of incentive salience toward drug-associated stimuli. The incentive motivational effects of drugs and their cues become stronger (sensitized) with repeated exposure due to increased activity of the mesolimbic dopamine system and neuroadaptations of brain circuits that mediate classical conditioning of incentive motivational processes (Robinson & Berridge, 2008). Thus, exposure to these stimuli elicits extreme incentive motivation (or craving) that can last for years or decades, even well into recovery.

To better understand incentive sensitization, let us return to the general motivating system described earlier in this chapter (refer again to Figure 5-3). Stimuli that activate the mesolimbic dopamine system—either because they are natural reinforcers such as food, or because they are cues that, through learning, have become associated with reinforcers—are said to have incentive salience: (a) The stimulus is easily noticed and attended to by the organism, and (b) the stimulus motivates behavior that is directed toward it. When a stimulus with incentive salience, such as food, is presented to a hungry animal, the food is noticed immediately. The animal becomes more active, and that activity is directed toward the food—the animal approaches the food and eats it. You might say that this activation makes the animal *want* the food. Because drugs activate the mesolimbic system, they are also *wanted*, and this makes the drug a positive reinforcer. With repeated use, a drug will acquire greater incentive value (and be a stronger reinforcer) because of sensitization. Chronic use of amphetamine, cocaine, morphine, heroin, nicotine, or alcohol increases the strength of excitatory glutamatergic input onto dopamine neurons in the ventral tegmental area (Saal, Dong, Bonci, & Malenka, 2003; Ungless, Whistler, Malenka, & Bonci, 2001). Similar neural changes are involved in learning and memory, suggesting that such synaptic adaptations may be an important step in the development of addiction. Even limited drug exposure can have surprisingly long-lasting consequences on the brain's reward system. For example, in healthy volunteers, sensitization of the dopamine-enhancing effects of amphetamine in the nucleus accumbens can be seen a full year following only three administrations of amphetamine over a 5-day period (Boileau et al., 2006).

Repeated presentation of a reinforcer will also cause the stimuli associated with it to have greater incentive salience. Thus, whenever a reinforcing drug—or, more importantly, stimuli paired with a reinforcing drug—is experienced, the mesolimbic dopamine system becomes active and creates motivation to approach these stimuli. PET analysis of dopamine activity in the ventral striatum of healthy volunteers shows that administering a placebo pill (one that resembles an amphetamine capsule previously taken by the volunteers) increases dopamine activity to a similar extent as that of amphetamine (Boileau et al., 2007). This finding helps explain why, during abstinence, simply visiting the location where they typically administered their choice drug can induce craving and cause individuals to relapse into drug taking. Even *unseen* drug-related cues (presented so quickly that individuals are not consciously aware of having perceived them) greatly activate the nucleus accumbens and other limbic areas of cocaine addicts (Childress et al., 2008). Visual cues are not the only stimuli capable of altering dopamine activity. Olfactory cues, such as the smell of beer and whiskey, can also increase ventral striatal dopamine activity (Kareken et al., 2004).

Cognitive processing of drug-related cues is also biased in current and former drug users. That is, drug-related stimuli are more attention grabbing and receive excessive focus, as incentive sensitization theory predicts. For example, research measuring visual attention (eye tracking) of heavy social drinkers toward alcohol-related cues revealed an attentional bias, as measured by initial orienting of the eyes toward those cues and a delay in disengaging from viewing those cues (Field, Mogg, Zetteler, & Bradley, 2004). This bias is even more pronounced following stress (Field & Quigley, 2009). It has also been demonstrated that social users of both alcohol and marijuana are more sensitive to stimuli related to alcohol and marijuana, respectively; they were faster to detect changes that involved drug-related items in a picture of a variety of objects, indicating an information processing bias toward drug-related items (Jones, Jones, Blundell, & Bruce, 2002; Jones, Jones, Smith, & Copley, 2003).

Subjective reports of craving are linked with presentation of drug-related cues and corresponding changes in the activity of motivational circuitry and dopamine. For example, in recovering long-term alcoholics, presentation of alcohol-related pictures induced craving for the drug and increased activity in the prefrontal and anterior cingulate cortices. Recall that these cortical areas are involved in many high-level executive functions, including attention, response competition, impulse inhibition, and judgment. Furthermore, PET analysis revealed lower dopamine D_2 receptor density in the ventral striatum (including the nucleus accumbens) of alcoholics, which correlated negatively with severity of craving and fMRI-measured brain activation. These results are shown in Color Plate B. The authors suggest that the dysfunction of dopamine in the ventral striatum may lead alcoholics to attribute increased amounts of attention to alcohol-related cues and experience greater motivation to consume alcohol (Heinz et al., 2004). Cue-induced activation of the dopamine system also occurs after a relatively short (1- to 2-year) history of alcohol abuse. Blood oxygen level–dependent MRI revealed greater limbic activation in teenaged drinkers, which correlated positively with the degree of reported craving for alcohol (Tapert et al., 2003). Even internal cues (memories) can have an effect. Eliciting drug-related memories in abstinent opiate addicts, by listening to a short autobiographical script describing a past episode when the participant was experiencing craving for opiates, induced craving in most participants. PET imaging revealed a positive correlation between the intensity of drug craving and the degree of cerebral blood flow in the orbitofrontal cortex (Daglish et al., 2001).

Thus, through neuroadaptations of learning and motivational circuitry and sensitization of the mesolimbic dopamine system, attraction toward drug-associated stimuli is increased. According to incentive sensitization theory, the subjective consequence of activation of this system is *wanting*, and the subjective experience of a sensitized system is intense wanting or *craving*.

Incentive sensitization theory can explain many aspects of drug use. First, it describes how drug addiction might develop. When a drug is first used or administered casually, it may not be a very strong reinforcer and may not be able to compete with other nondrug reinforcers to control a person's behavior. But with repeated administration, the drug acquires increased reinforcing properties—it has more pull. The more it is used, the more control it gains over motivational circuitry, and the more effective a reinforcer it becomes until it has the capacity to control a large amount of behavior.

The theory also explains why stimuli associated with a drug can evoke the craving to use the drug. Because sensitization of the dopamine system is relatively permanent and can become associated with specific stimuli, cravings—or the desire to use a drug—can last a very long time after drug use has stopped. Ex-addicts, even after many years of abstinence, are at a high risk of relapsing, and relapse is often triggered by stimuli associated with the use of the drug.

Sensitization of incentive salience can also explain the priming effect described earlier wherein a single exposure to a drug can restart more drug use even if it has been extinguished. In priming, a single drug administration stimulates a sensitized reward system that will increase the incentive of the drug and the incentive salience of stimuli associated with it; that is, it causes craving.

Robinson and Berridge are careful to point out that the subjective effect of activation in this brain system is a sensation of "wanting", not of "liking" or pleasure. Pleasure, they say, arises from the drug activating another neurotransmitters and brain regions. Repeated drug use sensitizes only the neural circuitry of the motivational system, not that of a system mediating the pleasurable effects or "liking" of drugs (Robinson & Berridge, 2008). In fact, pleasure tends to show tolerance, rather than sensitization, with repeated drug use. This explains the dissociation between "wanting" and "liking" in substance users—people often crave drugs even though they report that, at the same time, they are miserable and get little or no pleasure from the drug.

HEDONIC DYSREGULATION AND ADAPTATION

Another class of theories is based on the physical dependence model described previously. An example of such a theory was proposed by George Koob of the Scripps Research Institute and Michel Le Moal of l'Universitié de Bordeaux in France (Koob, 2000; Koob & Le Moal, 2001, 2008). Their theory is a hedonic, neurobiological/psychological dependence model of addiction based on a continually shifting balance between the activity of brain reward systems and the recruitment of antireward systems that results from recurrent drug use. They say that repeated drug administration results in a process similar to that described by Solomon and Corbit (1973), which is discussed in Chapter 3. Solomon and Corbit's theory proposes that the activation of euphoria or pleasure is an A process that generates a compensatory B process. The B process is dysphoric and cancels out the A process, causing tolerance to the euphoric effect of drugs. As you can see in Figure 3-2, the B process lasts longer than the A process; it is the cause of hangover after an acute administration and withdrawal after repeated administration of a drug. If we relate Solomon and Corbit's opponent process theory to that of Koob and Le Moal, the A process is driven by brain reward systems, the circuitry involved in positive reinforcement and that controls *happiness* and *pleasure*, and the B process is driven by brain antireward systems, the circuitry involved in negative hedonic balance and that limits the sensation of reward through *dysphoria* and *stress*. With repeated use of a drug, brain reward systems become dysfunctional and dysregulated—their level of activity does not return completely to normal, as illustrated in Figure 5-4. At the same time, brain antireward systems become increasingly recruited and their level of activity grows. Koob and Le Moal conceptualize this spiraling cycle of reward/antireward system dysregulation as an *allostatic process*.

Allostasis is a fairly new concept in stress physiology and medicine and stands in contrast to *homeostasis*, described in Chapter 3. Homeostasis presumes that physiological processes in the body have a set point, a level that is optimal for the animal, and that through a system of feedback, like a thermostat on a furnace, that level is maintained. Allostasis, on the other hand, refers to situations where the set point is not constant but changes in response to changes in the animal's environment (McEwan & Lashley, 2002). As you can see in Figure 5-4, with repeated drug use, new mood set points are established—the user becomes increasingly unhappy and depressed. This new allostatic set point means that a person must take larger and larger doses of the drug to achieve the same degree of euphoria or pleasure as he or she did from the first dose. In the short term, excessive drug use activates brain reward systems and suppresses brain antireward systems, temporarily alleviating the reward deficit. In the long term, however, repeated use of drugs causes further dysregulation of reward mechanisms and a progressive increase in the recruitment of antireward systems. This sets off a spiral where the user

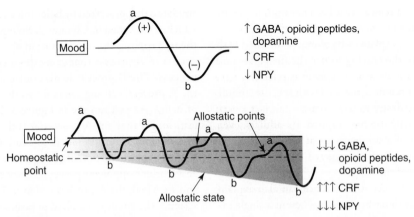

FIGURE 5-4   This graph is an elaboration of the Solomon and Corbit drawings in Figures 3-2 and 3-3 of Chapter 3. It shows what happens to the mood (hedonic) set point when a drug, such as cocaine, is repeatedly administered according to the hedonic dysregulation theory of Koob and Le Moal. (*Top*) This diagram represents the initial experience of a drug with no prior drug history. The *a-process* represents a positive hedonic or positive mood state, and the *b-process* represents a negative hedonic or negative mood state. The affective stimulus (state) has been argued to be the sum of both an *a-process* and a *b-process*. An individual experiencing a positive hedonic mood state from a drug of abuse with sufficient time between readministering the drug is hypothesized to retain the *a-process*. In other words, an appropriate counteradaptive opponent process (*b-process*) that balances the activational process (*a-process*) does not lead to an allostatic state. (*Bottom*) Changes in the affective stimulus (state) in an individual with repeated, frequent drug use that may represent a transition to an allostatic state in the brain reward systems and a transition to addiction. Notice that the apparent *b-process* never returns to the original homeostatic level before drug taking is reinitiated, thus creating a greater and greater allostatic state in the brain reward system. In other words, the counteradaptive opponent process (*b-process*) does not balance the activational process (*a-process*) but in fact shows a gradual lowering. Although these changes are exaggerated and condensed over time, the hypothesis here is that even during postdetoxification (a period of *protracted abstinence*) the reward system is still bearing allostatic changes. In the nondependent state, reward experiences are normal, and the brain stress systems are not greatly engaged. During the transition to addiction, the brain reward system is in a major underactivated state while the brain stress system is highly activated. In addition, the ability of all other reinforcers to cause pleasure is also diminished. *CRF*, corticotropin-releasing factor; *GABA*, γ-aminobutyric acid; *NPY*, neuropeptide Y.

becomes less and less happy using the drug and more and more depressed when they stop because the mood set point keeps diminishing. This motivates the user to seek and take larger and larger doses, lowering the set point even further.

As a neurobiological theory, Koob and Le Moal's model proposes that addiction involves disrupted neurotransmitter functioning and neuroadaptation in key brain regions that encompass reward and antireward systems. Many of these neurocircuits and their neurochemistry overlap. For example, both the acute, positive reinforcing effects of drugs and the negative motivational effects of withdrawal are proposed to involve increases or decreases in dopamine, opioid, cannabinoid, serotonin, GABA, and glutamate neurotransmission within the mesolimbic dopamine system (ventral tegmental area and nucleus accumbens) and the *extended amygdala* (which, in part, includes areas of the amygdala and nucleus accumbens; Koob & Le Moal, 2008). In addition to these *within-system* neuroadaptations, *between-system* changes take place in the neurocircuitry and neurochemistry that drive the stress response. For instance, during acute withdrawal, there are increases in stress hormones such as corticotropin-releasing hormone (CRH), adrenocorticotropic hormone (ACTH), and corticosterone/cortisol. Norepinephrine and dynorphin levels rise while GABA and neuropeptide Y levels fall, producing an increased sense of anxiety and dysphoria (Edwards & Koob, 2010). Neuroadaptation in these systems may also help understand why stress is a powerful factor in relapse to drug use, even following a prolonged period of abstinence.

Not only does neuroadaptation of brain reward/ antireward systems and a lowered set point alter the reinforcing effect of a drug, but the reinforcing value of other stimuli is also diminished. This makes participation in other nondrug activities less and less reinforcing, and eventually their control over behavior diminishes. The field is left open to the drug, which, because it is more powerful than other reinforcers, becomes the only event capable of acting as a reinforcer. This accelerates the spiral of addiction.

Koob and Le Moal acknowledge that sensitization of the reinforcement system takes place and that this increases the incentive value of drugs in the manner described by Robinson and Berridge, but they suggest that the sensitization contributes to the development of addiction only during the early stages where it stimulates drug intake. Eventually, they say that sensitization is overcome by the processes of *hedonic dysregulation*, the term they use to describe the lowering of the mood set point.

Koob and Le Moal's theory is an example of a modern dependence theory of addiction. It proposes that one of the withdrawal symptoms of all drugs of abuse is *dysphoria* (depression or unhappiness). Because this takes place in the brain and is normally only evident to the drug user, this dysphoria can be thought of as a *psychological withdrawal* syndrome that can be alleviated only by taking more drug, in larger quantities. This makes it a mechanism of psychological dependence. Because Koob and Le Moal have identified and measured the changes that take place in the extended amygdala and in the

hormone responses of the brain, they have avoided the circularity of many earlier ideas of psychological dependence described previously.

Another major difference between early drug dependency theories and hedonic dysregulation theory is the concept of allostasis, which suggests that the effects of withdrawal can last for a very long time. The concept of allostasis permits hedonic dysregulation theory to explain relapse long after the withdrawal symptoms created by homeostatic mechanisms have disappeared.

DISRUPTION OF BRAIN CONTROL CIRCUITS

Brain imaging techniques have greatly enhanced our understanding of how chronic drug use can produce long-lasting changes in the brain. This knowledge has contributed to the reconceptualization of addiction as a brain disease. One of the leading researchers in this area is Nora Volkow, director of the National Institute on Drug Abuse (NIDA) at the National Institutes of Health (NIH) in the United States.

Volkow and her colleagues have shown that all drugs of abuse activate the mesolimbic dopamine system, which plays a pivotal role in drug addiction. Substances including amphetamine, cocaine, morphine, heroin, alcohol, and nicotine elicit a temporary surge of dopamine release within the nucleus accumbens, which increases the saliency of drug-related stimuli and mediates the acute reinforcing effects of the drug. Volkow and colleagues suggest, however, that while these short-term increases in dopamine release are necessary for the development of drug addiction, they are not sufficient and cannot explain other traits that characterize compulsive substance use. They propose that drug addiction involves a dysfunction in information processing and integration among multiple brain regions that comprise four interrelated circuits. These circuits regulate *reward/ saliency* (e.g., nucleus accumbens and ventral tegmental area), *motivation/drive* (e.g., orbitofrontal cortex and motor cortex), *memory/conditioning* (e.g., amygdala and hippocampus), and *inhibitory control/executive function* (e.g., dorsolateral prefrontal cortex and anterior cingulate gyrus; Volkow, Fowler, Wang, Swanson, & Telang, 2007). All circuits receive direct input from dopamine neurons and are connected one to another, mostly by glutamatergic projections. During chronic drug use, these circuits undergo neuroplastic changes that give rise to many of the maladaptive behaviors that characterize addiction (Volkow et al., 2010).

One neuroadaptation associated with long-term drug use is a decrease in dopamine function. This manifests as both a downregulation of D_2-like receptors in the ventral striatum that persists even after months of abstinence and a reduction in ventral tegmental area dopamine neuron activity and transmitter release in the ventral striatum (Volkow et al., 2007). Volkow and colleagues suggest that this hypodopaminergic state might explain the lack of interest in social or recreational activities (natural rewards) that substance users previously enjoyed. Further, it might prompt additional drug use as a way to temporarily alleviate the deficit in dopamine activity so that the individual can feel normal.

In addition, neuroplastic changes take place in the prefrontal cortex. Addicts show deficits in metabolic activity and/or gray matter volume in a number of cortical areas, including the orbitofrontal cortex, anterior cingulate gyrus, dorsolateral prefrontal cortex, and insular cortex. These regions play important roles in motivation, attentional control, salience attribution, and inhibitory control; dysfunction of these areas leads to compulsion and impulsivity (Ersche et al., 2011; Volkow et al., 2007). Hypoactivity of the prefrontal cortex reduces decision-making ability and motivation toward natural rewards (Kalivas & Volkow, 2005).

Moreover, areas such as the orbitofrontal and anterior cingulate cortices send glutamate projections to regulate the release of dopamine within the nucleus accumbens (Kalivas & Volkow, 2005). Under baseline conditions (in the absence of drug and drug-associated cues), lack of prefrontal cortical activity and, subsequently, of glutamatergic stimulation of the nucleus accumbens might explain the loss of incentive salience of natural rewards. At the same time, however, the hypoactive prefrontal cortex is supersensitive to drug-associated stimuli. Exposure to drug cues elicits hypermetabolism of the dysfunctional prefrontal cortex and glutamatergic activation of nucleus accumbens dopamine neurons. The resultant surge of nucleus accumbens dopamine motivates the individual to compulsively seek and take the drug through stimulation of motivation/drive circuitry and further consolidates those drug-associated cues in memory/conditioning circuits. Normally, activation of these circuits would be kept in check by the prefrontal cortex. However, a dysfunctional prefrontal cortex cannot properly regulate dopamine neuron activity, and, therefore, the motivational/drive and memory/conditioning circuits are left uninhibited, resulting in compulsive drug intake.

Brain imaging studies provide intriguing insight into addiction as a brain disease. Cortical dysfunction and deficits in higher-order processing may also shed light on why so many substance users *deny* the presence or severity of their addiction. In 2009, of the roughly 21 million individuals in the United States whose substance use disorder remained untreated, only 5% felt they needed treatment and just over one-third of those individuals made some effort to get treatment (Substance Abuse and Mental Health Services Administration, 2010). Researchers suggest that this *denial* may actually be the product of dysfunctional cortical circuits that mediate insight and self-awareness. For example, the insular and anterior cingulate cortices, which exhibit reductions in gray matter volume in addicts, mediate interoception, self-awareness, behavioral monitoring, and response selection (Goldstein et al., 2009). One of the greatest challenges in treating substance addiction, therefore, may be to find ways of overcoming the cognitive deficits that prevent the individual from realizing that he or she needs treatment in the first place.

TREATING DRUG ADDICTION

Principles of Effective Treatment Programs

Drug addiction affects all aspects of an individual's life—physical, psychological, financial, and social—and increases the risk for other mental and physical illnesses that may develop as a direct result of the drug itself or the behaviors and lifestyle drug use promotes. Chronic drug use affects multiple brain circuits and preempts the motivation and sense of reward one might otherwise gain from social and recreational activities, driving compulsion to drug seeking and relapse. Addiction does not simply disappear overnight. Treatment is long-term and individualized, and maintaining abstinence requires life-long effort and commitment. The most effective treatments for drug addiction focus on all aspects of functioning that have been disrupted by drug use, helping the individual maintain a drug-free lifestyle and reestablish his or her place in the family, workplace, and society. Regaining control over one's life is the ultimate goal.

Based on decades of scientific research and clinical practice, the National Institute on Drug Abuse has proposed the following principles that should form the foundation of any effective treatment program for drug addiction (NIDA, 2009).

1. Addiction is a complex but treatable disorder that affects brain function and behavior. Drugs of abuse alter the brain's structure and function, resulting in changes that persist long after drug use has ceased. This may explain why drug abusers are at risk for relapse even after long periods of abstinence and despite the potentially devastating consequences.

2. No single treatment is appropriate for everyone. Matching treatment settings, interventions, and services to an individual's particular problems and needs is critical to his or her ultimate success in returning to productive functioning in the family, workplace, and society.

3. Treatment needs to be readily available. Because drug-addicted individuals may be uncertain about entering treatment, taking advantage of available services the moment people are ready for treatment is critical. The earlier treatment is offered in the disease process, the greater the likelihood of positive outcomes.

4. Effective treatment attends to multiple needs of the individual, not just his or her drug abuse. To be effective, treatment must address the individual's drug abuse and any associated medical, psychological, social, vocational, and legal problems. It is also important that treatment be appropriate to the individual's age, gender, ethnicity, and culture.

5. Remaining in treatment for an adequate period of time is critical. The appropriate duration for an individual depends on the type and degree of his or her problems and needs. Research indicates that most addicted individuals need at least 3 months in treatment to significantly reduce or stop their drug use and that the best outcomes occur with longer durations of treatment. Recovery from drug addiction is a long-term process and frequently requires multiple episodes of treatment. Because individuals often leave treatment prematurely, programs should include strategies to engage and keep patients in treatment.

6. Counseling—individual and/or group—and other behavioral therapies are the most commonly used forms of drug abuse treatment. Behavioral therapies vary in their focus and may involve addressing a patient's motivation to change, providing incentives for abstinence, building skills to resist drug use, replacing drug-using activities with constructive and rewarding activities, improving problem-solving skills, and facilitating better interpersonal relationships. Also, participation in group therapy and other peer support programs during and following treatment can help maintain abstinence.

7. Medications are an important element of treatment for many patients, especially when combined with counseling and other behavioral therapies.

8. An individual's treatment must be assessed continually and modified as necessary to ensure that it meets his or her changing needs during the course of treatment and recovery. In addition to counseling or psychotherapy, a patient may require medication, medical services, family therapy, parenting instruction, vocational rehabilitation, and/or social and legal services.

9. Many drug-addicted individuals also have other mental disorders. Because addiction often co-occurs with other mental illnesses, patients presenting with one condition should be assessed for the other(s). Treatment should address both (or all), including the use of medications as appropriate.

10. Medically assisted detoxification is only the first stage of addiction treatment. Although medically assisted detoxification can safely manage the acute physical symptoms of withdrawal and, for some, pave the way for effective long-term addiction treatment, detoxification alone is rarely sufficient to help addicted individuals achieve long-term abstinence. Thus, patients should be encouraged to continue drug treatment following detoxification.

11. Treatment does not need to be voluntary to be effective. Sanctions or enticements from family, employment settings, and/or the criminal justice system can significantly increase treatment entry, retention rates, and the ultimate success of drug treatment interventions.

12. Drug use during treatment must be monitored continuously, as lapses during treatment do occur. Knowing their drug use is being monitored can be a powerful incentive for patients and can help them withstand urges to use drugs. Monitoring also provides an early indication of a return to drug use, signaling a possible need to adjust an individual's treatment plan to better meet his or her needs.

13. Treatment programs should assess patients for the presence of infectious diseases as well as provide targeted risk-reduction counseling to help patients modify or change behaviors that place them at risk of contracting or spreading infectious diseases. Targeted counseling specifically focused on reducing infectious disease risk can help patients further reduce or avoid substance-related and other high-risk behaviors.

Treatment Programs

There are several program options available to individuals seeking addictions treatment. Some are short term and focus on the immediate physical and psychological symptoms of drug use and withdrawal. Others are long term and place emphasis on improving the outlook of the individual through employment counseling and family therapy. These programs and the therapies they offer are not mutually exclusive; treatment outcomes are improved when individuals avail of more than one therapeutic approach on the road to rehabilitation. What follows are some of the most effective treatment programs and approaches, as described by NIDA (2009).

DETOXIFICATION AND MEDICALLY MANAGED WITHDRAWAL. Detoxification is the process by which the body clears itself of drugs and is often accompanied by unpleasant and sometimes even fatal side effects. Medications are available to lessen the potentially dangerous physiological effects of withdrawal; therefore, it is referred to as *medically managed withdrawal*. Detoxification is generally considered a precursor to or a first stage of treatment as it does not address the psychological, social, and behavioral problems associated with addiction and therefore does not typically produce lasting behavioral changes necessary for recovery. Detoxification should be followed by a formal assessment and referral to subsequent drug addiction treatment.

OUTPATIENT TREATMENT PROGRAMS. Outpatient treatment varies in the types and intensity of services offered. Such treatment costs less than residential treatment and often is more suitable for people with jobs or extensive social supports. Although low-intensity programs may offer little more than drug education, other outpatient models, such as intensive day treatment, can be comparable to residential programs in services and effectiveness. Individualized drug counseling helps the patient develop coping strategies and tools to abstain from drug use and focuses on related areas of impaired functioning, such as employment status, illegal activity, and family/social relations. Many therapeutic settings use group therapy to capitalize on the social reinforcement offered by peer discussion and to help promote drug-free lifestyles. Research has shown that when group therapy is offered in conjunction with individualized drug counseling, positive outcomes are achieved. Outpatient programs may also treat patients with medical or other mental health problems and make referrals for needed supplemental medical, psychiatric, employment, and other services.

SHORT-TERM RESIDENTIAL TREATMENT. Short-term residential programs provide intensive but relatively brief treatment based on a modified 12-step approach (see Treatment Approaches). The original residential treatment model consisted of a 3- to 6-week hospital-based inpatient treatment phase followed by extended outpatient therapy and participation in an aftercare self-help group, such as Alcoholics Anonymous, which helps to reduce the risk of relapse once a patient leaves the residential setting.

LONG-TERM RESIDENTIAL TREATMENT. The best-known long-term residential treatment model is the *therapeutic community* (TC), which provides 24-hour a day care with planned lengths of stay between 6 and 12 months. TCs focus on the *resocialization* of the individual. Addiction is viewed in the context of an individual's social and psychological deficits, and treatment focuses on developing personal accountability and responsibility as well as socially productive lives. Treatment is highly structured with activities designed to help residents examine damaging beliefs, self-concepts, and destructive patterns of behavior and adopt new, more harmonious and constructive ways to interact with others. Many TCs offer comprehensive services, which can include employment training and other support services, on site.

Treatment Approaches

The following treatment approaches are designed to address certain aspects of drug addiction and its consequences for the individual, family, and society. Oftentimes, treatment programs will include more than one approach, such as behavioral therapy and medications. Treatment approaches that are specific to a single class of drugs will be described as appropriate in the chapters that follow.

Behavioral Treatments

Behavioral therapies are designed to engage people in treatment, provide incentives for them to remain abstinent, modify their attitudes and behaviors related to drug use, and increase their life skills to handle stressful circumstances and environmental cues that may trigger intense craving for drugs and relapse. The treatments outlined next have proven effective in helping individuals overcome addiction to a variety of substances, including alcohol, nicotine, marijuana, stimulants, and opiates.

COGNITIVE–BEHAVIORAL THERAPY (CBT). CBT was originally developed as a relapse prevention strategy and is based on the theory that learning processes play a critical role in the development of maladaptive behavioral patterns. Individuals learn to identify and correct problematic behaviors through techniques intended to enhance self-control by exploring the positive and negative consequences of continued use, self-monitoring to recognize drug cravings early on and to identify high-risk situations for use, and developing strategies for coping with and avoiding high-risk situations and the desire to use. A central element of this treatment is anticipating likely problems and helping patients develop effective coping strategies. The skills individuals learn through CBT approaches remain after the completion of treatment.

CONTINGENCY MANAGEMENT INTERVENTIONS/ MOTIVATIONAL INCENTIVES. Contingency management interventions are based on operant conditioning principles of reinforcing drug-free urine samples with low-cost incentives such as prizes or vouchers exchangeable for food items, movie passes, and other personal goods. Incentive-based interventions are highly effective in increasing treatment retention and promoting abstinence from drugs.

MOTIVATIONAL ENHANCEMENT THERAPY (MET). MET is aimed at helping individuals resolve ambivalence about engaging in treatment. Motivational interviewing principles are used to strengthen motivation to stop drug use and build a plan for change. The therapist and patient devise coping strategies for high-risk situations, and the therapist monitors change, reviews cessation strategies being used, and continues to encourage commitment to change or sustained abstinence. In general, MET seems to be more effective for engaging drug abusers in treatment than for producing changes in drug use.

12-STEP FACILITATION THERAPY. Twelve-step programs, such as those of Alcoholics Anonymous and Narcotics Anonymous, are some of the most well-known behavioral treatments for addiction. One of the goals of these self-help groups is to increase the likelihood of drug abstinence through affiliation and active engagement in a social community. Three key aspects predominate: *acceptance*, which includes the realization that drug addiction is a chronic, progressive disease over which one has no control, that life has become unmanageable because of drugs, that willpower alone is insufficient to overcome the problem, and that abstinence is the only alternative; *surrender*, which involves giving oneself over to a higher power, accepting the fellowship and support structure of other recovering addicted individuals, and following the recovery activities laid out by the 12-step program; and *active involvement* in 12-step meetings and related activities. While 12-step programs have proved effective in treating alcohol addiction, the efficacy of 12-step programs for treating other abused drugs, such as methamphetamine and cocaine, is ongoing.

BEHAVIORAL COUPLES THERAPY (BCT). BCT is a therapy for drug addicts with partners as an add-on to individual and group therapy. BCT uses a sobriety contract and behavioral principles to reinforce abstinence from drugs. BCT also has been shown to produce higher treatment attendance, adherence to medication therapy, and rates of abstinence than individual treatment, along with fewer drug-related, legal, and family problems.

BEHAVIORAL TREATMENTS FOR ADOLESCENTS. Adolescent drug abusers have unique treatment needs, and family involvement is a particularly important component of treatment for youth. *Multidimensional Family Therapy* (MDFT) for adolescents is an outpatient approach that views adolescent drug use in terms of a network of influences (individual, family, peer, community). Treatment includes individual and family sessions held in the clinic, in the home, or with family members at the family court, school, or other community locations. During individual sessions, the therapist and adolescent work on decision-making, negotiation, problem-solving, and communication skills to better deal with life stressors. Parents examine their parenting styles and learn to distinguish *control* from positive and developmentally appropriate *influence* on their children. *Brief Strategic Family Therapy* (BSFT) targets family interactions that are thought to maintain or exacerbate adolescent drug abuse and other co-occurring problem behaviors such as oppositional behavior, delinquency, associating with antisocial peers, aggressive and violent behavior, and risky sexual behavior. BSFT is based on a family systems approach to treatment, where family members' behaviors are assumed to be interdependent such that the symptoms of any one member (e.g., the drug-abusing adolescent) are indicative, at least in part, of what else is going on in the family system. The role of the BSFT counselor is to identify the patterns of family interaction that are associated with the adolescent's behavior problems and to assist in changing those problem-maintaining family patterns. *Multisystemic Therapy* (MST) addresses the factors associated with serious antisocial behavior of adolescents who abuse drugs. These factors include characteristics of the adolescent (e.g., favorable attitudes toward drug use), the family (poor discipline, family conflict, parental drug abuse), peers (positive attitudes toward drug use), school (dropout, poor performance), and neighborhood (criminal subculture).

Pharmacological Treatments

Drug addiction is a chronically relapsing disorder. In recovering addicts, abstinence is a life-long goal requiring continuous effort. There are, however, a number of pharmacotherapies that can help combat addiction. Details of specific pharmacotherapies will be explained in subsequent drug chapters, but they can be broadly categorized as medications that reduce the aversive (withdrawal) effects of drug cessation or reduce drug reward, craving, and the likelihood of relapse (O'Brien, 2008).

REDUCING WITHDRAWAL. If chronic drug use was simply a means of avoiding withdrawal, treatment for addiction would be fast, easy, and extremely effective. The drug of abuse could be replaced with a gradually decreasing dose of a pharmacologically similar, longer-acting medication until the individual was drug free. These *substitution* or *replacement* therapies are quite common. For example, nicotine patches or gums are used as a substitute for cigarettes; methadone is used to treat heroin addiction; benzodiazepines are administered to combat the potentially fatal symptoms of alcohol withdrawal. These therapies prevent or lessen the discomfort of detoxification, making withdrawal more tolerable. But, of course, addiction is not cured in this way. Addiction results from drug-induced neuroadaptations, and these brain changes create vulnerability for relapse. Pharmacotherapies that help alleviate the discomfort of withdrawal are a good first step, but they are not sufficient. Unfortunately, detoxification is the only treatment received by the majority of addicts (McLellan, Weinstein, Shen, Kendig, & Levine, 2005).

REDUCING DRUG REWARD, CRAVING, AND RELAPSE. Some of the substitution therapies used to reduce the symptoms of withdrawal may be administered long term to reduce the rewarding effects of drugs of abuse and prevent relapse. These drugs may be full agonists, such as the nicotine patch or methadone, which activate the same neurotransmitter receptors as the drug of abuse. It may seem counterproductive to replace one drug with another similar-acting drug as a means of treating addiction. Keep in mind, however, that replacement therapies are most often medically supervised and administered under controlled conditions and by a safer route, through transdermal absorption or oral administration, for example. Also, when highly addictive drugs are administered through these routes, their pharmacokinetic profiles are changed dramatically. They enter the brain more slowly; fail to produce the fast, high surge of nucleus accumbens dopamine; and lose their reinforcing effects. Even methylphenidate (Ritalin) and amphetamine fail to produce a sense of high when they are administered orally (Volkow et al., 2010). Stable levels of the medication are maintained within the brain so that the user does not experience the fluctuations of a *high* followed by a *crash*. This reduces craving for the drug of abuse and increases the likelihood of abstinence.

Finally, these agonists may produce cross-tolerance so that if relapse to drug use occurs, the individual may be less sensitive to its euphoric effects. Partial agonists, such as buprenorphine (Subutex), have also been shown to decrease craving and relapse. These therapeutic drugs bind to the same receptors as those activated by the drug of abuse, but produce only limited effects. Antagonist treatments, such as naltrexone, block neurotransmitter receptors so that, if taken, the drug of abuse cannot act on its receptors, and its euphoric effects are prevented. Naltrexone is available as an injectable, slow-release preparation as a treatment for opiate or alcohol addiction. An additional approach is to administer a medication, such as disulfiram (Antabuse), which creates an aversive effect in the user if the drug of abuse (in this case, alcohol) is consumed. You will learn more about Antabuse in the Chapter 6.

THE FUTURE OF PHARMACOTHERAPY. The ultimate goal of addiction pharmacotherapy is to develop a medication capable of preventing or reversing the pathological neuroadaptations that result from chronic drug use. This drug has yet to be developed, but there is hope. Acamprosate, which was approved for use in the United States in 2004, reduces craving for alcohol by altering the expression of the glutamate receptor gene thereby decreasing the neuronal hyperactivity that results from chronic alcohol use (Kranzler & Gage, 2008). N-acetylcysteine (NAC), which affects glutamate function and protects against methamphetamine-induced downregulation of dopamine transporter proteins, shows promise for the treatment of stimulant addiction (Dean, Giorlando, & Berk, 2011). Other neurotransmitter systems are also being investigated for their contribution to addiction, including leptin, a feeding peptide known to interact with the mesolimbic dopamine system (Opland, Leinninger, & Myers, 2010), the histaminergic system (Brabant, Alleva, Quertemont, & Tirelli, 2010), and the endocannabinoid system (Parolaro & Rubino, 2008), to name a few.

A new approach to addiction treatment through immunization is in the advanced stages of clinical testing. Vaccinations are developed by chemically bonding a tiny amount of a drug to a protein against which the immune system builds antibodies. With multiple vaccinations, when the drug of abuse is ingested, antibodies latch on to the drug molecules forming a complex that is too large to pass through the blood–brain barrier. With enough antibodies, most drug molecules will be prevented from reaching their sites of action and the individual will not experience any drug effects. These vaccinations are proving quite effective in helping recovering addicts remain abstinent and in reducing euphoria and psychoactive drug effects upon relapse. Currently, vaccines are being developed and tested for the treatment of cocaine, nicotine, phencyclidine (PCP), methamphetamine, heroin, and morphine addiction (Martell et al., 2009; Orson et al., 2008).

6

Alcohol

SOURCE OF ALCOHOL

Alcohol is a chemical term that describes a wide range of substances, very few of which are commonly consumed. Some members of this class are *isopropyl alcohol*, used as rubbing alcohol; *methanol* (*methyl alcohol*) or wood alcohol; and *ethanol* (*ethyl alcohol*), the alcohol we drink. The other alcohols can be consumed and have behavioral effects similar to those of ethanol, but they are rather toxic and are normally consumed only by accident. In this book, as in most others, the term *alcohol* will be used to refer to ethanol. Where other alcohols are discussed, they will be mentioned by name.

Fermentation

The alcohol we drink is made largely by *fermentation*. When sugar is dissolved in water and left exposed to the air, the mixture is invaded by microorganisms called *yeasts*. Yeasts consume the sugars and multiply rapidly. The metabolic processes of the yeasts convert the sugar into ethanol and carbon dioxide (CO_2), which rises to the top in bubbles, and the alcohol remains. More and more yeasts produce more and more alcohol until all the sugar is used up or the yeasts are unable to continue.

The type of beverage resulting from fermentation is determined by the source of the sugar. Almost any vegetable material containing sugar may be used, but the most common are grape juice, which is fermented to make wine, and grains, which are fermented to make beer. Modern fermentation is done with special yeasts rather than the wild variety. Yeasts are living organisms; they have been bred and selected over the centuries for particular types of fermentation. Because yeasts can tolerate only low levels of alcohol, fermented beverages do not have alcohol levels much above 10 to 15%.

Distillation

The Chinese were likely the first to distill alcohol as long ago as 3000 BCE. For a long time, the process, known only to alchemists, was a jealously guarded secret, and little was committed to writing until much later. The process of distillation is quite simple. It starts with ordinary fermentation of a sugary substance. When fermentation is completed, the mixture is heated. Because alcohol has a lower boiling point than water, the vapor or steam given off will have a higher content of vaporized alcohol than the original product. When this vapor is condensed after cooling, the resulting fluid will also contain a higher percentage of alcohol. There is no reason why the condensed spirits cannot be redistilled again and again until the resulting fluid has the desired level of alcohol. The traditional method among moonshiners for determining whether they have distilled their product sufficiently is to take a teaspoon of the stuff and set it on fire. When the fire has burned off all the alcohol, the spoon is tipped, and if more than a drop of water remains, the liquid is distilled again.

Brandy is the result of distilling wine, and whiskey is distilled from fermented grains. Brandy and whiskey were the first popular spirits. Today, we have rum, distilled from fermented molasses, and schnapps, which traditionally is distilled from fermented potatoes. Gin and vodka are made from a mixture of water, flavoring, and pure alcohol distilled from any source. Distilled spirits, or hard liquor, usually have an alcoholic content of about 40 to 50% by volume. In addition to these hard liquors are the liqueurs, which are sweetened and flavored. Some well-known liqueurs are crème de menthe, which is flavored with mint; Cointreau, which has an added flavor of oranges; and the famous Greek drink ouzo, which has an anise flavor.

Midway between the distilled and fermented beverages are the fortified wines, such as sherry, port, madeira, and muscatel, which were developed during the Middle Ages. These are blends of wine with extra alcohol added to boost the alcohol content to about 20%. Vermouth is a flavored fortified wine developed in Turin in the eighteenth century.

ORIGIN AND HISTORY

Alcohol has probably been a part of the human diet and that of our hominin ancestors for millions of years. Many of these ancestors, human and otherwise, consumed fruit, which has a high sugar content and therefore would have been an excellent food. However, because of the sugar and the presence of yeasts, all fruit, even ripe fruit, contains a small amount of alcohol, and as it matures, the alcohol content increases. The taste and smell of alcohol then would have been associated with food and nourishment throughout a significant proportion of our evolutionary history. As we shall see later, this long-term association has probably had a big influence on physiological and behavioral responses to alcohol (Dudley, 2000, 2002).

While people have likely been brewing alcohol since agriculture began about 10,000 years ago, they undoubtedly did so on a small scale, and there is no record of it. The earliest proof of humans fermenting alcohol involves large earthenware jugs found in China that date back 9,000 years. Analysis of the contents has shown that they once stored a wine made from rice, honey, and fruit (McGovern et al., 2004).

The earliest written set of laws, the Code of Hammurabi, written in 2225 BCE in Assyria, sets forth some rules for the keeping of beer and wine shops and taverns. The ancient Egyptians were also known for their drinking. The Egyptian Book of the Dead, from about 3000 BCE, mentions the manufacture of a drink called *hek*, a form of beer made from grain (Bickerdyke, 1971). Herodotus, the Greek historian, narrated how, at a rich man's feast in ancient Egypt, it was the custom to have a man carry around the image of a corpse in a coffin and show it to all the guests saying, "Drink and make merry, but look on this for such thou shalt be when thou are dead" (McCarthy, 1959, p. 66). The ancient Egyptians, as well as the Assyrians and the Babylonians, drank beer primarily (their climate was more suitable for the growing of grains than grapes), but they also drank a great deal of wine.

There is much evidence that the Greeks, who were supposed to be "temperate in all things," may not always have been so temperate where wine was concerned. Plato had much to say about the effects of alcohol. In *The Laws*, Plato wrote:

> When a man drinks wine he begins to be better pleased with himself, and the more he drinks the more he is filled full of brave hopes, and conceit of his powers, and at last the string of his tongue is loosened, and fancying himself wise, he is brimming over with lawlessness and has no more fear or respect and is ready to do or say anything. (Laws I, 649a–b; translation in Jowett, 1931, p. 28)

Although the early Romans had little trouble with wine, there was a great deal of insobriety and debauchery in the declining years of the Roman Empire for which the later Roman emperors, such as Nero, Claudius, and Caligula, became notorious. The fall of the Roman Empire has been blamed on the consumption of wine, not so much as a result of the alcohol, but because wine at the time was fermented and stored in vessels made of lead, and a lead-based additive was put into the wine to enhance flavor and stop fermentation. It is believed that most of the Roman nobility who drank wine suffered from mental instability as a result of lead poisoning (Nriagu, 1983).

Before the Romans brought grapes and wine to the British Isles, the main alcoholic beverages were beer made from barley, mead made from fermented wild honey, and cider made from fermented apples. The Romans introduced grapes to Britain, but the vines never thrived in the British climate, and wine, as today, was primarily imported. After the Romans left Britain, the Saxons carried on the tradition of heavy drinking with mead, ale, and cider. Taverns and alehouses were established in about the eighth century and quickly acquired a bad reputation.

After the Norman Conquest in 1066, drinking became more moderate, and wine was reintroduced, but the English were still heavy drinkers. "You know that the constant habit of drinking has made the English famous among all foreign nations," wrote Peter of Blois (French, 1884, p. 68).

Although distillation had been known for some time, its presence was not felt in England until the sixteenth century when a number of Irish settlers started manufacturing and distributing *usquebaugh*, which, in English, became known as whiskey. Brandy imported from France was also becoming popular. After the restoration of the monarchy in 1660, distilleries were licensed, and the popularity of gin spread like an epidemic (gin is raw alcohol flavored with juniper berry).

Between 1684 and 1727, the annual consumption of distilled spirits in England increased from about half a million gallons to over 3.5 million gallons (French, 1884). These figures do not include the large quantities of rum and brandy smuggled into the country to avoid paying high duties and tariffs. This epidemic raised such concern that the government passed a desperate series of laws aimed at curtailing the use of liquor, but nothing had much effect.

The English propensity for strong drink was transported across the Atlantic to the colonies. Colonial Americans were hearty drinkers, and alcohol played a large part in their lives.

How highly did the colonies prize strong drink? Their statutes regulating its sale spoke of it as "one of the good creatures of God, to be received with thanksgiving." Harvard University operated its own brewery, and commencements grew so riotous that rigid rules had to be imposed to reduce "the Excesses, Immoralities and Disorders." Workmen received part of their pay in rum, and employees would set aside certain days of the year for total inebriety (Benjamin Rush, quoted in Kobler, 1973).

Before the American Revolution, there had been some success in regulating taverns and drinking, but this control weakened after independence from England was gained. Americans connected liberty from the crown to the freedom to down a few glasses of rum. As a consequence, drinking houses emerged from the war with increased vitality and independence, and the legal regulation of licensed premises waned (Rorabaugh, 1979). Consumption continued to increase to prodigious levels, but a precipitous decline followed between 1830 and 1860. This decline can be attributed to the singular efforts of the temperance movement.

In both England and the United States, there had always been people who openly condemned the use of alcohol, and there were organized movements against drinking and alcohol consumption. In the late 1700s in the United States, the champion of temperance was Dr. Benjamin Rush, a physician who wrote widely about the dangerous physical, social, and moral effects of alcohol and published one of the first influential temperance documents, *An Inquiry into the Effects of Ardent Spirits.*

Although Rush's writings were not heeded at the time, they inspired the American temperance movement of the early nineteenth century, which was more successful than any similar movement before or since. The temperance movement was successful because it was philosophically in tune with the moral tenor and ideals of the new republic. Socially, it filled exactly the same function as drinking. "Some men sought camaraderie at the tavern, others in their local temperance organization" (Rorabaugh, 1979, p. 189). In addition, a religious revival was sweeping the United States at the time. Total abstinence from alcohol provided a symbolic way to express conversion and faith.

The temperance movement was not content to rely on the force of moral persuasion to dry up the country, however. During this period, the movement attracted enough power to have alcohol prohibition laws enacted in 11 states and two territories. Soon, a national Prohibition party was founded, and the temperance reformers set their sights on the federal government. Their vigorous campaign culminated in 1917 with the ratification of the Eighteenth Amendment to the U.S. Constitution. Prohibition was passed with little opposition, as most legislatures had their attention focused on World War I.

Because it did not have widespread public support, the law was virtually unenforceable and provided a vehicle for the rapid development and funding of mobsters and organized crime. Alcohol that was not manufactured in the United States was smuggled in from Canada and elsewhere in vast quantities. It became apparent to both presidential candidates, Herbert Hoover and Franklin Roosevelt, in the 1932 presidential election that Prohibition did not have popular support. One month after Roosevelt's victory, an amendment to the Constitution was drafted that would void the Eighteenth Amendment. Within 2 months, it was passed by both the House and the Senate, and on December 5, 1933, it was ratified and signed into law. Prohibition had lasted almost 14 years.

After Prohibition ended, alcohol consumption rates increased steadily until they peaked in about 1979. Spurred by movements such as Mothers Against Drunk Driving (MADD), consumption has begun to decline in response to an increasing concern with health and a decreasing public tolerance of drugs in general because of the harm that they do. David Musto, a medical historian at Yale University, is among those who predict that history is likely to repeat itself and that this decline will continue into the early twenty-first century but that it will then be followed by another drinking backlash (Kolata, 1991).

Figure 6-1 shows that American consumption of alcohol appears to go through cycles. Consumption peaks every 60 to 70 years, and these peaks have been followed by declines in use. Historians have pointed out that these periods of decline were accompanied by preoccupation with health and morality and by public concern over the harm that alcohol was doing, but fairly sharp increases in consumption followed. It appears as though the United States is now well into a phase of decreasing alcohol use.

MEASURING ALCOHOL LEVELS IN THE BODY

Alcohol levels are usually measured in terms of the concentration of alcohol in whole blood. This is known as the blood alcohol concentration (BAC), or blood alcohol level (BAL). The BAC may be measured directly by taking a blood sample, but more often a breath sample is taken and analyzed using a device known as a Breathalyzer. It has been established that alcohol concentration in the breath reflects the concentration in the blood fairly reliably, and so the results of a Breathalyzer are reported as "*blood* alcohol concentration" rather than "*breath* alcohol concentration."

Metric Measurements and Percentage

BAC is usually expressed in terms of milligrams (mg) of alcohol per 100 milliliters (ml) of whole blood (a milligram is 1/1,000 gram; a milliliter is 1/1,000 liter; 100 ml

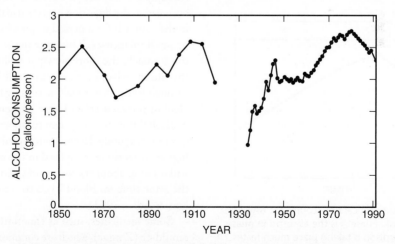

FIGURE 6-1 Yearly alcohol consumption, in gallons per person, of raw alcohol from 1850 to 1990 in the United States. Note that there are three peaks in consumption, about 60 years apart. The gap in the early part of the twentieth century is due to Prohibition. Note the short-lived increase in consumption in the years following World War II. (Williams, Clem, & Dufour, 1993)

is equal to a deciliter [dl]). The BAC may also be reported as a percent of alcohol in the blood. Fortunately, conversion between these measures is not difficult; it involves only moving the decimal point three places to the right or left. For example, a BAC of 80 mg of alcohol per 100 ml of blood (or 80 mg/dl) is equivalent to 0.08%.

SI Units

There has been a recent trend in the scientific literature toward reporting drug concentrations in *SI units* (Système International d'Unités). This measure makes it easy to compare the concentration of different drugs in the blood because it takes into account the molecular weight of the drug. If the concentration expressed in SI units is the same for two different drugs, then there will be the same number of molecules of each drug per liter. The SI unit of concentration is millimoles of alcohol per liter of blood (mmol/l). For example, 80 mg per 100 ml is equivalent to 17.4 mmol/l of blood.

ROUTE OF ADMINISTRATION AND PHARMACOKINETICS

Figure 6-2 shows the theoretical time course for the level of alcohol in the blood after taking a single drink. This curve can be considered as being made up of several

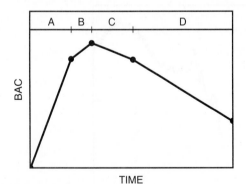

FIGURE 6-2 The theoretical time course for BAC after taking a single drink. Phase A is the absorption phase during which absorption is taking place much faster than elimination. Phases B and C form the plateau phase during which absorption tapers off and elimination starts to lower blood alcohol concentration. During this phase, blood concentration peaks. During the elimination phase, D, absorption is complete, and alcohol is eliminated from the body at a constant rate.

phases. The part of the curve labeled A is the absorption phase, during which absorption is taking place much more rapidly than excretion. The plateau phase, labeled B and C, is when absorption tapers off and excretion starts to lower alcohol levels. During this phase, blood alcohol levels peak. If absorption has been rapid, there may also be a brief period, immediately following the peak, when the decline in blood levels is rapid as a result of the distribution of alcohol out of the blood to other parts of the body. In the excretion phase, D, alcohol is eliminated from the body at a constant rate.

ABSORPTION

Alcohol is normally administered orally, and absorption takes place in the digestive tract. Because the molecules of alcohol cannot be ionized, neither the pH of the digestive system nor the pH of the blood has an effect on absorption.

Alcohol readily dissolves in water, and it may pass into the blood from the stomach, intestines, or colon. However, it is absorbed most rapidly from the small intestine. As long as alcohol stays in the stomach, it is exposed to fairly high levels of *alcohol dehydrogenase*, the main enzyme that breaks down alcohol. The stomach is where *first-pass metabolism* of alcohol occurs, catalyzed by alcohol dehydrogenase. After solid food has been eaten, the digestion process usually keeps the food in the stomach for a period of time before it is released in small quantities. Thus, the longer alcohol stays in the stomach, the more slowly it will be absorbed into the blood. Also, more alcohol will be broken down through *first-pass metabolism*, causing the overall level of alcohol released to be lower. In general, absorption of alcohol is faster on an empty stomach, and more will get into the body. Even though peak blood levels are higher when there is no food in the stomach, the peak will occur at about the same time, and it will take about the same time for blood levels to return to zero (Watkins & Adler, 1993).

Some medicines, such as cimetidine (Tagamet) and ranitidine (Zantac), which are commonly used to reduce stomach acidity, can increase BAC. These drugs, known as *histamine H_2-receptor antagonists*, are widely prescribed for ulcers and heartburn. Zantac 75 is ranitidine in nonprescription strength and is available over the counter. These H_2-receptor antagonists reduce stomach levels of alcohol dehydrogenase, and this significantly re-duces the amount of first-pass metabolism. One study found that the amount of alcohol entering the blood was increased by 17% after a single week of ranitidine treatment (DiPadova et al., 1992). The effect appears even greater with cimetidine. The effects of cimetidine and ranitidine are greatest when alcohol is taken on a full stomach. On an empty stomach (or in the case of alcoholics), there is little first-pass metabolism in the digestive system (DiPadova, Worner, Julkunnen, & Lieber, 1987).

There also appear to be gender differences in first-pass metabolism. Compared to men, women have lower levels of alcohol dehydrogenase in the stomach; consequently, more alcohol enters the blood, resulting in a higher BAC for women than the same amount of alcohol would produce in a man of similar size (Frezza et al., 1990; Whitfield & Martin, 1994).

Interestingly, abstainers appear to reach lower peak BACs than moderate drinkers. The reason for this difference is not clear, but it may have to do with different degrees of first-pass metabolism in people who never drink (Whitfield & Martin, 1994).

The time to reach the maximum blood alcohol level after drinking is highly variable between individuals and situations, but the time to reach the beginning of the plateau (B in Figure 6-2) is usually about an hour, with the peak about 15 minutes later. After a few drinks, however, absorption rates seem to increase, and the peak and plateau will be reached 20 to 25 minutes sooner (Ditmar & Dorian, 1987).

Beer passes out of the stomach more slowly than other alcoholic beverages. For this reason, beer creates lower BACs than the same amount of alcohol consumed in some other beverage. The passage of alcohol through the stomach may also be facilitated by carbonation. Sparkling wines such as champagne and rosé frequently have more "kick" than still wines (Vogel-Sprott, 1992).

The concentration of the alcohol also contributes to the speed of absorption. Diffusion rates increase with increases in concentration; therefore, the alcohol from beverages with high alcoholic content diffuses into the blood faster than the same amount of alcohol mixed in a weaker concentration. There is, however, an upper limit to this effect. High alcohol concentrations slow down the rate at which the stomach empties its contents into the intestine and, thus, can interfere with absorption. It is likely not a coincidence that most rapid absorption occurs at about 40% alcohol, the concentration of most hard liquors.

It has also been suggested that expectancy may have an effect on BAC when drinking. In a recent study, subjects who expected alcohol reached a higher average BAC than subjects who were given alcohol unexpectedly (Cole-Harding & Michels, 2007).

DISTRIBUTION

Because alcohol dissolves much more readily in water than in fat, alcohol is distributed almost entirely in body water. Therefore, individuals with different proportions of body fat, even though they may weigh exactly the same, may reach different BACs after drinking identical amounts of alcohol. Males, for example, have a lower percentage of body fat than females. Thus, if a man and a woman weigh exactly the same and drink the same amount of alcohol, the woman will have a higher BAC (assuming similar first-pass metabolism). The alcohol she drinks will be more highly concentrated in her blood because her body has less water to dilute it.

For males, age also makes a difference, as their body fat percentage generally increases until age 50 or 60. Even though their total body weight may not change, the same amount of alcohol will result in higher BACs as men get older. Women show a much smaller change in body composition with age.

It is possible to calculate the BAC for an individual after the consumption of a given amount of alcohol. Box 6-1 shows how to make these calculations for any individual.

Alcohol is distributed rather evenly throughout body water, and it crosses the blood–brain barrier, as well as the placental barrier, without difficulty. Consequently, alcohol levels in most tissues of the body, including the brain and a fetus (if present), accurately reflect the blood alcohol content of the drinker. Alcohol in the blood circulates through the lungs and vaporizes into the air at a known rate, which is why it is possible to measure the alcohol level in the blood and the rest of the body by measuring the alcohol vapor in exhaled air using a Breathalyzer, as described earlier.

BOX 6-1 Calculating Blood Alcohol Concentrations

Calculating the BAC is relatively simple. You have to know the weight and sex of the individual and the amount of alcohol consumed. To illustrate, let us calculate the BAC of a 175-pound man who has ingested 1 ounce of spirits. Because the BAC is usually given in milligrams per 100 ml of blood, it is easier to do the calculations in metric units rather than in pounds and ounces.

First, we convert the body weight (175 pounds) to kilograms by dividing by 2.2 (1 kg = 2.2 lb). This equals 80 kg. This weight must then be adjusted because not all of the body is capable of absorbing alcohol. The percentage that can absorb alcohol is estimated to be 75% in men and 66% in women. Therefore, an 80-kg man will have 60 kg to absorb alcohol (80 × 0.75 = 60); 60 kg = 60,000 g or 60,000 ml of fluid because 1 ml of water weighs 1 g.

Next, we must convert alcohol to milligrams. One ounce of spirits (100 proof, or 50% by volume) will contain 11.2 g of alcohol (0.5 fluid ounce of water weighs 14 g), and alcohol has a specific gravity of 0.8 (14 × 0.8 = 11.2); 11.2 g is 11,200 mg.

Now we can divide the 11,200 mg of alcohol by 60,000 ml of body fluid and multiply by 100. This calculation yields the BAC: 18.6 mg per 100 ml. Our 175-pound man will raise his BAC by 18.6 mg per 100 ml of blood with every ounce of spirits.

Beer is usually about 5% alcohol by volume and comes in 12-ounce bottles. One such bottle would contain 13.5 g of alcohol, or 13,500 mg. When this is spread around a 60,000-ml body, it gives a concentration of about 22.5 mg per 100 ml. Our 175-pound man would raise his BAC by 22.5 per 100 ml with each beer. The accompanying table gives the alcohol content of various common drinks so that you can do the appropriate calculations for different sources of alcohol.

To calculate how each of these drinks would affect you, take your weight in pounds and convert it to kilograms by dividing by 2.2. Next calculate the body weight (for your sex) that is capable of absorbing alcohol: male, 75%; female, 66%. This figure must then be converted to milligrams (and milliliters) by multiplying by 1,000.

Now calculate the amount of alcohol consumed in milligrams, divide it by your weight in milligrams, and multiply by 100. Because the body metabolizes alcohol at a rate of about 15 mg per 100 ml per hour, you can subtract 15 mg per 100 ml for each hour that has passed since your drinking started. Caution: These estimates of your BAC using this technique are just that—estimates. Two factors in this equation are approximations: the percentage of the body that will absorb alcohol and the rate of alcohol metabolism. Both depend on many factors, such as age, health, build, experience with alcohol, and even other drugs in your system. The figures given here are population averages that might not apply to you. In general, however, this technique tends to overestimate BAC, so it should be reasonably safe for most people most of the time. It is not recommended, however, that you bet your life or your driver's license on it.

Alcohol Contents of Some Beverages

Beverage	Alcohol Content Percent (volume)	Alcohol Content (mg)
Spirits (1 fl. oz.*)		
(100 proof)	50	11,200
(89 proof)	43	9,600
(80 proof)	40	8,900
Beer (12 fl. oz.)	5	13,500
Wine (2.5 fl. oz.)	12	8,400

*A shot is 1.25 oz., so that these figures must be increased by 25% if "shots" are being used to mix drinks.

ELIMINATION

Alcohol may be eliminated in breath, sweat, tears, urine, and feces, but between 90 and 98% of all alcohol consumed is metabolized by the liver (the remaining portion is eliminated by the kidneys, lungs, and through the skin). Because humans have been consuming alcohol throughout a long period of our evolution, we have developed an efficient means of eliminating alcohol and using it as a source of energy. The usual route of metabolism is shown in Figure 1-10. It involves two steps. In the first step, the *rate-limiting step*, alcohol is converted to *acetaldehyde* by the enzyme alcohol dehydrogenase. This is the slowest step in alcohol metabolism. Consequently, the rate at which this conversion takes place limits the speed of the entire process. The rate of conversion of alcohol to acetaldehyde is determined by the amount of alcohol dehydrogenase available and is relatively independent of the concentration of alcohol. The metabolism of alcohol, then, usually takes place at a steady rate throughout most BACs (this rate may vary between individuals and from species to species).

In the second step, the acetaldehyde is converted into *acetyl coenzyme A* by several enzymes, the most common of which is *aldehyde dehydrogenase*. Acetyl coenzyme A is converted mainly into water and carbon dioxide through a series of reactions known as the *citric acid cycle*, during which usable energy is released to the body. Acetyl coenzyme A is also used in a number of bodily processes, such as the production of fatty acids and steroids. As a result, alcohol consumption and its consequent metabolism can alter a great deal of body chemistry.

Between individuals, there is considerable variability in elimination rates. The range found in one study was from 5.9 to 27.9 mg per 100 ml of blood per hour, with a standard deviation of 4.5 (Dubowski, 1985). For the majority of individuals, the range is usually accepted to be between 10 and 20 mg per 100 ml per hour, with a mean of 15. The rate of metabolism of alcohol also seems to be influenced by drinking experience. Nondrinkers metabolize alcohol at a slightly slower rate (12–14 mg/100 ml per hour) than light to moderate drinkers (15–17 mg/100 ml per hour; Goldberg, 1943; Whitfield & Martin, 1994).

It has also been demonstrated that food can have an effect on the rate of alcohol metabolism as well as its absorption. Ramchandani, Kwo, and Li (2001) have shown that eating speeds up the rate of alcohol metabolism from 25 to 45%. The increase does not seem to depend on the type of food eaten and is probably a result of increased blood flow to the liver caused by a food in the stomach.

Although most alcohol is handled by the alcohol dehydrogenase system, another system appears to be in operation as well. This is known as the *microsomal ethanol-oxidizing system* (MEOS). The MEOS normally handles only 5 to 10% of the metabolism of alcohol, but its activity increases at higher levels of blood alcohol. The activity of the MEOS may be doubled or even tripled by continuous alcohol consumption. This increase may account for 50 to 65% of the increased alcohol metabolism induced by heavy drinking, a change that partly accounts for alcohol tolerance. The MEOS is important for another reason: It is also responsible for the metabolism of a number of other drugs, such as barbiturates (see Chapter 7). Therefore, if the MEOS is stimulated by continuous alcohol use, the metabolism of these other drugs will also be speeded up, and vice versa (Leiber, 1977; Leiber & De Carli, 1977). Thus, alcoholics usually have a great deal of resistance to the effects of barbiturates and other drugs.

NEUROPHARMACOLOGY

The neuropharmacology of alcohol is complex and involves a number of systems. One interesting aspect of alcohol intoxication is that a much higher concentration of alcohol is required than most other drugs. Most drugs discussed in this book produce their effects in blood concentrations in the nanomolar (nM) or micromolar range (μM), but effects of alcohol are seen only at the millimolar (mM) range, that is, 1,000 to 1,000,000 times greater than most drugs (these concentrations are given in SI units and reflect the number of drug molecules per liter so that they can be compared with other drugs of different molecular weights). Because its effects seemed to require such high concentrations, alcohol was initially thought to act on the nervous tissue through a physical effect like causing the neural membranes to swell or become distorted. However, it is now known that alcohol works by altering neural transmission at receptor sites and ion channels in a manner similar to other drugs.

The effects of alcohol are not confined to one receptor; alcohol affects many systems at the same time, and it can have different effects on different systems at different concentrations. The puzzle of how alcohol affects neurophysiology is only now being untangled, and there is a great deal that is still not known. The principal neurotransmitter systems that mediate the behavioral effects of alcohol are GABA and glutamate, but alcohol affects other systems as well, including glycine, serotonin, acetylcholine, dopamine, and the endogenous opioid system.

GABA

GABA is the principal inhibitory transmitter in the brain. PET-detected decreases in brain activity appear to be related to alcohol-induced stimulation of GABA receptors; interestingly, such stimulation is more pronounced in men than in women (Wang et al., 2003). There are two types of GABA receptors: $GABA_A$ and $GABA_B$. Alcohol is known to affect both, but in a different manner. The $GABA_A$ receptor is part of a *receptor–ionophore complex*; it contains a ligand-gated channel permeable to chloride (Cl^-) ions (*ionophore* is sometimes used as a synonym for *ion channel*). $GABA_A$ receptors are *pentameric*—made up of five subunits surrounding the central pore, as can be seen in Figure 7-1 in Chapter 7. Each subunit is a protein or chain of amino acids folded into a complex unit. There is considerable variability in the composition of subunits, each of which is created by a different gene.

There are eight major types of $GABA_A$ receptor subunits, designated alpha (α), beta (β), gamma (γ), delta (δ), epsilon (ϵ), theta (θ), pi (π), and ro (ρ). Some of these subunits are further divided into a number of varieties: There are six varieties of the alpha subunit (α_{1-6}), and three varieties each of beta (β_{1-3}), gamma (γ_{1-3}), and ro (ρ_{1-3}). The remaining four subunits (δ, ϵ, θ, and π) each have only one variety. Every $GABA_A$ receptor complex is made up of five of the possible 19 subunits put together in a variety of combinations, making many different types of $GABA_A$ receptors possible. The most common type of $GABA_A$ receptor is made up of two alpha subunits, two beta subunits, and one gamma subunit, and the most common receptor subunit varieties are $\alpha_1\beta_2\gamma_2$, $\alpha_2\beta_3\gamma_2$, and $\alpha_3\beta_3\gamma_2$ (Nutt & Stahl, 2010). Different $GABA_A$ receptor subunit configurations are found in distinct areas of the brain, which suggests that both the location and the variety of $GABA_A$ receptor

complex may determine its function and how it is affected by alcohol and other GABAergic drugs.

There are two actual receptor binding sites for the GABA transmitter molecule, each located between the interface of an alpha and a beta subunit (see Figure 7-1). These sites are referred to as *orthosteric* sites, where the natural ligand (GABA) binds to its specific receptor site. When an orthosteric site is activated, the ion channel that forms the central pore of the $GABA_A$ receptor complex opens and permits an influx of Cl^- ions, hyperpolarizing the postsynaptic membrane and inhibiting the cell. The $GABA_A$ receptor complex also contains what are called *allosteric* binding sites. When a drug binds to an allosteric site, it is able to alter the function of the receptor complex by creating conformational changes in the receptor that, in turn, affect the functioning of the orthosteric sites. $GABA_A$ receptor complexes contain an allosteric site for benzodiazepines, located between the alpha and gamma subunits, and other allosteric sites for alcohol, barbiturates, neuroactive steroids, picrotoxin, and general anesthetics, all of which are located on the membrane-spanning portion of the receptor complex. In most cases, activation of these allosteric sites does not open the Cl^- ion channel to cause hyperpolarization. Instead, it alters the binding affinity (i.e., the forming of a receptor–ligand complex) and efficacy (i.e., the elicitation of a biological response) of GABA to open the ion channel. Activation of allosteric sites can either enhance the effects of GABA or lessen those effects. If there is an enhancement of GABA, the drug is called a *positive allosteric modulator*; if the effects of GABA are diminished, the drug is a *negative allosteric modulator*. Alcohol is a positive allosteric modulator.

Different configurations of the $GABA_A$ receptor complex are associated with different parts of the brain and mediate different functions (Möhler et al., 2004). In addition, $GABA_A$ receptors made from different subunit combinations are differentially sensitive to different allosteric modulators.

Alcohol is known to act only on $GABA_A$ receptor complexes that contain a delta subunit in combination with alpha 4 or alpha 6 subunits (Tomberg, 2010). Alcohol functions at these receptor complexes as a positive allosteric modulator, enhancing the ability of GABA to open the ion channel. $GABA_A$ receptor complexes with delta subunits are unusual types of $GABA_A$ receptors. They are very sensitive to low levels of GABA and alcohol and appear to have specialized functions outside synapses. They are believed to be located in two places in relation to the neuron. One is in postsynaptic membranes, but not at a GABA synapse. These receptor complexes are normally activated by spillover GABA that diffuses from a GABA synapse. It is believed that their function is to enhance a tonic or long-term inhibition of the cell (Santhakumar, Wallner, & Otis, 2007; Tomberg, 2010). The other location of these *extrasynaptic* receptors is on a presynaptic membrane where they enhance transmitter release into the cleft, thus intensifying the inhibitory effect of GABA.

Alcohol-sensitive GABA$_A$ receptors containing the delta subunit are located in the cerebellum, a part of the brain responsible for balance, coordination, and motor control. Purkinje neurons, which are responsible for cerebellar output, are stimulated by low concentrations of alcohol, but, at higher doses, alcohol releases GABA from connecting cells, and this inhibits the Purkinje neurons. These alterations in Purkinje cell output cause many of the impairments in motor control caused by alcohol.

Whereas GABA$_A$ receptors maintain an inhibitory tone in the nervous system and are in operation all the time in response to a fairly constant level of GABA, GABA$_B$ receptors are metabotropic. They are not directly linked to an ion channel, but rather use a second messenger and indirectly control the functioning of a K$^+$ channel (see Chapter 4). There are three varieties of GABA$_B$ receptors that serve different functions. One variety works as an autoreceptor on the presynaptic membrane of GABA synapses where it stimulates GABA release. Another variety, located on postsynaptic membranes, blocks the release of other neurotransmitters by altering calcium channels (Kelm, Criswell, & Breese, 2011). GABA$_B$ receptor activity is also implicated in levels of cyclic AMP, which can alter synaptic plasticity. Alcohol is also known to alter the function of some subtypes of GABA$_B$ receptors, particularly at dopamine synapses stimulating the release of dopamine.

Glutamate

Glutamate is used throughout the brain as an excitatory transmitter, and alcohol blocks glutamate transmission. The level of excitability of the central nervous system (CNS) is maintained by a delicate balance between GABA and glutamate. It has been shown, in several parts of the brain, that acute doses of alcohol at concentrations achieved by normal drinking depress the functioning of the ion channel controlled by glutamate at the NMDA receptor. The NMDA receptor binding site for alcohol is within the ion channel itself, and alcohol molecules have the effect of blocking the ion channel. Just like GABA receptors, the NMDA receptors are composed of many different subunits, and there are specific NMDA subunit configurations that are particularly sensitive to alcohol.

The effects of alcohol on glutamate and GABA converge. GABA stimulation depresses neural activity, and the effect of glutamate diminishes excitability. Together they lead to a suppression of neural activity in particular locations of the CNS. As a result of chronic exposure to alcohol, the brain upregulates NMDA receptor–ion channel functioning; that is, the brain becomes more sensitive to glutamate as a means of compensating for prolonged depression by alcohol. It is believed that this increase in sensitivity to the excitatory transmitter glutamate may be responsible for alcohol withdrawal symptoms that occur when alcohol is no longer being consumed (Sanna & Harris, 1993).

Among many other functions, the hippocampus is responsible for memory formation. The effect of alcohol on NMDA receptors is known to interfere with long-term potentiation, a mechanism necessary for the formation of memories in the hippocampus. In addition, ethanol is known to prevent the formation of new neurons (neurogenesis) in the hippocampus. Both of these effects probably contribute to the effects of alcohol on memory, discussed later in this chapter (Tomberg, 2010).

The prefrontal cortex is responsible for many higher cognitive abilities including impulse control, attention, planning, and problem solving. The effects of alcohol are similar to the effects of brain damage to the prefrontal cortex and include impulsivity and impaired impulse control. The prefrontal cortex consists mostly of glutamatergic pyramidal projection neurons, which send axons throughout the rest of the brain, and inhibitory GABAergic interneurons, which suppress the activity of the pyramidal neurons. Considering the effects of alcohol on glutamatergic and GABAergic functioning, it is not surprising the alcohol can impair many cognitive processes (Tomberg, 2010).

Dopamine

These aforementioned and other changes in neural functioning can explain the effects of alcohol on specific areas of the CNS responsible for many of the behavioral effects of alcohol. The reinforcing effects of alcohol, like most reinforcing drugs, arise from increased activity in the mesolimbic dopamine system, specifically heighted dopamine release in the nucleus accumbens. Under normal conditions, the activity of mesolimbic dopamine neurons is inhibited by GABAergic interneurons synapsing on dopaminergic cell bodies within the ventral tegmental area (see panel B of Figure 12-1). These GABA interneurons are themselves innervated by GABAergic neurons projecting from the nucleus accumbens and ventral pallidum. When alcohol is consumed, nucleus accumbens and ventral pallidum neurons release increased quantities of GABA onto the inhibitory interneurons within the ventral tegmental area, and this decreases their activity. As a result, these interneurons release less GABA, thereby diminishing the inhibition of ventral tegmental dopaminergic neurons—enabling (in a roundabout way) an increase in firing and in the level of dopamine output in the nucleus accumbens (Tomberg, 2010). Glutamate activity likely also plays a role. The nucleus accumbens contains GABAergic medium spiny neurons, a special type of inhibitory cells that integrate the myriad of signals coming into the nucleus accumbens. These neurons receive glutamatergic input from the prefrontal cortex, amygdala, and hippocampus and send output to the nucleus accumbens and ventral pallidum. Ethanol's effects on GABAergic, glutamatergic, and dopaminergic cells converging in the nucleus accumbens are key to its reinforcing effects. Serotonin input is known to further increase activity in ventral tegmental area dopamine neurons (Tomberg, 2010).

ALCOHOL ANTAGONISTS

For thousands of years, people have been searching for a substance that would reverse the effects of alcohol. The ancient Greeks believed that the amethyst, a semiprecious stone, had this property, and the term *amethystics* has been used to describe these supposed agents.

In 1985, researchers at Hoffmann–La Roche reported that they had synthesized a substance called *RO 15-4513*, which seemed to be able to antagonize the effects of alcohol. Careful research has shown that the drug antagonizes only some of the effects of alcohol mediated by GABA (including self-administration; June et al., 1992), because it appears to be a competitive antagonist to alcohol at its allosteric binding site on GABA$_A$ receptors that contain the delta subunit (Hanchar et al., 2006; Wallner & Olson, 2008). There is little likelihood that RO 15-4513 could have any medical use. Although it blocks some of the effects of alcohol, it does not antagonize alcohol's lethal effects, so it cannot be used to treat alcohol overdose. In addition, RO 15-4513 may cause convulsions, making it unsuitable for treating alcoholism.

A common misconception is that coffee can sober someone up; systematic studies have found little evidence to support this belief. An early study suggested that caffeine might reverse some of the impairing effects of low levels of alcohol (less than 100 mg alcohol/100 ml blood) on driving, but could not do so at higher blood alcohol levels (Muskowitz & Burns, 1981). A more recent study examining the effect of 200 to 400 mg caffeine on impairments produced by alcohol (at about 80 mg/100 ml blood) found that caffeine was unable to alter a number of alcohol effects, including the subjective effects. These caffeine doses were able to cause a partial reversal of slowed braking speed caused by alcohol, but did not return braking speed to normal levels (Liguori & Robinson, 2001).

Because alcohol has so many effects on so many different sites within the body, it is unlikely that a single substance could antagonize all of its effects.

EFFECTS OF ALCOHOL

Effects on the Body

Alcohol in low and moderate doses causes dilation of capillaries in the skin. This is why individuals who drink heavily tend to have a flushed face. In addition, drinking alcohol creates a temporary sensation of warmth. A traditional medical use for alcohol was as a remedy for people exposed to cold. However, because alcohol dilates the capillaries, heat is lost from the skin more quickly and the body cools down faster, to the point where core temperature can become dangerously low in extreme cold.

By inhibiting antidiuretic hormone (ADH) secretion, alcohol causes increased urination and loss of water, though this occurs only while BAC is steady or falling.

EFFECTS ON HUMAN BEHAVIOR AND PERFORMANCE

Perhaps an indication of the cultural impact of inebriation is the vast number of synonyms for being drunk. In 1737, Benjamin Franklin compiled 228 terms commonly used for being drunk. The *American Thesaurus of Slang*, published in 1952, lists almost 900 such terms. Most of them suggest some sort of violence or damage, such as *smashed, hammered, crashed, pissed, bombed, loaded, plastered, tanked, paralyzed,* and *wiped out*, to cite just a few. Some terms are very old. *Soused*, for example, dates back to sixteenth-century England, and *cut* was used as long ago as 1770 (Levine, 1981).

What does it mean to be hammered or smashed? The body of literature on this subject, dating back to the time of Aristotle, is so vast that it is almost impossible to characterize it in this short space. Systematic observation of drinkers has shown that at BACs between 50 and 100 mg per 100 ml, people are more talkative, use a higher pitch of voice, and show mild excitement. At about 100 to 150 mg per 100 ml, subjects appear even more talkative and cheerful, and are often loud and boisterous; later, they become sleepy. At BACs above 150 mg per 100 ml, subjects frequently feel nauseous and may vomit. This phase is followed by lethargy and, in some cases, stupor. At doses between 200 and 290 mg per 100 ml, subjects may enter a stupor, experience a loss of understanding, memory blackout, and unconsciousness.

The problem with dose-related descriptions such as these is that there is such variability in the responses of individuals, depending on drinking history, environment, tolerance, and the rapidity of alcohol consumption, that they very seldom describe the behavior of any one individual on any single drinking occasion.

Subjective Effects

Many researchers report that alcohol causes a biphasic effect with regard to time and dose. At low doses and while blood levels are rising, alcohol has a stimulant effect, and people describe elation and euphoria; but at high doses and when the blood levels are falling, subjects report primarily feelings of sedation, anger, and depression (Babor, Berglas, Mendelson, Ellingboe, & Miller, 1983). With regard to aggressive behavior that sometimes ensues in people following high doses of alcohol, laboratory research using mice trained to self-administer alcohol has shown that heightened levels of aggression are due, at least in part, to GABA modulation in the dorsal raphe nuclei (Takahashi, Kwa, Debold, & Miczek, 2010).

Research has also indicated, however, that not everyone experiences the stimulation effect; some subjects experience only the sedating effects. Interestingly, those who describe stimulant-like effects also report a greater *drug liking* for alcohol and show more impairment on the digit symbol substitution test. It has been speculated that such individuals may be at greater risk for alcohol abuse (Holdstock & de Wit, 1998).

Perception

Alcohol has a detrimental effect on vision. It increases both absolute and difference thresholds, but usually only at high doses. A decrease in visual acuity, indicated by a lowering in the critical flicker fusion threshold, is caused by a BAC of about 70 mg per 100 ml. Decreases in peripheral vision have also been reported. Decreases in sensitivity to taste and smell occur at low doses, and a decrease in pain sensitivity is common at BACs above 80 to 100 mg per 100 ml. Changes in visual perception after acute alcohol consumption may be due to a decrease in lateral inhibition wherein an excited neuron reduces that activity of neighboring neurons (Johnston & Timney, 2008). This has the effect of accentuating the contrast between areas of high and low stimulation at edges and boarders. Lateral inhibition is an essential process used by many sensory organs to process incoming information.

Performance

Alcohol slows reaction time by about 10% at BACs of 80 to 100 mg per 100 ml, and large consistent deficits are evident with larger doses. Complex reaction-time tasks that require the subject to scan and integrate stimuli from several sources before responding show that, at lower doses, both the speed and the accuracy of performance decrease. Deficits are also seen in hand–eye coordination tasks, for example, in which the subject is required to maintain a marker over a moving target. PET analyses show that alcohol consumption decreases blood flow to the cerebellum, a region that controls voluntary movement and coordination and that contains $GABA_A$ receptors with the alcohol-sensitive delta subunit (Volkow, Mullani, Gould, Adler, & Krajeswski, 1988). In general, the more complex the task, the greater the impairment seen at lower doses. Small deficits occur at doses as low as 10 to 20 mg per 100 ml.

Before the Breathalyzer, police used the *Romberg sway test* to detect impairment. The subject is asked to stand with eyes closed and feet together. BACs as low as 60 mg per 100 ml can cause a 40% decrease in steadiness as measured by the amount of swaying. This lack of steadiness makes it difficult for a person to stand on one foot with eyes closed. At higher BACs, the lack of steadiness degenerates into staggering and reeling. The increase in sway appears to be a result of the effect of alcohol on the sensitive organs of balance in the inner ear, which causes *nystagmus*, eye movements responsible for the sensation that the room is spinning around. Alcohol's effect on the cerebellum may also contribute to this effect. Lack of steadiness can also bring on nausea and vomiting (Money & Miles, 1974).

Many people have demonstrated the impairing effects of alcohol on many tasks, but these effects may be dependent upon the expectations and motivations of the individual. Vogel-Sprott (1992) has shown that, at low doses (less than 100 mg/100 ml blood), many response deficits will disappear if subjects are paid or provided with an incentive to overcome the effects of the drug. In addition, subjects who expect that the drug will have an effect are often more impaired than those who do not (Fillmore & Vogel-Sprott, 1998).

Memory

Alcohol is also known to have a detrimental effect on memory. Low and moderate levels of alcohol have been shown to affect attention, encoding, storage, and the retrieval of information, but the storage function seems to be more strongly affected (Birnbaum & Parker, 1977). Rising BACs in the range of 87 mg/100 ml do not increase errors in a short-term (2-minute delay) verbal memory task, but do impair the accuracy of long-term (20-minute delay) verbal memory. Accuracy in both short- and long-term visual memory is not affected by rising BACs, but errors increase during the declining phase of blood alcohol (Schweizer & Vogel-Sprott, 2008).

Working memory was tested by the memory scanning task. In this test, participants are shown an array of two, four, or six items (letters); they are later shown an item; and then they must indicate whether that item was or was not present in the original array. Alcohol at a BAC of 74 mg/100 ml has little effect on recall if two items were used, but alcohol at this dose lengthens reaction time and decreases accuracy when four and six items were tested (Grattan-Miscio & Vogel-Sprott, 2005).

In long-term alcohol abusers, PET analyses using 2-deoxy-2[^{18}F]fluoro-d-glucose show that deficits in verbal and visual memory, as well as attention, correspond with decreased functioning in the dorsolateral prefrontal cortex and the anterior cingulate cortex (Goldstein et al., 2004).

BLACKOUTS. Heavier drinking may also cause periods of amnesia or *blackouts* where people may be unable to remember events that occurred while they were intoxicated. Research indicates that individuals with a BAC of 310 mg per 100 ml blood or greater have a 0.50 or greater probability of experiencing an alcoholic blackout (Perry et al., 2006). There are two different varieties of blackout. The first type is called a *grayout* or a *fragmentary blackout* and is the most common form of alcohol amnesia. When a grayout occurs, the drinker is able to remember only bits and pieces of events that occurred while drinking. The missing memories usually return if the drinker is reminded of these events or if he or she returns to the place where they occurred. This shows that the problem is primarily one of retrieval—the memories were formed and stored in the brain, but the person has trouble accessing them later when the alcohol is gone. Grayouts are thought to result from dissociation (Overton, 1972).

En bloc blackouts are more serious but less frequent. In this type of blackout, the drinker is usually able to remember events of a drinking episode up to a particular time and then remembers nothing until another well-defined point in time, usually when he or she wakes up the next morning. All events that occurred during that block of time are not remembered. In fact, there is no evidence that these memories were ever put into long-term storage because they never return, even when the person is reminded. Interestingly, during the period when a blackout is happening, the drinker's behavior may appear to be perfectly normal. He or she can carry on a conversation and carry out many normal behaviors. They can recall what happened in the past, before they began drinking, but cannot remember what happened 20 minutes ago (Ryback, 1970). They are able to hold things in short-term storage or working memory, but they are unable to form long-term memories.

Effects on Driving

Studies of the effects of alcohol on driving, in simulators and in real cars on closed tracks, have generally confirmed that alcohol begins to affect performance at about 50 to 80 mg per 100 ml (Mitchell, 1985; Starmer, 1990). At 80 mg alcohol per 100 ml blood, participants in a simulated driving study drove at higher average speeds and exhibited performance deficits, which increased the likelihood of collisions.

More recently, fMRI has been used to simultaneously scan the brains of people in a driving simulation task and assess the effects of alcohol on both driving and brain functioning. Initially, it is necessary to determine the normal patterns of activity and connectivity between different brain areas and establish critical networks that are activated in response to different driving tasks, and then examine the effect of alcohol on those functional networks. Calhoun and Pearlson (2012) have conducted and reviewed such studies and demonstrated that alcohol significantly disrupts most of the brain networks involved in driving in a dose-dependent manner, depending on the specific task involved. They conclude that acute alcohol impairs cognitive control through a decrease in cortical activation and in regions implicated in error monitoring, such as the anterior cingulate and inferior frontal gyrus.

These performance deficits correspond with decreased activation of the orbitofrontal cortex and certain motor regions of the brain (Calhoun, Pekar, & Pearlson, 2004). Unsurprisingly, it is clear that divided attention (i.e., using a cell phone or texting), when coupled with alcohol impairment, causes far more impairment than does alcohol alone (Harrison & Fillmore, 2011). The neural basis of this effect involved alcohol's influence on the hippocampus, anterior cingulate, and dorsolateral prefrontal cortex. These areas are associated with attentional processing and decision making. Consequently, intoxicated drivers are less able to orient and detect novel or sudden stimuli such as road obstacles while driving. The effect of alcohol on the hippocampus is also important as it processes visuospatial memory, which likely underpins the ability to remember the vehicle's spatial location on the road prior to the distracting events (Calhoun & Pearlson, 2012).

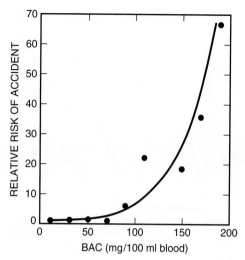

FIGURE 6-3 The relationship between BAC and the relative risk of being involved in a traffic accident. The relative risk of an accident with a BAC of 0.0 is 1.0. (Organization for Economic Cooperation and Development, 1978)

Figure 6-3 shows the relative probability of being responsible for a fatal crash at various BACs. The curve starts to rise between 50 and 100 mg per 100 ml. At 100 mg per 100 ml, the probability of being responsible for a fatal crash is seven times greater than if the BAC had been 0. After this point, the curve rises sharply. At a BAC of 200 mg per 100 ml, a driver is 100 times more likely to cause a fatal crash (Organization for Economic Cooperation and Development, 1978).

Statistics such as these establish the rationale for setting legal limits on BAC for driving. In most jurisdictions, the limit is between 80 and 100 mg per 100 ml of blood, the point at which the curve starts to rise sharply. It is important to remember, however, that these curves underestimate the risk for young inexperienced drivers, older drivers, and people unaccustomed to drinking. Their risk of being involved in an accident is considerably elevated even at BACs below the legal limit. Figure 6-4 shows similar curves for people of different ages (Organization for Economic Cooperation and Development, 1978).

Disinhibition and Behavior Control

One of the common behavioral effects of alcohol is *disinhibition*, a term that refers to the loss of restraint or an inability to withhold behavior under the influence of alcohol.

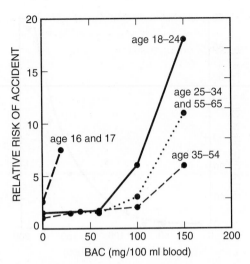

FIGURE 6-4 The relationship between BAC and the relative risk of being involved in a traffic accident for people of different age groups. The relative risk of an accident with a BAC of 0.0 is 1.0. (Organization for Economic Cooperation and Development, 1978)

Intoxication frequently causes disregard for personal risk, social norms, and long-term consequences in favor of short-term gratification. It is interesting that disinhibition may actually improve performance on tasks in which anxiety or conflict is interfering with behavior. In these cases, alcohol in low doses can actually be beneficial to performance.

Studies examining alcohol and behavioral control often use a *go–stop* task. In this task, a subject is required to make a response when a particular signal, the *go* signal, is presented but must withhold that response if the *go* signal is followed by a *stop* signal. Studies have shown that alcohol at moderate doses does not interfere with responding to the *go* signal, but it selectively interferes with the ability of the *stop* signal to inhibit behavior (Schweizer & Vogel-Sprott, 2008). Furthermore, fMRI studies of brain activity during these tasks show that alcohol weakens the connections between the frontal areas of the cortex and the striatum, a motor area of the brain (Vogel-Sprott, Easdon, Fillmore, Finn, & Justus, 2001).

Though disinhibition is usually associated with alcohol's physiological effects, it has been suggested that it may be equally attributed to socially conditioned expectations about alcohol consumption. In a recent study, when participants were exposed to alcohol-related images, they exhibited a tendency to associate images with

provocative terms rather than neutral ones. This suggests that even alcohol-related stimuli can cause disinhibition without alcohol being consumed (Freeman, Friedman, Bartholow, & Wulfert, 2010).

EFFECTS ON THE BEHAVIOR OF NONHUMANS

Conditioned Behavior

For various reasons, few studies have been done on the effects of alcohol on positively reinforced behavior, but those that have been done show that the effects are dose dependent. On both fixed interval (FI) and fixed ratio (FR) schedules, alcohol increases the rate of responding at low doses and decreases the rate at higher doses.

The effect of alcohol on punished responding is similar to that of the barbiturates and benzodiazepines (see Chapter 7) but not quite as striking. In an early experiment, Conger (1951) trained rats to run down a runway for food, but gave their paws a shock when they began to eat. He adjusted food deprivation and shock levels until the rats were willing to run partway down the runway but would not touch the food. He found that alcohol would cause the rats to approach and eat the food immediately, but rats given a placebo required many trials. Since then, several researchers have found that ethanol will increase response rates that are suppressed by an administered shock. This result is similar to the finding in humans that alcohol tends to loosen inhibitions and therefore reduces the control of consequences on behavior.

DISCRIMINATIVE STIMULUS PROPERTIES

Animals can be trained very easily to discriminate alcohol from saline. Donald Overton showed that at a dose of 3,000 mg/kg, rats reach criterion discrimination performance in just three trials. Of the drugs tested, the only drugs that were discriminated more quickly were phenobarbital and pentobarbital (Overton, 1982; Overton & Batta, 1977).

Using the electrified T-maze, Overton found that rats trained to discriminate alcohol from saline generalized the alcohol response when given a barbiturate and vice versa, indicating that the two drugs produce a similar subjective state. However, in a later series of experiments, he was able to train rats to discriminate between the two, showing that although the effects of barbiturates and alcohol are similar, they can be discriminated. It has been found that the alcohol response is not generalized to chlorpromazine, amphetamine, or atropine (Barry & Kubina, 1972) though it can be generalized to several anesthetics.

The stimulus properties of alcohol can be blocked by serotonin 5-HT$_3$ receptor blockers but not by haloperidol, a dopamine D$_2$ blocker—an indication that serotonin rather than dopamine may mediate the subjective effects of alcohol (Grant & Barrett, 1991). The discriminative effects of alcohol can be blocked by mu-selective doses of the opioid receptor blocker naltrexone, showing that the opioid system is also involved in the subjective effects of ethanol. Alcohol is known to increase the release of endogenous opioids (Platt & Bano, 2011).

More recent research has shown that the alcohol stimulus is complex and made up of several elements shared with other drugs. Porcu and Grant (2004) used a three-choice discriminative task to separate these elements. They trained rats to discriminate between water, ethanol, and the benzodiazepine midazolam (a positive GABA$_A$ modulator). Because ethanol is also a positive GABA$_A$ modulator, this forced the rats to discriminate ethanol on the basis of some other property. In this situation, the alcohol cue generalized to dizocilpine, an NMDA receptor blocker, showing that the effects of ethanol on both GABA and NMDA glutamate receptors have separate stimulus effects that can be differentiated experimentally.

TOLERANCE

Acute Tolerance

Several studies have shown that many of the effects of alcohol are more pronounced while the BAC is rising than later when the BAC is falling. The phenomenon of acute tolerance, when tolerance develops during a single administration, is illustrated in Figure 3-1. In the first study of this type, done many years ago, it was shown that while the BAC was rising, subjects first appeared intoxicated at 150 mg per 100 ml, but while the BAC was falling, they appeared sober at 200 mg per 100 ml (Mirsky, Piker, Rosebaum, & Lederer, 1945). Many

effects of alcohol also show acute tolerance, but some do not. Schweizer and Vogel-Sprott (2008) found that the speed of cognitive performance usually recovers from impairment to drug-free levels during declining BACs, whereas alcohol-increased errors fail to diminish.

Acute tolerance of alcohol effects on cognitive functioning vary depending on many factors. Some of these include dose and prior alcohol exposure (Hiltunen, 1997). A genetic component has been implicated in acute tolerance as well. Hu and colleagues (2008) isolated several possible genes in mice that may be responsible for the similar effects of acute tolerance in humans.

Chronic Tolerance

Chronic tolerance to alcohol appears to develop fairly rapidly in both nonhumans and humans. The extent and speed of observed tolerance depends on the species studied and the effect measured. Maximal tolerance develops in a few weeks in humans and reaches a point at which dose increases of 30–50% are required to attain similar effects. Tolerance disappears in rats after 2 or 3 weeks of abstinence but develops again more quickly with repeated exposure (Kalant, LeBlanc, & Gibbins, 1971).

Metabolic Tolerance

One effect of heavy drinking is the stimulation of both alcohol dehydrogenase, the major enzyme responsible for the breakdown of alcohol, and the MEOS, a secondary pathway for ethanol metabolism. As described in the section on Absorption, light to moderate drinkers are able to metabolize alcohol somewhat faster than abstainers (Goldberg, 1943; Whitfield & Martin, 1994). Also, it appears that metabolic tolerance develops over time in adult rats, but not in adolescent rats (Broadwater, Varlinskaya, & Spear, 2011). It is unknown whether this difference also exists in adolescent and adult humans.

Behavioral Tolerance

Repeated exposure and practice seem to be important in the development of tolerance to the behavioral effects of alcohol. In one experiment, a group of rats was given alcohol and placed on a treadmill. The rats quickly developed tolerance to the disruptive locomotor effects of the drug, presumably due to practice. Those given a similar amount of alcohol without the treadmill sessions did not show any tolerance when tested on the treadmill later under the influence of alcohol (Wenger, Tiffany, Bombardier, Nicoins, & Woods, 1981).

Tolerance also depends on expectancy. In one experiment, two groups of participants received equal doses of alcohol, either in the familiar form of beer, or in an unfamiliar drink (a blue peppermint mixture). Participants who received the alcohol in the unfamiliar drink showed poorer performance on cognitive and motor tasks and rated themselves as more intoxicated than participants who received beer (Remington, Roberts, & Glautier, 1997).

It has been suggested that voltage-gated calcium and potassium channels may be partly responsible for behavioral tolerance. Mice that have had the genes for these ion channels *knocked out* through experimental manipulation develop much more rapid tolerance at the cellular and behavioral levels than mice with active channels. It is apparent that the action of ethanol on calcium and voltage-gated potassium channels has a direct effect on behavior, though the mechanism is not clear (Martin et al., 2008).

WITHDRAWAL

As with most of the depressant drugs, chronic consumption of alcohol can cause withdrawal symptoms. Although the distinction may not always be appropriate, it is customary to think of two separate stages of alcohol withdrawal: (a) the early minor syndrome and (b) the late major syndrome, also known as *delirium tremens* or the *DTs*. The early minor symptoms usually appear about 8 to 12 hours after the end of a drinking bout, although many aspects of withdrawal may be seen during the latter part of long drinking sessions even while the drinking is still going on. Withdrawal starts in the form of agitation and tremors; other symptoms, such as muscle cramps, vomiting, nausea, sweating, vivid dreaming, and irregular heartbeat, may also be seen. This stage is usually over within 48 hours.

Studies of patients admitted to the ER with alcohol withdrawal syndrome indicate a 2% mortality rate overall and an 8% mortality rate for those patients who develop delirium (Ferguson, Suelzer, Eckert, Zhou, & Dittus, 1996). Fewer than 5% of patients hospitalized for alcohol withdrawal go on to show the late major withdrawal symptoms. After 2 days of the minor symptoms, patients show increasing agitation, disorientation, confusion, and hallucinations. Seizures may also occur (Wolfe & Victor, 1972). These major symptoms may last as long as 7 to 10 days. Alcohol withdrawal hallucinations do not usually take the form of the proverbial pink elephant. They frequently involve smaller animals, such as rats, bats, or insects, and can be quite terrifying.

In general, the most effective treatment of alcohol withdrawal is a combination of supportive care and the administration of another depressant drug such as diazepam, which suppresses the withdrawal symptoms and has a long duration of action. Other specific symptoms may also be treated with other drugs; for example, hallucinations can be controlled with haloperidol, an antipsychotic. Effective supportive care consists of measures such as reducing sensory stimulation by placing the patient in a dimly lit, quiet room; providing adequate food and water to prevent dehydration; keeping the patient warm and comfortable; and providing reassurance (Naranjo & Sellers, 1986).

SELF-ADMINISTRATION IN NONHUMANS

Oral Self-Administration

When alcohol is freely available to rats and monkeys, they will drink the alcohol but not in quantities sufficient to cause obvious intoxication or physical dependence. This type of drinking resembles typical human drinking patterns, but the thrust of this research has been to provide a model of human alcoholism. Because alcoholics tend to consume much more alcohol than these moderate amounts, there has been considerable research over the years to find what factors can cause this consumption to increase. Research using oral administration has been hampered because alcohol has a disagreeable taste that most nonhuman species prefer to avoid, and the effects on the CNS are somewhat delayed because of slow absorption from the digestive system (Meisch, 1977).

One way to increase intake is to subject the animal to a period of forced consumption when its only source of food or water is laced with alcohol. After a rat has been forced to consume the alcohol, its voluntary intake may increase. Depriving the animal of food or water will also induce it to consume higher levels of alcohol. Intake will sometimes remain high even after the food or water is returned (see Chapter 5). Other induction methods include putting the alcohol in water sweetened by sucrose and then *fading* the sucrose and delivering single small food pellets at regular intervals.

The animal will learn to press a lever on a reinforcement schedule for access to oral alcohol. Although some reports claim that food deprivation and other induction procedures are not necessary, they are often used.

The genetic basis for alcohol use has been studied by breeding rat and mice strains that will either prefer or avoid the free consumption of alcohol. This research, however, presents problems because it is not clear that the behavior system being selected has anything to do with alcoholism. For example, it may be that oral consumption is normally suppressed by a learned aversion to alcohol, a phenomenon called *conditioned taste aversion* (CTA). By selectively breeding alcohol-preferring rats, you may be selecting rats that are unable to learn the CTA, rather than ones who have a genetic disorder similar to alcoholism in humans (Green & Grahame, 2008).

Intravenous Self-Administration

Induction procedures are generally not necessary when alcohol is administered through a cannula implanted in the bloodstream. Providing alcohol this way avoids the issues of bad taste, CTA, and slow CNS effects, and most mice and monkeys rapidly learn to self-administer. Rats, however, are difficult to train to self-administer alcohol intravenously, but do readily learn to press a lever to receive access to water containing alcohol in various concentrations which they can drink.

When alcohol infusions are freely available, the pattern of self-administration is somewhat erratic. Periods of high-level intake are followed by self-imposed abstinence lasting 2 to 4 days, when withdrawal symptoms may occur. These periods do not seem to follow any regular pattern. (Compare this with stimulants such as cocaine; see Figure 10-6). Figure 5-2 (bottom panel) shows the intake of a rhesus monkey pressing a lever for intravenous alcohol over a period of 90 days in the laboratory of Jim Woods and his colleagues (Griffiths et al., 1980). The similarity of this pattern to human alcohol intake has already been noted.

SELF-ADMINISTRATION IN HUMANS

Laboratory Studies

In the laboratory, the pattern of alcohol self-administration is fairly consistent when alcohol is freely available. Alcohol is consumed at high levels for several days. It is then followed by a self-imposed period of low consumption lasting 2 or 3 days. During this time, withdrawal symptoms may appear. Figure 5-2 (top panel) shows the drinking pattern of alcoholic volunteers who worked on an operant schedule of button pushing to earn drinks. This pattern is very similar to that of a rhesus monkey under similar conditions, and to the typical pattern of many chronic alcoholics under natural conditions (Griffiths et al., 1980).

Factors That Affect Consumption

CULTURE. Cross-cultural studies in numerous societies in which alcohol is consumed have revealed some interesting patterns that appear to be consistent across cultures, including our own. Alcohol consumption is generally a male activity that is practiced socially outside the home among peer groups and not in the company of family members or people of higher status. Drinking is generally more acceptable among those who engage in physical labor and must grapple with the environment than among individuals who are charged with preserving tradition, such as priests, mothers, and judges (Robinson, 1977).

But differences also exist—among individuals and cultures, many drinking patterns have been identified. The spree drinker, common in Finland, binges occasionally but stays relatively sober otherwise. In France, on the other hand, it is more common for individuals to consume a fixed amount of alcohol every day steadily over the course of the day and exhibit few symptoms of intoxication. Such differences in national drinking patterns do not seem to influence certain consequences of consumption, such as rate of alcoholism or alcohol-related diseases. However, the difference may be significant when acute intoxication is important; for example, one beer a day may not ever cause a traffic accident, but the same quantity of beer, if consumed on one occasion every 2 weeks, could easily be responsible for traffic accidents.

GENDER. In a survey of nearly 300 undergraduate students, men reported a mean of 7.27 drinking occasions per month during which they consumed an average of 6.82 drinks per occasion. Woman reported a mean of 5.77 drinking occasions per month and an average of 5.05 alcoholic beverages per occasion (Balodis, Potenza, & Olmstead, 2009). Although heavy drinkers are more likely to be male, this fact does not mean that women reach a lower level of intoxication than men. Studies have shown that women do consume less alcohol than men; however, when adjustments are made for differences in body size and the ability to absorb alcohol, it turns out that women social drinkers achieve the same BACs as men (McKim & Quinlan, 1991; Vogel-Sprott, 1984).

AGE. A number of studies have shown that, although people drink just as frequently as they age, they tend to drink less on each occasion (Vogel-Sprott, 1984), so their total consumption declines. Unlike the difference in consumption between genders, this age-related decline in consumption per occasion cannot be explained by changes in body composition with age (McKim & Quinlan, 1991).

ALCOHOLISM

When the social reform movement of the nineteenth century was campaigning for better treatment of people who drank too much, it adopted the position that excessive drinking was a disease. Previously, alcohol intoxication was known by such terms as *inebriety* or *intemperance*, but more medical-sounding terms were developed, including *alcoholism*, *dipsomania*, and *narcomania*. *Alcoholism* survived and is now used widely (Barrows & Room, 1991). It is, however, not used by the current *DSM*. The *DSM-IV-TR* (2000) defines substance dependence and substance abuse using established criteria listed in Chapter 5 (see Box 5-1). These are the same criteria no matter which substance is being discussed. If the substance is alcohol, the diagnosis would be "substance abuse or dependence of the alcohol type" not "alcoholism."

As discussed in Chapter 5, alcoholism was the first form of drug addiction accepted as a disease, and theories of alcoholism have had a considerable influence on how we understand addiction in general. Also, the Alcoholics Anonymous movement has adopted and widely endorses the original disease theory of alcoholism that was proposed by E. M. Jellinek in the 1950s and 1960s.

Jellinek's (1960) theory was published in his book *The Disease Concept of Alcoholism*. Jellinek was associated with the *Alcoholics Anonymous* movement, which, along with Jellinek's arguments, was effective in convincing both the American Medical Association and the World Health Organization to declare alcoholism a disease. One of the more important assumptions of this disease theory is that alcoholism is not caused by alcohol. Alcoholism is a genetic disease, and people are alcoholics from the time they are born. Everyone, both alcoholic and nonalcoholic, starts drinking in the same way, in a moderate, social manner. But there are some who progress to drink more and more heavily, and, eventually, they enter the *prodromal phase* of alcoholism, which is characterized by frequent blackouts. Many such people are not *alcoholics*. They are *problem drinkers* who either stay that way or eventually stop drinking. Some individuals progress to become *gamma alcoholics* (Jellinek's term). The change from being a problem drinker to a gamma alcoholic is marked by two symptoms: (a) a loss of control over drinking, and (b) physical dependence indicated by high levels of tolerance and withdrawal symptoms such as seizures, hallucinations, and the delirium tremens. It is worth noting that the distinction between problem drinkers and alcoholics is the presence or absence of physical dependence and loss of control, not the amount consumed. Problem drinkers may actually consume more than alcoholics, but they are not considered alcoholics, and they do not have the disease. Any research on the disease of alcoholism, therefore, must be done on alcoholics, not on problem drinkers. This distinction is responsible for many arguments over data between supporters and opponents of the disease model.

Genetics of Alcoholism

Jellinek's insistence that alcoholism is a genetic disease stimulated a great deal of research in the hope that the nature of the disease could be more precisely defined. Evidence is clear that the risk of becoming an alcoholic is increased as much as fourfold if a close relative (mother, father, or sibling) is an alcoholic. It is known that the amount of drinking of identical twins (who are, genetically, clones) is more similar than the drinking behavior of fraternal twins (who have the same genetic similarity as normal siblings). Thus, the closer the genetic makeup, the more similar the drinking pattern. It is clear from years of research that genetic factors can explain about half of the variance in vulnerabilities leading to heavy drinking and associated problems (Li, Hewitt, & Grant, 2004; Schuckit, 1992, 2009).

There appear to be four characteristics under genetic control that contribute to such vulnerabilities: (a) a flushing response to alcohol; (b) a low level of response to alcohol; (c) personality characteristics that include impulsivity, sensation seeking, and neuronal and behavioral disinhibition; and (d) psychiatric symptoms. It is clear that there is no single alcoholism gene; however, genome linkage studies have identified several chromosome regions that are associated with each of these four factors. Genes encoding enzymes associated with the metabolism of alcohol are the most well-established genes that have polymorphisms associated with alcohol dependence (Kimura & Higuchi, 2011). For example, the flushing response is a result of a genetically controlled inability to metabolize acetaldehyde.

While genetics clearly plays a major role, additional factors cannot be neglected, as a person with an identical twin who is an alcoholic has only a 60% chance of being alcoholic. Genetics controls physiological factors including aspects of body chemistry, personality, and brain function that increase the probability that a person will drink in an alcoholic manner in a particular environment. A variety of genetic susceptibilities to alcohol may cause problems only in particular environments. The right combination of environment and genetics is necessary to make a person drink in an alcoholic manner.

FHP Versus FHN

One method that could be useful in understanding the nature of the disease of alcoholism might be to compare alcoholics with nonalcoholics on a number of measures; any consistent difference in the biochemistry, personality, or response to alcohol could give a clue as to the nature of alcoholism. A problem with this approach is that any differences found might be caused by the alcohol consumed, not the alcoholism. One widely used strategy to avoid this difficulty is to compare people who are likely to become alcoholics with those less likely, before they start drinking, and to note the differences (remember that, according to Jellinek's theory, an alcoholic is an

alcoholic before he or she starts drinking). We know that people who come from families in which there is a history of alcohol problems (*family history positive* [FHP]) are at a greater risk of becoming alcoholic than those who have a family history without alcohol problems (*family history negative* [FHN]). One interesting line of research has attempted to compare high-risk (FHP) and low-risk (FHN) individuals to see whether it is possible to detect differences in these groups that might be able to identify potential alcoholics or shed some light on what makes people drink excessively and become alcoholics.

Although early studies were encouraging, there appear to be few consistent differences between FHP and FHN individuals in terms of pharmacokinetics and metabolism of alcohol, and no clear-cut differences have been established in cognitive and neuropsychological measures of personality (Searles, 1988) or in alcohol preference, alcohol-liking scores, BACs, or alcohol-induced impairment (de Wit & McCracken, 1990).

Some studies, however, have detected differences between FHN and FHP subjects in electroencephalographic responses, and in some experiments, FHP subjects may show a greater sensitivity to the subjective and motor-impairing effects of alcohol than FHN subjects (Porjesz & Begleiter, 1987; Schuckit, 1987, 1992). As well, researchers using fMRI have demonstrated that FHP individuals differ in their sensitivity of the reward circuit (Andrews et al., 2011). In a meta-analysis, Quinn and Fromme (2011) found confirming evidence that the overall subjective effect of alcohol is less in FHP males than FHN males demonstrating the "low level of response" characteristic proposed by Schuckit (2009).

Loss of Control

According to the disease model, one of the defining characteristics of alcoholism is *loss of control*. It is assumed that exposure to even one or two drinks of alcohol will cause, in the alcoholic, an uncontrollable craving to drink more and more. For this reason, it was considered that someone who was an alcoholic could never be a moderate or social drinker, and therefore the only therapy for alcoholism must be total and complete abstention from alcohol, forever.

Since the time it was proposed, the loss-of-control theory has never received significant experimental support. In fact, most research has disconfirmed the basic notion (Finagrette, 1988). A number of studies in England (Davis, 1962) and the United States (Armor, Polach, & Stambul, 1978) have found many cases of alcoholics who have reverted from excess drinking to moderate social drinking and have maintained that level for years. These studies caused a storm of controversy, and many alcoholism experts denounced them as unscientific and attacked them on various grounds.

Some have argued that most of these studies were done with problem drinkers, not with populations of gamma alcoholics, as defined by other characteristics such as physical dependence. In addition, it has been argued that most studies showing that alcoholics can return to controlled drinking do not allow enough time to detect whether controlled drinking is possible (Maltzman, 1994).

In addition to the research with alcoholics in treatment, laboratory studies have repeatedly shown that alcoholics are perfectly capable of moderating their alcohol intake in response to such manipulations as increased cost, and they virtually never lose control (Mello & Mendelson, 1972). Such laboratory studies are also challenged on the grounds that the laboratory is too artificial and irrelevant to alcohol use in a natural setting.

As Schuckit (2009) suggested, it is also likely that lack of impulse control is a major factor under genetic control in the development of alcoholism.Rogers, Moeller, Swann, and Clark (2010) demonstrated recently that many individuals who develop alcohol dependence also have neurological problems which lead to poor impulse–behavior control. For people with such problems, it is probably best that they avoid even social drinking, but there is little evidence that *loss of control* is the inevitable consequence of taking even one drink.

Related to the concept of loss of control is the phenomenon of reinstatement or priming (see Chapter 5). Reinstatement is when a learned drug self-administration response is extinguished to the point where all responding has stopped, and administration of a noncontingent dose of the drug causes the drug self-administration response to resume. de Wit and Chutuape (1993) have shown that social drinkers are much more likely to choose an alcoholic drink and report an increased craving for alcohol after they have been given a dose of alcohol. This study was later replicated (Chutuape, Mitchell, & de Wit, 1994), but a later study was able to show that

a drink of alcohol increased only desire for alcohol; it did not increase choice of alcohol among social drinkers (Kirk & de Wit, 2000). Reinstatement has also been demonstrated in laboratory animals. While reinstatement looks like loss of control, it is not clear whether it is analogous to what Jellinek's theory would call loss of control. Reinstatement is a fairly universal phenomenon that can be seen in many species with many different reinforcers, while loss of control as described by Jellinek is seen only for alcohol and only in alcoholics.

HARMFUL EFFECTS OF AN ACUTE ADMINISTRATION

On July 23, 2011, English singer/songwriter Amy Winehouse was found dead in her London home. The coroner's report, released in late October, ruled that her death had been due to alcohol poisoning. It stated that Winehouse's blood alcohol content was 416 mg per 100 ml blood at the time of her death (*The Guardian*, 2011). There was no evidence of any other drug present in the singer's body. Unfortunately, alcohol-related deaths are not uncommon. Thousands of people are admitted to hospital, and hundreds die each year from acute alcohol poisoning. University students appear to be a particularly vulnerable population, perhaps largely because of a drinking culture that encourages binge drinking at institutes of higher learning. Between 1999 and 2008 in the United States, hospitalization rates for alcohol overdoses, in young adults alone, increased 25% reaching 29,412 cases in 2008 (Oster-Aaland, Lewis, Neighbors, Vangsness, & Larimer, 2009; White, Hingson, Pan, & Yi, 2011).

A single dose of alcohol, if large enough, can be lethal. A BAC of about 300 to 400 mg per 100 ml of blood will usually cause loss of consciousness. In a study of alcohol poisonings, Kaye and Haag (1957) reported that without therapeutic intervention, people whose BACs reached 500 mg per 100 ml of blood died within an hour or two. The world record for high BAC is thought to be 1,500 mg per 100 ml, reported in a 30-year-old man whose life was saved by vigorous medical intervention. Later, he reported that he had drunk 4.23 liters of beer and an undetermined number of bottles of liquor in the space of 3 hours (O'Neil, Tipton, Prichard, & Quinlan, 1984).

As with most depressant drugs, death by alcohol usually results from respiratory failure. Alcohol is a toxic substance, and the lethal dose is uncomfortably close to the usual social dose. A 150-pound male would have to drink 7.5 ounces of liquor to have a BAC of 150 mg per 100 ml of blood. These numbers are at the upper levels of an acceptable social high. Around 25 ounces of liquor would produce a BAC of 500 mg per 100 ml of blood, probably a lethal dose for most people. Thus, the therapeutic index for alcohol is about 3.3 (25 ÷ 7.5).

Fortunately, alcohol has built-in safety features: Vomiting or unconsciousness will usually occur before death. People who die from alcohol poisoning usually have to drink a large amount quickly and in high concentrations in order to get a lethal dose into their bodies before they lose consciousness.

Hangover

The problem of how to avoid a hangover from alcohol has occupied some of history's best minds, as this passage from Plato's *The Dialogues* illustrates:

> They were about to commence drinking, when Pausanias said, "And now, my friends, how can we drink with the least injury to ourselves?" I can assure you that I feel severely the effect of yesterday's potations, and must have time to recover; and I suspect that most of you are in the same predicament, for you were of the party yesterday. Consider then: "How can the drinking be made easiest?" (Symposium 176a–b, translation in Jowett, 1931)

Like the ancient Greeks, most drinkers have, at some time, suffered the next day for having had too much the night before. There are several explanations for a hangover. They suggest that hangover results from alcohol-produced effects, such as low blood sugar levels, dehydration, and irritation of the lining of the digestive system. There is no doubt that most effects of alcohol contribute to discomfort the next day, but it is probably best to think of a hangover as a miniature withdrawal from alcohol—a rebound excitation of an alcohol-depressed nervous system.

For most drinkers, hangovers are not physiologically serious, but for people with epilepsy, heart disease, or diabetes, hangovers can have serious medical consequences (Gauvin, Cheng, & Holloway, 1993).

The Greeks never did answer Pausanias's question "How can the drinking be made easiest?" apart from concluding that "drinking deep is a bad practice." But over the centuries, a number of cures have been suggested, including eating a spoonful of sugar or drinking lots of water. To the extent that a hangover can be thought of as a withdrawal from alcohol, one cure is to take a "hair of the dog that bit you." Consuming more alcohol relieves the hangover by depressing this rebound excitability in the same way that other depressant drugs are used to treat withdrawal. A small amount could be effective, but if too much is consumed it will only postpone the withdrawal.

Alcohol-Induced Behavior

Apart from the self-inflicted physical harm that can be done by an acute administration of alcohol, the drug can be responsible for changes in behavior that cause untold social, psychological, financial, and physical harm to the drinker and others. It is not possible to catalog all the manifestations of harm, but most people have been made aware of them in some form. They include accidents caused while drunk or hung over not only while driving but also in industry and at home (Gutjahr, Gmel, & Rehm, 2001), crimes committed under the influence of alcohol, and damage done to families and social relationships. All these effects are difficult to quantify, and some may not be a direct result of alcohol. They are nonetheless real and must be included in any assessment of the harmful effects of alcohol.

Reproduction

A well-known quote from Shakespeare's *Macbeth* states that drink "provokes the desire, but takes away the performance" in matters sexual. The bard's analysis is essentially correct. Acute alcohol consumption may increase interest by diminishing inhibitions, but, in higher doses, it reduces sexual arousal in both males and females. In males, lower doses (BAC less than 100 mg/100 ml) may increase the duration of erections and thus provide increased opportunities for fulfillment of the partner. This fact may explain why alcohol is often perceived as enhancing sexual performance (Mello, 1978; Rubin & Henson, 1976). As well, it has been found that males experience a decreased sensitivity to female social cues and that they are less able to differentiate between friendliness and sexual interest (Farris, Treat, & Viken, 2010). In females, higher doses of alcohol (100 mg/100 ml blood) reduced genital arousal, but moderate levels (80 mg/100 ml blood) did not (George et al., 2011).

One study using rats showed that increasing doses of alcohol caused increasing disruptions of copulation of male rats with receptive females. In addition, low doses of alcohol that disrupted copulation with receptive females caused male rats to attempt to copulate with unreceptive females, something they would not normally attempt. These findings support the speculation that low doses of alcohol adversely affect uninhibited sexual performance but can stimulate sexual behavior that is normally inhibited (Pfaus & Pinel, 1988).

HARMFUL EFFECTS OF CHRONIC CONSUMPTION

The Liver

Prolonged drinking of alcohol damages the liver. The damage usually starts with a buildup of fatty acids in the liver cells, or *steatosis*. Alcoholics frequently contract alcoholic hepatitis, which usually develops into *cirrhosis*, which means *scarring*. The liver cells swell and experience cellular hardening, membrane damage, and eventually cell death. Once the liver becomes filled with scar tissue and is no longer able to function, the condition is often fatal, especially if alcohol consumption is not stopped.

Cirrhosis occurs in approximately 8% of chronic alcoholics; among nonalcoholics, the condition affects only 1%. Alcohol consumption accounts for somewhere between 40 and 90% of liver cirrhosis deaths in the United States. Generally, alcohol consumption of more than five drinks a day for at least 5 years is necessary for the development of cirrhosis.

The Nervous System

Some alcoholics and heavy drinkers may show a cluster of symptoms that includes a loss of memory for past events, an inability to remember new material, and disorientation and confusion. These symptoms are collectively known as *Korsakoff's psychosis*, *Wernicke's disease*, or *Wernicke–Korsakoff syndrome*. They are a result of damage in certain parts of the brain first noted by Carl Wernicke. The condition seems to result from deficiency of thiamin (vitamin B1), which is common among many alcoholics (Victor, Adams, & Collins, 1971). Many of the conditions suffered by alcoholics can be traced to vitamin deficiencies, chiefly because people who drink

large quantities of alcohol do not normally have a balanced diet. In addition, alcohol can damage the digestive system and interfere with the normal absorption of some nutrients.

The Wernicke–Korsakoff syndrome is not the only neurological damage associated with heavy drinking. A number of other disorders of both the central and peripheral nervous systems are attributable, either directly or indirectly, to excessive alcohol use and do not appear to involve dietary deficiencies. These include epilepsy, cerebellar syndrome, and alcoholic dementia (Marsden, 1977). In alcoholic dementia, patients show a gradual progressive decline in cognitive functions involving much more than just memory. Alcohol-related dementia probably accounts for more than 10% of all cases of dementia (Gupta & Warner, 2008). It is diagnosed after alcohol consumption of 35 drinks per week for males and 28 for females for more than 5 years and seems to be associated with binge drinking.

MRI analysis of chronic alcohol users shows decreases in cerebral blood flow (Demir, Ulug, Lay Ergun, & Erbas, 2002) and widespread reduction in brain tissue, including loss of glial cells and neurons in the prefrontal cortex, hypothalamus, cerebellum, and hippocampus (Brust, 2010; Gazdzinski, Durazzo, & Meyerhoff, 2005; Mann et al., 2001). Neurodegeneration occurs primarily during intoxication, due to the increased oxidative stress and proinflammatory proteins, which are neurotoxic (Crews & Nixon, 2009). It may also arise from glutamate excitotoxicity, in which high levels of glutamate lead to cell death. Alcohol itself can protect the brain from glutamate excitotoxicity through blockade of NMDA receptors and glutamate activity, but frequent alcohol use causes an upregulation of glutamate transmission and excessive glutamine release during hangover and withdrawal. These changes are partially reversed with prolonged abstinence from alcohol, with the greatest increases in brain volume noted within the first month of withdrawal (Gazdzinski et al., 2005).

You do not have to drink heavily for years to show evidence of neurotoxic effects of alcohol. In a study of drinking by university students (18 to 20 years old), students whose intake was characterized by sporadic consumption of large quantities of alcohol in short periods (binge drinking) had problems on a battery of memory tests, showing a deficit in declarative verbal memory. Such findings are characteristic of damage to the hippocampus (Parada et al., 2011).

Cancer

The use of alcohol is causally related to cancers of the mouth, throat, colon, and liver—parts of the body that are directly exposed to high alcohol concentrations and susceptible to alcohol damage (Boffetta & Hashibe, 2006). This may be a result of the acetaldehyde molecule, which is a first metabolite of alcohol and is thought to have a *genotoxic* effect. That is, it can cause damage to the genetic code, which in turn may lead to cancer. The role of alcohol as a solvent for tobacco carcinogens, and the *reactive oxygen species*, which are chemically reactive byproducts of alcohol metabolism, may also contribute to alcohol's carcinogenic effects.

There is conflicting evidence relating alcohol consumption with breast cancer in women. In general, there appears to be a weak association, but alcohol does appear to increase breast cancer incidence in populations that are otherwise at risk, such as those who have a family history of breast cancer or those postmenopausal women taking estrogen replacement therapy (Gunzerath, Faden, Zakhari, & Warren, 2004). Increased estrogen and androgen levels in women who consume alcohol appear to be significant factors in the development of breast cancer. However, alcohol cannot be exclusively blamed in many cases, as genetic predisposition, dietary choices, and lifestyle habits all contribute to the development of any type of cancer (Singletary & Gapstur, 2001).

Reproduction

In males, chronic alcohol consumption is known to cause impotence, shrinking of the testicles, and a loss of sexual interest. Although there have been few studies of the effects of chronic alcohol consumption in females, there is evidence that it can cause menstrual dysfunctions, such as amenorrhea, dysmenorrhea, and premenstrual discomfort (Mello, 1987).

Since ancient times, people believed that alcohol might be teratogenic (responsible for birth defects). In ancient Carthage, drinking on wedding days was forbidden; it was believed that it might cause an abnormal child to be born (Jones & Smith, 1975). Aristotle warned against drinking during pregnancy, and later, at the time of the gin epidemic in England, it was noted that there was an increase in infant deaths. Similar effects associated with alcohol consumption have been reported in the medical literature, and the extent of the problem is now fully appreciated. It is now recognized that the use of alcohol during pregnancy can harm the developing fetus and may result in a number of behavioral, anatomical, and physiological irregularities, which are known as *fetal alcohol syndrome* (FAS), in their more severe form, or *fetal alcohol effects* (FAE), *alcohol-related birth defects* (ARBD), or *alcohol-related neurobehavioral disorder* (ARND) if only a few behavioral or neurological symptoms are present. In 1983, the term *fetal alcohol spectrum disorder* (FASD) came into use as an umbrella term identifying the wide range of outcomes from prenatal alcohol exposure (Riley, Infante, & Warren, 2011).

The manifestations of FAS are mental retardation, poor coordination, loss of muscle tone, low birth weight, growth deficiency, malformation of organ systems, and characteristic facial features, such as small eyes, smooth philtrum (the area between the nose and the upper lip), and a thin upper lip (see Figure 6-5; NIAAA, 2004). These symptoms do not always appear together, but the chances for development of any or all of these effects increase according to the amount of alcohol consumed during pregnancy.

The incidence of FAS depends on the criteria used to diagnose it. Using strict diagnostic guidelines, FAS prevalence is believed to be between 0.5 and 2.0 cases per 1,000 live births in the United States, but the incidence of FASD has been estimated to be as high as 10/1,000 live births and, in some places in the world, 68 to 89/1,000 live births (Riley et al., 2011).

The mechanism by which alcohol affects the developing fetus is not precisely known, but studies with nonhumans have shown that in the developing brain alcohol

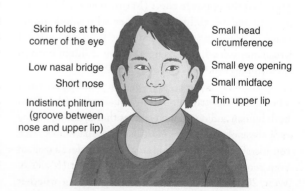

Skin folds at the corner of the eye

Low nasal bridge

Short nose

Indistinct philtrum (groove between nose and upper lip)

Small head circumference

Small eye opening

Small midface

Thin upper lip

FIGURE 6-5 Typical facial characteristics of a child with fetal alcohol syndrome. (Adapted from National Institute on Alcohol Abuse and Alcoholism, 2004)

can disrupt neurogenesis, cell migration, cell adhesion, neuron survival, axon outgrowth, synapse formation, and neurotransmitter function (Brust, 2010). As we have seen in Chapter 4, all these processes are vital to the proper development of the central nervous system. Functional disruption of neural organization may occur particularly in the formation of the cortex. It appears that alcohol disrupts cell migration during cortical development; only four layers, rather than the usual six layers, are formed. In addition, neurons may end up migrating to the wrong layer (Abel & Sokol, 1989). Structural abnormalities are seen in other brain regions including the corpus callosum, basal ganglia, hippocampus, and cerebellum (Niccols, 2007).

Many normal, healthy children are born to women who have drunk heavily during pregnancy, so alcohol alone cannot be entirely responsible. As Abel and Sokol (1989) suggest, alcohol is a necessary but not sufficient condition for FAS or FAE. Other factors that have been associated with the likelihood of FAS or FAE include (a) having previous children, (b) being black, (c) having a high score on an alcohol screening test, and (d) having a high percentage of drinking days. It also seems clear that occasional high levels of consumption do more damage than the same amount of alcohol consumed at chronic low levels (Abel & Sokol, 1989; Maier & West, 2001).

Apart from FAS, maternal alcohol consumption can affect other aspects of fetal development, including growth. Mothers who consumed greater than 12 grams of alcohol (approximately the equivalent of one standard drink) per day had a greater risk of having a low-birth-weight baby, whereas lower consumption on weekends produced the opposite effect (Mariscal et al., 2006). At ages 10 and 14, children of women who drank an average of one drink a day during the first 3 months of pregnancy were 4 pounds lighter than children born to nondrinking mothers (Day et al., 2002).

There does not appear to be any time during pregnancy when it is completely safe to drink, but it seems clear from both human and nonhuman studies that drinking during early stages of pregnancy is most likely to be harmful. In fact, considerable harm can be done to the fetus before a woman even recognizes that she could be pregnant (Maier & West, 2001). There is also no clear agreement whether there is a safe level of alcohol consumption during pregnancy. The Surgeon General of the United States and the British Department of Health recommend complete abstinence from alcohol during pregnancy (and during times when becoming pregnant is possible) as the only way to be certain of avoiding ill effects.

Heart Disease

Degeneration of the heart muscle, known as *alcoholic cardiomyopathy*, results directly from the chronic consumption of alcohol. This condition most likely arises from the effect alcohol has on the metabolism of the membrane of the cells of the heart muscle. The result is very similar to cirrhosis of the liver and was once described as "cirrhosis of the heart" (Myerson, 1971, p. 183). It appears that moderate consumption of alcohol can reduce the risk of developing heart disease, but binge and irregular heavy drinking seems to be correlated with an increased risk (Bagnardi, Zatonski, Scotti, La Vecchia, & Corrao, 2008). Based on these findings, patterns of alcohol consumption seem to be a major consideration in terms of health risks and benefits.

Other Effects

Chronic use of alcohol may also be responsible for a number of other pathologies. These include diseases of the digestive system such as ulcers and cancer, inflammation and other disorders of the pancreas, pneumonia and other diseases of the lungs and respiratory system, abnormalities of the blood, and malnutrition.

It has been observed for some time that alcoholics are more susceptible to many infectious diseases and less responsive to treatment. The reasons for this susceptibility include differences in lifestyle, nutrition, liver functioning, and the adverse effects of excessive consumption of alcohol on many aspects of the immune system.

That being said, a low to moderate dose of certain alcoholic drinks, such as beer and wine, may trigger a sort of protective effect on the immune system in healthy adults (Romeo et al., 2007). The cause of this protective effect is difficult to attribute to alcohol, however, as it may be due to other compounds present in the wine or beer.

BENEFITS OF ALCOHOL CONSUMPTION

It is not unusual for substances that are physiologically stressful and toxic at high doses to be beneficial at low doses. This effect is called *hormesis* (Dudley, 2002).

It may reflect an evolutionary adaptation to substances that an organism is naturally exposed to at low doses. The sort of exposure to alcohol experienced by our frugivore ancestors may have favored the evolution of metabolic adaptations to alcohol that maximize its benefits and minimize its harm.

Historically, alcohol has been used as a medicine. Avicenna, the tenth-century Persian physician, recommended wine for his older patients, although he cautioned his younger patients to drink it in moderation. Arnaud de Villeneuve, who reputedly invented brandy in the thirteenth century, hailed it as the water of immortality and called it *aqua vitae*, "water of life." He was convinced that it would increase longevity and maintain youth (McKim & Mishara, 1987).

Generally speaking, there is a U-shaped relationship between alcohol consumption and mortality among adults over the age of 45. There has been a great number of epidemiological studies that have plotted daily dose of alcohol against the *relative risk* of one health problem or another. Relative risk is calculated by dividing the incidence of a disease in people who use a given amount of alcohol by the incidence of that disease in people who do not consume any alcohol at all. Thus, if 5% of alcohol abstainers get cancer and 10% of heavy drinkers get cancer, then the relative risk for heavy drinkers is 2.0; that is, they are twice as likely to get cancer as abstainers. The relative risk of abstainers is always 1.0, and numbers less than 1.0 indicate a reduced risk of the disease. Figure 6-3 shows a plot of the relative risk of having an automobile accident against various BACs.

When alcohol consumption is plotted against relative risk of coronary heart disease, the result is in the form of a "J" curve or a "U" curve, depending on the range of doses reported; that is, relative risk drops to numbers less than 1.0 for moderate consumption (usually defined as one or two drinks a day) but increases to higher numbers as daily consumption increases (Brust, 2010; Gunzerath et al., 2004). The relative risk of myocardial infarction (heart attack) is reduced by 25% in men who consume up to two drinks a day. In fact, it has been suggested that if all drinking of alcohol ceased, there would be about 80,000 more deaths from coronary heart disease each year in the United States (Pearson & Terry, 1994). This protective effect of alcohol is likely a result of the ability of alcohol to lower levels of low-density cholesterol and increase high-density cholesterol. The

type of alcoholic beverage consumed may also be a factor as red wine and dark beers have been found to provide more protection than liquor (Mann & Folts, 2004).

Another J-shaped risk curve with alcohol consumption has been reported for diabetes. Most studies indicate that moderate drinking reduces the incidence of type 2 diabetes and is associated with improved glycemic control in those with the disease. One study showed a 60% reduction associated with two drinks a day, but at three drinks a day this protective effect disappeared. And the incidence of diabetes increased as alcohol consumption increased above that level (Gunzerath et al., 2004).

Because alcohol reduces blood clotting and levels of low-density cholesterol that can clog arteries, it might be expected that alcohol would be able to reduce the risk of ischemic strokes (caused by clots blocking arteries in the brain). In fact, a J-shaped curve has been shown for risk of ischemic strokes in the elderly, with two drinks a day giving the best protection but seven drinks a day increasing relative risk to 3.0 (Gunzerath et al., 2004; Reynolds et al., 2003). Figure 6-6 illustrates the relative risk of stroke for men and women (and overall risk) related to daily alcohol consumption. Data are plotted according to the number of grams of alcohol consumed per day. A standard drink (12 oz of beer, 5 oz of wine, 1.5 oz of 80-proof distilled spirits of liquor such as gin, rum, vodka, or whisky) generally contains about 12.0 to 14.0 grams (0.4 to 0.5 oz) of pure alcohol. The risk of stroke decreases at low levels of consumption (one to three or so drinks per day), but increases rapidly at high levels (five or more drinks per day). Notice that this effect is most evident in women than in men (Reynolds et al., 2003). Low levels of alcohol consumption appear to offer protection only against ischemic stroke (where an artery to the brain is blocked), not from hemorrhagic stroke where the blood vessels rupture and bleed into the brain.

Alcohol, in low doses, may also offer some protection against age-related dementias. One meta-analysis found that small amounts of alcohol reduce incidence of dementia (risk ratio 0.63) and Alzheimer's disease (risk ratio 0.57), but not vascular dementia and cognitive decline (Peters, Peters, Warner, Beckett, & Bulpitt, 2008).

In general, it appears that there are some beneficial effects of low and moderate levels of alcohol consumption, but it seems that most of the conditions where alcohol is beneficial are those associated with aging. Young people are at relatively low risk of coronary heart disease,

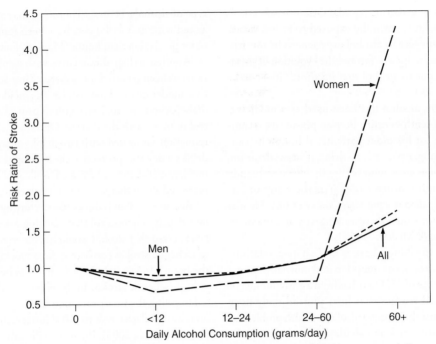

FIGURE 6-6   The relative risk of stroke for men and women related to average daily alcohol consumption. This is an example of a "J" curve mentioned in the text. The risk of stroke decreases at low levels, but increases rapidly at high levels. Note that this effect appears much more pronounced in women than in men. (Data from Reynolds et al., 2003)

ischemic stroke, and diabetes. Therefore, they are not likely to gain from any of the beneficial effects of alcohol but are exposed to all the risks of alcohol consumption, whereas older people are more likely to get some benefit. Research has shown that for those under 60, increased alcohol consumption is related to increased risk of dying from any cause (no J curve), but for those over 60, the relative risk of dying was less for light and moderate drinkers than for heavy drinkers and abstainers. This relationship was the same for both sexes (Rehm & Sempos, 1995). It is possible that all this was foreseen a thousand years ago by Avicenna when he recommended wine for his older patients.

If alcohol has so many health benefits, should it be *prescribed* to abstainers? One article summed up the dilemma this way: "Nowhere in medicine is the double edged sword so sharp on both sides" (Sandridge, Zylstra, & Adams, 2004, p. 670). These authors believe that the beneficial effects could be offset by the risks of addiction, especially in people with a family history of alcoholism. They believe that patients should be informed of all the

pros and cons and then be allowed to make an informed decision.

It must also be remembered that all this research is correlational, not experimental. It is possible that there is some third factor, such as general health or sociability, that correlates with alcohol consumption. It may be, for example, that people who are healthy tend to drink and abstainers may not drink because they do not feel well. This would make it look like moderate drinking makes you healthy. Timothy Naimi and his colleagues at the Centers for Disease Control and Prevention in Atlanta, Georgia, analyzed the findings of a large-scale population health study and found many factors that correlated with both moderate alcohol consumption and reduced risk of cardiovascular disease. They point out that many of these confounding factors are not measured in studies indicating that moderate alcohol consumption is associated with a lowered risk of cardiovascular disease, so there is no way of assessing their involvement in the relationship (Naimi et al., 2005). On the other hand, most modern studies attempt to avoid this criticism by measuring general health and accounting for its effects. Another criticism is that the group of abstainers used to establish the relative risk may contain former alcoholics who have stopped drinking, but may have increased their risk in the past by drinking heavily. This would not give an accurate picture of the risk of true lifetime abstainers. Many recent studies have addressed this criticism by excluding former drinkers from the abstinent group.

TREATMENTS

Because there has been little agreement about what alcoholism really is and why people drink, many types of treatments have been developed to help those who want to reduce their alcohol intake. It is generally agreed upon that the first step must be to eliminate physical dependence if it is present. This is usually done in a hospital or a detoxification center where the alcoholic goes through withdrawal under medical supervision until all withdrawal symptoms are over. Following detoxification, an active treatment phase may or may not be followed by a long-term program to prevent relapse.

The nature of the therapy and its outcome goals are determined by how the therapist defines alcoholism. If alcoholism is considered a genetic disease, as described by Jellinek, no *cure* is possible, and the aim of therapy should be complete and total lifetime abstinence. On the other hand, if excessive drinking is a result of environmental factors interacting with genetic vulnerabilities, it may be possible to moderate drinking without eliminating it altogether.

In Chapter 5, various behavioral and social approaches to the treatment of addictions (including alcoholism) were discussed. These include cognitive behavioral therapy, contingency management, motivational enhancement, and family therapy, and can involve individual or group therapeutic techniques. One technique, Alcoholics Anonymous (AA), was initially developed as a method to help alcoholics stay sober. The AA approach, also known as the 12-step approach, has been adapted by many other support groups for people who have problems controlling gambling, overeating, and the use of other drugs.

Because of its prominence and its influence on the treatment of all addictions, we will take a brief look at the history and philosophy of AA.

Alcoholics Anonymous

Alcoholics Anonymous was founded in 1935 by Dr. Bob Smith and Bill Wilson. It grew out of the Oxford Movement, a popular Protestant religious movement in which small groups met weekly for prayer, worship, and discussion, with the aim of self-improvement. One Oxford group meeting in Akron, Ohio, was attended by an alcoholic stockbroker and an alcoholic physician, both of whom were seriously but unsuccessfully trying to stop drinking. They found that their fellowship and that of the group helped them to stop drinking. They brought other alcoholics into the group, and many had similar success. In fact, helping other alcoholics to stay sober seemed to be making an important contribution to the maintenance of their own sobriety. As the meetings got bigger, new groups were formed, and eventually they broke away from the Oxford Movement and became AA (Alcoholics Anonymous, 1980).

The organization has grown rapidly and spread around the world. In 1982, there were 20,000 groups in 100 countries, and the estimated world membership was well over 1 million (Maxwell, 1984). Currently, AA estimates that there are almost 116,000 groups and a membership of over 2 million, half of which are in the United States (Alcoholics Anonymous, 2012). Although AA broke away from the Oxford Movement, it has retained many of the elements that seemed to be responsible for its effectiveness, including spirituality, although this aspect can be moderated to suit each individual.

At every meeting of AA, someone reads the 12 steps and the 12 traditions that explain the basic principles and processes the organization has found to be effective over the years. Most AA members believe that to control drinking, the individual must first admit to being "powerless over alcohol" and unable to control drinking without help. AA members believe that drinking can be controlled only by relying on a greater power, often identified as "God" or "God as we have come to understand Him" (or Her) for people who are uncomfortable with the concept. They feel that there is no cure; there are only alcoholics who drink and alcoholics who do not drink. For this reason, members are expected to attend regular meetings for extended periods of time. It is not unusual for new members to attend more than six meetings a week (in fact, there is a tradition of new members doing "90 meetings in 90 days"). In addition to attending meetings, members often see each other socially outside of meetings and frequently talk on the phone, especially if stress or desire for alcohol is threatening a member's resolve (Maxwell, 1984). For many people, AA is not a treatment at all; it is a long-term commitment and a way of life. It has been estimated that AA is currently helping as many alcoholics in the United States as all medical facilities combined. It has been estimated that about 5% of all alcoholics are affiliated with AA (Finagrette, 1988).

Although AA has reported that 64% of participants drop out of the program within their first year, there is no doubt that AA is effective for many drinkers. In fact, it has been claimed that participation in AA is the most effective treatment, but this is a difficult claim to test, largely because AA does not permit itself to be subjected to the same close scientific evaluation that other treatment techniques must undergo. In addition, the people who try and stick with AA are most likely to have a high socioeconomic status and a stable social situation, are highly motivated to quit, are between ages 40 and 45, and have spouses who help with the treatment (Baekeland, 1977). These are the best candidates for help, no matter what the treatment (Ogbourne & Glaser, 1981).

Vaillant has suggested that one reason why AA works is that it provides alternative sources of reinforcement and keeps the alcoholic busily engaged in activities that are incompatible with drinking alcohol. AA provides a busy schedule of social and service activities with supportive former drinkers, especially at times of high risk (e.g., holidays). AA requires members to "work the program" and encourages returning again and again to group meetings and to sponsors who provide an external conscience (Vaillant, 1992, p. 52).

Pharmacotherapies for Alcoholism

The U.S. Food and Drug Administration has approved only four agents for the treatment of alcoholism, which are usually used in conjunction with other behavioral and social therapies. These pharmacotherapies are disulfiram, acamprosate, and oral and extended-release naltrexone. Numerous other drugs are being tested as well.

ANTABUSE (DISULFIRAM).   The effect of disulfiram was described in Chapter 1. As shown in Fig 1-10, it blocks the action of aldehyde dehydrogenase, the enzyme which breaks down acetaldehyde. Drinking alcohol without this enzyme leads to a buildup of acetaldehyde in the body and makes a person feel very sick. Thus, taking disulfiram regularly prevents people from drinking because, if they do, they will become very ill. Extensive clinical trials with disulfiram have shown that it offers some protection from unplanned or spontaneous drinking, but a patient who wants to drink can simply stop taking the drug. There is, in fact, a very high rate of noncoherence in patients—up to 80% do not take Antabuse as directed (Garbutt, 2009). People who are motivated enough to take disulfiram regularly are also motivated enough to avoid alcohol without taking disulfiram. However, the drug does appear to be effective if it is taken under some sort of supervision, usually in conjunction with another therapy. The supervisor needs to be trained in supervisory techniques and educated in evasion behaviors used by patients with alcohol dependence (Brewer, 1992).

ACAMPROSATE.   Acamprosate (Campral) is effective in suppressing glutamate activity, which is hyperactive in the postwithdrawal phase of alcoholics. The major goal of this therapy is to reduce the aversiveness of withdrawal and thereby diminish the motivation to resume drinking (Rosner et al., 2010). Results of acamprosate clinical trials have been mixed, with trials in Europe showing that the drug is effective, while trials in the United States show no such effect. The difference may be due at least in part to a difference in procedure. In the U.S. trials, patients were tested a short time after detoxification, whereas in the European trials a longer period of time had elapsed between detoxification and the drug trial (Garbutt, 2009).

NALTREXONE.   Naltrexone is an opioid receptor antagonist (see Chapter 11). Two formulations have been approved by the FDA for use in the United States. They are oral naltrexone and an extended-release injection that remains effective for a month. Naltrexone blocks activity in the opioid system and has been shown to reduce the normal *high* or level of intoxication after alcohol consumption. It is also reported to reduce craving for alcohol in abstinent heavy drinkers. There have been numerous studies that show that oral naltrexone is modestly effective in reducing the likelihood of relapse to heavy drinking and enhances the possibility of complete abstinence from alcohol. While the therapeutic effects are generally modest, clinical experience has shown that some patients have a strong therapeutic response. It has not been clearly established which patients respond well to naltrexone, but they seem to be patients with a positive family history of alcoholism and a higher baseline rate of craving for alcohol (Garbutt, 2009). It has also been shown that patients who reliably take their naltrexone are also more likely to show improvement. For this reason, an extended-release formulation has been developed and tested. The extended-release injection has undergone several clinical trials and been shown to be effective, particularly in men and patients who are abstinent for 4 or more days before receiving the naltrexone (Garbutt, 2009).

Naltrexone may cause side effects, which include vomiting, diarrhea, and somnolence. The extended-release injection has been reported to cause nausea, decreased appetite, dizziness, and some injection-site pain. These are generally well tolerated, but may contribute to some noncompliance.

OTHER PHARMACOTHERAPIES. Tiapride is a D_2 dopamine receptor blocker approved for use in France. It has been shown to be effective in a limited number of clinical trials, but may have serious side effects, particularly in young people. Other dopaminergic agents have been used, particularly antipsychotic drugs such as clozapine, aripiprazole, and olanzapine. These appear to be especially effective in patients with schizophrenia and bipolar disorder. Other drugs that have been tested, and that have shown some promising results, are anticonvulsants such as topiramate and valproic acid/divalproex (Depakote or Depakene) (Garbutt, 2009).

Anxiolytics and Sedative-Hypnotics

THE NATURE AND NEUROPHYSIOLOGY OF ANXIETY

Anxiety is a normal part of life. The sense of apprehension or nervousness we feel when getting ready for a first date, sitting in a job interview, preparing to write an exam, or calculating whether there is enough money in the bank account to cover the month's rent—these anxieties are common and normal. But when anxiety is unrelenting, unreasonably exaggerated given the circumstances, and interrupts one's ability to meet the everyday demands of life, that degree of anxiety is not normal.

Anxiety disorders are the most common of all psychiatric conditions, with a lifetime prevalence estimated to be as high as 28.8% (Kessler, Berglund, et al., 2005). Women are up to twice as likely as men to suffer from anxiety, and there appears to be a genetic component, as anxiety disorders tend to run in families. The *DSM-IV-TR* includes five classes of anxiety disorders, and research links them with abnormal brain physiology, especially in the limbic system and in regions communicating with it.

Generalized anxiety disorder is characterized by excessive and relentless worry whereby an individual feels irritable, keyed up or on edge, tense, easily fatigued, and has trouble concentrating attention on daily tasks. The source of the anxiety is often vague or unrealized, so the person cannot easily confront it directly, and the anxiety persists. Functional MRI (fMRI) studies show hyperactivity of the amygdala, whereas the ventromedial prefrontal cortex, which suppresses amygdalar activity, tends to be underactive (Damsa, Kosel, & Moussally, 2009).

Social phobia or *social anxiety disorder* is the most frequently experienced anxiety disorder. It is the fear of being scrutinized, rejected, or embarrassed in public. Oftentimes, sufferers will avoid social interactions to prevent distress. Like those with generalized anxiety disorder, social phobia is marked by hyperactivity of the amygdala and also of the orbitofrontal cortex (Damsa et al., 2009).

The category *specific phobia* refers to the extreme anxiety that results when confronting or even thinking about certain objects or situations. Some common phobias include fear of specific animals (spiders, dogs), natural environments (heights, storms), blood–injection–injury (needles, medical procedures), and situations (elevators, flying). fMRI studies of people presented with or even anticipating a feared stimulus (such as a spider) show heightened activity of many brain regions: visual areas, supplementary motor regions, thalamus, amygdala, anterior cingulate cortex, and insular cortex (Damsa et al., 2009).

Panic disorder is associated with panic attacks—seemingly unprovoked, quickly mounting, full-blown alarm reactions marked by heightened sympathetic nervous system activity. Racing heartbeat, sweating, trembling, chest pain, difficulty breathing, nausea, and a sense of losing control or detachment from reality are all features of panic attack. Sufferers may fear they are having a heart attack or a stroke, or are dying. A specific phobia, called *agoraphobia*, often coincides with panic disorder. This is the fear of being in a place or situation from which it would be difficult to escape or get help if a panic attack were to occur, such as on an airplane or in an empty parking garage. Although agoraphobia is not one of the five major classes of anxiety disorders according to the *DSM-IV-TR*, it is proposed to become its own diagnosable disorder in the *DSM-5*. MRI studies of individuals with panic disorder show structural brain abnormalities, specifically a reduction in the volume of the anterior cingulate cortex and an increase in gray matter within the insula, superior temporal gyrus, midbrain, and pons (Damsa et al., 2009).

Other considerations for the *DSM-5* include the reclassification of the two final anxiety disorders—obsessive compulsive disorder and posttraumatic stress disorder—into separate diagnostic categories. *Obsessive compulsive disorder* is characterized by persistently nagging, uncontrollable, anxiety-provoking thoughts that often involve checking, counting, avoiding, or cleaning (obsessions) that a person attempts to relieve or dispel by engaging in some repetitive behavior (compulsion). One common obsession is the fear of contamination, which an individual may try to relieve with compulsive, excessive washing and scrubbing of the skin. Individuals with obsessive compulsive disorder exhibit a reduction in the volume of the hippocampus and amygdala and increased volume in the anterior cingulate cortex; deformities of the thalamus; decreased activation of the orbitofrontal cortex, thalamus, and basal ganglia; and increased activation of the caudate and frontal and parietal cortices (Damsa et al., 2009).

Posttraumatic stress disorder can develop after experiencing a traumatic event, such as a natural disaster, abuse, or military combat, where one's safety or life was threatened. The sufferer may reexperience the event in dreams or illusions and lose his or her sense of safety, pleasure in life, and connectedness to loved ones and friends.

Structural brain abnormalities associated with posttraumatic stress disorder include a reduction in the volume of the hippocampus, anterior cingulate cortex, and insula and dysfunctional activation of other regions including the amygdala and prefrontal cortex (Damsa et al., 2009).

The anxiety disorders are highly comorbid (co-occurring) with depression and are often treated with medications more commonly thought of as antidepressants (see Chapter 13). An interesting genetic similarity between individuals with anxiety and those with depression is an increased likelihood of possessing one or two short alleles (gene forms) of the promoter region of the serotonin (5-HT) transporter gene, which regulates the number of 5-HT transporter proteins. As is the case with depression, possessing the short form of this portion of gene is associated with heightened risk of developing an anxiety disorder (Caspi, Hariri, Holmes, Uher, & Moffitt, 2010).

Insomnia, which includes difficulty falling asleep or getting a full night of restful sleep, is considered a risk factor for both anxiety and depression, and up to 80% of individuals with insomnia experience other psychiatric symptoms (Jansson-Fröjmark & Lindblom, 2008; Stewart et al., 2006). Some of the drugs discussed in this chapter are also used in the treatment of insomnia.

INTRODUCTION TO ANXIOLYTICS AND SEDATIVE-HYPNOTICS

The term *anxiolytic* (or, more historically, *tranquilizer*) is applied to drugs that are used therapeutically to treat agitation and anxiety disorders. The term *sedative-hypnotic* refers to drugs that are used to sedate and aid sleep (i.e., sleeping pills). There are several categories of drugs that have anxiolytic and sedating effects. The most common in use today is the *benzodiazepines*. Before that, the *barbiturates* were widely used. A number of other substances that are neither barbiturates nor benzodiazepines have also been used as sedative-hypnotics or anxiolytics. They include older drugs like *meprobamate* (Miltown) and *methaqualone* (Quaalude), which were widely used in the 1960s but are no longer used today. More newly developed classes of drugs include the *nonbenzodiazepines* such as *abecarnil* and *alpidem* (these have similar therapeutic and side effects as the benzodiazepines, but have significantly different chemical structures) and a class of drugs introduced since the late 1990s called the

Z drugs, which include *zolpidem, zopiclone, zaleplon*, and *eszopiclone* (these have increasingly become the accepted treatment for insomnia, as they have a shorter duration of action and are associated with less risk of tolerance and abuse [Richey & Krystal, 2011]).

The hypnotic, sedating, and tranquilizing properties of all these drugs arise from similar neural mechanisms; that is, their principal mechanism of action is the modulation of GABA$_A$ receptor activity—but they have different binding affinities, potencies, and efficacies at specific receptor subunits, which may result in discrete and specific pharmacological effects, depending on the drug (more about this in the section on neurophysiology). For the most part, the medical use of the drug (i.e., whether a drug is prescribed as an anxiolytic or as a sedative-hypnotic) is determined mainly by other factors, such as the speed of action and the duration of effect. Fast-acting drugs with short duration of action are useful as sedative-hypnotics, and longer-acting drugs are used as anxiolytics. Before the introduction of benzodiazepines, one problem with using long-acting barbiturates as anxiolytics was the impairment caused by their sedating actions. The newer drugs and the Z drugs, however, are now able to target specific symptoms, diminishing some of the unpleasant side effects associated with older drugs.

Anxiolytics and sedative-hypnotics share some properties with alcohol (see Chapter 6), with inhaled solvents, and with other substances generally called depressants or general anesthetics. *GHB* (gamma-hydroxybutyrate) is a peculiar substance that occurs naturally in the body and shares many properties with the sedative-hypnotics. It could well have been included in this chapter, but it also has many unique properties that have caused some to suggest that it is a unique pharmacological entity. For this reason it will be discussed in Chapter 15.

HISTORY OF ANXIOLYTIC AND SEDATIVE-HYPNOTIC DRUG DEVELOPMENT

Before the development of the barbiturates, physicians of the nineteenth century had only a few substances that they could use to calm people or aid sleep. These were alcohol (usually in the form of brandy), bromides, chloral hydrate (otherwise known as chloral),

and opium. For the most part, these were marginally effective and had unwanted side effects. Barbiturates were first synthesized in 1864, and, for over 100 years, they were one of the most useful drugs in the physician's black bag for the treatment of anxiety and insomnia, replacing brandy, bromides, and opium as tranquillizers. Barbiturates were essentially the only drugs used as sedatives and tranquillizers from the 1920s to mid-1950s (López-Muñoz, Ucha-Udabe, & Alamo, 2005).

During the twentieth century, more than 2,500 different barbiturates were synthesized, and about 50 have been marketed and used clinically (examples of these can be found in Table 7-1; some drugs may no longer be used or may not be approved for use in parts of Europe or North America). Compounds containing barbiturates have been recommended in the treatment of nearly 80 different disorders ranging from arthritis to bed-wetting (Reinisch & Sanders, 1982). In 1936 in the United States alone, 70 tons of barbiturate pills were sold, and dependence became widespread. By the 1990s, however, benzodiazepines had largely replaced barbiturates in almost all medical uses, mainly because of their improved therapeutic index. But barbiturate use has not disappeared completely. The long-acting drug phenobarbital is still prescribed to prevent epileptic seizures and to antagonize adverse stimulating effects of some drugs such as ephedrine, d-amphetamine, and theophylline. Butalbital is an intermediate-acting barbiturate combined with drugs such as aspirin, caffeine, acetaminophen, and codeine in analgesic preparations such as Fioronal and Fioricet for the treatment of headaches. Some ultrashort-acting barbiturates, such as thiopental, are given intravenously prior to surgery as anesthetic inducers. Since the 1970s, barbiturates have been used to reduce intracranial pressure following traumatic brain injury. Although not as commonly as before, amobarbital, aprobarbital, butabarbital, pentobarbital, and secobarbital are all still prescribed for the treatment of insomnia (López-Muñoz et al., 2005).

In the 1960s, barbiturates were sold illicitly on the streets as *downers*. Almost all illicit barbiturates were diverted from medical use, and as the medical use of barbiturates has declined, so has their availability and, consequently, their illicit use.

TABLE 7-1 Anxiolytic and Sedative-Hypnotic Drugs

Generic Name	Trade Name
Barbiturates	
amobarbital	Amytal
aprobarbital	Oramon
butabarbital	Butisol
butalbital	Axotal, Fioricet, Fioronal
mephobarbital	Mebaral
pentobarbital	Nembutal
phenobarbital	Luminal
secobarbital	Seconal, Quinalbarbitone
thiopental	Pentothal
Benzodiazepines	
alprazolam	Xanax
centrax	Prazepam
chlordiazepoxide	Librium
clonazepam	Rivotril, Klonopin
clorazepate	Tranxene, Novo-Clopate
diazepam	Valium
flunitrazepam	Rohypnol
flurazepam	Dalmane
lorazepam	Ativan, Temesta
nitrazepam	Mogadon
oxazepam	Serax
temazepam	Restoril
triazolam	Halcion
Z drugs and others	
abecarnil	ZK-112,119
alpidem	Ananxyl
buspirone	Buspar
eszopiclone	Lunesta
zaleplon	Sonata, Starnoc
zolpidem	Ambien, Stilnox
zopiclone	Imovane, Zimovane

The first synthesis of the benzodiazepines was a combination of good science and good luck. In the 1930s, Leo Sternback synthesized several substances known as *heptoxdiazines* while working on the chemistry of dyes in Krakow, Poland. But not until the 1950s, when he was working at the Hoffman–La Roche laboratories in the United States, did Sternback and his colleagues do further work with these compounds. Their research was stimulated by an attempt to find

a new, safe drug that could be used as an anxiolytic. Their approach was simple; they would pick a class of biologically active chemicals that was simple to make and easy to change and that no one else had studied. They would then make and test as many derivatives as they could, hoping to discover a useful drug by chance. The heptoxdiazines fitted this description perfectly, so the researchers started to synthesize all sorts of new variations and had them tested for their biological properties.

None of the derivatives they tested had any biological effect. However, one of these derivatives, identified as Ro 5-0690, was not tested at that time; it was assumed to be inactive and was set aside. Not until 1957, after it had been taking up needed space on the worktable for 2 years, was it finally sent for testing. In fact, one story has it that the reason it was sent for testing rather than being thrown out was that it had "such pretty crystals." To everyone's surprise, the pretty crystals were found to have sedative properties (Sternback, 1973). The researchers finally decided to call Ro 5-0690 *chlordiazepoxide*. After further testing, it was marketed as Librium (Greenblatt & Shader, 1974).

In the years that followed, many more drugs of this type, known as the benzodiazepines, were synthesized and tested, and a number were eventually marketed as anxiolytics, sedative-hypnotics, muscle relaxants, and seizure suppressants (examples of these can also be found in Table 7-1). One of the benzodiazepines was *diazepam* (Valium), which was also developed by Sternback and marketed in 1963. Although all the benzodiazepines have very similar effects in humans, they differ in their relative potency. Some are more potent as sedative-hypnotics, and some are more potent as anxiolytics; they also differ in their speed of action. Apart from diazepam and chlordiazepoxide, common anxiolytic benzodiazepines are *lorazepam* (Ativan), *clorazepate* (Tranxene), *alprazolam* (Xanax), and *oxazepam* (Serax). Sedative-hypnotic benzodiazepines are *nitrazepam* (Mogadon), *flurazepam* (Dalmane), *triazolam* (Halcion), and *temazepam* (Restoril). *Clonazepam* (Rivotril) is used as an anticonvulsant.

Although recreational use of the benzodiazepines is not as extensive as that of the barbiturates, benzodiazepines do have addictive qualities and are liable to be abused. One benzodiazepine piqued public interest in the mid-1990s since it was reported to be widely used on the street—*flunitrazepam* (Rohypnol). The World Health Organization reported in 1995 that illicit use of flunitrazepam was higher than for any other benzodiazepine. As a result, the UN Commission on Narcotic Drugs increased restrictions on flunitrazepam (Mintzer & Griffiths, 1998).

Rohypnol is sold in parts of Europe, Mexico, and South America, but it has never been marketed in the United States. It is smuggled from Mexico to the southern states, and, by 1995, it was being used quite extensively by young people, especially in conjunction with alcohol. It is known as *Mexican Valium, roaches,* or *roofies.* Flunitrazepam now has the status of a club drug—a drug used at dance clubs, bars, and all-night dance parties, or *raves.* Because of its powerful amnesic effects, Rohypnol also gained the reputation of being a *date rape drug* that is slipped into the drinks of young women who are then sexually assaulted. Laboratory blood tests of date rape victims throughout the United States suggest, however, that the use of Rohypnol for this purpose is not as common as publically believed. Other classes of drugs, such as alcohol and cannabis, and other benzodiazepines, such as diazepam, oxazepan, and lorazepam, are more commonly associated with date rape (ElSohly & Salamone, 1999).

The barbiturates, benzodiazepines, and nonbenzodiazepines (e.g., methaqualone, meprobamate, Z drugs) combat anxiety and insomnia principally through their actions at $GABA_A$ receptors. A variety of other drugs, used for similar purposes but with different mechanisms of action, deserve brief mention. Over-the-counter sleep aids, such as Nytol, Sominex, Sleepinal, Compoz, Unisom, and Nighttime Sleep Aid, contain the antihistamines doxylamine or diphenhydramine, which are also found in allergy and cold medications such as Benadryl or NyQuil. Antihistamines cause drowsiness by antagonizing histamine H_1 receptors in the brain and blocking the action of acetylcholine. In an attempt to regulate circadian (day/night) rhythm, some people take capsules containing melatonin, a hormone released by the pineal gland. Although not a lot of data support its effectiveness as a sedative-hypnotic, there are some indications that it may help speed the onset of sleep (Richey & Krystal, 2011). The hypocretin/orexin system has also become a target of pharmacological

research; dysfunction of this system occurs in the sleep disorder *narcolepsy*.

Prescription medications most commonly considered antipsychotics (see Chapter 12) and antidepressants (see Chapter 13) offer promise as anxiolytics. In a recent study, the atypical antipsychotics quetiapine and risperidone fared better than a placebo in the treatment of generalized anxiety disorder and obsessive compulsive personality disorder (Maher et al., 2011). However, the same adverse side effects associated with these medications in the treatment of schizophrenia also occurred in their use as anxiolytics. A number of antidepressant medications of various classes, including the selective serotonin reuptake inhibitors (SSRIs), serotonin–norepinephrine reuptake inhibitors (SNRIs), monoamine oxidase inhibitors (MAOIs), and reversible inhibitors of monoamine oxidase A (RIMAs), have also proven useful in the treatment of anxiety disorders (Reinhold, Mandos, Rickels, & Lohoff, 2011; Schneier, 2011). You will notice in Table 7-1 that a drug called buspirone (Buspar) is listed under Z drugs and Others. This medication is widely used in the treatment of anxiety disorders, but is not a benzodiazepine and does not modulate GABA activity. Instead, buspirone is a serotonin agonist, acting specifically at the $5\text{-}HT_{1A}$ receptor subtype. Its major benefit over the benzodiazepines is that it reduces anxiety without producing sedation or muscle relaxation, common effects of the benzodiazepines. Drugs such as clonidine and propanolol, which decrease sympathetic nervous system activity but antagonize noradrenergic activity, are helpful in the treatment of posttraumatic stress and panic disorder.

According to a study by the U.S. Drug Testing Advisory Board that compared pharmacy dispensing of prescription anxiolytics and sedative-hypnotics in the decade spanning 1997–2008, barbiturate prescriptions have decreased, by 22% (representing 820,000 fewer prescriptions) for phenobarbital and 61% (381,000 prescriptions) for butalbital. During the same time period, the dispensing of prescription benzodiazepines increased, by 114% for clonazepam (representing 10.9 million additional prescriptions), 71% for alprazolam (17.6 million prescriptions), 30% for temazepam (1.9 million prescriptions), 24% for lorazepam (4.2 million prescriptions), and 17% for diazepam (2.1 million prescriptions). Since their introduction in the late 1990s, prescriptions for the Z drugs have also been increasing as these drugs are slowly replacing the benzodiazepines in the treatment of insomnia, especially in North America.

NEUROPHYSIOLOGY

The neurophysiology of the barbiturates and benzodiazepines is fairly well understood. Their effects are mediated primarily by their ability to modify transmission of the inhibitory transmitter GABA, specifically at the $GABA_A$ receptor (it might be helpful, at this point, to review the information related to GABA and its receptor subtypes found in Chapters 4 and 6).

A prototypical $GABA_A$ receptor complex is illustrated in Figure 7-1. Although $GABA_A$ receptors exist in a variety of forms, the most common type of subunit combination is $\alpha_1\beta_2\gamma_2$, which comprise approximately

60% of all $GABA_A$ receptors in the brain. GABA receptors are found all throughout the central nervous system (CNS), both at synapses and elsewhere, and seem to maintain a general level of activity that creates an *inhibitory tone* in the brain, preventing excessive excitation that could result in seizures.

The barbiturates, benzodiazepines, and nonbenzodiazepines do not modify $GABA_A$ receptor activity by altering levels of GABA or by interacting directly with GABA's receptor binding site. Instead, these drugs are positive allosteric modulators—they have their own binding sites on the $GABA_A$ receptor complex that, when occupied, enhances the effects of GABA binding. Some drugs, like abecarnil and alpidem, have a low affinity for the benzodiazepine receptor binding site and have a weak effect. Others, like diazepam, flunitrazepam, midazolam, and triazolam, have a high affinity and a correspondingly greater effect. Some compounds that act as

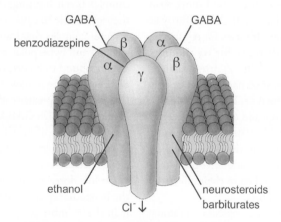

FIGURE 7-1 A schematic drawing of the $GABA_A$ receptor complex indicating the location of some of its ligand binding sites. The receptor complex is composed of five subunits: most typically two alpha (α) subunits, two beta (β) subunits, and a gamma (γ) subunit. The location of receptor binding sites is illustrated: There are two GABA (orthosteric) binding sites located at the interface of alpha and beta subunits; the benzodiazepine (allosteric) binding site is located at the interface of an alpha and a gamma subunit; and other allosteric sites for ethanol, barbiturates, and neuroactive steroids (among others) are located internal to (in the membrane-spanning portion of) the receptor complex. When the ion channel (located in the central pore of the complex) is open, it permits chloride ions (Cl^-) to pass into the cell, hyperpolarizing it and making it more difficult for excitatory neurotransmitters to depolarize the membrane and create an excitatory postsynaptic potential.

allostatic modulators of the benzodiazapine binding site have been shown to alter GABA activity dramatically, by more than 700%.

The binding site for benzodiazepines (and the Z drugs) is formed at the interface of one of the alpha subunits (α_1, α_2, α_3, or α_5) and the gamma subunit (usually γ_2, which is present in about 90% of $GABA_A$ receptor complexes; Rudolph & Knoflach, 2011). However, the high affinity and activity of benzodiazepines at α_1, α_2, α_3, and α_5 $GABA_A$ receptor subtypes is not standard in the Z drugs; their affinity for these alpha subunits differs, which may be the cause of their distinct therapeutic profiles (Nutt & Stahl, 2010).

Alpha 1 receptor subunits are found throughout the CNS. The most prominent effect of their activation is sedation, although they are also responsible to a lesser degree for the amnesic and anticonvulsant effects of benzodiazepine drugs such as diazepam (Rudolph & Knoflach, 2011). Among the Z drugs used short term to treat insomnia, zolpidem has the highest affinity at the $GABA_A$ α_1 subunit, lower affinities for α_2 and α_3 subunits, and essentially no affinity for α_5 subunits (Rudolph & Knoflach, 2011). Other Z drugs, such as zaleplon, zopiclone, and eszopiclone, have similar or only slightly lower affinities for the α_1 subunit but significantly higher affinities at α_2, α_3, and α_5 subunits, compared to zolpidem; Nutt & Stahl, 2010). For this reason, zolpidem is referred to as an α_1-selective drug (Rudolph & Knoflach, 2011). Importantly, the addictive properties of benzodiazepines have been linked to their effects on the α_1 subunit of $GABA_A$ receptors.

Activation of $GABA_A$ receptor complexes containing α_2 and α_3 subunit types also produces sedation, and, in addition, these subunits are thought to regulate brainwave activity during sleep and the transition between sleep and wakefulness. Muscle relaxation also results from the activation of these alpha subunits. However, the primary effect of α_2 and α_3 subunit activation is anxiolysis (anxiety reduction) and alteration of mood. Large numbers of α_2 and α_3 subunits are located in the cortex, dorsal raphe nucleus, limbic system, and interrelated structures that are known to regulate emotion.

Alpha 5 subunits play some role in muscle relaxation and sedation, but appear to be more highly involved in learning and memory; concentrations of $GABA_A$ receptor complexes containing α_5 subunits are found in the hippocampus (Nutt & Stahl, 2010). Activation of α_5 subunits is likely related to the amnesic effects of anxiolytic drugs. Tolerance to the sedative actions of benzodiazepines has also been linked to the α_5 subunit.

With different alpha subunits playing varying roles, it is possible that the therapeutic and side effects of GABAergic drugs are related to their distinctive selectivity for particular subunits. A major problem with using GABAergic drugs as anxiolytics is the co-occurring, unwanted sedation. A major goal of anxiety research is to create drugs that will selectively and preferentially activate alpha subunits responsible for producing anxiolysis rather than those primarily involved in sedation and sleep.

The benzodiazepines show lower affinity and activity at α_4 and α_6 $GABA_A$ receptor subunits, and this pattern is also seen with the Z drugs.

When benzodiazepines and Z drugs bind, their ability to modulate the function of the $GABA_A$ receptor complex is self-limiting; that is, these drugs are not, on their own, able to cause conformational changes in the receptor complex that lead to the opening of the Cl^- ion channel and hyperpolarization of the cell. GABA must also be bound to its orthosteric binding site if the benzodiazepines are to have any effect on the receptor's ion channel. The copresence of benzodiazepine increases the affinity with which GABA binds to its site and enhances the conductance of the Cl^- ion channel; the conductance is of a similar degree as if high concentrations of GABA alone were present.

At low doses, the barbiturates have similar effects to the benzodiazepines. The binding site for barbiturates is in the membrane-spanning portion of the receptor complex. At high doses, barbiturates are quite different in their effects on the $GABA_A$ receptor complex—they are able to open the Cl^- ion channel by themselves, without the co-presence of GABA binding. Therefore, there is an upper limit on the inhibitory effect of the benzodiazepines and Z drugs on the brain, but no upper limit on the inhibitory effect of the barbiturates. High doses of benzodiazepines can cause extreme sedation and grogginess but are not life threatening. High doses of barbiturates produce unconsciousness and anesthesia (Richards, 1980), and they depress breathing by inhibiting the autonomic centers in the brainstem. The respiratory depression caused by barbiturates is similar to the depression caused by alcohol. Barbiturates cause slow, shallow breathing and, at high doses, may prevent breathing altogether. This depression of breathing and a similar depression of the cardiovascular system are the main cause of death in cases of barbiturate overdose. The difference in the potential to cause lethal overdose is the major difference between the barbiturates and the benzodiazepines and is one of the main reasons why the benzodiazepines have replaced the barbiturates as anxiolytics and long-term sedative-hypnotics.

Why would the brain have receptor sites for benzodiazepines? It is likely that the body has endogenous substances that use these receptors. A search is under way to find an endogenous benzodiazepine. It is thought that such a substance might be responsible for modulating anxiety. In fact, it has been demonstrated that there is an enhancement in the receptivity of benzodiazepine receptors immediately following periods of stress in laboratory animals. Such an increase would make an endogenous benzodiazepine more effective and would increase inhibitory tone, making the organism less sensitive to the physiological and possibly cognitive effects of stress and distress (Hommer, Skolnick, & Paul, 1987; Martin & Acre, 1996).

An endogenous benzodiazepine, however, might have exactly the opposite effect. We know that there are some benzodiazepines that work as *inverse agonists* or *negative GABA_A modulators*. They act opposite to the usual benzodiazepine effect; that is, they decrease GABA's ability to open the Cl^- ion channel, and they increase feelings of tension, anxiety, and panic (Carvalho, de Greckshk, Chapouthier, & Rossier, 1983; Squires & Braestrup, 1977; Stephenson, 1987). Likewise, there are barbiturate inverse agonists that act in opposition to GABA to induce seizures (Ticku & Olsen, 1978).

Even though many of the effects of the benzodiazepines and barbiturates can be understood in terms of their ability to modulate GABA activity, their neurophysiology is complex, and other transmitters and neuromodulators may be involved. For example, the benzodiazepines are known to enhance the effects of adenosine, another inhibitory transmitter, by blocking its reuptake and permitting its accumulation (Phillis & O'Regan, 1988), an effect directly opposite to that of caffeine (see Chapter 9).

Benzodiazepines, though considered safer and less addicting than the barbiturates, are known to have abuse potential. Dependence, defined by high-dose use over a prolonged period, is not common among individuals who are prescribed these medications, but abuse is prevalent among individuals who obtain the drugs without prescription and who are also dependent upon alcohol and other drugs (Kan, Breteler, van der Ven, Timmermans, & Zitman, 2001). Like all addictive drugs, benzodiazepines influence the transmission of dopamine in the mesolimbic dopamine pathway, which projects from the ventral tegmental area to the nucleus accumbens and prefrontal cortex. If you refer to Figure 12-1 in Chapter 12, you will notice that glutamate, dopamine, and GABA neurons all converge within the ventral tegmental area. Benzodiazepines increase dopamine activity by binding to α_1-containing $GABA_A$ receptors and inhibiting GABAergic interneurons that synapse upon dopamine cell bodies within the ventral tegmental area. The net result is a reduction in GABA neuron firing and a disinhibition (freeing) of dopamine neurons that are normally suppressed by GABA interneuron activity. This disinhibition of dopamine activity leads to neuroplastic changes within the mesocortical pathway, specifically in the firing of excitatory glutamatergic neurons that synapse upon dopamine cell bodies in the ventral tegmental area. Glutamate activity is amplified, driving dopamine cell firing even higher. In laboratory research using mice, just a single administration of diazepam or zolpidem resulted in neuroplastic changes in glutamate activity (Heikkinen, Möykkynen, & Korpi, 2009).

ROUTE OF ADMINISTRATION AND ABSORPTION

Both barbiturates and benzodiazepines are weak acids. Benzodiazepines have a pKa of about 3.5 to 5.0, and they are readily absorbed from digestive and parenteral administration. The choice of route depends on the purpose for which the drug is given. If a rapid effect is needed, an intravenous injection would be indicated, but can sometimes result in local irritation (Lader, 2011). If a long-term effect is wanted, as when diazepam is used to treat anxiety, the oral route is appropriate. Absorption from the digestive system is more rapid than absorption from an intramuscular site, probably because the drugs tend to bind to protein and do so more readily at an injection site than in the digestive system. There are reports that flunitrazepam can cause very rapid effects when the tablets are ground into a powder and administered intranasally (Woods & Winger, 1997).

There is a range of lipid solubility in the benzodiazepines and a resulting difference in the speed of absorption of different benzodiazepines. Diazepam, one of the fastest-acting benzodiazepines, reaches a peak in about 30 to 60 minutes. Other fast-acting benzodiazepines are midazolam, temazepam, flunitrazepam, and triazepam. Oxazepam is slower acting and may take several hours to peak (Busto, Bendayan, & Sellers, 1989). Among individuals, there is a great deal of variability in the rate of absorption and the peak blood levels obtained after a given dose of a benzodiazepine. A dose of diazepam given to one person may cause a blood level 20 times higher than the same dose in another person (Garattini, Mussini, Marcucci, & Guaitani, 1973).

Absorption from the digestive system may be greatly increased by the drinking of alcohol. After small amounts of alcohol are ingested, the blood levels of diazepam can be nearly doubled (Laisi, Linnoila, Seppala, & Mattila, 1979).

The Z drugs are readily absorbed from the digestive system and reach a peak in about an hour. There is considerable first-pass metabolism of zaleplon.

DISTRIBUTION AND EXCRETION

Once a barbiturate or benzodiazepine is in the blood, distribution and, consequently, duration of action are determined by the lipid solubility of the particular drug. The highly lipid-soluble drugs pass through the blood–brain barrier quickly, and their effects on the brain are seen quickly. However, the effects can disappear rapidly because their levels in the brain soon fall. This decrease occurs because highly lipid-soluble drugs become redistributed to areas of the body that contain fat. From these fat deposits, the drug is released slowly into the blood and metabolized by the liver. Thus, fast-acting drugs also tend to have a short duration of action, even though they may still circulate at low levels in the blood for a period of time (Busto et al., 1989; Mark, 1971).

The redistribution of the benzodiazepines in body fat creates a two-phase excretion curve. During the first phase, there is a rather rapid drop in blood level as the drug is redistributed. This phase has a half-life of 2 to 10 hours. In the second phase, the blood level drops more slowly because the drug remaining in the blood is being metabolized, and, as it is metabolized, it is being replaced by the drug slowly being released from

body fat. The half-life during this phase varies from 27 to 48 hours, although the half-life of some benzodiazepines, such as triazolam, is much faster, about 2 to 4 hours (Lader, 2011; Wilder & Bruni, 1981). There is considerable variability in the half-lives of benzodiazepines from individual to individual.

The duration of the effect of the benzodiazepines, however, is not always determined by their half-lives because the metabolites of some of the older benzodiazepines (e.g., diazepam, chlordiazepoxide, and flurazepam) are also active. These metabolites have even longer half-lives and may have somewhat different effects. In the development of newer benzodiazepines, consideration has been given to the elimination of these active metabolites. The newer benzodiazepines—oxazepam, triazolam, alprazolam, clonazepam, and lorazepam—do not have any active metabolites (American Society of Hospital Pharmacists, 1987; Rickels, 1983).

The benzodiazepines and barbiturates also cross the placental barrier easily, and they appear in the milk of nursing mothers.

The metabolism of benzodiazepines can be slowed by the consumption of alcohol. It has been shown that the half-life of chlordiazepoxide is increased by 60% after a small drink of alcohol (Desmond, Patwardham, Schenker, & Hoyumpa, 1980). Zaleplon has an extremely short half-life of about 1 hour (Julien, 2001).

EFFECTS ON THE BODY

Apart from a depression in respiration and a slight drop in blood pressure, barbiturates have few physiological effects at low doses. Unlike the barbiturates, the benzodiazepines do not produce significant depression of respiration in healthy individuals, even at high doses. They also have little effect on heart rate or blood pressure. The benzodiazepines are also reported to increase appetite, and weight gain is sometimes a consequence of continuous use (Greenblatt & Shader, 1974; Haney, Comer, Fischman, & Foltin, 1997).

Outside the CNS, the benzodiazepines have very few effects. They have muscle-relaxant properties that are clinically useful and appear to result from the effect of the drug on the brain rather than on the muscles themselves. These properties have made benzodiazepines useful in treating increased muscle tone caused by multiple sclerosis, Parkinson's disease, and brain injury. The benzodiazepines are also reported to be useful in the treatment of backache and muscle strain. When taken for anxiolytic or sedative-hypnotic purposes, ataxia and tremor are unwanted side effects.

The benzodiazepines are anticonvulsants, and they are useful in treating *petit mal* seizures and infantile spasms; however, for long-term control of epilepsy, the benzodiazepines are not likely to replace the barbiturate and barbiturate-like drugs now commonly in use.

Effects on Sleep

The benzodiazepines are effective in treating insomnia; flurazepam is widely used in the United States, and nitrazepam is used in Europe for this purpose. Zolpidem is also one of the most widely used hypnotics. These drugs decrease latency to fall asleep, decrease wakefulness during the night, and increase total sleeping time. Unfortunately, benzodiazepines, like the barbiturates, decrease the percentage of time spent in REM as well as in stage 3 and stage 4 sleep. This effect diminishes with continued use, and when the drug is discontinued, after as little as 2 weeks, there is a withdrawal rebound (Griffiths & Sannerud, 1987). With nitrazepam, this rebound reaches a peak about 10 days after the drug is stopped and may last for several weeks. With the increase in REM comes an increase in rebound insomnia, that is, bizarre dreaming, restlessness, and wakefulness during the night (Oswald, Lewis, Tangey, Firth, & Haider, 1973). The desire to resume taking the drug to get a good night's sleep increases accordingly.

This rebound appears to be a withdrawal symptom that can be eliminated simply by returning to the use of the sleeping pill. As a result, once people have started to use sedative-hypnotics for sleep, they find it difficult to stop. After periods as short as a week, they find that they cannot get a good night's sleep without their pill, and every time they try to stop, the same thing happens. They do not realize that they must go through a period, sometimes as long as a month, of poor sleep before they can sleep well without their pill.

Zopiclone is reported to have little, if any, rebound effect after short-term use (Hajak, 1999), and no withdrawal or rebound effects were found with zaleplon after 2 to 4 weeks of use (Elie, Ruther, Farr, Emilien, & Salinas, 1999). A number of studies have failed to demonstrate any rebound insomnia after flunitrazepam

(Woods & Winger, 1997). Zaleplon, because it is relatively fast acting, reduces the time to go to sleep but does not increase total sleeping time (Elie et al., 1999).

EFFECTS ON THE BEHAVIOR AND PERFORMANCE OF HUMANS

Subjective Effects

Many (although not all) studies of the subjective effect of the benzodiazepines have shown that subjects report euphoria and liking along with sedation and fatigue (de Wit & Griffiths, 1991; Evans, Griffiths, & de Wit, 1996). In one experiment, diazepam and a placebo were given to volunteers who were asked to fill out a Profile of Mood States form at that time and at 1, 3, and 6 hours later. Compared with a placebo, doses of 5 and 10 mg of diazepam caused a decrease in feelings of arousal and vigor and an increase in fatigue and confusion. These effects were seen only at 1 hour with the low dose but were generally seen for up to 3 hours with the high dose. These feelings were considered unpleasant by the participants, few of whom voluntarily took the drug again when they were given the chance (Johanson & Uhlenhuth, 1980). Positive effects and increased liking scores for benzodiazepines are more likely to be seen in people with a history of sedative or alcohol abuse, moderate alcohol use, or opioid use, including those on methadone maintenance (Evans et al., 1996). Flunitrazepam seems more likely than other benzodiazepines to increase "liking" and "take again" scores in normal healthy volunteers and in people on methadone maintenance (Garek et al., 2001; Mintzer & Griffiths, 1998).

Effects on Performance

The benzodiazepines and barbiturates increase the critical frequency of fusion threshold, indicating a deficit in visual functioning. Some studies have also reported that the auditory flicker fusion threshold is diminished by the benzodiazepines (Vogel, 1979).

The benzodiazepines can have severe effects on memory; they cause anterograde amnesia, a loss of memory for events that occurred while under the influence of the drug (Lader, 2011). These problems occur at low doses that do not cause sedation or impair alertness or motor functioning. Memory problems are sometimes observed in patient populations taking benzodiazepines for anxiety or insomnia. Benzodiazepine users consistently perform worse on verbal memory tasks than nonusers (Barker et al., 2004).

Memory effects do not seem to show tolerance and may persist for months after the drug is discontinued. One reason why benzodiazepines are reputedly sometimes used as date rape drugs is because the victim often has trouble remembering incidents surrounding the assault.

Psychologists who study memory sometimes use benzodiazepines as a tool to explore memory processes (Pompéia, Gorenstein, & Curran, 1996). It is often observed that, even at low doses, benzodiazepines cause deficits in *explicit memory* but not in *implicit memory*. That is, if people are asked to *use* information they acquired after taking a benzodiazepine (implicit memory), they can do that. But if they are explicitly asked to *recall* that information (explicit memory), they have trouble. There is some evidence that this distinction is a result of the fact that there are usually no retrieval cues in explicit memory tasks, but there are such cues in implicit memory tasks. In any case, it has been shown that benzodiazepine-caused memory problems can often be overcome by providing recall cues and reminders of what happened (Pompéia et al., 1966) in a manner similar to alcohol grayout (see Chapter 6).

Even though the benzodiazepines have a clear effect on the ability to acquire new information, they do not appear to alter the ability to recall information acquired prior to their administration (Taylor & Tinklenberg, 1987).

At higher blood levels, sedation occurs that can be detected by tests such as the digit symbol substitution test (which shows a decrease in working or short-term memory), by tests of attention, and by psychomotor performance tests such as reaction time. These effects can be reversed by the administration of the benzodiazepine receptor blocker flumazenil (Bareggi, Ferini-Strambi, Pirola, & Smirne, 1998).

Attention and psychomotor effects may start as soon as 1 hour after oral administration for diazepam or 3 hours for lorazepam. The duration of the impairment will vary, depending on the dose, but can last up to 24 hours. The time course of the impairment does not reflect the concentration in the blood, and shorter-acting benzodiazepines may actually cause a longer-lasting

effect than long-acting benzodiazepines. The degree of impairment is not always evident to the individual, who will frequently report that he or she feels fine (Roache & Griffiths, 1987; Taylor & Tinklenberg, 1987).

It should also be remembered that the benzodiazepines can actually improve performance in some people. Improvements are usually seen in individuals who were highly anxious or were in difficult and stressful situations where anxiety might be expected to interfere with performance (Janke & DeBus, 1968).

Residual Effects

Benzodiazepines are widely used at bedtime to induce sleep. Many have such a long half-life that they are still in the body for some time the next day. Because sleeping pill users may drive to work, operate equipment, and engage in other activities that might be impaired by the drug, it is important to determine whether these residual levels of the drug can affect performance the next day. Many, but not all, studies show next-day residual effects of benzodiazepines. Not surprisingly, higher doses are more likely to have residual effects than lower doses (Woods & Winger, 1997). In an attempt to reduce these residual effects, the benzodiazepines and nonbenzodiazepines with short-elimination half-lives are now being more widely used as hypnotics.

The residual effects of benzodiazepines also greatly enhance the effect of a single drink of alcohol (Saario & Linnoila, 1976).

Among the newer sedative-hypnotics, no residual effects on reaction time, driving, or memory were seen with zopiclone, even when it was administered 4 to 6 hours before in the middle of the night (Verster et al., 2002).

Effects on Driving

Extensive research by a group at the University of Helsinki in Finland has shown that a 10-mg dose of diazepam will increase collisions in a simulated driving task. This impairment is also greatly worsened by alcohol (Linnoila & Hakkinen, 1974). A recent meta-analysis of publications examining the influence of benzodiazepines on driving supports this early research. Benzodiazepines increased the risk of traffic accident by 60 to 80%, and the likelihood of *accident responsibility* rose by 40%. Risk was greater in drivers under the age 65.

Combining alcohol with a benzodiazepine resulted in a 7.7-fold increase in accident risk (Dassanayake, Michie, Carter, & Jones, 2011). In general, evidence shows that there is a considerable risk of an automobile accident in first-time users of benzodiazepines. The risk is probably amplified by the fact that the individual is often not able to detect the impairment (Taylor & Tinklenberg, 1987). Although some tolerance may develop to this effect, driving impairments and next-day sleepiness have been seen with lorazepam after 7 days of use (van Laar, Volkerts, & Verbaten, 2001). Driving impairments in patients receiving diazepam for anxiety are still apparent 3 weeks into treatment (van Laar, Volkerts, & Willigenberg, 1992). The nonbenzodiazepine drug, zopiclone, also significantly impaired driving ability during the first 2 to 4 weeks of treatment (Dassanayake et al., 2011).

Many studies show that the benzodiazepines and Z drugs may have residual effects on driving the next morning. One study showed that flunitrazepam and, to a lesser extent, zopiclone had effects of driving at 9:00 A.M. the day after being used, but zolpidem did not. By 11:00 A.M., flunitrazepam still had effects, but neither zolpidem nor zopiclone did (Bocca et al., 1999). Similar residual effects have been reported with flurazepam but not lormetazepam, which does not have any active metabolites (Brookhuis, Volkerts, & O'Hanlon, 1990).

In spite of the foregoing evidence, the presence of benzodiazepines in the blood was not found to be a contributing factor in a large sample of road accidents after the effects of alcohol had been accounted for (Benzodiazepine/Driving Collaborative Group, 1993).

EFFECTS ON THE BEHAVIOR OF NONHUMANS

Unconditioned Behavior

One of the first effects noticed in the early screening tests of the benzodiazepines was a *taming* effect. The research animals became more placid, and fighting behavior induced by electric shocks was reduced. It has since been demonstrated that chlordiazepoxide and diazepam are effective in reducing only defensive aggression, that is, aggression induced by an attack or provoked by a painful stimulus like a shock. Unprovoked aggression or attack behavior does not seem to be altered at lower-than-toxic doses (DiMascio, 1973). It has been suggested that this

change in provoked aggression is a result of the ability of the benzodiazepines to diminish anxiety. Defensive aggression is presumably a result of anxiety or fear caused by being attacked. Attack itself is not motivated by anxiety (Hoffmeister & Wuttke, 1969).

Conditioned Behavior

Benzodiazepines show the classical profile of drugs that are therapeutically useful in the treatment of anxiety. Heise and Boff (1962) showed that doses of benzodiazepine that decrease avoidance responses are one-fourth to one-sixth the size of doses that have any effect on escape responding.

The benzodiazepines also have a spectacular effect on behavior suppressed by punishment: They cause an increase in punished behavior at doses that decrease or have little effect on positively motivated behavior (Hanson, Witloslawski, & Campbell, 1967; Kleven & Koek, 1999). Animals injected with barbiturates continue to make responses that are punished by electric shock at normal, unpunished rates. The reason for their unchanged behavior does not appear to be that they no longer feel the shock; they jump and flinch when it happens, but they nevertheless continue to make the punished response.

DISCRIMINATIVE STIMULUS PROPERTIES

Laboratory animals can be readily trained to discriminate all benzodiazepines from saline. Flunitrazepam and triazolam appear to be more potent than other benzodiazepines (Woods & Winger, 1997).

Animals trained to discriminate a benzodiazepine will generalize the response to other benzodiazepines and barbiturates but not to the antipsychotics or ketamine. The discriminative stimulus effects of benzodiazepines cannot be blocked by stimulant drugs such as amphetamine, caffeine, cocaine, and the hallucinogen mescaline, but they can be blocked by drugs that block the benzodiazepine receptor (Colpaert, 1977; Lelas, Gerak, & France, 1999).

Although the benzodiazepine cue will generalize to the barbiturates, it has been shown that rats can be trained to discriminate chlordiazepoxide from barbiturates and alcohol but not from diazepam. This finding indicates qualitative differences between the subjective effects of all these drugs, even though they are similar enough to generalize to each other (Barry, McGuire, & Krimmer, 1982). Alcohol will, however, potentiate the discriminative effects of flunitrazepam (Schechter, 1998). There is some evidence from rats that zolpidem may have slightly different discriminative effects from the benzodiazepines since there is only partial generalization to many benzodiazepines, and no generalization occurs in rats trained to discriminate alcohol (Rush, 1998).

Humans can easily learn to discriminate benzodiazepines. In one experiment, six women and seven men were able to reliably discriminate a dose of 0.375 mg of triazolam. There was no gender difference in the participants' ability to discriminate this drug, nor in their ratings of sedation or impairment of performance (Vansickel, Hays, & Rush, 2006).

TOLERANCE

Acute Tolerance

Tolerance to the effects of benzodiazepines can develop during a single administration. Such tolerance seems to be limited in humans to the effect of benzodiazepines on behavior such as digit symbol substitution and tracking and may not be seen in physiological effects. It has also been shown that the acute tolerance can develop to the motor-impairing effects of midazolam (Coldwell et al., 1998). Similarly, studies have shown that phenobarbital has a more powerful effect at a given concentration as the blood level is rising than when the blood level is descending (Ellenwood et al., 1981).

Chronic Tolerance

With repeated administration, benzodiazepines become less and less effective in their ability to modulate the effects of GABA. There is some disagreement, however, whether this is a result of a reduction in the capacity of the benzodiazepines to alter the effect of GABA or whether the sensitivity of the GABA receptor to GABA is reduced. In any case, many behavioral effects of the benzodiazepines show tolerance (Hutchison, Smith, & Darlington, 1996).

In laboratory animals, tolerance develops to many of the behavioral effects of the benzodiazepines, including their locomotor, ataxic, muscle relaxant, and anticonvulsant effects. Tolerance to the disruptive effects of chlordiazepoxide on avoidance develops in rats when the drug is administered every day for 6 weeks (Masuki & Iwamoto, 1966). Tolerance to the anxiety-reducing effects in humans is variable and appears to be related to the dosing regime and the specific benzodiazepine used (Hutchison et al., 1996).

Tolerance also develops slowly to the anticonvulsant effects of the benzodiazepines as well as to the drowsiness that is seen sometimes at therapeutic doses. Although there are some data to suggest that tolerance does not develop to the hypnotic effects of benzodiazepines and to zolpidem in particular, other work has shown that tolerance to the sleep-producing effects of these drugs develops after about 4 weeks (Rush, 1998). As mentioned earlier, there has been a tendency to prescribe short-acting benzodiazepines and nonbenzodiazepines as sleeping pills to avoid next-day residual effects, but it seems that these drugs have a tendency to develop tolerance faster than the longer-acting benzodiazepines. In addition, they also seem to cause more frequent and more intense rebound insomnia. Among the short-acting hypnotics, however, there are differences. Triazolam appears to cause more rebound insomnia than either midazolam or zolpidem (Soldatos, Dikeos, & Whitehead, 1999).

Cross-Tolerance

There is cross-tolerance between the benzodiazepines and other depressant drugs. The drowsiness sometimes produced by higher therapeutic doses of the benzodiazepines is less often seen in people who have a recent history of barbiturate and alcohol abuse (Greenblatt & Shader, 1974).

One study has shown that tolerance develops after only one exposure to the motor-impairing effect of alcohol, barbiturates, and benzodiazepines in mice. Animals that are tolerant to the barbiturates are cross-tolerant to alcohol and the benzodiazepines, and benzodiazepine-tolerant animals are tolerant to the effects of alcohol but show only weak or partial tolerance to the barbiturates. This suggests that the tolerance to barbiturates and benzodiazepines may arise from mechanisms that are similar but not identical (Khanna, Kalant, Chau, & Shah, 1998).

WITHDRAWAL

In laboratory animals, it has been shown that many benzodiazepines will cause physical dependence similar to barbiturates, and there is a cross-dependence between phenobarbital and many benzodiazepines; that is, withdrawal from phenobarbital can be blocked by benzodiazepines (Gerak et al., 2001). Nevertheless, the symptoms of barbiturate withdrawal can be much more severe than those of benzodiazepine withdrawal, as described later.

In humans, barbiturate withdrawal was first described in the medical literature in 1905, 2 years after the introduction of the first barbiturate into medical practice. In spite of this early report, the medical literature on barbiturate withdrawal was contradictory until the 1930s, when the weight of evidence could no longer be denied.

The benzodiazepines have been used widely in medical practice since the early 1960s, but, as with the barbiturates, years passed before their ability to cause physical dependence at therapeutic doses become widely acknowledged. It has been known for some time that withdrawal from relatively high doses of benzodiazepines taken for a long time will cause symptoms similar to those of withdrawal from barbiturates and alcohol: agitation, depression, abdominal pain, delirium tremens, insomnia, and seizures (Greenblatt & Shader, 1974; Hollister, Motzenbecker, & Degan, 1961). Such dependence was believed to be rare, and most physicians were confident that there was no chance of physical dependence in their patients who received low therapeutic doses. An early study estimated that physical dependence occurred in only 1% of patients receiving diazepam for various emotional disorders (Bows, 1965). In fact, physical dependence was considered so unlikely that one group of researchers concluded, "It is time to dispel the myth that the unsuspecting housewife must be protected from the careless prescribing of dangerous drugs likely to produce lifelong addiction" (Rickels, Downing, & Winokur, 1978, p. 403). It soon became apparent, however, that therapeutic doses of benzodiazepines could cause rather unpleasant withdrawal symptoms and could lead to excessive use by some individuals.

In a classic study by Cosmo Hallstrom and Malcolm Lader (1981), four patients were gradually weaned from a high daily dose (average of 135 mg) of diazepam, and six patients were weaned from a low daily dose (average of 20 mg/day). After the drug was withdrawn, patients in both groups showed symptoms that included anxiety, sleep disturbances, intolerance to bright lights and loud noises, weight loss, unsteady gait, and numbness or tingling feelings. There were also changes in brainwave activity and duplication of the increase in the electrical activity of the cortex that follows a loud noise (auditory evoked potential). These changes were similar in both the high- and low-benzodiazepine subjects. Most of the symptoms peaked in intensity after 5 days and were gone within 2 weeks. Other researchers found similar withdrawal effects with therapeutic doses (Crawford, 1981; Petursson & Lader, 1981). Therapeutic doses were clearly causing problems.

David E. Smith of the Haight-Ashbury Free Medical Clinic and Donald R. Wesson (1983) suggested, on the basis of extensive clinical experience, that there are actually two types of withdrawal from benzodiazepines: *sedative-hypnotic withdrawal* and *low-dose withdrawal*. Each has a different set of symptoms (Griffiths & Sannerud, 1987). Each type has a different time course, and the occurrence of both types of withdrawal may overlap.

Sedative-Hypnotic Withdrawal

The sedative-hypnotic type of withdrawal involves tremors, delirium, cramps, and, possibly, convulsions. These are similar to the symptoms of barbiturate and alcohol withdrawal (described in Chapter 6), and they are the symptoms described in studies of the effects of high doses of benzodiazepines. Sedative-hypnotic withdrawal can be expected in people who have taken the drug in higher-than-recommended therapeutic doses for at least a month. Generally, the withdrawal symptoms start within a few days of abstinence and are gone within about 10 days. These withdrawal symptoms are more likely to be seen with benzodiazepines that have short half-lives because blood levels of these drugs fall more rapidly than blood levels of the longer-acting drugs.

Low-Dose Withdrawal

Low-dose benzodiazepine withdrawal symptoms are seen in some individuals after low therapeutic doses have been taken for longer than 6 months. They emerge more slowly and include anxiety, panic, irregular heartbeat, increased blood pressure, impairment of memory and concentration, feelings of unreality, muscle spasm, and a sensitivity to lights and sounds. Patients consistently report feeling as though they are walking on cotton wool, in a mist, or wearing a veil over their eyes. There are frequent reports of perceptual difficulties, such as sloping walls or floors, and distortion of reality and self-perception: "Everything feels unreal or distant"; "I feel I'm not really me"; "My head feels like a huge balloon" (Ashton, 1984, p. 1138).

Very often, these feelings come in cycles or waves; their frequency may vary with each symptom (Ashton, 1984). Smith and Wesson (1983) suggest that many symptoms cycle every 10 days. There are no consistent data on the duration of withdrawal. It has been reported to last as briefly as 2 weeks (Owen & Tyrer, 1983) and as long as a year (Ashton, 1984; Smith & Wesson, 1983).

It is not clear how many users of benzodiazepines at therapeutic doses have withdrawal symptoms; estimates range from 15 to 44% (Higgitt, Lader, & Fonagy, 1985). It is also not clear why certain people may be more susceptible than others.

As with most withdrawal symptoms, both the sedative-hypnotic type and the low-dose type of symptoms disappear quickly when the withdrawn drug is resumed. The low-dose withdrawal symptoms are especially sensitive to resumption of treatment and can be controlled with only a few milligrams of benzodiazepine.

The benzodiazepine receptor antagonist flumazenil can precipitate these low-dose symptoms in long-term users of benzodiazepines at therapeutic doses (the equivalent of 11.2 mg diazepam/day). The precipitated symptoms are similar to nonprecipitated symptoms except that they are more likely to include panic attacks. The magnitude of the withdrawal symptoms was correlated with the daily dose of benzodiazepine but was not related to the duration of use (Mintzer, Stoller, & Griffiths, 1999).

Individuals who have taken high doses of benzodiazepines for longer than 6 months may well experience both types of withdrawal (see Figure 7-2). Note that other changes may occur when the benzodiazepines are stopped. These changes are due to symptom

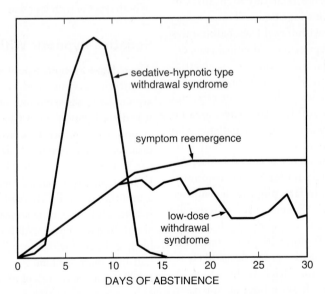

FIGURE 7-2 Two types of withdrawal symptoms that may be seen after use of the benzodiazepines. The sedative-hypnotic type of withdrawal has severe symptoms but lasts only a few days. The low-dose benzodiazepine withdrawal symptoms are less intense but last much longer and seem to come and go in cycles. Also shown is the reemergence of symptoms that were there before the benzodiazepine was started and may reappear, causing more distress. (Adapted from Smith & Wesson, 1983, p. 89)

reemergence—the expression of symptoms that were present before the drug was started and were suppressed while the drug was being used. Often these reemergent symptoms are more intense than the original symptoms experienced before taking the drug (Lader, 2011). Reemerging symptoms are not really withdrawal symptoms, but their presence contributes to and complicates benzodiazepine withdrawal.

SELF-ADMINISTRATION IN HUMANS

Laboratory Studies

CHOICE EXPERIMENTS. In a study that used normal human participants and has been replicated several times, Johanson and Uhlenhuth (1980) gave people a choice between capsules of different colors. In an earlier part of the experiment, participants had been given each of the capsules twice, so they knew what effect each colored capsule would have, even though they did not know what each capsule contained. In this experiment, the participants chose capsules containing amphetamine much more often than a placebo, but they did not choose diazepam more often than a placebo (Griffiths et al., 1980). In a similar procedure, lorazepam was not chosen more often than a placebo; in fact, at higher doses, participants chose a placebo more frequently than lorazepam or diazepam (de Wit, Johanson, & Uhlenhuth, 1984; Johanson & Uhlenhuth, 1980).

In a similar study, participants were selected for high anxiety levels and given the choice between diazepam and a placebo. The highly anxious participants reported that the capsules containing the diazepam reduced their anxiety, but they did not choose the diazepam capsule more frequently than a placebo. This finding suggests that relief from anxiety is not a motivation for benzodiazepine self-administration and that highly anxious people are not particularly at risk for benzodiazepine abuse (de Wit & Johanson, 1987), although other experiments have not found this latter effect (McCracken, de Wit, Uhlenhuth, & Johanson, 1990).

It has been demonstrated that moderate alcohol users and people with a history of sedative-hypnotic and alcohol abuse would choose benzodiazepines more frequently than a placebo (de Wit & Griffiths, 1991; Evans et al., 1996). In another study, people chose benzodiazepines when the choice was reliably followed by a task

that required relaxation and earned them some money (Silverman et al., 1994).

SELF-ADMINISTRATION EXPERIMENTS. In a study conducted by Roland Griffiths and colleagues (Griffiths, Bigelow, & Lieberson, 1979) at the Johns Hopkins University School of Medicine, pentobarbital was made available to male volunteers in an experimental hospital ward setting. The participants, all of whom had a history of sedative drug abuse, could earn an administration of a drug by riding an exercise bicycle for 15 minutes. Five of the seven participants continued to self-administer doses of 90 mg (a high level) of pentobarbital over the 10 days of the experiment, indicating that the drug acted as a positive reinforcer in humans. The same experiment also showed that participants would not self-administer a placebo. Diazepam was self-administered by some participants but not as frequently or as reliably as the barbiturate.

Outside the Laboratory

Outside the laboratory, humans show two patterns of benzodiazepine self-administration apart from use for legitimate medical conditions. In the legal or *iatrogenic* (physician-caused) pattern, the drug is prescribed for its effects as an aid to sleep or anxiety problems and is then continued unnecessarily, or the dose is escalated. In the street-use pattern, the drugs are obtained illegally and are taken at high doses. Of these two patterns, the first is more common.

IATROGENIC USE. Benzodiazepines are widely prescribed for a variety of symptoms. In many cases, the prescription and use are entirely consistent with appropriate treatment of medical conditions; however, the use of these drugs often changes in nature and may cause problems for the patient in a couple of different ways. As we have seen, if they are prescribed at too high a dose or for too long, they can cause physical dependence and require special treatment to avoid withdrawal when the drug is discontinued. In addition, a patient may become motivated by the reinforcing effects of the drug and may start exhibiting an inappropriate amount of behavior toward obtaining the drug in increasing amounts. Such a patient may learn exactly how to tailor a medical history so that a physician will predictably prescribe the desired drug or may go "doctor shopping" to find a compliant physician. Some patients may refuse to stop taking a drug and not consider alternative therapies, even though the drug is causing adverse side effects or the doctor recommends stopping. Other signs include a tendency to escalate doses, requests for early refills of the prescription because the prescription was "lost," and so on.

According to the popular stereotype, the typical Valium user is a well-educated, middle-class, suburban housewife who is denied personal or professional fulfillment by her husband and family. In fact, this does not appear to be the case. The Balter survey found that typical long-term users of anxiolytic benzodiazepines tended to be over 50, female, and suffering from substantial anxiety and some significant chronic health problem, such as heart disease or arthritis. This survey showed that, in general, most of the people who are receiving long-term benzodiazepines are receiving them for legitimate medical reasons—usually anxiety. Mellinger, Balter, and Uhlenhuth (1984) showed that at least half of long-term users suffered from high levels of psychic distress (anxiety).

Survey results indicate that large numbers of people who report severe symptoms of anxiety do not report the use of benzodiazepines. Given this information, some observers have concluded that benzodiazepines are underused rather than overused because there appear to be many people who could benefit from benzodiazepine use but are not receiving benzodiazepine treatment (Uhlenhuth, de Wit, Balter, Johanson, & Mellinger, 1988).

The extent of abuse or misuse of the benzodiazepines is not well understood. In one study, 176 people were referred to an outpatient clinic for assessment of benzodiazepine abuse. Fifty-six percent used benzodiazepines in clinically appropriate doses but did so longer than recommended by their physician. Others who took doses larger than prescribed did so in combination with other substances, such as alcohol, opioids, and cannabis (Juergens, 1993). In another study of 136 clinic clients who were found to be benzodiazepine abusers, less than 0.5% abused benzodiazepines alone. Most were well-educated Caucasian females more than 30 years old, and they received their benzodiazepines legally from a physician. Diazepam was the preferred benzodiazepine, particularly by primary cocaine and opioid users (Malcolm, Brady, Johnston, & Cunningham, 1993). The

use of alprazolam and diazepam is a particular problem for many people on methadone maintenance (Sellers et al., 1993), although some research shows that heroin addicts and those on methadone maintenance have a distinct preference for flunitrazepam (Woods & Winger, 1997).

Because flunitrazepam appears to be different from other benzodiazepines in terms of its potential for recreational use, a number of researchers have attempted to discover if there is anything different about it that causes this effect. So far, no special property of flunitrazepam has become apparent (Mintzer & Griffiths, 1998; Woods & Winger, 1997).

STREET USE. When used for recreational purposes, the benzodiazepines are most often taken in conjunction with some other drug. Often that drug is alcohol, but, surprisingly, it has been reported that 60 to 70% of patients on methadone maintenance use benzodiazepines (often to boost the effects of the methadone). Laboratory data also support the claim that diazepam will enhance the subjective and physiological effects of opioids (Griffiths & Sannerud, 1987), although one study showed that diazepam did not alter the blood levels of methadone and vice versa (Preston, Griffiths, Clone, Darwin, & Gorodetzky, 1986).

Figure 7-3 shows the use of sedative-hypnotics (barbiturates; Panel A) and anxiolytics (Panel B) by male and female college students in the United States from 1980 to 2010. The graphs represent the number of students who reported using this class of drugs within the past year when it was not prescribed to them by a physician. Use of both sedatives and tranquilizers was high in the early 1980s but then declined until the mid-1990s. Following that decline, drug use rose steadily until the mid-2000s before it again started to decline. Prevalence of reported use is similar between men and women (Johnston, O'Malley, Bachman, & Schulenberg, 2011).

SELF-ADMINISTRATION IN NONHUMANS

Like humans, rats and monkeys will readily work to give themselves infusions of all types of barbiturates, although it appears that the short-acting barbiturates may maintain higher rates of responding than the longer-acting barbiturates (Winger, Stitzer, & Woods,

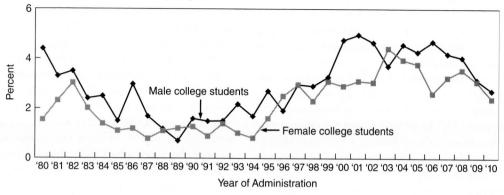

A. Sedative-Hypnotic use in the past year

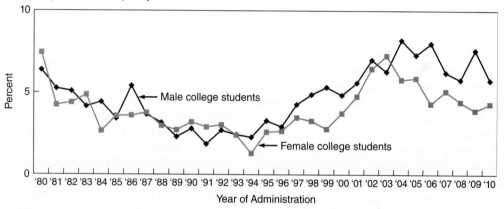

B. Anxiolytic use in the past year

FIGURE 7-3 Trends in the number of male and female college students who reported using a sedative-hypnotic (barbiturate) or an anxiolytic within the past year without a prescription from a doctor. Panel A (top) shows sedative-hypnotic use, and Panel B (bottom) shows anxiolytic use. (Data from Johnson et al., 2011)

1975). Response patterns maintained by barbiturates on fixed interval (FI) and fixed response (FR) schedules are similar to typical response patterns maintained by other reinforcers and take place at doses that do not appear to cause physical dependence (Kelleher, 1976).

Laboratory animals will also self-administer benzodiazepines both intravenously and orally (Rowlett, Platt, Lelas, Atack, & Dawson, 2005; Stewart, Lamaire, Roche, & Meisch, 1994). Currently, there are many demonstrations of self-administration of both short- and long-acting benzodiazepines (Gerak et al., 2001; Griffiths, Lucas, Bradford, Brady, & Snell, 1981), although short-acting benzodiazepines like triazolam maintain higher rates of responding than long-acting benzodiazepines (Griffiths et al., 1981). Where comparisons have been made, the

positive reinforcing effects of benzodiazepines are not as robust as those of barbiturates (Griffiths, Lamb, Sannerud, Ator, & Brady, 1991) and benzodiazepines that do not modulate activity of α_1-containing $GABA_A$ receptor complexes are less reinforcing than those that do (Rudolph & Knoflach, 2011). In intravenous self-administration studies using rhesus monkeys, Rowlett and colleagues (Rowlett et al., 2005; Rowlett & Leas, 2007) found that the breaking point on a progressive ratio schedule of reinforcement was highest for the α_1-subunit modulating drugs, diazepam, midazolam, and zolpidem, and lower for a drug (L-838417) that antagonizes α_1 subunits but acts as a partial agonist at α_2, α_3, and α_5 subunit-containing $GABA_A$ receptor complexes. This finding suggests that anxiolytics and sedative-hypnotics that selectively target

α_1 subtype-containing $GABA_A$ receptors may be more reinforcing and have higher abuse potential, although efficacy at α_2 and α_3 subtypes has also been shown to play a role in benzodiazepine abuse (Ator, Atack, Hargreaves, Burns, & Dawson, 2010).

The reinforcing effects of the benzodiazepines, even long-acting ones, can be enhanced by a period of exposure to the drug or to other barbiturates or benzodiazepines. In one study, Harris, Glaghorn, and Schoolar (1968) gave rats a choice between drinking a solution of chlordiazepoxide and drinking pure water. The rats always chose water. Then, for 25 days, the rats had to drink the chlordiazepoxide in order to obtain food. After this period of forced consumption, the rats showed a preference for the chlordiazepoxide, even when the alternate choice was water. Other research has shown that the effect of prior exposure does not depend on the development of physical dependence (Ator & Griffiths, 1992).

Taken together with the human choice and self-administration laboratory studies that show reinforcing effects in people with a history of sedative-hypnotic abuse, it appears that, at least for the longer-acting benzodiazepines administered orally, a period of forced consumption greatly enhances the reinforcing effect of the drug. In this respect, benzodiazepines are very different from the barbiturates, which are very powerful reinforcers right from the start in humans and nonhumans.

Subjective reports and epidemiological studies suggest that flunitrazepam may have a higher potential for use than any other benzodiazepine because it is preferred by many users, but self-administration and drug discrimination studies with laboratory animals have been unable to find any difference between the effects of flunitrazepam and other short-acting benzodiazepines like midazolam and triazolam (Gerak et al., 2001). It has also been noted that people on methadone maintenance seem to use benzodiazepines to "boost" methadone's subjective effect. In one study using baboons, self-administration of flunitrazepam was enhanced in animals who were administered methadone concurrently (Ator, Griffiths, & Weerts, 2005).

HARMFUL EFFECTS

Reproduction

Initially, it was thought that the benzodiazepines interfered with the menstrual cycle and fertility in women, but such concerns have not been substantiated. In males, chlordiazepoxide has been reported to cause a failure to ejaculate, but this does not appear to be a common problem (Greenblatt & Shader, 1974). In fact, there have been reports that the benzodiazepines improve reproductive success in previously infertile couples.

Early epidemiological studies suggested that the benzodiazepines might cause birth defects in humans. These effects have not been confirmed (Eros, Czeizel, Rockenbauer, Sorensen, & Olsen, 2002), but there is evidence of behavioral teratogenic effects in rats. In one study with rats, pups born to mothers injected with diazepam during the third (last) week of gestation showed absence of locomotion responses and the acoustic startle responses seen in normal rats (Kellogg, Tervo, Ison, Paisi, & Miller, 1980). In fact, it appears that exposure to benzodiazepines in utero affects the reaction of animals to various stressors, and these effects may be different at different developmental stages throughout the life span and may even extend into old age (Kellogg, 1988).

Withdrawal symptoms have been reported in infants when the mothers used normal therapeutic doses of diazepam during pregnancy. The withdrawal symptoms—tremors, irritability, and hyperactivity—are similar to withdrawal from opioids. They start 2.5 to 6 hours after delivery and can be treated with barbiturates (Rementiria & Bhatt, 1977). Even benzodiazepines given during labor have been reported to affect the newborn infant by depressing respiration, creating a reluctance to feed, and decreasing the ability to maintain normal body temperature (floppy baby syndrome). Apgar scorers (ratings of cardiac and respiratory functioning at birth) are also depressed. The drug has been detected in the blood of a baby up to 8 days after delivery (Cree, Meyer, & Hailey, 1973).

As with most drugs, it is probably unwise to take benzodiazepines at any time during pregnancy or even if pregnancy is possible. This could be a serious problem because benzodiazepines are prescribed much more frequently for women than for men.

Overdose

The main reason why benzodiazepines have replaced the barbiturates is that they are much safer. The major danger from barbiturate use is overdose, either accidental or deliberate. At one time, more than 15,000 deaths per year in the United States resulted from barbiturate overdose; without doubt, the majority of these were suicides.

Benzodiazepine overdoses are not as dangerous as barbiturate overdoses. About 12% of drug overdose emergencies in the United States involve the benzodiazepines, but because benzodiazepines do not cause significant respiratory depression, the outcomes of benzodiazepine overdoses are seldom fatal, and there seem to be no lasting effects. Doses as high as 2,250 mg of chlordiazepoxide have been tolerated with symptoms of sleep and drowsiness. There is no deep coma or severe respiratory depression, and the victims can usually be awakened (Greenblatt & Shader, 1974). Most symptoms disappear within 48 hours. Deaths due solely to benzodiazepine overdose are more likely to result from the shorter-acting drugs like nitrazepam, temazepam, and flunitrazepam (Drummer & Ransom, 1996). Hospital emergency rooms will often use flumazenil, the benzodiazepine receptor antagonist, to treat benzodiazepine overdoses.

Although the benzodiazepines are relatively safe by themselves, they intensify the effect of other depressants, such as alcohol and the barbiturates. The benzodiazepines can be, and frequently are, fatal when combined with high doses of alcohol (Torry, 1976).

TREATMENT

Anyone wishing to discontinue using the benzodiazepines after a long period of use should not attempt it alone because the withdrawal can be severe and may involve convulsions, which require medical treatment. Withdrawal should be done under medical supervision with the aid of a physician who appreciates the problem. Although withdrawal can usually be accomplished on an outpatient basis, hospitalization may be necessary, especially for patients with a history of seizures, psychotic episodes, or high doses of the drug (Higgitt et al., 1985).

The approach to detoxification from a benzodiazepine is similar to detoxification from other sedative drugs and alcohol. The best way to proceed is to gradually reduce the daily dose of the benzodiazepine, a technique called *GDR, gradual dose reduction*. Withdrawal should be conducted over an 8 to 12 week period and be completed in no more than 6 months (Lader, 2011). This is most successfully done in conjunction with counseling, group therapy, or Cognitive Behavioral Therapy, and careful monitoring of the patient's withdrawal symptoms. It is important that the patient be told exactly what symptoms to expect and how long they will last. It is sometimes helpful to also seek social support from self-help groups and members of the family. The patient should be taught various strategies for coping, not only with the withdrawal but also with the re-emergence of the symptoms for which the benzodiazepine was prescribed in the first place (Colvin, 1983). The most intense withdrawal and the greatest anxiety and panic are experienced while the last few milligrams of the drug are being withdrawn (Lader, 2011; Smith & Wesson, 1983). Treatment of iatrogenic physical dependence is usually successful: 88 to 100% of patients stop their benzodiazepine use (Higgitt et al., 1985).

When withdrawal has been managed, various therapies may be attempted, but it is important to match the patient with an appropriate therapeutic strategy. Options include group therapies with people who have similar problems, education, family involvement, a 12-step program similar to Alcoholics Anonymous in which participants are encouraged to "work" a program of recovery, and the support of peer groups and a physician who understand the process.

An illegal user seldom abuses benzodiazepines except as an adjunct to some other addiction, such as alcohol, heroin, or amphetamine, and treatments usually focus on the primary addiction.

Tobacco and Nicotine

Tobacco is the only known natural source of *nicotine*, and it is now clear that nicotine is the active ingredient in tobacco. The tobacco plant belongs to the nightshade family of plants (*Solanaceae*). The genus *Nicotiana*, of which there are two subgenera, *rustica* and *tabacum*, is used for its nicotine content. Both subgenera contain many species and varieties that differ quite widely in physical characteristics. By far, the principal source of tobacco today is *N. tabacum*, which is cultivated in temperate climates all over the world. Species of *N. rustica* are not widely grown commercially. While it has a higher nicotine content (up to 9%), it is reputedly harder to cultivate. Wild *N. rustica* has been widely used as a medicine and for shamanistic rituals by native peoples of North and South America. In addition to nicotine, it contains other psychoactive substances such as the hallucinogen *harmine* (see Chapter 15). Cultivated strains of tobacco have much higher nicotine content than any wild members of the same genus. The actual nicotine content of the cured tobacco leaf may reach as high as 6.17%.

Although some scholars have claimed that tobacco originated in Africa or Asia, we are now certain that its origins are exclusively American and that the aboriginal peoples of North and South America were the first and only users of the drug at the time of the European discovery of the New World. The earliest known illustration of smoking is reproduced in Figure 8-1. This stone carving from a Mayan temple shows a priest smoking what appears to be a cigar or a reed cigarette.

The plants of *N. tabacum* are usually about 2 meters tall and have long, broad, pointed leaves that are harvested two or three at a time from the bottom of the plant as they mature, although for some types of curing the entire plant is cut at one time. In 1809, a French chemist, Louis Nicolas Vauquelin, claimed to have discovered the active ingredient in tobacco (he called it *nicotianine*), but his extracts were not pure. It was not until 1828 that pure nicotine was isolated by the German chemists L. Posselt and F. A. Reimann.

PREPARATIONS

The leaves of the tobacco plant are cured and prepared in different ways, depending on the intended use of the tobacco. The vast bulk of tobacco is consumed as cigarettes or cigars and in pipes. After harvesting, tobacco for burning is usually dried or cured and then fermented, a process that is not really fermentation as described in Chapter 6, but oxidization. Drying and fermenting cause a change in the chemistry of the plant and influence the taste and other characteristics of the tobacco.

Tobacco for chewing is specially processed and flavored. Traditional tobacco snuff is made by drying the leaves, grinding them to a very fine powder, and mixing the powder with various aromatic and flavoring agents. Dry snuff was usually snorted into the nostrils in the form of a dry powder, but this practice is no longer used. Modern snuff is sometimes called *moist snuff*. It is not inhaled, but placed in the mouth and tucked under the tongue or between the lip and the gums. It is not chewed and, unlike traditional chewing tobacco, does not require therapies for the treatment of smoking addictions. These will be discussed in more detail later in this chapter. They include nicotine gum, nicotine nasal spray, nicotine inhaler, nicotine patches, and lozenges.

The latest addition to the arsenal of nicotine delivery devices is the e-cigarette, a battery-operated device that resembles a traditional cigarette and simulates tobacco smoking. It consists of a disposable or refillable cartridge containing nicotine mixed with propylene glycol and, in some cases, flavors, and an electronic heating device that can aerosolize the nicotine solution. When air is drawn in through the mouthpiece, it triggers the aerosolizing device and a nicotine aerosol is released and drawn into the mouth and lungs.

HISTORY

Every early European explorer, from Columbus on, commented on one aspect of the life of the native peoples of North America: their use of tobacco. At San Salvador, the site of Columbus's first landfall in 1492, the local inhabitants presented him with some "dry leaves," which Columbus concluded "must be a thing much appreciated among them." Later members of his expedition went ashore in search of the Great Khan. They found no Khan, but they did observe the natives smoking cigars, something that they did not appreciate or understand. They reported that the natives were "perfuming themselves" and that they "drink smoke." One of these men, Rodrigo de Jerez, would later become all too familiar with the significance of the activity; he took up smoking and was imprisoned by the court of the Inquisition for this "devilish habit."

Jean Nicot, the French ambassador to Portugal, became convinced of the medical usefulness of the plant and sent seeds to the royal family in France. Because of his great interest in this plant, Nicot's name was given to the genus *Nicotiana* and subsequently to the alkaloid nicotine.

Tobacco use spread as a wonder cure, but it did not take long to catch on as a recreational activity, although many users were quick to point out that they were really using it to prevent diseases, such as the Plague. When Samuel Pepys, the British diarist, encountered houses where victims of the Great Plague had perished, he felt "an ill conception of myself and my smell, so that I was forced to buy some roll-tobacco to smell and to chew, which took away the apprehension" (Brooks, 1952, p. 40). This association of tobacco with healing lasted into the Victorian era.

FIGURE 8-1 A priest smoking a cigar or reed pipe: Carving found in a Mayan temple. Native American priests and shamans used tobacco in sacred rituals. Their rituals centered on foretelling the future and curing illness.

spitting. Sometimes additives are used for flavor and to enhance absorption of the nicotine. Often tobacco used as moist snuff is not fermented, but pasteurized, a process where the product is steamed. There are numerous varieties of moist snuff including dipping tobacco and a product from Sweden called *snus*.

More recently, other nicotine delivery systems have been developed, mostly as nicotine replacement

The English were among the last Europeans to take up tobacco. In the late sixteenth century, British sailors and sea captains, among them Hawkins, Drake, and Raleigh, carried the habit home from the West Indies. Raleigh's name has long been associated with tobacco not only because he is credited with the introduction of smoking to the English court but also because he founded the colony at Virginia that was later to owe its survival and prosperity to tobacco cultivation.

Although the British were late to take to the drug, they made up for their tardiness in the popularity tobacco acquired. By the end of the sixteenth century, the demand for the leaf was beginning to cause concern in some quarters. In 1604, King James I published an antitobacco essay titled *A Counterblaste to Tobacco*, in which he refuted all the arguments claiming medical benefits from smoking. As a matter of fact, James I anticipated most of the modern antismoking campaigns, even to claiming that smoking affects "the inward parts of man, soiling and infecting them with a vicious and oily kind of Soote, as hath been found in some great tobacco takers, that hath after their death opened" (Arber, 1895, p. 111).

The tobacco that the English were smoking all this time (and that so angered the king) was imported from Spain at great expense, but the English colony at Virginia was to change all that. The colonists, under John Rolfe, had gotten off to a very bad start. They suffered shipwreck and starvation and were at the point of quitting when Rolfe decided to try growing some Spanish tobacco seeds (*Nicotiana tabacum*) in the soil of Virginia. The experiment was a great success. The plants prospered, and in 1616 a shipload of Virginia tobacco was sent to Britain. At first, the English were skeptical, but the quality of Virginia tobacco was obvious, and within a decade it had replaced the Spanish imports. In spite of the king's taxes and other attempts to discourage the tobacco trade, the colony flourished and secured the English colonial presence in North America.

Smoking has been the primary means of administering tobacco throughout most of its European history, but for a time, it was eclipsed by snuffing. Powdered tobacco was either pinched between the fingers or placed on the back of the hand and then sniffed into the nostrils. The result was usually a vigorous sneeze. The early use of snuff was associated with the clergy (Pope Urban VII was an ardent snuffer), who preferred it to smoking because it was not outlawed in churches and its use could be better concealed from disapproving parishioners.

Tobacco chewing was a North American contribution. It was first observed as a habit of North American native people, but chewing was never very popular in Europe. In the early part of the nineteenth century, however, there was a strong nationalist sentiment in the new United States and a deliberate rejection of European habits and fashions; snuff was rejected, and chewing tobacco was adopted with patriotic fervor. Chewing was democratic; snuff was aristocratic. Snuff and the pipe had "filtered down from the leaders of fashion to the common folk, while chewing was a practice which . . . seeped from the common man upward into the higher ranks of society" (Robert, 1967, p. 103). The popularity of chewing prompted one Englishman, Charles MacKay, to suggest that the national emblem of the United States should be a spittoon rather than an eagle.

Like tobacco chewing, cigarette smoking had its beginnings in America. Early Spanish explorers reported that Mexican Indians smoked tobacco through *reeds*. These were hollow canes filled with tobacco and lighted so that they "burned themselves out without causing a flame." For centuries, cigarette smoking was confined to the Spanish and Portuguese empires, and, even there, it accounted for only a small part of tobacco use. Quite suddenly, in the 1840s, it became very popular in France, especially among French ladies, and it was chiefly the enthusiasm women showed for this means of smoking that stimulated its general acceptance. It was also about this time that flue-cured, or *bright*, tobacco was discovered in North Carolina. This low-nicotine, sweet, mild smoke was perfectly suited to the cigarette. Some people considered cigarettes a novelty—a fad that would soon pass—but they were wrong.

Tobacco smoking persisted unabated until the 1960s, when tobacco was dealt a severe but not fatal blow. The U.S. Surgeon General's Report of 1964, for the first time, definitively linked smoking to cancer and other diseases. This was followed in 1971 by a similar report of the Royal College of Physicians of London. The truth could no longer be hidden or ignored: Tobacco smoking was unhealthy. These statements, combined with the environmentalist and naturalist movements, were actually able to halt the growth of smoking and start a decline.

The prevalence of smoking among U.S. adults has generally declined, from 24.7% in 1997 to 19.9% in

2010 (Ward, Barnes, Freeman, & Schiller, 2010). This declining trend is shared with other developed nations around the world and is expected to continue. Based on data from the Organization for Economic Cooperation and Development (OECD), an investment firm, Citi Investments, published a report in 2011 projecting the year when smoking rates would be zero in different member states. Based on current smoking rates, it speculated that this would occur in the United States in 2046 and in the United Kingdom and Canada in 2040. Sweden, which has a current smoking rate of 15%, is projected to have no smokers by the year 2018.

Although the use of tobacco in industrialized nations is declining, tobacco consumption has been rising in the developing countries of the world by about 1.4% per year. It appears that tobacco manufacturers, discouraged by the shrinking of their traditional market, have turned their attention to populations not so well educated about the health risks of smoking (Greenlees, 2005). In response, many developing countries have been resisting aggressive marketing with stringent rules and controls but find themselves in frequent court battles (Wilson, 2010). If current trends continue, by the mid-2020s, about 85% of the world's smokers will be in poor and developing countries (American Lung Association, 2006).

Legal Status

In the United Kingdom, tobacco is not governed by the Medicines Act, and until recently, nicotine tobacco products were not regulated by the U.S. Food and Drug Administration (FDA). The FDA is entitled to regulate drugs in the United States, and a drug is defined as a substance intended by its makers (a) to affect the structure or functions of the body or (b) for use in the diagnosis, cure, mitigation, treatment, or prevention of disease. The tobacco industry had escaped FDA control by claiming that tobacco products were sold only for smoking pleasure and not for the effect of nicotine.

In February 1994, after years of planning, the commissioner of the FDA formally requested that the FDA be given the power to regulate cigarettes as drugs. This request led to a series of hearings before a subcommittee of the U.S. House of Representatives. In the course of the hearings, the commissioner outlined the argument that nicotine was addicting and presented evidence that cigarette manufacturers had knowingly

manipulated nicotine delivery of tobacco products (Kozlowski & Henningfield, 1995; Schwartz, 1994) and that, in fact, cigarettes were "nicotine delivery systems." The arguments of the FDA did not convince Congress to give it the power to regulate tobacco, but in 1996 the administration of President Clinton gave the FDA authority to reduce the access and appeal of tobacco products to children and adolescents. In 1997, a provision went into effect prohibiting sales of tobacco products to anyone under the age of 18, a measure that was ruled legal by a federal district court decision. However, in 2000, the U.S. Supreme Court ruled in a 5 to 4 decision that the FDA cannot regulate tobacco products until given authority by the Congress.

In June 2009 the U.S. Senate passed the Family Smoking Prevention and Tobacco Control Act, which finally put tobacco products under FDA control in the United States (Mundy & Etter, 2009, June 12). This bill enables the FDA to regulate the marketing and promotion of tobacco products and to set performance standards for tobacco products in order to protect the public health, but the FDA cannot ban these products. It can regulate nicotine content if there is a public health concern, but it cannot eliminate nicotine entirely. The FDA does have the authority to approve products that were introduced after February 15, 2007, and to force tobacco manufacturers to pay fees to fund FDA product reviews. The act applies to cigarettes, "roll your own" tobacco, and smokeless products. It does not, however, cover e-cigarettes as several courts have ruled that because e-cigarettes are not sold as therapeutic devices for smoking cessation, they are not "tobacco products" and are not covered by the Act (Cobb & Abrams, 2011; Peterson, 2011).

ROUTE OF ADMINISTRATION

Unlike cocaine from the coca leaf or morphine from opium, until recently nicotine from tobacco was never self-administered in its pure form. Nicotine is a highly toxic poison, and doses must be controlled precisely; too high a dose will have quite unpleasant effects. Because of its diluted concentration in tobacco, precise control of dosage can more easily be achieved when the nicotine is in its natural form. Forms of tobacco delivery that have been developed more recently, such as the patch, gum, and others, are constructed to deliver precise amounts and avoid toxic doses of nicotine.

Tobacco products have been traditionally consumed in three ways. First, the tobacco is burned, and the smoke is inhaled as with cigars, cigarettes, and pipes. A second method also uses inhalation, but the tobacco is not burned. Instead, the plant is dried and ground into fine particles, and the particles are inhaled, as with dry snuff. The third means of consuming tobacco is by putting it in the mouth, but not swallowing it, as is done with chewing tobacco and moist snuff.

Inhaling Tobacco Smoke and Tobacco

When tobacco is burned, nicotine vaporizes and can be found in the smoke and particles of ash that dissolve in the mucous membranes on the inside surface of the lungs. About 90% of inhaled nicotine is absorbed into the blood in this way (Pierce, 1941). The amount of nicotine actually delivered to the smoker is determined more by the way the cigarette is smoked than by the actual nicotine content of the cigarette; the delivered amount can vary between 0.3 and 3.2 mg per cigarette (Benowitz & Henningfield, 1994). The average cigarette contains 8 to 9 mg of nicotine, of which a typical smoker absorbs about 1 mg in the course of taking 10 puffs per cigarette (Jones, 1987). The major determinant of nicotine absorption is the volume of smoke inhaled per puff. Increasing the duration of the inhalation does not significantly increase nicotine absorption (Zacny, Stitzer, Brown, Yingling, & Griffiths, 1987).

Nicotine from tobacco smoke may also be absorbed through membranes of the mouth (*buccal membranes*), but because nicotine is a weak base with a pKa of about 8.0, absorption by this route is determined by changes in the pH of saliva. In general, cigarettes are made from flue-cured tobacco, which has an acidic smoke. This lowers the pH of saliva to about 5.3. In acidic saliva, nicotine is ionized and absorption reduced. To be absorbed, the nicotine from cigarette smoke must be inhaled into the lungs, which are so efficient that pH has no effect on absorption. By contrast, pipe and cigar tobacco is usually air-cured, and this process results in a more basic or alkaline smoke. This raises the pH of saliva to about 8.5, well within the range where ionization of nicotine is less than 50%, and absorption is rapid (see Chapter 1). Consequently, nicotine in the smoke from cigars and pipes can be absorbed from the mouth, and inhalation is not necessary (Armitage, 1973; Jones, 1987).

Nicotine absorbed from the lungs is carried directly to the heart; from there, much of the nicotine-containing blood goes straight to the brain. Because of this direct route, the nicotine does not get a chance to dissipate, so the high concentration in the lungs after a puff or rapid inhalation of smoke tends to remain in the blood as a nicotine bolus until it reaches the brain (Russell, 1976). Because nicotine is absorbed much more slowly from the capillaries of the mouth and nose, no such bolus occurs if the smoke is not inhaled.

A long-standing theory is that the bolus causes a sudden delivery of concentrated nicotine to the brain and that this is responsible for the strength of nicotine addiction, but the presence of the bolus has largely been theoretical. Jed E. Rose of Duke University Medical Center and his colleagues attempted to examine the absorption kinetics of nicotine during cigarette smoking using PET imaging with a 3-second temporal resolution and radiolabeled ^{11}C-nicotine loaded into cigarettes. He used both nicotine-dependent smokers (DS) and nondependent smokers (NDS) and scanned them while they took 10 puffs on the cigarette with 48 seconds between each puff (Rose et al., 2010).

The results are shown in Figure 8-2. The most interesting finding was that nondependent smokers absorbed nicotine faster than did the dependent smokers (see Panel A). For both groups, the effect of each puff can be seen in the form of an increase in the slope of the absorption curve, which was much more noticeable in the nondependent smokers. Panel B shows the range of brain nicotine accumulation in study participants by illustrating data for four individuals—the two DS-group participants and the two NDS-group participants with the most extreme (smallest and largest) oscillations, or changes in the slope of the line, in nicotine absorption.

Note that nicotine concentrations in the blood continue to accumulate after each puff and do not fall back as would be expected by the nicotine bolus theory. This finding was unexpected and means that the nicotine bolus theory needs to be reconsidered.

Tobacco taken in the form of traditional dry snuff is sniffed into the nostrils. With this route of administration, most of the nicotine is absorbed through the mucous membranes of the nasal cavity, although some tobacco eventually gets into the stomach and lungs. Since dry snuff is not commonly used in modern times, absorption from this route of administration has not been extensively studied.

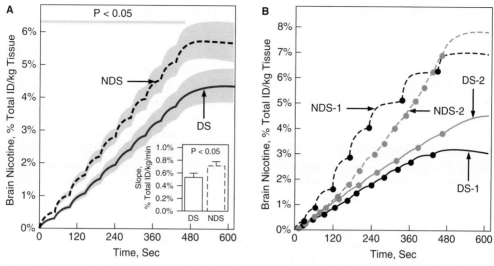

FIGURE 8-2 Panel A shows the averaged brain nicotine accumulation curves calculated for the conditions of 10 puffs with 48-second inter-puff intervals for dependent smokers (DS) and nondependent smokers (NDS). Shaded areas represent mean ± SEM. The insert shows the averaged slopes of nicotine accumulation over 7 min. Panel B gives examples of the brain nicotine accumulation curves for four smokers, two DS and two NDS, calculated for conditions when the individual number of puffs per cigarette and inter-puff intervals were measured during unrestricted smoking of one cigarette. Black dots show the time points when subsequent puffs were taken. (Rose et al., 2010)

Absorption from the Mouth and Digestive System

When tobacco is chewed or taken in the form of moist snuff, the nicotine is absorbed through the buccal membranes in the cheeks and under the tongue. With traditional chewing tobacco, the tobacco juice is spit out, so chewing is not a form of oral administration. However, with moist snuff where spitting is uncommon, nicotine in saliva that is not absorbed through the membranes of the mouth is swallowed. Nicotine is a weak base, so it will not have many lipid-soluble molecules when dissolved in solutions with a pH lower than 6. Consequently, this nicotine is not readily absorbed from the acidic digestive system. Swallowed nicotine has another disadvantage because the blood from the capillaries of the digestive tract must pass through the liver before it achieves general circulation throughout the body. Because nicotine is metabolized rapidly in the liver, much of the nicotine that is swallowed is metabolized during this first pass before it can get to the rest of the body. Although nicotine is not normally self-administered orally, a large number of poisonings occur each year among children who eat tobacco. Fortunately, the nicotine that gets into the blood in high levels induces vomiting, and the swallowed tobacco is frequently expelled before the nicotine reaches toxic levels.

Buccal absorption of nicotine can be fairly rapid, but the rate of absorption depends on the pH of the saliva, and, like tobacco smoke, that can be influenced by the properties of the tobacco. Different brands of moist snuff can create variations in the pH of the saliva. One study examined several common brands of moist snuff and found that the pH varied between 6.9 and 8.6. Later research confirmed that absorption was considerably faster from the more basic product, the one with the higher pH (Fant, Henningfield, Nelson, & Pickworth, 1999; Henningfield, Radzius, & Cone, 1995). In addition to differences in pH, there is considerable variation in the nicotine content of different products, which ranged from 7.5 to 11.4 mg/g. As a result, smokeless tobacco users who dip or chew 8 to 10 times a day could be exposed to the same amount of nicotine as people who smoke 30 to 40 cigarettes a day (Centers for Disease Control and Prevention, 1999).

Newer Forms of Nicotine Administration

Newer forms of nicotine administration have been developed for the purpose of nicotine replacement therapy for people who have given up smoking. Nicotine chewing gum was the first of these. The fact that nicotine can be absorbed transdermally (through the skin) allowed for the development of the *patch*. Nicotine-containing patches are placed on the skin, and they release nicotine in various concentrations for a period of time. Nicotine nasal sprays and lozenges have also been developed.

The patch causes a slow buildup of nicotine in the blood and maintains it at a constant level for hours. The gum will cause rises and falls in blood nicotine levels in response to its use; as a result, it causes patterns in blood nicotine that more closely resemble those caused by smoking, although peak levels reach only one-third that of smoking (Keenan, Henningfield, & Jarvik, 1995). The nasal spray causes the most cigarette-like changes in blood levels. Within 2.5 minutes of administration, nicotine reaches 85% of peak levels in the blood (Sutherland et al., 1992). Figure 8-3 shows the blood level of nicotine for 1 hour after administration by these routes.

E-cigarettes have been tested and do not appear to be efficient or reliable. There is considerable puff to puff variability in nicotine availability, and they generate minimal blood nicotine concentrations. Absorption is through the membranes of the mouth rather than the lungs and is therefore slow like nicotine gum (Cobb & Abrams, 2011).

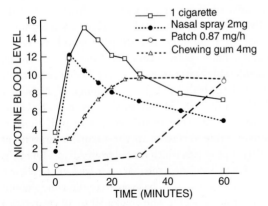

FIGURE 8-3 Nicotine blood levels for 1 hour after the administration of nicotine from various sources. (From de Wit & Zacny, 1995, p. 459)

DISTRIBUTION

The patterns of nicotine distribution in the body depend on the route of administration and the time after administration. When initial high concentrations circulate in the blood, as happens after inhalation, a high concentration is apparently retained in the brain. After about 30 minutes, the nicotine leaves the brain and is concentrated in the liver, kidneys, salivary glands, and stomach (Schmiterlow & Hanson, 1965).

Nicotine crosses most barriers, including the placenta, and may be found in the sweat, saliva, and milk of nursing women.

EXCRETION

Two pathways in the liver metabolize nicotine into two inactive metabolites, *cotinine* and *nicotine-1'-N-oxide*. The primary enzyme responsible is the cytochrome P450 2A6 (abbreviated CYP2A6) enzyme. The half-life of nicotine is variable, but is estimated to be between 90 and 150 minutes. There is evidence that smokers are able to metabolize nicotine faster than nonsmokers and that females clear nicotine from their bodies faster than males. Nicotine elimination speeds up during pregnancy and slows with age. Because nicotine metabolism occurs primarily in the liver, it speeds up after a meal because eating causes an increase in blood flow to the liver. Menthol, which is added to some cigarettes, has been shown to slow nicotine metabolism (Hukkanen, Jacob, & Benowitz, 2005).

There appear to be genetic differences in the way people metabolize nicotine. About 16 to 25% of the population has a genetic defect in the ability to metabolize nicotine. A given dose of nicotine will reach higher levels and last longer in those people. This appears to offer some protection from becoming a smoker; people with this genetic defect are less likely to become smokers, and if they do smoke, they consume fewer cigarettes (Pianezza, Sellers, & Tyndale, 1998).

The amount of nicotine excreted by the kidneys depends on the pH of the urine, as described in Chapter 1. Acidic urine (pH less than 7) tends to ionize nicotine and reduce its reabsorption through the nephron wall. Consequently, as much as 30 to 40% of administered nicotine may be eliminated in the urine. Reduced ionization at an alkaline pH increases reabsorption into the blood, and the efficiency of the kidneys is reduced, thereby shifting the load of excretion to the enzymes of the liver.

Nicotine will accumulate in the body of a smoker over the course of a day, and if smoking continues until bedtime, there also will be a day-to-day accumulation (Hukkanen et al., 2005).

NEUROPHYSIOLOGY

Acetylcholine (ACh) is a neurotransmitter used widely in both the peripheral nervous system (PNS) and central nervous system (CNS). Recall from Chapter 4 that there are two basic receptors for ACh: *muscarinic* and *nicotinic*, named after the substances first known to be agonists at each receptor, muscarine and nicotine, respectively. Nicotinic receptors (nAChRs) are located in both the CNS and PNS. In the PNS where they were first discovered, they act at neuromuscular junctions of striated muscles and control voluntary muscle action. Nicotinic

receptors are blocked by curare, a poison used on arrow and spear points by some South American tribes. Curare blocks the ability of nerves to cause muscle contraction, and this creates paralysis.

Nicotinic receptors are located in many centers in the CNS as well and participate in many brain functions. Nicotinic receptors are primarily ionotropic meaning that they regulate ion channels directly rather than through a second messenger system. Each nicotinic receptor is made up of five subunits, each one encoded by a specific gene. The five subunits are organized as a ring around a central pore. When activated by an agonist, the configuration of all five subunits changes and the pore is opened, allowing the flow of positively charged ions, primarily Na^+ and K^+ to pass through, thus they create an excitatory postsynaptic potential (see Figure 8-4). They also increase the permeability of Ca^{2+} ions, and

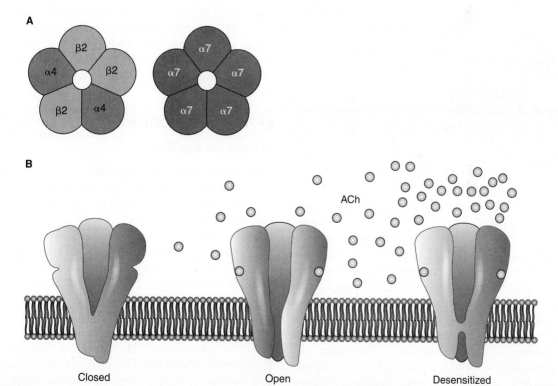

FIGURE 8-4 Panel A shows the makeup of two nAChRs. One is made up of two alpha$_4$ units and three beta$_2$ units, which is the most common hetromeric nAChR in the mammalian brain. The other, made up of seven alpha units, is the most common homomeric nAChR in the mammalian brain. Looking down from above you can see that these subunits surround a central pore or channel. Panel B illustrates a side cut-away view of the nAChR showing the subunits arranged around the central pore that passes through the membrane. There are three main configurations of the nAChR: closed pore at rest, the basal state; open pore with two acetylcholine (ACh) molecules bound to the agonist binding sites; and closed pore in the desensitized state with two ACh molecules bound. (Redrawn from Dani & Balfour, 2011)

when the receiver is located presynaptically this causes the release of neurotransmitters. Thus, nAChRs are involved in excitatory synaptic transmission when they are located postsynaptically and function as neuromodulators, stimulating transmitter release, when they are located presynaptically.

The receptive and functional characteristics of each nAChR are determined by the specific combination of the subunits of which it is composed. There are 17 different receptor subunits that have been identified, 12 of which are used by nAChRs in neurons, so a great many types of nicotinic receptors are possible. In neurons, the subunits are named alpha 2 to 10 (α_2–α_{10}) and beta 2 to 4 (β_2–β_4). These receptors can be *homomeric* (composed of receptor subunits that are all the same), but most are *heteromeric* (composed of different types of subunits). A homomeric receptor might be described as $(\alpha_7)_5$ if it is made up of five α_7 subunits. A heteromeric receptor could be described as $(\alpha_4)_2(\beta_2)_3$ if it is made of two α_4s and three β_2s. The different combinations of subunits of nAChRs determine many of their properties including sensitivity to nicotine, which ions are permitted through the ion channel, and the rate they can pass through.

The nAChR can take on three different configurations. First, there is a *basal* state with high affinity for antagonists, and the ion channel is closed. Second, there is an *active* state, with the channel open, and there exists a low affinity for agonists and antagonists. Third, there is a *desensitized* state with the ion channel closed. These are illustrated in Figure 8-4. When an agonist occupies its receptor sites (there are two for acetylcholine), located between an alpha subunit and a neighboring subunit, the nAChR enters its *active* configuration and the ion channel opens. When the agonist leaves the receptor sites, the nAChR returns to its *closed* configuration. If the receptor is repeatedly activated, the receptor will enter its *desensitized* configuration in which its receptor sites are occupied, and it is not sensitive to agonists and antagonists. It will return to its inactive or basal state after a period of time when there is no agonist bound to the receptor. The change from the resting to active states is fast (milliseconds), and the change to the desensitized state is slow (tens of milliseconds to minutes). The return to its normal, sensitized state may take hours. The change to the desensitized state can account for acute tolerance to nicotine.

When high concentrations of agonist cause the nAChRs on a membrane to stay in their desensitized state for a long period of time, this leads to upregulation—an increase in the number and sensitivity of nAChRs, so that when the levels of agonist drop, there is an excess number of highly sensitive nAChRs on the membrane. Such a mechanism may be responsible for some withdrawal effects of nicotine and an increased response to nicotine in the morning after waking.

As mentioned earlier, curare is an antagonist at nicotinic receptor sites, but because of the properties of the subunits, it antagonizes only nAChRs at neuromuscular junctions and has no effect on neuronal nAChRs. On the other hand, a drug called mecamylamine is an antagonist primarily at neuronal nAChRs. This drug is useful in research with nicotine because if a nicotine effect can be blocked by giving mecamylamine, it is reasonable to conclude that the nicotine effect was a result of its action on nAChRs.

Because of all these changes of state and upregulation, it becomes extremely difficult to know what effect an agonist is going to have on a synapse at any given time. Its effect will depend not only on the concentration of the agonist and the nature of its subunits, but on the current configuration of the nAChRs, and that depends upon the concentration of the agonist at various times in the past.

EFFECTS OF NICOTINE

Effects on the Body

PERIPHERAL NERVOUS SYSTEM. In the PNS, nicotinic receptor sites are located in the neuromuscular junctions of striated or voluntary muscles. The poisonous effects of curare result because the drug blocks these junctions, and the muscles become paralyzed; the victim can no longer breathe and dies of suffocation.

Acetylcholine is important in the functioning of both the sympathetic and parasympathetic divisions of the autonomic nervous system. The preganglionic transmission in both systems depends on nicotinic receptors so that stimulation and blocking of nAChRs can alter functioning of both the sympathetic and parasympathetic divisions. The receptor subtypes found in parasympathetic ganglia are largely alpha$_3$ and beta$_4$ subtypes.

The biphasic effect of nicotine on cholinergic transmission is reflected in the ability of nicotine to stimulate, and then inhibit, transmission of autonomic ganglia as nicotinic receptors enter their desensitized state. These two effects, however, are modified because nicotine causes the release of other neurotransmitters that affect the PNS. One such neurotransmitter is epinephrine, which produces sympathetic stimulation. When this is combined with neuromuscular and parasympathetic stimulation and blocking, the result is a very complicated array of PNS changes.

In general, at doses encountered in tobacco smoking, nicotine produces increases in heart rate and blood pressure and causes a constriction of blood vessels in the skin. This constriction causes a drop in skin temperature and is probably responsible for the cold touch that smokers have and the reason that the skin of smokers tends to wrinkle and age faster than that of nonsmokers (Daniell, 1971). The reduced blood flow to the skin also explains why smokers do not blush easily. This lack of skin color prompted one judge in the 1930s to accuse cigarettes of "deadening the sense of shame" and corrupting the morals of young people.

Nicotine also inhibits stomach secretions and stimulates the activity of the bowel. For this reason, especially for someone with little tobacco tolerance, a cigarette can act as a laxative.

CENTRAL NERVOUS SYSTEM. The effects of nicotine in the CNS are complicated. Apart from its direct effects on synapses, nicotine also stimulates the release of epinephrine from various sites in the PNS, including the adrenal glands, causing CNS arousal. Arousal is also produced by direct stimulation of the reticular activating system. Respiration is increased because of both direct and indirect stimulation of the respiration center in the brainstem. Respiratory arrest caused by an overdose of nicotine results from a block of these centers as well as of the neuromuscular junctions that control the muscles used in breathing.

Nicotine can cause muscular tremors. One British surgeon, H. J. Johnson (1965), was motivated to quit smoking when he noticed that an extra cigarette before surgery caused a fine hand tremor. In addition, there may be an inhibition of some reflexes. There is a decrease in the patellar reflex (knee jerk) after a cigarette. This effect, which is due to a lowering in the tone of voluntary muscles, appears to be a direct result of stimulation of inhibitory cells in the motor pools in the spinal cord (Domino, 1973).

Another brainstem center that is stimulated both directly and indirectly by nicotine is the vomiting center.

This effect is most noticeable in naive smokers who have no tolerance and do not have the experience to control dosage appropriately. Their initial experience with tobacco makes most young people nauseous and "green about the gills." This effect is subject to tolerance, but even experienced smokers can feel a bit "green" if they consume more than their accustomed amount of tobacco.

Higher in the brain, nicotine causes a general release of NE, DA, and other neurotransmitters, and activates systems that use these transmitters. Photon emission tomography (PET) imaging using $[^{11}C]$raclopride, which binds to D_2 receptors, demonstrates a relationship between the pleasurable effects of smoking and binding potential of the radiotracer. Participants who reported increases in euphoria while smoking their usual brand of cigarette during a PET scanning session also demonstrated significant decreases in $[^{11}C]$raclopride binding potential in the caudate region of the dorsal striatum (Barrett, Boileau, Okker, Pihl, & Dagher, 2004). Decreases in radiotracer binding potential demonstrate that receptor sites are occupied by dopamine. Conversely, participants who reported experiencing smoking-induced decreases in euphoria demonstrated increased $[^{11}C]$raclopride binding in the caudate.

Nicotine is known to increase dopamine activity in the nucleus accumbens. This effect is caused by direct stimulation of dopamine neurons in the nucleus accumbens and by the ability of nicotine to potentiate excitatory glutamatergic connections to dopaminergic neurons in the ventral tegmental area and nucleus accumbens. Nicotine increases the activity of glutamatergic neurons by boosting glutamate release through presynaptic receptors and by increasing depolarization of postsynaptic neurons (Dani & Balfour, 2011). It has been shown that nAChRs on dopaminergic neurons projecting from the ventral tegmental area to the nucleus accumbens contain the $beta_2$ subunit. It is possible to breed mice that do not have a particular gene that codes for this subunit. These are referred to as *knockout* (KO) mice. Knockout mice that do not have the gene that contains instructions for making $beta_2$ subunits ($beta_2$ KO mice) do not show a surge in dopamine in the nucleus accumbens when the ventral tegmental area is stimulated and do not self-administer nicotine.

In one study, Maskos and colleagues (2005) restored $beta_2$ subunits in nAChRs in the ventral tegmental area of $beta_2$ KO mice. As a result, these mice showed increased dopamine activity in the nucleus accumbens when the ventral tegmental area was stimulated and self-administered nicotine in the same manner as normal mice. The mice also showed improved cognitive functioning and exploratory behavior, suggesting that the presence of beta$_2$ subunits is important in cognition as well. Similar results have been found for the alpha$_4$ subunit, confirming that nAChRs containing alpha$_2$, alpha$_4$, and beta$_2$ subunits mediate nicotine reinforcement.

The presence of the alpha$_5$ subunit nAChRs appears to be associated with the aversive effects of nicotine seen at higher doses. Alpha$_5$ KO mice will self-administer much higher doses of nicotine compared to normal mice. It is known that people who carry a particular form of the gene that makes alpha$_5$ subunits with diminished function are at a much greater risk of being smokers and of suffering from respiratory disease (Tuesta, Fowler, & Kenny, 2011).

EFFECTS ON THE BEHAVIOR AND PERFORMANCE OF HUMANS

Subjective Effects

ACUTE EFFECTS. Smoking is a pleasurable experience for many people (de Wit & Zacny, 1995). In one study, nicotine was administered either by tobacco smoke inhalation or by intravenous infusion to volunteers, and their subjective responses were measured using the Addiction Research Center Inventory (ARCI). Smokers reported increased liking scores and subjective effects similar to those caused by morphine and amphetamine. These effects peaked about 1 minute after administration and were gone within a few minutes. Nonsmokers, however, did not enjoy the experience (Henningfield, Miyasato, & Jasinski, 1985; Jasinski, Johnson, & Henningfield, 1984). These subjective effects were blocked by mecamylamine (Henningfield, Miyasato, Johnson, & Jasinski, 1983). In another experiment, smokers were deprived of smoking beginning in the evening and given cigarettes with different levels of nicotine on the morning after. They were permitted to smoke the cigarettes themselves and were asked to push a button when they experienced "a rush, a buzz, or a high." Nineteen of twenty-two subjects experienced at least one such sensation. Frequency and duration of sensations were related to blood nicotine levels. These sensations lasted for about 11 seconds and

occurred with a delay of about 30 seconds after a puff (Pomerleau & Pomerleau, 1992).

CHRONIC EFFECTS. A survey in the United Kingdom has shown that smokers have lower levels of psychological well-being than nonsmokers and ex-smokers (West, 1993). In addition, even though it is typically found that mood worsens when a person stops smoking, it slowly returns to the normal smoking level after 3 or 4 weeks. What's more, it then continues to improve even further during the following 10 weeks, so the person's mood becomes even better than it was while he or she was smoking (Hughes, Higgins, & Hatsukami, 1990).

Effects on Performance

Over the years, a considerable amount of research has explored the effect of nicotine on motor and cognitive performance; the results have been inconsistent. This is partly because many experiments have not been well designed and have had shortcomings that make the results difficult to interpret. For example, if an improvement in performance is reported for participants who smoke, it is important to be able to rule out the possibility that this was not a result of nicotine improving performance that had been degraded by withdrawal. Thus, such research needs to be conducted either on smokers who have not been deprived of nicotine or on nonsmokers. A recent meta-analysis reported that 40% of studies published between 1994 and 2008 used participants who were smokers deprived of nicotine for more than 4 hours (Heishman, Kleykamp, & Singleton, 2010).

Another common problem is that many studies do not use a placebo control and do not have a double-blind design so that expectancy and placebo effects cannot be ruled out. In a 1994 review, Heishman, Taylor, and Henningfield found that 74% of studies did not use a placebo smoking condition. This situation seems to be improving, however, because in 2010, Heishman and colleagues found that this percentage had decreased to only 30% (Heishman et al., 2010). Another factor that has allowed for improvement in the design of recent studies examining the effects of nicotine on performance is that nicotine can now be administered in various forms, such as in nicotine gum, whereas most studies conducted prior to 1994 used *ad labium* smoking, which meant that the dose of nicotine was impossible to control.

To help make sense of all this research, Heishman et al. (2010) gathered articles that met their stringent criteria, which included (a) that the study participants be either nonsmokers or smokers who were not deprived of nicotine and (b) that the study use both a placebo control condition and a double-blind design. Heishman and colleagues (2010) assessed the studies' findings related to motor control, attention, and memory and were able to make some interesting conclusions, which reflect the current state of knowledge about the effect of nicotine on these functions. These conclusions are outlined below.

FINE MOTOR ABILITIES. These included finger tapping, handwriting movements, and pegboard performance. The finger tapping test measures the fastest rate at which a participant is able to tap his or her finger, and in the pegboard task, the participant must place small plastic pegs into drilled holes on a board as quickly as possible. In these measures, nicotine consistently improved performance.

ACCURACY AND SPEED OF ALERTING ATTENTION. This is measured by tests such as Choice Reaction Time (CRT), the Continuous Performance Task (CPT), and the Rapid Visual Information Processing (RVIP) task. The CRT is similar to the Clock Test, described in Chapter 2. In the CPT and RVIP, single digits are presented in quick succession (100 or 200 digits/min) on a computer screen, and detection of target sequences of numbers is indicated by a button press. In these measures, nicotine had a positive effect on both the accuracy and speed of attention.

ACCURACY AND SPEED OF ORIENTING ATTENTION. In these tasks, the participant must detect a particular target object in an array of other objects that are distractors, such as the letter "B" in a page of "P"s. Accuracy of orienting attention did not seem to be affected by nicotine, but speed of identifying the target was improved by nicotine.

ACCURACY OF SHORT-TERM AND LONG-TERM EPISODIC MEMORY. Episodic memory is memory for events, times, and places one can describe and talk about. The most common test is to show the participant a list of words and then ask him or her to recall the words or recognize them some time later. In this case, short term is a time period of less than 3 minutes, and in long-term tests, the time interval is greater than 10 minutes. The results of this task showed that nicotine did improve short-term episodic memory, but had no effect on long-term episodic memory.

WORKING MEMORY ACCURACY AND SPEED. Working memory is often tested by using the n-back test. In this test, researchers present participants with a visual display of constantly changing letters in which a target letter appears from time to time. When the target letter appears, participants are asked to report which letter had been presented either immediately before, two letters before, or three letters before the target letter. Increasing the number of letters that must be remembered increases cognitive load by taxing working memory. Nicotine had a negative effect on the accuracy of working memory, but it was not significant. Response times, however, were improved by nicotine.

This meta-analysis reaffirmed findings from the 1994 review that nicotine has a positive influence on fine motor performance and attention. An additional benefit of the 2010 review was confirmation of the beneficial effects of nicotine on memory processes. Heishman and colleagues conclude that this new evidence is a result of improved testing methodology, such as the n-back test, which had not been developed earlier. They note that their analysis found positive effects of nicotine on speed of alerting and orienting attention and working memory, but did not find significant effects on accuracy in orienting attention, long-term episodic memory, and accuracy of working memory, which suggested that these effects were mediated by nicotine's influence on the motor system.

Interestingly, nicotine has been shown to improve various aspects of cognitive functioning in patients with Alzheimer's disease and in aging laboratory rats and monkeys (Levin, 1992).

EFFECTS ON THE BEHAVIOR OF NONHUMANS
Unconditioned Behavior

Spontaneous motor activity (SMA) of rats is initially depressed by 0.8 mg/kg of nicotine, but, after 7 days of testing, this dosage produces an increase in SMA that, during repeated testing, gets greater until the increase is similar to that produced by 0.8 mg/kg of amphetamine.

It is believed that the initial depression is a result of the effect of nicotine on ACh transmission in the brain, an effect that disappears with tolerance after a few days. Once the ACh effect decreases, the increase in epinephrine causes an increase in SMA in a manner similar to amphetamine (Morrison & Stephenson, 1972b; Stolerman, Fink, & Jarvik, 1973).

Conditioned Behavior

After an initial suppression of all behavior at higher doses, the effects of nicotine on both positively and aversively motivated behavior are similar to amphetamine: The effect is dependent on control rate; high rates are depressed, and low rates are increased (Morrison, 1967; Pradhan, 1970). Like amphetamine, nicotine does not appear to increase responses that have been suppressed by response-contingent shock (Morrison & Stephenson, 1972a).

Nicotine does disrupt the ability of rats to withhold responding on a DRL (differential reinforcement of low response rate) schedule in a manner similar to amphetamine; although this effect does not appear on the initial exposure to the drug, it takes 10 repeated doses (Kirshenbaum et al., 2011). This effect can be blocked by the nAChR antagonist, mecamylamine.

This great similarity between the effects of nicotine and amphetamine on operant behavior suggests that many of these effects are likely brought about by a similar mechanism. Because amphetamine increases activity at catecholamine synapses and nicotine causes the general release of epinephrine and stimulates DA and NE synapses, it is possible that many of these behavioral effects of nicotine are a result of the release of catecholamines (Pradhan, 1970). This increase in catecholamine activity, however, depends on the action of nicotine at its receptor sites because most of these behavioral effects can be blocked by with mecamylamine (Morrison, 1967).

Because nicotine has been shown to improve certain cognitive tasks in humans, there has been considerable interest in the effects of nicotine in laboratory animals on tasks that model various aspects of human cognition. Popke, Mayorga, Fogle, and Paule (2000) used a number of such tasks to examine the effects of nicotine on cognition of rats. In one test, a repeated incremental acquisition task, rats were required to learn a sequence of lever presses on three levers. The session started with presses on one lever producing reinforcement, but eventually required the rat to learn a specific pattern of six lever presses on the three levers to earn reinforcement. On this task, there is no effect of nicotine on accuracy, but speed of responding was increased at moderate doses. Similarly, nicotine enhanced speed of performance on a conditioned discrimination task, which is like a matching to sample task. In this task, animals are presented with one of two stimuli (e.g., either a loud sound or a soft sound). After a delay, they are required to press a particular lever for reinforcement. The animal must remember which stimulus was presented to know which lever to press. Increasing doses of nicotine increased the speed of pressing the lever, but had no effect on accuracy.

Another test used by Popke and colleagues (2000) was a timing test, in which rats were required to hold down a lever for 10 to 14 seconds in order to earn a reward. This task was disrupted by nicotine administration, even at the lowest dose. Nicotine had a similar effect on DRL, which required that the rat withhold responding for 10 seconds, but not more than 14 seconds, in order to receive reinforcement. Nicotine disrupted accuracy of DRL responding by causing the rats to respond too soon. Thus, it appeared that nicotine had no effect on learning tasks but interfered with timing tasks and the ability to withhold responding (Popke et al., 2000). Based on these results, the researchers suggested that nicotine may not be useful in the treatment of cognitive deficits in humans, especially in conditions where there is a deficit in inhibiting responding such as in attention deficit hyperactivity disorder (ADHD).

The Popke et al. study did not find that nicotine improved working memory using the delayed matching to sample task, but others have found that nicotine facilitated working memory in the radial arm maze. The radial arm maze consists of a central platform with arms (usually eight, but there can be more) radiating from it. A food cup is located at the end of each arm, but, from the center of the maze, the rat cannot see if there is food in the cup. After the rat finds food in one arm, it must return to the center and try another arm until it finds all the food. The rat normally does not enter an arm from which it has already retrieved the food. This means that it must remember the arms it has already visited. When a rat enters an arm for the second time, this is considered an error. Many researchers have found that nicotine improves performance on this task and increases the number of arms the rat enters before making an error. Not only is this effect seen after a single acute administration of nicotine, but during chronic administration for 21 days. This improvement in performance can last for 2 weeks after the end of the chronic administration (Rezvani & Levin, 2001).

It has also been shown that withdrawal from 0.4 mg/kg of nicotine can disrupt the ability of rats to avoid a shock in the same manner that nicotine withdrawal can interfere with the behavior of humans (Morrison, 1974).

DRUG STATE DISCRIMINATION

In a drug state discrimination task, nicotine is an effective cue in a dosage range similar to that which alters operant behavior. It has been shown that 0.2 mg/kg of nicotine can be used as a cue and will not generalize to various doses of epinephrine, pentobarbital, physostigmine, chlordiazepoxide, or caffeine. The stimulus properties of nicotine can be blocked by mecamylamine (Morrison & Stephenson, 1969; Stolerman, Pratt, & Garcha, 1982).

In experiments with rats, low doses of ethanol can block nicotine discrimination (Korkosz et al., 2005), but alcohol does not seem to affect nicotine discriminations in humans (Perkins, Fonte, Blakesley-Ball, Stolinski, & Wilson, 2005). Caffeine is able to potentiate the discrimination of nicotine in rats (Gasior, Jaszyna, Munzar, Witkin, & Goldberg, 2002).

As mentioned earlier, humans sometimes describe the effect of intravenous nicotine as being similar to that of cocaine. Similarly, nicotine will fully substitute for cocaine in rats, but the effect is not bidirectional; cocaine will only partially substitute for nicotine in trained animals. Desai, Barber, and Terry (2003) used various antagonist drugs to further explore this relationship and concluded that nicotine's ability to mimic cocaine is due to its stimulation of dopamine release, an effect it shares with cocaine. The subjective similarity is not because cocaine has an effect on cholinergic systems that would also be affected by nicotine.

In an attempt to determine the locations in the brain responsible for nicotine's discriminative properties, Miyata, Ando, and Yanagita (2002) trained rats to discriminate nicotine and then tested the generalization of the nicotine response when nicotine was administered into various locations in the brain. They found that the nicotine response generalized fully to nicotine

administrations into the medial prefrontal cortex and only partially to administrations into the nucleus accumbens and the ventral tegmental area. Administrations into the dorsal hippocampus and the medial habenular nucleus did not generalize at all, showing that the discriminative stimulus properties of nicotine are primarily mediated by effects in the cortex and that reinforcement systems are only partially involved.

It has been shown that humans can discriminate between identical cigarettes that are different only in nicotine content (Kallman, Kallman, Harry, Woodson, & Rosecrans, 1982), although it is not known whether this is done by taste or through a central mechanism. Humans can easily detect nicotine in nasal spray. This effect is centrally mediated because it is blocked by mecamylamine and cannot be blocked by a PNS blocker of nAChRs. Men appear to be more sensitive to the stimulus properties of nicotine than women (Perkins, 2009).

WITHDRAWAL SYMPTOMS

When most tobacco users attempt to give up their habit, they experience withdrawal symptoms in varying degrees of intensity. Withdrawal from nicotine is not as physically severe as withdrawal from heroin, but it is just as stressful psychologically (Sigmund Freud, during one of his many attempts to quit cigar smoking, was described by his doctor as suffering "torture beyond human power to bear"; Jones, 1953, p. 311). Indeed, many ex-heroin addicts who have also quit smoking report that they found it harder to give up tobacco than heroin. While this chapter has focused primarily on the effects of nicotine on dopamine, nicotinic receptors are involved in the modulation of virtually every major neurotransmitter in the brain. After chronic exposure to nicotine, all these systems show adaptation. Smoking cessation disrupts this new equilibrium and leads to a constellation of physiological changes in all parts of the brain as systems readjust to the absence of the effects of nicotine. Nicotine withdrawal is the manifestation of all these changes (Paolini & De Biasi, 2011).

Systematic studies of nicotine withdrawal in chronic smokers reliably show the following symptoms: decreased heart rate; increased eating causing weight gain; an inability to concentrate; increased awakenings from sleep; craving for cigarettes; and mood changes including anxiety, anger, aggression, and depression (Hughes, Gust, Skoog, Keenan, & Fenwick, 1991; Hughes, Higgins, & Bickel, 1994). Other reported symptoms include nervousness, drowsiness, light-headedness, headaches, dizziness, tremor, and nausea (Jarvik, 1979). Nicotine-dependent individuals who abstain from tobacco for 10 to 24 hours show a slowing in brainwave activity to levels normally seen during drowsiness or light sleep (Herning, Jones, & Bachman, 1983).

Withdrawal symptoms develop over the first 3 days of abstinence, peak at about 1 week, and then gradually decrease. Most of these symptoms, except for weight gain and craving, are over within 1 to 6 months. Intense cravings for tobacco are often triggered by exposure to social and environmental cues. Such cravings become less frequent with time, but may persist indefinitely (Chandler & Rennard, 2010).

Withdrawal symptoms can be relieved by the administration of nicotine via other sources such as gum and transdermal patches. Symptoms of nicotine withdrawal can also be reduced, at least temporarily, by the taste and smell of tobacco or the act of smoking itself. One study showed that tobacco withdrawal symptoms were relieved if smokers were allowed to smoke a denicotinized cigarette that delivered no nicotine at all to the smoker (Butschky, Bailey, Henningfield, & Pickworth, 1994).

Nicotine withdrawal can interfere with performance on various cognitive and motor tasks. Functional magnetic resonance imaging (fMRI) studies provide an illustration of the cognitive impairments caused in chronic smokers by nicotine abstinence. Using BOLD imaging, researchers tested participants using the n-back test described earlier and in Chapter 2. If the participants had smoked nicotine within 1.5 hours prior to testing, activity in the dorsolateral prefrontal cortex was significantly lower when reporting which letter had directly preceded the letter X (one-back) compared to when reporting which letter had occurred two or three letters before X (two-back and three-back). However, following 14 hours of nicotine abstinence when participants were experiencing nicotine withdrawal, BOLD imaging showed that participants exhibited high levels of activity in the dorsolateral prefrontal cortex, regardless of which letter they were asked to report. In other words, during nicotine withdrawal, the previously simple one-back task required as much brain activity as the two- and three-back tasks. The researchers also found that participants made more errors on all three tasks during nicotine withdrawal (Xu et al., 2005). These effects are shown in Color Plate C.

Unlike most other drugs that cause physical dependence, withdrawal severity of nicotine does not seem to be related to dose; heavy and light smokers report equally severe withdrawal. Nor is withdrawal severity related to length of time smoking, previous attempts at quitting, sex, age, education, or alcohol and caffeine use (Hughes et al., 1991). However, severity of withdrawal does seem to be related to speed of nicotine metabolism. Fast metabolizers show more severe withdrawal than slow metabolizers (Rubinstein, Benowitz, Auerback, & Moscicki, 2008).

In studies of laboratory animals, nicotine withdrawal is associated with reduced dopamine in the nucleus accumbens. This seems to be mediated by connections to the accumbens and the ventral tegmental area from the lateral habenula, which inhibit dopamine neurons in the mesolimbic dopamine system. This suppression of the reward system is associated with aversiveness and a state of anhedonia, where there is a decrease in motivation to engage in normally pleasurable activities. The lateral habenula is normally rich in $alpha_3$ and $beta_4$ subunits of nAChRs. These subunits, along with $alpha_2$ and $alpha_5$ subunits, are also known to be associated with the aversive effects of high doses of nicotine (Dani & Balfour, 2011; Paolini & De Biasi, 2011).

Nicotine withdrawal has widespread effects on laboratory animals on many tests of performance and emotionality. Nicotine withdrawal increases the threshold for the rewarding effects of electrical brain stimulation, indicating a depression of the reward system. Nicotine withdrawal will create a conditioned place aversion in rats; that is, rats will avoid places where they have experienced nicotine withdrawal. Fear is also enhanced; rats experiencing nicotine withdrawal avoid the open arms of an elevated plus maze (see Chapter 2). $Beta_2$ and $alpha_6$ subunits appear to be involved in these and other effects showing increased anxiety during withdrawal (Paolini & De Biasi, 2011).

SELF-ADMINISTRATION IN NONHUMANS

Because self-administration of nicotine in humans is so persistent and widespread, it is surprising that laboratory animal self-administration is much less robust and restricted to a limited set of conditions. There are some anecdotal accounts of tame monkeys smoking. Indeed, Charles Darwin, in *The Descent of Man* (1882), claimed to have seen monkeys "smoke tobacco with pleasure" (p. 7). Darwin used these observations to support his contention that the sense of taste and the nervous systems of humans and monkeys are similar. Surprisingly, however, early systematic research from laboratories found monkeys to be reluctant smokers (Jarvik, 1973). Monkeys have been taught to inhale cigarette smoke, but the procedure involved a period of forced consumption in which the thirsty monkeys were reinforced with drinking water for sucking on a tube through which they received tobacco smoke. After this training, some animals seemed to prefer sucking on a tube that delivered tobacco smoke over one that delivered only air. It is doubtful whether this procedure represents a situation similar to human tobacco use. Animals do not normally initiate smoking on their own (Jarvik, 1973).

It has now been widely demonstrated that laboratory animals will work for intravenous infusions of nicotine, but early studies had difficulties showing reliable self-administration. It is now known that these early difficulties were due to several factors. The first was that there is a rather narrow range of doses at which nicotine is a reinforcer. Doses that are too low are not reinforcing, and doses that are too high have adverse effects and tend to be avoided. This is because higher doses stimulate nAChRs in the interpeduncular nucleus and the medial habenula. These receptors contain alpha$_5$ subunits, which are known to create aversive effects (Dani & Balfour, 2011; Fowler, Arends, & Kenny, 2008).

But even after appropriate doses were determined, self-administration did not appear to be as robust as it should have been, considering its persistence in humans. It was noticed, however, that responding for nicotine was much more persistent if a second-order schedule was used. For example, Goldberg, Spealman, and Goldberg (1981) demonstrated reliable intravenous self-administration in monkeys using a second-order schedule where the nicotine infusion was preceded by a colored light. They found that monkeys would respond at a higher rate for the combination of light and nicotine infusion than the nicotine infusion alone. They also showed that the monkeys would persistently respond for the light alone, even if it was only occasionally paired with the nicotine infusion.

It appears that the presence of conditioned reinforcement arising from stimuli paired with nicotine infusions

is very important in the reinforcing properties of nicotine. Anthony Caggiula at the University of Pittsburgh, Eric Donny at Johns Hopkins School of Medicine, and their colleagues have extensively explored this effect. They designed a series of experiments where rats were trained to lever press for a combination of a cue light and nicotine infusions, and then each of these elements was removed and systematically replaced (Caggiula et al., 2001). They trained rats to lever press on an FR5 schedule for an infusion of nicotine. Each nicotine infusion was paired with a 1-second cue light and was followed by a 1-minute time-out period where the house light (the overhead light in the chamber) was turned off. After 20 days of training on the FR5 schedule there was a 12-day extinction period. The extinction period was different for each of three groups of rats. For one group (the "saline + cues" group), saline was substituted for the nicotine infusion, but presentation of the cue light continued during the saline infusion. For another group (the "nicotine + no cues" group), the nicotine infusion continued, but there were no changes in the house light and cue light. For the third group of rats (the "saline + no cues" group), both nicotine and the cue- and house-light changes were discontinued.

Figure 8-5 shows what happened to responding in each of the three groups of rats during the extinction phase. As you can see, during the last five sessions of the acquisition phase (left side of Panels A, B, and C; the "cues + nicotine"), all groups were responding at a rate of over 20 infusions per session. When both the cues and nicotine were removed, responding dropped to less than five infusions (middle of Panel C; the "no nicotine + no cues"). When either nicotine alone (middle of Panel B; the "nicotine only") or cues alone (middle of Panel A; the "cues + saline") were presented, responding dropped to around 10 infusions per session and remained relatively stable.

In Phase 3 of the experiment, the reacquisition phase, conditions were restored. As you can see in Panel A (right side) of Figure 8-5, when the nicotine infusions were restored, responding returned to its original level after a few sessions. Panel B (right side) shows that when cues were restored to rats receiving only nicotine, responding returned and even exceeded original response rates. Panel C (right side) shows what happened when nicotine and cues were restored separately to rats that had received neither drug nor cue during extinction. Restoring nicotine alone increases responding slightly, but not significantly above extinction

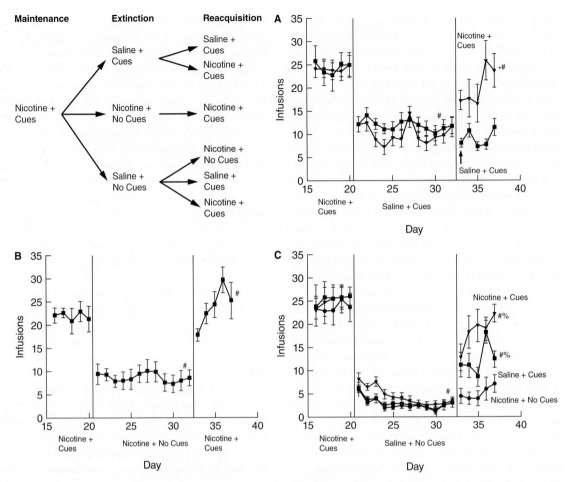

FIGURE 8-5 The design of this experiment is shown in the top left panel. In the maintenance phase of the experiment, groups of rats were trained to press a lever on an FR5 schedule for an infusion of nicotine, which was accompanied by a 1-second cue light and followed by a 1-minute timeout period where the house was turned off. The maintenance phase was followed by a 12-day extinction period. The extinction period was different for each of the three groups of rats. In one group, the nicotine was replaced by an infusion of saline (Saline + Cues), but the cues were not changed. In another group (Nicotine + No cues), the nicotine infusion continued, but it was not accompanied by any visual cues. In the third group (Saline + No cues), both nicotine and the cues were discontinued. Finally, during the reacquisition phase, various combinations of nicotine and cue lights were made available to the rats. The left side of Panels A, B, and C (the "Cues + Nicotine") shows responding during the last five sessions of the maintenance phase. The middle section of each graph shows responding during the extinction phase. The right section shows responding during reacquisition. (Redrawn from Caggiula et al., 2001)

levels. However, restoring the cue, either with saline or in combination with nicotine, did cause significant increases in responding. It appears that reestablishing the cues associated with nicotine delivery, but not simply restoring the nicotine delivery alone, elevated infusion rates above extinction levels (Caggiula et al., 2001). This experiment shows that conditioned cues associated with nicotine delivery play a crucial role in the maintenance and reestablishment of nicotine self-administration and demonstrates that simply replacing nicotine may not be enough to discourage smoking in smoking cessation treatments.

SELF-ADMINISTRATION IN HUMANS

There is little doubt that nicotine is a reinforcer in human smokers. In one study, smokers were attached to an intravenous catheter and could self-administer infusions of nicotine by pressing a lever on an FR10 schedule. Responding increased on this lever when the nicotine was available and was extinguished when saline infusions were substituted. It was also shown that when larger doses were used, subjects administered fewer infusions, and they increased infusions when the dose was decreased (Henningfield et al., 1987; Henningfield, Lucas, & Bigelow, 1986). This research shows that humans are sensitive to changes in nicotine concentration and are capable of adjusting doses, but the nature of the change in blood nicotine levels that is responsible for these adjustments is not clear. One possibility is that smokers are trying to maintain a constant level of nicotine in the blood; another is that they are trying to achieve sudden high doses delivered to the brain.

Constant Blood Level Theory

One assumption often made about smoking behavior is that the smoker is attempting to maintain a constant blood level of nicotine; that is, a dose high enough to avoid withdrawal symptoms, but below a level that has toxic or aversive effects.

For some time, it had not been clearly established that nicotine is the ingredient in tobacco that is responsible for tobacco consumption. To show that it is, researchers used the strategy of changing the nicotine content of cigarettes and noting whether the amount of smoking changed as a consequence. Would smokers adjust (titrate) their consumption to achieve a constant nicotine blood level?

Early studies had trouble demonstrating dose compensation when researchers measured dose by simply counting the number of high- and low-nicotine cigarettes a person smoked. They soon learned that people control nicotine intake, not by changing the number of cigarettes they smoke, but by changing their smoking behavior; that is, they compensate for low-nicotine cigarettes by taking deeper and more frequent puffs on the cigarette. These variables can be measured precisely by having subjects smoke through a special cigarette holder connected to a computer that monitors total smoke inhalation. Using these techniques, it has been demonstrated that smokers will compensate for increased or reduced doses by increasing and decreasing their puffing behavior, but the compensation is not as complete as when intravenous infusions are used.

One of the predictions of the constant blood level theory is that the first few puffs on a cigarette will be rapid and deep as the smoker tries to raise blood nicotine levels that have fallen since the previous cigarette was smoked. As the nicotine level increases, the puff rate will decrease, and few puffs will be taken near the end of the cigarette. This change in puff rate has been reported by several researchers (Chait & Griffiths, 1982). In addition, the theory predicts that people will be highly motivated to smoke when their blood levels are low after a period without smoking. The lowest levels occur after a night of sleeping. A British study showed that 14% of smokers light up within 5 minutes of waking in the morning, and 50% do so within 30 minutes.

Even though human smokers attempt to prevent their nicotine blood level from falling to the point where withdrawal symptoms occur and make adjustments for the amount of nicotine delivered by their cigarette, they are unable to compensate completely. Their blood levels then become higher than normal when nicotine content is increased and lower than normal when it is decreased. In addition, nicotine replacement therapy is not as effective as one might expect if maintaining constant nicotine blood level and withdrawal avoidance were all that mattered. Factors other than constant blood level must be controlling nicotine intake as well.

Nicotine Bolus Theory

The *nicotine bolus theory* was proposed by M. A. H. Russell of the Maudsley Hospital in London to explain some aspects of smoking behavior. Careful observation of a cigarette smoker will show that when smoke is inhaled into the lungs, it is frequently done with one rapid inhalation rather than gradually, as with a normal breath. This sudden filling of the lungs with smoke tends to saturate the blood in the capillaries of the lungs with nicotine at the moment of inhalation. This concentration of nicotine in the blood, known as the *nicotine bolus*, stays together as the blood returns to the heart and is pumped to the brain. This theory suggests that the sudden high level of nicotine in the brain intensifies the pleasure and enhances its reinforcing effect. This is what makes cigarette smoking so much more addicting than other, slower routes of administration and keeps the smoker smoking (Russell, 1976). A similar theory has been proposed to explain the addictive nature of intravenous injections of heroin (Dole, 1980) and is consistent with the general finding that the reinforcing properties of many drugs can be greatly enhanced by delivering them to the brain rapidly and in high concentrations. When drug absorption in the brain is slowed, the pleasurable effects are greatly blunted (Parasrampuria et al., 2007).

It is possible that these spikes in nicotine concentration might be able to generate an enhanced activation of nAChRs. As we saw earlier, nAChRs enter a desensitized configuration if they are continuously exposed to high concentrations of an agonist and will revert to their basal configuration only when the concentration drops. If nicotine were delivered to the receptor as a series of spikes created by each puff, then the rising edge of the spike would be able to activate the nAChRs and have a large effect on the cell before the receptors enter their desensitized configuration (refer to Figure 8-4). Then, during the declining edge of the spike, nicotine concentrations drop allowing the nAChRs to return to their basal configuration in time for the next spike (Rose et al., 2010).

Careful examination of Figure 8-2 shows that this series of events cannot happen because there is no spike. There is merely an increase in the concentration of nicotine caused by the nicotine bolus, but the levels never drop before the next puff. This does not mean that the nicotine bolus is not important; it only shows that the mechanism of action cannot incorporate a decrease in desensitization of nAChRs. It is still clear that after each pulse, nicotine concentrations rapidly increase, and rapid increases in drug concentration usually have an intensified effect, although, in this case, the mechanism for such an effect is not apparent from what we know about the properties of nAChRs.

Because a nicotine bolus can be achieved only by smoking, this theory explains why the craving for the drug is worse in smokers than in those who take tobacco by other means, but it cannot account for the great popularity of tobacco in its other forms throughout history.

Non-Nicotine Factors

In the experiment by Caggiula and colleagues described earlier and illustrated in Figure 8-5, it was shown in rats that cues associated with nicotine infusions can acquire reinforcing properties and maintain self-administration. It is possible that many of the sensory experiences associated with smoking, such as the smell, taste, and the motor activities of smoking, can also acquire reinforcing properties and may be important in both maintaining smoking and in relapse to smoking after quitting. We have seen as well that smokers report considerable satisfaction from smoking denicotinized cigarettes, which can relieve craving and other symptoms of nicotine withdrawal, despite a lack of drug.

It is important to understand the role of these non-nicotine-related factors in smoking because one strategy of treating tobacco addiction is *nicotine replacement therapy* (NRT) where nicotine is provided via other routes of administration, such as the patch or a nicotine inhaler. NRT can provide substitute nicotine, but does not provide the sensory cues of smoking. The role of sensory and motoric cues in smoking has been explored extensively by Jed Rose and his colleagues at Duke University (Rose, 2006). In one experiment, over a 4-hour period, Rose administered nicotine intravenously to smokers, either by continuous infusion or in 2-second burst infusions designed to mimic the dose of nicotine one would get from taking a puff of a cigarette. At the same time, some participants inhaled computer-programmed puffs of either denicotinized cigarettes or normal cigarettes (their usual brand), while other participants in the no-smoking condition did not puff on any form of cigarette. This 4-hour period was the "satiation phase" of the experiment. Then, 1 hour later, participants from all groups were allowed to smoke their usual brand of cigarette *ad lib* (without restriction) for 3 hours, and their total smoke inhalation was monitored via a special cigarette holder.

In comparing smoke inhalation during this *ad lib* phase across all groups of participants, Rose found that prior IV nicotine alone, whether infused continuously or in pulses during the satiation phase of the experiment, had very little effect on *ad lib* cigarette smoking behavior. In contrast, the combination of IV nicotine and the opportunity to puff on denicotinized cigarettes during the satiation phase reduced *ad lib* smoking significantly. This and other studies show that components of smoking, other than nicotine, play a significant role in cigarette addiction and that simply replacing nicotine, as is done in NRT, may not be a sufficient smoking cessation treatment strategy in and of itself.

There has been considerable research to try to identify which non-nicotine factors associated with cigarette smoking are important in maintaining smoking behavior. It has been shown that anesthetizing the throat and airways so that the smoker cannot taste the smoke or experience its effects significantly attenuates smoking satisfaction in habitual smokers and that adding an irritant (citric acid) to mimic the effects of smoke on the airways can enhance the pleasure of inhaling nicotine aerosol (Caggiula et al., 2001). It is likely that the taste, smell, and other properties of tobacco smoke are important factors in the motivation to smoke.

The Dual Reinforcement Model

Caggiula and colleagues (2009) have proposed a theory to account for the ability of non-nicotine stimuli to enhance the reinforcing effects of smoking. They call it the *dual reinforcement model*. They propose that there are actually three processes at work during nicotine reinforcement. First, there is the primary reinforcement caused by nicotine that arises from its effect on the mesolimbic dopamine system, described earlier. Second, they say that non-nicotine-related stimuli, such as the taste and smell of the tobacco smoke, acquire secondary reinforcing properties through conditioning, because they are paired with the primary reinforcement derived from the nicotine administration. They also propose a third factor—they hypothesize that nicotine has "reinforcement enhancing" properties, that is, the ability to make a weak reinforcer stronger, and that these properties enhance the effect of the non-nicotine stimulus. The sum of all these processes results in making nicotine administrations through smoking a much more powerful reinforcer than would be predicted by nicotine's own primary reinforcing effect.

To illustrate the "reinforcement enhancing" effect, Caggiula and colleagues (2009) performed an experiment in which rats were placed in an operant chamber with two levers. One lever produced the same visual stimuli used in the nicotine studies described earlier (the onset of a 1-second cue light and the offset of the house light for 1 minute) but no infusion of nicotine. The other lever caused an infusion of nicotine but no change in visual stimuli (cue or house light). For one group of rats, only the stimulus lever was active (pressing on the nicotine lever produced no results); for a different group, only the nicotine lever was active (pressing it produced no changes in visual stimuli). The researchers found that, in both groups of rats, the "active" lever supported low levels of responding. You may find it surprising that visual stimuli alone would be reinforcing given that they had never been paired with nicotine, but it has been known for some time that sensory changes (changes in illumination and sounds) function as weak reinforcers for laboratory animals (this is called sensory reinforcement). It appeared that the reinforcing effect of the light changes and the reinforcing effect of nicotine infusions were roughly equivalent; rats press either lever at about the same rate.

An interesting thing happened, however, when another group of rats was permitted to press both levers in the same session (i.e., both levers were made "active"). In this group, responding on the nicotine lever was just as low as it was in the group that was permitted to press only that lever; however, these rats responded for the visual stimuli at a much higher rate than before. It appears that the nicotine infusions received after pressing the nicotine lever greatly enhanced the reinforcing properties of the visual stimuli produced by pressing the other lever. Drawing an analogy to human smoking, the ability of nicotine to enhance the reinforcing properties of the smell and taste of tobacco smoke and the combination of this reinforcement with the primary reinforcement from nicotine alone add up to make tobacco smoking a much more powerful reinforcer than nicotine alone.

These three explanations—the constant blood level theory, the nicotine bolus theory, and the dual reinforcement model—are not mutually exclusive explanations. They may all be correct to some extent in different smokers, and the same smoker at different times may be motivated by the need to create a nicotine bolus, avoid nicotine withdrawal, or experience the taste and smell of tobacco smoke. The ability of nicotine to enhance the reinforcing effects of other reinforcers no doubt enhances these motivations and perhaps other reinforcers not yet considered.

HARMFUL EFFECTS
Heart Disease

Smoking increases the risk of heart disease by two to four times that of a nonsmoker and doubles the risk of stroke (Centers for Disease Control and Prevention,

2012). Heart disease caused by tobacco smoke appears to be due largely to the combined action of nicotine and carbon monoxide. Carbon monoxide is present in smoke, and, when breathed into the lungs, it binds with hemoglobin in the blood, reducing the ability of the blood to carry oxygen and, consequently, reducing oxygen supply to the heart itself. Nicotine increases the workload of the heart by releasing catecholamines. These effects are further complicated by the fact that other constituents in the smoke reduce the lungs' ability to absorb oxygen (see the next section on lung disease), so the heart must work even harder to pump more blood through the lungs and satisfy the oxygen needs of the body. In addition, there is a relationship between atherosclerosis and the number of cigarettes smoked per day. Atherosclerosis is a disease wherein plaques, or deposits, build up in blood vessels and eventually stop the circulation of blood. When the blood flow to the heart itself is stopped in this manner, the heart muscle dies, and a heart attack occurs. Figure 8-6 summarizes how smoking cigarettes contributes to heart disease.

Chronic obstructive pulmonary disease (COPD) is the co-occurrence of chronic bronchitis and emphysema.

In COPD, air passages into and throughout the lungs become obstructed, and airflow is restricted. This causes shortness of breath and other breathing difficulties. It is usually caused by breathing noxious particles or gases, which triggers an abnormal inflammatory response in the lung (Rabe et al., 2007).

When tobacco smoke is inhaled, the ash and tars are deposited on the moist membranes on the inside surface of the lung, through which oxygen and carbon dioxide must pass to and from the blood. Normally, particles are cleared from the lungs by small hairs called *cilia*, which agitate and work the pollutants upward until they are ejected by coughing. Another line of defence against inhaled particles is the action of *phagocytes*. The phagocytes attack, surround, and destroy foreign matter in the lungs. Smoking reduces the actions of both the cilia and the phagocytes, leaving the lungs more vulnerable to the toxic effects of inhaled pollutants and infections by bacteria and viruses. As a result, smokers are more susceptible to COPD.

COPD can be caused by air pollution and industrial exposure to dust and airborne chemicals, but in the United States, 80 to 90% of cases of COPD are a result of

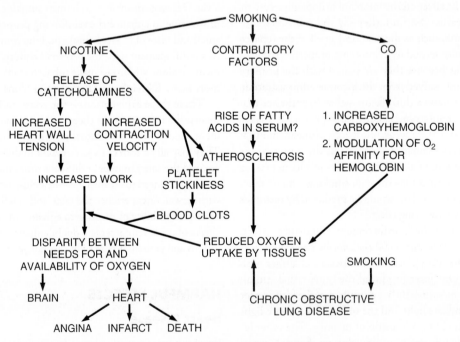

FIGURE 8-6 The mechanisms by which smoking contributes to heart disease. Smoking increases the demand on the heart by increasing its workload while at the same time decreasing the oxygen the heart muscle receives by increasing carboxyhemoglobin and causing atherosclerosis and COPD. (From Van Lancker, 1977, p. 252)

smoking. COPD is the third leading cause of death in the United States (Murphy, Janquan, & Kochanek, 2012).

There is no cure for COPD, but, among smokers, smoking cessation is one of the most important factors in slowing down the progression of the disease. Quitting smoking can significantly reduce the rate of deterioration in lung function and delay the onset of disability and death.

Cancer

According to the American Cancer Society, smoking is responsible for 30% of all cancer deaths and 87% of all lung cancer deaths in the United States. The risk of developing lung cancer in male smokers is 23 times higher than in nonsmokers, and, in females, the risk is 13 times higher. Lung cancer is not the only cancer associated with smoking. Smoking increases the risk of many other forms of cancer: nasopharynx, nasal cavity and paranasal sinuses, lip, oral cavity (a form of cancer that Freud suffered), pharynx, larynx, esophagus, pancreas, uterine cervix, kidney, bladder, stomach, colorectum, and blood (leukemia) (American Cancer Society, 2011; Sasco, Secretan, & Straif, 2004).

It should be no surprise that smoking causes cancer because tobacco smoke is known to contain many recognized carcinogens including arsenic, benzene, beryllium, 1,3–Butadiene, cadmium, chromium, ethylene oxide, nickel, Polonium-210, and vinyl chloride (National Cancer Institute, 2011).

Smoking also greatly increases the risk of cancers produced by other known carcinogens, such as pollutants, asbestos, and alcohol. For example, the risk of smokers getting cancer of the mouth and pharynx is two to six times greater in heavy drinkers than in nondrinkers (Rothman & Keller, 1972).

The risk of lung cancer can be greatly decreased by quitting smoking, and the risk lessens considerably over time after a person stops. The extent to which this happens is determined by factors such as the length of time and the number of cigarettes smoked, the age at which the person began smoking, and whether or not he or she was already ill at the time of quitting (U.S. DHHS, 2004).

Reproduction

It is now clearly established that smoking can decrease fertility in both men and women. In women, smoking interferes with many of the processes involved in becoming pregnant, and in men, smoking reduces sperm count (Soares & Melo, 2008). Women who smoke more than 20 cigarettes per day are 1.7 to 3.2 times more likely to be infertile than nonsmokers. It appears, though, that this effect is reversible: Fertility returns to normal after cessation of smoking (Baird, 1992).

Maternal smoking increases the risk of a baby being born with a birth defect. This risk can be measured in terms of an *odds ratio* (OR)—the success rate of the treatment group (or, in this case, the maternal smoking group) divided by the success rate of the control group (or, in this case, the maternal nonsmoking group). An odds ratio greater than "1.0" indicates that a birth defect is more likely in mothers who smoked during pregnancy. In a review of 101 studies involving over 173,000 birth-defect cases compared with 11.7 million controls, it was shown that maternal smoking was positively and significantly correlated with many birth defects: cardiovascular/heart defects (OR = 1.09); musculoskeletal defects (OR = 1.16); limb reduction defects (OR = 1.26); missing/extra digits (OR = 1.18); clubfoot (OR = 1.28); craniosynostosis (an abnormally shaped head; OR = 1.33); facial defects (OR = 1.19); eye defects (OR = 1.25); orofacial clefts (OR = 1.28); gastrointestinal defects (OR = 1.27); and undescended testes (OR = 1.13). There was a reduced risk for hypospadias (having the urinary opening on the underside of the penis, rather than at the end; OR = 0.90) and skin defects (OR = 0.82). For all defects combined, the OR was 1.01, due to including defects with a reduced risk and those with no association (Hackshaw, Rodeck, & Boniface, 2011).

Many years of research have clearly established that babies born to women who smoke during pregnancy are likely to be anywhere from 150 to 200 grams lighter at birth than babies born to nonsmoking mothers. This effect is dose dependent and is estimated to be a loss of birth weight of 11 grams per cigarette smoked per day by the mother. The weight loss may occur because smokers do not put on as much weight during pregnancy as nonsmokers do; therefore, their babies are lighter. Another possibility might be that the developing fetus receives less oxygen from the body of a smoking mother because of the reduced oxygen-carrying capacity of her blood (Russell, Taylor, & Law, 1968). In any case, women who smoke during pregnancy are more likely to spontaneously abort and have babies prematurely, and their children are also more likely to be ill and die (Kramer, 1987; U.S. DHHS, 1989, 1990).

It has been estimated that if maternal smoking could be eliminated altogether, the overall infant death rate could be reduced by 10% (Haglund & Cnattingius, 1990).

Environmental Tobacco Smoke

Smoking is unhealthy, not only for smokers, but also for those who work and live with them. In 1992, the U.S. Environmental Protection Agency (U.S. EPA) released a document reviewing what was known at that time about the dangers of being exposed to *environmental tobacco smoke* (ETS), also known as *secondhand smoke*. Breathing this smoke is referred to as *passive smoking* or *involuntary smoking*.

ETS comes from two sources: (a) *mainstream smoke* (MS), which the smoker inhales and then breathes back out into the atmosphere, and (b) *sidestream smoke* (SS), which issues from a burning cigarette between puffs. MS is created when the smoker draws air through the cigarette. The flame that creates MS is 200 to 300 degrees hotter than the flame that creates SS. Both types of smoke contain the same carcinogens and toxic substances, but the combustion differences mean that the concentration of these substances is much higher in SS than in MS. For example, the concentration of one carcinogen, 4-ABP, is 30 times greater in SS than in MS. Levels of 4-ABP in the blood of nonsmokers have been measured at 10 to 20% that of smokers, even though the smoke they inhale is much less concentrated (U.S. EPA, 1992).

The U.S. Surgeon General estimates that living with a smoker increases a nonsmoker's chances of developing lung cancer by 20 to 30%, and there is evidence that secondhand smoke may increase the risk of breast cancer, nasal sinus cavity cancer, and nasopharyngeal cancer in adults and the risk of leukemia, lymphoma, and brain tumors in children (U.S. DHHS, 2006).

Exposure to secondhand smoke irritates the airways and has immediate harmful effects on a person's heart and blood vessels. It may increase the risk of heart disease by an estimated 25 to 30% (U.S. DHHS, 2006, 2010). In the United States, secondhand smoke is thought to cause about 46,000 heart disease deaths each year (California Environmental Protection Agency,

2005). There may also be a link between exposure to secondhand smoke and the risk of stroke and hardening of the arteries; however, additional research is needed to confirm this link.

Even though the health dangers of ETS are present for all age groups, children are particularly vulnerable. The report also concludes that ETS is responsible for between 150,000 and 300,000 cases of bronchitis and pneumonia in infants up to 18 months of age and that ETS exposure worsens the severity of asthma symptoms in 200,000 to 1 million children per year (Spitzer et al., 1990; U.S. EPA, 1992). The report also finds a strong link between ETS and *sudden infant death syndrome* (SIDS; infants die suddenly and unexpectedly between the ages of 1 month and 1 year). The risk of SIDS death is between 1.6 and 7.7 times greater for babies of smoking mothers than for babies of nonsmokers. The risk is higher for babies in homes where the mother smokes more than 20 cigarettes per day (Nicholl & O'Cathain, 1992; U.S. EPA, 1992). It has been estimated that there would be a 27% decrease in SIDS if maternal smoking were eliminated (Haglund & Cnattingius, 1990).

The low birth weights created by smoking while pregnant can also occur in nonsmoking women if they are exposed to several hours of ETS daily (U.S. EPA, 1992).

More recently, the 2006 Surgeon General's report has raised concern about what it calls *thirdhand smoke*. It has been shown that a significant level of tobacco toxins remains in a home after a period of active smoking. These toxins take the form of dust and soot that get deposited in a layer on every surface in the home and that give off volatile toxic compounds for months after smoking (U.S. DHHS, 2006).

TREATMENTS

Compulsion to Smoke

Perhaps one of the most tragic examples of the strength of the tobacco habit is that of the founder of psychoanalysis, Sigmund Freud. Freud smoked cigars (upward of 20 per day) for most of his life, despite the fact that he suffered from heart pains and cancer of the mouth as a direct result. Toward the end of his life, he was in constant pain after undergoing 33 operations for his cancer yet was still unable to quit. Freud died of cancer at the age of 83. He had tried to quit for 45 years but was unable to do so for any more than a year or so (Brecher & Editors of *Consumer Reports*, 1972, p. 215).

Freud, of course, is not alone. In his Statement on Nicotine-Containing Cigarettes in 1994 before the House Subcommittee on Health and the Environment, David Kessler, the commissioner of the FDA, made the following points: (a) Two-thirds of adults who smoke say that they wish they could quit, and (b) 17 million try to quit each year in the United States, but fewer than 1 out of 10 succeed. Three out of four adult smokers say they are addicted, and eight out of ten smokers say they wish they had never started.

As Freud's case shows, tobacco smoking can be a difficult habit to break, but his case is not typical. Perhaps he was a fast metabolizer of nicotine or had a genetic abnormality of nAChR subunits, which amplified his withdrawal from nicotine. A large British survey conducted in the late 1980s, before there were many smoking cessation therapies and no pharmacotherapies, found that quitting is not all that bad; 53% of ex-smokers reported that stopping was "not at all difficult," 27% said it was "fairly difficult," and only 20% said it was "very difficult." Between two-thirds and three-quarters of ex-smokers were able to stop smoking without the benefit of any treatment (Chapman & MacKenzie, 2010), but for those who need help, a great variety of therapies is now available. One of the most common and most effective is nicotine replacement therapy (NRT).

Nicotine Replacement Therapy

This treatment is the most commonly used smoking cessation strategy. It is based on the same strategy as methadone maintenance with heroin addicts (see Chapter 11). It substitutes a relatively safe source of the drug, such as a nicotine patch, gum, nasal spray, lozenge, sublingual tablet, or nicotine inhaler, for the more harmful source: tobacco smoke. In addition, it blunts the pleasurable effect of inhaled nicotine. Most NRT vehicles create relatively low nicotine blood levels with slow absorption (see Figure 8-3), but the nasal spray and inhaler are more rapidly absorbed and more closely mimic tobacco smoke.

All forms of NRT have been shown to increase the chances of quitting to a greater extent than a placebo. A meta-analysis of 110 studies has shown that the rate of quitting at 6 months with a placebo is about 10%, but with NRT, the rate is 17%. This gives an odds ratio of 1.7. Another meta-analysis of the different forms of NRT showed that nicotine gum and the patch are the least effective, while the inhaler, the lozenge/sublingual tablet, and the nasal spray are the most effective, doubling the chances of abstinence over a placebo. Success rates have been further increased by combining a constant rate delivery system, like the patch, with a rapid delivery system like the nasal spray, which can be used to control *breakthrough* cravings (McNeil, Piccenna, & Ioannides-Demos, 2010).

Nicotine replacement may not always lead to smoking cessation, but even if it succeeds only in reducing the number of cigarettes smoked, as it often does, it will have achieved partial success (Keenan et al., 1995). Nicotine replacement therapy should continue for 3 to 6 months with a gradual weaning of dose, although many people continue to use it for a much longer period of time. Those who stop may find it necessary to revert to the use of the gum or a patch in circumstances where relapse is likely.

Bupropion

Bupropion is another pharmacological treatment for smoking, but is not a nicotine replacement therapy. Bupropion was originally developed as an antidepressant and sold as Wellbutrin. It is considered a third-generation antidepressant as it acts primarily as a reuptake inhibitor of norepinephrine and dopamine (see Chapter 13). After being marketed as an antidepressant, it was shown that bupropion seemed to be able to help people quit smoking. With further testing, it was marketed as a smoking cessation aid and sold as Zyban. In addition to its ability to act as a reuptake inhibitor of monoamines, bupropion is also an antagonist at nAChRs that contain the $alpha_3$, $alpha_4$, $alpha_7$, $beta_2$, and $beta_4$ subunits. Action at $alpha_4$, $alpha_6$, $alpha_7$, and $beta_2$ receptors involves the release of dopamine, and, by inhibiting these receptors, bupropion diminishes the primary reinforcing effect of nicotine. $Alpha_3$ and $beta_4$ subunits are primarily located in the habenular nuclei, which have antireward functions and cause unpleasant symptoms of nicotine withdrawal. Thus, bupropion is capable of reducing both the rewarding effects of nicotine and the aversive effects of nicotine withdrawal (McNeil et al., 2010).

Bupropion is typically begun 1 to 2 weeks before smoking is stopped, and the dose is increased to about

300 mg/day in two 150 mg administrations (slow release formulations are also commonly used). The recommended duration of treatment is 7 to 12 weeks, but this may be extended to prevent withdrawal. Bupropion appears to be about as effective as standard NRT (OR = 1.9). The OR of bupropion is increased to 2.9 when it is combined with NRT (Paolini & De Biasi, 2011).

As is typical of the antidepressants, many people report side effects with bupropion. Insomnia is frequently reported, although one benefit of bupropion is that there is decreased weight gain compared to placebo (Chandler & Rennard, 2010; McNeil et al., 2010).

Varenicline

Varenicline was approved as a pharmacotherapy for smoking cessation in the United States and the European Union in 2006. It is sold as Chantix in the United States and Champix in Canada, Britain, and Europe. Varenicline was developed from *cytisine*, an alkaloid found in the leaves and seeds of the golden rain tree (*Cytisus laburnum*), which were dried and smoked as a tobacco substitute during World War II.

Varenicline is a partial agonist at the alpha$_4$beta$_2$ nicotinic acetylcholine receptor. That is, it partially stimulates the receptor and also, by occupying the receptor, blocks other agonists such as nicotine from having any effect. This action partially mimics that of nicotine, but blocks any effect of nicotine molecules if they are present. By partially stimulating the alpha$_4$beta$_2$ nAChR, varenicline causes some of the primary reinforcing effects of nicotine in the mesolimbic dopamine system and alleviates some of the nicotine withdrawal effects. At the same time, it blocks any reinforcing effects of nicotine delivered by smoking. Like many antidepressant drugs, varenicline is also a serotonin reuptake blocker, but it is not known whether this action contributes in any way to its smoking cessation properties (McNeil et al., 2010).

Treatment with varenicline should start 7 days before quitting smoking. Over 8 days, the dose should be increased from 0.5 mg/day to 1.0 mg twice/day. This regime is designed to reduce nausea, the main side effect of varenicline. The recommended duration of treatment is 12 weeks and, if the patient is successful in smoking cessation, should be continued for an additional 12 weeks to prevent relapse.

Most testing trials find that people using varenicline are about 2.3 times more likely than those in a placebo control group to be abstinent from smoking 6 months to 1 year after quitting. One meta-analysis found that varenicline-treated patients were 1.5 times more likely to be abstinent at 1 year than those using bupropion, and 1.3 times more likely than those using NRT (McNeil et al., 2010). Whereas a combination of bupropion and NRT has been shown to be more effective than bupropion alone, it is not likely that there would be any improvement by combining varenicline with NRT because of the nicotine antagonist properties of varenicline.

Since the drug was approved in 2006, it has been reported that some people taking varenicline exhibit aggressive, erratic behavior and suicidal ideation. This has led to inclusion of a warning on the label, prompting caregivers and physicians to watch for such symptoms (Chandler & Rennard, 2010).

Pharmacological Interventions in Those Not Interested in Quitting

All of these studies of pharmacotherapies have used participants who want to stop smoking, but is there anything that can be done for those who are not ready to quit? The Clinical Practice Guidelines of the U.S. Public Health Service recommend that people who are not ready to quit be given a brief "motivational intervention." One such strategy might be an attempt to reduce smoking rather than stopping it altogether, but there are concerns about such a strategy. These include (a) uncertainty that smoking reduction has any health benefits, (b) concern that any smoking reduction may only be temporary, and (c) concern that such attempts will undermine future attempts to stop. These concerns have been addressed in a systematic review of studies examining attempts to reduce smoking in people who claim that they are not ready to quit. Six such studies were reviewed which included ten trials: Six tested pharmacological interventions (five NRT and one bupropion), one examined a behavioral intervention, and three tested combined interventions. The effect of these interventions on abstinence at 6 months was analyzed (Asfar, Ebbert, Klesges, & Relyea, 2011).

The study authors found that these interventions were able to increase the probability of being abstinent from smoking at 6 months. Compared to controls, those receiving pharmacological interventions were 2.33 times more likely to be abstinent, and those receiving combined interventions were 2.14 times more likely to be abstinent. These findings demonstrate that for people who claim to be unwilling to quit smoking, pharmacological interventions at least can be as effective as they are in people who claim to be motivated to quit.

Other Pharmacotherapies

There are other drugs with numerous different pharmacological actions that have been used to treat smoking, with varying degrees of success. The tricyclic antidepressant nortriptyline (Pamelor) has been shown to be about as effective as bupropion and NRT in some trials, but has more undesirable side effects, which include sedation and a dry mouth (Chandler & Rennard, 2010). Naltrexone, an opioid receptor blocker, has also been used in combination with NRT in the hopes that one of its side effects, weight loss, would counter the weight gain often seen when people stop smoking. This combination has been shown to be effective, and weight gain was indeed reduced. Further research is needed (O'Malley et al., 2006).

The nicotinic receptor blocker mecamylamine has also been tested and shown to be effective in combination with the nicotine patch, but studies are limited and more research is needed. It has been suggested that nAChR antagonists like mecamylamine should eliminate not only the direct reinforcing effects of nicotine, but also the conditioned reinforcing effects associated with the taste and smell of tobacco smoke, as well as the reward enhancement effect proposed by the dual reinforcement model. It has been shown that, initially, smoking increases as the smoker tries to overcome the loss of reinforcing effects, but continued administration leads to a decrease in smoking due to extinction. Consequently, the most effective way to use mecamylamine would be to initiate the drug well before the smoking cessation. This would provide the opportunity for extinction of both primary and conditioned reinforcement (Caggiula et al., 2009; Rose, 2006) and should make quitting easier.

Other drugs that have been assessed for their ability to reduce smoking behavior include moclobemide, an MAO-A inhibitor, selegiline, an MAO-B inhibitor, and bromocriptine, a dopamine D_2 and serotonin agonist (McNeil et al., 2010).

Immunization

Two pharmaceutical companies, one in England and the other in the United States, have developed and have started clinical trials of a tobacco vaccine. The

---

TABLE 8-1 Comparison of the Odds Ratios (OR) of Different Smoking Cessation Interventions Derived from 23 Meta-Analyses and Reviews, Which Together Pooled the Results of 598 Studies Published from 2000 to 2007

Intervention	Control Group	Number of Studies	Odds Ratio
Group behavior therapy	No intervention	55	2.17
	Self-help		2.04
Bupropion	Placebo	24	2.06
Physician advice		39	
Intensive	Control		2.04
Minimal	Control		1.74
Intensive	Minimal advice		1.24
NRT	Placebo	123	1.77
Telephone counseling	Minimal intervention	27	1.56
Nursing intervention	Standard care	29	1.47

Source: Lemmens et al. (2008).

vaccines, known as Nicotine-Qb (NicQb), TA-NIC, and NicVAX, stimulate the body's immune system to create antibodies for molecules of nicotine. The antibodies then surround the nicotine molecules and block them from crossing the blood–brain barrier. This effect has been demonstrated in laboratory animals. Rats were exposed to tobacco smoke for 10 minutes, and brain levels of nicotine were reduced by 90% in vaccinated animals (Pravetoni et al., 2011).

Keeping nicotine out of the brain should greatly diminish its ability to act as a reinforcer and should cause smoking behavior to extinguish. The vaccine would need to be given in four or five doses at monthly intervals and would require a booster shot every few months.

A clinical trial has shown that the vaccine is effective in helping people quit smoking but only in those for whom the vaccine was able to create high levels of nicotine antibodies. Before more trials can be conducted, it will be necessary to find a way to increase the ability of the drug to create nicotine antibodies in a greater percentage of immunized people (Cornuz et al., 2008).

Other Interventions

Many behavioral interventions have been developed for the treatment of addictions (many of which have been described in Chapter 5). They include counseling, group therapy, motivational therapy, behavior management, and many others. All of these treatments have been adapted in one form or another to treat tobacco addiction, and the effectiveness of most has been evaluated. In a 2008 review, Lemmens and colleagues (2008) attempted to summarize the effectiveness of various intervention strategies for nicotine addiction. Table 8-1 summarizes their results, providing odds ratios for the effectiveness of each treatment.

As you can see, in this analysis of 55 studies, group behavior therapy appeared to be the most effective form of therapy with an OR of 2.17 compared to a no-intervention control group. Bupropion and intensive physician advice showed ORs of about 2.0. NRT had an OR of 1.77. What this table shows is that pharmacotherapy is often no more effective than many other more traditional forms of therapy, including advice from a physician or a nurse.

Caffeine and the Methylxanthines

Coffee is useless since it serveth neither Nourishment nor Debauchery.

—ANONYMOUS, 1650 (AUSTIN, 1985, P. 236)

Caffeine is the best-known member of a family of drugs known as the *xanthine stimulants* or the *methylxanthines*. Although there are many methylxanthines besides caffeine, only two others occur naturally and are widely self-administered. These are *theophylline* and *theobromine*. The three have similar molecular structures and similar behavioral and physiological effects. The methylxanthines occur naturally in a number of species of plants belonging to 28 genera and over 17 families, but their most common sources are coffee, tea, and chocolate. Caffeine is also typically added to soft drinks and is an ingredient in many over-the-counter painkillers, cold remedies, stimulant pills, and, more recently, energy drinks.

Caffeine was first isolated from coffee in 1820 by Ferdinand Runge, a German chemist, who called it *Kaffeebase*. It has been suggested that Runge's interest in coffee was stimulated by Wolfgang von Goethe, the author of *Faust*, who was a close friend of Runge and a great coffee lover. No one is sure where the name *caffeine* came

from, but a medical dictionary first used the term in 1823. Theobromine was isolated in 1842 and theophylline in 1888. Most of the basic chemistry of the methylxanthines was worked out and published in 1907 in a book by Emil Fischer, a Nobel prize–winning organic chemist.

SOURCES OF METHYLXANTHINES

Caffeine is available from a wide variety of sources. Table 9-1 gives a summary of some of these sources and an estimate of the amount of caffeine and other methylxanthines they contain.

Coffee

Coffee is made from the fruit of a bush or small tree of the genus *Coffea*. The two most common species are the *arabica* and the *canephora* (also called *robusta*), which together account for 99% of the world's coffee. They are native to Ethiopia but are now widely cultivated in Africa and South America and in tropical climates all over the world. The coffee bean is a seed kernel of the coffee berry (or cherry), which grows in clumps along the branches. Each berry contains two seeds within its pulp. Usually, the berry is picked and dried briefly in the sun before the seeds are removed from inside the pulp.

TABLE 9-1 Sources of Methylxanthines

Source	Serving Size	Caffeine (mg)		Other Methylxanthines
		Mean	Range	
Coffee				
Instant	8 oz	93	27–173	
Brewed (drip)	8 oz	133	102–200	
Decaffeinated	8 oz	8	3–8	
Espresso	1 oz	40	30–90	
Starbucks brewed coffee (grande)	16 oz	320		
Tea				
Brewed	8 oz	53	40–120	thophylline
Chocolate				
Hot chocolate (drink)	8 oz	9	3–13	thophylline
Milk chocolate	1 oz	6	11–15	thophylline
Unsweetened chocolate (baking)	1 oz	35	18–118	thophylline (150–300 mg)
Sweetened chocolate	1 oz	20	15–35	thophylline
Chocolate milk	8 oz	5	2–7	theobromine (75–100 mg)
Soft drinks				
Coca-Cola Classic	12 oz	35		
Diet Coke	12 oz	47		
Pepsi	12 oz	38		
Diet Pepsi	12 oz	36		
Mountain Dew	12 oz	54*		
Jolt Cola	12 oz	72		
Energy drinks and energy shots**				
Spike Shooter	8.4 oz	300		
Cocaine	8.4 oz	300		
AMP	8.4 oz	74		
Red Bull	8.3 oz	80		
Rockstar	8 oz	80		
Nitro2Go	2 oz	***		
ZipFizz	4 oz	120		
5 Hour Energy	2 oz	138		
6 Hour Power	2 oz	125		
Over-the-counter analgesics				
Excedrin (extra strength)	1 tablet	65		
Anacin (maximum strength)	1 tablet	32		
Vanquish	1 tablet	32		
Over-the-counter stimulants				
No-Doz (maximum strength)	1 tablet	200		
Vivarin	1 tablet	200		
Wake Ups	1 tablet	100		
Ban Drowz	1 tablet	100		

*In Canada, Mountain Dew contains no caffeine.

**Caffeine content posted does not include the caffeine content of other additives such as guarana.

***The manufacturer lists only the ingredients, not the caffeine content.

Sources: Barone and Roberts (1984); Gilbert (1976); Heckman et al. (2010); Mumford et al. (1994); www.espinet.org/new/cafchart.htm (accessed September 2011); http://www.energyfiend.com/ (accessed September 2011)

In preparation for making coffee, the beans are roasted. Roasting serves no function other than to enhance the flavor. The roasted beans are then crushed or ground and mixed with boiling water. The caffeine content of a cup of coffee can vary considerably because of a number of factors: the caffeine concentration in the coffee beans (*robusta* has about twice the caffeine content of *arabica*), method of brewing (although most brewing methods extract nearly all the available caffeine), and, not surprisingly, the size of the cup. Most sources will tell you that the average cup of coffee contains 100 mg of caffeine, but this is likely an underestimate. It is based on a 5-ounce (oz) cup, which is the size often used in restaurants and hospitals. Cups used at home and work are typically bigger, closer to 8 or 9 oz. Cups of coffee sold at coffee shops are even larger. Actual surveys have shown that the caffeine content of an 8-oz cup of drip brewed coffee may range between 100 and 200 mg, but the mean is closer to 133 mg. Table 9-1 gives caffeine content in an 8-oz cup.

Tea

Tea is made from the leaves of *Camellia sinensis*, which in its natural form is a large tree, but in its commercial cultivated form is more like a bush. For the best-quality teas, only the bud and first two leaves of each twig are plucked. Inferior-quality teas are made from the third and fourth leaves. Caffeine content, as well as quality, decreases in leaves the further they are from the bud.

A drink may be made from the raw green leaves, but such concoctions are rather bitter. Most of the tea consumed outside of Asia is *black* or *fermented tea* (the process is not really fermentation but *oxidation*). The green leaves are dried slightly and then crushed and left to oxidize. The crushing or rolling breaks the membrane and releases enzymes that cause the oxidation. This turns the leaf black and gives it a particular taste. In *semifermented* or *oolong tea*, the oxidation process is stopped, before it is completed, by roasting. In *green Chinese tea* or *unfermented tea*, the leaves are steamed soon after picking and before drying to prevent oxidation. Consequently, green tea has quite a different taste from black tea. In the Orient, teas are frequently scented with flower petals. *Jasmine tea* is an example.

The amount of caffeine in a cup of tea varies, but is likely less than that found in a cup of coffee. One study showed a median of 27 mg per 5-oz cup with a range of 8 to 91 mg. In addition to caffeine, tea contains theophylline and theobromine (Gilbert, 1976; Graham, 1984).

Cocoa

Cocoa is made from seeds found in the seedpods of the *cacao tree, Theobroma cacao*, which is native to the dense, tropical Amazon rain forest. (The name *cacao* refers to the tree and its seeds; the term *cocoa* is used to refer to the processed products of the bean. Care should be taken not to confuse either of these terms with *coca*, the bush that is the source of cocaine; see Chapter 10.) Cocoa is now cultivated mainly in Central and South America, the West Indies, and West Africa. The mature tree grows seedpods from the trunk and main branches. These pods, about 6 to 10 inches long and 3 to 4 inches in diameter, contain 20 to 40 seeds surrounded by pulp. The seeds are removed and put in boxes or piles for fermentation. During this process, which lasts 5 to 6 days, the pulp ferments, becomes very watery, and separates from the seed; fermentation heats the beans, causing them to germinate, and then kills them. The beans are then dried in the sun or in commercial driers. This entire process takes place on the plantation.

After drying, the beans are shipped to manufacturing plants for further processing. They are roasted for enhanced flavor and then crushed, and the husks of the shells are removed. The result is sold as unsweetened chocolate, a product that has a high fat content and is not very appealing. In 1828, in the Netherlands, a Dutchman, C. J. Van Houten, invented a press that could remove most of the fat, or cocoa butter, from the unsweetened chocolate. This turned out to be a major breakthrough in the processing of cocoa. In addition to inventing the press, the Dutch learned to *alkalize* cocoa, which gives it a stronger flavor and a darker color and makes the powder disperse better in water.

In the production of cocoa powder, the unsweetened chocolate is pressed into cakes. This process removes a large portion of the cocoa butter. The cakes are then ground to produce the dry cocoa powder. Chocolate is made by mixing the roasted, alkalized, and refined beans with sugar and cocoa butter and, in the case of milk chocolate, with milk or milk solids. The details of the mixing process are complicated and vary according to the type and proposed use of the chocolate being produced (Minifie, 1970).

Chocolate contains both caffeine and theobromine in varying concentrations. It has been estimated that 1 oz of semisweet (baking) chocolate may contain between 150 and 300 mg of combined methylxanthines, and a cup of chocolate milk may contain 75 to 100 mg.

Other Natural Sources of Methylxanthines

Other natural sources of caffeine are the *ilex plant* of the Amazon region of South America and the *cassina* of North America. The ilex plant, *Ilex paraguariensis*, is a holly (related to the Christmas holly) that contains between 1 and 2% caffeine. A tea-like drink called *maté* is made from its leaves and is popular in South America. Each morning, men of the Peruvian Achuar Jivaro tribe are reported to drink a strong herbal tea made from the ilex that contains the caffeine equivalent of five cups of coffee, after which they vomit in order to avoid overdose symptoms. It is considered to be part of a macho ritual passed down through the ages (Science News, 1992).

Cassina is another type of holly, *Ilex vomitoria*, from which a beverage known as *yaupon, cassina tea*, or *black drink* is made. Yaupon is not used today, but at one time it was widely consumed by native peoples of the southeastern United States. It was considered a noble beverage, and its use was restricted to great men and chiefs. Cassina tea enjoyed a revival during the American Civil War and World War I, when coffee and tea were either not available or very expensive.

Guarana is a paste made from the seeds of *Paullinia cupana*, which, at 2 to 6% caffeine, is the most potent of the natural sources of caffeine. The plant grows in regions of the Amazon, Orinoco, and Negro rivers in South America. The paste is molded into sticks or bars or even sculptures and dried in the sun. For use, it is powdered and mixed with water. Because it has an acrid taste, like chocolate, it is usually sweetened with sugar.

There are a number of species of the genus *Cola*, a small evergreen tree native to southern Nigeria. Its nuts (*kola nuts*) are edible and contain caffeine and theobromine. Cola trees are now cultivated all over western Africa, and chewing the nut is a widespread habit. The nut is sold commercially to the United States, where it is used to flavor cola beverages such as Coca-Cola and Pepsi-Cola. Most of the caffeine in these beverages, however, does not come from the kola nut but is added later. Energy drinks may contain guarana, maté, and kola nut.

Medicines and Food Additives

In addition to being added to cola beverages, caffeine is added in small quantities for flavor to pudding mixes, baked goods, dairy desserts, and candy (Barone & Roberts, 1984). Caffeine can also be found in hundreds of prescription and over-the-counter medicines. Table 9-1 lists a few of these. They include common analgesics such as Anacin, weight control aids, allergy relief compounds, and stimulants.

Both theophylline and caffeine are used as a respiratory stimulants for newborn babies and people suffering from asthma.

Soft Drinks and Energy Drinks

Caffeine has been a constituent of Coca-Cola since it was first manufactured in 1885. The original source was the kola nut. Since that time it has been added to numerous other soft drinks, as can be seen in Table 9-1. In most cases, these drinks are sold in a 12-oz can or bottle that contains 35 to 50 mg of caffeine. In the 1980s, Jolt cola, containing 71 mg of caffeine, was introduced in the United States. In the United States, the Food and Drug administration (FDA) regulates soft drinks and imposes a limit of 71 mg of caffeine in a 12-oz serving. In the 1990s, to get around this regulation, several manufacturers started marketing caffeinated drinks as a dietary supplement, a product not regulated by the FDA. These products are generally known as *energy drinks*.

Energy drinks may contain between 50 and 300 mg of caffeine in an 8.4-oz (or smaller) serving, but they also contain other additives that include taurine, vitamins, and sugar or artificial sweeteners. They may also contain herbal supplements, such as ginkgo, guarana, kola nut, maté, and cocoa—some of which also provide additional caffeine and other methylxanthines. This extra caffeine content is not included on the label, or in the caffeine amounts given in Table 9-1, so it is impossible to know the exact dose of caffeine contained in an energy drink.

In the 2000s, energy drinks have become exceedingly popular, and sales increased drastically. Energy drinks are now the fastest growing sector of the United States beverage market, and sales are expected to surpass 9 billion dollars in the United States alone in 2011 (Seifert, Schaechter, Hershorin, & Lipshultz, 2011). In Canada, energy drinks are regulated by Canada's National Health Product Regulation, which oversees labels and marketing, but not caffeine content.

HISTORY OF METHYLXANTHINE USE

Coffee

The coffee bush is native to Ethiopia. Its properties were discovered sometime between the twelfth and fifteenth centuries. From Ethiopia, its use spread across Arabia, Egypt, and North Africa, around the Mediterranean into Turkey, and then to Europe.

William Harvey, the first person to describe the circulation of the blood, was one of the first coffee drinkers in England, and he promoted the beverage for its therapeutic benefits. Two of his students believed that it was a cure for drunkenness (Austin, 1985). The first English coffeehouse opened in Oxford in 1650, and the concept soon spread throughout England. Coffeehouses were referred to as "schools of the cultured," and coffee was "the milk of chess players and thinkers." Coffee, and the intellectual tradition associated with coffeehouses, soon spread throughout Europe. At one time, coffee drinking gained such popularity in England that the consumption of alcoholic beverages, particularly cheap gin, started to decline. Coffee has remained popular throughout Europe, but in Great Britain it was eventually replaced by tea.

Although tea was the preferred drink in colonial America, coffeehouses were as common as in England and filled the same social function: a meeting place for intellectual and political discussion. Boston coffeehouses such as the Brown, the North End Coffee-House, and the Exchange served as headquarters for Whigs and Tories and were the scenes of much plotting and fighting. One famous coffeehouse, the Green Dragon, is still marked by a plaque at the site where "such adventurous and ardent patriots as Otis, Joseph Warren, John Adams, Samuel Adams, Cushing, Pitts, Molyneux, and Paul Revere met nightly to discuss public affairs" (Cheney, 1925, p. 233).

Tea

There are many legends about the origins of tea. One tale credits the discovery of the beverage to the Chinese emperor Chen Nung. It is known that tea was cultivated and sold commercially in China by 780 C.E. when the book *Ch'a Ching*, or *Tea Classic*, was written. The book was sponsored by a group of merchants, and its purpose was to promote tea drinking (Forrest, 1973).

Tea was first mentioned in print in Europe in 1559, but it was not until 1606 that the Dutch actually shipped some to Europe. In the 1630s, the Dutch started shipping tea on a regular basis to satisfy a growing demand in their country as well as in Germany and France. Tea was also becoming popular in Portugal, which had an extensive Oriental trade of its own. In the 1640s and 1650s, tea enjoyed a brief phase of popularity in France, but the French turned to coffee in the 1660s.

During all this time, tea was not extensively consumed in England. It did not become fashionable until Charles II married the Infanta Catherine, who brought tea drinking with her from Portugal in 1662. Tea also became popular in the 13 British colonies of North America. In fact, by 1760, tea was the third largest export from England to the colonies, and this figure represented only a quarter of the total tea imported; the rest was smuggled. Smuggling was due to the tea tax imposed by the English Parliament at Westminster on all tea imported into Britain. When the tea was later shipped to America, the price included this import tax. In 1767, this indirect tax was removed, and a direct tax was imposed. These taxes angered the colonists, and when the British East India Company tried to export a tea surplus to the colonies in 1773, the angry colonists dumped it into Boston Harbor. This *tea party* was the first of many, and it set the stage for the American Revolution.

Cocoa

The Mayans of the Yucatán Peninsula, the Aztecs of Mexico, and the Incas of Peru cultivated the cacao tree long before the European discovery of North America. They believed it to be a gift of the gods. This belief is the origin of the genus name of the cacao bush, *Theobroma*, which is Greek for *food of the gods*. Among the Central American Indian tribes, chocolate was a food generally reserved for the wealthy and powerful. It was believed to be an aphrodisiac and was used at wedding feasts and by wealthy noblemen who could afford to support, and had to satisfy, many wives. It has been reported that Montezuma, emperor of the Aztecs at the time of Cortés, consumed 50 golden goblets of the drink each day. He called it *chocolatl*, but what he downed must have been quite different from modern chocolate. The Aztecs' concoction included maize and spices, such as peppers, but no sugar or milk.

Cortés introduced the drink to the Spanish court in 1520 with the addition of vanilla and sugar, and this sweetened form eventually gained popularity all over Europe. The Spanish managed to keep the source of chocolate secret for 100 years, but eventually the Dutch introduced the plant into the Philippines and Ceylon (now Sri Lanka).

Chocolate was introduced in Europe before coffee and tea and enjoyed a brief popularity, but because it was expensive, its use was restricted to the wealthy and the nobility. In every case, it was displaced by coffee, which remains the most popular xanthine-containing beverage today (with the exception of England, where coffee was replaced by tea). In time, chocolate did become cheaper and more readily available. The first chocolate factory in England was founded by S. J. Fry in 1728, when chocolate had become more plentiful, but by that time, tea was the indisputable beverage of the people. Even though chocolate did not make it as a popular drink, the development of better processing techniques made it successful as a confection.

Today, the bulk of the world's supply of cocoa comes from West Africa rather than South America. It is also grown commercially in Indonesia and Sri Lanka. It is perhaps ironic that cocoa, which is native to South America, is now a more profitable crop in Africa. The South Americans, however, have had their revenge many times over. Coffee, a native African plant, is now grown primarily in South America.

EXTENT OF METHYLXANTHINE USE

Caffeine and the other methylxanthines are probably the most widely self-administered drugs in the world. It has often been claimed (in earlier editions of this text and elsewhere) that coffee is the second most valuable traded commodity in the world after oil. This may have been true many years go, but it is not the case today. United Nations International Merchandise Trade Statistics for 2009 are presented in Table 9-2. This table shows the export value of a selected sample of diverse commodities and products. Crude oil from various sources is clearly the most valuable at 1.4 trillion U.S. dollars. The total of all products that contain methylxanthine (including coffee, tea, cocoa, and maté) is 65.2 billion U.S. dollars. Methylxanthines are clearly outtraded by many other

TABLE 9-2 Total Values of Some Internationally Exported Commodities in 2009 According to the United Nations International Merchandise Trade Statistics

Product or Commodity	Value of World Exports (in U.S. Dollars)
Crude oil from various sources	1.4 trillion
Medicines and pharmaceuticals	1.2 trillion
Automobiles	434.4 billion
Paper products	98.2 billion
Pearls and precious stones	89.5 billion
Textiles	38.0 billion
Food and Agricultural Products	
Meat	101.4 billion
Dairy products (milk and cheese)	54.5 billion
Vegetables (fresh, frozen and tubers)	86.4 billion
Fish	68.4 billion
Coffee and products containing methylxanthines	65.2 billion
Alcoholic beverages	57.2 billion
Wheat products	36.1 billion
Tobacco	34.2 billion

Source: http://comtrade.un.org/pb/CommodityPagesNew.aspx?y=2009

products including cars, jewels, copper, coal, and others not shown. But among agricultural and food exports, products containing methylxanthines are fifth behind meat, dairy products, and vegetables, and they are only slightly behind the world's total export of fish and fish products.

The average caffeine consumption of the world's population is about 70 mg per person per day, 90% of which is consumed in the form of coffee and tea. The Scandinavian countries are the world's greatest partakers of coffee. Their per capita consumption is about 7 to 9 kg of green coffee beans annually. In North America, Canadian consumption is about 6.3 kg and in the United States, 4.1 kg. Middle Eastern, North African, and Asian countries are at the bottom of the list of coffee consumers (International Coffee Organization, 2012). Ireland and Great Britain are the greatest per capita consumers of tea, about 10 times that of the United States and Canada. European countries, including the Scandinavian countries, are at the bottom of the tea list (Food and Agriculture Organization of the United Nations online database; http://faostat.fao.org/site/291/default.aspx).

In the late 1990s, U.S. average daily consumption of caffeine from all caffeinated beverages was 120 mg. The 90th percentile was 287 mg (this means that 10% of the population consumed more than this amount per day). Sources of caffeine were coffee (53%), soft drinks (28%), tea (18%), and others, including cocoa (1%). Older individuals consumed a higher proportion of coffee and tea, while younger individuals consumed more soft drinks (Knight et al., 2004). These data were collected before energy drinks and shots became popular, and these sources have caused a significant change in patterns of caffeine consumption, especially among younger people (Seifert et al., 2011).

ROUTE OF ADMINISTRATION

When consumed in natural products, the methylxanthines are normally taken orally without difficulty. But when given for medical reasons, the purified drugs sometimes cause nausea and gastric irritation, especially in children. In such cases, the drugs may be given in the form of a rectal suppository or by intramuscular or intravenous routes.

ABSORPTION

Although the methylxanthines are absorbed from the stomach, absorption is much more rapid through the walls of the intestine. Factors that decrease stomach-emptying time, such as the presence of food, will slow methylxanthine absorption. The methylxanthines are bases; consequently, when they are dissolved in the acidic environment of the digestive system, they might be expected to be highly ionized and not lipid soluble. However, these drugs have a very low pKa—about 0.5. Consequently, at the pH of the digestive system and any other pH encountered in the body, the methylxanthines will not be ionized at all and will be free to dissolve in any tissue in accordance with their lipid solubility. The methylxanthines are quite lipid soluble and dissolve poorly in water.

The caffeine in coffee, tea, and chocolate exists and is consumed in its alkaloid form, but for medicinal purposes, the methylxanthines are usually given as salts, which can be absorbed much more readily. Aminophylline (a bronchodilator used to treat asthma) is the most widely used methylxanthine preparation. It is a mixture of theophylline and *ethylenediamine*. The latter substance is considered therapeutically inert, but it increases the amount of dissolved theophylline 20 times and thereby speeds absorption. *Oxtriphylline* (Choledyl or choline theophylline) is also widely used.

After drinking coffee or tea, a person completely absorbs caffeine from the digestive system. Peak blood levels of caffeine are reached in about 30 minutes. Peak blood levels of caffeine after drinking colas and chocolate are between 1.5 to 2.0 hours. There is no significant first-pass metabolism (Arnaud, 2011).

DISTRIBUTION

Caffeine crosses the blood–brain and placental barriers without difficulty and reaches all body organs, although the rates of entering and leaving the organs may vary. About 10 to 30% of caffeine in the blood becomes bound to protein and trapped in the circulatory system (Arnaud, 1993; Axelrod & Reisenthal, 1953). Caffeine is present in all body fluids, including breast milk. Theophylline and theobromine are less lipid soluble than caffeine and are slower getting through the blood–brain barrier.

EXCRETION

In humans, less than 2% of caffeine is excreted unchanged in the urine (Arnaud, 1993). The remainder is converted to paraxanthine and other metabolites in the liver (Bonati & Garattini, 1984; Burg, 1975). For a given individual, the half-life of caffeine is fairly constant, but this may vary from 2.5 to more than 4.5 hours in different individuals, with a mean of 3.5 hours. The half-lives of theophylline and theobromine are considerably longer than caffeine at 6.2 and 7.2 hours (Arnaud, 2011). There is evidence that the half-life may be dose dependent; that is, the larger the dose, the longer the half-life (Kaplan et al., 1997). In spite of its long half-life, caffeine does not appear to accumulate in the body over days if it is not consumed after 6:00 P.M. (Axelrod & Reisenthal, 1953). In nonhumans, the half-life varies considerably, from 11 to 12 hours in the pig and squirrel monkey to 2 hours in the rat (Kihlman, 1977).

There appear to be individual genetic differences that determine the rate of caffeine metabolism. Caffeine is metabolized by one of the cytochrome P450 enzymes, and the CYP1A2 gene carries instructions for building this enzyme. There are two forms of the CYP1A2 gene. Individuals who express the CYP1A2*1A form of the gene are *rapid* caffeine metabolizers. Those who carry the CYP1A2*1F form of the gene are *slow* caffeine metabolizers. The same amount of caffeine will therefore have a greater effect on a slow metabolizer of caffeine than a fast metabolizer and may be more likely to have adverse effects.

The CYP1A2 enzyme can also be stimulated or inhibited by medicines and foods. For example, caffeine metabolism is slowed by alcohol and grapefruit juice but speeded by broccoli, and smokers eliminate caffeine twice as fast as nonsmokers (James, 1991; Parsons & Neims, 1978). The fluoroquinolones, a family of antibiotic drugs, can also slow caffeine metabolism by inhibiting the CYP1A2 enzyme.

In women, metabolism of caffeine is closely related to hormone levels. Caffeine half-life in women is longer during the luteal phase (after ovulation) than during the follicular phase (before ovulation) of the menstrual cycle (Arnaud, 1993). The half-life in women taking oral contraceptives is twice that of women ovulating regularly (Callahan, Robertson, Branfman, McCormish, & Yesair, 1983). Caffeine elimination is also slowed during pregnancy (Neims, Bailey, & Aldrich, 1979). These changes appear to be due to alterations in enzyme levels.

It has also been shown that newborns cannot metabolize caffeine well. They excrete about 85% of it unchanged in the urine, with the result that the half-life is about 4 days. The adult pattern of caffeine metabolism is not developed until 7 to 9 months of age (Aldrich, Aranda, & Neims, 1979).

In nonhuman species, caffeine is metabolized differently, using different enzymes and creating different metabolites (Arnaud, 2011; Berthou et al., 1992). For this reason, one must always approach nonhuman studies of the methylxanthines with caution. Some metabolites created in other species may be more active or toxic than those created in humans (Stavric & Gilbert, 1990).

NEUROPHYSIOLOGY

The effects of methylxanthines on neural functioning are now fairly well understood. Most of the effects of the methylxanthines appear to arise from the fact that they are *adenosine receptor blockers*. Adenosine has many functions in the body. It acts as a neurotransmitter at postsynaptic synapses and as a neuromodulator at presynaptic sites where it works mostly by inhibiting the release of a number of neurotransmitters. In general, its effect is to inhibit neurotransmission in many synapses in the brain.

There are four types of adenosine receptors—A_1, A_{2A}, A_{2B}, and A_3—and the methylxanthines appear to be effective blockers of the A_1 and, most potently, A_{2A} types. A_1 receptors are distributed widely in the brain, while A_{2A} receptors are primarily located in the striatum. Both A_1 and A_{2A} receptors appear to modulate levels of dopamine in the brain, and, because they block these adenosine receptors, the methylxanthines increase dopamine levels. It is this increase in dopamine that is responsible for most of the behavioral and reinforcing effects of the methylxanthines.

The means by which methylxanthines increase dopamine activity is complex and involves some newly discovered neural mechanisms. The receptors for adenosine often participate in the formation of *receptor mosaics* where two or more receptors become attached to each other and consequently influence one another's operation (Fuxe, Marcellino, Guidolin, Woods, &

Agnati, 2008). Such receptor mosaics can involve the same types of receptors or several different types of receptors. The operation of receptor mosaics involving A_1, A_{2A}, D_1, and D_2 receptors has been studied in the striatum where they determine dopamine effects by integrating the activity of dopamine and glutamate on GABAergic neurons (Ferre, 2008). The effects of methylxanthines on activity in the striatum are further complicated by the presence of cannabinoid CB_1 receptors, which sit on striatal GABAergic neurons. The sensitivity of these receptors can be enhanced by chronic caffeine administration (Rossi et al., 2010). The net result of these effects is an increased transmission at D_2 receptors and modulation of the release of dopamine, glutamate, and acetylcholine (Fredholm, Bättig, Holmén, Nehlig, & Zvartau, 1999).

In addition to their effect on adenosine, caffeine and the methylxanthines are known to block benzodiazepine receptors, but this effect seems to require higher doses of caffeine than those that normally cause behavioral effects. At a dose roughly equivalent of 10 cups of coffee, as many as 20% of benzodiazepine receptors are blocked (Paul, Marangos, Goodwin, & Skolnick, 1980). Among the different methylxanthines, however, there does not seem to be a correlation between the ability to block benzodiazepine receptors and the drug's effects (Snyder, 1984). It is not known whether this ability to block benzodiazepine receptors has any behavioral significance.

Not long ago, it was shown that three substances that occur naturally in chocolate resemble anandamide, the endogenous transmitter that works at cannabinoid receptors (see Chapter 14). In addition, other compounds have been found in chocolate that block the metabolism of anandamide (di Tomaso, Beltramo, & Piomelli, 1996). Although these compounds do not exert effects great enough to cause a noticeable high, their presence might contribute to the enjoyment and popularity of chocolate, beyond those effects predicted by the presence of caffeine.

EFFECTS OF CAFFEINE AND THE METHYLXANTHINES

Effects on the Body

Because the methylxanthines cause the release of epinephrine from the adrenal gland, there is a resultant stimulation of the sympathetic nervous system.

However, much of caffeine's effect outside the central nervous system is due to its direct effect on the muscles; smooth (involuntary) muscles tend to relax, and striated (voluntary) muscles are strengthened.

The smooth muscle relaxation results in dilation of the bronchi of the lungs and a decrease in airway resistance. Theophylline is the most potent methylxanthine in producing this effect; as a result, it is used clinically in the treatment of asthma. Methylxanthines also reduce the susceptibility of striated muscles to fatigue (see the section on athletic performance).

Caffeine has different effects on blood flow in different parts of the body. It causes a constriction of blood vessels in the brain but dilation in the rest of the body. By constricting blood flow to the brain, caffeine is able to reduce headaches caused by high blood pressure. For this reason, caffeine is found in many over-the-counter headache remedies.

High levels of caffeine stimulate the spinal cord. This manifests first as an increase in excitability of spinal reflexes. Higher doses lead to convulsions, which are sometimes lethal. The regulatory centers of the medulla are also stimulated by high doses, producing an increase in the rate and depth of breathing. This ability of the methylxanthines to stimulate respiration makes them useful in the treatment of babies born with breathing difficulties.

Effects on Human Performance and Behavior

Caffeine has long been associated with improvements in cognitive function and performance. Textbooks have claimed that the effects of caffeine at low doses (100 to 200 mg) typically cause "greater sustained intellectual effort and a more perfect association of ideas" or "a keener appreciation of sensory stimuli" (Ritchie, 1975, p. 367). However, it is not clear what these terms actually mean. Research into the effects of caffeine can be tricky and must take into account a number of factors that are not always obvious. To begin with, we know that caffeine improves mood and makes tasks seem easier. This often leads research participants to believe that performance has improved, when it actually has not. This means that subjective reports are not reliable.

In an early experiment by Goldstein, Kaizer, and Warren (1965), participants were asked to rate the effects of caffeine on their alertness, physical activity, and wakefulness. Then they were given caffeine and tested on their ability to detect a number in an array of numbers flashed on a screen for 1/32 second. They were also tested on coordination in a line-drawing task. The participants' assessment of their alertness and physical activeness did not correlate with their real abilities as measured by these various tasks; though all participants thought they were doing better, caffeine produced no improvement.

The effect of caffeine on performance may also be influenced by placebo effects, so careful placebo controls are important and instructions to participants must be worded so as to avoid creating expectations (Fillmore & Vogel-Sprott, 1992; Harrell & Juliano, 2009). A double-blind procedure, as described in Chapter 2, should be used.

Since the vast majority of people consume caffeine daily, it is also necessary to account for the effect of the experimental participant's usual dietary consumption of caffeine. This is often done by instructing participants to avoid caffeine-containing products for a period of time to be sure that all participants are caffeine-free at the beginning of the experiment. This, however, creates another problem: the effect of caffeine withdrawal. If someone is a regular coffee drinker and is deprived of coffee overnight, or even for a number of hours, he or she will experience caffeine withdrawal, which interferes with cognition and performance on various tasks. Thus, if you give him or her caffeine and performance improves, you cannot be sure whether this represents an improvement in baseline performance or whether you are seeing a decrease in withdrawal effects in the group treated with caffeine (Heatherley, 2011; Rogers & Dernoncourt, 1998; Rogers et al., 2005).

Typically, researchers have found that caffeine is capable of reversing decrements in performance caused by boredom and fatigue, drugs, caffeine withdrawal, and the common cold (Lara, 2010). Caffeine improves attention and speeds both simple and choice reaction times. Some studies have demonstrated that caffeine is also capable of improving the performance of normal, alert individuals on attention and working memory tasks at doses equivalent to a single cup of coffee (Smith, 2009). Improvements have also been seen in reaction times on visual, cognitive, and verbal reasoning tasks in regular coffee users who were not experiencing caffeine withdrawal as well as in non–coffee consumers (Haskell, Kennedy, Wesnes, & Scholey, 2005). One researcher concluded that "despite the development of tolerance and withdrawal reactions to some extent, caffeine can produce these effects [improvements in performance] in regular users without abstinence and in non regular users." (Lara, 2010, p. S243)

Effects on Athletic Performance

Caffeine, in doses of about 6.5 mg/kg (450 mg in a 155-pound person), has been shown to improve some types of athletic performance. It does not seem to improve performance in events that require muscle strength, such as weight lifting, nor does it improve performance that requires intense output over a short duration, such as sprinting and throwing. It does, however, improve performance in tasks that require submaximal output for an extended period of time, such as cross-country skiing, running, or cycling (Nehlig, Daval, & Debry, 1992; Ryu et al., 2001). However, even in these events, results are far from consistent, and the effect is moderated by other factors such as body composition.

It was once thought that the reason for improved performance on these tasks is that caffeine increases blood levels of fatty acids that can be used as fuel by the muscles. As a result, the muscles use less glycogen, their normal fuel; it is kept in reserve, so the muscles are not fatigued as quickly in endurance events (Tarnopolsky, 1994). However, it has since been shown that caffeine does not have this effect. It does, however, lower the threshold for exercise-induced beta-endorphin and cortisol release, which may contribute to the reported benefits of caffeine on exercise endurance.

Because of the possibility that caffeine is an athletic performance enhancer, for many years caffeine was banned by the International Olympic Committee (Lombardo, 1986) in urine in concentrations higher than 12 mg per litre (Tarnopolsky, 1994). Only one athlete has ever been disqualified from Olympic competition for exceeding the caffeine limit—a member of the Australian pentathlon team in the 1988 Summer Olympics at Seoul (James, 1991). The World Anti-Doping Agency lifted this restriction in January 2004, and there are now no legal restrictions on caffeine.

Effects on Sleep

There is little doubt that the methylxanthines can produce insomnia. Their effect seems to be in increasing the "stability of wakefulness" by increasing the length of time it takes to fall asleep and reducing total sleep time. In one study, 300 mg of caffeine increased the latency of sleep onset from 18 to 66 minutes and reduced total sleep time from 475 to 350 minutes compared to control participants (Brenesova, Oswald, & Loudon, 1975). As can be seen in Table 9-1, caffeine is a major ingredient in many over-the-counter stimulant pills, most of which contain 100 mg of caffeine.

In general, people who take caffeine before going to bed report sleeping less soundly and feeling less rested. Caffeine also lowers the acoustic arousal threshold while sleeping; people wake up more easily in response to a sound in the night. This effect is variable among individuals; habitual coffee drinkers are less affected than coffee abstainers. This difference is probably due to tolerance rather than a preexisting difference between coffee drinkers and coffee abstainers. After 7 days of exposure to a 400-mg daily dose of caffeine, total sleep time and awakenings had returned to baseline levels (Bonnet & Arand, 1992).

It has also been demonstrated that caffeine can counteract the sleep-inducing effects of pentobarbital (a tranquilizing medication). A usual sleep-inducing dose of pentobarbital, 100 mg, when given in combination with 250 mg of caffeine, produces the same effect on sleep as a placebo (Forrest, Bellville, & Brown, 1972).

Although the mechanisms that cause sleep are still not fully understood, numerous brain regions are known to be involved. One, which is located in the subcortical preoptic region called the *ventrolateral preoptic nucleus* (VLPO), is a sleep-inducing center. When it is active, it causes sleep by generating synchronous activity in the cortex, which shows up on an EEG as slow waves. There are several other centers in the brainstem and midbrain that are waking centers. They arouse and desynchronize cortical activity, which wakes up the brain and keeps it active. The waking centers and the sleep center send inhibitory axons to each other so that control of the cortex tends to flip-flop between these centers. After you have been awake for a period of time, the sleep center is triggered to become active, it inhibits the wakefulness centers, and you sleep. After you have slept for a period of time, the wakefulness centers take over, they inhibit the sleep center, and you wake up. There are numerous environmental, neural, and chemical events that can trigger the flip-flop, but a build up of adenosine is one trigger that can activate the sleep center.

Caffeine blocks or suppresses this activation by blocking adenosine receptors with the result that you can stay awake longer (Luppi & Fort, 2011).

Effects on Behavior of Nonhumans

UNCONDITIONED BEHAVIOR. Caffeine will increase spontaneous motor activity of mice in an open field with maximum effects appearing at 20 to 40 mg/kg doses. A dose of 80 mg/kg will greatly decrease spontaneous motor activity. Increases in activity are also produced by theophylline at similar doses, but there is some evidence that theophylline may be slightly more potent than caffeine (Scott & Chen, 1944). Interestingly, chronic treatment with caffeine results in a depression of spontaneous activity (Fredholm, 1995).

The LD_{50} of caffeine for both rats and mice is somewhere around 250 mg/kg by intraperitoneal administration (Barnes & Elthrington, 1973). Death may be due to convulsions. Some animals die at lower doses from bleeding as a result of attacking themselves. Automutilation has been observed in rats when caffeine was given at a dose of 185 mg/kg for 14 days. The rats bit their tails and paws, even though they seemed to retain their normal sense of pain. When a ball of wire was placed in their cage, they temporarily attacked it but soon returned to biting themselves. When picked up, they did not bite the hand of the experimenter, but they did attack other rats placed with them in a cage (Peters, 1967).

OPERANT AND RESPONDENT CONDITIONED BEHAVIOR. The first person to experiment with the effects of caffeine on conditioned behavior was Pavlov (1927). He showed that the drug could disrupt conditioned discriminations by increasing responses to the negative stimulus. After ingesting caffeine, the animals responded to stimuli that did not signal food in the same way that they had responded to stimuli that did signal food. He concluded that the drug produced "an increase in excitability of the Central Nervous System."

The profile of effects of caffeine on operant behavior is very similar to, but not exactly the same as, the profile caused by the psychomotor stimulants such as amphetamine (McKim, 1980). This similarity is probably a result of the increased catecholamine release and dopamine activity caused by caffeine (Garrett & Griffiths, 1997).

There is some evidence that caffeine at 30 mg/kg in a rat will increase food-reinforced responding that has been suppressed by punishment with electric shock (Morrison, 1969). If this observation is true, it makes this effect of caffeine more similar to the barbiturates than to amphetamine. In general, caffeine appears to increase avoidance responding. Increases were seen on nondiscriminated avoidance responding of squirrel monkeys at a dosage of 1 to 30 mg/kg of caffeine; these increases were almost as great as those seen with amphetamine (Davis, Kensler, & Dews, 1973).

Although the effects of caffeine and the other methylxanthines on conditioned animal behavior have not been extensively investigated, it appears that they are very different from the effects of amphetamine on some types of behavior and very similar to amphetamine on others. These data clearly show that caffeine cannot be thought of as a mild amphetamine; its behavioral properties are quite distinctive and difficult to classify with any other category of drug.

DISCRIMINATIVE STIMULUS PROPERTIES

At a dose of 32 mg/kg, rats can be trained to discriminate between caffeine and saline in a two-lever Skinner box. Rats generalize the state produced by caffeine to lower doses of caffeine and higher doses of theophylline, but there is no generalization to nicotine (Modrow, Holloway, & Carney, 1981).

As with human subjective effects, caffeine appears to share some of the subjective effects of cocaine and amphetamine, at least at low doses. There is partial generalization to cocaine and amphetamine in rats trained to discriminate low but not high doses of caffeine and vice versa. Caffeine will increase the discriminative effects of low doses of cocaine. Dopamine receptor blockers will block the discriminative effects of low but not high doses of caffeine (Garrett & Griffiths, 1997).

For some time, there has been a concern over what are known as *look-alike* or *turkey drugs*. These preparations look, in all regards, like controlled psychoactive drugs, such as amphetamine, but instead contain a drug or a combination of drugs that are not prescribed or controlled substances. Turkey drugs designed to mimic amphetamine or cocaine often contain caffeine in combination with other substances such as *ephedrine* and *phenylpropanolamine*. One study has shown that, in rats at least, this combination of drugs can mimic the discriminative stimulus effects of 10 mg/kg of cocaine (Gauvin et al., 1989).

Although there is considerable individual variability, humans can discriminate the presence of caffeine in capsules at very low doses. In one experiment, a dose of 1.8 mg of caffeine was detected by one participant, although two others detected a dose of 10 mg, and one participant needed 178 mg. In the same experiment, the same participant who was able to detect 1.8 mg of caffeine detected a dose of 100 mg of theobromine, but two participants out of seven were unable to discriminate 1,000 mg of theobromine (Mumford et al., 1994).

The discriminative effects of caffeine can be blocked by antagonizing dopamine receptors (Garrett & Griffiths, 1997). Adenosine A_1 receptor blockers can prevent caffeine discrimination, but the presence of an A_{2A} receptor blocker does not alter caffeine's discriminative effects. In fact, it counteracts the ability of the A_1 receptor blocker to interfere with the stimulus effects of caffeine (Solinas et al., 2005).

Subjective Effects

Early studies on the subjective effects of caffeine were confusing. In some studies, participants reported increased anxiety, jitteriness, and nervousness, but other studies reported no subjective effects at all. Later studies found that participants experience an array of positive effects, such as increases in feelings of well-being, alertness, energy, motivation for work, and self-confidence. Griffiths and Mumford (1995) and Rush, Sullivan, and Griffiths (1995) report that positive effects are more reliably detected under a restricted set of conditions. First, they are seen when caffeine is administered to people who are not caffeine users or to caffeine users who have been deprived at least overnight. The fact that positive effects are seen in coffee abstainers indicates that these effects are not simply a matter of alleviating caffeine withdrawal (Childs & de Wit, 2006; Richardson, Rogers, Elliman, & O'Dell, 1995). Second, positive effects are more likely to be seen at low doses (from 20 to 200 mg). The higher the dose, the more likely it is that unpleasant effects will be reported. Finally, positive effects are most likely to be reported by individuals for whom caffeine acts as a positive reinforcer.

In a study by Mumford and colleagues (1994), participants were given 178 mg of caffeine, and scores on a mood scale were determined at various time points thereafter. The drug caused increases in well-being, magnitude of drug effect, energy, affection for loved ones, motivation to work, self-confidence, social disposition, alertness, and concentration, and decreases in *sleepy* and *muzzy* feelings. These changes were evident within 30 minutes and remained higher than placebo levels for at least 8 hours.

The same study also examined the subjective effects of theobromine. A dose of 100 mg produced positive changes in energy, motivation to work, and alertness but to a much smaller extent than caffeine. The time course for these changes was similar to caffeine, but at 5 to 10 hours after ingestion, participants reported unpleasant effects such as headache and lethargy.

In another experiment, participants who had experience with street drugs, including cocaine, were given intravenous doses of caffeine, and the subjective effects were measured. There was a dose-related increase in ratings of "liking," "drug effect," "high," and "good effects." These feelings occurred 2 minutes after injection and decreased over the following 60 minutes. At high doses, caffeine was identified as "a stimulant (like cocaine or amphetamine)." Most participants were reasonably certain that they had been given cocaine (Rush et al., 1995).

Tolerance

Chronic administration of caffeine causes an upregulation in the number of adenosine receptors, presumably as in an attempt to restore the influence of adenosine prior to caffeine (Hirsh, 1984).

Tolerance to the behavioral effects of caffeine has been demonstrated in rats. One study showed that a 100-mg/kg injection of caffeine could depress bar pressing on an FI schedule to about 40% saline control rates (Wayner, Jolicoeur, Rondeau, & Barone, 1976). After eight injections of caffeine, this dose could only depress responding to 75% of baseline. It has also been demonstrated, in a study of operant responding in rats, that chronic treatment with caffeine shifted the caffeine dose–response curve to the right by a factor of 6. This means that after exposure to caffeine, a six-fold increase in dose was required to produce the same effect as before the exposure (Carney, 1982).

A number of studies using human participants have shown that caffeine has less effect on heavy drinkers of coffee than on nondrinkers. In one experiment, 150 to 300 mg of caffeine produced complaints of jitteriness, nervousness, and upset stomach in nonusers, but users reported increased alertness, decreased irritability, and a feeling of contentedness (Goldstein, Kaizer, & Whitby, 1969). It should be pointed out that studies like these, while probably demonstrating tolerance, may simply be showing that individuals who are resistant to the effects of caffeine are the ones who become heavy coffee drinkers.

To demonstrate tolerance to a drug effect, an experimenter must give the drug to one group of participants and a placebo to a second group for some period of time. The effect must diminish in the drug-exposed group. Furthermore, the placebo group must show the effect when switched to the drug. Tolerance to several effects of caffeine has been demonstrated using this design. Different effects of caffeine show tolerance at different rates; for example, cardiovascular effects fade within 2 to 5 days, but caffeine-induced increases in urination may take considerably longer or never show complete tolerance. Similarly, tolerance to various physiological effects has been demonstrated (Griffiths & Mumford, 1995). We have seen that the sleep-disrupting effects of 400 mg of caffeine show tolerance within 7 days. The subjective effects of 300 mg are tolerated within 4 days (Evans & Griffiths, 1992). In general, many effects of caffeine seem to disappear within a week at usual levels of consumption. Some acute effects of caffeine—the effect on spontaneous motor activity and susceptibility to convulsions—actually reverse with chronic treatment.

WITHDRAWAL

Laboratory animals appear to suffer from caffeine withdrawal, although the main symptom is a decrease in locomotor activity and a disruption of ongoing operant responding. In humans, there have been a number of documented cases of caffeine withdrawal dating back to 1833. The most common symptom is headache. In addition, people report drowsiness, decreased energy, and fatigue that can be described as weakness, letdown, or lethargy. People also report decreased motivation for work and impaired concentration, decreased feelings of well-being and self-confidence, increased irritability, and flu-like symptoms such as aches and muscle stiffness, hot and cold spells, heavy feelings in the limbs, and nausea (Griffiths & Mumford, 1995). The severity of symptoms is directly related to dose. In one study, deprivation of normal caffeine consumption in the morning (12 to 28 hours of deprivation) produced withdrawal symptoms at lunchtime testing (e.g., decreased feelings of vigor and well-being and increased feelings of fatigue and light-headedness). No changes in psychomotor performance or reaction time were detected, however (Lane, 1997; Phillips-Bute & Lane, 1998).

Doses as high as 600 mg per day can cause physical dependence after only 6 to 14 days of exposure. Withdrawal symptoms can also be seen at daily exposures of as little as 100 mg per day over a longer period of time (Griffiths & Mumford, 1995).

Withdrawal symptoms usually start within 12 to 28 hours of the last coffee intake, peak at 20 to 51 hours, and last 2 to 9 days (Griffiths & Mumford, 1995; Griffiths & Woodson, 1988; Juliano & Griffiths, 2004). Figure 9-1 shows the time-course incidence of headache and scores on an "energy/active" scale of participants maintained on 100 mg of caffeine and switched to a placebo. As you can see, it took nearly 2 weeks for these scores to return to normal (Griffiths & Mumford, 1995).

U.S. studies have shown that, among coffee consumers who have gone without coffee for 24 hours, 27 to 52% report experiencing headaches. Estimates of the number of people who are exposed to caffeine withdrawal (i.e., the number who consume more than 100 mg a day) are enormous. Caffeine withdrawal is often overlooked as a possible diagnosis when people report headache, fatigue, and mood disturbances in circumstances where normal diet, including caffeine, is disrupted. Such circumstances might include fasting before various laboratory tests, operations, or procedures such as endoscopies.

On a more mundane level, caffeine withdrawal may well be responsible for the behavior of people who are grouchy and impossible to get along with until they have had their first cup of coffee in the morning. It is probably also responsible for illnesses and headaches that occur during holidays or weekends or when people interrupt normal routines that include coffee drinking.

In the *DSM-IV-TR* (2000), caffeine withdrawal was included on an experimental basis to encourage research into its clinical significance. The category Caffeine Withdrawal has been recommended for inclusion

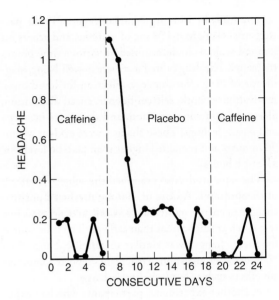

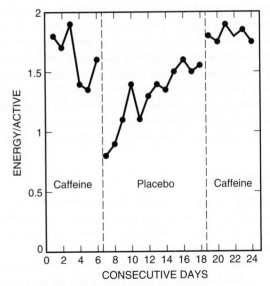

FIGURE 9-1 Changes in frequency of reported headaches and scores on an "energy/active" scale of participants for 24 days while they consumed 100-mg caffeine capsules, then a placebo, and then switched back to caffeine. Caffeine withdrawal caused increases in reported headaches and a decrease in energy and activity that lasted as long as a week. (From Griffiths et al., 1990)

in the *DSM-5*. It has also been included as an official diagnosis in the *ICD-10* (World Health Organization, 1993). However, in 2002, it was suggested that withdrawal symptoms from caffeine could be explained by nonpharmacological factors such as expectation or placebo effects, as described in Chapter 2 (Dews, O'Brien, & Bergman, 2002). This possibility was investigated by Juliano and Griffiths (2004), who reviewed the literature. They pointed out that most of the studies that have found clinically significant withdrawal from caffeine were double-blind studies where the participants did not know that they were experiencing caffeine withdrawal; expectancy and placebo effects were not likely to have caused the withdrawal symptoms. In fact, in some studies, participants did not know that the experiment involved caffeine at all.

SELF-ADMINISTRATION IN NONHUMANS

In laboratory animals, caffeine is not a robust reinforcer. It can serve as a reinforcer, but only under limited circumstances, and it does not seem to be able to support a lot of behavior. In one study where bar pressing delivered an intravenous caffeine infusion, only two out of six monkeys self-administered the caffeine spontaneously. The four monkeys that did not voluntarily self-administer caffeine were then given automatic infusions of caffeine for a period of time.

This procedure succeeded in establishing caffeine as a reinforcer in three of the four remaining monkeys (Deneau, Yanagita, & Seevers, 1969). The pattern of self-administration was irregular, with periods of voluntary abstinence, and there was no tendency to increase the dose over time. Other researchers have also demonstrated modest reinforcing effects with caffeine, but they were limited to specific doses and particular animals (Griffiths, Bigelow, & Lieberson, 1979). Other studies have not been able to demonstrate reinforcing effects of caffeine at all, although these studies used only one dose of caffeine or tested for only a short time (Hoffmeister & Wuttke, 1973).

Figure 9-2 shows the pattern of caffeine self-administration in a baboon (Griffiths & Mumford, 1995). This animal is typical of most. Caffeine is administered erratically, and irregular periods of abstinence occur. The reinforcing nature of caffeine is demonstrated, however, because rates of responding decline to near zero when a placebo is substituted.

Similar results have been found in rats. When given the opportunity to consume caffeine orally, few spontaneously do so, and a period of forced consumption is usually required before caffeine is self-administered (Vitiello & Woods, 1975).

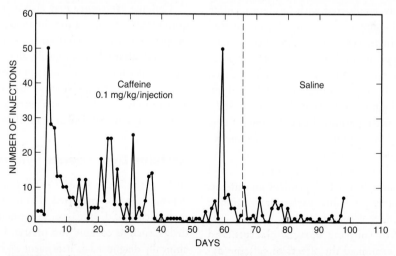

FIGURE 9-2 Intravenous self-injection rates of caffeine for a baboon with a history of self-administering numerous sedative and stimulant drugs. Caffeine was available on an FR 2 schedule, and a maximum of 50 administrations were available each session. The dotted line indicates the point at which a saline placebo injection was substituted for caffeine. (From Griffiths & Mumford, 1995)

Even though it may not be a robust reinforcer on its own, caffeine has been shown to potentiate the reinforcing effects of cocaine (Horger, Wellman, Morien, Davies, & Schenk, 1994), and it will act as a primer for cocaine; that is, an injection of caffeine will reinstate previously extinguished cocaine self-administration in rats (Worley, Valdez, & Schenk, 1994). This effect can be blocked by the administration of dopamine receptor blockers.

SELF-ADMINISTRATION IN HUMANS

A number of human self-administration studies have reported a preference for caffeinated coffee and capsules containing caffeine, suggesting that caffeine serves as a reinforcer. In one such study, participants were given a choice between capsules containing caffeine and capsules containing a placebo. Of the 12 participants, four showed a clear preference for caffeine capsules (Griffiths & Woodson, 1988). If caffeine truly is a reinforcer, you may be wondering why only one-third of participants preferred the caffeinated capsules. Although, in this study, coffee consumption prior to the experiment did not seem to be related to caffeine preference, other research suggests that the reinforcing value of caffeine may indeed be determined by one's state of physical dependence.

One such study, conducted with moderate coffee drinkers, revealed a distinct preference for caffeinated coffee over decaffeinated coffee. This preference could be detected in some people at doses as low as 25 mg per cup and was greatest when the participants reported caffeine withdrawal (Hughes, Higgins, Bickel, & Hunt, 1989; Hughes, Higgins, Gulliver, & Mireault, 1987). In another study, when permitted to consume caffeine freely for 1 week prior to preference testing, people reliably preferred caffeinated coffee. However, people who were not permitted to have any caffeine for 1 week and were presumably not physically dependent on caffeine, showed considerable individual variation in caffeine preference (Griffiths & Woodson, 1988).

Using a within-subjects design, Garrett and Griffiths (1998) examined the effects of caffeine dependence by maintaining participants, for 9 to 12 days, on a daily dose of caffeine (300 mg/70 kg per day; *caffeine-dependent* phase) or on a daily dose of a placebo (*caffeine-nondependent* phase). When switched from the caffeine-dependent to the caffeine-nondependent phase

of the experiment, participants demonstrated typical withdrawal symptoms (e.g., fatigue and shifts in mood). Caffeine-dependent participants were also willing to forfeit money to avoid placebo administration and to pay more money for caffeine compared to participants in the nondependent phase. When dependent, they were twice as likely to take a dose of caffeine versus a placebo as when they were nondependent. This study clearly shows that people actively avoid caffeine withdrawal and seek the effects of caffeine.

In both humans and nonhumans, the reinforcing properties of caffeine seem to vary considerably from individual to individual, and several factors have been identified as contributing to choosing caffeine. Being physically dependent is one. Another is that the people who usually report positive subjective effects from caffeine also show a caffeine preference and people who report adverse effects usually avoid it (Griffiths & Woodson, 1988). But these characteristics are not essential. In one experiment, a person who was otherwise a coffee abstainer showed a definite preference for caffeine over a placebo (Griffiths & Mumford, 1995).

Higher doses are not as reinforcing as lower doses. Increasing doses beyond 100 mg usually decreases the rate of self-administration, and doses in the 400- to 600-mg range are usually avoided.

Caffeine preference may also be related to task requirements after ingestion. In an experiment in which people were required to participate in a computer vigilance task after taking a capsule, all participants showed a preference for caffeine-containing capsules. However, when ingesting a capsule was followed by a relaxation activity, only two of the seven participants preferred the caffeine capsule (Silverman et al., 1994).

Caffeine Dependence Syndrome?

In Chapter 5, the *DSM-IV-TR* criteria for *substance dependence* were discussed. These criteria are used to make a clinical diagnosis of dependence on a variety of drugs, such as cocaine and heroin. Is it possible to be clinically diagnosed as *dependent* on caffeine? Evidence from case histories suggests that it is. One study, published in the *Journal of the American Medical Association* in 1995, reported on clinical interviews with a number of people, recruited through newspaper notices, who thought that they were dependent on caffeine. They were assessed by a psychiatrist using a structured clinical interview, and 16 were identified as meeting the *DSM-IV-TR* criteria of caffeine *dependence*. Of these 16, 94% reported symptoms of withdrawal, 94% reported continued use of caffeine despite knowledge of persistent or recurrent physical or psychological problems that were likely caused or exacerbated by caffeine use, 81% reported persistent desire or unsuccessful attempts to cut down or control use, and 75% reported tolerance. These people reported ingesting doses of caffeine that ranged between 129 and 2,548 mg per day. Three people diagnosed as caffeine-dependent consumed daily doses that were lower than the average daily consumption in the United States. Seven of the 16 primarily consumed soft drinks, one drank tea, and the remainder drank coffee (Strain, Mumford, Silverman, & Griffiths, 1995).

HARMFUL EFFECTS

Reproduction

At high enough levels, caffeine will damage chromosomes. It appears, however, that such effects do not occur at concentrations normally found in the human body, and caffeine is generally considered safe in this regard. There is some speculation, though, that caffeine might enhance the chromosome-damaging activity of other agents, such as X-rays (Kihlman, 1977). Even though it does not damage chromosomes, caffeine can affect the fetus via other mechanisms. For example, caffeine raises the levels of circulating catecholamines, which could reduce blood flow to the fetus.

Studies in animals have shown that low levels of caffeine slow both embryonic and neonatal growth (Dunlop & Court, 1981). The effects of caffeine on human reproduction and fetal growth have recently become a growing concern, thanks to new evidence. A large British prospective study, examining more than 2,600 pregnancies, found that maternal caffeine intake was related to retardation in fetal growth (CARE Study Group, 2008). Caffeine consumption of less than 200 mg per day was associated with a reduction in birth weight of 60 to 70 grams, and the reduction was greater with higher caffeine consumption. This study controlled for tobacco and alcohol use throughout pregnancy.

In a review of the effects of caffeine consumption on reproductive outcomes, Peck, Leviton, and Cowan (2010) pointed out a common problem with such studies: Caffeine consumption during pregnancy is often confounded with morning sickness and nausea experienced during the first trimester. It is known that women who experience these symptoms are more likely to have normal pregnancies and healthy babies. They are also the women who are most likely to reduce their consumption of coffee, tea, and other distinctive tasting beverages because they feel sick and develop aversions to caffeine-containing drinks. This could make it look like there is a positive relationship between caffeine consumption and negative pregnancy outcomes. As Peck and colleagues point out, few studies take this factor into account.

Nevertheless, in the British study described earlier, there was a group of 100 women who voluntarily reduced caffeine consumption, from 300 mg to less than 50 mg per day, in the first few weeks of pregnancy. These women had babies weighing an average of 161 g heavier than women who did not reduce their caffeine consumption. This does not constitute a true experimental study, but it is evidence that there is likely a causal relationship between maternal caffeine consumption and birth weight. Unfortunately, the research did not determine whether the voluntary reduction in caffeine consumption was due to increased morning sickness.

The above-mentioned review by Peck and colleagues looked at all research into the effects of caffeine consumption on reproductive success from 2000 to 2009. They found that most studies examining the relationship between caffeine consumption and spontaneous abortion, prematurity, fetal death, and fetal malformations did not adequately control for the confounding effect of morning sickness. As a result, and owing to the fact that many studies used flawed measures of caffeine consumption, Peck and colleagues concluded that there was no convincing evidence that caffeine has any detrimental effect on reproductive success.

It should be remembered, however, that no matter how carefully these studies are conducted, as described in Chapter 2, it is impossible to demonstrate a causal effect using correlational methodology. It is also true that, even though a harmful effect has not been demonstrated, it has also not been demonstrated that caffeine is safe. For this reason, some suggest that women of reproductive age should limit caffeine consumption to 300 mg per day (Heckman, Weil, & Gonzalez de Mejia, 2010). But the majority of expert opinion suggests that, until a safe level of consumption can be established, it is probably wiser for pregnant women to abstain from all caffeine-containing beverages and medicines (James, 1991).

Methylxanthines are also found in considerable concentrations in breast milk. Considering that the rate of methylxanthine metabolism in newborns is extremely slow, even small amounts acquired in breast milk could accumulate, possibly to toxic levels. Therefore it is probably prudent to limit caffeine consumption while breast feeding as well.

Cardiac Disease

The epidemiological evidence linking caffeine consumption to heart disease is still equivocal. In the early 1970s, the Boston Collaborative Drug Surveillance Program published two studies showing that drinking more than six cups of coffee a day doubled the risk of heart attack. Since that time, numerous studies have failed to replicate the finding. Contradictory results abound. For example, one study of more than 85,000 women in the United States concluded that coffee was not an important cause of heart attacks (Willett et al., 1996); another study of more than 800 women in Boston found that heavy coffee consumption (more than five cups per day) did increase the risk of heart attack (Palmer, Rosenberg, Rao, & Shapiro, 1995).

These divergent findings might be explained, at least in part, by the fact that caffeine consumption is usually not measured accurately, and, as a result, risk is consistently underestimated (James, 1991). Another possible explanation might be related to the manner in which coffee is prepared. One study has shown that boiled coffee contains a substance that raises cholesterol levels, but filtered coffee does not contain this factor (Pirich, O'Grady, & Sinzinger, 1993). A further confound in this research is the possibility that the link may be genetically determined and may exist only for specific populations. Cornelis, El-Sohemy, Kabagambe, and Campos (2006) showed a positive relationship between caffeine consumption and cardiovascular disease, but only in individuals with the "slow metabolizing" form of the CYP1A2 enzyme gene (i.e., the CYP1A2*1F form). These individuals excrete caffeine slowly. While the issue is far from settled, the bulk of recent research has not found an association between caffeine consumption and cardiovascular disease for most people (Lopez-Garcia et al., 2006, 2008).

Bone Density

Of increasing concern is the effect of caffeine on bone density in postmenopausal women. One study showed that daily consumption of two to three cups of coffee accelerated bone loss in the spine and body of postmenopausal women who consumed less than the recommended daily dietary source of calcium (Harris & Dawson, 1994).

Caffeinism and anxiety

At doses of 5 to 10 cups per day, caffeine can cause sensory disturbances, such as ringing in the ears and seeing flashes of light, as well as mild delirium and excitement. These are symptoms of a disorder sometimes called *caffeinism*. The *DSM-IV-TR* does not use this term, but recognizes *caffeine intoxication*. It describes mild symptoms, which can be seen after as little as 100 mg. The symptoms of caffeinism are more severe, brought on by consumption of more than 1 g of caffeine per day, and also include psychomotor agitation, twitching, rambling flow of thoughts and speech, irregular heart rhythm, and periods of inexhaustibility.

Higher doses of caffeine, more than 300 mg, are known to induce anxiety (Lara, 2010). Caffeine can also cause panic attacks and increase anxiety in people with panic and anxiety disorders, but does not have this effect in normal individuals unless used excessively (Carroll, 1998). The ability of caffeine to generate anxiety is associated with a particular phenotype of A_{2A} adenosine receptor, suggesting that this effect is mediated by the actions of caffeine on adenosine receptors (Lara, 2010).

Lethal Effects

The lethal dose of caffeine in humans has been estimated at between 3 and 8 g (roughly 30 to 80 cups of coffee or stay-awake pills) taken orally. Death results from convulsions and respiratory collapse. Between 2006 and 2008, the American Association of Poison Control Centers reported that more than 46,000 cases of caffeine toxicity were treated in the United States. Of these, 45 had life-threatening symptoms, and three people died (Seifert et al., 2011).

BENEFICIAL EFFECTS

There is evidence that coffee consumption may have protective effects against Parkinson's disease. In one large prospective study in men, consumption of caffeine from a variety of sources, but not decaffeinated coffee, appeared to reduce the incidence of Parkinson's (Ascherio et al., 2001). Caffeine can also reduce some symptoms of Parkinson's such as tremors and the deterioration of motor skills (Blandini, Nappi, Tassorelli, & Martignoni, 2000; Trevitt, Kawa, Jalali, & Larsen, 2009). The connection between caffeine and Parkinson's might be expected in light of the fact that Parkinson's disease is caused by a deficiency of dopamine-producing cells in the substantia nigra, and caffeine increases dopamine activity by blocking adenosine receptors.

It has been speculated that caffeine may cause weight loss, or at least prevent weight gain and obesity, because of its ability to increase metabolic activity and increase energy expenditure (Greenberg, Boozer, & Geliebter, 2006; Turk et al., 2009).

A 2005 review of published studies concluded that the consumption of coffee was related to a reduced risk of developing Type 2 diabetes, but it is not entirely clear whether this is because of caffeine or some other ingredient in coffee (van Dam & Hu, 2005). Other studies that compared caffeinated and decaffeinated coffee found that the decaffeinated coffee also offered some protection against Type 2 diabetes. The effect was not as strong as in the caffeinated coffee, but significant enough to suggest that something else in coffee might be the active agent (Heckman et al., 2010). Clearly more investigation is required.

EPILOGUE

What Do We Really Know About Caffeine?

As we have seen, selling caffeine-containing beverages is big business—even bigger than the tobacco industry. You can be sure that any threat to the profits of the coffee industry would be met with resources similar to those that the tobacco industry has put forward in defending itself against the increasing public awareness of the dangers of smoking. Perhaps that threat already has been met.

In an editorial in the British journal *Addiction*, one of the world's foremost caffeine researchers, Jack James of La Trobe University in Bundoora, Australia, warned that the coffee industry has been subtly directing caffeine research away from areas of health problems and manipulating the dissemination of health information about caffeine for many years (James, 1994). The coffee industry established something called the International Life Sciences Institute (ILSI). This sounds as though it should be a scholarly organization with lofty aims, but in reality it was established to make sure that caffeine retained its status of "generally recognized as safe" by the U.S. Food and Drug Administration. In this regard, it has been successful. Despite increasing numbers of studies that have provided reason for doubt, caffeine is still considered a *safe* food additive.

How does the ILSI work? Its influence may be seen in the pages of this book. According to James, the ILSI sponsors international invitation-only conferences attended by prominent scholars and then publishes the results. According to James, however, in publications that deal with the health hazards of caffeine, "evidence is consistently interpreted in a way that is favourable to the interests of the book's sponsors." This approach is given credibility because other publications that do not deal with health issues are balanced, erudite, and scholarly.

In addition, the caffeine industry sponsors research, but are careful to limit sponsorship to *safe* areas, such as the study of coffee compounds other than caffeine. As James says, "Under the guise of public interest, the industry actively supports continuing research on noncaffeine constituents of coffee, knowing fully that nothing untoward (and nothing of particular interest to the public) is likely to be revealed" (James, 1994, p. 1579).

Psychomotor Stimulants

The drugs known as psychomotor stimulants have one effect in common: They stimulate transmission at synapses that use epinephrine (E), norepinephrine (NE), dopamine (DA), or serotonin (5-HT) as transmitters. These transmitters are called *monoamines* (MAs) or *biogenic amines*. The first three—E, NE, and DA—are very similar. As you learned in Chapter 4 (and saw in Figure 4-15), the body manufactures E from NE in one chemical step, and NE is made by changing the structure of DA slightly. Together, these three are called *catecholamines* (CAs). The odd monoamine is 5-HT. It is an *indoleamine*, which is chemically different from the CAs but is influenced by many of the same drugs and destroyed by many of the same enzymes (see Chapter 4).

The term *sympathomimetic* is sometimes used to refer to this class of drugs. This term is used because epinephrine is the primary transmitter in the sympathetic nervous system, and these drugs stimulate sympathetic synapses to some extent and mimic sympathetic arousal.

SOURCES

Some psychomotor stimulants occur naturally and have been used for centuries, and some are very new synthetic drugs. The *amphetamines* are synthetic and do not occur naturally; *d-amphetamine* (dextro-amphetamine or dex-amphetamine) and *l-amphetamine* (levo-amphetamine) have exactly the same chemical structure, but the molecules are mirror images of each other (technically, they are called *optical isomers*). In the amphetamines, the d- isomer is more potent than the l- isomer for most central effects. When the term *dl-amphetamine* or just *amphetamine* is used, it refers to a mixture of the two isomers. The trade name of dl-amphetamine is Adderall; it is used in the treatment of *Attention Deficit Hyperactivity Disorder* (ADHD) and the sleep disorder *narcolepsy*. Dexedrine is a common trade name of d-amphetamine, which is also used to treat ADHD and narcolepsy. Another similar drug is *methamphetamine*, which differs slightly from the other two in structure and effect. It is sold under the trade names Methedrine or Desoxyn and used to treat ADHD and obesity. Its medical use is not widespread; in 2009, only 10,000 prescriptions were issued in the United States (U.S. Department of Justice, 2011). Methamphetamine can be synthesized from material legally available, which includes cold medication that contains ephedrine or pseudoephedrine, iodine, hydrochloric acid, ether, and ammonia. It is currently manufactured in large quantities in illegal laboratories and sold in a waxy form known as base or paste or in a tablet or powder. When the powder is recrystalized, it is sold as *crystal, ice,* or *crystal meth.*

Cocaine is extracted from the leaf of a small tree known as the *coca bush* (*Erythroxylum coca*), which is native to South America. It prefers high elevations and thrives on the slopes of the Andes Mountains. It grows in both wild and cultivated forms from northwestern Argentina to Ecuador. Only slightly different chemically from cocaine are two synthetic drugs, *methylphenidate* (Ritalin) used to treat ADHD and *pipradrol* (Meratran), used in Europe to treat symptoms of senile dementia, but not widely used in the United States.

Cathinone is another naturally occurring cocaine-like drug found in the leaves and shoots of *Catha edulis*, a shrub-like plant that grows in the countries of eastern Africa and southern Arabia. It is called *khat* in Yemen (also spelled *quat* or *qat* and pronounced *cat*). It is also known as *tscaht* in Ethiopia and *miraa* in Kenya (Kalix, 1994). Cathinone is not stable; it degrades shortly after the plant is harvested. For this reason, the plant is used primarily in the area where it is grown, and, unlike cocaine, it is not exported for use elsewhere (United Nations, 1980). There are a number of synthetic derivatives of cathinone. One is bupropion, a drug used as both an antidepressant and a smoking cessation aid. Others that have been used recreationally are methylone, methcathinone (ephedrone), 4-methoxymethcathinone (methedrone), and 4-methylmethcathinone (mephedrone).

Another psychomotor stimulant is a naturally occurring drug *ephedrine*. Ephedrine comes from the herb *ma huang* (*Ephedra vulgaris*), which has been used as a medicine in China for centuries. There are also North American varieties of *Ephedra*.

HISTORY

Cocaine

For centuries, coca leaves have been chewed by various Indian tribes in South America. No one knows how long the coca plant has been used, but it is of great antiquity. Legends of some tribes of Colombian Indians tell how their people came from the Milky Way in a canoe drawn by an anaconda. In addition to a man and a woman, the canoe contained several psychoactive plants, including coca (Schultes, 1987). Coca leaves have been found in burial middens in Peru that date back to 2500 BCE. Large stone monolithic idols found in Colombia and dating to 500 BCE have the puffed-out cheeks of the coca chewer. The Incas started to use the plant when they conquered the region in about the tenth century. Under the Incas, coca became sacred. It was used primarily by the priests and nobility for special ceremonies and was not consumed daily by the common folk.

When the Spanish conquered the Incas, at first they banned coca use, considering it to be idolatrous and pagan, but they changed their minds when they found out how useful it could be. The Spanish did not use coca themselves, but they learned that it had great value as payment for labor in the gold and silver mines in the Andes. In addition to finding coca an item of commerce, the Spanish realized that the Indians could work harder and longer and required less food if they were given coca.

As the Spanish grew more interested in the plant, attempts were made to classify it. In 1749, samples were sent to Europe, where Linnaeus gave the plant its own family, Erythroxylaceae. In 1786, Lamarck named the most important species *Erythroxylon coca* (Aldrich & Baker, 1976).

Europeans remained unaware of either the medicinal or psychological effects of the plant, probably because samples sent from South America had deteriorated from age. It is also likely that Europeans were averse to chewing the leaves in the manner of the South Americans. Not until the form of the drug was changed did they show any interest in coca. The first change involved identifying the active ingredient. Earlier attempts had been made with partial success, but the credit for isolating and naming cocaine goes to Albert Niemann of the German university town of Göttingen, who published his results in 1860.

For several years, cocaine was a drug without a medical use until Sigmund Freud became interested and proposed many uses of cocaine, including the treatment of addictions and depression, but it was one of his colleagues, Karl Köller, who discovered the only real medical use of cocaine—it was the world's first local anesthetic.

The isolation of cocaine not only stimulated a search for medical uses for the drug but also made it available in a form that the upper-middle class could inject along with morphine, which was popular at the time (see Chapter 11). Around the turn of the twentieth century, cocaine gained favor with writers and intellectuals. Robert Louis Stevenson is reported to have written *The Strange Case of Dr. Jekyll and Mr. Hyde* with the aid of cocaine. Sherlock Holmes, the fictional detective created by Sir Arthur Conan Doyle, was a prototype of the intellectual cocaine user of the time. Over the cautions and objections of the good Dr. Watson, he injected the drug to keep his keen mind stimulated.

In 1863, Angelo Mariani, a Corsican chemist, patented a wine containing coca that became exceedingly popular (it was even endorsed by the Pope) and made Mariani a very wealthy man. It was probably Mariani's success that inspired a Georgia pharmacist, John S. Pemberton, to produce an American version called "French Wine of Cola, Ideal Tonic." Later, in 1886, he removed the alcohol and replaced it with a kola nut extract, added soda water, and called it Coca-Cola. In its early days, Coca-Cola was promoted as a remedy and a health drink, and it is probably for this reason that soda fountains developed in drugstores in the United States. Around the turn of the twentieth century cocaine was removed from Coca-Cola. To this day, Coca-Cola is made from coca leaves from which the cocaine has been removed.

In the early part of the twentieth century, in the United States there was a growing backlash against cocaine and other drugs. Cocaine was being injected by professionals and intellectuals, but the drug was associated with corruption and crime in the popular mind. It was no surprise that cocaine was included with morphine and opium in the Harrison Narcotic Act of 1914, which effectively banned its use. As a result of this inclusion of cocaine in the U.S. law and the influence of the United States on the development of international narcotics control, cocaine was also included with morphine in all international treaties aimed at the control of narcotics and in the internal legislation of many other countries.

The Harrison Act drove cocaine underground, where it was used by the "unconventional rich and the unconventional poor": party-going, decadent, wealthy whites, and gamblers, musicians, and artists of all colors. For decades, cocaine was not a part of the lives of the vast majority of the population of the United States. Then, during World War II, amphetamines were introduced and widely used by the military, so the idea of a stimulant or an *upper* was no longer new and foreign. In the 1960s, things started to change. The use of cocaine increased along with a general increase in the use of other drugs popular at the time, including marijuana and hallucinogens (Grinspoon & Bakalar, 1976).

Amphetamines

Ephedrine, in the herb *ma huang*, has been used in China for more than 5,000 years. Legend has it that its medicinal properties were first identified by the Emperor Chen Nung, who was also credited with the discovery of tea. Ephedrine was isolated from the herb in the 1880s, but not until 1924 were its properties investigated by two Americans, Ko Kuei Chen and C. F. Schmidt. They pointed out that the structure and actions of ephedrine were similar to those of the neurotransmitter epinephrine, which was known to be a stimulant of the sympathetic nervous system. Epinephrine was used at the time to treat asthma because one of its effects was to dilate the airways in the lungs and make breathing easier. Epinephrine, however, was very unstable; it had to be administered by injection, and its effects were very brief. Ephedrine was far superior because it could be taken in pill form, had a longer duration of action, and was less toxic. The use of ephedrine became so widespread that there were fears that supplies would run out, and a search was begun for a synthetic substitute. As it happened, such a substitute had already been discovered, but no one knew it. Many years earlier, in 1887, a German chemist, L. Edeleano had synthesized what we now know as amphetamine, but he had failed to explore its properties, and it remained untested until 1910, when G. Barger and Sir H. H. Dale (the proposer of Dale's law; see Chapter 4) published a technical paper showing the effects of amphetamine and other sympathomimetic drugs on the body. The significance of Barger and Dale's paper was not grasped until 1927, when Gordon Alles, a young chemist at a research laboratory in Los Angeles, suggested that amphetamine would probably be the best and cheapest substitute for ephedrine.

In 1937, the American Medical Association sanctioned the use of amphetamine for the treatment of narcolepsy and as a mild "pick-me-up" or stimulant for depression. By 1943, at least half the sales of the drug were prescribed for weight reduction and diet control, antidepressant or stimulant effects, or extended periods of alertness. Amphetamine was also marketed in inhalers for the treatment of asthma and sold over the counter without a prescription. The pharmaceutical company Smith, Kline, and French held the patents for amphetamine and was doing so well that other companies wanted some of the market, too. It was not long before the Ciba Company started marketing methylphenidate as a *nonamphetamine* stimulant (Grinspoon & Hedblom, 1975). To control the indiscriminate prescribing of amphetamines by physicians, most countries now limit the medical conditions for which amphetamines may be prescribed. These conditions are narcolepsy and the treatment ADHD and do not include obesity or the need to stay awake. The production and marketing of amphetamines are now carefully monitored.

As medicinal sources of amphetamines dried up, more amphetamine and methamphetamine were being made in illicit labs, which are now the primary source.

Cathinone (Khat)

Khat use has been known since antiquity. Alexander the Great sent khat to General Harrar to cure his melancholia, and it has been mentioned repeatedly by Arab physicians as a remedy for a variety of disorders. Amda Sion, a fourteenth-century ruler of Ethiopia, was the first recorded khat addict. Khat has been known in Europe since the early 1600s but has only recently been used there because of difficulties transporting the leaf.

The first case of khat psychosis in the United States was reported in 1982. Since then, cases have been reported in the United Kingdom (Giannini, Miller, & Turner, 1992), Europe (Kalix, 1994), and Canada (Kalix, 1994).

Khat and cathinone are illegal in the United States and Canada, but is still legal in the United Kingdom, although the matter is under close study.

The synthetic derivatives of cathinone have been used for recreational purposes for many years. Methcathinone (ephedrine) originally became popular in Russia where it has been called *jeff*, *Jee-cocktail*, or *cosmos*. It has been a problem in Eastern Europe since the early 1980s. In the early 1990s, it appeared in the illicit drug market and was found in clandestine labs in the United States as *cat*. In 1992, it was classified as a Schedule-1 substance (the highest restriction a drug can receive) under the Emergency Scheduling Act (Glennon, Young, Martin, & Dal Cason, 1994).

Mephedrone was first synthesized in 1929 and rediscovered in 2003. It was soon being made in clandestine labs and became widely known as *meow meow*. Even though in many countries cathinone derivatives were illegal, this only applied if the drug was sold for human consumption. To get around this, it was sold over the Internet as *plant food* or *bath salts* and came with the caution "Not For Human Consumption." In the late

2000s in the United Kingdom, a number of deaths were attributed to the drug, and in April 2010, methadrone and all derivatives of cathinone were given Class B Status under the Misuse of Drugs Act—the same status as marijuana. A number of other European countries have passed similar legislation. Similarly, many U.S. states have made it illegal, but it is still legal in Canada.

ROUTES OF ADMINISTRATION AND ABSORPTION

The amphetamines are weak bases and have a pKa of between 9 and 10. When taken orally, they tend to be ionized in the digestive system, which slows the rate of absorption. The drug is more potent when administered by injection, inhalation, or snorting. When given for medicinal purposes or to prevent sleep and fatigue, amphetamines are always taken orally, and the decrease in potency can be compensated for by increasing the dose. The oral route has the advantage that blood levels may be kept fairly constant without too much variation over time. When amphetamines are taken for the rush they produce, they are administered by injection, which causes the sudden high blood levels required for this effect.

The same is true for cocaine, which has a pKa of 8.7. Traditionally, the Indians of the Andes rolled coca leaves into a ball, stuck a wad in the cheek, and sucked it. It is also common for those who take coca in this manner to mix the leaves with lime in the form of wood ashes (Schultes, 1987) or ground shells; this practice raises the pH of the saliva and the digestive system and, consequently, reduces ionization and increases absorption. It is very unusual for pure cocaine to be taken orally. It is nearly always injected or sniffed to improve absorption, but recently it has become popular to smoke cocaine, both as a hydrochloride salt and as a freebase.

Most of the cocaine sold in the United States is the salt cocaine hydrochloride (cocaine HCl). It may contain various impurities from the refining process and be deliberately diluted or *cut*. One method that was used to determine the purity of this drug was to place some of the powder on a sheet of tinfoil and heat it until it vaporized; pure cocaine HCl leaves little residue. It soon became apparent to those who performed this test that inhaled cocaine has an effect similar to injected cocaine. Soon this method of smoking, called *tooting*, became popular, as did other methods, such as mixing cocaine with tobacco or marijuana.

Crack is cocaine HCl mixed with a solution of baking soda (sodium bicarbonate). The water is evaporated, leaving crystalline chunks or *rocks* that are heated in pipes or other devices, and the vapors are inhaled. The baking soda is a base, which removes the ionic charge from the molecules of cocaine and increases its lipid solubility.

After oral administration of amphetamines, the absorption rate is determined by factors such as the presence of food in the stomach and the degree of physical activity. Peak blood levels may be reached in 30 minutes to 4 hours (Brauer, Ambre, & de Wit, 1996; Vree & Henderson, 1980). After intranasal administration (sniffing) of cocaine, peak blood levels are achieved in 10 to 20 minutes (Javaid, Musa, Fischman, Schuster, & Davis, 1983). The rate of absorption of vaporized cocaine HCl and cocaine from vaporized freebase or crack has not been studied, but it is likely extremely rapid because both processes release the cocaine molecule in unionized form, making it highly lipid soluble. In fact, crack is a variation on the ancient technique used by the Incas, who mixed coca leaves with lime. This made the saliva basic and enhanced the absorption of the cocaine from the coca leaves using the same chemical principle.

Traditionally, cathinone is taken orally by chewing the leaves of the khat plant in much the same manner as the natives of the Andes have used coca. In Russia, methcathinone is usually administered by injection, but in the United States, sniffing of methcathinone powder seems to be preferred (Glennon et al., 1994). Mephedrone, when sold as *bath salts* and *plant food*, is sold as a powder, tablets, or capsules and may be taken orally, injected, or snorted.

DISTRIBUTION

The amphetamines, cocaine, and other drugs in this class cross the blood–brain barrier and are concentrated in the spleen, kidneys, and brain.

EXCRETION

The excretion of the amphetamines depends to a very great extent on the pH of the urine. Because it is ionized at acid pHs, amphetamine is not reabsorbed from the nephron in acidic urine, but as the urine becomes more basic, more of the drug is reabsorbed, and more of the burden of excretion is carried by metabolism in the liver. The half-life of amphetamine may be as short as 7 to 14 hours when the urine is acidic. When the urine is basic, excretion is shifted to metabolic processes, and the half-life may be 16 to 34 hours (Creasey, 1979). Amphetamine is also excreted in sweat and saliva (Britton, El-Wardany, Brown, & Bianchine, 1978; Vree & Henderson, 1980).

Amphetamines that are not excreted unchanged are metabolized through several routes that use a variety of enzymes. Many of the metabolites are also behaviorally active and have very long half-lives (Brookes, 1985).

Cocaine is excreted much faster than the amphetamines. It has a half-life of from 45 to 75 minutes (Javaid et al., 1983), although this also depends on the pH of the urine.

Cathinone has a half-life of about 90 minutes, intermediate between cocaine and amphetamine (Kalix, 1994). Little is known about the pharmacokinetics of mephedrone apart from the fact that it is metabolized by three separate pathways in the liver and some of its toxic effects may be due to an accumulation of toxic metabolites (Meyer, Wilhelm, Peters, & Maurer, 2010).

NEUROPHYSIOLOGY

All the drugs in this chapter are grouped together because they have a common effect on synapses that use a monoamine (MA) as a transmitter, but the mechanisms by which they stimulate these synapses differ (it may be useful at this point to review the discussion of MA synapses in Chapter 4).

The action of MAs is terminated both by the presence of specific enzymes such as MAO and COMT in the synapse and by reabsorption back into the presynaptic neuron. The reabsorption is caused by special transporter molecules (called *monoamine transporters*; MATs), which actively move the monoamine across the membrane into the cell. Each monoamine has a special transporter on the membrane; there is a dopamine transporter (DAT), a norepinephrine transporter (NET), and a serotonin transporter (SERT). DATs and NETs are not always specific; DATs will transport norepinephrine, and NETs will also transport dopamine, but the transmitters have a lower affinity for each other's transmitter so they mostly transport their own monoamine.

These transporters are large protein molecules that span the membrane of the postsynaptic cell. They belong to a family of transporters called *Na⁺/Cl⁻ dependent substrate-specific neuronal membrane transporters*. Each has a receptor site located outside the membrane that binds the relevant monoamine along with Na⁺ and Cl⁻ ions. In the case of DATs, the dopamine is transported along with two Na⁺ and one Cl⁻ ion. NETs and SERTs transport one Cl⁻ and one Na⁺ ion along with each molecule of serotonin or norepinephrine. When the monoamine and the relevant ions are bound to the transporter, the configuration of the transporter changes so that the monoamine and the ions are moved to the inside of the membrane where they are released. The transporter then returns to its original configuration and is able to perform the operation again. Normally, the monoamines are then stored in vesicles by the action of another transporter in the membrane of the synaptic vesicle called the *vesicular monoamine transporter* (VMAT). This prevents them from being destroyed by enzymes in the axon terminal and protects organs inside the cell from being damaged by the monoamine until such time as the vesicle releases the transmitter back into the cleft in response to depolarization of the membrane.

The psychomotor stimulant drugs are able to alter the functioning of these transporters in two different ways. Cocaine is an example of a *reuptake inhibitor*. It simply binds to the receptor site of a transporter and stays there so that the transporter is unable to transport its monoamine back into the presynaptic neuron. This causes the monoamine to remain in the cleft longer and in higher concentrations and have a greater effect on the postsynaptic membrane (see Figure 10-1, Panels A & B). The amphetamines, on the other hand, are *substrate-type releasers* whose actions are more complicated. Because they are structural analogues (i.e., they are similar) to monoamines, amphetamines can enter the presynaptic neuron by binding to the transporter, along with Na⁺ and Cl⁻ ions, in the same manner as a monoamine. Once inside the axon terminal, the amphetamines get packaged into synaptic vesicles along with the monoamine.

The reabsorption of monoamines into the presynaptic cell is slowed because amphetamines compete to occupy the transporter, but that is just the beginning of the story. Entry of amphetamines and other substrate-type releasers into the presynaptic neuron and its vesicles has several effects within the cell. Once they enter the synaptic vesicles, amphetamines disrupt the vesicular pH balance, which triggers the vesicles to release monoamine into the cytoplasm of the axon terminal—they do so by reversing the direction of VMAT action. This also inhibits VMAT function and the repackaging of monoamine into vesicles. Additionally, in conjunction with the increased levels of Na⁺ in the cell, the amphetamines cause transporter proteins to work in reverse, moving the monoamine from the cytoplasm of the presynaptic terminal into the extracellular space. Amphetamines can also cause the transporter to act briefly as an open channel, allowing monoamine to move out of the cell at a high rate. Thus, substrate-type releasers cause both a slow, steady release of the transmitter by the reverse action of the transporter and rapid, brief bursts of transmitter (Torres, Gainetdinov, & Caron, 2003; see Figure 10-1, Panel C). In addition, amphetamines inhibit the activity of MAO, the enzyme that normally degrades any molecules of monoamine that float free in the cytoplasm of the cell (Egashira, Yamamoto, & Yamanaka, 1987). By inhibiting MAO activity, monoamines are protected from being degraded, and their levels in the axon terminal increase substantially.

Substrate-type releasers like amphetamines are also able to block VMAT and prevent the storage of monoamines in vesicles, and cause the release of these molecules from the vesicle into the cytoplasm of the cell. Once there, they are available to be transported outside the cell by the reverse action of DATs, NETs, or SERTs (Kahlig & Galli, 2003; Kahlig et al., 2005).

Another difference between the blockers like cocaine and the substrate-type releasers is that the presynaptic membrane normally contains autoreceptors, which detect the level of monoamine outside the membrane and inhibit the release of the transmitter if the level gets too high. This system works to modulate the effect of transporter blockers, but has no effect on the substrate-type releasers like amphetamine.

Different drugs have different affinities for each transporter and consequently have different effects on various monoamines. Cocaine binds with comparable affinity to NETs, DATs, and SERTs and therefore at a given dose has a similar effect on dopamine, norepinephrine, and serotonin. Methylphenidate is equally effective at NETs and DATs, but much higher concentrations are required to block SERTs. Amphetamine and methamphetamine are most potent at NETs, compared to which they are

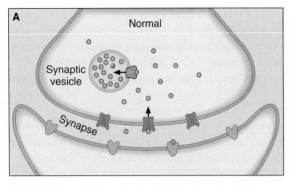
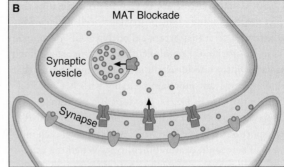
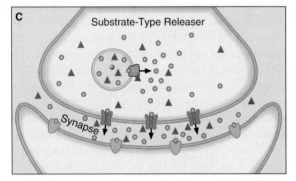
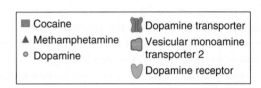

FIGURE 10-1   Panel A shows the normal operation of a monoamine transporter (MAT). A molecule of the monoamine attaches to the MAT and is moved into the cell. This reduces the concentration of the monoamine in the synaptic cleft. Once inside the cell, the MA is transported into the synaptic vesicle by a vesicular monoamine transporter (VMAT). Panel B shows the action of a MAT blocker such as cocaine. The blocker prevents the MAT from moving monoamines into the cell, and the level of monoamines builds up in the synaptic cleft. Panel C shows the operation of substrate-type releasers like amphetamine. The molecules of the substrate-type releaser are taken through the membrane by the MAT. Once inside, they cause the vesicle to release stored monoamines into the cytoplasm of the cell and the MATs to work in reverse, moving monoamines into the synaptic cleft. Substrate-type releasers can also cause the channel of the MAT to stay open, allowing monoamines to diffuse out rapidly.

five to nine times less potent at DATs and 200 to 500 times less potent at SERTs (Han & Gu, 2006).

In Chapter 13 on Antidepressants, you will read about medications called SSRIs and SNRIs. The terms *SSRIs* and *SNRIs* stand for selective serotonin reuptake inhibitors and serotonin–norepinephrine reuptake inhibitors. The reuptake inhibitors work in exactly the same way as cocaine; they are blockers of SERTs and NETs, and, at high doses, some (such as venlafaxine) also block DATs. The tricyclic antidepressants are also monoamine transport blockers. Each of these has a varying effect on DATs, NETs, and SERTs as well.

Because cocaine blocks SERTs and NETs the same way as antidepressants, it should also have antidepressant

properties—but it does not. The reason for this is not entirely clear. It has been speculated that there may be other as-yet undiscovered receptors for cocaine (Rothman & Bauman, 2003), which eliminate any antidepressant effects and are responsible for cocaine's abuse potential.

Methcathinone and cathinone are substrate-type monoamine transporter blockers and have effects very similar to amphetamine. They are classed as psychomotor stimulants, but mephedrone and methylone, even though they are also substrate-type monoamine transporter blockers, have quite different effects. They are considered to be more like entactogens or club drugs and are discussed in Chapter 15. Also, MDMA (ecstasy), another entactogen, is also a substrate-type monoamine transporter blocker. It is likely that the reason why these drugs have such different effects is because they have a different profile of affinities for DATs, NETs, and SERTs; the entactogens have a much greater effect at serotonin synapses than do amphetamine and methcathinone, and a lower affinity for DATs (Cozzi, Sievert, Shulgin, Jacob, & Ruoho, 1999; Nagai, Nonaka, & Satoh Hisashi Kamimura, 2007).

In the central nervous system, all monoamine systems are known to be affected by the psychomotor stimulants, but most of the behavioral effects appear to be a result of their effect on dopamine systems (see Chapter 4). Recall that the nigrostriatal dopamine system, running from the substantia nigra to the striatum, is important in the control of motor activity and that the mesolimbic dopamine system, running from the ventral tegmental area to the nucleus accumbens, controls reinforcement and motivation. Psychomotor stimulants are known to increase the release of dopamine in these systems. Positron emission tomography (PET) studies suggest that between 60 and 77% of dopamine transporters are blocked by doses of cocaine commonly abused by humans and that at least 47% of transporters must be blocked for users to experience a cocaine-induced high (Volkow et al., 1997).

Another DA system (the tuberoinfundibular pathway) exerts some control over the secretions of the pituitary gland. This DA system inhibits the secretion of *prolactin*, a hormone that controls the release of milk during breast feeding, and also suppresses male sexual activity.

In the peripheral nervous system, the stimulants excite synapses that use epinephrine, the transmitter in the sympathetic nervous system, and cause sympathetic arousal (the fight-or-flight response).

In addition to its abilities as an MA stimulant, cocaine has the ability to block Na^+ ion channels in membranes. This blocks the conduction of action potentials along nerve axons and is the basis of cocaine's ability to act as a local anesthetic. The local anesthetic action, however, has nothing to do with the MA-stimulating effect of the drug and requires much higher concentrations. Cocaine is seldom used for this purpose today. Procaine (Novocaine), a synthetic substitute that has the local anesthetic action of cocaine without its stimulant properties, was developed for this purpose. Even though procaine lacks the stimulant properties of cocaine, it nevertheless acts as a positive reinforcer in rats and monkeys (Ford & Balster, 1977; Yokel, 1987).

The influence of cocaine is still felt in the naming of local anesthetic drugs. It is common to use the ending *-caine* in the formulation of generic and trade names to indicate that the drug has local anesthetic action.

EFFECTS OF PSYCHOMOTOR STIMULANTS

Effects on the Body

Because the psychomotor stimulants activate the sympathetic nervous system, they cause an increase in heart rate and blood pressure, *vasodilation* (a dilation of the blood vessels), and *bronchodilation* (dilation of the air passages in the lungs). Bronchodilation is medically useful for people suffering from asthma. This was the primary motivation for the invention and development of the amphetamines in the first place. However, most of the sympathetic effects are not considered pleasant by people who inject amphetamines for psychological effects. They generally prefer methamphetamine, which has stronger CNS effects and fewer peripheral effects than d- or l-amphetamine.

Studies of laboratory animals have shown that some of the effects of amphetamine are greater if animals are tested in groups rather than alone. One study with humans showed that amphetamine has a tendency to cause higher increases in blood pressure and body temperature when people were tested in groups rather than alone (de Wit, Clark, & Brauer, 1997).

It has been known for a long time that amphetamine and other psychomotor stimulants reduce appetite and food consumption in laboratory animals. The exact mechanism responsible is not well understood, but it seems that this effect is achieved secondarily. In laboratory animals, amphetamine reduces food consumption because it stimulates the animal to engage in many behaviors other than eating. The missed food consumption is compensated for by excessive eating later. Anorectic drugs are capable of creating a satiety response, which generates a sequence of behavior that, in rats, involves grooming and resting and, in humans, the feeling of having had a full meal. It is thought that activity at serotonin 5-HT_{1B} and 5-HT_{2C} receptors may be involved. It is possible that some stimulants may activate these receptors (Rodgers, Holch, & Tallett, 2010).

Effects on Sleep

One reason for the widespread use of amphetamines during World War II and in the 1950s was that they prevented sleep. In addition to their ability to block fatigue, amphetamines increase concentration, which makes them popular among students as a study aid (Hall, Irwin, Bowman, Frankenberger, & Jewett, 2005) and among long-distance truck drivers and military pilots on extended missions (Emonson & Vanderbeek, 1995). Systematic studies have shown that amphetamine use does cause insomnia. Amphetamine, methylphenidate, and modafinil are used in the treatment of narcolepsy, a sleep disorder that causes excessive sleepiness and frequent daytime sleep attacks.

EFFECTS ON THE BEHAVIOR AND PERFORMANCE OF HUMANS

Subjective Effects

When cocaine and amphetamine are given intravenously, their effects are identical (Fischman et al., 1976). One of the most noticeable effects of the amphetamines is that they make people feel good; they improve mood. From the earliest occasions when amphetamines were given to humans, positive mood changes were recorded. There were reports that the drug caused "a sense of well-being and exhilaration," feelings of "high spirits," and "bubbling inside." Most subjects felt a decrease in fatigue and an increase in energy; a clear, organized mind; and a desire to get to work and accomplish things (Grinspoon & Hedblom, 1975, p. 62). Later, systematic double-blind studies confirmed these reports (Gunne & Anggard, 1972; Johanson & Uhlenhuth, 1980).

Figure 10-2 shows the results of such a study. It shows the effect of various doses of methamphetamine, d-amphetamine, methylphenidate, and triazolam on rating scales for "liking the drug" and for feeling "talkative and friendly;" "stimulated;" and "sluggish, fatigued, and lazy." Triazolam (Halcion) is a benzodiazepine with sedative and anxiolytic properties. As you can see, all three psychomotor stimulants have similar effects: They cause a large increase in the positive rating scales of drug liking and feeling talkative and friendly, and they decrease feelings of sluggishness, fatigue, and laziness. Triazolam, on the other hand, at high doses caused a small increase in most positive scales and a very large increase in the sluggishness scale (Sevak, Stoops, Hays,

& Rush, 2009). These effects peaked at 2 hours for the amphetamines and at 3 hours for methylphenidate. Even at the higher doses, the effects were nearly gone at 5 hours.

Some of the subjective effects of amphetamine are greater if the subject is expecting to receive the drug (Mitchell, Laurent, & de Wit, 1996), but the effects appear to be similar in subjects tested alone or in social groups (de Wit et al., 1997).

PET studies using radioactive glucose have shown that cocaine-induced euphoria is correlated with a 14% global reduction in glucose metabolism in all areas of the neocortex as well as in the basal ganglia, thalamus, midbrain, and hippocampus (London et al., 1990), indicating a decrease in neural activity. Glucose metabolism rebounds to above-normal levels during the first week of withdrawal (Volkow et al., 1991).

Acute tolerance to pleasurable effects occurs after one administration or with repeated doses within a single session. Subjective effects tend to be greater when blood levels are rising than when they are falling (Brauer et al., 1996). In one study, humans were permitted to administer cocaine intravenously every 10 minutes for 1 hour. Feelings of positive mood increased after the first infusion but did not increase throughout the session, even though the blood levels of cocaine rose steadily with repeated infusions (Fischman & Schuster, 1982).

In addition to making people feel good, amphetamine at high doses after intravenous or intranasal administration produces intense feelings of euphoria and pleasure, called *rushes*. Rushes are not exclusive to intravenous administration, but this route is extremely efficient at delivering high drug levels to the brain and increasing their intensity. The rush has been described as "being lifted into the air with feelings of extreme happiness." Another account claims, "The heart starts beating at a terrible speed and his respiration is very rapid. Then he feels as if he was ascending into the cosmos, every fiber of his body trembling with happiness." Many people report that the rush has a strong sexual component. "The shot goes straight from the head to the scrotum," as one user put it (Rylander, 1969, p. 254).

The effects of cocaine are similar but shorter acting. Within a couple of minutes after cocaine is snorted, there is a numbing sensation called the *freeze*, which is followed after 5 minutes by a feeling of exhilaration and well-being. As with amphetamine, there is a feeling of energy and a sensation of clear thoughts and perceptions. This lasts for 20 to 30 minutes and is followed by a mild depression called the *crash* or *comedown*.

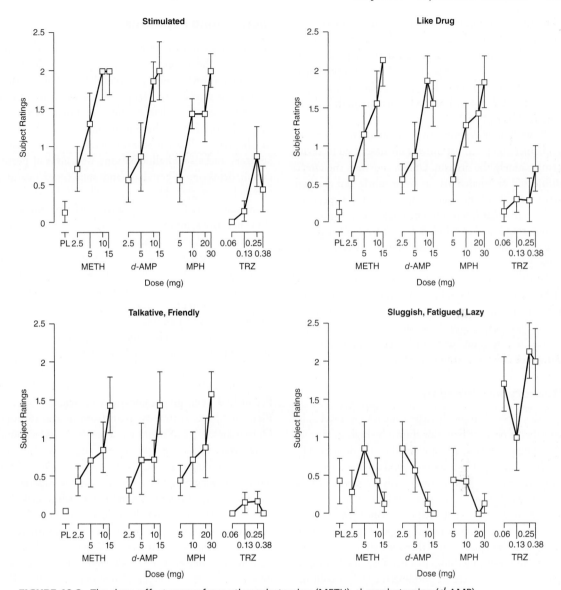

FIGURE 10-2 The dose–effect curves for methamphetamine (METH), d-amphetamine (*d*-AMP), methylphenidate (MPH) and triazolam (TRZ) for average subjective ratings of feeling "stimulated," "liking the drug effects," "talkative and friendly," and "sluggish and fatigued." The scale was from 0 = "no effect" to 4 = "extremely." (From Sevak et al., 2009, figure 3, p. 1014)

When cocaine is injected, there is also a rush that may be felt within seconds and lasts about 45 seconds. This is illustrated in the following experiment. Electroencephalographic (EEG) recordings allow researchers to correlate subjective reports with neurophysiological changes. Since head movements can interfere with EEG recordings, participants used a microswitch-equipped joystick to report when the effects of cocaine could be detected and when the participant was experiencing cocaine-induced euphoria or dysphoria. Using this technique, researchers discovered that whereas cocaine was *detected* for approximately

75 minutes postinjection, cocaine-induced euphoria occurred only during the first 10 to 15 minutes and correlated with increased alpha activity over the parietal and occipital lobes. During the 20 to 30 minutes postinjection, euphoria was replaced with dysphoria and correlated with a below-baseline level of activity in these brain regions (Lukas, 1991).

As with amphetamine, the rush associated with cocaine injection is almost universally described in sexual terms, namely, the orgasm. Unlike snorting, the effects of injected or inhaled are far from subtle and gradual; they take hold of the user immediately. The experience is so intense that it tends to encompass and engross the shooter totally and cuts him or her off from other people who might be nearby (Waldorf, Murphy, Renarman, & Joyce, 1977).

With repeated administrations, cocaine-produced rushes show rapid tolerance. When intravenous injections of cocaine were given 70 minutes apart, reports of rushes disappeared over the session, but other measures, such as "feeling good," were unchanged (Kumor, Sherer, Muntaner, Jaffe, & Herning, 1988).

Stereotyped Behavior

In 1965, a Swedish psychiatrist named Gosta Rylander described a peculiar behavior shown by high-dosage users of phenmetrazine, an amphetamine-like drug used for weight reduction. These users ground up phenmetrazine pills and injected them intravenously to experience the rush. The behavior Rylander noticed was what the users called *punding*—the repetitive performance of some (usually useless) act for an extended period. Typical acts were taking apart and putting together a watch or a telephone, sorting and resorting things in a handbag, or cleaning an apartment. When users are punding, they will usually not eat or drink or even go to the bathroom, and they become annoyed if the activity is interrupted (Rylander, 1969). Similar behavior is common among amphetamine users. Punding is considered the human equivalent of stereotyped behavior seen in laboratory animals after high-dose injections of amphetamines (stereotyped behavior of nonhumans will be described shortly).

It is quite likely that both punding and stereotyped behavior are caused by stimulation of the nigrostriatal DA system, which has input into the extrapyramidal motor system (see Chapter 4).

Monoamine Psychosis

At high doses and after repeated use, cocaine, cathinone, and the amphetamines can cause psychotic behavior in otherwise normal people (Bowers, 1987). This is called *monoamine psychosis* or MA psychosis. MA psychosis is virtually indistinguishable from true, full-blown paranoid schizophrenia, which is discussed in more detail in Chapter 12. The symptoms of MA psychosis include auditory and visual hallucinations, delusions of persecution, delusions of grandeur, and, sometimes, hostility and violence triggered by a paranoid belief that danger is imminent. In addition, symptoms of MA psychosis include negative symptoms, which include flattened affect, depression, and anxiety (Srisurapanont et al., 2011).

Stimulant psychosis can occur in individuals who have no history of psychotic behavior and will cause a worsening of symptoms when given to people already experiencing psychotic symptoms. It usually clears in several hours to several days, depending on the dose and duration of exposure, without residual effects (Angrist & Sudilovsky, 1978; Curran, Byrappa, & McBride, 2004).

One commonly reported symptom of MA psychosis is a tactile hallucination first noticed by Sigmund Freud. Freud had been giving cocaine to a friend, Dr. von Fleischl-Marxow, to treat pain from neural tumors. During the course of treatment, Fleischl-Marxow found it necessary to increase the dose to high levels, and he started showing the signs MA psychosis. One of the most distressing symptoms Fleischl-Marxow experienced was the feeling of creatures—in his case, white snakes—crawling over him. Others have described the feeling as bugs crawling around just under the skin (Brecher & the Editors of *Consumer Reports*, 1972, p. 275). These are known as *cocaine bugs* (or *crank bugs*, if they are caused by amphetamine). This phenomenon is formally called *formication*, from the Latin *formica*, meaning *ant*.

VIOLENCE. Violent behavior has been associated with continued amphetamine use. The violent behavior usually results from changes in the user's personality, which becomes hostile, paranoid, and defensive. Although violent episodes are not especially frequent, they are unpredictable and sudden. Rylander (1969) described one such case:

One addict who had just taken a shot stopped his car in a street, not feeling well, leaned backwards and put his feet up on the instrument panel. A bypasser asked if he was sick and offered his help. The addict drew a knife, got out and chased the helpful man. He stumbled and fell just when the addict tried to slash his back. (Rylander, 1969, p. 263)

Sensory Effects

Amphetamines have been reported to lower the critical frequency of fusion threshold, indicating an increase in visual acuity (Simonson & Brozek, 1952). Slight improvements have been reported in auditory flicker fusion as well (Besser, 1967). The passage of time is underestimated; 1 second seems longer than it really is (Goldstone, Boardman, & Lhamon, 1958).

Effects on Performance

The Spanish conquistadores may not have believed the claims of the South American Indians that coca made them stronger, but there seems to be little doubt that amphetamines and cocaine can improve performance on a number of tasks and skills. Most of the early work of this nature was done by the armed forces of several countries during World War II. They found that endurance could be increased and the effects of fatigue could be diminished by amphetamines. In fact, amphetamines are still used in the military for this purpose. They are commonly referred to as *go pills* (see Box 10-1).

Amphetamine will improve reaction time under normal circumstances (Fleming, Bigelow, Weinberger, & Goldberg, 1995). Amphetamine has also been shown to improve performance on the Digit Symbol Substitution test (DSST) and digit span which are tests of short-term memory and response speed (de Wit, Enggasser, & Richards, 2002). While it is well established that amphetamine can greatly improve vigilance and attention, deficits have been noted in tasks of divided attention where the participant is expected to attend to more than one thing at the same time. Amphetamine appears to induce *tunnel vision* in which attention becomes overwhelmed and this decreases the ability to

---

BOX 10-1   Tarnak Farm Incident

On the night of April 17, 2002, during the Afghanistan conflict, two American F-16 fighter jets were flying at 23,000 feet, returning at night from a 10-hour patrol when the pilots saw muzzle flashes on the ground below them. They reported what they thought was surface to air fire, but what they had actually seen was a Canadian Forces antitank and machine-gun exercise, which was taking place below them near Kandahar on a former Taliban firing range called Tarnak Farm. The wingmen believed that their flight leader was under attack. The flight leader radioed flight control for permission to fire his 20-mm cannons at what he believed to be an antiaircraft or multiple launch rocket system below. He was told to "stand by" and then 2 minutes later to "hold fire." Four seconds after the hold fire order, the wingman reported he was "rolling in, in self-defense," and 35 seconds later dropped a laser-guided 500 lb bomb on the Canadian soldiers. He then said "I hope I did the right thing." Minutes later, flight control replied "Friendlies, Kandahar" (Wikipedia, 2011; Tarnak Farm Incident; http://en.wikipedia.org/wiki/Tarnak_Farm_incident).

The Canadian soldiers were from the Third Battalion of Princess Patricia's Canadian Light Infantry. Five were killed, and eight were wounded.

Later at the hearings, it was revealed that the two pilots were told by their superiors to use *go pills* on their missions, and the airmen blamed the incident on the drugs. This was a significant part of the defense of the two pilots, but the military did not accept this explanation, citing the lack of similar incidents.

On July 6, 2004, the wingman who dropped the bomb was found guilty of dereliction of duty in what the U.S. military calls a *nonjudicial hearing* before a senior officer. He was fined nearly $5,700 in pay and reprimanded. The reprimand said he had "flagrantly disregarded a direct order," "exercised a total lack of basic flight discipline," and "blatantly ignored the applicable rules of engagement." The flight leader was reprimanded for leadership failures and allowed to retire.

This incident attracted a great deal of attention to the widespread practice of using amphetamines by military pilots and the general belief that they improve performance without having any undesirable effects. When you finish reading this chapter, you will be in a position to form an opinion about the extent to which go pills might have contributed to the deaths of five Canadian soldiers and whether the two U.S. pilots were treated fairly by the U.S. Air Force.

gather information effectively. People then focus their attention on only one event and miss other things happening in the environment (Easterbrook, 1959).

There are many examples of the effectiveness of amphetamine in overcoming fatigue. In a simplified simulated flying task, where subjects are required to move a joystick in order to keep dials from moving off center, the performance of subjects given a placebo deteriorated over a 4-hour period, but the scores of subjects given 5 mg of amphetamine actually stayed above their normal levels for the test (Weiss, 1969). Amphetamine has the ability to improve performance in tasks that require vigilance or prolonged attention. One measure of vigilance is the *clock test*. In this test, the subject faces a large dial around which a pointer moves in discrete steps. Every once in a while, the pointer moves two steps rather than one, and the task of the subject is to detect when such events occur. Over a period of 2 hours, the performance of normal subjects deteriorates from 95 to 80% accuracy. Subjects given 10 mg of amphetamine prior to this test show no deterioration in accuracy over the 2-hour period (Weiss, 1969). Amphetamine can also overcome deterioration in performance caused by other factors, such as decreased oxygen levels.

ADHD. Because psychomotor stimulants like amphetamine and methylphenidate at low doses are known to improve attention, they have become widely used in the treatment of ADHD, a disorder that afflicts about 5% of children in the United States and Canada. Children (and adults) with ADHD have trouble focusing and are often hyperactive or impulsive. In 2005, an estimated 9% of boys and 4% of girls in the United States were taking stimulant medications as part of their treatment for ADHD. Most take methylphenidate (Ritalin), although amphetamines (Adderall) are also used.

It may seem strange that a "stimulant" might be useful to treat a "hyperactivity" disorder, but ADHD appears to arise from a deficit in monoamine functioning in the prefrontal cortex, specifically in areas that mediate attention and the ability to inhibit inappropriate behaviors. Psychomotor stimulant drugs are able to increase dopaminergic and noradrenergic activity in these areas and improve attention and impulse control.

PERFORMANCE DEFICITS. Although stimulant drugs can improve performance, this improvement may be limited to simple tasks like the vigilance test or overlearned and overpracticed tasks like reaction time. Some investigators have suggested that stimulants may actually impair performance requiring flexibility and the ability to adopt new strategies (Judd, Squire, Butters, Salmon, & Paller, 1987). As we have seen earlier, even at low doses, amphetamine may create a tunnel vision effect by concentrating attention on only one feature of the environment. At higher doses, most of the beneficial effects of stimulants are lost, and people become impatient, are more easily distracted, and show impaired judgment.

EFFECTS ON DRIVING. Epidemiological studies have shown that people under the influence of amphetamines are 2.3 times more likely to be killed in an automobile accident (Drummer et al., 2004). Observed behaviors of drivers under the influence of amphetamines include drifting out of the lane, erratic driving, weaving, speeding, and an increased risk of high-speed collisions (Logan, 1996). Such epidemiological studies, however, provide little in the way of information on dose and cannot make a causal connection between the drug and driving problems.

In one experiment by Silber and colleagues (2005), participants were tested on a driving simulator after being given an oral dose of either 0.42 mg/kg of d-amphetamine (average of about 30 mg per person) or a placebo. When tested in a simulated nighttime scenario, amphetamine did not appear to have any effect, but during a simulated daytime scenario, amphetamine caused a decrease in driving ability measured by a failure to stop at a red light and slow reaction times. The authors concluded that these findings were consistent with amphetamine-induced narrowing of attentional focus, which caused participants to miss significant stimuli, such as a red light that appeared on the visual periphery.

ATHLETIC PERFORMANCE. In one early study, Smith and Beecher (1959) gave amphetamine to competitive swimmers who were then timed while performing in the event for which they were training. They found that amphetamine could produce a 1% improvement in the swimmers' best drug-free times. Although 1% does not sound like much, in the highly competitive sport of swimming, athletes may train many months to reduce their times by 1%. Similar improvements have been seen in such track events as the 600- and 1,000-yard runs and the mile and in such field events as the shot put.

Because the psychomotor stimulants improve athletic performance, their use by athletes is banned by most national sports federations, and urine samples supplied by athletes at sporting events are screened for these drugs. As mentioned earlier, ephedrine is a psychomotor stimulant closely related to amphetamine. Ephedrine and similar drugs act as *bronchodilators* and are found in many cold preparations, cough syrups, and decongestants. Athletes undergoing drug testing should be aware of the contents of these medicines before they take them because they could cause urine to test positive for a banned substance. Some banned substances found in cold medicines include norpseudoephedrine, methoxyphenamine, isoprenaline, isoproterenol, and methylephedrine.

EFFECTS ON THE BEHAVIOR OF NONHUMANS

Unconditioned Behavior

At low and intermediate doses, amphetamines increase spontaneous locomotor and exploratory activity in rats. At higher doses, there is an increase in locomotion at first, but after about an hour, the animals start to show increased sniffing and a variety of stereotyped behavior. The stereotyped behavior is usually some simple, short act with no particular function; it is repeated over and over to the exclusion of other behavior. In rodents, it may take the form of bobbing the head up and down, sniffing in a corner, rearing on the hind legs, or gnawing and biting.

In monkeys, there is a decrease in locomotor activity, and the stereotyped behavior is generally more complex than in rodents. It is also different in different subjects. One monkey may examine its hands; another may move sideways. These behaviors will reappear in the same animals when the drug is given at a later date. In humans, stereotyped behaviors, described earlier as punding, are more complex.

After high doses of amphetamines and cocaine, it is common for both rodents and monkeys to chew and bite at their own bodies. This self-directed biting is called *automutilation*. Animals may sometimes bite off their fingers, toes, or paws. It is likely that automutilation is a form of stereotyped behavior because it appears to be repetitious; but it may also be a result of formication, the sensation of bugs

crawling under or on the skin is a symptom of amphetamine or cocaine psychosis in humans. The same sensation, experienced by animals, could cause them to pick at or cut their skin in an attempt to let the bugs out.

Even at low doses, amphetamines and cocaine decrease consumption of both food and water in most species. This is probably a combination of (a) the effect of the drug on the part of the brain that controls appetite and (b) the fact that the drug increases other behavior sequences and reduces the time available for eating and drinking. We know that appetite suppression is not related to the reinforcing effects of these drugs because fenfluramine, a drug similar to amphetamine, is very effective in suppressing appetite but does not appear to have any reinforcing effects (Brady et al., 1987). In fact, fenfluramine antagonizes the reinforcing effects of amphetamine and cocaine (Wee & Woolverton, 2006). As mentioned earlier, it is possible that this effect is mediated through changes in serotonin function.

Conditioned Behavior

In one of the earliest experiments on the effects of amphetamines on operant behavior, Peter Dews (1958) gave methamphetamine to pigeons responding on several schedules of reinforcement for food. Dews found that the drug increased responding on the fixed interval (FI) schedule but decreased fixed ratio (FR) responding at exactly the same dose. In his paper, Dews first demonstrated a relationship between the effect of amphetamine and the rate at which the pigeon was responding. He noticed that methamphetamine increased the rate of responding if it was low, as in the FI, but slowed responding that was normally fast, as in the FR. This effect became known as the *rate dependency effect*. It has since been demonstrated that this rule applies across all amphetamine-type drugs and many others, across many species, and across many types of behavior and schedules of reinforcement (Dews & Wenger, 1977). The significance of this observation cannot be overestimated. It was one of the first demonstrations that a drug interacts dynamically with ongoing behavior. It also showed that it was not appropriate to understand the effect a drug might have by simply classifying it as a "psychomotor stimulant." Whether the drug stimulates or depresses motor activity is a result of the behavior being observed and not entirely determined by the properties of the drug alone.

The rate dependency principle appears not to apply to the effect of amphetamine on behavior suppressed by punishment. Punishment-suppressed behavior usually occurs at a low rate, but most amphetamines and cocaine do not increase the rate.

The effects of cocaine are similar to those of amphetamine, but the rate-increasing effects of cocaine are not as great (Smith, 1964).

DISSOCIATION AND DRUG STATE DISCRIMINATION

It has been demonstrated that amphetamine causes dissociation; animals trained under the influence of amphetamine cannot completely remember what they learned when the amphetamine has worn off. This may be bad news for people who use amphetamines to help them stay awake and cram for exams (Roffman & Lal, 1972).

Rats can learn to discriminate amphetamine and cocaine from saline with moderate ease, although they are not as easily discriminable as barbiturates or benzodiazepines (Overton, 1982). Animals generalize the amphetamine response to cocaine, methylphenidate, cathinone, and some monoamine oxidase (MAO) inhibitors (Glennon, 1987; Glennon, Young, Martin, & Dal Cason, 1995; Huang & Ho, 1974; Porsolt, Pawelec, & Jalfre, 1982; Schechter & Glennon, 1985). In rats, amphetamine responses do not generalize to caffeine, nicotine, the barbiturates, chlorpromazine, atropine, or any of the common hallucinogens (Seiden & Dykstra, 1977).

The discriminative effects of amphetamine can be blocked by dopamine D_1 and D_2 receptor blockers in the mesolimbic dopamine system. Dopamine activity in the nigrostriatal system does not appear to be involved (Callahan, De La Garza, & Cunningham, 1997). It does not appear that norepinephrine or serotonin plays a significant role in amphetamine discrimination (Brauer et al., 1997).

Humans can also readily learn to discriminate amphetamine from a placebo (Chait, Uhlenhuth, & Johanson, 1986). In one experiment, human participants were trained to discriminate a capsule containing 10 mg of methamphetamine from a placebo capsule for a monetary reward. After the training phase, they were tested with 2.5, 5, 10, and 15 mg capsules of methamphetamine and d-amphetamine and capsules of methylphenidate containing 5, 10, 15, and 30 mg. They were also tested with capsules containing 0.06, 0.13, 0.25 and 0.38 mg of triazolam. The test doses of these drugs were chosen to be within the range of doses recommended when these drugs are taken therapeutically. The results can be seen in Figure 10-3. The methamphetamine response generalized completely to d-amphetamine and methylphenidate showing that the participants could not distinguish between them (Sevak, et al., 2009). The triazolam was easily discriminated.

TOLERANCE

Acute Tolerance

As described earlier, with continuous use, sniffing every 20 or 30 minutes for 10 or 12 hours, cocaine quickly loses its ability to cause rushes and gradually becomes incapable of improving mood. This phenomenon, sometimes known as a *coke-out*, is usually why runs come to an end (see the section on self-administration of cocaine later in this chapter). This acute tolerance dissipates rapidly and may be gone within 24 hours (Waldorf et al., 1977). Even though acute tolerance develops to the subjective effects, it does not appear to develop to the effects on blood pressure and heart rate. This suggests that people who increase the frequency of dose of amphetamine or cocaine to maintain a subjective effect may be in danger of reaching levels that could be toxic (Brauer et al., 1996).

Tolerance has been demonstrated for the discriminative effects of amphetamine in rats. Rats trained to discriminate amphetamine were given a single administration of either 1.5 or 3.0 mg/kg of amphetamine, and then a dose–response curve for the discriminative properties of amphetamine was determined 24 hours later. Compared to rats given saline, the dose–response curve was shifted to the right in a dose-dependent manner for rats given the amphetamine the day before. The peaks of the dose–response curves were the same, indicating that pre-exposure to amphetamine decreased potency, but not effectiveness, of the amphetamine as a discriminative stimulus (Barrett, Caul, & Smith, 2004).

Chronic Tolerance and Sensitization

Some effects of cocaine and amphetamines become tolerated with repeated administration. In humans, the appetite-suppressing effect usually disappears in about

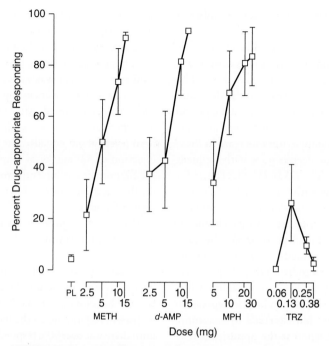

FIGURE 10-3 Dose–effect curves for methamphetamine (METH), d-amphetamine (*d*-AMP), methylphenidate (MPH), and triazolam (TRZ) for percentage of methamphetamine-appropriate responding of humans trained to discriminate methamphetamine. Statistical analysis showed that the curves for METH, *d*-AMP, and MPH did not differ from each other and that all three curves were different from TRZ. (Sevak et al., 2009, figure 1, p. 1011)

2 weeks, and the effects on the heart and blood pressure also diminish. The lethal effects also show tolerance, and chronic amphetamine users are able to increase their dose to extremely high levels. In one such case, a 15,000-mg dose of amphetamine was administered in a 24-hour period; this was 1,000 times the normal therapeutic dose and several times the estimated LD_{50} for nontolerant humans. Some effects, such as the blocking of sleep, show no tolerance.

For some effects, reverse tolerance or sensitization takes place. Stereotyped behavior and psychotic behavior appear more frequently after repeated doses in humans. In rats, chronic administration of cocaine lowers the threshold for convulsions, and some electrical activity within the brain increases with continued use (Stripling & Ellinwood, 1976). With continued administration of cocaine, stereotyped behavior and spontaneous motor

activity also increase in frequency and intensity (Post, Weiss, Pert, & Uhde, 1987). As described in Chapter 3, this sensitization is a result of increased sensitivity of the mesolimbic dopamine system (Pierce & Kalivas, 1997).

WITHDRAWAL

Amphetamine and cocaine are not associated with a severe or medically serious withdrawal when use is discontinued. Depression seems to be the most prominent characteristic of psychomotor stimulant withdrawal.

After a single dose of amphetamine or cocaine, the high is usually followed by a *crash* or *comedown*—a period of depression and lethargy that can be thought of as a withdrawal symptom. The depression is immediately relieved by another administration of the drug. The withdrawal occurs within half an hour after taking cocaine, but its appearance is delayed for a number of hours after amphetamines.

After chronic heavy use, abrupt discontinuation of amphetamine or cocaine use will cause withdrawal symptoms within 24 hours of the last dose. The severity of the depression is related to the dose and the duration of the intake period. If the intake period has been long enough to interfere with sleep and eating, there will also be a compensatory increase in these behaviors. The quality of sleep is poor with frequent dreams and awakenings. The *DSM-IV-TR* criteria for diagnosing amphetamine withdrawal include depression, fatigue, vivid or unpleasant dreams, insomnia or hypersomnia, increased appetite, and psychomotor agitation or retardation. The depression may be quite severe and may be accompanied by suicidal thoughts and suicide attempts (Meredith, Jaffe, Ang-Lee, & Saxon, 2005; Scott et al., 2007). Amphetamine withdrawal depression is similar to psychiatric depression except that the latter is characterized by insomnia and decreased appetite, whereas the opposite is true for the amphetamine-induced depression (Angrist & Sudilovsky, 1978). Both can be successfully treated with antidepressant drugs.

The initial phase of withdrawal can last for a week, but the increased appetite, sleep disturbances, and depression may continue for weeks or months (Gawin & Kleber, 1987; McGregor et al., 2005).

Withdrawal from psychomotor stimulants can also disrupt performance. In the early stages of abstinence, methamphetamine addicts demonstrate decision-making dysfunctions on tasks that require switching from a losing to a winning strategy in a two-choice procedure. This performance deficit correlates with reduced dorsolateral prefrontal cortex activation and failure to activate the ventromedial cortex, as measured by functional magnetic resonance imaging (fMRI; Paulus et al., 2002). Following at least 1 year of amphetamine abstinence, PET imaging continued to demonstrate decreased dorsolateral prefrontal cortex activation in association with decision making in risky situations (Ersche et al., 2005).

Whereas most drug discrimination studies using psychomotor stimulants have focused on exploring the drugs' primary effect, one interesting experiment explored the properties of psychostimulant withdrawal. In this experiment, rats were trained to discriminate between a 0.25 mg/kg s.c. injection of amphetamine and a 0.033 mg/kg s.c. injection of haloperidol (haloperidol is an antipsychotic drug known to block D$_2$ receptors; see Chapter 12). Using a two-lever Skinner box task, food reinforcement was associated with pressing only one of two levers, depending on which drug the rat had been administered. After this discrimination training, when rats were given a saline injection they pressed both levers about equally. The rats were then given an injection of 3.0 mg/kg of amphetamine and tested in the Skinner box at intervals from 6 to 72 hours following the injection. The rats' lever-pressing behavior can be seen in Figure 10-4.

Panel A of Figure 10-4 shows performance after discrimination training. As you can see, a test dose of 0.25 mg/kg of amphetamine prompted over 90% responding on the amphetamine lever, but as the test dose decreased, so too did the percent of responding on the amphetamine lever. As the test dose of haloperidol increased, responding on the haloperidol lever increased until there was over 90% responding at a dose 0.35 mg/kg haloperidol.

Panel B shows the result of testing at various periods after a 3.0 mg/kg injection of amphetamine. At 6 and 8 hours following injection, almost all responding was on the amphetamine lever indicating that the rats were still experiencing the effects of the amphetamine. As time passed, the rats began responding on the haloperidol lever. This indicates that the rats experienced withdrawal from amphetamine as subjective state similar to that of a haloperidol injection. Finally, at 72 hours, responding returned to the 50% level (Barrett et al., 2004).

This type of finding is exactly what might be expected by the Opponent Process Theory of Solomon and Corbit described in Chapter 3 and illustrated in Box 3-1.

SELF-ADMINISTRATION IN HUMANS

Cocaine

Cocaine has a long history of self-administration, starting with the native people of South America who consumed the drug orally, as noted earlier in this chapter. Their pattern of use was very different from the modern North American patterns of self-administration of pure cocaine or amphetamines. With pure cocaine,

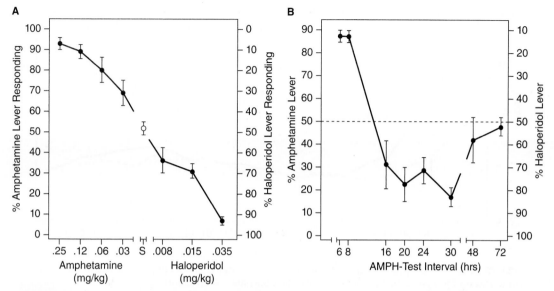

FIGURE 10-4 Panel A shows the percent of responding on the amphetamine lever and on the haloperidol lever for rats trained to discriminate amphetamine from haloperidol in a two-lever Skinner box. As you can see, the rats responded at the 50% level when neither drug is administered ("S" = saline). Panel B shows the time course for responding on the amphetamine and haloperidol levers for 72 hours after a dose of 3.0 mg/kg of amphetamine. You can see that, for the first 8 hours after the amphetamine injection, the rats responded on the amphetamine lever, indicating that they were experiencing the effects of amphetamine. As time passed, however, rats responded on the haloperidol lever, showing that the subjective experience of withdrawal (or hangover) from amphetamine was similar to an injection of haloperidol. (Adapted from Barrett et al., 2004, figures 2 and 3, p. 765)

continuous use is rare. When snorted or injected, cocaine is usually taken in large quantities for brief periods of time that are followed by periods of abstinence. This is sometimes called the *run–abstinence* cycle. This pattern is also seen with crack addicts.

Cocaine is often taken in conjunction with other drugs. The most usual mix is the *speed ball*, a combination of cocaine (or amphetamine) and heroin. Users claim that the heroin reduces the jitteriness that cocaine arouses by stimulating the sympathetic nervous system, and the cocaine diminishes the sleepiness or *nod* caused by heroin. Cocaine is also regularly mixed with sedatives such as benzodiazepines or with hallucinogens such as ketamine or PCP for the same reason.

Amphetamines

Like cocaine, amphetamines are self-administered sporadically in run–abstinence cycles rather than continuously, but the pattern may depend on the effect for which the drug is taken. Because it is longer lasting than cocaine, amphetamine allows constant blood levels to be maintained more easily for an extended period of time—for example, when the drug is used by truck drivers or students cramming for finals to enhance behavior or prevent sleep. When the need is over, the drug is usually discontinued, and the person then recovers by making up for the lost sleep.

When amphetamines are used for their euphoric effects, usually much higher doses are taken, and the administration is frequently intravenous or inhalation. In the 1960s, this type of use was characterized by the *peak user* or *speed freak* who typically injected amphetamine every few hours for days at a time. During such *runs*, users do not sleep, they eat very little, and they may show symptoms of amphetamine psychosis, such as punding and paranoia. Eventually, when they are too exhausted to continue or they run out of the drug, they *crash*—they sleep for an extended period (24 to 48 hours). When they wake up, they are very hungry and will eat

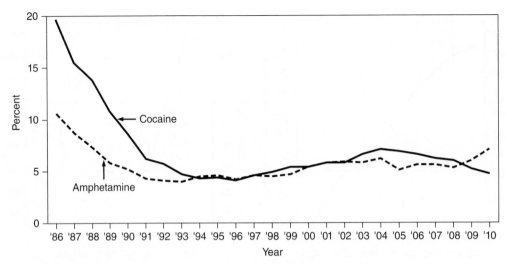

FIGURE 10-5 Changes in the annual prevalence rates for cocaine and amphetamine use in the United States for ages 19 to 28. (Johnston, O'Malley, Bachman, & Schulenberg, 2011)

ravenously before going out to search for more drugs in order to begin another run.

Trends in Use

Figure 10-5 shows the annual prevalence of cocaine and amphetamine use (the percentage of those who report having used these drugs within the past year) for people ages 19 to 28 in the United States from 1986 to 2010. There was a large spike in cocaine use (solid line) in the early 1980s and then a gradual decline until the mid-1990s when use seemed to level off. There was a mild resurgence in the mid-2000s, but use has now declined to the level of the 1990s. A similar pattern can be seen for the amphetamines (dashed line) with widespread use throughout the 1980s and then a decline during the early 1990s. There was a slight resurgence in the use of amphetamines in the early 2000s, but, unlike cocaine use, there has been no decline (Johnston et al., 2011).

Self-Administration in Nonhumans

In 1968, Roy Pickens and Travis Thompson, then at the University of Minnesota, published the first detailed account of cocaine self-administration in nonhumans (the first cocaine self-administration experiments were actually done by G. A. Deneau and his colleagues at the University of Michigan, but these

were not published until 1969). Pickens and Thompson, using two rats implanted with intravenous catheters, showed that the rats would bar press on an FR schedule for cocaine (this experiment is described in Chapter 5). For several reasons, this was an important milestone. It was the first demonstration of self-administration of a drug other than morphine, and it established that a drug with no apparent withdrawal symptoms could be a reinforcer, confirming that the reinforcing effect of drugs was not a result of fear of withdrawal. Since the time of this experiment, there have been many demonstrations of cocaine self-administration in many species.

Figure 10-6 shows data published by Deneau et al. (1969) and demonstrates the erratic pattern of cocaine self-administration in monkeys when the drug is freely available, 24 hours a day. A monkey quickly learns to give itself the drug and is soon administering the drug at levels high enough to cause convulsions. The record shows that there is considerable fluctuation from day to day. On some days, no drug is taken; on others, massive quantities are infused. This pattern of self-administration of cocaine is similar to the binge–abstinence cycles shown by human stimulant users. If no restrictions are placed on cocaine intake and the drug is freely available, laboratory animals will often administer cocaine to the point of killing themselves (Bozarth & Wise, 1984).

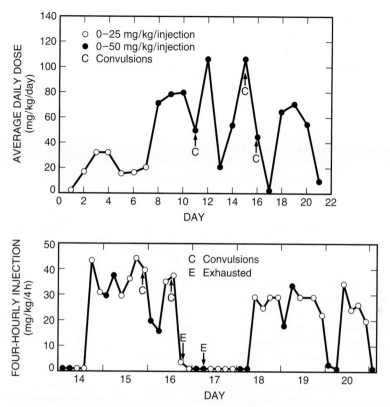

FIGURE 10-6 The pattern of cocaine self-administration in the monkey. *Top*: Daily intake for 21 days. *Bottom*: Intake in 4-hour periods from day 14 to day 21, illustrating the cycles of intake and abstinence. (Adapted from Deneau, Yanagita, & Seevers, 1969)

Figure 10-6 illustrates the typical run–abstinence cycle of a monkey self-administering cocaine. In this case, the monkey actually stopped responding for a 28-hour period on day 17 before resuming injections on day 18.

The pattern of self-administration is quite different when daily access to cocaine is limited; that is, there is a long time-out after each infusion, or the access to cocaine is limited to brief sessions during the day. Under these conditions, laboratory animals self-administer cocaine in a steady and regular manner, precisely controlling the amount of drug they receive on any given day (Ahmed & Koob, 1998; Bass, Jansen, & Roberts, 2010). When rats are restricted to three opportunities to administer cocaine per hour, they do not show bingeing and do not consume all the cocaine

available to them. Rather, their consumption throughout the day fluctuates with circadian rhythm whereby self-administration occurs mostly during the dark phase of the cycle. When cocaine is available five times per hour, the circadian rhythms are overwhelmed, and the rats take every cocaine infusion available for days in a row (Roberts, Brebner, Vincler, & Lynch, 2002).

Nonhumans readily self-administer all the psychomotor stimulants, using a variety of routes of administration. The patterns and rates are similar to those for cocaine. Extinguished cocaine self-administration can be reinstated by an infusion of other psychomotor stimulants and by other drugs such as morphine and caffeine. In addition, cocaine self-administration is enhanced by stress, previous experience with cocaine, and the concurrent administration of caffeine, heroin, and alcohol. Self-administration is decreased by the concurrent availability of alternative reinforcers such as sweetened water (Carroll & Bickel, 1998).

David Roberts of Wake Forest University and his colleagues have explored the factors that can increase responding of rats on a progressive ratio schedule (PR). This research is described in Box 10-2.

BOX 10-2   How to Make a Rat Addicted to Cocaine

As described in Chapter 5, addiction is the progression from simple self-administration of a drug, what we might call casual use, to a compulsive disorder with characteristics described by the *DSM-IV-TR*. One such characteristic is outlined in criterion 5: spending a great deal of time on activities necessary to obtain the substance, use the substance, or recover from its effects (see *DSM-IV-TR* criteria for substance dependence in Box 5-1 of Chapter 5). Roberts, Morgan, and Liu (2007) point out that simple self-administration of drugs in laboratory animals may be useful as a model for casual drug use, but may not be a useful way to model addiction. This is because, in most cases, responding stabilizes quickly and shows no progressive increase over time, as is symptomatic of addiction. They suggest that the Progressive Ratio (PR) schedule may be a useful way to model behaviors outlined in criterion 5 of the *DSM-IV-TR* symptoms of addiction.

In the PR schedule, a rat is required to press a lever on a ratio schedule that keeps increasing. For example, it might be required to press a lever once for the first infusion of a drug, twice for the second, four times for the third, eight times for the fourth, and so on. Eventually, the rat will stop responding because the requirement for reinforcement is too great. This is called the *breaking point* or *break point* (see Chapter 2). The break point is a good analogue of criterion 5 because it measures "spending a great deal of time on activities necessary to obtain the substance." David Roberts and his colleagues noted that, in many cases, the break point for cocaine self-administration in rats can be increased by various experimenter-administered pretreatments, such as pre-exposure to cocaine and other stimulants. These experiments show that the motivation to use cocaine can be manipulated, but Roberts and colleagues wanted to explore which conditions of self-administration could cause break points to increase.

Human cocaine users often show binge–abstinence cycles during which they use the drug excessively for a period of time and then crash and remain abstinent for a few days. Roberts set up an experiment to mimic this pattern. First, he determined the break points for cocaine for a group of rats. Then, he exposed the rats to a procedure wherein they were given access to self-administered infusions of cocaine four times per hour for 10 days on an FR5 schedule. Following this, rats were deprived of cocaine for 7 to 10 days. Under these conditions, there was a dramatic increase in PR breaking points when the rats resumed testing on a PR schedule. Surprisingly, break points were not increased if the drug was available continuously on an FR1 schedule, or if there was only a 1-day deprivation period after the 10-day binge. These findings suggest that the increased break point for cocaine could be caused by self-administration factors, but are sensitive only to a restricted and particular set of conditions. Roberts and colleagues then set out to explore what those conditions might be.

In addition to mimicking the binge–abstinence cycle, Roberts found that progressive ratio testing that immediately followed training to self-administer a 1.5 mg/kg injection of cocaine on an FR1 schedule also led to a steady increase in break point over a 2-week period. This demonstrates that imposing extra work demands for the drug (having rats respond on a PR as opposed to an FR1 schedule) increases motivation to self-administer cocaine.

Another important factor was cocaine dose. If rats were initially trained to self-administer a 0.75 mg/kg injection, subsequent testing on the PR schedule demonstrated increasing break points only when rats were tested using 0.75 and 1.5 mg/kg injections of cocaine, not with a higher dose (3.0 mg/kg) or a lower dose (0.38 mg/kg) injection.

Roberts and colleagues also showed that the motivation to administer cocaine, as determined by PR break points, was sensitive to previous PR testing with a smaller dose, and by speed of injection: A drug dose administered over a 5-second period was more effective at increasing break points than the same dose administered over 25 or 59 seconds.

This series of experiments shows that changes in the motivation to use cocaine, an indication of the development of addiction in humans, can be modeled through the use of the progressive ratio schedule, and that the results are not always what you might expect; high doses and easy availability actually decrease the motivation to use the drug, whereas low doses and restrictions on availability seem to increase motivation.

HARMFUL EFFECTS

Direct Effects

When methylphenidate is given chronically at low levels in the treatment of hyperactivity in children, it sometimes causes a transient reduction in growth velocity (Brookes, 1985).

There are reports that the Andean Indians who chew the coca leaf regularly seem to have few health problems. It has been noted, however, that these and other regular users of cocaine have a sallow or yellowish complexion, which may be attributable to mild jaundice caused by liver disease. Chronic cocaine use has also caused liver damage in experimental animals (Caldwell, 1976). Chronic cocaine sniffing can cause inflammation and ulceration of the mucous membranes in the nose. This damage can even progress to the extent that openings appear in the septum (the membrane separating the nostrils). Because cocaine is a local anesthetic, this discomfort in the nose will be relieved by sniffing more cocaine, and in this way it will contribute to the motivation to continue sniffing the drug.

As mentioned earlier, when cocaine is freely available it leads to bingeing behavior, which continues until the drug runs out or the user becomes exhausted. During such runs, it is not unusual for vast sums to be spent on the drug (Siegel, 1982). People have been known to sell their houses and cars to finance a binge. Not only do such binges consume personal finances, but many users report disturbing physiological and psychological symptoms: paranoid feelings, visual hallucinations, cravings, antisocial behavior, attention and concentration problems, blurred vision, and weight loss.

The use of oral amphetamine for short periods (e.g., to stay awake while driving or studying) can have undesirable effects as well including restlessness, excessive talking, confusion, and dizziness. If use is continued for too long, paranoid psychotic behavior starts to appear, which is complicated by the lack of sleep. Punding and irrational thinking may also emerge, and these are not likely to improve one's ability to drive or study. In susceptible individuals, the increased blood pressure can cause strokes (Rumbaugh, Bergeron, Fang, & McCormick, 1971). In addition, when the drug is stopped, the period of recovery is characterized by depression with suicidal tendencies, lethargy, and sleep disturbances.

High-level chronic stimulant use, especially if associated with intravenous administration, is potentially quite harmful. The effects are both direct and indirect. Amphetamines have a strong direct effect on the heart and circulatory system; the irregular heartbeat and increased blood pressure they cause can result in internal bleeding and strokes (Grinspoon & Bakalar, 1979a). Irreversible brain damage has also been reported as a result of deterioration and rupturing of small blood vessels in the brain (Rumbaugh et al., 1971).

In addition, amphetamine appears to have a neurotoxic effect on some parts of the brain, especially those cells in the brain that release dopamine. Nonhuman primate studies demonstrate that damage to brain dopamine neurons can result from only four administrations of methamphetamine at doses comparable to those used recreationally by humans. PET imaging with a radiolabeled dopamine transporter ligand revealed that total doses of 2, 4, or 8 mg/kg of methamphetamine injected into baboons over 8 hours on a single day resulted in significant reductions in dopamine transporter density in the striatum, 2 to 3 weeks later. This indicates the death of dopamine cells (Villemagne et al., 1998). The results of this study are shown in Color Plate D.

As described earlier, high doses and continuous use of stimulants can cause MA psychosis.

Indirect Effects

As with so many excessively used drugs, many of the harmful effects of amphetamine are indirect and arise from the user's lifestyle. Because intravenous users rarely use sterile injection apparatuses, they frequently contract diseases, particularly hepatitis and HIV/AIDS. Their ability to fight diseases is reduced by (a) the poor diet associated with the appetite-suppressing effects of the drug, and (b) the fact that they seldom sleep. High-dose amphetamine users are suspicious, antisocial, and prone to violence (Rylander, 1969).

The death rate from all causes among amphetamine and cocaine users has been found to be about six times higher than that of the general population. It is slightly higher for intravenous users and for those who also show psychiatric symptoms (Arendt, Munk-Jørgensen, Sher, & Jensen, 2011).

Reproduction

Both amphetamine and cocaine have been used to enhance sexual activity. It has been reported that low doses prolong erections and delay ejaculation in males and enhance desire and enjoyment of orgasm in females. These changes, along with the decrease in sexual inhibitions caused by the drug, sometimes lead to changes in sexual practices while taking these drugs. People who would not normally do such things sometimes engage in marathon sexual acts, group sex, and same-sex experiences (Smith, Buxton, & Dammann, 1979). Continuous high doses, by inhalation of crack or freebase or by injection of cocaine, often lead to a disruption in sexual activity in males and periods of disinterest in sex (Siegel, 1982).

Like cocaine, khat initially increases sex drive in males, but continued use can cause decreased sexual interest and impotency (Giannini, Burge, Shaheen, & Price, 1986). It can also inhibit milk production in nursing mothers who continuously abuse the plant.

There have been some studies of the effects of amphetamine-like drugs on fetal abnormalities. Most of these studies were done on women who used these drugs to control their appetite during pregnancy. They provided some evidence linking this chronic, oral, low-dose use with a higher-than-average incidence of birth abnormalities. Evidence from animal studies also indicates that amphetamine used during pregnancy can cause behavioral and physical problems in offspring (Grinspoon & Hedblom, 1975).

Many studies, but not all, have found that maternal cocaine use does retard fetal growth; babies are smaller and more likely to be premature (Zuckerman & Frank, 1994). Other studies, however, have found that babies born to mothers who reported using cocaine while pregnant were almost 10 times more likely to have *abruptio placentae* (the placenta detaches prematurely; Shiono et al., 1995). Studies of possible long-term developmental and behavioral effects of prenatal exposure to cocaine are plagued with methodological difficulties, not the least of which is accurately measuring cocaine exposure and separating its effect from other confounding factors such as the use of other drugs and the quality of pre- and post-natal care (Zuckerman & Frank, 1994). It is now becoming clear that such exposure does not necessarily lead to reduced intelligence, as was once thought. Several studies, however, have concluded that children whose mothers used cocaine while pregnant have more behavioral problems, including a decreased ability to pay attention and stay focused, increased aggression, and irritability (Vogel, 1997).

Overdose

Cocaine users who take large doses commonly experience muscle weakness and respiratory depression. The user may be unable to stand up or may collapse but not lose consciousness (Crowley, 1987).

The lethal dose of cocaine depends to a large extent on the route of administration. Individuals vary greatly, but the LD_{50} in a 150-pound man is about 500 mg. When the drug is taken intranasally, the LD_{50} may be as low as 30 mg. The absolute dose may not be the important variable in determining the lethality; rather, what seems to be important is the sudden increase in drug levels in the brain.

The cocaine-related deaths of several prominent athletes and celebrities have emphasized that cocaine has intense cardiovascular effects that can be fatal when the drug is injected or inhaled in concentrated form, causing the cocaine sudden-death syndrome. As noted earlier, it is not unusual for laboratory animals to self-administer lethal doses of cocaine. George and Goldberg (1989) showed that between individual strains of rats and mice, there is considerable variability in sensitivity to various effects of cocaine. One strain of rats, for example, seemed insensitive to the reinforcing effects of usual doses of cocaine but was very sensitive to the lethal effects of cocaine on the heart. If there are similar genetic variations in humans, it is possible that certain individuals might be highly resistant to the euphoric effects of the drug. Such people would be at a considerable risk from cocaine because attempts to reach euphoric doses could easily drive blood levels into the lethal range. Such genetic variations in sensitivity may account for the cocaine sudden-death syndrome (George & Goldberg, 1989).

The cocaine overdose or *caine reaction* has two phases: An initial excitement is followed by severe headache, nausea, vomiting, and then severe convulsions. This phase is followed by a loss of consciousness, respiratory depression, and cardiac failure causing death. Death may be very rapid, within 2 to 3 minutes, or it may take as long as half an hour. Someone who survives the first 3 hours is likely to recover, but if breathing has been depressed too long, there may be brain damage from loss of oxygen (Gay & Inaba, 1976).

Seizures caused by cocaine overdose can be treated with diazepam, and respiratory depression or arrest can be treated with artificial respiration. Chlorpromazine, an antipsychotic, is also very effective as an antagonist of the toxic effects of cocaine (Crowley, 1987).

TREATMENT

As with treatments of most drugs that cause physical dependence, there is usually a detoxification stage where the addicted person goes through withdrawal. Acute withdrawal symptoms of amphetamine and cocaine were described earlier. Because a single use of amphetamine or cocaine can eliminate these symptoms and cause a sense of well-being, relapse during this period is common. It is important, therefore, to find drugs that are able to mitigate these withdrawal symptoms, and many attempts have been made. The drug amineptine (a tricyclic antidepressant that inhibits dopamine and, to a lesser extent, norepinephrine) reduced treatment dropout rates, but did not appear to diminish symptoms of withdrawal or craving. This drug has not been made available for treatment because of concerns that it has potential for abuse. Another drug, mirtazapine, has been tested with mixed results (Shoptaw, Kao, Heinzerling, & Ling, 2009). It has a complex pharmacology, acting as an inverse agonist at many adrenergic and serotonergic receptors, and is also a NET blocker.

Behavioral Therapies

The most widely used behavioral treatments of both cocaine and amphetamine addiction are cognitive behavioral therapy, contingency management, and community reinforcement, or a combination of these (Ciccarone, 2011; see Chapter 5). Cognitive behavioral therapy teaches strategies to think rationally, avoid maladaptive behavior, and prevent relapse. In a recent meta-analysis, cognitive behavioral therapy was shown to be effective in reducing methamphetamine use and in creating other positive changes in behavior after only two to four sessions (Lee & Rawson, 2008). Contingency management and community reinforcement use operant techniques to reward clients for continued abstinence from the drug. Contingency management uses conditioned rewards such as vouchers for goods and services, while community reinforcement uses social reinforcement such as praise and encouragement from one's family and social group (Lussier, Heil, Mongeon, Badger, & Higgins, 2006). Contingency management often works better than community reinforcement during treatment, but the therapeutic effect of contingency management is often diminished when the rewarding contingencies are stopped so that both treatments are equally effective at the end of

the treatment period. Combined treatment works better than either treatment alone (Ciccarone, 2011).

Pharmacotherapies

Many attempts have been made to find a drug that can act as a maintenance drug for the psychomotor stimulants. As described in Chapter 5, such drugs should block withdrawal symptoms, reduce craving for psychomotor stimulants, and block the effect of a psychomotor stimulant if it should be taken. Ideally, such a drug should not be addicting itself, but if it is, it should be taken orally and have a long half-life. These properties will keep blood levels steady and eliminate fluctuations in the body, which could create addiction.

MODAFINIL. Modafinil has a complex pharmacology—it stimulates dopamine, norepinephrine, and glutamate transmission as well as the release of histamine. It is used as a cognitive enhancer, to treat ADHD, and to treat sleepiness in people with narcolepsy. It appears to have limited abuse potential. It is also considered to be an athletic performance enhancer and was classed as a prohibited stimulant by the World Anti-Doping Agency in 2004. Several clinical trials have assessed modafinil in the treatment of cocaine and methamphetamine dependence. There have been encouraging but inconclusive results with cocaine treatment (Dackis, Kampman, Lynch, Pettinati, & O'Brien, 2005), and results with methamphetamine addicts have been variable (Karila et al., 2010).

BUPROPION. Bupropion is an antidepressant, sold as Wellbutrin, and also widely available as a smoking cessation aid as Zyban (see Chapters 8 and 13). It is a DAT and NET blocker, but has little effect on SERT. It also is an antagonist at nicotinic cholinergic receptors. In clinical trials with methamphetamine users, it was shown to reduce craving, but was only effective in reducing the use of methamphetamine in light users, not in heavy users (Karila et al., 2010).

METHYLPHENIDATE. This drug is sold under the trade name Ritalin and is widely used to treat ADHD. It is a cocaine-like blocker of DATs and NETs with little effect on SERTs and is reported to have less abuse potential than cocaine and the amphetamines. It has been shown to reduce amphetamine use in heavy intravenous users.

ORAL D-AMPHETAMINE. There have been several studies testing the effectiveness of oral amphetamine as a maintenance drug for both amphetamine and cocaine users. It may seem odd to be using amphetamine as a treatment for amphetamine abuse, but the advantage lies in substituting oral amphetamine for injected amphetamine. Oral is a safer route of administration, and there would be no huge fluctuations in blood level, which is what causes rushes and euphoria. In one Australian study, a sustained-release formulation of amphetamine (dexamphetamine) often used to treat ADHD, when given at a dose of 20 to 110 mg/day, increased treatment retention (86.3 days compared with 48.6 days for those receiving placebo). It also decreased methamphetamine consumption in a group of methamphetamine users. At follow-up, the degree of methamphetamine dependence was significantly lower in the dexamphetamine group than in the placebo group. Dexamphetamine maintenance was not associated with serious adverse events (Longo et al., 2010).

NALTREXONE. Naltrexone is an opioid antagonist, and the endogenous opioid system has been implicated in the mechanisms of reinforcement (see Chapter 5). Naltrexone has been shown to reduce the cue-induced reinstatement of methamphetamine self-administration in laboratory animals and to block the subjective effects of d-amphetamine and craving in amphetamine-dependent addicts. In a double-blind, placebo-controlled trial, naltrexone was effective in reducing amphetamine use in addicted outpatients (Jayaram-Lindström, Hammarberg, Beck, & Franck, 2008).

OTHER DRUGS. In addition to those mentioned earlier, many other drugs have been tested as pharmacotherapies for psychostimulant abuse and have failed to produce any benefit. These include aripiprazole, a second-generation antipsychotic, which acts as a dopamine D_2-like receptor partial agonist; risperidone, a second-generation dopamine and serotonin antagonist; baclofen, gabapentin, gamma-vinyl-GABA, and topiramate, which potentiate GABA transmission by various means; rivastigmine, a cholinesterase inhibitor; fluoxetine and other SSRI antidepressants; ondansetron, an antiemetic that is a $5\text{-}HT_3$ receptor antagonist; and isradipine and amlodipine, calcium channel blockers (Karila et al., 2010).

In spite of a tremendous effort to find an effective drug to treat psychostimulant addiction, there has been very little success. Only three drugs, apart from oral d-amphetamine, have been successful in double-blind placebo trials: bupropion, modafinil, and naltrexone, and even for some of these drugs there have been conflicting results. To this point, behavioral and psychosocial treatments remain the cornerstone of treatment for psychostimulant addiction, and drug therapy should be regarded as an adjunct rather than a replacement for these approaches (Rose & Grant, 2008).

Immunization

In the 1970s, Bob Schuster, a pioneer in the field of behavioral pharmacology, suggested that it might be possible to make a vaccine that would stimulate the immune system to create antibodies that would bind to molecules of cocaine. This would prevent the cocaine molecules from passing through the blood–brain barrier to enter the central nervous system, thereby blocking their effect. It was originally envisioned as a means to prevent people from using and becoming addicted to cocaine, but it would also be useful in the treatment of cocaine addiction by blocking the reinforcing effect of the drug. That concept was expanded, and nicotine vaccines have been developed (see Chapter 8). Work has also proceeded on the development of a vaccine against cocaine.

One of the difficulties with developing a vaccine for a drug is that the immune system normally only creates antibodies for large protein molecules, and drugs like cocaine are small molecules. Drug vaccines are created by bonding a molecule of the drug to a fragment of a virus, and this combination is injected into the body. The immune system then creates antibodies to both the virus fragment and the drug at the same time so that when the drug enters the body again, the immune system will attack it and block its action. Over the years, a number of different virus fragments have been attached to molecules of cocaine. Most have been able to generate cocaine antibodies, but it usually takes a number of vaccinations, and the immune response lasts only for a few months, so frequent booster shots are needed. In addition, not everyone is capable of creating enough antibodies for the vaccine to be effective. Remember that drugs like cocaine are injected suddenly and in large quantities, and there would need to be enough antibodies present to handle all of the drug before it can get to the brain.

In one study, the effectiveness of a cocaine vaccine was evaluated in a sample of cocaine-using individuals regularly visiting a methadone maintenance clinic. The vaccine worked in about 38% of the participants, who developed high antibody levels in their blood. These participants showed a reduction in positive urine tests for cocaine. Unfortunately, though, this effect lasted only 2 months before antibody levels dropped (Martell et al., 2009). This and other studies show that cocaine vaccine treatment has the potential to be very effective if a vaccine could be developed that created more cocaine antibodies in more people and lasted for a longer time.

The study just described used vaccine created from a B-subunit of cholera toxin. In 2011, a paper was published reporting the development of a new cocaine vaccine created by attaching a cocaine analog to an adenovirus (Ad) gene transfer vector—a virus that has been modified so that it can carry a gene into cells, but that does not contain the DNA needed for its own reproduction. The Ad transfer vector is widely used for gene replacement therapy. This new vaccine has been shown to create high and persistent levels of cocaine antibodies in mice (Hicks et al., 2011). It has not been tested on humans, but fosters hope that a more effective treatment for cocaine and amphetamine addiction may soon be developed.

CHAPTER

11

Opioids

The patience of a poppy.
He who has smoked will smoke.
Opium knows how to wait.

—Jean Cocteau (1968, p. 36)

The drugs in this class are referred to either as *opiates* or *opioids*. These terms refer to any drug, natural or synthetic in origin, with properties similar to opium or its main active ingredient, morphine (technically, the term *opiate* should be used only to refer to drugs of natural origin, that is, derived from opium, and *opioid* should be used in reference to all opiate-like drugs, including synthetic and semisynthetic opiates, but often this distinction is not made). This text will use the term *opioid* in a generic sense to refer to all drugs in this class.

This family of drugs is also frequently referred to as *narcotic analgesics* or just *narcotics*. Technically, a narcotic is a drug that causes sleep. The narcotic analgesics produce *analgesia* (a loss of sensitivity to pain) and make a person sleepy. This name distinguishes these drugs from *non-narcotic analgesics*, such as aspirin, which do not cause sleepiness. One difficulty with the word *narcotic* is that, over the years, it has acquired a new meaning and is now commonly used to refer to the habit-forming property of a drug. It has also developed a distasteful connotation; calling a drug a narcotic immediately conjures

up visions of degenerate and depraved addicts who are slaves to the drug and its suppliers. This misuse of the term has been given legal sanction, further increasing the confusion. In the United States, the Harrison Narcotic Act of 1914 defined both marijuana and cocaine as narcotics, along with opioids. In Canada, the Narcotic Control Act regulates the use of many habit-forming drugs, some of which, like marijuana, are not narcotics at all in the sleep-producing sense, but in a legal sense they have become *narcotics*.

Because it has so many meanings and connotations, the term *narcotic* will be avoided here. The term *opioid* will be used instead.

ORIGINS AND SOURCES OF OPIOIDS
Natural and Semisynthetic Opioids

The main natural source of *opium* is a poppy called *Papaver somniferum*. This poppy had its origins in Asia Minor but is now grown throughout the world in countries with similar climates. On only 10 days in its life cycle, the plant manufactures opium, which must be gathered during those days. Opium is the sap that exudes out of scratches made in the seedpods of the poppy after the petals have fallen off (this can be seen in Figure 11-1). The scratches are made one day; the next day, the sap is scraped off and compressed into cakes and dried. This is *opium*.

FIGURE 11-1 Opium poppy (*left*) and a seed pod that has been scratched (*right*). The white sap running from the cuts in the seedpod is opium.

There are several active ingredients in opium. The two main ones are *morphine*, which accounts for 10% of the weight of opium, and *codeine*, which makes up only 0.5%. *Thebaine* is also present in much lower quantities. Morphine was first isolated from opium by the German chemist Frederick Serturner. He called it *morphium* after Morpheus, the Greek god of dreams, and published his findings in 1803. The significance of the finding was not immediately recognized, but in 1831 he was awarded a prize by the Institute of France for his discovery. Also in the 1830s, morphine was first manufactured and sold commercially. Codeine was isolated in 1821 by the French chemist Pierre J. Robiquet while he was experimenting with a new process for isolating morphine.

Heroin (*diacetylmorphine* or *diamorphine*) is a semisynthetic opioid made by adding two acetyl groups to the morphine molecule. Heroin is about 10 times more lipid soluble than morphine and, therefore, gets to the brain faster and in higher concentrations. Morphine

is widely used in medicine and is usually sold as a salt under its generic name *morphine sulfate*. In the United States, morphine and codeine are legally available only by prescription. In Canada, the same is true for morphine, but codeine is available in small quantities without a prescription in some over-the-counter painkillers and cough medicines. Heroin is illegal and cannot be prescribed or used in the United States. For some restricted purposes, it may be used in Canada on an experimental basis. It may also be prescribed in the United Kingdom under certain conditions.

Thebaine, also known as *paramorphine*, is a minor constituent of the opium poppy and is not used therapeutically, but is the source of many semisynthetic opioids including *oxycodone*. It is sold as Percocet (if it is mixed with acetaminophen) or Percodan (if it is mixed with aspirin). A much more notorious formulation of oxycodone is OxyContin, a tablet that contains many times the oxycodone of a regular tablet but in a slow-release form. It is designed to give long-term pain relief to arthritis sufferers, but if the tablet is crushed, dissolved, and injected, the entire dose can be experienced at once. Used this way, it is highly addicting and frequently causes accidental overdoses. In 2011, a new tamper-proof formulation of OxyContin (OxyNEO in Canada and OxyContin OP in the United States) was put on the market. In Canada, the standard OxyContin tablet will be phased out completely. Other opioids synthesized from thebaine include buprenorphine, nalorphine, and naloxone.

Hydrocodone may be derived from either codeine or thebaine. It is mixed with acetaminophen and sold as Vicodin, an analgesic, but is also widely used illegally as a recreational drug.

Synthetic Opioids

A number of drugs bear little chemical resemblance to morphine but appear to have similar pharmacological and behavioral effects and to work at the same receptor. They are not all as effective at the receptor as morphine, and some are much more effective. The best known of these is *meperidine* (Demerol), called *pethidine* in the United Kingdom. It is similar to morphine but shorter acting. *Methadone* (Dolophine) and *LAAM* (levo-α-acetylmethadol) have a much longer duration of action than morphine and are much more effective when given orally. Methadone is used as a maintenance drug for heroin addicts. LAAM was widely used for the same purpose until it was withdrawn from European and North American markets in the early 2000s because of adverse side effects, including causing dangerous heart arrhythmia.

Other synthetic opioids include *fentanyl* (Sublimaze), *levorphanol* (Levo-Dromoran), *pentazocine* (Talwin), *phenazocine* (Narphen), and *propoxyphene* (Darvon).

Buprenorphine, developed in the 1970s, can be administered sublingually (under the tongue) and is useful in treating postoperative and cancer pain. More recently, it has proved useful in treating opioid addiction because it has long-lasting effects, which reduce the severity of withdrawal. All of these drugs are available only by prescription in most countries.

Over the years, clandestine laboratories have synthesized many *designer drugs* based on the fentanyl molecule, *China White* being the best known. Another notorious designer drug, called *MPTP*, was created accidentally in an attempt to synthesize meperidine. MPTP is metabolized into a neurotoxin that destroys the substantia nigra, part of the extrapyramidal motor system that provides dopamine stimulation to the basal ganglia. The result was what has been called the *frozen addict*, a person with severe symptoms of Parkinson's disease.

HISTORY

It is believed that the opium poppy was being cultivated in the western Mediterranean region in the sixth millennium BCE, and opium capsules found in grass bags in Neolithic burial sites in northern Spain date to about 4200 BCE (Rudgley, 1995). The earliest written reference to opium is a Sumerian idiogram that is translated as "joy plant". The use of this symbol has been dated to about 4000 BCE. Opium is also mentioned frequently in Assyrian medical tablets dating from the seventh century BCE. These tablets are probably copies of earlier manuscripts. Originally wild, the opium poppy was being cultivated in Assyria and Babylon by the second century BCE. By this time as well, opium use had spread throughout the Middle East and North Africa. It was mentioned in the *Ebers Papyrus*, early Egyptian medical scrolls dating to 1550 BCE. In these early writings, the poppy is considered primarily as a medicine, but the nonmedical properties of the plant were certainly appreciated.

The ancient Greeks knew of opium as well. The Greek physician Hippocrates recommended the use of opium for a number of conditions, as did the Roman physicians Pliny and Galen and the Arabian physician Avicenna, who recommended it for diseases of the eye and diarrhea.

The use of opium spread from the Middle East in every direction with the expansion of the Islamic religion. It was carried east to India by Arab traders in the ninth century and then from India to China, where it was used primarily as a medicine and taken orally. Later, when tobacco smoking was banned by a Chinese emperor in 1644, the Chinese filled their pipes with opium and invented the practice of opium smoking, a very efficient drug delivery system that ensured the popularity of the drug in that country.

The Arabs traded opium, along with spices and other goods, with the merchants of Venice. In the early part of the sixteenth century, Europeans became aware of opium primarily through the efforts of traveling physicians. A Swiss doctor known as Paracelsus traveled throughout Europe and carried opium in the pommel of his saddle. He called it "the stone of immortality". Other physicians quickly adopted the drug and prescribed it in various forms to their patients, with great success. John Sydenham, an English physician, wrote in 1680, "Among the remedies it has pleased Almighty God to give to man to relieve his sufferings, none is so universal or so efficacious as opium."

Throughout the seventeenth and eighteenth centuries in Britain, the popular use of opioids grew steadily, but in the nineteenth century, there was a drastic increase in the British consumption of opium. In 1825, the opium consumption rate was between 1 and 2 pounds per 1,000 population, but at its peak in 1875 the rate was greater than 10 pounds per 1,000 population. Opium was available in many formulations from food stores, pubs, and even peddlers on the streets. The most popular form in which opium was sold was tincture of opium, or *laudanum*, which was opium dissolved in alcohol.

About this time, morphine became available. Morphine, however, remained more under the control of the medical profession and, unlike opium, was never widely sold in shops. This restriction did not hinder its popularity; physicians generally prescribed it when requested. Because the lower classes seldom saw a doctor, morphine was more commonly used by the middle and upper classes.

Although many people were openly addicted to the drug, it was not perceived as a medical or social problem at the beginning of the nineteenth century. Not until the 1830s did all this opium use generate any concern, and not until 1868 was any legislative effort made to control it. The regulatory change was brought about by the development of social and political ideas rather than medical research or theory.

The availability of the drug was recognized as the main problem. In 1868, the British Parliament passed the Pharmacy Act, which made pharmacist shops the only legal source of opioids and was the first of several laws that slowly brought the use of opioids under the control of the medical profession and out of the hands of

the people. It also marked the start of the belief—a new idea at the time—that addiction was a medical problem and should be handled by physicians.

The story of opioid use in the United States is somewhat different. Americans were just as fond of opioids as the British. In 1870, when British consumption peaked at over 10 pounds per 1,000 population, American consumption rates were greater than 13 pounds per 1,000. It was in part consumed orally in the form of patent medicines, but a great deal of it was refined into morphine and injected by means of the recently developed hypodermic syringe. This route of administration may have become popular because of the wide use of morphine injections to treat wounded soldiers during the Civil War. In 1914, Congress passed the Harrison Narcotic Act, which, in effect, made it illegal to be an addict and illegal for physicians to prescribe opioids to addicts.

Heroin

Heroin was invented in 1898 by Heinrich Dreser who worked as the head of drug safety and efficacy testing for Bayer Company of Germany. Earlier that year, researchers at Bayer had discovered that if an acetyl group is added to salicylic acid (an effective painkiller and fever remedy that, unfortunately, was corrosive and produced terrible gastric side effects), the corrosive properties are diminished. The result was acetylsalicylic acid (ASA, originally trademarked as *Aspirin*). In search of a miraculous pain killer that would be his claim to fame, Dreser thought he might try the same trick with the morphine molecule and made *diacetylmorphine* (or diamorphine), which the Bayer company marketed as *Heroin*. The name was derived from the German *heroisch*, meaning *heroic*, to imply concentrated power. Early tests showed that heroin was much more effective than morphine as an analgesic but did not cause as much nausea and vomiting. It was advertised in newspapers and magazines, and, in 1899, Bayer Company produced more than a ton of heroin, which it exported to more than 20 different countries. Bayer also claimed that heroin was not addictive, and, surprisingly, this was believed by the medical profession for many years. This was the first of many attempts to find the "holy grail" of opioid research: A drug that would have the valuable analgesic effects of morphine without the undesirable side effects of respiratory depression and addiction. In the search for this holy grail, thousands of new opioids have been developed. Unfortunately, for all the drugs developed so far, addiction potential has always been positively correlated with analgesic potency (Corbett et al., 2006).

It did not take long for morphine users to discover heroin. They soon found that heroin could be sniffed into the nostrils and did not always require injections. This fact and the relative lack of nausea must have enhanced its appeal to casual users. By the 1920s, the newspapers in the United States associated heroin with crime, industrial unrest, and a series of Bolshevik bombings, so in 1924 it was banned totally by Congress. It became illegal for doctors to prescribe it for any reason. This law and the Harrison Narcotic Act are still in effect today in the United States.

ROUTES OF ADMINISTRATION

Morphine is a base with a pKa of about 8. Consequently, it is not rapidly absorbed from the digestive system because most of its molecules are ionized in acid pHs and not lipid soluble. Even though opium eating (or drinking) is common and morphine is frequently given in oral medications, opioids that are bases when given by the oral route are much less effective than the same dose given parenterally. In addition, there is significant first-pass metabolism of morphine. Enzymes in the digestive system destroy significant amounts of morphine; only 15% is available for absorption if ingested orally. Compare that to methadone of which 80 to 90% is available for absorption after first-pass metabolism. In addition to extensive metabolism in the digestive system, morphine given orally is subject to significant metabolism on its first pass through the liver before it can get to the brain (Goth, 1984). Opioids are frequently given orally as analgesics, and the slowness of the absorption from the digestive system is an advantage because slow absorption makes it easier to maintain constant drug levels in the blood (Melzack, 1990; see Chapter 1).

When the drug is administered for its subjective effects, most users prefer parenteral routes, which cause sudden high levels that appear to be the most reinforcing. Heroin, but not morphine, can be taken intranasally in the form of snuff. Many years ago, the Chinese developed a method of smoking opium in a pipe. More recently, the AIDS epidemic has made many people reluctant to use needles, and a newer form of smoking has been developed called "chasing the dragon". Oil-rich, relatively pure heroin is heated on metal foil until it vaporizes. The user then inhales it through a tube or straw, chasing the smoke so as not to miss any (Strang, Griffiths, & Gossop, 1997). This appears to be an efficient way to get the drug into the body. Up to 90% of heroin is vaporized, depending on whether it is a salt or freebase, on the temperature, and on the airflow (Meng et al., 1997). The term "chasing the dragon" is also used as a metaphor for the elusive search for the perfect heroin experience that leads to heroin addiction.

Synthetic opioids have different chemical properties, and their pharmacokinetics may be quite different from the natural and semisynthetic opioids.

The two most important opioid antagonists, nalorphine and naloxone, are poorly absorbed from the digestive system and are usually administered parenterally. Maximum brain levels are reached in 15 to 60 minutes.

DISTRIBUTION

After absorption into the blood, most opioids are concentrated in the lungs, liver, and spleen, and a large percentage is bound to blood proteins. Opioids pass readily through the placental barrier to the fetus, but most are slow getting through the blood–brain barrier because they have poor lipid solubility.

The heroin molecule is an exception—it is highly lipid soluble and, therefore, gets into the brain quickly and in high concentrations. The heroin molecule is inactive in the brain, but it is rapidly converted into its metabolites, morphine and monoacetylmorphine, in high concentrations. As a result, heroin is about 10 times more potent than morphine (Inturrisi et al., 1983). Codeine also appears to have little direct action on receptors in the brain and has its effect through metabolites, the main one being morphine.

It also appears that the brain is able to eliminate opioids by an active transport mechanism. These two factors combine to keep brain levels of opioids low relative to the levels in other body tissues. Within the brain, opioids are concentrated in the basal ganglia, the amygdala, and the periaqueductal gray, an area closely associated with the sensation of pain. The opioid antagonists enter the brain much more quickly than morphine and reach higher concentrations there.

EXCRETION

About 10% of morphine is excreted in the urine unchanged. The remainder is turned into various metabolites that are eliminated in the urine and in the feces through concentration in the bile. The half-life of morphine is about 2 hours; the half-life of codeine is about 3 to 6 hours. Ninety percent of morphine is eliminated within 24 hours of administration (Creasey, 1979).

Meperidine is extensively metabolized in the liver, and the metabolites are eliminated by the kidneys. It has a half-life of 3.5 hours. Methadone is not completely metabolized; about 10% is eliminated unchanged in the urine. Compared to other opioids, it has an extremely long half-life of 10 to 25 hours because methadone becomes bound extensively to blood proteins and is not available for metabolism. This long duration of action makes methadone ideal for maintenance therapies. At low doses, methadone is excreted primarily in the feces, but at higher doses, more and more methadone is found in the urine. An even longer half-life has been reported for another synthetic opioid, l-alpha-acetylmethadol (LAAM). LAAM itself is not active, but two of its metabolites are.

Naloxone is completely metabolized in the liver and has a half-life of about 1.5 hours, although its effects may be shorter than this since the drug is rapidly redistributed to body fat. This may be of concern when naloxone is being used to treat an opioid overdose. Its effects may rapidly disappear, and the opioid overdose effects may unexpectedly return (Clarke, Dargan, & Jones, 2005).

NEUROPHYSIOLOGY

Scientists had been certain for many years that opioids worked at receptor sites because their activity seemed to be related to their molecular configuration, and there was competitive antagonism of their effects. But until the early 1970s, no one had ever found an opioid receptor in the body, nor had any endogenous substance been found in the brain that might work at an opioid receptor. In 1973, however, three laboratories independently identified specific receptors for opioids in the brains of rats. This discovery stimulated considerable research, and there has

been a veritable explosion of data on opioid receptors since that time. Opioid receptors have now been found in the brains of most vertebrates, from hagfish to humans.

If the brain is equipped with receptors for opioids, it is likely that the brain has opioid-like substances of its own, that is, endogenous ligands. A search for such a substance was begun. Within 2 years of the discovery of opioid receptors, six naturally occurring opioids had been isolated from the brains of several different species of animals, including humans. One of the researchers, Eric J. Simon (1981), proposed the name *endorphins* for these substances. He derived this name from the words *endogenous* and *morphine*. Other opioid ligands are called *enkephalins*, meaning *in the head*. The endogenous opioids are derived from a polypeptide: a string of amino acid molecules. These and other endogenous ligands are discussed in Chapter 4.

Opioid Receptors

There appear to be at least four types of opioid receptors, referred to as mu (μ), kappa (k), delta (δ), and the more recently discovered "opioid receptor–like" receptor (ORL$_1$). Over the years, several systems of opioid receptor naming have been used, so you may see these receptors referred to by various names depending on the year of the publication and the source (Corbett et al., 2006). Table 11-1 provides a summary of these names. This text will use the original Greek name terminology: mu, kappa, delta, and ORL$_1$.

At one point, another receptor called the sigma (σ) receptor was included with the opioid receptors, but it has since been established that this is not a receptor for opioid molecules. It is known instead to be a binding site for the hallucinogen PCP (phencyclidine), located on the NMDA glutamate receptor (see Chapter 15).

Opioid receptors are all G-protein-coupled receptors and release second messengers, which have several effects on the cell and on the cell membrane. They activate a variety of potassium channels in the membrane and inhibit high-threshold voltage-gated calcium channels. Through these and other mechanisms, activation of all four types of opioid receptors causes inhibition at postsynaptic membranes, and, on presynaptic neurons, they inhibit the release of many different neurotransmitters such as glutamate, GABA, glycine, norepinephrine, dopamine, and acetylcholine. This means that opioids are both

TABLE 11-1 Summary of Opioid Receptor Names and Recommended Name Changes

Original Name	Greek Letter	IUPHAR* (1996)	International Narcotics Research Conference	IUPHAR* (1999)
Mu	μ	OP$_3$	MOR	MOP
Delta	δ	OP$_1$	DOR	DOP
Kappa	k	OP$_2$	KOR	KOP
ORL$_1$	-	OP$_4$	NOR	NOP

*International Union of Basic and Clinical Pharmacology (IUPHAR).
Source: Adapted from Cox et al. (2011); used with permission.

inhibitory neurotransmitters and inhibitory neuromodulators of many other neurotransmitters. Opioid receptor activation is also known to inhibit the production of the second-messenger cyclic AMP (cAMP), an effect that can inhibit membrane excitability and transmitter release.

In addition to these effects, opioid receptors can do other things inside the cell. It has been shown that in some cases, when the receptor is occupied, the receptor–ligand complex moves inside the membrane through a process called *endocytosis* where it can activate kinases directly. This in turn can alter the activity of transcription factors, which change the expression of genes in the cell nucleus and create longer-term changes in neural transmission (Corbett et al., 2006; Keith et al., 1998).

Opioid Action

WHY DIFFERENT OPIOIDS HAVE DIFFERENT EFFECTS.
There are many different opioids, each of which has a different pattern of agonism or antagonism at the various receptor types. Some opioids are primarily mu agonists or antagonists; these may have very little or no effect on other receptor types. Some opioids may act as agonists or antagonists at two or more receptor types. When a drug has agonistic effects on two or more receptor subtypes, it may be called a *mixed agonist*. These different opioids have different effects on the brain and behavior. This is because different receptor types are distributed in different parts of the brain. Activation of all types of opioid receptors has the same effect on all cells, but the location of the cell determines what effect the opioid will have in the brain and on behavior.

The mu receptor has a diffuse distribution throughout the limbic system, including the hippocampus and the amygdala, and throughout the thalamus, the locus coeruleus, and the ventral tegmental area. The delta receptor is also located in the limbic system, including the hippocampus and the amygdala, but in regions that do not overlap with the mu receptor distribution. Delta receptors are also located in the cortex, the hypothalamus, the nucleus accumbens, and some regions of the medulla. The kappa receptor has a third distinct distribution that includes the nucleus accumbens, the ventral tegmental area, the hypothalamus, and specific regions of the thalamus (Mansour et al., 1994).

PARTIAL AGONISTS.
The mu receptor is responsible for most of the effects of morphine and the drugs described in this chapter. Solomon Snyder and his colleagues have demonstrated that not all opioids bind to mu receptors with the same affinity; some have a strong attraction for the receptor, and some have a much weaker attraction. In general, those with the weakest attraction at the receptor have the greatest effect on the receptor. Morphine, for example, does not have a strong attachment to mu receptors but has a strong effect when it binds with them. In contrast, nalorphine has only a weak effect on the receptor but binds strongly to it. When these two drugs are mixed together, the nalorphine will be the one to have an effect because it will displace the morphine from the receptor. Because the effect of the nalorphine is only slight, there will be little opioid effect, even though morphine is present. Thus, the nalorphine acts as a competitive antagonist to the morphine, turning off the effect of the morphine and substituting its own

mild effect. In this sense, it acts as an antagonist because it blocks the morphine, but it is also an agonist because it stimulates the receptor in a mild, morphine-like way.

An opioid with these properties is known as a *partial agonist* (or sometimes as a *mixed opioid agonist–antagonist*). Nalorphine, pentazocine, and cyclazocine belong to this category. They will terminate the activity of more potent agonist drugs and at the same time have a milder effect of their own (Snyder, 1977). It happens that many of these drugs are also mixed agonists and also have agonistic effects on kappa receptors.

OPIOID ANTAGONIST. Naloxone is a pure antagonist at mu, kappa, and delta receptors (Corbett et al., 2006). It will displace any other opioid from the mu receptor but has almost no agonistic effect of its own. It is used to treat victims of opioid overdose because it will immediately terminate the action of all agonists. If naloxone is given to an individual who is physically dependent on opioids, it will immediately cause withdrawal symptoms. Opioid antagonists are used in some forms of treatment of opioid addiction described later in this chapter. Naloxone is very important in opioid research because it provides a way of making sure that the effect of a drug is due to its interaction with opioid receptors. This can be established simply by giving naloxone and seeing whether the effect is blocked (Garfield, 1983).

Sites of Action in the CNS

ANALGESIA. The opioids appear to produce their analgesic effects by several mechanisms. They affect areas of the spinal cord that transmit dull, burning pain, and it is believed that they block this incoming sensory information. The periaqueductal gray is an area of the brain known to be important in the perception of pain and rich in opioid receptors. When the body undergoes stress and pain, this system is activated, and the pain is reduced as described in Chapter 4.

The sensory component of pain can be broken into several separate sensations. We may experience *thermoceptive pain* (pain caused by extreme heat or cold), *mechanical pain* (pain due to physical damage to the muscles and skin), and *visceral nociception* (pain associated with organ damage). These types of pain can be acute or chronic or may even appear to arise from limbs that have been amputated (*phantom limb pain*). Mu agonists seem

to be effective against a broad range of pain, including all the acute types and some chronic types but not phantom pain. Delta agonists are effective against thermal and mechanical pain but are ineffective against visceral pain. Kappa agonists can be used against visceral pain but are effective only against low-intensity thermal and mechanical pain (Millan, 1986, 1990; Schmauss & Yaksh, 1984).

Pain is a complicated phenomenon. Not only does it have a sensory component, but it has emotional aspects as well. We not only know that a sensation is painful; we also know that we really do not like it. Opioids also reduce the aversive emotional aspect of pain. This effect may be mediated through opioid receptors located in various areas of the limbic system, such as the amygdala. It is believed that in addition to these lower centers, there are opioid systems in the frontal cortex through which opioids relieve pain.

REINFORCEMENT. Functional magnetic resonance imaging (fMRI) BOLD research in rats demonstrates heroin-induced increases in signal intensity in the mesolimbic system, amygdala, and hippocampus. These effects are completely prevented by pretreatment with naloxone, suggesting they are most likely caused by activation of mu receptors (Xu et al., 2000). This increase in mesolimbic activity, particularly in the ventral tegmental area and nucleus accumbens, is responsible for the reinforcing properties of opioids at the mu receptor. It has been shown that laboratory animals will learn to press a lever to deliver minute quantities of morphine directly into the ventral tegmental area. In the ventral tegmental area, mu agonists inhibit GABA release from interneurons, which, in turn, disinhibits dopamine neurons that project to the nucleus accumbens, thereby increasing dopamine release. Thus, the extent to which an opioid acts as a mu agonist is positively correlated with its reinforcing effect and its abuse potential. On the other hand, kappa agonists appear to directly inhibit dopamine release in the nucleus accumbens and do not have any reinforcing properties.

VITAL LIFE FUNCTIONS. Mu-agonist opioids depress three important centers in the brainstem. They depress the respiratory center and cause slow, shallow breathing. Death from opioid overdose is usually a result of respiratory depression. The vomiting center is also depressed, and so is the center that causes coughing. This suppression of the cough center is one reason why opioids have been included in cough medicines for centuries. At one time, most over-the-counter cough medicines contained codeine, but now they often contain dextromethorphan (Atweh & Kuhar, 1983).

DEPENDENCE. The development of physical dependence to mu opioid agonists does not appear to directly involve the mesolimbic reward system because it has been shown that repeated injection of morphine into the periventricular gray, but not the ventral tegmental area, will cause the development of physical dependence (Bozarth & Wise, 1984).

EFFECTS OF OPIOIDS

Effects on the Body

When opioids are first administered, two of their most notable effects are nausea and vomiting. These are caused by the stimulation of an area of the brain known as the *chemoreceptor trigger zone*, which detects impurities in the blood and stimulates a center that causes vomiting. Opioids also depress this vomiting center, and this action blocks vomiting. The result of these two effects is that nausea and vomiting are usually seen only after the first administration of the drug. With continuing doses, these symptoms decrease.

Because opioids constrict the pupils of the eyes, many opioid users have small pupils, and this effect diminishes only slightly with tolerance. Pinpoint pupils are also a symptom of opioid overdose. Opioids have little effect on the functioning of the heart, but there is some lowering of blood pressure due to dilation of the peripheral blood vessels. This dilation causes the face and neck to become flushed and warm and may cause sweating. Profuse sweating is one of the unpleasant side effects of methadone.

One of the first medical uses of opium was in the treatment of diarrhea and dysentery, and it is still used for this purpose. Opioids do not decrease the overall action of the stomach and intestines, but they seem to disrupt the coordination of digestive activity, causing the food to pass very slowly through the system. This effect stops diarrhea but produces constipation instead, and it can be a serious medical complication of opioid addiction. Opioids also interfere with urination by causing contractions of the bladder sphincter, making it difficult to pass urine.

Opioid use is known to decrease the level of sex hormones in both men and women, and this lowered hormone level is thought to be responsible for males' difficulty in maintaining erection and for the reduced sex drive and diminished fertility of both male and female opioid users. Heavy use may even cause atrophy of secondary sex characteristics in males and stop menstruation in women. It has been suggested that opioid addiction is common among prostitutes because opioids have historically been used as a birth control measure.

Effects on Sleep

In spite of the fact that morphine is named after the god of dreams, opioids do not increase sleep. They cause a sleepy sensation and nodding, under normal circumstances, but acute administration of morphine and heroin actually causes insomnia and does not increase sleeping time (Bellville, Forrest, Shroff, & Brown, 1971). The user may doze off but will soon awaken with a start and will not feel rested. When subjects do sleep, they show increased muscular tension, spend more time in the lighter sleep stages, and experience a decrease in slow-wave and REM sleep (Kay, Eisenstein, & Jasinski, 1969). However, because of their analgesic properties, opioids are useful in promoting sleep in people who are kept awake by pain.

EFFECTS ON HUMAN BEHAVIOR AND PERFORMANCE

Subjective Effects

Many literary figures were known to be users of opium. One of the first people to write about the effects was Thomas De Quincey, the English essayist, critic, and writer, author of the now famous *Confessions of an English Opium-Eater*, published in 1821. De Quincey used opium for much of his life and wrote about its effects on his mind and on his life in *Confessions*. Like most people in the nineteenth century, he first took opium as a medicine but quickly appreciated its euphoric effects. After his first dose, his reaction was as follows:

> In an hour, O heavens! What a revulsion! What a resurrection from its lowest depths, of the inner spirit! .... That my pains had vanished was now a trifle in my eyes; this negative effect was swallowed up in the

immensity of those positive effects which had opened before me, in the abyss of divine enjoyment thus suddenly revealed . . . . Here was the secret of happiness, about which philosophers had disputed for so many ages, at once discovered; happiness might now be bought for a penny, and carried in the waistcoat-pocket; portable ecstasies might be had corked up in a pint-bottle and peace of mind might be sent down by the mail. (De Quincey, 1901, pp. 169–170)

De Quincey reported that he had an increased sensitivity in both hearing and vision. The increase was not so much in the loudness of noises and brightness of lights as in the ability of the mind "to construct out of raw organic sound an elaborate intellectual pleasure" (De Quincey, 1901, p. 179).

And finally, the dreams. Opioids at higher doses induce a sleepy, trancelike state called a *nod*, during which the user sees visions or dreams (hence the expression "pipe dreams"). Unlike the hallucinations from drugs such as LSD, these are more like vivid daydreams:

Whatsoever things capable of being visually represented I did but think of in the darkness . . . which once traced in faint and visionary colour. . . . They were drawn out by the fierce chemistry of my dreams into insufferable splendor that fretted my heart. (De Quincey, 1901, p. 224)

Nor are the dreams always visual. Samuel Taylor Coleridge always claimed that the words to the famous poem *Kubla Khan* came to him in a trance after he had taken opium. Users of opium are firmly convinced that the creative processes are helped by the drug. As Jean Cocteau, the French poet, playwright, and artist, said,

All children possess the magic power of being able to change themselves into what they wish. Poets, in whom childhood is prolonged, suffer a great deal when they lose this power. This is undoubtedly one of the reasons which drives the poet to use opium. (Cocteau, 1968, p. 71)

De Quincey took opium orally, and though he enjoyed the experience well enough, he missed a subjective effect that is usually experienced only by people who inject morphine or heroin or who smoke opium: the rush. This intense momentary feeling of pleasure is experienced after injecting the drug and is a result of the high concentrations delivered suddenly to the brain. Rushes are usually described as sexual, rather like an orgasm in the stomach or in the entire body. As one 17-year-old addict described it, "It's just the most intense wonderful feeling . . . . I worry that I will always be tempted to feel the heroin rush again, because nothing else I've tried comes close to it" (Weil & Rosen, 1983, p. 87).

Systematic Studies of Mood

Many authors who write about the subjective effects of opioids stress the euphoric effects and the "divine enjoyment" that the drug offers. Such writings and other accounts have frequently led theorists to speculate that the origin of the attraction of opioids is the relief of anxiety and depression, but most of the experiments in which mood and emotional behavior are measured objectively find that positive feelings do not last and are replaced with mood changes and emotions that are mostly negative. In one study conducted at the McLean Hospital in Belmont, Massachusetts, by Roger Meyer, Steven Mirin, and their associates (Meyer & Mirin, 1979), male adult heroin addict volunteers were admitted to the hospital and kept in a ward for 42 days. During that time, for a period of 10 days, they were allowed to earn heroin injections. During their entire stay, the ward staff kept track of their aggressive and social behaviors, and they were administered standardized psychological tests and asked to complete mood scales. This study found that during the first few days of heroin administration, before significant tolerance developed, heroin relieved tensions and produced euphoria. However, as use continued, there was a shift to unpleasant mood states and increased psychiatric symptoms. These unpleasant feelings were relieved for only a brief period of 30 to 60 minutes after each injection. In addition to this deterioration in mood, there was a decrease in physical activity and social interaction and an increase in aggressive behavior and social isolation. These effects diminished when the participants were maintained on methadone and when the self-administered heroin was blocked by an opioid antagonist.

The effects on mood also differ according to whether the drug is given to experienced users or naive participants. In a classic study, Lasagana and his colleagues at

Harvard (Lasagana, Felsinger, & Beecher, 1955) investigated the changes in mood and subjective effects in different populations and found that former addicts were more likely to experience positive feelings after opioids, whereas nonusers reported sedation, mental clouding, and feelings of sickness. In this experiment, 17 out of 30 former users said that they would like to repeat the experience of morphine a second time, whereas only 2 out of 20 nonusers wanted to repeat. Other researchers have not been able to find consistent reports of positive feelings experienced after mu agonists such as heroin (Zacny & Walker, 1998, p. 353).

The subjective effects of morphine are different when given to people experiencing pain. Conley, Toledano, Apfelbaum, and Zacny (1997) gave morphine to participants who were experiencing the pain of having their arms immersed in icy water. They found that the pain diminished the feelings of being "spaced out," "high," "sleepy," and "light-headed," which were normally caused by morphine in individuals not experiencing pain.

At low doses, the mixed opioid agonist–antagonist pentazocine produces subjective effects similar to those of morphine (i.e., increases in euphoria). At higher doses, however, people report sedation and dysphoria and feeling "confused" and "having difficulty in concentrating." These unpleasant effects are reported by nondependent opioid users and, to an even greater extent, nonusers. Other mixed opioid agonist–antagonists that have a strong affinity for kappa receptors, such as cyclazocine, produce quite unpleasant subjective effects including depersonalization, hallucinations, and many symptoms of psychosis in both opioid abusers and nonabusers (Zacny & Walker, 1998).

Performance

In a review of the effects of opioids on human performance, Zacny (1995) concluded that acute administration of opioids to those with little or no experience of the drug can have a moderate effect on performance. In general, performance seems to slow down but does not become more erratic. Partial agonists, or mixed agonist–antagonists such as propoxyphene, cause more impairment than full agonists such as morphine (Zacny, Hill, Black, & Sadeghi, 1998). Cognitive performance seems to be less impaired than psychomotor performance.

For most types of tasks, it appears that tolerance develops, and that, with moderate dosages of heroin or morphine, addicted individuals can maintain good health and productive work for extended periods. There are numerous cases of individuals who administered opioids in one form or another for years but were still able to pursue successful and even brilliant careers. One such individual was Dr. William Stewart Halstead, one of the founders of Johns Hopkins Medical School and one of the most brilliant surgeons of his day. He pioneered the development of aseptic surgical techniques and the use of cocaine as a local anesthetic and was known as the "father of modern surgery." Yet during his career, he was addicted to morphine, a fact that he was able to keep secret from all but his closest friends (Brecher & the *Editors of Consumer Reports*, 1972, p. 35).

These observations, that tolerance to the detrimental effects of opioids occurs in chronic users, have been confirmed. Longtime opioid-dependent users show little, if any, impairment caused by either morphine or the mixed agonist–antagonists. It is still not entirely clear, however, whether this is true for those who use opioids for long-term pain relief, although it has been shown that the detrimental effects of opioids on performance are diminished when given to people experiencing pain (Conley et al., 1997).

Opioid Withdrawal

The only time Dr. Halstead's habit caused him any trouble was when he was attempting to reduce his dosage and started to show withdrawal symptoms. This is similar to the finding by Thompson and Schuster (1964) that food-seeking and shock-avoidance behavior of monkeys was not disrupted while monkeys self-administered morphine but was disrupted when they were not allowed access to morphine and started to experience withdrawal (this research will be discussed later in this chapter).

EFFECTS ON THE BEHAVIOR OF NONHUMANS

Unconditioned behavior

Morphine has a biphasic effect on spontaneous motor activity (SMA). At low doses, there is an increase in movement, but at higher doses, there is a decrease. In mice, this low-dose stimulation causes "running fits" where the mice run blindly and continuously. This effect can be blocked by nalorphine. In rats, low doses cause an increase in SMA. At higher doses, this behavior takes the form of stereotyped responses that differ from the stereotyped behavior caused by amphetamine (see Chapter 10). Morphine-produced stereotyped behavior covers a wide range of behaviors, including social behavior, whereas stereotyped behavior caused by psychomotor stimulants involves only nonsocial behaviors of short duration (Schörring & Hecht, 1979). Still higher doses produce a type of *catalepsy*; the animal's body becomes rigid and can be molded into almost any position, which it will maintain for extended periods. In primates, there does not seem to be an excitatory phase. The main effect is a depression of behavior.

Conditioned behavior

At low doses, opioids tend to increase response rates of most species of animals responding for positive reinforcers at a low rate, but high doses decrease response rates (Thompson, Trombley, Luke, & Lott, 1970). The rate-decreasing effects of opioid agonists can be blocked by low doses of antagonists, but these antagonists at higher doses have effects very similar to agonists.

As with fixed interval (FI) response rates, there are reports that opioids increase both discrete trials and continuous avoidance of electric shocks at low doses, which is not what might be expected from an analgesic, but at higher doses, opioids slow avoidance behavior without disrupting escape responding (Heise & Boff, 1962), an effect similar to alcohol and the tranquilizers.

It might be expected that a drug with noted analgesic properties would increase behavior suppressed by punishment, but this is not the case. Opioids usually only decrease response rates already diminished by response-contingent shock (Geller, Bachman, & Seifter, 1963). It would appear that the ability of opioids to diminish pain is not one of the mechanisms by which the drugs change avoidance behavior.

Effects of Self-Administered Opioids

Travis Thompson and Charles Schuster (1964) conducted one of the earliest experiments in which monkeys were maintained on a schedule of self-administered morphine. Monkeys could give themselves intravenous morphine for a brief period every 6 hours. After the self-administration behavior was acquired, Thompson and Schuster placed the monkeys on a fixed ratio (FR) 20 for food and a discrete-trials shock-avoidance schedule between periods of morphine availability. They found that the behavior of the monkeys on these schedules was not impaired by the self-administered drug, even though the doses reached rather high levels. The only time they noticed deterioration in the avoidance or the FR was when the morphine was no longer available and the monkeys were going through withdrawal. This is similar to the experience of Dr. Halstead, the addicted surgeon described earlier.

DRUG STATE DISCRIMINATION

Opioids are readily discriminated from saline by both rats and monkeys. Morphine is not as discriminable as the barbiturates or marijuana, but it is more easily discriminable than the hallucinogens and the stimulants (Overton, 1973).

Animals trained to discriminate morphine will generalize to all other mu opioid agonists, such as methadone and codeine, but only partly to mixed opioid agonist–antagonists, such as cyclazocine. In addition, rats can be trained to discriminate between morphine and cyclazocine. Discriminative stimulus control of morphine and cyclazocine can be blocked by opioid antagonists, but cyclazocine requires a dose of antagonist 10 to 30 times higher than morphine. This evidence suggests that these drugs have effects on different populations of opioid receptors (Zacny & Walker, 1998). Morphine works at the mu receptor, which can be blocked easily by opioid antagonists, but cyclazocine works as a partial agonist at mu receptors and as a full agonist at kappa receptors, so its effects can only be partly blocked by the mu antagonist (Dykstra, Preston, & Bigelow, 1997).

It has been shown that tolerance to the discriminative effects of morphine in rats can develop in 1 to 3 days and increases with higher doses (Young, Steigerwald, Makhay, & Kapitsopoulos, 1991).

TOLERANCE

As we have seen with many of the behavioral effects of opioids in humans, there is rapid and extensive tolerance to most of their effects. Figure 11-2 shows the increasing dose self-administered by two species. Within 3 or 4 months of

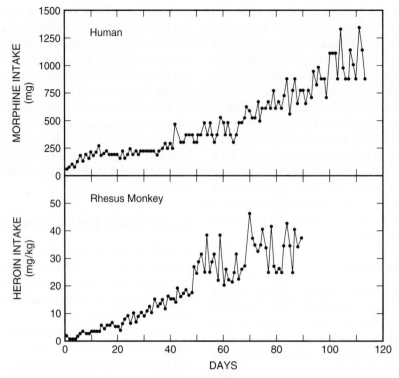

FIGURE 11-2 Daily intake of morphine (top) and heroin (bottom) in a human and a rhesus monkey when allowed free access to the drug. In both species, intake slowly increases over time, and there are no periods of abstinence or voluntary withdrawal. (Adapted from Griffiths et al., 1980)

regular use, consumption will increase 10-fold or more. In fact, doses taken by a regular user may be sufficiently high to kill a nontolerant individual several times over. Tolerance to different effects develops at different rates and disappears at different rates. For example, complete tolerance to the analgesic effects may develop, but the constriction of the pupils only partially disappears with continued opioid use, and the constipating effects never go away.

There are many mechanisms of tolerance to opioids. Some involve changes in opioid metabolism, and some are the result of changes in the properties of opioid receptors. We know that opioid receptors, through the process of endocytosis, are often removed from the membrane when they are activated. This quick reduction in the number of membrane receptors is thought to be a mechanism of acute tolerance (von Zastrow, 2010).

It is also known that mu, delta, and ORL$_1$ opioid receptors (but not kappa receptors) are constantly being recycled and replaced (Corbani, Gonindard, & Meunier, 2004) and that, in this process, their sensitivity to opioids may be altered—they may be either desensitized or resensitized. This process is believed to play a role in the development of longer-term tolerance.

Tolerance can also be context dependent; it can depend on the environment in which the drug is given (Siegel, 1983). This shows that learning and behavioral mechanisms are involved (see the discussion of conditioned tolerance in Chapter 3).

Cross-Tolerance

Generally, when tolerance has developed to any mu opioid agonist drug, there will be tolerance to all others. This cross-tolerance does not extend to the depressants, stimulants, or hallucinogens, but there is some degree of cross-tolerance between opioids and alcohol.

Withdrawal

Opioid withdrawal is probably one of the most misunderstood aspects of drug use, largely because of the images of withdrawal that have been portrayed in the movies and popular literature for many years. The popular notion of the severity of heroin withdrawal probably came about in the 1920s and 1930s, when heroin addicts had easier access to cheaper sources of the drug and took it in much greater quantities than are common now. Few addicts these days are able to take enough drug to cause the severe withdrawal symptoms that are shown in the movies. Even in its most severe form, however, opioid withdrawal is not as dangerous or terrifying as withdrawal from barbiturates or alcohol. In fact, withdrawal from alcohol can be fatal, but withdrawal from heroin or any other opioid is never fatal.

Classic heroin withdrawal proceeds in predictable stages. It starts 6 to 12 hours after the last administration of the drug, peaks at 26 to 72 hours, and, for the most part, is over within a week. The first signs are restlessness and agitation. Yawning soon appears and may become quite violent. The person is able to stay still only briefly and paces about with head and shoulders stooped over. The user experiences chills, with an occasional hot flash, and breathes with short, jerky breaths. During this time, goose bumps appear on the skin, which takes on the appearance of the skin of a plucked turkey (this is the origin of the expression "going cold turkey"). At this point, the addict becomes drowsy and will often fall into a deep sleep known as the *yen sleep*, which may last 8 to 12 hours. After awakening, there is vomiting, diarrhea, and cramps in the stomach, back, and legs. There may also be twitching of the extremities, which causes the hands to shake, and a kicking of the legs (this is the origin of the expression "kicking the habit"). There is also profuse sweating; the person's clothes and bed may become saturated with sweat. These symptoms become progressively less severe and soon disappear altogether.

The severity of the withdrawal depends on the daily dose of the addict and is seldom as drastic as this description. For most individuals, withdrawal resembles a bad case of the flu. Even though heroin withdrawal is not life threatening, it is extremely uncomfortable and is not undertaken lightly.

Withdrawal is similar for all opioids that operate primarily at the mu receptor, although it is usually less severe with the less potent opioids such as codeine or propoxyphene. The withdrawal symptoms can be stopped almost instantly, at any stage, by the administration of any of the opioid mu-agonist drugs. Opioid withdrawal symptoms can also be reduced by alcohol (Ho & Allen, 1981). Withdrawal in a physically dependent individual can be generated almost instantly by the administration of a mu opioid antagonist.

Mu opioid withdrawal causes a rebound in cyclic AMP levels, which leads to an enhancement of the release of numerous neurotransmitters. During withdrawal, there is an increase in the activity of the periaqueductal gray. If this is inhibited, the withdrawal symptoms are diminished (Corbett et al., 2006). In addition, repetitive infusions of heroin into the periventricular gray will cause physical dependence in rats. This indicates that the *central gray*, a region in the central brain composed of the periaqueductal gray and the periventricular gray, is involved in producing opioid withdrawal. The central gray is also known to be involved in pain transmission and modulation and is a site of action for the analgesic effects of mu opioids.

Withdrawal from opioids, like cyclazicine, that are active at kappa receptors is milder and is not associated with craving or drug-seeking behavior (Haertzen, 1970).

SELF-ADMINISTRATION IN HUMANS

We tend to think of all heroin users as addicts, but this assumption is certainly not true. Many people appear to be able to maintain what is called an *ice cream habit* or *chipping* in which heroin is taken occasionally when the drug and opportunities to take it are available. Chipping is a reality, but its extent is unknown because chippers are difficult to detect. They appear to be able to maintain a normal lifestyle and seldom require treatment.

We know a great deal more about the pattern of addicted heroin use, which has been extensively studied. In this pattern, the user is often (though not always) physically dependent and attempts to consume sufficient heroin to experience the rush and to avoid withdrawal—usually at least one injection a day. The addict is preoccupied with *taking care of business* or *scoring*—obtaining and taking the drug. This usually requires most of the addict's attention and money, leaving little time and resources for anything else. A heroin addict typically chooses friends and associates who are also heroin users.

The first exposure to heroin is usually motivated by curiosity and approached with caution. Frequently, the new user is introduced to the drug by someone he or she trusts. Surveys show that the majority of addicts were first given the drug by a friend. Very few were given the drug by a *pusher* or someone unknown to them. It is extremely unlikely that someone could be made into an addict, against his or her will, by an unscrupulous pusher trying to develop new markets.

We have already seen that the initial experience with heroin is considered unpleasant by the majority of first-time users, and it probably requires considerable persistence to acquire a physical dependence. It is not known how many people exposed to opioids do not become addicts and avoid the addicted lifestyle.

At the other end of addiction, there appears to be a *maturing out* of heroin use. Studies have indicated that many addicts spontaneously discontinue use of the drug (Winick, 1962). These addicts usually reach this point in their 30s or 40s after some 5 to 10 years of heroin use. The longer a person has used heroin, the less the chance of maturing out. It is difficult to determine the number of addicts who eventually mature out; estimates range from more than two-thirds (Winick, 1962) to less than a quarter (Ball & Snarr, 1969). A great many heroin addicts never do manage to leave the habit behind, and they survive into old age still using heroin. Addiction workers are reporting an increasing number of heroin-addicted seniors (Jones, 2005). In fact, in the United States, the proportion of those over 50 enrolled in heroin treatment programs tripled between 1994 and 2004, and the number is expected to double again by 2020. These figures have led some to suspect that maturing out may have been restricted to studies done in the 1950s and 1960s (Darke, 2011). More recent long-term research on cohorts of Vietnam War veterans reveals that addiction to many drugs, including opioids, shows high levels of spontaneous remission, that is, recovery without medical intervention. Over a 25-year period, 59 out of 136 heroin users attempted to stop on their own, and, of these, 52 were successful (Price, Risk, & Spitznagel, 2001).

LABORATORY STUDIES

Laboratory studies of human opioid self-administration show that opioids act as reinforcers in opioid abusers by a number of different routes of administration. Different drugs have different reinforcing potential. Morphine appears to be more reinforcing than codeine, and both are more reinforcing than propoxyphene. Propoxyphene would be self-administered only in situations where it was available at little or no cost. Not surprisingly, heroin does not function as a reinforcer in opioid abusers when they are pretreated with an opioid antagonist. A study by Lamb and colleagues (1991) showed that nondependent drug users would self-administer intramuscular morphine at doses so low that the drug had no detectable subjective effect.

There are few studies of self-administration in non-drug-abusing populations. This is because it is considered unethical to give drugs like heroin to nonusers as doing so could potentially lead them to more extensive use and eventually to become addicts. One such study using fentanyl (which is permitted for use as an analgesic and, therefore, considered ethical to study its effects on people experiencing pain) showed that it would not be self-administered unless the participant was experiencing pain from immersing his or her arm in cold water (Zacny & Walker, 1998). Thus, it appears that in non–drug users, opioids function as reinforcers only in the presence of pain. This is not surprising given the results of the Lasagana et al. (1955) study mentioned earlier, but more research needs to be done with this population.

Patterns of Use

Studies of nonhumans and humans have shown very similar patterns. In both cases, when the drug is freely available, the amount of self-administered drug is carefully regulated. The daily dose increases gradually and regularly until it reaches a peak and then remains steady. There are no intake–abstinence cycles as with alcohol and stimulants, and withdrawal symptoms are not seen. Figure 11-2 shows data from similar studies. In one study, a human heroin addict self-administered morphine intravenously; in the other, a rhesus monkey gave himself heroin via the same route (Griffiths, Bigelow, & Henningfield, 1980). For the most part, this pattern is similar to that of the opioid addict who attempts to maintain a fairly constant blood level and avoids withdrawal when it is at all possible to do so.

It is tempting to speculate that the gradual increase in dose is a result of tolerance, but this may not be the case. As we have seen in Chapter 3, with repeated administrations, the reinforcing effects of many drugs,

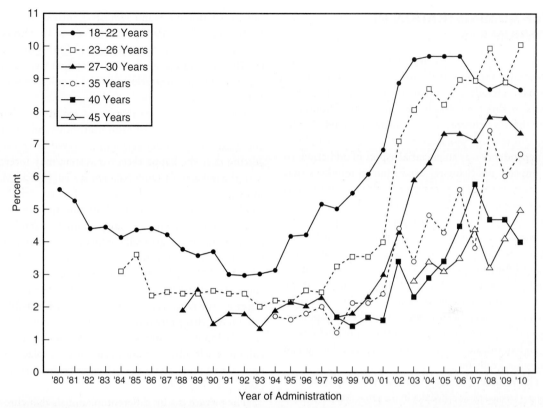

FIGURE 11-3 Percent of people surveyed in the United States who reported having used an opioid analgesic within the past year, outside the care of a physician. Data are broken down by age groups. (Adapted from Johnston, O'Malley, Bachman, & Schulenberg, 2011; used with permission)

including heroin, become sensitized rather than diminished. The increase in self-administered drug may be a result of increased reinforcing properties of the drug since it has been shown that, up to a point, larger doses are more reinforcing than smaller doses.

Extent of Use

Rates of heroin use in the United States have been relatively stable since the 1990s. Annual prevalence rates are highest in younger, compared to older, age groups, with the highest use among 18- to 22-year olds. But the picture is quite different if the illegal use of prescription opioid drugs is included. Figure 11-3 shows annual rates of analgesic opioid use since 1980 reported by the Monitoring the Future Survey. This figure shows the percentage of people in different age classes who, in the past year, report using analgesic opioids other than heroin outside medical supervision. You can see a large increase in the illicit use of these opioids starting in the mid-1990s, and, 10 years later, use had leveled off for all age groups. The increase was greatest in the younger age categories (under 30) and reaches as high as 10% for some groups in 2009 and 2010 (Johnston et al., 2011). The most popular of these prescription drugs were Vicodin (hydrocodone and acetaminophen) and OxyContin (oxycodone).

According to the 2010 National Survey on Drug Use and Health (Substance Abuse and Mental Health Services Administration, 2011), 1.9 million prescription narcotic users meet diagnostic criteria for opioid abuse or dependence, which is second only to marijuana, which sits at 4.3 million. The number of new users of prescription opioids is roughly the same as the number of new users of marijuana. Most (more than 80%) prescriptions for opioids were obtained, originally, from a physician. For those individuals who take opioids that were prescribed, but not to them, more than 56% got the drugs from a friend or relative.

SELF-ADMINISTRATION IN NONHUMANS

Morphine was the first drug for which intravenous self-administration was demonstrated in nonhumans. We have already discussed one of the first experiments of this type, conducted by Travis Thompson and Charles Schuster and published in 1964. At the time this research was done, it was assumed that physical dependence was an essential aspect of addiction, so Thompson and Schuster used squirrel monkeys that had been made dependent on morphine by injections four times a day for 30 days. The monkeys were then given the opportunity to bar press for morphine four times a day. The monkeys were placed on an FI–FR chain schedule; to receive the drug, the monkeys were on an FI 2-minute schedule while a tone was turned on. The first response made after 2 minutes turned off the tone and turned on a white light. While the white light was on, the animals were required to make 25 responses. When this requirement was completed, a red light came on, and an infusion of morphine was given through an intravenous catheter.

The monkeys readily learned this response, and they performed these schedules in the same manner as they would for any other reinforcer. Thompson and Schuster (1964) also demonstrated that both deprivation from morphine and injections of nalorphine would increase the amount of morphine the monkeys would administer. In later research, they demonstrated that nondependent monkeys would also self-administer morphine (Schuster & Thompson, 1969).

As shown in Figure 11-2, when opioids are freely available, they are self-administered by laboratory animals with great regularity on a daily basis, and the daily dose slowly increases.

All the mu receptor agonists are self-administered by laboratory animals, although the mixed agonist–antagonists are not as reinforcing as morphine and heroin. The reinforcing effects of the opioids can be blocked by mu antagonists. Full antagonists, like naloxone and naltrexone, and partial agonists, like cyclazocine, are not self-administered. In fact, laboratory animals will learn to respond to avoid administrations of mu antagonists and kappa agonists (Zacny & Walker, 1998). Kappa agonists are not reinforcers, but some delta agonists are, although they do not appear to be as reinforcing as mu agonists (vanRee, Gerrits, & Vanderschuren, 1999). More recently, though, Stevenson, Folk, Rice, and Negus (2005) found that the SNC80, a highly selective delta agonist, did not support self-administration, nor did it enhance heroin self-administration.

There are also reports that kappa agonists can block the reinforcing effects of both morphine and cocaine and a number of other self-administered drugs, suggesting that the kappa receptor system may interact with the mu agonist reinforcement system (Glick, Maisonneuve, Raucci, & Archer, 1995). More recently, Wee and Koob (2010) reviewed the literature and concluded that in nondependent laboratory animals, stimulation of kappa receptors generally antagonizes the reinforcing effects of cocaine, morphine, heroin, and ethanol, whereas blocking kappa receptors has no effect. They concluded that kappa agonists do not have any direct effect on the reinforcement system, but are capable of enhancing drug-motivated behavior because kappa stimulation causes stress, and it is known that stress enhances self-administration, conditioned place preference, and reinstatement of drug self-administration (Wee & Koob, 2010).

The picture is a bit different in animals that chronically self-administer mu opioid agonists and are in a physically dependent state. In this case, kappa receptor antagonists reduce the increased self-administration of ethanol and cocaine. Wee and Koob (2010) argue that kappa receptors are involved in the development of the negative emotional state created by physical dependence, and, consequently, blocking kappa receptors reduces severity of withdrawal and thereby the motivation to self-administer drugs (see Koob and LeMoal's theory of hedonic dysregulation in Chapter 5).

HARMFUL EFFECTS

Acute Effects

At very high doses, opioids produce a comatose state with pinpoint pupils and severe depression of breathing, which eventually causes death. Unlike barbiturates, opioids lower the seizure threshold and may also cause convulsions at high doses. Opium has been used historically as a poison, so it is not surprising that people die from time to time from accidental overdoses

BOX 11-1   What Was the Mysterious Gas Used by the Russians to End the Moscow Theater Hostage Taking?

On October 23, 2002, at about 9:00 p.m., 41 Chechen terrorists invaded a popular Moscow theater. They took over 800 people hostage and demanded that the Russians withdraw their troops from Chechnya. The terrorists threatened to start shooting their hostages and blow up the theater with explosives strapped to their bodies. The Russian government refused to negotiate. The standoff lasted 57 hours. Early on the morning of October 27, the Russian Federal Security Service pumped a gas into the theater and then stormed it and took it by force. The gas was effective—it knocked the terrorists out so fast that they were not able to detonate their explosives. Unfortunately, the gas proved lethal to many; 129 of the hostages and all but two of the terrorists were killed by the gas.

At the time, the Russians would not say what gas they had used, but in response to international pressure they announced several days later that the gas had been a fentanyl derivative, but questions still remain. There are several derivatives of fentanyl that could have been used, but the most likely would have been carfentanil, which is more than 30 times more potent than fentanyl and 10,000 times more potent than morphine. Potency would have been an important consideration. Fentanyl and its derivatives like morphine are not normally a gas at room temperature, so the carfentanil must have been nebulized and made into an aerosol, that is, turned into very fine particles and dispersed into the air—a complicated process. The more potent the drug, the less nebulization would have been needed.

But another question remains. Why did so many people die? It turns out that carfentanil and other fentanyl derivatives have a fairly high therapeutic index (TI) compared to morphine. The TI of morphine is about 70, while the TI of carfentanil is 10,600. These numbers suggest that these drugs should have been quite safe. There are two possible answers to this question. The first is that the dose received by each individual would have varied greatly, depending on where each person was. The aerosol was introduced into the theater by the ventilation system, and those close to the air vents would have received a much higher dose. This inability to control the dose is an inherent problem with using gases and aerosols in this manner. But there is another possibility: Another agent may have been mixed with the fentanyl derivative.

One advantage of using an opioid drug is that there is a very effective and fast-acting antidote available, naloxone. After the raid, many victims were treated in nearby hospitals that had been warned to stock up on their supplies of naloxone; unfortunately, the doctors were not told that the gas was an opioid, so many did not use the naloxone. In many cases, however, when it was used, it did not seem to be effective. This has led many to speculate that another agent had been mixed with the fentanyl derivative. Many suspect that it might have been the gaseous anesthetic halothane. Many survivors reported a sweet smell as the gas took effect. This is a property of halothane. In addition, a toxicological analysis of a German survivor after returning to Germany showed traces of halothane. If halothane were mixed with the fentanyl derivative, it might explain why there were so many deaths. Halothane has a very low therapeutic index, and, additionally, it does not have any antidote.

In these days of terrorism and hostage taking, there is little doubt that many militaries around the world are developing "calmative" or rapidly acting agents that can incapacitate a person rapidly but not be lethal. Normally such research is never made public, so this incident provides us with a speculative glimpse of where this field may be going (Wax, Becker, & Curry, 2003).

---

of opioids. Box 11-1 describes how a derivative of fentanyl was used by the Russian security forces on Chechen rebels who seized a Moscow theater in 2002. The drug killed both the hostage takers and many hostages.

Between 1999 and 2002, the number of U.S. death certificates citing opioid analgesic poisonings rose more than 91%, and, during this time, poisoning from opioid analgesics surpassed both cocaine and heroin poisoning as the most frequent type of drug poisoning (Paulozzi, Budnitz, & Xi, 2006). Opioids account for nearly half of overdose deaths in the United States; accidental death/overdose data from 2005 show that methadone accounts for 16.2% of all overdoses, other opioid pain killers for 22%, and heroin for 7.7% for a total of almost 46% of overdose deaths attributable to opioids (Paulozzi et al., 2006).

Heroin overdose is the leading cause of death among heroin users. In fact, in some communities, it is the leading cause of death in males between the ages of 25 and 54. In Australia, it has been estimated that every year about 2% of heroin users die and the majority of these deaths are due to overdose (Gerostamolous, Staikos, & Drummer, 2001). Most heroin overdose deaths occur in people with 5 to 10 years of experience with using the drug; only about 17% are new users. These deaths do not seem to be related to changes in the purity of street heroin (Sporer, 2003).

One mystery related to heroin overdose is that, many times, the victim has not used more heroin than usual or more heroin than other people using the drug at the time (Brecher & the Editors of *Consumer Reports*, 1972). If these deaths were not overdoses, what could be killing so many addicts? There are several explanations. One possibility is quinine, a drug used to cut or dilute the heroin before it is sold on the streets. Quinine can be lethal when given intravenously, and these overdose victims frequently show signs of quinine poisoning, such as frothing from the nose and mouth. Another explanation is the mixing of heroin with other drugs. One study showed that 85% of those dying from heroin overdose were using another central nervous system depressant, 45% were using benzodiazepines, and 36% were using alcohol (Gerostamolous et al., 2001). These drugs potentiate the effects of heroin and may make an otherwise normal dose of heroin lethal. Many famous celebrities and musicians—Jim Morrison of The Doors, Hillel Slovak of The Red Hot Chili Peppers, rocker Janis Joplin, and actor River Phoenix, and others—have succumbed to the effects of heroin or a mixture of heroin and alcohol.

Another possible cause of an unexplained overdose is a loss of tolerance to the drug. Often this loss is due to a period of abstinence. Addicts have seven times the risk of overdose during their first 2 weeks after their release from residential treatment (Sporer, 1999). During treatment, they have lost their tolerance to the lethal effects of the drug, so their usual dose is now fatal. Loss of tolerance may be due to conditioned tolerance effects. As described in Box 3-2 of Chapter 3, some tolerance may depend on the specific environment in which the drug is normally given. If the drug is used in a new environment, tolerance is diminished, and what is a normal dose for an addict may suddenly be transformed into a lethal dose.

Chronic Effects

HEALTH. Surprisingly few medical problems arise as a direct result of chronic heroin use. One of these is constipation. Somewhat more serious is a direct link between opioids and cancer. Opioids interfere with the body's ability to repair damaged DNA, and this effect makes them cancer promoters; they enhance the cancer-causing effects of other substances that damage DNA. Like alcohol use, heroin use greatly increases the chance of bladder cancer caused by smoking (Falek, Madden, Shafer, & Donahoe, 1982).

CNS EFFECTS. Opioids do not appear to alter the structural anatomy of the brain. However, SPECT data suggest that chronic heroin use is associated with widespread reductions in cerebral blood flow to the frontal, parietal, and temporal lobes of patients within the first week of heroin withdrawal. These effects may not be long lasting since perfusion deficits show marked improvement following 3 weeks of heroin abstinence (Rose et al., 1996). Opioid users and former users do show abnormal brain activation patterns during decision making on the *Cambridge risk task*. This task involves choosing among two computer-based decks of cards, one associated with an unlikely high reward and one associated with a likely low reward. Brain imaging studies using positron emission tomography (PET) and fMRI show that, similar to stimulant addicts, opioid addicts have reduced activation of the anterior cingulate cortex during errors made while completing the task (Forman et al., 2004). It is not clear whether this difference was caused by the drug or whether it is a preexisting condition in opioid addicts.

REPRODUCTION. In males, chronic opioid use reduces levels of the male sex hormone testosterone. This effect leads to a decrease in sex drive and fertility and may also cause changes in secondary sex characteristics. In women, alteration in hormone levels causes menstrual irregularities, amenorrhea, and a consequent decrease in fertility.

Pregnancies are also complicated by direct and indirect effects of opioids and opioid withdrawal. During pregnancy, the ability of the body to eliminate opioids is increased. The subsequent reduction in circulating levels of opioids leads to increased demand for the drug, and the probability of withdrawal is greater if the drug supply is irregular or uncertain. It is believed that opioid withdrawal during pregnancy can harm the fetus because it causes a decrease in blood oxygen levels. Numerous other medical complications during the pregnancies of addicted women may arise from the problems of the addicts' lifestyle. These complications, which occur in

40 to 50% of pregnant addicts, include anemia, cardiac disease, swelling, liver disease, hypertension, pneumonia, tuberculosis, and infections of the urogenital system, such as bladder infections and venereal disease (Kreek, 1982).

Babies born to addicted mothers have low birth weights and are more likely to be premature and to experience illness and complications after birth. In general, these problems are less likely in methadone-maintained mothers than in those using street heroin.

One big problem for babies born to dependent mothers is that right after birth, they have to go through withdrawal because they are no longer exposed to the opioid in the mother's blood. Withdrawal in neonates is similar to adult withdrawal. The symptoms include irritability, respiratory distress, yawning, sneezing, tremors, difficulty in sucking and swallowing, and a peculiar high-pitched cry. Some may even experience seizures. These symptoms start within 72 hours of birth and may last 6 to 8 weeks (Finnegan, 1982).

LIFESTYLE EFFECTS. Although opioids cause some direct health problems, most of the harm done by opioids is indirect and arises from the lifestyles most addicts are forced to adopt. Heroin is expensive and requires a lot of money to support the habit. Because getting the drug takes such priority, housing and nutrition suffer, and so does health. Added to these difficulties is the greatly increased exposure to disease caused by the practice of *shooting up* the drug. These injections are seldom done with clean needles and syringes; many people often use the same equipment, providing direct access into the body for diseases such as hepatitis and HIV/AIDS. Being a heroin addict is not healthy.

In a 33-year study of 581 heroin-addicted criminal offenders admitted to the California Civil Addict Program between 1962 and 1964, it was found that by 1997, nearly half the group had died. This represents a death rate 50 to 100 times the death rate among the general population of men the same age. Accidental poisoning and drug overdose were the most common cause of death (21.6%). Nineteen and a half percent were homicide, suicides, and accidents. Liver disease, cancer, and cardiovascular disease accounted for the remaining deaths (Hser, Hoffman, Grella, & Anglin, 2001). Nearly 40% of those surviving used heroin within the past year, and nearly 10% were in methadone treatment.

Years of Potential Life Lost

Being a heroin addict is dangerous. Death rates from many causes are higher in heroin addicts than the general population, and these deaths are all the more tragic because they tend to occur in younger people early in their lives and careers. This is tragic, not only for the individual and their families, but also for the community, which loses many years of productivity when a death is premature. To take into account deaths that occur in younger persons, it has become common to report these rates in terms of *years of potential life lost* (YPLL, although you will sometimes see PYLL for *potential years of life lost*). Rather than merely report the number of deaths in a population per 1,000 individuals, the YPLL method calculates the number of years of potential life that were lost in a population per 1,000 individuals. This method of reporting fatalities emphasizes the tragedy of deaths in younger people.

In these studies the researchers pick a reference age (say, 65), and then, for every death due to a certain cause, they determine how many years of potential life were lost by subtracting the age at death from 65. This is the YPLL. The YPLLs for individuals are added and reported as total years of potential life lost per 1,000 people.

In a study published in 2007 in the journal *Preventative Medicine*, Breda Smyth and her colleagues (Smyth, Hoffman, Fan, & Hser, 2007) analyzed the data from the 33-year follow-up study of heroin addicts released from the California Civil Addict Program from 1962 to 1964 (reported earlier; Hser et al., 2001) in terms of YPLL. Table 11-2 shows the YPLL for several causes of death in this group compared with the general population in 1997. As you can see, unintentional injury was the main cause of death among addicts, costing 42.6 lost years of life per 1,000 people. This is almost four times higher than the general population. *Unintentional injuries* include heroin overdose, poisoning/injury, and accidents. Heroin overdose was the leading cause of deaths in this category, accounting for 49 of the 282 deaths and a total of 1,153 of YPLL. More than half of these overdose deaths occurred less than 15 years after admission to the study.

The second leading cause of premature deaths in this study was chronic liver disease, which was probably due to high rates of hepatitis B and C caused by needle sharing and heavy drinking. The high death rate from cancer is not likely due to heroin use alone but, rather, tobacco. The rate of smoking in the sample was 98%.

TABLE 11-2   Years of Potential Life Lost Due to Various Causes for Heroin Addicts, 1962 to 1997

Cause of Death	Addicts YPLL/1000	U.S. Population 1997 YPLL/1000
Unintentional injuries*	42.64	11.95
Liver disease	31.14	1.32
Heart disease	26.26	8.29
Cancer	15.91	7.50
Homicide	43.22	4.38
Suicide	38.40	4.56
Stroke	31.57	1.17
TOTAL	**229.14**	**39.17**

*Includes heroin overdose, poisoning injury, and accidents.

Source: Adapted from Smyth et al. (2007); used with permission.

PHARMACOLOGICAL TREATMENT OF OPIOID ADDICTION

Detoxification

One approach to treating opioid addiction is to eliminate the physical dependence by helping the addict get through withdrawal. At one point, when it was widely believed that physical dependence was the cause of addiction, detoxification was thought to be an effective treatment for addiction. It is now understood that extensive drug use can cause changes in the brain that last much longer than the overt physical changes precipitated by withdrawal, and that many withdrawal symptoms can be evoked by conditioning mechanisms (see Chapter 5). Therefore, eliminating the physical dependence does not *cure* the addiction. Nevertheless, there are other long-term treatments that address these problems and require abstinence from opioids. Detoxification is therefore necessary before such treatments can be started.

There are two approaches to detoxification. In the abrupt approach, withdrawal is initiated suddenly by abstinence or administration of an opioid antagonist. Another approach is to switch from the illicit opioid to methadone or buprenorphine and then slowly taper the dose so that withdrawal symptoms are alleviated.

In the abrupt approach, the aim is to mitigate the severity and discomfort of withdrawal and to get it over with as quickly as possible. The fastest way to accomplish this is to give an opioid antagonist, such as naloxone. Opioid antagonists will shorten the duration of withdrawal, but intensify the symptoms. One way to reduce the aversiveness of withdrawal is to make the patient unconscious by giving an anesthetic or to heavily sedate them. This method can reduce withdrawal to just a few days or even a few hours, but is not recommended because it increases the risk of cardiac and respiratory arrest.

In the tapering procedure, patients are switched to an opioid agonist like methadone, or a mixed agonist/antagonist like buprenorphine, and the dose is systematically reduced, a procedure that can take from 10 to 28 days. To reduce the severity of withdrawal, patients may be given a drug such as clonidine or lofexidine, which are alpha$_2$-adrenergic receptor agonists often used to lower blood pressure. Alpha$_2$-adrenergic receptors are located on the presynaptic neuron of noradrenergic synapses, and, when they are activated by an agonist like clonidine, they inhibit the release of norepinephrine. This blocks activity in the sympathetic nervous system, and it is this activity that causes many of the unpleasant effects of withdrawal, such as sweating. Many other opioid withdrawal symptoms are caused by the activation of the locus coeruleus, a center in the brainstem that contains the cell bodies of most of the NE neurons in the brain. Clonidine and lofexidine effectively diminish this activity. They also cause sedation, which is helpful during withdrawal. Lofexidine appears to work better than clonidine, and detoxification may be achieved in as little as 5 days (Lobmaier, Gossop, Waal, & Bramness, 2010).

Maintenance Therapies

Maintenance therapies are based on the philosophy that the real harm done by opioids arises from the fact that they are expensive and illegal. It follows that if addicts have a cheap, reliable source of the drug, they will remain healthy, be free to pursue careers and normal lives, and not be forced into a criminal lifestyle. In maintenance therapies, addicts are provided with an opioid agonist, which is made continuously available. Methadone, buprenorphine, LAAM, and even heroin itself have all been used.

HEROIN. In the United Kingdom, where it is legal for physicians to prescribe heroin, heroin became the first maintenance drug and is still used that way to some extent, but it has significant disadvantages and is not widely used any more. One problem is that heroin is short acting, and several doses are required every day. It must also be injected, so it is necessary to give the addict the heroin and injection apparatus to take home, and the drug may be shared with other people or sold on the street.

METHADONE. In the United States, various laws made it impossible for doctors to prescribe heroin to addicts (or anyone else), so methadone has been used to maintain addicts since the first clinic opened in 1974 (Nyswander, 1967). Methadone has several advantages over heroin as a maintenance drug: (a) it can be taken orally, (b) it prevents withdrawal symptoms for 24 hours, and (c) it acts as an antagonist to heroin. Because it can be taken orally, it is easy to administer and does not have all the associations of shooting up. The fact that it lasts for 24 hours means that it can be administered once a day in a clinic, and the user does not need to take it home. And because it blocks the effects of heroin, addicts on methadone will experience few euphoric effects

or rushes if they decide to try heroin. This is probably because methadone occupies mu receptors and has a higher affinity to the receptor, and this blocks other mu agonists like heroin. Methadone continues to occupy mu opioid receptors in the thalamus, caudate, anterior cingulate cortex, and temporal and frontal cortices at 22 hours post-administration in former heroin users on maintenance therapy. PET imaging with [18F]cylcofoxy, which binds to mu receptors, shows that receptor availability is reduced by 19 to 32% in these regions (Kling et al., 2000). It is also likely that a decrease in sensitivity to heroin that occurs following methadone therapy arises from cross-tolerance between methadone and heroin.

Substitution of methadone for heroin is not considered a therapeutic end in itself. Methadone is always used in conjunction with psychological or social treatments. In fact, the success of methadone treatments depends heavily on the addict's having a good, trusting relationship with a well-trained staff (Weddington, 1995).

In a typical methadone maintenance clinic, patients are screened to ensure that they really are physiologically dependent on heroin. Then, over a period of several weeks, a dosage of methadone is worked out that will maintain the patients free from withdrawal symptoms. Typically, patients must return to the clinic every day for a drink of methadone. In some programs, addicts who demonstrate that they have been free of heroin and other problems are permitted to take the drug home and are required to attend only two or three times a week.

Over the years when methadone has been used as a maintenance drug in the United States, it has been demonstrated that it reduces sickness and death associated with illicit drug use (Sporer, 2003), normalizes disruptions of immune and endocrine functions, reduces the transfer of HIV/AIDS, and reduces criminal activity (Ling, Rawson, & Compton, 1994; Veilleux et al., 2010).

Many addicts choose to stay maintained on methadone indefinitely, but as normal lifestyles develop, there are pressures to detoxify altogether. Methadone patients are discriminated against in insurance, licensing, employment, and housing, and the pressures to attend clinics regularly interfere with travel and vacations. Then, too, methadone has uncomfortable side effects, such as sweating, sexual dysfunction, and constipation. When patients appear ready and motivated to discontinue the drug, doses of methadone are slowly decreased over a period of no less than 6 months, so that withdrawal is minimized. This process is best accomplished at a very gradual rate that is decided on by the user. Even when the methadone reduction is gradual, detoxification becomes difficult when the dosage gets low.

BUPRENORPHINE.   Buprenorphine was originally used as an analgesic, but now is widely used for opioid maintenance. It can be taken orally and has a long half-life. Buprenorphine is a partial mu agonist. This means that it is quickly bound to mu receptors, is slow to detach, and only has a partial effect; that is, there is a ceiling to its agonistic ability. It also displaces other agonists like heroin. Because of this, buprenorphine is safer than methadone and has fewer side effects. It cannot cause overdose and blocks the effects of other agonists like heroin. Withdrawal from buprenorphine is not as severe as withdrawal from a pure agonist. Therefore, it is much easier to stop taking buprenorphine than methadone, and it is easier to switch to antagonist therapies without experiencing withdrawal (Ling et al., 1994).

In normal circumstances, buprenorphine is given every day, but it has been shown that buprenorphine is just as effective when given three times a week (Schottenfield et al., 2000). One problem with buprenorphine pills is that they are sometimes crushed and injected for a more intense effect. To prevent this, naloxone is added to the oral buprenorphine pills, which are administered sublingually (under the tongue). This way, the buprenorphine is absorbed, but the naloxone is not. If crushed and injected, the naloxone will be absorbed and will block the effect of the buprenorphine.

Antagonist Therapies

Maintenance therapies were originally developed at a time when it was widely believed that fear of withdrawal was the primary motivation for taking opioids. We now understand that being physically dependent is not a crucial factor in addiction, rather it is the reinforcing effects of the drug that motivate use and, in the case of treatment, relapse. The primary benefit of maintenance therapies is that they are a legal, cheap, and reliable form of positive reinforcement that substitutes for an expensive and illegal one, which requires an unhealthy, risky lifestyle. For many people, this is not enough. They want to become completely abstinent. Antagonist therapies were developed as an abstinence-focused intervention.

Patients are first detoxified from the opioid they are addicted to by using one of the methods described earlier and kept abstinent for 7 to 10 days. This stage can be difficult, and the dropout rate is very high. This is followed by the relapse–prevention phase. As early as possible, addicts are given daily doses of the antagonist, naltrexone, when they come for therapy. This is usually at an outpatient day program where they also have educational seminars, recreational activities, and group therapy. Naltrexone is a pure antagonist, like naloxone, which is more often used as an emergency treatment for opioid overdose. Naltrexone can be taken orally, has no abuse potential, and reduces opioid craving. But the most important property of naltrexone is that it completely blocks all of the effects of opioids including the euphoric and reinforcing effects. A person taking naltrexone can shoot up even large doses of heroin and feel nothing. In theory, this should discourage opioid use and even cause the opioid-seeking response to extinguish.

Even though early results were encouraging (Kleber, 1974), an unexpected difficulty has arisen. When drug users know that they have taken an antagonist, they seldom try to shoot up heroin because they know that it will not have an effect. When they start taking the antagonist, they usually stop using heroin so suddenly that the positive reinforcing effects of the heroin on heroin-seeking behavior never get a chance to extinguish. It seems that taking the naltrexone becomes a discriminative stimulus, signaling that the reinforcing effect is not available. When they want to take heroin, they simply stop taking the naltrexone. For this reason, antagonist therapies have high noncompliance and dropout rates. These compliance problems can be partially addressed by using alternative administrations of naltrexone, such as long-lasting sustained release depot injections and naltrexone implants. Studies have shown that these extended release naltrexone administrations lengthened treatment and seemed to lower heroin craving (Comer et al., 2006).

Success rates with antagonist therapies are much higher in people who are extremely motivated to quit, have strong family support, and have legitimate professional careers to pursue or who have been ordered by a court to discontinue heroin use (Jaffe, 1987; Veilleux et al., 2010).

CHAPTER

12

Antipsychotic Drugs

Canst thou not minister to a mind diseased;
pluck from the memory a rooted sorrow; raze
out the written troubles of the brain; and
with some sweet oblivious antidote cleanse
the stuff'd bosom of that perilous stuff which
weighs upon the heart?

—Macbeth

Macbeth asked this question of the doctor treating Lady Macbeth. The doctor's answer was no. Modern physicians are a bit better off when it comes to ministering to a "mind diseased". In fact, modern psychiatry has been revolutionized by many "antidotes" in the form of anxiolytics, antipsychotics, antidepressants, and antimanics. They are not as wonderful as Macbeth envisioned them; they have troublesome side effects, and they do not always work well, but they are probably a good deal better than the treatment that Lady Macbeth was offered. In this chapter, you will learn about the antipsychotics—drugs used to treat the psychoses, of which schizophrenia is the most well-known.

THE NATURE OF SCHIZOPHRENIA

Psychotic disorders are characterized by a loss of touch with reality; people with psychosis reach a state where they grossly misunderstand and misinterpret events going on around them, and they respond inappropriately in both an intellectual and emotional sense. They may experience bizarre hallucinations, and their behavior may be guided by *delusions*—beliefs that have no basis in reality. Psychosis may be brief, brought on by drugs or some toxin, or it may be a life-long battle. Psychotic behavior may arise early in adulthood or later in life from diseases such as Alzheimer's.

Schizophrenia and Other Psychotic Disorders, as the category exists in the *DSM-IV-TR* (2000), encompasses a variety of psychoses. The most well-known of these, *schizophrenia*, is often misunderstood. The word is derived from the Greek *schizein*, "to split," and *phren*, "mind." The splitting, however, does not refer to two different personalities in the same individual. It is, instead, a separation between thought, emotion, and behavior—different aspects of a single personality.

The *DSM-IV-TR* diagnostic criteria for schizophrenia are presented in Box 12-1.

At the time of evaluation, the clinician would also specify the subtype of schizophrenia, based on the combination of symptoms exhibited. Box 12-2 presents a case study of a patient suffering from the catatonic subtype of schizophrenia. One major revision suggested for the *DSM-5* is that these subtypes no longer be included.

The symptoms of schizophrenia are often classified into two types: positive and negative. *Positive symptoms* are traits that are abnormally present in psychosis. These include hallucinations, most often auditory or visual, and delusions or irrational beliefs that can be very

BOX 12-1   DSM-IV-TR Diagnostic Criteria for Schizophrenia

A. *Characteristic Symptoms*: Two (or more) of the following, each present for a significant portion of time during a 1-month period (or less if successfully treated):

1. delusions
2. hallucinations
3. disorganized speech (e.g., frequent derailment or incoherence)
4. grossly disorganized or catatonic behavior
5. negative symptoms, i.e., affective flattening, alogia (poverty of speech), or avolition (inability to initiate and persist in goal-directed activities)

Note: Only one Criterion A symptom is required if delusions are bizarre or hallucinations consist of a voice keeping up a running commentary on the person's behavior or thoughts, or two or more voices conversing with each other.

Source: Reprinted with permission from American Psychiatric Association. © 2000, DSM-IV-TR Diagnostic Criteria for Schizophrenia.

BOX 12-2   Schizophrenia: A Case Study

This account of a schizophrenic episode was published in the *Journal of Abnormal and Social Psychology* in 1955 ("An Auto-biography,"). The author is not identified by name, but we are told that she is a college-educated social caseworker and was a 36-year-old mother of three children when she experienced her first schizophrenic episode. Her experience with schizophrenia was at a time before antipsychotic drugs were available, and common treatments were barbiturates (amobarbital) and shock treatment. Compare the symptoms this woman describes with the description of schizophrenia provided in Box 12-1. Do you feel that she fits the criteria for schizophrenia?

Most of what follows is based on an unpublished autobiography written in the spring of 1951 shortly after I returned home from the second of the three episodes of my schizophrenic experiences. . . .

Shortly after I was taken to hospital for the first time in a rigid catatonic condition,* I was plunged into the horror of a world catastrophe. I was being caught up in a cataclysm and totally dislocated. I myself had been responsible for setting the destructive force into motion, although I had acted with no intent to harm, and defended myself with healthy indignation against the accusations of others. If I had done anything wrong, I was suffering the consequences along with everyone else. Part of the time I was exploring a new planet (a marvelous and breathtaking adventure) but it was too lonely. I could persuade no one to settle there and I had to get back to earth somehow. The earth, however, had been devastated by atomic bombs and most of its inhabitants killed. Only a few people—myself and the dimly perceived nursing staff—had escaped. At other times I felt totally alone on the new planet.

After the first few weeks of extreme disorganisation, I began to acquire some relatively stable paranoid delusions. . . .

During the paranoid period I thought I was being persecuted for my beliefs, that my enemies were actively trying to interfere with my activities, were trying to harm me, and at times even trying to kill me. I was primarily a citizen of the larger community. I was trying to persuade people who did not agree with me, but whom I felt could be won over, of the correctness of my belief. . . .

In order to carry through the task which had been imposed upon me, and to defend myself against the terrifying and bewil-dering dangers of my external situation, I was endowed in my imagination with truly cosmic powers. The sense of power was not always truly defensive but was also connected with a strong sense of valid inspiration. I felt that I had power to determine the weather, which responded to my inner moods, and even to control the movement of the sun in relation to other astronomi-cal bodies. . . . I was also afraid that other people had power to read my mind, and thought I must develop ways of blocking my thoughts from other people. . . .

(continued)

BOX 12-2   (Continued)

A mixture of sexual and ethical motivation became apparent during phases when I felt myself to be carrying through a predominantly maternal role and to be symbolically identified with Mary, the Mother of Christ. This identification was poetic; that is, I knew that I was myself and was Mary only in the figurative sense. The "Christ-Child" was apparently the human baby in general, the infant as the symbol of humanity, but I doubt that I would have made this identification if all my children had been girls.

Catatonic schizophrenia is characterized by a state of immobility in which the individual assumes a position without moving for extended periods of time.

---

complex and highly organized. Feelings of grandeur ("I am being spoken to by God") or paranoia ("The CIA is plotting to kill me because I know too much") may be involved. There may also be incoherent thought and speech, involving a loosening of associations between ideas where thoughts skip from one subject to a completely unrelated subject and the speaker is unaware that the topics are unconnected. This type of speech has been described as "word salad." There may be excessive motor activity that serves no apparent purpose or, in contrast, a lack of movement in which individuals maintain odd mannequin-like postures for hours.

Negative symptoms are traits that are abnormally absent in psychosis. These include *affective flattening* where the person's face is immobile and unresponsive, and he or she shows a diminished range of emotional expressiveness. *Anhedonia*, in which a person feels no pleasure, may also occur. Another negative symptom is *alogia*, or impoverished speech, where replies are brief and uncommunicative and seem to reflect diminished thinking. *Avolition* is an inability to initiate or engage in goal-directed activities. The person remains unmotivated for long periods of time and shows no interest in participating in work, social activities, or even personal hygiene. The person may also withdraw, socially. These negative symptoms do not appear exclusively in schizophrenia—they may be exhibited in a variety of other disorders, such as major depressive disorder or with brain injury.

In addition to the positive and negative symptoms, there are cognitive deficits that include an inability to sustain attention, problems with learning and memory, difficulties with problem solving and abstract thinking, and slowing of neuromuscular actions.

The symptoms of schizophrenia appear gradually, usually over a period of 3 to 5 years. The first symptoms are typically negative, followed by an onset of positive symptoms that may take some years to emerge. Men and women are equally likely to be affected by schizophrenia, although men typically experience signs and symptoms beginning at a slightly earlier age (late teens or early twenties) than do women (twenties or thirties).

Worldwide, the incidence of schizophrenia is approximately 1%, and rates are remarkably similar regardless of race, culture, society, or the region in which a person lives. However, having a close relative with schizophrenia, such as a sibling or parent, increases one's risk of developing the disorder by up to 10 times; having an identical twin with schizophrenia increases one's risk nearly 50 times. This is irrefutable evidence that genetic makeup plays a pivotal role in rendering individuals susceptible to developing schizophrenia. No one particular gene has been flagged as the "schizophrenia gene" and probably never will. Instead, genetic analysis has pinpointed a number of gene mutations on many chromosomes that, together, create vulnerability to develop schizophrenia. These genes are involved in such processes as neuronal migration during prenatal brain development, neuronal differentiation and growth, axonal projection, and the formation of receptors and synapses (Doherty, O'Donovan, & Owen, 2011; Walsh et al., 2008).

If schizophrenia were caused purely by genetics, we would expect identical twins (who are genetic clones of one another) to either both exhibit schizophrenia or for neither to be affected. In fact, the likelihood of both identical twins exhibiting schizophrenia, when one is affected, is only about 45%. We can conclude, then, that environmental influences must also play an important role in activating or promoting the expression of genes implicated in schizophrenia. Many environmental factors have been discovered. If a mother contrasts a virus while pregnant, especially during the second trimester, brain development of the fetus can be affected, either by the virus itself or by the mother's immune system response to the virus. In large cities, where viruses are spread more readily, schizophrenia rates are approximately three times higher than those in rural areas. Schizophrenia rates are also higher in individuals whose gestation occurred during the winter flu season. During the dark winter months, levels of vitamin D (the "sunshine" vitamin) also tend to be lower. In pregnant women, vitamin D deficiency may predispose the developing offspring to schizophrenia as vitamin D is important for normal brain development. Other influential environmental factors include birth complications and a lack of oxygen to the child during labor and delivery, early childhood infection, head trauma, stress, and use of drugs such as cannabis or methamphetamine.

THEORIES OF SCHIZOPHRENIA

Our understanding of the etiology of schizophrenia has progressed in leaps and bounds over the past few decades. Various conceptions of the illness can be summed up as follows: Schizophrenia is the result of a genetic predisposition triggered by environmental factors. The positive symptoms of schizophrenia result from hyperactivity at mesolimbic dopaminergic synapses; the negative and cognitive symptoms result from degenerative processes in the brain that lead to hypoactivity at mesocortical dopaminergic synapses. Dysfunctional glutamate neurotransmission also occurs in schizophrenia. Other neurotransmitter systems, including serotonin, GABA, acetylcholine, and histamine, have all been implicated as well.

Next, you will find details supporting these claims and how, when they are pieced together, our understanding of the etiology of schizophrenia becomes much clearer.

Brain Structural and Functional Abnormalities in Schizophrenia

When the brains of individuals with schizophrenia are examined, either postmortem or using brain imaging technology, we see significant structural abnormalities; inherently, these lead to functional disturbances as well. One of the most noticeable abnormalities is the size of the lateral and third *ventricles*, cavities in which cerebrospinal fluid is produced and flows to cushion, cool, and nourish the brain. In individuals with schizophrenia, these ventricles are nearly twice as large as those of individuals unaffected by the illness. Most likely, a loss of brain tissue leads to this enlargement—the cerebrospinal-fluid-filled ventricles take over space opened due to the deterioration of neurons.

Compared to nonschizophrenic controls, individuals with schizophrenia have less brain tissue volume in up to 50 different brain regions (Kubicki et al., 2007). This deterioration is most pronounced in the corpus callosum, cerebellum, and areas of the frontal and temporal lobes, including structures of the limbic system, such as the hippocampus, amygdala, and cingulate gyrus (Borgwardt, McGuire, & Fusar-Poli, 2011). The deficits in brain volume are small in the beginning stages of the illness but become progressively greater as symptoms worsen. For example, MRI research shows that, as the cingulate gyrus deteriorates, there is a corresponding decrease in the ability to function socially (i.e., to perform social cognition, to attribute emotion to facial expressions; Fujiwara et al., 2007). Loss of volume in the dorsolateral prefrontal cortex is associated with impaired cognitive functioning and deficits in working memory (Volk & Lewis, 2010).

When does brain tissue loss begin, and what pathological processes are at play? Researchers suggest that the abnormal neurophysiological processes that underlie schizophrenia may begin even before birth and continue throughout childhood and adolescence. Children who have a parent with schizophrenia, and who are, thereby, at increased risk for developing the illness, often exhibit cognitive and behavioral warning signs of neurophysiological abnormalities. For example, high-risk individuals who, as adults, developed schizophrenia, showed speech and neuromotor deficits and delays, a lack of motor coordination, problems with social adjustment and competence, cognitive deficits, poor academic performance, attentional problems, short-term and verbal memory deficits, and problems with smooth-pursuit eye movements in childhood (Erlenmeyer-Kimling et al., 2000; Nicolson et al., 2000; Niemi, Suvisaari, Tuulio-Henriksson, & Lönnqvist, 2003; Schiffman et al., 2004, 2009).

During childhood and adolescence, the brain undergoes a period of *synaptic pruning* where weak, unused synapses are pruned out and strong, frequently used synapses remain and grow even stronger. Some researchers believe that, in schizophrenia, this process is pathologically exaggerated so that too many connections are pruned and certain populations of neurons dwindle in number. These populations include, but are not necessarily limited to, dopaminergic and glutamatergic neurons, which you will learn more about shortly.

The Dopamine Hypothesis of Schizophrenia

Before discussing the dopamine hypothesis of schizophrenia, it might be helpful to do a quick review. Recall from Chapter 4 that there are multiple dopamine pathways in the brain. The nigrostriatal pathway contains dopamine neurons whose cell bodies reside in the substantia nigra and project to the dorsal striatum of the basal ganglia, which contains the caudate nucleus and the putamen. This dopaminergic system is important for the integration of smooth movements (it is the extrapyramidal motor system). When there is a deficiency of dopamine at these synapses, people show symptoms that resemble those of Parkinson's disease—tremors, slowed motor functions, stiff limbs, and trouble maintaining balance. These are called *extrapyramidal signs and symptoms (EPS)*. Antipsychotic medications (especially the typicals) block the activity of dopamine in the nigrostriatal pathway, often producing serious EPS that make taking the medication intolerable.

In addition, two other dopamine systems are highly implicated in the development of schizophrenia. They have cell bodies that reside in the ventral tegmental area and send projections to release dopamine in the cortex (this is the mesocortical pathway) and in the nucleus accumbens and limbic structures, including the hippocampus and amygdala (this is the mesolimbic pathway).

The *dopamine hypothesis* has been the dominant theory of the neurological basis of schizophrenia from the 1960s to this day. The basic tenet of this theory, in its original form, was that schizophrenia and other psychoses result from excessive dopamine activity in the brain. Support for this assumption was based mainly on two important observations: (a) drugs that increase dopamine function (e.g., cocaine or amphetamine) can, in high doses or with chronic administration, produce a state almost indistinguishable from the positive symptoms of schizophrenia, and (b) the antipsychotics available at the time (i.e., the typicals) were all dopamine antagonists (more on this later).

As research into the role of dopamine in schizophrenia progressed, other lines of supporting evidence emerged. Available antipsychotic medications, such as chlorpromazine and reserpine, that were effective in reducing symptoms of schizophrenia, also produced severe EPS; in the 1960s, researchers already knew that Parkinson's disease was related to a depletion of dopamine in the brain, and so they extrapolated that antipsychotics must be exerting a similar effect. Also, the most effective antipsychotic drugs were found to be those with the greatest ability to block dopamine receptors. In fact, the correlation between the therapeutic dose of a typical antipsychotic and the drug's affinity for the dopamine receptor was found to be almost perfect (Seeman, Lee, Chau-Wong, & Wong, 1976). The weaker the drug's affinity for the dopamine receptor, the larger the dose required to produce a therapeutic effect.

With the discovery and marketing of haloperidol in the late 1960s, however, came a problem. Haloperidol was more effective than the other typicals in alleviating the positive symptoms of schizophrenia, yet its affinity for dopamine receptors seemed to be lower. How could this be? The answer came in the late 1970s with the discovery that dopamine (and antipsychotic medications) could bind to more than one subtype of dopamine receptor. Some of the typicals, like chlorpromazine, which belongs to a group of chemicals known as the *phenothiazines*, have a high affinity for both D_1 and D_2 receptor subtypes. Others, like haloperidol, which belongs to the pharmacologically similar group of chemicals known as the *butyrophenones*, have a high affinity for the D_2 (but not the D_1) receptor subtype. There does not appear to be any relationship between the therapeutic effect of an antipsychotic and its affinity for the D_1 receptor (Seeman, 2002). In fact, many of the typical antipsychotics have a higher binding affinity for D_2 receptors than dopamine itself. They bind more tightly and have lower *dissociation constants*, compared to molecules of dopamine. A dissociation constant is a measure of the ease with which a ligand, such as a drug molecule, will dissociate or separate from the receptor to which it is bound. A lower dissociation constant entails stronger binding, and a higher dissociation constant entails weaker binding. With this discovery, the dopamine hypothesis was revised: Schizophrenia and other psychoses result from excessive dopamine activity, specifically at D_2 receptors. The most effective antipsychotics, then, were those with a high affinity for D_2 receptors.

The dopamine hypothesis, even in its revised form, still could not fully explain the etiology of schizophrenia. For one, there are inconsistencies in the research comparing D_2 receptor densities in individuals with and without schizophrenia, and no strong evidence that dopaminergic circuits progressively deteriorate along with other neurotransmitter circuits. Also, if schizophrenia were due simply to an overabundance of dopamine, antipsychotic drugs (which block dopamine activity as soon as they reach their site of action) should work immediately. Instead, the therapeutic effect may be delayed for several weeks, suggesting that alleviation of psychotic symptoms involves a more complex mechanism than simply blocking excessive dopamine activity (Carlsson, 1994). It may also involve the slow and long-lasting changes in the electrical properties or connectivity of cells, as discussed in Chapter 4. Finally, the negative and cognitive symptoms of schizophrenia do not improve with D_2 receptor blockade, suggesting that hyperactivity of D_2 receptors does not fully account for schizophrenia symptoms. Some researchers have suggested that perhaps D_3 or D_4 receptor dysfunction is also involved, as these receptor subtypes act similarly to D_2 receptors—their activation inhibits, rather than excites, second messenger activity.

An additional revision to the dopamine hypothesis, which has garnered a lot of support, states that excessive dopamine activity, specifically in the mesolimbic pathway, does indeed explain the positive symptoms of schizophrenia. However, the negative and cognitive symptoms of schizophrenia result from a lack of dopamine activity, specifically in the mesocortical pathway, as well as the structural abnormalities (and, thereby, functional deficits) resulting from the degeneration of various brain regions, as described earlier. As you will soon learn, when we put all of the pieces together, hypoactivity of the frontal lobes may actually be the driving force behind hyperactivity of the mesolimbic dopamine system.

The Glutamate Hypothesis of Schizophrenia

The original dopamine hypothesis of schizophrenia was supported by the discovery that stimulant drugs, like cocaine and amphetamine, produced effects that mimic the positive symptoms of schizophrenia. The *glutamate hypothesis* of schizophrenia was borne of a similar coincidental discovery (see Moghaddam & Javitt, 2012, for a review). In the late 1950s, researchers synthesized two dissociative drugs, phencyclidine (PCP) and ketamine (known by the street name Special K; see Chapter 15). These drugs produced symptoms similar to not only the positive but also the negative and cognitive symptoms of schizophrenia.

Some years later, researchers discovered that the PCP binding site (to which ketamine also binds) sits within the ion channel of the glutamate NMDA receptor (see Chapter 4 for a review). The ability of various compounds to produce schizophrenia-like symptoms is directly related to the affinity with which these drugs bind to the NMDA receptor's PCP binding site and, thereby, their ability to antagonize glutamate function. Antagonizing the NMDA receptor's binding sites for glutamate or for glycine produces similar effects.

In contrast to dopaminergic neurons, which exist in distinct pathways and brain regions, glutamatergic neurons are nearly ubiquitous in the brain. This is not all that surprising, given that glutamate is the major excitatory neurotransmitter in the central nervous system. All neural information leaving the cortex, travelling between cortical areas, and most information entering the cortex does so through glutamate neurons. So the repercussions of glutamate dysfunction are widespread.

According to early conceptions of the glutamate hypothesis, genetic factors predispose individuals to glutamate hypoactivity, specifically at the NMDA receptor. Many of the genes believed to contribute to the development of schizophrenia influence glutamate neuron connectivity, synaptogenesis, and neurotransmission at the NMDA receptor. The dysfunction may be the result of neurodevelopmental abnormalities in which NMDA receptor synapses do not form properly, or it may result from synaptic overpruning of glutamate neuronal connections during childhood and adolescence.

Despite its appealing simplicity, the original glutamate hypothesis could not explain some puzzling findings. If schizophrenia results from a lack of glutamate neurotransmission, why are measures of cerebrospinal fluid glutamate levels similar between individuals with schizophrenia and those without? An additional problem for the original glutamate hypothesis came from animal research showing that injections of NMDA receptor antagonists at doses that produce schizophrenia-like symptoms actually increased, rather than decreased, glutamate release in the prefrontal cortex. Recall that glutamate also binds to another receptor subtype, the AMPA receptor. Researchers also discovered that blockade of AMPA receptors reversed the effects of the NMDA receptor antagonists. So glutamate dysfunction in schizophrenia might be the result of two combined processes: NMDA receptor hypoactivity and AMPA receptor hyperactivity.

How can it be that NMDA receptor blockade increases glutamate activity in the prefrontal cortex? This makes sense if we consider that neurons in the cortex are inhibited by GABA interneurons—if they were not, excitation of some glutamate neurons would set off a domino effect of ever-increasing cortical activation. Blockade of NMDA receptors present on these GABA interneurons decreases their firing; in other words, there is an *inhibition of inhibition*, or excitation, and increased glutamate release and activation of AMPA receptors. This would not be so at NMDA receptors, since they are antagonized through blockade of the PCP binding site. This disorganized pattern of glutamate neurotransmission may produce a state of noise and disruption in which the cortex is unable to properly assess information (Moghaddam & Javitt, 2012). One goal of antipsychotic drug development is to stabilize NMDA and AMPA receptor glutamate neurotransmission in the cortex. NMDA itself, or direct NMDA agonists, cannot be used as antipsychotic medications because they increase the risk of seizure and brain damage resulting from *excitotoxicity*, when neurons die from excessive stimulation. However, indirect NMDA agonists, such as glycine and d-serine (an agonist at the NMDA receptor glycine binding site), facilitate NMDA receptor activity and hold great promise.

Putting the Pieces Together

As you have learned, schizophrenia develops gradually, usually with the emergence of negative and cognitive symptoms followed, perhaps years later, by the onset of positive symptoms. This course of symptom development provides us with insight into the neuropathology of schizophrenia.

Deterioration of brain regions, including limbic structures and prefrontal regions, likely begins *in utero* and continues throughout childhood, getting fast-tracked during the synaptic pruning that takes place

prior to and during adolescence. This process likely leads to a progressive and substantial loss of glutamate synapses, resulting in NMDA receptor hypoactivity and glutamate dysregulation. To understand the implications of glutamate dysfunction on dopamine systems, you must understand that NMDA receptor activity regulates dopamine function.

In the prefrontal cortex sit the cell bodies of glutamate neurons whose axons project to the ventral tegmental area. There, they synapse with dopaminergic neurons that form both the mesocortical and mesolimbic pathways. Recall that the most current conceptions of the dopamine hypothesis of schizophrenia state that the negative and cognitive symptoms of schizophrenia result from hypoactivity of the mesocortical pathway. Normally, cortical glutamate neurons projecting to the ventral tegmental area produce a tonic excitation of mesocortical dopamine neurons. These dopamine neurons, in turn, project their axons back to the prefrontal cortex (this is the mesocortical pathway) where they release dopamine in response to this excitation. This glutamate–dopamine interaction is illustrated in Figure 12-1, panel A.

Additionally, prefrontal cortical glutamatergic neurons form synapses with GABAergic interneurons within the ventral tegmental area. The axons of these GABAergic interneurons project to and inhibit the activity of the dopaminergic neurons that, in turn, project their axons to the nucleus accumbens (this is the mesolimbic pathway). Stimulation of glutamate neurons in the prefrontal cortex results in the inhibition of dopamine neurons that form the mesolimbic pathway, due to the presence of the GABAergic neurons that act as a chronic braking system. This glutamate–dopamine interaction is illustrated in Figure 12-1, panel B. Recall that the positive symptoms of schizophrenia are believed to be the result of hyperactivity of the mesolimbic dopamine pathway.

When cortical glutamate activity is diminished, due to PCP or ketamine blockade of NMDA receptors or due to neurodevelopmental pathology, resulting in a loss of NMDA receptors or glutamate connectivity, ventral tegmental area dopamine neurons are understimulated. As a result, the mesocortical dopamine pathway becomes hypoactive, and, at the same time, the mesolimbic dopamine pathway becomes hyperactive. These glutamate–dopamine interactions may explain why,

A

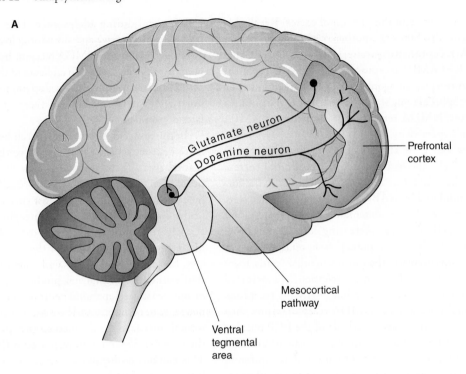

B

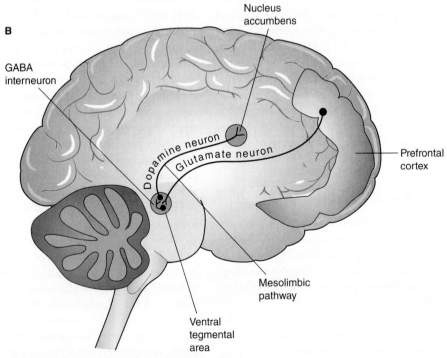

FIGURE 12-1 Glutamate–dopamine interactions.

with progressive deterioration of neurons and glutamate functionality, we see the emergence of negative and cognitive, followed by positive, symptoms of schizophrenia.

Other Neurotransmitter Systems Implicated in Schizophrenia

In addition to dopamine and glutamate, there may be other neurotransmitter systems that are rendered dysfunctional in schizophrenia. These include, but are not limited to, serotonin (Rasmussen et al., 2010), GABA (Lewis, Hashimoto, & Volk, 2005), acetylcholine (Lester, Rogers, & Blaha, 2010), and histamine (Ito, 2009). Research into neurotransmitter systems and their interactions continues to advance our understanding of the mechanisms of schizophrenia.

DISCOVERY OF ANTIPSYCHOTIC MEDICATIONS

Like most of the therapeutically useful drugs described in this book, drugs that treat the symptoms of schizophrenia were discovered by accident. In the 1950s, a French military surgeon, Henri Laborit, was looking for a preoperative medicine that would relieve patients' anxiety and reduce the high death rate that was associated with *surgical shock*, an acute and sometimes fatal state of weakness and reduction in vital functions that occur during surgery. Laborit theorized that shock was caused by excessive release of transmitters such as epinephrine, acetylcholine, and histamine; therefore, he tried out drugs known to block these substances to see if they would reduce the incidence of surgical shock. The drugs he tried included atropine, curare, and antihistamines. The first antihistamine Laborit tested was *promethazine*, which was supplied by the Rhône-Poulenc company. Like most antihistamines, it has sedating properties. Laborit was encouraged by the results he got with promethazine. In 1951, Rhône-Poulenc asked Laborit to try another antihistamine that it had synthesized several years earlier but had rejected because its sedating properties had been too strong. This was chlorpromazine.

The results were impressive. Laborit's patients did not lose consciousness but became sleepy and lost interest in everything going on around them (the sedating or tranquilizing effect) and could be anesthetized with a reduced dose of anesthetic. Laborit described the state

induced by chlorpromazine as *artificial hibernation*. He recognized the significance of this effect and immediately suggested to some psychiatrist friends that the drug might be useful in treating agitated mental patients. Two Parisian psychiatrists named Delay and Deniker learned about these trials and requested samples from Rhône-Poulenc. They administered the drug in higher doses and did not mix it with other drugs as other psychiatrists had been doing. In 1952, they reported some amazing successes; in 1953, the drug was marketed in Europe as Largactil (Sneader, 1985; Snyder, 1986; Spiegel & Aebi, 1981).

Chlorpromazine was marketed in the United States in 1955 as Thorazine and was very successful. At that time, the number of patients in mental hospitals had been climbing steadily, but with the introduction of chlorpromazine, it started to decline dramatically. In the next 3 decades, the resident population of mental institutions in the United States dropped by 80% (Hollister, 1983), largely as a result of the use of antipsychotics.

The drugs that are useful in treating the symptoms of schizophrenia are called by several names, derived from three major effects of this class of drugs on behavior. In North America, they are often referred to as *antipsychotics* because their most useful effect is to diminish the symptoms of psychosis that appear in schizophrenia.

The term *major tranquilizer* is sometimes used to refer to the antipsychotics because they have a sedating effect, not only in agitated psychotic patients but also in healthy people. This name is inappropriate because it suggests that these drugs are useful only because they *tranquilize* agitated patients. Even though there is a tranquilizing effect, these drugs seem to produce their antipsychotic effect by directly blocking the symptoms of psychosis. Rather than simply making psychotic people more tranquil or sedated, they cause psychotic people to be less psychotic and, in many cases, less agitated. Another problem is that the term major tranquilizer implies that they are just a stronger version of *minor tranquilizers*, a term sometimes applied to drugs such as the benzodiazepines or barbiturates (see Chapter 7). This terminology is misleading because it implies that both drugs have a similar effect and that one class is more powerful than the other. In fact, there is very little similarity, in chemistry or effect, between the barbiturates and benzodiazepines on the one hand and the antipsychotics on the other.

In Europe, the term *neuroleptic* is preferred. Neuroleptic means *clasping the neuron*. It refers to a capacity of these drugs to cause EPS, such as rigidity in the limbs and difficulty of movement, similar to those symptoms seen in people suffering from Parkinson's disease. This property of these drugs is a persistent and bothersome side effect, and it is indeed strange that a family of drugs should be named after a side effect rather than its most useful therapeutic effect. This name may have been chosen because at one time it was believed that both effects were related; that is, people believed that these drugs would not relieve psychosis unless they were causing neuroleptic effects as well. It is now known that the two types of effects are independent (Creese, 1983). In fact, we now have drugs that seem to be effective antipsychotics but have few, if any, neuroleptic (EPS) effects. Although the term *neuroleptic* is probably more common than *antipsychotic*, we use the latter term here because it seems more appropriate to think of drugs in terms of their useful effects rather than their side effects.

COMPARING TYPICAL AND ATYPICAL ANTIPSYCHOTICS

A distinction is drawn between *typical* (or *first-generation*) and *atypical* (or *second-generation*) antipsychotic medications. Examples of both types can be found in Table 12-1 (some of these may not have gained approval or may no longer be approved, for use in parts of Europe or North America).

The older drugs, the *typical antipsychotics*, were all developed before 1975 and are either phenothiazines or butyrophenones. They are primarily D_2 receptor blockers and are most effective in treating the positive symptoms of psychosis, rather than the negative or cognitive symptoms (which, in fact, may even be worsened). Approximately one-third of individuals with schizophrenia experience no improvement of symptoms when taking typical antipsychotics (Wiersma, Nienhuis, Slooff, & Giel, 1998). Adverse EPS are *typical* of these drugs, hence the name. The neuroleptic side effects range from being inconvenient, for some individuals, to producing major, life-long physical disability for others. For this reason, it is often difficult for individuals to comply with taking their prescribed dose.

More recently developed schizophrenia medications, and those currently in development, are pharmacologically

TABLE 12-1 Examples of Typical and Atypical Antipsychotic Drugs

Generic Name	Trade Name
Typical antipsychotics	
acetophenazine	Tindal
carphenazine	Proketazine
chlorpromazine	Thorazine, Largactil
chlorprothixene	Taractan, Tarasan
fluphenazine	Prolixin
haloperidol	Haldol
loxapine	Loxitane, Loxapac
mesoridazine	Serentil
molindone	Lindone, Moban
perphenazine	Trilafon, Etrafon**
pimizide	Orap
prochlorperazine	Stemetil, Compazine
promazine	Sparine
reserpine	Serpasil
thioridazine	Mellaril
thiothixene	Navane
trifluoperazine	Stelazine
triflupromazine	Vesprin
Atypical antipsychotics	
amisulpride	Solian
aripiprazole	Abilify
clozapine	Clozaril
olanzapine	Zyprexa
paliperidone	Invega
quetiapine	Seroquel
raclopride	Dogmatil
remoxipride*	Roxiam
risperidone	Risperdal
sertindole	Serlect
ziprasidone	Zeldox; Geodon
zotepine	Nipolept

*Found to have dangerous side effects and is not used therapeutically but is still used in nonhuman experimentation.
**Etrafon is a combination of perphenazine and the tricyclic antidepressant amitriptyline.

unlike the typicals. These are the *atypical antipsychotics*. Although their individual profiles vary considerably, they share an important property: a very weak affinity for the

D_2 receptor—they bind to D_2 receptors very loosely and have dissociation constants that are significantly higher than that of dopamine or the typicals (Seeman, 2002). Because of this, adverse EPS are *atypical* effects of these drugs.

Panel A of Figure 12-2 compares the D_2 receptor dissociation constants of a number of typical and atypical antipsychotic medications.

Positron emission tomography research reveals that about 60 to 80% of D_2 receptors must be occupied in the striatum of the basal ganglia to produce EPS (Seeman, 2002). Because of their weak affinity for the D_2 receptor, atypical antipsychotics avoid the problem of blocking dopamine in the nigrostriatal system and, therefore, produce far fewer EPS compared to the typicals. They are also more effective than the typicals in treating a wider range of schizophrenic symptoms.

Instead, the atypicals have high affinities for D_3 and D_4 receptors. Neither of these receptor subtypes is found in high quantities in the basal ganglia. The D_3 receptor is localized largely in the nucleus accumbens, the terminal point of the mesolimbic projection, with many fewer receptors in the basal ganglia (Landwehrmeyer, Mengod, & Palacios, 1993). The D_4 receptor is localized largely in the cortex, amygdala, and hippocampus—the regions that are important in cognition, emotion, and learning. There are very few, if any, D_4 receptors in human motor systems (Primus et al., 1997). Thus, it is possible for the atypical antipsychotics to depress dopamine activity in the mesolimbic system and treat psychoses without having a great effect on the nigrostriatal system and causing Parkinsonian side effects.

Another major difference between the typicals and the atypicals is the extent to which they bind to 5-HT receptors, especially the 5-HT_{2A} subtype. Both classes of antipsychotics have some 5-HT_{2A} blocking ability, but this activity is much higher for the atypicals. Panel B of Figure 12-2 illustrates the dissociation constants of typical and atypical antipsychotics for D_2 receptors as compared to 5-HT_{2A} receptors. Overall, the typicals tend to have greater effects at D_2 receptors than at 5-HT_{2A} receptors, and the opposite is true for atypical antipsychotic drugs, although there are some notable exceptions to this rule, such as remoxipride.

There is another reason why the effects of atypical antipsychotics on 5-HT_{2A} receptors may be important. Drugs like LSD and psilocybin are agonists at 5-HT_{2A}

receptors and produce psychotic symptoms such as hallucinations. Metabotropic glutamate (mGlu) receptors interact with 5-HT_{2A} receptors to create a functional receptor complex that, when activated by hallucinogenic drugs, triggers unique cellular responses in the cortex (González-Maeso et al., 2008). In untreated schizophrenia, there is an upregulation of 5-HT_{2A} receptors and a downregulation of mGlu receptors, suggesting that an imbalance of 5-HT_{2A} to mGlu receptors may create vulnerability to psychosis. In addition, mGlu knockout mice (mice genetically engineered so that the gene coding for the mGlu receptor is inactivated, i.e., *knocked out*) fail to demonstrate behavioral effects of hallucinogenic drugs (Moreno, Holloway, Albizu, Sealfon, & González-Maeso, 2011). As such, mGlu receptors and, specifically, the 5-HT_{2A}–mGlu receptor complex may be ideal targets for antipsychotic medications.

In addition to their actions on DA and 5-HT, the atypicals affect other neurotransmitter systems, including acetylcholine, histamine, norepinephrine, and peptide transmitters such as GABA (Pira, Mongeau, & Pani, 2004). These additional actions may contribute to their therapeutic efficacy and side effect profiles. For example, the anticholinergic effects of some atypicals, such as olanzapine and clozapine, provide an additional mechanism for reducing EPS. However, some of these additional actions may cause unpleasant or even dangerous effects on the body, as you will read later in this chapter.

The first atypical to come onto the market was *clozapine* (Clozaril), which alleviates the positive, negative, and cognitive symptoms of schizophrenia. Clozapine has a high affinity for D_4 receptors, as well as multiple 5-HT receptor subtypes, muscarinic acetylcholine receptors, and alpha$_1$ adrenergic receptors. As with the other atypicals, clozapine has only a weak affinity for D_2 receptors. Its primary therapeutic effects are thought to result from antagonism of D_4 and 5-HT_{2A} receptors (Meltzer, 1994). Clozapine, and the many other atypicals that have since been developed, are often first used in the United Kingdom or other European countries and are slow to be approved for use in the United States and Canada.

In 2002, the FDA approved a new drug, aripiprazole (Abilify) for the treatment of schizophrenia. This drug is unlike its predecessors and, for that reason, is sometimes referred to as a third-generation antipsychotic. Aripiprazole has a mechanism of action unlike the other

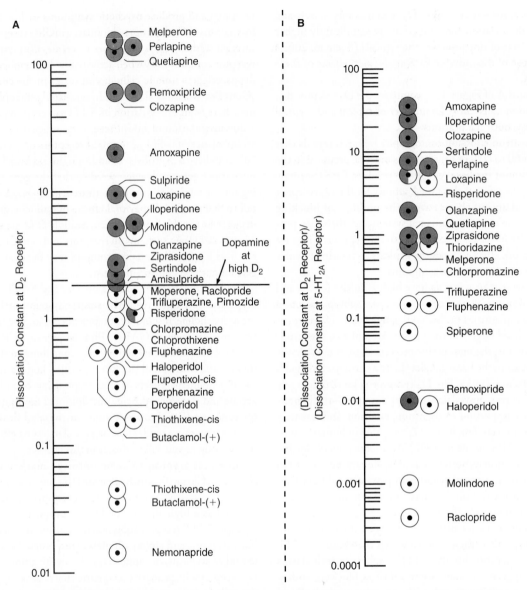

Typical antipsychotics are represented by unshaded rings; atypical antipsychotics are represented by shaded rings. Risperidone, a weak atypical, is half shaded, half unshaded.

FIGURE 12-2 Typical and atypical antipsychotic dissociation constants. Typical antipsychotics are represented by unshaded rings; atypical antipsychotics are represented by shaded rings. Risperidone, a weak atypical, is half shaded, half unshaded. *Panel A*: Typical antipsychotics bind more tightly than dopamine to the D_2 receptor (in its functional high-affinity state), with dissociation constants lower than that of dopamine. The atypical antipsychotics bind more loosely than dopamine to the D_2 receptor, with dissociation constants higher than that of dopamine. Out of the 31 antipsychotics illustrated, there are two or three apparent exceptions to this rule. *Panel B*: Typical and atypical antipsychotics' dissociation constants at D_2 vs. 5-HT_{2A} receptor subtypes. In general, typical antipsychotics have lower dissociation constants at D_2 receptors than at 5-HT_{2A} receptors, and the reverse is true of atypical antipsychotics. However, of the 20 antipsychotics illustrated, there are three or four apparent exceptions. Remoxipride is one of these. (Adapted from Seeman, 2002, Figure 4A and 4B, p. 54; reprinted with permission.)

atypicals. It is a DA receptor partial agonist—it modulates, rather than blocks, dopamine activity at D_2, D_3, and D_4 receptor subtypes. Recall from Chapter 4 that a partial agonist has a high affinity for the receptor to which it binds, but it activates that receptor to a lesser degree than would the natural ligand (i.e., dopamine). Because of this, in regions of the brain where dopamine activity is too low (i.e., in the prefrontal cortex where the mesocortical pathway terminates), aripiprazole acts as an agonist by binding to and increasing the activation of DA receptors. In regions of the brain where dopamine activity is too high (i.e., in the nucleus accumbens where the mesolimbic pathway terminates), aripiprazole acts as an antagonist by preventing DA from binding to its receptors and activating those receptors to a lesser degree. Aripiprazole also acts as a partial agonist or antagonist at various 5-HT receptor subtypes and affects histamine and alpha-adrenergic receptor function. Because aripiprazole stabilizes dopamine activity, it is able to treat positive, negative, and cognitive symptoms of schizophrenia.

In terms of their efficacy in relieving positive, negative, and cognitive symptoms of schizophrenia and their ability to increase quality of life and improve one's overall mental state, the atypicals are not overwhelmingly superior to the typicals. In some cases and for certain symptoms, they may be less efficacious (Leucht, Kissling, & Davis, 2009; Melnik, Soares, Puga, & Atallah, 2010). Overall, their greatest benefit is the lack of EPS they produce.

ROUTES OF ADMINISTRATION

The antipsychotics are usually taken orally, but preparations are available to be given in intramuscular or intravenous injections. They are seldom injected when given as antipsychotics, but they are injected when used as a presurgical or preanesthetic medication because the sedating effects appear more quickly when given parenterally. Intravenous injection also avoids any irregularities or delays in effect arising from erratic absorption from the digestive system. It is doubtful, however, that antipsychotic effects can be significantly speeded by giving the drug parenterally; the antipsychotic effects take several days or weeks to develop. The antipsychotics may be injected in circumstances where it may be difficult to induce agitated schizophrenic patients to take the drugs orally.

Because antipsychotic drugs are often taken chronically and patients do not always take them reliably, they are sometimes given in the form of a slowly dissolving *depot injection* , as described in Chapter 1. Typical antipsychotics (e.g., fluphenazine, haloperidol, and perphenazine) can be dissolved in an oily base, such as sesame, coconut, or synthetic vegetable oil, and injected intramuscularly. Newer atypical antipsychotics administered as depot injections are not suspended in oil. For example, risperidone can be encapsulated in a biodegradable polymeric microsphere preparation, which erodes slowly to release the drug. Olanzapine and paliperidone can be combined with the salt form of pamoic acid (pamoate salt) and suspended in water. Following intramuscular injection, the pamoate salt slowly dissolves to release the drug into the body (Haddad, Lambert, & Lauriello, 2011). A single depot injection of oil-, microsphere-, or crystalline-salt-based preparation may be effective for as long as 4 weeks (Haddad et al., 2011).

ABSORPTION AND DISTRIBUTION

Most antipsychotics are readily absorbed from the digestive system. Once absorbed, they are distributed throughout the body and easily cross placental and blood–brain barriers. Blood protein binding is considerable, and the drugs tend to be absorbed into body fat and released very slowly. Oil-based depots can take weeks or months to reach steady-state levels with regular injections and are slowly eliminated. Depot injections of the atypicals, because they are not dissolved in oil, do not accumulate in body fat over time. Long-acting risperidone reaches peak release at about 28 days. Long-acting olanzapine and paliperidone show peak blood levels after about 2 to 4 days (Haddad et al., 2011).

EXCRETION

The typicals and atypicals undergo extensive metabolism prior to excretion in urine and feces (Sheehan, Sliwa, Amatniek, Grinspan, & Canuso, 2010). There is considerable individual variability in the metabolism of antipsychotics and in the optimal blood concentration. Finding the best dose for any individual is largely a matter of trial and error. Because of their strong protein binding and tendency to stay in body fat, typical antipsychotics have very long half-lives of 11 to 58 hours, and metabolites can be found in the urine months after treatment. This is not the case for the atypicals. Cytochrome P450 enzymes play a major role in the metabolism of antipsychotics. This can be problematic for individuals taking a variety of additional medications, such as antidepressants, mood stabilizers, or anxiolytics, as many of these drugs also rely on cytochrome P450 enzymes for their metabolism. Individuals taking antipsychotics are also at increased risk of renal failure.

EFFECTS OF ANTIPSYCHOTICS

Effects on the Body

The effects of antipsychotics are widely variable, both within an individual taking different drugs and between individuals taking the same drug. Each drug's effectiveness as an antipsychotic and the sorts and intensity of side effects vary considerably from person to person. This is one reason why so many of these drugs are on the market. Psychiatrists may try giving an individual a number of different drugs at different doses until one is found that produces the most favorable therapeutic effect with the fewest side effects.

There is no cure for psychosis, and treatment is lifelong. With prolonged use, antipsychotic medications can take a significant toll on one's body. As we have already seen, the most pronounced side effect of the typical antipsychotics is EPS—alterations in movement that resemble the symptoms of Parkinson's disease. This effect is reported in about 40% of patients on typical antipsychotics. It includes a dulled facial expression, rigidity and tremor in the limbs, loss of coordinated movement, weakness in the extremities, and a slowing of movements. Anti-Parkinson's medications are frequently given to combat these EPS. In addition, about 20% of patients show *akathisia*, a condition characterized by uncontrolled restlessness, constant compulsive movement, and sometimes a protruding tongue and facial grimacing.

Because the typicals accumulate in brain tissue, prolonged use can lead to a neurological condition called *tardive dyskinesia*. It is characterized by involuntary, tic-like, repetitive movements of the face, such as muscle twitching, smacking of the lips, or flicking of the tongue, sometimes dozens of times per minute. Unfortunately, for some individuals, the symptoms of tardive dyskinesia are permanent and do not go away even after the drug is stopped (Enna & Coyle, 1983). Rates of tardive

dyskinesia tend to be higher in elderly individuals and in women. In contrast to the typicals, the atypicals are far less fat-soluble and bind only briefly to D_2 receptors. As a result, their likelihood of causing tardive dyskinesia is extremely low (Seeman, 2002).

With regard to clozapine specifically, a major problem is increased risk of a disorder called *agranulocytosis*, a potentially fatal loss of white blood cells and decline in immune system function due to the suppression of bone marrow activity. It occurs in 1 to 2% of all patients receiving clozapine and can happen at any time. For this reason, patients taking clozapine must be carefully and continuously monitored with frequent blood testing. This serious side effect kept clozapine off the market for many years.

Antipsychotics also seem to cause the body to have trouble regulating temperature, which becomes easily influenced by changes in the environment. In hot environments, patients are more susceptible to heat stroke; in cold climates, they are more vulnerable to hypothermia. The skin also develops an oversensitivity to the sun so that it burns quickly.

Other side effects of typical antipsychotics include weight gain, changes in cardiac function and blood pressure (due to the effect of these drugs on NE receptors), dry mouth, impaired vision, dizziness, constipation (due to anticholinergic effects), and jaundice. In certain susceptible individuals, there is an increased risk of seizures.

Although they produce far fewer EPS than do the typicals, the atypicals have their own set of problematic or even life-threatening side effects. Like the typicals, long-term use of atypicals is associated with disturbances in glucose metabolism and fat regulation, significant weight gain, and onset of diabetes (Üçok & Gaebel, 2008). Increases in triglycerides and cholesterol have also been found in individuals taking clozapine and olanzapine. Like the typicals, the atypicals can produce abnormal cardiac function that can be life threatening, especially in older adults (Mehta, Chen, Johnson, & Aparasu, 2011). The U.S. Food and Drug Administration warns against treating dementia-related psychotic symptoms in the elderly with olanzapine or risperidone due to a near doubling of risk of death related to cardiac dysfunction or respiratory infections. People taking atypical antipsychotics also experience thermodysregulation, dry mouth, dizziness, nausea, and are more prone to developing cataracts.

Aripiprazole has a relative absence of most of the side effects mentioned earlier and, for that reason, has a higher compliance rate compared to typicals and many of the atypicals. Its most significant side effects are nausea and dizziness (Melnik et al., 2010).

Effects on Sleep

Antipsychotics at therapeutic doses have very little effect on sleep, but some antipsychotics that have sedating effects (e.g., chlorpromazine, quetiapine) will increase sleep time when given at high doses or when first administered. The antipsychotics do not alter sleep cycles or REM sleep (Spiegel & Aebi, 1981). There is evidence that the atypicals may increase the risk of obstructive sleep apnea (Shirani, Paradiso, & Dyken, 2011).

Lethal Effects

The antipsychotics produce many side effects, but these drugs are not lethal. In fact, they are extremely safe and have a high therapeutic index (see Chapter 1), about 100. For some antipsychotics, the therapeutic index is as high as 1,000 (Baldessarini, 1985). It is practically impossible to use antipsychotics to commit suicide.

EFFECTS ON THE BEHAVIOR AND PERFORMANCE OF HUMANS

Subjective Effects

Chlorpromazine, when given to healthy subjects, causes a very pronounced feeling of tiredness. Subjects report slower and confused thinking, difficulty concentrating, and feelings of clumsiness. They also report a need for sleep, dejection, anxiety, and irritability. Simple tasks such as walking seem to take great effort.

Haloperidol is not as sedating as chlorpromazine, but, along with other atypical antipsychotic drugs, it makes subjects feel internally aroused and externally sedated at the same time; that is, they feel restless and want to do something but also feel restrained and have difficulty moving (Spiegel & Aebi, 1981).

The subjective experience of antipsychotics is never described as pleasant. This fact is probably responsible for the poor compliance rates with these drugs; patients often do not take them. This does not appear to be true, however, of many of the atypical antipsychotics, such as clozapine (Meltzer, 1990).

Effects on Performance

Reports on the effects of typical antipsychotics on attention and cognitive performance have been variable. Most studies of the acute effects show impairment probably related to sedative effects. Tolerance to these effects has also been reported to occur within 14 days. Clozapine and remoxipride, both atypical antipsychotics, have been shown to interfere with performance. The findings with sulpride, however, have been mixed (King, 1993).

Surprisingly, few studies of the effects of antipsychotics on cognitive functioning have been conducted. Those that were done have been inconclusive, reporting no effect, deficits, or improvements (Judd et al., 1987).

EFFECTS ON THE BEHAVIOR OF NONHUMANS

Effects on Unconditioned Behavior

Unlike the antianxiety drugs, such as the benzodiazepines, the most remarkable effect of the antipsychotic drugs is that they suppress spontaneous movement in an open field, and higher doses render most laboratory animals immobile. In fact, these animals take on a sort of *plastic immobility*. Their limbs will remain in any position in which they are placed, as though the animals were made out of modeling clay. This immobility gave rise to the name *neuroleptic*.

At doses that do not seem to produce these neuroleptic effects, antipsychotic drugs diminish the frequency and intensity of attack behaviors in most species. This decrease in aggression coincides with an overall decrease in activity, so it is possible that it results from an overall debilitation in motor abilities (Miczek & Barry, 1976).

Effects on Conditioned Behavior

In general, the antipsychotic drugs cause a decrease in responding on schedules maintained by positive reinforcement, although at lower doses there are reports that low response rates may be increased. This rate-dependent effect is similar to the effect seen with many other drugs, including amphetamine.

As far back as 1953, when chlorpromazine was first being tested on humans by Laborit, Simone Courvousier and her associates at the Rhône-Poulenc company (Courvoisier, Fournel, Ducrot, Kolsky, & Koetschet, 1953) discovered that the drug would decrease avoidance at doses that would have no effect on escape from a shock, an effect now known to be shared by anti-anxiety drugs such as barbiturates and benzodiazepines. In fact, this was the first time that this technique had been adopted for use in testing drugs, and it has since become one of the most widely used screening devices for new psychotherapeutics (Laties, 1986).

DRUG STATE DISCRIMINATION AND DISSOCIATION

It has been demonstrated that chlorpromazine will cause dissociation. In one study, rats trained on an avoidance task under the influence of chlorpromazine were unable to remember what they had learned when tested under saline but could recall the task when returned to the drug state again (Otis, 1964). This finding has caused some concern among psychotherapists because psychotherapy involves learning, and patients often receive psychotherapy while they are being treated with these drugs. Consequently, when they are taken off the drugs, they may not recall what they learned in psychotherapy.

In drug state discrimination studies, the antipsychotics are not well discriminated. For an antipsychotic to act as a discriminative stimulus, large doses are required, and many more training trials are needed, compared with most other behaviorally active drugs (Overton, 1987; Overton & Batta, 1977).

Once an animal has been trained to discriminate an antipsychotic, the response will generalize to most other antipsychotics at sufficiently high doses. There are some exceptions. For example, a rat trained to discriminate clozapine will not generalize to haloperidol or chlorpromazine (Goas & Boston, 1978). There is no generalization between the antipsychotics and the antidepressants or any other class of drugs (Stewart, 1962).

TOLERANCE

Once a therapeutic dose has been established for a patient, it is often maintained for years without any decrease in effectiveness. Haloperidol's ability to increase dopamine release in the cortex does decline with prolonged use; clozapine does not show tolerance of this sort (Advokat, 2005). Tolerance seems to develop to the sedating effects of antipsychotics when first given, and tolerance also seems to develop to the EPS.

WITHDRAWAL

Physical dependence, if it occurs at all, is rare or mild. There are reports of muscular discomfort, exaggeration of psychotic symptoms and movement disorders, and difficulty sleeping when some antipsychotics are suddenly withdrawn, but such effects are not normally seen even after years of use at normal doses. It is possible that the failure to notice withdrawal symptoms is due to the extremely slow excretion of the drug from the body (Baldessarini, 1985). In an examination of 28 patients who abruptly discontinued clozapine use, 11 showed no withdrawal symptoms at all, 12 showed mild symptoms that included headache and nausea, 4 experienced more significant symptoms including vomiting and diarrhea, and 1 experienced a rapid reemergence of psychotic symptoms (Shiovitz et al., 1996).

SELF-ADMINISTRATION IN HUMANS AND NONHUMANS

As we learned in Chapter 5, some drugs have aversive properties, and antipsychotic drugs appear to be included in this group. In one experiment, monkeys learned to bar press to avoid infusions. At first, the monkeys did not respond to avoid chlorpromazine; after a week, they were successfully avoiding 90% of the programmed infusions. It appears that the aversive properties of chlorpromazine develop slowly, with repeated doses (Hoffmeister & Wuttke, 1975).

Experience with humans is similar. The antipsychotics are never abused; in fact, they are a class of drugs that have considerable compliance problems. *Compliance* refers to the extent to which a patient adheres to a regimen of medical treatment. In the case of typical antipsychotics, most schizophrenic patients show poor compliance; they often stop taking their medication, with the usual result that their symptoms reappear. For this reason, various administration techniques have been developed that do not depend on the patient's compliance. Among them is administration of depot injections, which slowly release the drug and maintain the appropriate blood levels. Noncompliance is slightly less of a problem with the atypical antipsychotics.

HARMFUL EFFECTS

Reproduction

Antipsychotics can have serious effects on reproductive functions. In males, antipsychotics reduce sexual interest, an effect that may arise from their sedative properties. Sexual performance may also be impaired. The primary difficulty is a failure to ejaculate; erection and orgasm are unaffected. These problems arise from cholinergic, adrenergic, histaminergic, and dopaminergic properties of the antipsychotics and their effect on hormone levels (Üçok & Gaebel, 2008; Woods, 1984). Recall from Chapter 4 that, in the *tuberoinfundibular pathway,* dopamine acts as a neurohormone to inhibit the release of prolactin from lactotroph cells of the pituitary. Prolactin suppresses male sexual activity. Drugs like cocaine, which activate this system, can stimulate male sexual performance by suppressing prolactin release, but the antipsychotics, which block D_2 receptors on lactotroph cells, cause excess release of prolactin. This is less of a concern with the atypicals, although risperidone elicits elevations in prolactin levels to a similar extent as the typicals (Üçok & Gaebel, 2008).

In females, there may be abnormal menstrual cycles and infertility. In both males and females, there is sometimes an enlargement of the breasts and fluid discharge from the nipples (Woods, 1984).

OTHER THERAPEUTIC EFFECTS OF ANTIPSYCHOTIC DRUGS

Antipsychotic drugs are useful in the treatment of other medical problems and forms of mental illness. They are effective *antiemetics*; that is, they prevent nausea and vomiting and are useful in the treatment of motion sickness. In addition, they were originally developed by Laborit as presurgical and preanesthetic medications and are still used for that purpose.

A number of movement disorders thought to result from excessive dopamine activity in the brain can, not surprisingly, be treated effectively with antipsychotics. These disorders include *Huntington's chorea*, an inherited degenerative disease. Huntington's is fatal, but antipsychotics help control some of the symptoms. Antipsychotics are also useful in treating *Tourette's syndrome*; Tourette's patients show involuntary muscle tics, twitches, and vocalizations. Surprisingly, antipsychotics are also used to treat tardive dyskinesia.

Antipsychotics have also been used to treat hiccups, stuttering, delirium tremens caused by alcohol withdrawal, and psychotic behaviors induced by psychomotor stimulants, LSD, and other hallucinogens. Atypicals, including aripiprazole, have been used in the treatment of major depressive disorder, bipolar disorder, mania, and irritability in autistic children.

Antidepressants

THE NATURE OF DEPRESSION

From time to time, we all feel sad or "depressed" as a result of things that happen to us or to those we love, but this condition is not usually accompanied by physical symptoms, and it does not last. For some people, depression is much more serious; there may be no apparent cause in their environment, but their depression is deep, and either it does not go away or it keeps returning for no obvious reason. These people may also experience a loss of appetite, loss of interest in normally pleasurable activities (this is called *anhedonia*), lack of energy, problems sleeping, exaggerated feelings of worthlessness and guilt, and haunting thoughts of death and suicide. The symptoms just described are typical of a *major depressive episode*, which is the defining feature of *major depressive disorder*. Major depressive disorder, or more colloquially *depression*, is currently categorized in the *DSM-IV-TR* as a *mood disorder*, and Box 13-1 presents a summary of the *DSM-IV-TR* symptoms for major depressive episode.

As you learned in Chapter 5, the American Psychiatric Association plans to publish a new edition of the *DSM* (the *DSM-5*) in 2013. The *DSM-5* will include revisions to the diagnostic criteria for major depressive episode (see the *DSM-5* Web site at: www.dsm5.org/ProposedRevisions/Pages/proposedrevision.aspx?rid=427#). One proposed revision is the removal of criterion E, related to symptoms of bereavement. This decision is based on findings that depression brought on by bereavement is similar to depression triggered by any other stressful experience. Failure to acknowledge, diagnose, or treat depression because it stems from the loss of a loved one is therefore inappropriate (Kendler, Myers, & Zisook, 2008).

Individuals who chronically experience a mildly depressed state but do not meet the full criteria for major depressive episode may be diagnosed with *dysthymic disorder*. An additional proposed change for the *DSM-5* is to split and rename the mood disorders category, shifting major depressive disorder and dysthymic disorder into a new category called *depressive disorders*.

Another interesting characteristic of depression is that it can occur in persons who do not actually feel depressed. Often older people show many of the physical symptoms of depression—insomnia, weight loss, and so on—but do not seem to feel sad. They may, however, show anhedonia. This type of depression can also be treated with antidepressant medications.

Traditionally, mild depression was labeled *neurotic depression*, and serious depression accompanied by physical symptoms was considered a *psychosis*. *DSM-IV-TR* no longer makes this distinction or considers depression to be psychotic, but it does recognize that depression may be associated with schizophrenia. In such cases, the depressed person will also exhibit hallucinations, delusions, or other symptoms of psychosis.

Recorded accounts of depression span millennia, from the ancient Greeks to contemporary cultures and societies. Because large segments of the population experience

BOX 13-1   *DSM-IV-TR* Criteria for Major Depressive Episode

A. Five (or more) of the following symptoms have been present during the same two-week period and represent a change from previous functioning; at least one of the symptoms is either (1) depressed mood or (2) loss of interest in pleasure.

  1. depressed mood most of the day, nearly every day, as indicated by either subjective report (e.g., feels sad or empty) or observation made by others (e.g., appears tearful)
  2. markedly diminished interest in pleasure in all, or almost all, activities most of the day, nearly every day
  3. significant weight loss when not dieting or weight gain (e.g., a change of more than 5% body weight in a month) or decrease or increase in appetite nearly every day
  4. insomnia or hypersomnia nearly every day
  5. psychomotor agitation or retardation nearly every day
  6. fatigue or loss of energy nearly every day
  7. feelings of worthlessness or excessive or inappropriate guilt nearly every day
  8. diminished ability to think or concentrate, or indecisiveness, nearly every day
  9. recurrent thoughts of death (not just fear of dying), recurrent suicidal ideation without a specific plan, or a suicide attempt or a specific plan for committing suicide

B. The symptoms do not meet the criteria for a Mixed Episode.*

C. Symptoms cause clinically significant distress or impairment in social, occupational, or other important areas of functioning.

D. Symptoms are not due to direct physiological effects of a substance (e.g., a drug of abuse or medication) or a general medical condition.

E. Symptoms are not better accounted for by bereavement, i.e., after the loss of a loved one, the symptoms persist for longer than 2 months or are characterized by marked functional impairment, morbid preoccupation with worthlessness, suicidal ideation, psychotic symptoms, or psychomotor retardation.

*A mixed episode is where both manic and depressive symptoms occur at the same time.

Source: Reprinted with permission from American Psychiatric Association. © 2000, *DSM-IV-TR* Criteria for a Major Depressive Episode.

---

it at some time in their lives, depression has been called the "common cold of mental illness". In Western cultures, depression is ever more prevalent in each generation since World War II. The World Health Organization is projecting that, by the year 2030, depression will be the leading cause of premature mortality and disability leading to loss of productive life; currently, it is the second leading cause. In the United States, Canada, and Europe, approximately 13 to 17% of the population will experience depression at some point in their lifetime (Kessler, Chiu, Demler, Merikangas, & Walters, 2005). The prevalence is much lower in Eastern cultures, such as Korea or Taiwan, where depression estimates are approximately 4% (Chang et al., 2008).

Women are twice as likely as men to suffer depression (depression affects approximately 24% of women and 12% of men), and the symptoms of depression also typically differ between the genders. Women with

depression are more likely to have feelings of sadness, worthlessness, and excessive guilt whereas, men are more likely to be very tired and irritable, lose interest in once-pleasurable activities, and have difficulty sleeping (Cochran & Rabinowitz, 2000). Men may be more likely than women to turn to alcohol or drugs when they are depressed. They also may become frustrated, discouraged, irritable, angry, and sometimes abusive. Compared to the general population, there is an increased overall mortality rate for depressed people, and the probability of suicide is estimated to be five times greater (Bostwick & Pankratz, 2000). More than 90% of individuals who attempt suicide and 60% of those who commit suicide suffer from some form of mood disorder (Beautrais et al., 1996). Although women report more thoughts and attempts at suicide, men more often die of suicidal injuries.

THEORIES OF DEPRESSION

Monoamine Theory of Depression

It has been known for some time that mood is related to the functioning of the monoamines, in particular, serotonin (5-HT) and norepinephrine (NE), although dopamine (DA) may also play a role. Recall that all of the monoamine neurotransmitters have centers in the midbrain or upper brainstem and send projections forward to various parts of the limbic system and the forebrain through the *medial forebrain bundle*: (a) NE fibers that arise in the *locus coeruleus* in the midbrain, (b) serotonergic fibers that originate in areas of the *raphe system*, and (c) dopaminergic fibers of the mesocorticolimbic system that originate in the *ventral tegmental area.*

The *monoamine theory* of depression, in its original form, suggested that depression was a result of reduced levels of activity in these monoamine systems. The theory was supported by observations that changing monoamine activity levels affected mood. Drugs like cocaine or amphetamine that enhance monoamine neurotransmission make people feel good. Alternatively, decreased transmission at monoamine synapses is associated with depression. Depression is the most common psychiatric condition in individuals with Parkinson's disease, which is marked by severe depletion of dopamine (Ravina et al., 2009). The drug reserpine, which was once used to treat high blood pressure, depletes monoamines by blocking the activity of vesicular transporter proteins that reside in the axon terminals where they fill synaptic vesicles with monoamines. Coincidently, individuals administered reserpine showed improvement in their hypertensive symptoms but developed severe depression (reserpine is no longer prescribed). Similarly, depleting 5-HT by ridding its amino acid precursor, tryptophan, from the body also produces depression. All of these findings support the monoamine theory of depression.

There are, however, some observations that cannot be explained by the monoamine theory, as it originally existed. For example, we know that antidepressant medications produce an immediate physiological effect. That is, as soon as the drug reaches monoamine synapses, it increases transmitter levels. But, as with antipsychotic medications, there is a substantial problem. The effect on monoamine activity is immediate, but antidepressants need to be taken continuously before any relief from depression is felt. This lag time between the start of antidepressant treatment and any alleviation of depressive symptoms can be 4 to 6 weeks and perhaps up to 12 weeks by the time antidepressants reach their full effectiveness. In the context of the original monoamine theory, which simply stated that depression is a result of diminished monoamine activity, this does not make sense. Another finding that cannot be explained by the original monoamine theory is that the above-mentioned correlation between tryptophan depletion and depression does not hold true for everyone. In individuals with no personal or family history of depression, tryptophan depletion has no effect on mood (Riedel, Klaassen, & Schmitt, 2002). This suggests that other physiological differences must exist between those individuals who are susceptible to depression and those who are not. Therefore, the monoamine theory, in its simple form, is no longer tenable—the neurophysiological changes associated with depression are much more complicated than first thought. A wealth of research has advanced our understanding of the role monoamines play in mood disorders, and the monoamine theory in its updated form, as described later, continues to receive much support and attention.

All of the three monoamines are probably involved in some aspect of mood, and they interact with each other in complex ways, but the monoamine that has received the most focus in the past couple of decades is serotonin. Decreased activity in the serotonin system, although it may not be the direct cause of depression, certainly appears to play a role in vulnerability to depression. Many lines of research support this idea. For example, individuals diagnosed with major depressive disorder have low cerebrospinal-fluid levels of 5-HT, its amino acid precursor tryptophan, and its major metabolite 5-H1AA. Below-normal levels of 5-H1AA also correspond with a nearly fivefold increase in suicide risk (Pompili et al., 2010). Treatments that have been shown to be effective in relieving depression ultimately increase transmission at serotonin synapses.

SPECT imaging data indicate that depressed individuals also exhibit decreased numbers of 5-HT reuptake transporter proteins in the brainstem (Malison et al., 1998). At first glance, this appears counterintuitive. Because reuptake transporter proteins rid 5-HT from the synapse, a reduction in their quantity would seem like a protective mechanism, decreasing vulnerability to depression. Moreover, antidepressants such as the SSRIs are effective because they inhibit the action of serotonin reuptake transporter proteins; with chronic treatment, SSRIs significantly reduce (i.e., by 30–40%) the amount of 5-HT transporter protein mRNA in the raphe nuclei (Lesch et al., 1993).

To understand this finding, we must consider the bigger picture—what this deficiency in 5-HT transporter proteins actually illustrates. Quite possibly, it indicates a pathological reduction in the sheer number of serotonin neurons (upon which the transporter proteins reside). Even a slight reduction in the number of raphe serotonergic neurons would translate into an exponentially greater loss of 5-HT release in projection areas, such as the cortex. It may also be an indication of a more widespread dysregulation of serotonin system function. In support of this explanation, genetic research has isolated a portion of a gene, found on chromosome 17, responsible for 5-HT transporter protein production. This portion of the gene, called a *promoter region*, regulates the number of 5-HT transporter proteins that get made. It comes in two forms—long and short. Possessing the short form of this portion of gene is associated with having significantly fewer 5-HT transporter proteins and a heightened risk of developing depression, whereas possessing the long form appears to create a protective effect. Finally, a reduction in 5-HT reuptake transporter protein quantity could indicate a compensatory mechanism, an attempt by neurons to overcome a preexisting state of synaptic 5-HT hypoactivity by reducing 5-HT reuptake activity (Malison et al., 1998).

Depressed individuals also exhibit abnormalities in the functioning and quantity of 5-HT receptors, particularly for the 5-HT$_{1A}$ receptor subtype. Much of this evidence comes from PET imaging studies that measure the *binding potential* of 5-HT$_{1A}$ receptors. Differences in receptor binding potential could indicate an upregulation or downregulation in the density of receptors present on neurons, a change in the sensitivity of the receptors to neurotransmitter molecules, or it could indicate an increase or decrease in the presence of neurons containing those receptors. This area of research is hotly debated because some evidence suggests increases and some suggests decreases in 5-HT$_{1A}$ receptor binding potential in depression. The debate may be, at least in part, due to the different brain regions analyzed by researchers and to the varying roles 5-HT plays in those brain regions.

Remember that 5-HT$_{1A}$ receptors act, not only as postsynaptic receptors, but also as autoreceptors. In the raphe nuclei, 5-HT$_{1A}$ receptors are mostly autoreceptors, located on the presynaptic neuron. Stimulation of those receptors inhibits cell firing and reduces 5-HT activity. In other brain regions, such as the hippocampus, hypothalamus, amygdala, and cortex, 5-HT$_{1A}$ receptors are located postsynaptically. Stimulation of those receptors increases serotonin neurotransmission. Changes in the sensitivity or number of 5-HT$_{1A}$ receptors could result from genetic makeup, rendering the individual more vulnerable to depression. Or, these changes might represent an adaptive response to depression—a way for the brain to compensate for abnormal levels of serotonin activity, perhaps triggered by some physiological or environmental event. As you can see, when it comes to serotonin and depression, it is very difficult to tease apart cause and effect among the myriad of influencing variables.

The increase in serotonin transmission produced by antidepressant medications appears to be a necessary, but not sufficient, condition for alleviating depression. It is believed that, in serotonergic synapses at least, increased levels of transmitter do not result in an immediate increase in cell firing. The presynaptic cell, through the action of autoreceptors, detects excessive amounts of transmitter in the cleft brought about by the antidepressant medication. When the autoreceptor detects increased amounts of transmitter, it actually inhibits the release of more 5-HT (typically by reducing the influx of calcium at the terminal). Thus, acute administration of reuptake inhibitors like the SSRIs does not cause an immediate increase in conduction at 5-HT synapses. It takes a few weeks for the autoreceptors to habituate to the presence of excess 5-HT, and only then does serotonergic conduction at the synapse actually increase. With chronic treatment, antidepressants are able to enhance the sensitivity and functioning of 5-HT$_{1A}$ postsynaptic receptors, leading to increased monoamine activity (Drevets et al., 2007). In addition, there is a downregulation and desensitization of 5-HT$_{1A}$ autoreceptors, which acts to decrease cell inhibition resulting from the antidepressant-induced rise in monoamine levels and thereby enhance monoamine neurotransmission. The delay experienced with other classes of antidepressants may result from similar adjustment mechanisms.

The bulk of evidence supports the theory that depression is a result of diminished activity in the 5-HT system in the brain, which runs from the raphe nuclei through the medial forebrain bundle to the forebrain. The situation is very complicated, however, and many other explanations of depression exist. In the mid-1990s, antidepressant medications that target both serotonin and norepinephrine were introduced. Like 5-HT, NE activity is also dysregulated in depression, and more recently developed antidepressants target the NE system. In addition, altered transmission of serotonin, and perhaps even norepinephrine and dopamine, may be caused by, and may in turn cause changes in, activity of other transmitter systems—even some that do not use monoamines. Alternate theories of depression cite the importance of different neurotransmitters, such as GABA, acetylcholine, opioid peptides, and cannabinoids, and the balance achieved among levels of these neurotransmitters (Uppal, Singh, Gahtori, Ghosh, & Ahmad, 2010). Activity at monoamine synapses may in fact be only one link in a long and complex chain of neurological deficiencies that cause mood disorders.

Still other theories suggest the involvement of second messengers, biological rhythms, hormone levels, and the immune system. Among these, one theory that has garnered substantial support and warrants attention is a theory based on stress—the glucocorticoid theory of depression.

Glucocorticoid Theory of Depression

A system that has become a major focus of depression research is the *hypothalamic–pituitary–adrenal* (HPA) axis, illustrated in Figure 13-1. It is an important part of the neuroendocrine system that controls the body's response to stress. Stress is the most influential environmental factor that predisposes an individual to depression, so it is not surprising that research would veer in this direction. The HPA-axis response to stress is organized hierarchically so that the physiological changes that take place are like a domino effect. The stress response starts in the hypothalamus where neurons

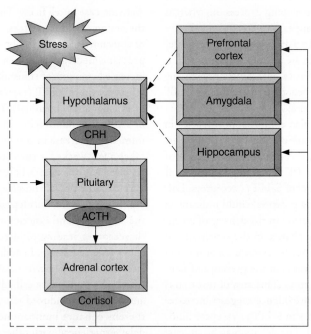

Solid lines indicate stimulation; Dashed lines indicate inhibition
CRH: corticotropin-releasing hormone; ACTH: adrenocorticotropic hormone

FIGURE 13-1   The hypothalamic–pituitary–adrenal axis and connections.

secrete corticotropin-releasing hormone (CRH). The release of CRH, in turn, initiates the release of adrenocorticotropic hormone (ACTH) from the anterior pituitary, which ultimately stimulates the secretion of glucocorticoids (cortisol in humans) from the cortex of the adrenal glands, which sit above the kidneys.

The stress response is important for our survival since it mobilizes us for fight or flight and helps us escape danger. Once a stressful experience ends, the HPA-axis response must be terminated. This is achieved through a series of negative-feedback loops—cortisol binds to glucocorticoid receptors in the pituitary, hypothalamus, and especially in the hippocampus, which then sends a signal to the hypothalamus to stop releasing CRH. In individuals who experience frequent or chronic stress, the HPA axis may become overactive. Animal research suggests that chronic-stress-induced hyperactivity of the HPA axis is due, at least in part, to a downregulation of glucocorticoid receptors in the hippocampus (Meyer, van Kampen, Isovich, Flügge, & Fuchs, 2001). Overactivity of the HPA axis, indicated by high levels of CRH and cortisol, is a frequent finding in patients with major depressive disorder and in suicide victims (Paez-Pereda, Hausch, & Holsboer, 2011).

Neurons that contain CRH are present, not only in the hypothalamus, but also in areas of the limbic system. Recall that the limbic system plays an important role in emotion and mood. One such limbic area is the prefrontal cortex, which, like the hippocampus, contains receptor sites for CRH and cortisol and sends inhibitory projections to the hypothalamus. Another limbic area is the amygdala, which, you will recall, plays an important role in fear and anxiety. The amygdala also contains receptors for HPA-axis stress hormones but sends excitatory projections to the hypothalamus. A very common finding in patients with depression is structural change in areas of the limbic system. These changes are believed to result from high levels of cortisol circulating through the bloodstream and entering the brain. In depression, both the prefrontal cortex and the hippocampus lose volume (i.e., they *atrophy*), whereas the amygdala increases in volume. Increases in metabolism and blood flow to the amygdala are related to the severity of depressive symptoms (Peluso et al., 2009).

Because the prefrontal cortex, hippocampus, and amygdala are interconnected with the hypothalamus, structural changes lead to a loss of balance between inhibition and excitation of the stress system, resulting in heightened stress hormone release. Heightened HPA-axis activity and resulting elevation of stress hormone levels substantially increases one's risk of depression and suicide. Investigation of the therapeutic potential of CRH receptor antagonists has produced mixed results. In some clinical trials, patients with major depressive disorder experienced significant reduction of depressive symptoms with CRH antagonists. In other trials, CRH receptor antagonists fared no better than a placebo. It may be that CRH antagonists benefit only those individuals whose depression is brought on by stress and resulting hyperactivity of the HPA axis (Paez-Pereda et al., 2011).

Two Sides of the Same Coin

You may be wondering whether the monoamine or glucocorticoid theory offers the best explanation of the physiological changes that take place in depression. It may be more appropriate, instead, to think about these theories as representing two sides of the same coin. This is because stress hormones interact in complex ways with monoamine systems, including DA, NE, and 5-HT. For example, dopamine and glucocorticoid receptors coexist in neurons of the ventral tegmental area that project to the nucleus accumbens (Ahima & Harlan, 1990). Under chronic stress, heightened cortisol levels encourage DA release and structural change within the mesolimbic DA system. One such change is an upregulation of DA receptors in the ventral tegmental area (Czyrak, Mackowiak, Chocyk, Fijal, & Wedzony, 2003).

CRH neurons originating in the amygdala are directly and indirectly connected to areas of the hindbrain and midbrain, including the serotonin-containing raphe nuclei and the norepinephrine-containing locus coeruleus. During stressful events, amygdala activity overrides that of the prefrontal cortex and activates stress pathways in the hypothalamus and brainstem, leading to increased levels of monoamines and perhaps even upregulation of their receptors. Therefore, any change in the structure or activity of the amygdala has the potential to produce changes in the functioning of monoamine systems.

Changes in glucocorticoid levels are also strongly associated with changes in 5-HT function. You have read that depressed individuals often demonstrate abnormalities in the number and function of 5-HT$_{1A}$ receptors, but the exact nature of this relationship is hotly debated. One finding that is well established is the link between stress, high levels of HPA-axis stress hormones, and a reduction in both number and function of postsynaptic 5-HT_{1A} receptors in the hippocampus (Drevets et al., 2007). Adrenalectomy (surgery to remove the adrenal glands and thereby rid the body of cortisol) increases 5-HT_{1A} receptor densities and binding (Grino et al., 1987), whereas 2 weeks of chronic stress (and elevated levels of cortisol) decreases 5-HT_{1A} receptor densities and binding in the rat hippocampus (López, Chalmers, Little, & Watson, 1998). This suggests that changes in 5-HT neurotransmission may actually be the result of hypersecretion of stress hormones, especially cortisol.

Research in patients with major depressive disorder suggests that abnormal HPA-axis function precedes the onset of clinical symptoms of depression. It may be that certain individuals are genetically predisposed to develop HPA-axis hyperactivity. In a study that spanned 2 decades, researchers discovered that the number of childhood and adolescent stressful experiences correlated with the development of depression and suicidal ideation. Moreover, this correlation was strongest in individuals with the short form of the 5-HT transporter protein gene (Caspi et al., 2003). Possessing the short form of the 5-HT transporter protein gene also makes people more susceptible to depression resulting from childhood maltreatment (Uher et al., 2011). The experience of stress, perhaps early in life, triggers and sensitizes the stress system so that when stressors occur later in life, the HPA axis overreacts.

Those patients who get relief from depressive symptoms are also those who show normalization of HPA-axis functioning. Antidepressant medications reduce HPA-axis activity by increasing the number of cortisol receptors to create more efficient negative-feedback loops. As a result, the stress-induced rise in glucocorticoid levels is blunted and shortened, and decreases in 5-HT_{1A} receptor densities and binding that occur with elevated stress hormone levels are prevented. This normalization of HPA-axis activity precedes the alleviation of depressive symptoms. Patients who show improvement with antidepressant medication but whose HPA-axis function fails to normalize are more likely to relapse into depression. This suggests that normalizing the stress response may be a necessary condition in order for antidepressants to work (Paez-Pereda et al., 2011). It is clear, then, that the interaction between HPA-axis stress hormones and monoamine neurotransmitters, perhaps especially 5-HT, is important in linking stressful events with the development of depression.

HISTORY OF ANTIDEPRESSANT MEDICATIONS

There are several types of antidepressants. The classes of antidepressant drugs discussed next, along with examples from each class, can be found in Table 13-1 (some of these may not be approved for use in parts of Europe or North America). The first drugs that were successfully used to treat depression were the *monoamine oxidase inhibitors* (MAOIs) and the *tricyclic antidepressants* (TCAs). Consequently, these two classes are referred to as *first-generation antidepressants*.

The first antidepressant ever marketed was an MAOI called *iproniazid*, developed in the late 1950s. Before its antidepressant properties were realized, iproniazid was used in the treatment of tuberculosis (TB). Physicians noticed a great improvement in the mood of TB patients that was separate from the relief of their TB symptoms, and the drug was redeveloped for its antidepressant properties. When MAOIs were first introduced, they became widely used. But in a few years, the initial enthusiasm waned because of several factors.

To begin with, iproniazid was taken off the market soon after it was released because of reports that it caused liver damage. It turned out that the liver damage occurred only because the doses used were too high. In addition, some clinical studies concluded that MAOIs were ineffective. Once again, these reports were unfounded. The studies used inadequate research design, and we now know that the doses studied were too low. It is now known that MAOIs are just as effective as any other treatment for depression. Up to 70% of patients who fail to respond to newer classes of antidepressants show improvements in mood with MAOIs. New MAOIs are more specific in their actions, they are reversible, they are much less likely to interact with diet (discussed later), and they do not cause liver damage at therapeutic doses. This class of drugs is regaining a role as an effective and relatively safe treatment for depression.

The tricyclic antidepressants are so named because their molecular structure contains three rings of atoms. The tricyclics were also discovered by accident, during research on antipsychotic drugs (see Chapter 12); the first of these was *imipramine*. In the late 1950s,

TABLE 13-1 First- and Second-Generation Antidepressants

Drug Class	Generic Name	Trade Name
Monoamine oxidase inhibitors (MAOIs)	iproniazid	Euphozid
	phenelzine	Nardil
	tranylcypromine	Parnate
	isocarboxazid	Marplan
	selegiline	Eldepryl
	moclobemide	Aurorix
Tricyclic antidepressants (TCAs)	imipramine	Tofranil
	amitriptyline	Elavil
	desipramine	Norpramin
	doxepin	Sinequan
	nortriptyline	Pamelor
	clomipramine	Anafranil
Selective serotonin reuptake inhibitors (SSRIs)	fluoxetine	Prozac
	citalopram	Celexa
	escitalopram	Lexapro
	paroxetine	Paxil
	sertraline	Zoloft

imipramine was tested on psychiatric patients, and although it did not improve symptoms of schizophrenia, it did elevate the mood of depressed patients. Because the tricyclics were considered safer than the early MAOIs, many more were developed, and their use became common in the treatment of depression.

The popularity of the tricyclics was overshadowed by the introduction of a newer class of drugs that worked differently from the MAOIs or TCAs. This diverse group of chemicals is often called *second-generation antidepressants* and includes the *selective serotonin reuptake inhibitors* (SSRIs). The first and probably most well-known SSRI to be marketed is *fluoxetine* (Prozac). Its structure is only slightly different from that of imipramine and the other TCAs. Yet the SSRIs appeared safer with fewer of the bothersome side effects of the first-generation antidepressants and could be used to treat a variety of psychiatric conditions, such as anxiety, that frequently co-occur with depression.

Prozac was introduced in the United States in 1987 and soon received considerable attention in the popular media because it was being used not to treat depression but as a means of altering personality (more on this

later). The media also carried reports that the drug could precipitate violent acts and suicide. If such adverse effects occur, however, they are extremely rare. Fluoxetine and other SSRIs are often a first-line treatment for depression. Although many second-generation antidepressants have been used in Europe, strict drug development laws have delayed or prevented their use in North America.

Riding on the success of second-generation antidepressants, the *third-generation antidepressants*, sometimes called the *atypicals*, are the more recently approved medications used to fight depression. These drugs include the *serotonin and norepinephrine reuptake inhibitors* (SNRIs) that affect the functioning of both of those monoamines. Enhancing NE activity, through stimulation of the reticular activating system, is helpful for those individuals who exhibit symptoms of fatigue and loss of energy associated with depression. Third-generation antidepressants do not alter the functioning of muscarinic acetylcholine receptors and therefore do not produce some of the side effects associated with older antidepressants. Some of the atypicals do affect nicotinic acetylcholine and histamine receptor functioning and influence the dopamine system. Examples of these drugs and their

TABLE 13-2   Third-Generation Antidepressants/Atypicals

Generic Name	Trade Name	Mechanism of Action
venlafaxine	Effexor	5-HT and NE reuptake blockade, DA reuptake blockade only at high doses
desvenlafaxine*	Pristiq	5-HT and NE reuptake blockade
duloxetine	Cymbalta	5-HT, NE, and DA reuptake blockade
mirtazapine	Remeron	NE α_2 autoreceptor and 5-HT$_{1A}$ autoreceptor blockade; 5-HT$_{2-3}$ receptor antagonist; histamine H1 receptor antagonist
nefazodone	Serzone	5-HT and NE reuptake blockade; 5-HT$_{2-3}$ receptor antagonist
amoxapine	Asendin	NE reuptake blockade
bupropion	Wellbutrin; Zyban	DA reuptake blockade; partial NE reuptake blockade; ACh nicotinic receptor antagonist
maprotiline	Ludiomil	NE reuptake blockade
reboxetine	Norebox, Edronax	NE reuptake blockade
trazodone	Desyrel	5-HT reuptake blockade, 5-HT$_2$ receptor antagonist

*Major metabolite of venlafaxine.

mechanisms of action can be found in Table 13-2 (some of these may not be approved for use in parts of Europe or North America).

NEUROPHYSIOLOGY

Antidepressants generally work by increasing activity in one or more of the monoamine systems of the brain. In addition, other transmitter systems may be affected. There are several ways that they can do this, and antidepressants are usually classified by their principal mechanism of action. Regardless of the class of antidepressant, alleviation of depressive symptoms comes weeks after treatment begins. It is believed that this lag time is the result of the neuroadaptations that must take place before symptoms (specifically, the downregulation of 5-HT$_{1A}$ autoreceptors and increase in serotonin system function; Uppal et al., 2010).

First-Generation Antidepressants: MAOIs and TCAs

All monoamine neurons produce the enzyme *monoamine oxidase* (MAO). This enzyme degrades monoamine molecules that float freely (i.e., those that are outside of vesicles) in the cytoplasm of the axon terminal, thereby depleting available neurotransmitter. The MAOIs do exactly what their name implies—they inhibit (block) the activity of monoamine oxidase so that molecules of DA, NE, and 5-HT that float freely in the cytoplasm are not destroyed but, instead, are available for vesicle storage and later release. Thus, MAOIs increase the availability and activity of DA, NE, and 5-HT. There are actually two types of MAO: *MAO-A* degrades all three monoamines, whereas *MAO-B* is most active in metabolizing DA. The effect of the older MAOIs was nonselective and irreversible–they inhibited both MAO-A and MAO-B, and their effects persisted for several days or weeks, even when the drug was not taken, until enzyme stores became replenished. Because both forms of MAO enzymes are present throughout the body, the nonselective MAOIs produced numerous unpleasant side effects. Some newer MAOIs, such as selegiline, act selectively on MAO-B at low doses and, at higher doses, affects MAO-A. In addition, some newer MAOIs are reversible, meaning that they can detach from MAO rather than deactivate it permanently.

Although they are grouped with the MAOIs as first-generation antidepressants, the tricyclics are actually more similar in function to the second- and third-generation SSRIs and SNRIs. Their principal mechanism of action is to block reuptake transporter proteins on the terminal buttons of 5-HT and NE neurons so that, after these monoamines are released into the cleft by an action potential, their reuptake is inhibited and their duration of action on the postsynaptic cell is prolonged. At one point it was believed that all tricyclics worked in the same way, but there are now many drugs that have the three-ring structure of the tricyclics but produce various effects on functioning of other monoamines (Ordway, Klimek, & Mann, 2002). In addition, the TCAs affect other transmitter systems—they act as anticholinergics, blocking muscarinic acetylcholine receptors, and they antagonize histamine and α_1 adrenergic receptors. Although the TCAs are a safer and sometimes more effective alternative to the MAOIs, these additional actions can produce unpleasant and even dangerous side effects in some people.

Second- and Third-Generation Antidepressants: SSRIs and SNRIs/Atypicals

As their name suggests, the SSRIs, through blockade of reuptake transporter proteins, diminish the ability of presynaptic cells to reabsorb and recycle 5-HT. This causes a buildup of 5-HT at synapses and prolongs postsynaptic receptor stimulation. This action is specific to 5-HT; the SSRIs have minimal effect on other monoamines or other neurotransmitters, such as histamine and acetylcholine. SSRIs are not selective as to which serotonin receptor they bind. It is believed that the antidepressant effects of the SSRIs result from changes to 5-HT_{1A} receptor functioning whereas the unpleasant side effects of the SSRIs may be due to activation of 5-HT_2 receptors.

The SNRIs and atypicals block the reuptake of 5-HT, NE, and in some cases DA. For example, bupropion, which blocks DA reuptake transporter proteins, is used to treat depression (Wellbutrin) and also as a smoking cessation aid (Zyban). In addition to its dopaminergic actions, bupropion affects the functioning of NE and ACh. Some newer antidepressants, like mirtazapine, act by antagonizing autoreceptors, specifically for NE and 5-HT, to prevent inhibitory feedback to the cell and thereby increase the amount of transmitter released. In addition, mirtazapine and some other atypicals block histamine receptors to induce sedation and drowsiness in those individuals who experience difficulty falling and staying asleep.

ABSORPTION

The MAOIs, tricyclics, and many second- and third-generation antidepressants have similar absorption pharmacokinetics. The TCAs reach maximal blood concentrations in 1 to 3 hours (although some TCAs may take as long as 8 hours). The absorption of SSRIs and SNRIs is slower; 4 to 8 hours are needed to reach maximum concentrations. Antidepressants generally have high levels of protein binding (over 95% for fluoxetine; DeVane, 1998).

A significant proportion of a dose of most antidepressants is destroyed by the digestive system and liver before it reaches the bloodstream. This first-pass metabolism is inhibited by alcohol; as a result, alcohol will greatly increase the amount of drug absorbed from a specific dose. Overdoses of TCAs are much more serious when taken in conjunction with alcohol. SSRIs and SNRIs are exceptions; they appear to have little interaction with alcohol. In fact, SSRIs have been suggested as a treatment for alcoholism (Lejoyeux, 1996).

DISTRIBUTION

Antidepressants readily cross the blood–brain and placental barriers. They tend to become concentrated in the lungs, kidneys, liver, and brain. Some antidepressants can be found in significant quantities in breast milk.

EXCRETION

The MAOIs have a short half-life of 2 to 4 hours (Preskorn, 1993). Some MAOIs may be taken once a day because they have an irreversible effect on MAO and their effects persist long after they are eliminated from the body. Newer MAOIs, like moclobemide, have a reversible effect, and two or three daily doses are required. The TCAs have a half-life of about 24 hours and, in most people, reach a steady-state level after about 5 days. Usually, only a single daily dose is needed.

Most second- and third-generation antidepressants have shorter half-lives than the tricyclics and often require more frequent dosing (Richelson, 2001). Newer SSRIs generally have a short to medium half-life (15 to 25 hours) and do not have active metabolites. With these drugs, a steady-state blood level can be achieved in a few days with single daily dosing. One major exception, fluoxetine, has an extremely long half-life and an active metabolite that blocks the enzyme responsible for its destruction. Fluoxetine has a half-life of nearly 4 days, and its active metabolite, norfluoxetine, has a half-life of 7 to 15 days (Richelson, 2001). It may take as long as 75 days for the drug and its metabolite to reach a steady-state level in the body. It can also take this long for the drug and its metabolite to be completely eliminated from the body after the drug is discontinued (Lane & Baldwin, 1997).

There is considerable variability between individuals in the pharmacokinetics of the antidepressants. After a fixed daily dose of a tricyclic, individual steady-state blood levels may be as much as 36 times higher in some individuals than in others because some people have a genetic deficiency in one of the enzymes the body uses to destroy these drugs. In these people, antidepressants can have extremely long half-lives (Preskorn, 1993; Rudorfer & Potter, 1987). Thus, doses vary for individuals, and, in many cases, blood levels must be monitored (Simpson & Singh, 1990). Swanson, Jones, Krasselt, Denmark, and Ratti (1997) have reported two deaths caused by tricyclics taken at normal clinical doses. The individuals seem not to have cleared the metabolites as rapidly as most people, and the metabolites built up to a toxic level. Like many other genetic factors, the distribution of the enzyme can be associated with ethnicity (Sramek & Pi, 1996).

EFFECTS OF ANTIDEPRESSANTS

Effects on the Body

MAOIs alone do not produce serious or life-threatening side effects. Some of their side effects include tremors, weight gain, blurry vision, dry mouth, and a lowering of blood pressure and *postural hypotension* (fainting or dizziness when moving to a standing position after being seated or lying down). Unfortunately, MAOIs can have dangerous side effects that result from interaction with other drugs or foods. Drugs like amphetamines, decongestants, and nose drops that cause the release of NE are potentiated by MAOIs because they block the breakdown of NE, which then accumulates. In some cases, they block the metabolism of other drugs or may interact with them in unexplained ways. Drugs potentiated by MAOIs include alcohol and some opioids.

Another problem with MAOIs is that MAO not only destroys the monoamines but is also responsible for the breakdown of some substances in food. One of these substances is *tyramine*, which is found in aged cheese, pickled herring, beer, wine, and chocolate. MAO-A, which is present in the intestine, normally metabolizes tyramine just after it is consumed. Any tyramine missed by intestinal MAO-A is destroyed by MAO-B in the liver and the lungs before it gets into general circulation throughout the body. Normally, less than 1% of tyramine gets past this MAO and into the system (Fitton, Faulds, & Goa, 1992). If tyramine-rich foods are eaten while taking MAOIs, the body is unable to break down the tyramine, and it accumulates. Tyramine causes effects that mimic sympathetic nervous system activation, such as sweating, nausea, and increased blood pressure, which in turn can cause headaches, internal bleeding, and even stroke or death. This is known as the *cheese effect*. As a consequence, people on MAOIs have always had to watch their diet.

The older MAOIs blocked both forms of MAO, but newer MAOIs are more selective. As an example, moclobemide selectively blocks MAO-A and has minimal effect on MAO-B. As a result, tyramine that gets past the inhibited MAO-A in the intestine can still be metabolized by the MAO-B in the liver and lungs. Selective MAO-A inhibitors are, therefore, much safer, and patients do not have to be as careful with their diet (Fitton et al., 1992). It also helps if the pill is taken well after eating, allowing any dietary tyramine to be metabolized before the MAOI has its maximum effect.

An additional danger associated with MAOIs, as well as the other types of antidepressants, is the development of *serotonin syndrome*, which is caused by an acute increase in serotonergic transmission. Oftentimes, it is the result of interaction between a drug and a food (such as those containing *tryptophan*, the 5-HT precursor amino acid) or the coadministration of multiple drugs, including herbal remedies, that increase serotonin levels. In some cases, an insufficient *washout time* (the time allowed for a drug to be eliminated from the body) when medications are changed can cause serotonin syndrome

(Lane & Baldwin, 1997). This may happen when patients are switched to another antidepressant from fluoxetine, which has a particularly long half-life. Serotonin syndrome may also result when patients taking antidepressants use psychostimulants such as amphetamine or cocaine. Serotonin syndrome is characterized by such cognitive symptoms as disorientation, agitation, and confusion. It is also life-threatening, mainly because of dysregulation of autonomic nervous system functions, leading to increased blood pressure, flushing, fever, shivering, irregular heartbeat, diarrhea, and shock. It may lead to coma and can cause death.

The tricyclics also affect autonomic nervous system function through their anticholinergic effects. Specifically, TCAs inhibit the parasympathetic division of the autonomic nervous system, which uses ACh as a transmitter. These effects are characterized by symptoms such as dry mouth, constipation, blurred vision, ringing in the ears, and retention of urine. Excessive sweating is also common. Tremors are seen in about 10% of patients taking tricyclics. Side effects are usually worse during the first 2 weeks of treatment or when the dose is increased suddenly. Older patients are also more likely to show confusion and delirium; incidence can be as high as 50% in patients over 70 (Baldessarini, 1985).

Extrapyramidal or Parkinsonian symptoms, similar to the side effects of antipsychotics (see Chapter 12), are unusual with tricyclics but have been reported (Gill, DeVane, & Risch, 1997). Dizziness, irregular heartbeat, and postural hypotension may develop because of the influence of TCAs on adrenergic receptor functioning. Patients taking the tricyclics often report increased appetite and preference for sweets, accompanied by weight gain. This may be due to the influence of TCAs on histamine activity. One study reported an increase of 1.3 to 2.9 pounds per month. In fact, excessive weight gain is a major reason why patients stop taking these drugs. An additional, dangerous side effect is reduction in seizure threshold, which can cause convulsions, especially in those with seizure disorders.

The SSRIs have fewer nonspecific actions on systems outside of serotonin and, therefore, have far fewer unpleasant side effects. SSRIs may cause nausea, gastrointestinal problems, headache, dizziness, sweating, nervousness, and agitation, but these symptoms tend to dissipate with time. These side effects likely result from SSRI effects on 5-HT$_2$ receptors. In contrast with the MAOIs, the SSRIs decrease appetite, cause weight loss, and are sometimes used to treat obesity (Boyer & Feighner, 1991).

Most of the side effects associated with third-generation antidepressants are due to this class's antagonism of acetylcholine and histamine receptors and enhancement of 5-HT$_{2-3}$ receptor activity. These side effects include increased appetite and weight gain, changes in blood pressure, dizziness, dry mouth, and gastrointestinal problems. Side effects associated with bupropion include restlessness and agitation, tremor, constipation, nausea, headache, dry mouth, and loss of appetite. An additional, dangerous side effect of bupropion is that, like some TCAs, it increases the risk of seizure. The reason nefazodone (Serzone) is no longer sold in Canada or the United States is because of the risk of liver damage. It is, however, available in other countries and in generic form in North America.

Effects on Sleep

All classes of antidepressants have been found to affect sleep. The MAOIs can cause either insomnia or sedation. Strangely, the tricyclics cause drowsiness, although this may have more to do with their anticholinergic properties than their monoamine-stimulating effects. Unlike the antidepressant effect, which takes days to develop, a single dose of a tricyclic can cause sleepiness and is sometimes prescribed to treat insomnia. The drug does not, however, increase total sleeping time. High doses of tricyclics at bedtime can cause nightmares.

Many antidepressants, like fluoxetine and venlafaxine, reduce REM (rapid eye movement) sleep time significantly. Reduction in REM sleep may be associated with a drug's antidepressant effects because sleep deprivation, particularly REM deprivation, has been shown to decrease symptoms of depression, and sleep can make depression worse (Janicak, Davis, Preskorn, & Ayd, 1993). The beneficial effects of REM deprivation build with time and even persist after deprivation ceases. Not all antidepressants reduce REM sleep time (Spiegel & Aebi, 1981), and bupropion actually increases it (DeVane, 1998).

Fluoxetine is reported by some patients to increase the vividness of their dreams. While some enjoy this side effect, others find it disturbing. Others experience insomnia while taking SSRIs. While some of the third-generation antidepressants, such as mirtazapine, have antihistaminergic actions and cause sedation and sleepiness, others, like bupropion, can produce insomnia.

EFFECTS ON THE BEHAVIOR AND PERFORMANCE OF HUMANS

Subjective Effects

The antidepressants do not produce euphoric or even pleasant effects. At low doses, imipramine's effects are similar to those of the antipsychotics. It causes feelings of tiredness, apathy, and weakness. Higher doses impair comprehension and produce confusion that is described as unpleasant. Amitriptyline causes feelings of calmness and relaxation (Spiegel & Aebi, 1981). Even the atypicals that increase dopaminergic activity do not produce euphoria. Recall, from Chapter 5, that both the magnitude and the rate of dopamine surge associated with a drug correspond with individuals' reports of euphoria and pleasure. Because increases in dopamine activity are achieved slowly, any pleasurable effect one might feel is greatly blunted.

Effects on Performance

Because impairments in memory, attention, and cognition are characteristics often experienced by individuals with major depression, it is difficult to determine whether declines in performance are due to the depression or the medication. Acute doses of the TCAs imipramine and amitriptyline appear to have detrimental effects on vigilance tasks and can cause cognitive, memory, and psychomotor impairment that seems to be related to sedation. These drugs should not be used by people who must drive, use heavy equipment, or do intellectual work. Some studies have shown improvement in cognitive functioning after chronic drug treatment, suggesting that these impairments show tolerance. Other studies, however, have not (Lickey & Gordon, 1991). An evaluation of SSRIs and SNRIs on episodic- and working-memory task performance, mental processing speed, and motor performance showed significant drug-induced improvements. SNRIs improved memory performance to a greater extent than did SSRIs (Herrera-Guzmán et al., 2009).

There is evidence that the MAOI moclobemide impairs psychomotor performance. An investigation of the influence of long-term SSRI or SNRI treatment on driving performance found poorer driving (more weaving) in medicated patients than controls, but attributed the impairment to depressive symptoms, not the medication (Wingen, Ramaekers, & Schmitt, 2006).

Effects on Personality

In 1990, fluoxetine (Prozac) attracted national attention by appearing on the cover of *Newsweek*. Quoted in that issue was a psychiatrist, Peter Kramer, who had written about giving fluoxetine to people not to treat depression but to modify their personalities. Prozac "seemed to give social confidence to the habitually timid, to make the sensitive brash, and to lend the introvert the social skills of a salesman" (Kramer, 1993, p. xv). Kramer quoted one of his patients as saying that the drug had made him feel "better than well." He also coined the term *cosmetic psychopharmacology*, suggesting that people could take drugs such as fluoxetine to cover, by neurochemical means, some aspect of their personality that they were not satisfied with in the same way that facial blemishes could be hidden by makeup or the shape of a nose could be made more attractive by cosmetic surgery.

It has been established that fluoxetine and other SSRIs are useful in treating people with diagnosed personality disorders, such as obsessive-compulsive personality, and with compulsive behaviors (Gitlin, 1993). However, the use of fluoxetine and SSRIs as a personality cosmetic for people who do not have a diagnosed disorder, but are just not happy with their personality, is a matter of some debate. It raises a number of interesting issues, not the least of which concerns the origins of personality. If a drug can cause such immediate and profound changes in personality, this effect has far-reaching implications for the way we view personality. Is our personality determined by our past, our childhood experiences, and the like, as many theorists have long believed, or is it determined by 5-HT levels in the raphe nuclei (Kramer, 1993)?

Effectiveness in Treating Depression

There is little doubt that antidepressant medications are an effective means of combating depression. Efficacy rates are roughly similar for all classes—MAOIs, TCAs, SSRIs, and SNRIs—although there are significant individual differences as to which class works best, as well as differences in the way that different types of depression respond to different antidepressants. It is likely that the neurochemical and neurophysiological manifestations of depression differ between individuals so that certain classes of antidepressants work better for some than others. The severity of the depression also influences whether antidepressants are effective in relieving symptoms (Fournier et al., 2010). The presence of a comorbid disorder, such as anxiety, is an additional important consideration since some newer antidepressants, like the SSRIs and SNRIs, are also used to treat other psychiatric conditions.

There are also considerable differences in the severity of side effects in different individuals. This is one reason why there are so many antidepressant drugs available. It is often necessary to change a drug treatment several times to find a drug and a dose that works for a specific person (Rush & Ryan, 2002). Advances in the development of antidepressant medications usually involve finding drugs with fewer side effects, rather than drugs with new or novel mechanisms of action, greater therapeutic effectiveness, or faster onset (Ordway et al., 2002).

We are not yet at the point where we can say that antidepressants are a cure-all for depression. Approximately 60 to 70% of individuals with major depression get some relief from antidepressant medications, but only 28 to 50% show full remission of symptoms (Trivedi et al., 2006). Moreover, much of the improvement associated with antidepressant treatment is also evident in patients treated with placebos. Placebo response rates are as high as 30%, which, compared to a 50% response rate in drug-treated individuals, means that the mere expectation of improvement can account for up to 75% of the improvement that actually occurs (Mora, Nestoriuc, & Rief, 2011). Placebo response rates vary according to the assessment method; physicians and clinicians are more likely to note improvement in depressive symptoms compared to when individuals self-report. Placebo effect rates have also grown across the past few decades; with millions of individuals having taken antidepressants, there is a growing belief that they work. So the expectancy that there will be improvement (and, therefore, the placebo effect) is increasing. When the effectiveness of tricyclics is compared to that of an *active placebo* (in this case, the anticholinergic drug atropine, which produces side effects similar to those of the TCAs), the active placebo is as effective in reducing depression as the TCA—patients are convinced they are

receiving the antidepressant medication, as opposed to the placebo, because they experience physiological symptoms. The expectation that they will feel better makes them feel better (Moncrieff, Wessely, & Hardy, 2004).

Our belief in the effectiveness of antidepressants over placebos is also influenced by the way in which research is published. Studies that fail to find benefits of a drug over a placebo frequently do not get published. Therefore, what we read in the literature are only the good-news stories. A recent analysis of published and unpublished data sets obtained from clinical trial research revealed that the placebo effect can account for up to 82% of the effectiveness of antidepressant medication treatment (Kirsh et al., 2008). Furthermore, in patients experiencing mild or moderate depression, placebos were no more effective than antidepressants. Only in the most extremely depressed patients was there a relatively small difference in treatment outcome between the placebo and drug groups, and this was due to a decreased effectiveness of the placebo rather than an increased effectiveness of the antidepressant (Kirsh et al., 2008).

There has been a considerable interest in the use of antidepressants in treating depression in children and adolescents. A number of studies have shown that the TCAs are generally not effective in this population, but the SSRIs do work. As with adults, children show a very high rate of placebo effect (between one-third and one-half of the patients in the placebo group improve). Fluoxetine is the only SSRI that has been shown to be effective at a higher rate than placebos, but there are problems. In these studies, there is a higher rate of adverse symptoms in the SSRI group than in the placebo group (1 to 6% vs. 0 to 4%). These include agitation, hyperactivity, and symptoms of mania. In 2004, the U.S. Food and Drug Administration issued a *black box* warning against prescribing antidepressants to children and adolescents. You will learn more about this in the upcoming section on violence and suicide.

EFFECTS ON THE BEHAVIOR OF NONHUMANS

Conditioned Behavior

Tricyclic antidepressants are more effective than methamphetamine at increasing operant response rates. They even appear to further increase high rates of responding, whereas amphetamine tends to decrease those rates (Dews, 1962).

The tricyclic antidepressants tend to decrease avoidance behavior at doses that have no effect on escape behavior (McMillan & Leander, 1976), thus making them similar to the antianxiety drugs and the antipsychotics. The tricyclics do not increase punishment-suppressed behavior. If anything, they tend to decrease it, making them similar to amphetamine and the psychomotor stimulants, in this regard.

DISCRIMINATIVE STIMULUS PROPERTIES

Neither the MAOIs nor the TCAs are discriminable at doses that produce most of their behavioral effects. However, at very high but sublethal doses, they can be discriminated. There does not appear to be any generalization between the antidepressants and the antipsychotics or any other drug class (Stewart, 1962).

The SSRIs and the SNRIs/atypicals, however, do have discriminate stimulus properties at therapeutic doses. Dekeyne and Millan (2003) trained rats to discriminate citalopram, bupropion, and reboxetine. They also found that antidepressants that blocked both serotonin and norepinephrine would substitute for either citalopram or reboxetine, but SSRIs generalize only to citalopram. Bupropion did not substitute for either citalopram or reboxetine. Taken together with the observation that the MAOIs and the TCAs do not appear to have any discriminable properties, this suggests that the stimulus properties of antidepressant drugs do not arise from their antidepressant properties.

The stimulus properties of citalopram were blocked by drugs that block $5\text{-}HT_{2C}$ receptors, and the reboxetine cue was blocked by NE α_1 antagonists, showing that the stimulus properties of these drugs arise from interactions with very specific receptors (Dekeyne & Millan, 2003).

TOLERANCE

There are reports that the therapeutic effectiveness of some drugs may show tolerance in some individuals after a few months of use, but the extent to which this happens and its clinical significance is not clear (Baldessarini, 1985). Tolerance to many of the side effects of the antidepressants usually occurs within several weeks, although tolerance may not develop to the tiredness reported with the SSRIs.

WITHDRAWAL

Sudden discontinuation of high doses of the tricyclics can cause withdrawal symptoms, which include restlessness, anxiety, chills, akathisia (a feeling of a compulsion to move), and muscle aches (Baldessarini, 1985). For this reason, these drugs should not be abruptly discontinued.

Withdrawal from SSRIs has been reported. The symptoms include dizziness, light-headedness, insomnia, fatigue, anxiety, nausea, headache, and sensory disturbances. These symptoms may last for 3 weeks and can be relieved by resuming antidepressant medication (Zajecka, Tracy, & Mitchell, 1997).

Withdrawal from SNRIs, especially venlafaxine, can be serious and include both bodily symptoms, such as heart palpitations and nausea, and psychiatric symptoms including delusions. Some individuals experience symptoms that are similar to stroke.

SELF-ADMINISTRATION IN HUMANS AND NONHUMANS

Neither the TCAs nor the MAOIs are self-administered unless prescribed by a physician for the treatment of depression. They are seldom sold illicitly on the street and do not appear to be used nonmedically. Apart from their medical application, neither of these classes appear to be reinforcing to either humans or nonhumans (Griffiths, Bigelow, & Henningfield, 1980).

To determine whether imipramine has aversive effects, an experiment was conducted in which monkeys were able to avoid infusions of various doses of imipramine by pressing a lever. Imipramine was avoided only at very high doses. It appears to be one of the few drugs tested that has neither positive nor negative reinforcing properties (Hoffmeister & Wuttke, 1975).

Interestingly, some of the second- and third-generation antidepressants have been successfully used to treat addiction to other drugs, including alcohol. Bupropion, as an antidepressant, is marketed as Wellbutrin, but it is also marketed as Zyban, a smoking-cessation aid.

Compliance

Because depression is a chronic disorder, it is important to find effective ways of preventing relapses. Chronic administration of therapeutic doses of most antidepressants has been shown to do just that. Patients, however, must be willing to tolerate the side effects of the drug over an extended period of time. Comparative trials have shown that the SSRIs are far superior to any other antidepressants in terms of patients' remaining compliant to chronic drug regimens. This success was due to the comparatively low rate of unwanted side effects of the SSRIs (Tollefson, 1993).

HARMFUL EFFECTS

Reproduction

Early studies indicated that the tricyclic antidepressants can interfere with male sexual functioning, but they suggested that the problems are not extensive (Harrison et al., 1986). A later study, however, found evidence that the problem may be more serious than it was first thought. Monteiro, Noshirvani, Marks, and Lelliott (1987) compared a group of men and women receiving the tricyclic clomipramine for obsessive-compulsive disorder with a placebo control group. In response to general questions about sexual functioning, there did not appear to be any difference between the drug group and the controls, but when questioned more closely in a structured interview about changes in sexuality, nearly all (96%) of the drug group reported severe difficulties in achieving orgasm. No difficulties were reported in the control group. This effect did not seem to be a result of sedation or fatigue and did not show any tolerance. Delayed or impaired ejaculation has also been reported with the MAOIs (Woods, 1984). Also, patients taking newer antidepressants, including the SSRIs and SNRIs, frequently report delayed ejaculation and loss of interest in sex. Because the atypical bupropion does not affect 5-HT function, it is unlike the others in that it is not associated with sexual dysfunction; it may, in fact, enhance sexual activity through its dopaminergic effects.

There is little evidence that the antidepressants cause any adverse effects to the fetus during pregnancy in humans, but a teratogenic effect has been noted in laboratory animals. As a general rule, antidepressants should be discontinued during pregnancy. In one study, pregnancy outcomes of women on fluoxetine and tricyclic antidepressants were compared with a matched control group. There were no differences in fetal malformations between the groups, but the women in the fluoxetine and tricyclic antidepressant groups were nearly twice as likely as controls to miscarry (Pastuszak et al., 1993).

Some antidepressants have been detected in breast milk of nursing mothers, but usually there is no evidence of the drug in the blood of the baby. It appears that the first-pass metabolism of the baby is able to get rid of the drug before it gets into his or her system.

Violence and Suicide

Soon after fluoxetine was introduced to the U.S. market, there were reports that it induced intense, violent, suicidal preoccupations in some patients (Teicher, Glod, & Cole, 1990). In fact, Prozac-induced violence became a defense in some courtrooms and was the subject of extensive coverage by television talk shows. There have since been many high-profile court cases where fluoxetine in particular has been blamed by the defense for causing many terrible crimes. Despite their increased safety over first-generation antidepressants and growing popularity, public health officials began to worry that the SSRIs may be having unintentional effects, especially on young people.

In 2004, the U.S. Food and Drug Administration (FDA) thoroughly reviewed clinical trial data, both published and unpublished, involving more than 4,000 children and adolescents. The review revealed that those taking antidepressant medications were twice as likely as those taking placebos to have suicidal ideations and attempt suicide (4% of those in the drug group vs. 2% in the placebo group). European and North American public health agencies issued warnings. The FDA mandated a *black box* warning, the most serious type of warning, to be placed on all antidepressant medications prescribed to children and adolescents. Friends and family members should closely monitor the young person for worsening depression, indications of suicidal thoughts, and changes in behavior. In 2007, this warning was widened to include young adults up to age 24. In subsequent studies, researchers did not find significant evidence that suicidal ideation increases with antidepressant drug use but, instead, that the benefits of antidepressant treatment for young people outweighed the risks (Bridge et al., 2007). Yet, European and North American warnings prompted discontinuation of antidepressant treatment in many children and adolescents, and far fewer new prescriptions were written. Between 2003 and 2005, suicide rates increased dramatically (by 14% in the United States; by 49% in the Netherlands) as young people were not treated for their depression (Gibbons et al., 2007).

One reason why there is such confusion around this issue is because it is inherently difficult to research. Antidepressant drugs are often prescribed for people who are very agitated, depressed, and suicidal anyway. Suicide and violence after taking an antidepressant drug may represent only a lack of effect—an inability to prevent a suicide, not a drug-induced effect (Walsh & Dinan, 2001). In addition, if a drug causes suicide and violence in only a small number of people but reduces these acts in most others, large-scale studies that average across everyone would not detect it.

After being taken for 3 to 4 weeks, fluoxetine may induce an activating effect with racing thoughts, nervousness, and tremor (Boyer & Feighner, 1991). Sometimes this develops to the point where it is called *akathisia*, a movement disorder characterized by restlessness, agitation, an inability to sit still, and a compulsion to be continuously active. Akathisia is also one of the movement disorders seen after the administration of antipsychotics (see Chapter 12). Reports of violence and suicide seem to be associated with akathisia in certain individuals (Rothschild & Locke, 1991). Even though many large-scale studies have not shown increased akathisia caused by fluoxetine in the general population, studies in teenagers and children have shown that it does occur more often after fluoxetine than a placebo (Vitiello & Swedo, 2005).

For most people, fluoxetine is relatively safe and effective, but, like any drug, it has the capacity to cause serious problems for some patients, and its use and dosage should be monitored closely, especially for the first few weeks.

Overdose

The SSRIs and SNRIs are considerably safer than first-generation antidepressants, and unintentional overdose is extremely rare. As described earlier, SSRIs in combination with other antidepressants or psychomotor stimulants can cause serotonin syndrome. If this syndrome is unrecognized and untreated, it can ultimately cause respiratory, circulatory, and kidney failure. Serotonin syndrome is relatively common in SSRI overdose, certainly compared to the incidence of seizures or coma. Both the SSRI citalopram and the SNRI venlafaxine appear to be more dangerous due to their influence on cardiac function (Christoph et al., 2010; Isbister, Bowe, Dawson, & Whyte, 2004).

The tricyclics are potentially dangerous medications. The toxicity of the tricyclics is due primarily to their effect on the contractility of the heart muscle. They have a therapeutic index of around 10 to 15. This is a serious concern, especially when these drugs are prescribed for people who are severely depressed and contemplating suicide. There is considerable variability in the death rates attributed to drugs within the same class. Among the tricyclics, clomipramine is relatively safe, but many deaths have been attributed to amitriptyline. Tranylcypromine, an MAOI, is responsible for a high rate of deaths, but the rate of isocarboxazid fatalities is low (Leonard, 1993).

OTHER TREATMENTS FOR DEPRESSION

Antidepressant medications are not the only treatments for depression. Some individuals choose herbal remedies, such as St. John's wort, which you read about in Chapter 1. Other herbal treatments, such as saffron stigma and petal, lavender, echium, and rhodiola, have been shown to be more effective at alleviating the symptoms of depression than a placebo and, in some instances, are as effective as the SSRI fluoxetine and the TCA imipramine (Dwyer, Whitten, & Hawrelak, 2011).

Electroconvulsive therapy (ECT), in which seizures are induced in anesthetized patients, is most often considered a therapeutic alternative for those who fail to respond to a variety of antidepressant medications. MRI studies show that ECT treatments and improvement in depressive symptoms are associated with neurogenesis (growth of new neurons) in the hippocampus. Recall from earlier in this chapter that atrophy (cell death) of hippocampal neurons is a hallmark of depression. It is thought to result, at least in part, from high circulating levels of cortisol and may, in turn, facilitate hyperactivity of the HPA-axis stress response in a sort of perpetually damaging feedback loop. In animal studies, electroconvulsive shock increases hippocampal levels of a protein, called *brain derived neurotopic factor (BDNF)*, in a dose-dependent, long-term manner (Bolwig, 2011). BDNF acts within the cell nucleus and performs vital roles in the growth and survival of existing and new neurons and receptors. Some researchers suggest that hippocampal degeneration associated with depression is the result of monoamine neurons failing to produce enough BDNF. Stress hormones, especially cortisol, contribute significantly to the loss of BDNF in the hippocampus and regions of the limbic system. ECT increases BDNF levels and neurogenesis in these regions, as do antidepressant drugs (Bolwig, 2011; Rojas, Fritsch, Rojas, Jara, & Fiedler, 2011).

Other methods of stimulating the brain have also proven effective in treating depression. These include *deep brain stimulation*, in which electrodes are chronically implanted within the prefrontal cortex, and *transcranial magnetic stimulation*, in which neuron depolarization is induced by applying a strong magnetic field to the scalp. Indirectly stimulating the brain, through electrical activation of the ascending fibers of the vagus nerve, which, in turn, excites regions of the brainstem, has also proven effective in some people.

Physical inactivity is recognized as a risk factor for depression, and a cost-effective and natural way to combat mild to moderate depression is through exercise. Exercise can also be used as an adjunct to boost symptom alleviation that results from antidepressant medications. Some of the proposed mechanisms by which exercise can ease depression include promotion of hippocampal neurogenesis, increases in 5-HT and BDNF levels, and a decrease in HPA-axis activity and cortisol production (Carek, Laibstain, & Carek, 2011).

Different forms of therapy, including cognitive behavioral therapy (CBT), psychodynamic therapy, and interpersonal therapy, have all proven effective in the treatment of depression. With symptom alleviation comes measurable physiological changes. For example, after several sessions of CBT or psychoanalysis, improvements in depressive symptoms correspond with reductions in cortisol to normal levels (Sharpley, 2010). Moreover, imaging studies reveal increases in blood flow to the hippocampus, normalization of amygdala activity, and improved PFC–limbic connectivity following therapy. Serotonin transporter protein levels also show normalization after a year of psychodynamic therapy (Sharpley, 2010).

It appears, then, that the way in which neurochemical and neurophysiological changes associated with depression become normalized is not as important as the fact that they do normalize.

Cannabis

*At first, a certain absurd, irresistible hilarity
overcomes you. The most ordinary words,
the simplest ideas assume a new and bizarre
aspect. This mirth is intolerable to you; but
it is useless to resist. The demon has invaded
you . . . .*

—CHARLES BAUDELAIRE

The hemp plant, or *Cannabis sativa*, was initially given
its name and classification by Carolus Linnaeus in
1753. The plant is indigenous to Central and Southern
Asia, and its use has been dated as far back as the third
millennium BCE. Many varieties of cannabis exist, from
small shrubs to much larger plants. These can be identified by their distinctive leaves, which are frequently long
and slender and have serrated edges. There are both male
and female plants, which can be differentiated based on
size and leaf structure. Female plants may grow taller
than males and tend to have denser leaf structure, while
male plants usually have thicker stems and fewer leaves.
The female plant must be fertilized by pollen from the
male flower to produce seeds. To help collect the wind-
borne pollen, the female exudes a sticky resin from its
flowering top, which also protects the seeds from heat
and insects.

Since Linnaeus first classified C. *sativa*, there has been
speculation about whether more than one species exists.
In 1785, Jean-Baptiste Lamarck classified a second species of cannabis, *Cannabis indica*, based on plant samples
collected in India. More recently, some botanists have
identified three species based on differences in form and
potency: C. *sativa*, C. *indica*, and C. *ruderalis* (Grinspoon &
Bakalar, 1993). Otherwise, it is speculated that there is
only one species, C. *sativa*, of which there are two phenotypes (subspecies or varieties). One is traditionally cultivated in northerly areas for its fiber. It matures rapidly,
has a low content of active ingredients, and is often called
hemp. The other type is slow maturing; is traditionally
cultivated in southerly, more tropical regions for its intoxicating properties; and has a relatively high content of
psychoactive ingredients (Small, 1979).

HISTORY

It is believed that cannabis originated in central Asia,
but its early history is difficult to trace because it was
cultivated and widely dispersed long before records were
made. The spread of cannabis appears to have occurred
in the middle of the second century BCE. The people
responsible were the Scythians, a warlike and mobile
Middle Eastern tribe related to the Semites. The word
cannabis is a Scythian word, and the Greek historian
Herodotus described the Scythians as having used

cannabis. He explained how the Scythians would enter their tents, throw hemp seeds on heated stones, inhale the vapors, and "howl with joy." This procedure was used as a cleansing ceremony after funerals (Benet, 1975).

The Scythians spread cannabis into Egypt by way of Palestine and northward into Russia and Europe, where the Scythian custom of burning cannabis seeds after funerals still remains (Benet, 1975).

In China, cannabis has been known since Neolithic times, about 6,000 years ago. The Chinese word for hemp, "ma", has been in use for at least 3,000 years. The plant was cultivated for its fiber; for its seed, which was a staple grain; for its intoxicating effects; and for its medicinal effects (Li, 1975).

Cannabis has been used for centuries in India. Its use spread there directly from China rather than from the Middle East. From India, the drug was introduced to Africa by Arab traders who sailed along the east coast of Africa in the twelfth century. It spread across Africa along with the cultural influence of Islam. In Africa, it is known as *bangi* or *dagga* (Earleywine, 2002). Hemp was introduced into Russia and Eastern Europe by the Scythians. From there, it spread into Western Europe, where it was grown for centuries without widespread recognition of its intoxicating properties. It was grown chiefly for its fiber, from which rope was made. It was also commonly used as a medicine.

Despite the fact that cannabis has been used as a folk remedy wherever it has been grown, scientific medical attention was not directed toward the drug until 1839 when W. B. O'Shaughnessy, a young chemistry professor at the University of Calcutta, tried it out on various ailments. He reported that hemp was an effective anticonvulsant and an appetite stimulant. There followed a series of papers that expounded the usefulness of hemp in the treatment of a number of disorders, including tetanus, neuralgia, dysmenorrhea, asthma, gonorrhea, and migraine. It was also reported to be useful in treating addiction to alcohol, opium, and chloral hydrate, and there were claims that hemp might be useful in the treatment of mental illness. One of the earliest of these claims was made in 1845 by the French physician J. J. Moreau de Tours, who used it to treat melancholia, hypomania, and other forms of mental illness (Moreau, 1973). In England, Sir John Russell Reynolds, president of the Royal College of Physicians and physician to Queen Victoria, used marijuana extensively in the treatment of neurological disorders (Consroe & Sandyk, 1992).

In general, the intoxicating effects of the drug remained unnoticed by Europeans until the publication of *Le Club des Hachichins* by the French writer Théophile Gautier in 1846. Gautier was a romantic and flamboyant writer who once offered a reward to anyone who could invent a new pleasure. The reward was earned (but we do not know whether he ever collected) by J. J. Moreau de Tours, the physician just mentioned. Dr. Moreau introduced Gautier to Le Club des Hachichins and gave him his first hashish with the words, "This will be subtracted from your share in Paradise." Gautier's account of the effects is now a classic description of the drug experience.

The drug that Gautier used was imported from the Middle East and North Africa. No one made the association between hashish and the quantities of hemp that were being grown at that time all over Europe to make rope. Even though he recognized that the two plants were related, Moreau believed that hemp and hashish were different (what the members of the club received was not cannabis resin or what we now call hashish—Moreau used the term *hashish* to refer to a product made by boiling the plant in butter).

In the era of European imperialism, rope was a very important item. Empires were built on naval strength, and ships could not sail without rope. Hemp did not grow well in England, so its production was encouraged in the American colonies. Sir Walter Raleigh was ordered to grow hemp in his Virginia colony, and consequently a crop was planted alongside tobacco in 1611, the colony's first season. American hemp proved to be of good quality, and hemp became a staple crop of the American colonies for more than 200 years. One of the better-known hemp growers was George Washington.

It is believed that the use of the cannabis plant for smoking and the word *marijuana* were introduced into the United States by Mexican laborers in the early twentieth century. Marijuana smoking spread slowly through the United States, primarily among racial minorities and jazz musicians. This association did much to shape the perceptions of white legislators and to motivate opponents. In the 1920s, marijuana started to attract the attention of the authorities and the public, which almost universally condemned it. Alarmist stories appeared in newspapers attributing criminal activity to the drug, especially crimes of violence.

Because there was a shortage of reliable scientific data to the contrary, these accusations went unchallenged. By

1937, most states had laws against marijuana, and the U.S. government had passed the Marijuana Tax Act, which imposed prohibitive taxes on possession and use, effectively eliminating the legitimate medical use of marijuana and driving recreational users underground. Soon, most other Western countries had antimarijuana laws. In Canada, marijuana is classed as a "narcotic" and included in the Narcotic Control Act with the opioid drugs (and cocaine).

The medical profession, represented by the American Medical Association, has always supported the position of the U.S. government. In 1970, one result was the Controlled Substances Act, which ignored the previous century of accumulating medical evidence and declared that marijuana had no potential medical use but had a high potential for abuse.

In spite of these laws (or perhaps because of them), the popularity of marijuana continued to grow until it reached its peak in the 1970s and started to level off. Throughout the 1980s and early 1990s, use in the United States declined considerably, but that decline may be coming to an end. Marijuana is currently the most common illicit drug in the United States, and its prevalence of use is increasing (Substance Abuse and Mental Health Services Administration, 2011).

In the United States, legislation to decriminalize the drug for recreational purposes has been passed in 10 states, though the nature of the legislation differs by state. Oregon was the first to decriminalize; possession of up to 1 ounce (28.45 grams) is currently punishable by either a $500 or $1,000 fine with no criminal penalty, though stricter penalties are in place for sale or cultivation. California, North Carolina, Colorado, Mississippi, New York, Nebraska, Ohio, Alaska, and Massachusetts have also passed laws to decriminalize cannabis possession. In Canada, there have been a series of failed attempts to legalize or decriminalize cannabis, and the drug's legal status remains the same in all provinces. In the United Kingdom as well, the drug remains illegal, though its legality has been the subject of debate by various administrations, and its legal status has fluctuated over the years.

THE CANNABINOIDS

The primary active ingredient in cannabis is *delta-9-tetrahydrocannabinol* (delta-9-THC or Δ^9-THC), but the chemistry of cannabis is much more complex.

An entire class of chemical compounds, called the *cannabinoids*, is found exclusively in cannabis, and each may contribute, directly or indirectly, to the behavioral effects of the cannabis plant. The cannabinoids belong to the chemical class of *terpenophenolics*, of which 85 have been identified in cannabis, including the most psychoactive and common cannabinoid, delta-9-THC (El-Alfy et al., 2010). Other cannabinoids include *cannabinol* (CBN) and *cannabidiol* (CBD). Although these cannabinoids were once believed to be devoid of any important behavioral effects, it now appears that CBD may have anxiolytic and/or antipsychotic properties (Zuardi, Crippa, Hallak, Moreira, & Guimarães, 2006). The story, however, is not quite this simple because the amount of active ingredients appears to depend on preparation and route of administration, and these "inactive" ingredients may alter the potency or metabolism of more active ingredients. New cannabinoids are created during burning, digestion (when the drug is taken orally), and metabolism. It is still not clear what effects each cannabinoid has, how much each contributes to behavioral effects, or how cannabinoids interact with each other. Consequently, the effect of a particular cannabis plant cannot be predicted simply on the basis of the results of an analysis of its ingredients. As if things were not complicated enough, the content of marijuana changes over time, especially if exposed to light and air. With time, THC may be converted into CBN (Mechoulam, Hanus, & Martin, 1976).

Extracted and Synthetic Cannabinoids

Pharmaceutical companies market medicines that contain cannabinoids. Some of these are natural cannabinoids extracted and purified from the cannabis plant. One such drug is Sativex, an oral spray developed by Bayer for the treatment of symptoms associated with multiple sclerosis and severe neuropathic-related cancer pain. Sativex contains THC, which the company calls *tetranabinex*, and cannabidiol, which it calls *nabidiolex*. Sativex is currently approved for use in the United Kingdom, Spain, Canada, and New Zealand. At this time, the FDA has not yet approved Sativex for use in the United States.

Several synthetic drugs similar to the cannabinoids have been developed, and some are licensed for commercial use. Synthetic cannabinoids may be more useful than naturally occurring ones because they may be more stable and effective or have greater selective effects. Nabilone (Cesamet) and dronabinol (Marinol) are synthetic cannabinoids now used clinically to treat anorexia and weight loss in patients with AIDS as well as to alleviate nausea and distress in patients receiving chemotherapy for cancer. Levonantradol, a synthetic cannabinoid about 30 times more potent than THC, has been developed but at this time is solely used in research and has not yet been marketed (Ben Amar, 2006). Another synthetic cannabinoid, WIN 55212-2, a receptor agonist, is now widely used in research. Rimonabant (Acomplia) is a synthetic antagonist to cannabinoids that blocks the main cannabinoid receptors in the central nervous system. Rimonabant was developed as an antiobesity drug, but approval of the drug was withdrawn in Europe in January 2009. Synthetic cannabinoids intended for recreational use have entered the market in the last decade. Such designer drugs are marketed as incense under names such as Spice and K2. As of March 2011, five recreational synthetic cannabinoids are illegal in the United States.

Cannabis Preparations

All parts of the cannabis plant contain THC, and the plant is prepared for consumption in various ways. The most familiar to North Americans is *marijuana*. The term "marijuana" is a Mexican–Spanish word that originally referred to a cheap tobacco but later came to refer to the dried leaves and flowers of the cannabis plant. Marijuana is usually smoked in a cigarette, cigar, or pipe but is sometimes baked into cookies or brownies.

In India, a distinction is made between *bhang* and *ganja*. Bhang is similar to marijuana. It is the dried leaves of uncultivated cannabis plants or female plants from which the resin has been removed. Generally, bhang is not very potent. Ganja, made from the tops of female plants from which the resin has not been removed, is three to four times more potent than bhang. In the West Indies, cannabis was imported directly from India, and the Indian term *ganja* rather than the North American *marijuana* is used. In Jamaica, ganja refers to the entire cannabis plant, and no distinction is made between ganja and bhang.

Hashish, also known as *charas* in India, refers to the dried resin from the top of the female plant. It is a pale yellow sap when harvested but turns almost black when dried. It may be consumed in a number of ways. Frequently, it is smoked, either alone or in a mixture with tobacco, or it may be baked into cookies.

A purified variation of hashish is *hash oil*, which is prepared by boiling the hashish in alcohol (or some other solvent), filtering out the residue, and then permitting the alcohol to evaporate. The cannabinoids are highly soluble in alcohol, which extracts them from the hashish and concentrates them. Depending on the degree of purity, hash oil may range from black or red to light amber. Hash oil is much more concentrated than hashish. It may contain up to 60% cannabinoids and is easier to smuggle. Hash oil may be consumed in several ways, such as placing a drop on the paper of a regular tobacco cigarette or on hot tinfoil and inhaling the smoke.

Marijuana samples seized in the 1960s contained, on average, 1.5% THC, but the average THC content has increased substantially over the past 50 years. In the 1980s, THC content in marijuana was approximately 3.0 to 3.5%; by the 1990s, it was 3.5 to 4.5%; by 2008, THC content rose to just over 10% (National Drug Intelligence Center, Domestic Cannabis Cultivation Assessment, July 2009). The increase in average potency is a result of improved cultivation methods and the increased frequency of sinsemilla and high-potency marijuana found in police seizures. The THC content in crossbred and hydroponically grown marijuana such as *sinsemilla* can be as high as 30% (Pijlman, Rigter, Hoek, Goldschmidt, & Niesink, 2005).

ABSORPTION

Oral Administration

THC is a weak acid with a pKa of 10.6; consequently, it is not ionized at the pH of body fluids. The cannabinoids are extremely lipid soluble—in fact, they will hardly dissolve in water. When marijuana is taken orally, the cannabinoids are absorbed from the digestive system rather slowly. Oral absorption may be aided by adding oil to the plant material before consumption. When THC is taken orally in the form of a pill (Marinol is a synthetic THC dissolved in sesame oil), absorption is also incomplete and erratic, and there is considerable first-pass metabolism (Smith, 1998). For this reason, the dose must be doubled or tripled to have the same effect as when inhaled (Institute of Medicine, 1982).

The peak effects after oral administration usually occur 1 to 3 hours following ingestion and may last 5 hours or longer (Agurell, Lindgren, Ohlsson, Gillespie, & Hollister, 1984; Paton & Pertwee, 1973). Oral administration is also more likely to cause nausea or vomiting (Grinspoon, 1971).

With an interest in the use of cannabinoids for medicinal purposes, pharmaceutical companies are developing ways of delivering cannabis preparations that have more rapid absorption. Sativex, for example, is delivered as a spray under the tongue, but absorption is still not as fast as with inhalation. Cannabis inhalers are being developed, but none are yet commercially available.

Inhalation

Smoking cannabis plant material is an efficient route of administration. Usually the material is hand-rolled in a paper, and the *joint* is consumed in the manner of a tobacco cigarette. Hashish is often mixed with tobacco and smoked as a joint, but more often it is smoked in a pipe. A water pipe known as a *bong* is often used. It cools the smoke and prevents the loss of the drug through sidestream smoke. Hash oil is placed on joints or tobacco cigarettes or heated on tinfoil, and the fumes are inhaled.

Normal smoking causes about 10 to 25% of the cannabinoids in a marijuana cigarette to enter the lungs, and virtually all of that enters the body (Agurell et al., 1986). Blood levels of THC peak within 15 minutes. Effects may begin to be felt within a few minutes and reach a peak after 30 to 60 minutes.

Because of a widespread belief that absorption increases with the duration of each puff, experienced marijuana smokers will take deep draws on the marijuana cigarette and hold the smoke in the lungs for 10 to 20 seconds. Actually, holding the smoke in the lungs may not contribute much to the absorption of THC. It appears that the depth of an inhalation is much more important than the duration in determining THC absorption (Azorlosa, Greenwald, & Stitzer, 1995).

As an alternative to conventional smoking, *vaporizers* have become a popular way to inhale cannabis smoke. The vaporizer heats the plant to a point where the active compounds (mainly delta-9-THC) reach their boiling point and can be inhaled as vapor. These cannabinoids vaporize at a lower temperature than tars and other carcinogens and therefore make up the majority of the vapor. Recent studies have shown that the use of a vaporizer allows pulmonary function to significantly improve without a reduction in drug use (Van Dam & Earleywine, 2010). After 1 month of occasional use, participants showed marked improvement in most measures of pulmonary function, which likely arose due to previous smoking. As well, it has been shown that vaporizing delivers similar amounts of THC as traditional smoking, but without many of the respiratory disadvantages associated with the burning of organic materials (Hazekamp, Ruhaak, Zuurman, van Gerven, & Verpoorte, 2006). These findings indicate that using a vaporizer is a safer and equally effective alternative when administrating cannabis for medical purposes.

DISTRIBUTION

Because of their high lipid solubility, the cannabinoids are distributed to all areas of the body according to blood flow but tend to become concentrated in the lungs, the kidneys, and the bile of the liver. Only about 1% of the administered dose at peak blood concentrations actually enters the brain. This amounts to 2 to 44 micrograms (Adams & Martin, 1996).

Figure 14-1 shows the rated *high* produced by different doses of THC administered by different routes. This peak high lags behind the peak blood levels of THC (Adams & Martin, 1996). The effect may be delayed because THC levels in the brain continue to increase for several hours after the drug has been consumed.

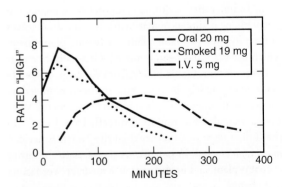

FIGURE 14-1 The time course for the intensity of the subjective "high" after consuming various doses of THC via different routes of administration. (Adapted from Agurell et al., 1986)

EXCRETION

Metabolism starts as soon as the cannabinoids enter the body. There is some metabolism in the lungs if the drug is inhaled and some in the intestines if the drug is taken orally, but most of the metabolism takes place in the liver. Delta-9-THC is converted primarily into 11-hydroxy-delta-9-THC, a substance that is believed to be more active than delta-9-THC and that penetrates the blood–brain barrier more easily (Adams & Martin, 1996). These substances are then rapidly converted into more than 100 other metabolites, some of which may have effects of their own. Some of these effects may be similar to those of THC, but others may be different. Most of these metabolites are less lipid soluble and are more easily excreted (Mechoulam et al., 1976).

CBD is thought to have only a slight effect of its own, but it appears to have a direct effect on the metabolism of THC in the liver. It blocks the enzyme that metabolizes delta-9-THC, slows its metabolism, and prolongs its duration of action. By contrast, CBN may speed the metabolism of THC (Mechoulam et al., 1976). It is also possible that CBD and CBN interact with THC in other ways. For example, these substances may alter the distribution of THC by displacing it from binding sites in the blood and increasing the amount of THC available for distribution to the brain (Siemens, Kalant, & deNie, 1976).

Blood levels of delta-9-THC and its main metabolites fall rather rapidly at first. This initial decline, due to redistribution, has a half-life of about 30 minutes in humans, but this is followed by a phase with a much slower rate of decline and a half-life of 20 to 30 hours (Agurell et al., 1986). During this phase, the rate of metabolism is limited by the rate at which the THC is released from body fat into the blood, which is quite slow. Traces may be detected in the body as long as 30 days later (Institute of Medicine, 1982; Smith-Kielland, Skuterud, & Mørland, 1999). The duration of time that cannabinoids can be detected depends to some extent on body composition. This period is shorter for people with the least amount of body fat.

It is still not clear whether regular cannabis users metabolize and excrete the cannabinoids faster than nonusers (Adams & Martin, 1996; Agurell et al., 1986). Research with laboratory animals has not shown that the development of tolerance is related to any change in cannabinoid absorption, distribution, or metabolism (Agurell et al., 1986; Dewey, Martin, & Harris, 1976). THC is excreted primarily through the feces (55%) and the urine (20%).

NEUROPHARMACOLOGY

Until the late 1980s, the mechanism by which cannabinoids alter neural functioning was a mystery. Evidence suggested they bind to certain receptor sites, but these receptors had never been identified. In 1990, a receptor for cannabinoids was identified by two scientists at the National Institute of Mental Health in Bethesda, Maryland.

Researchers in the laboratory of Miles Herkinham were working with levonantradol, a synthetic cannabinoid, labeled with a radioactive tracer. After tracking the radioactive molecule, researchers were able to create a map of where levonantradol was present in the brain and presumed that it was binding to a cannabinoid receptor at these sites. In the neighboring laboratory of Tom I. Bonner, Linda Matsuda had discovered a gene coding for a receptor. Her goal was to find a receptor for substances that modulate pain, but their receptor did not bind known pain neurotransmitters. Matsuda had mapped where these receptors were found. When compared with Herkinham's findings, it was apparent that the receptors were in the same brain areas where radioactive levonantradol was present. The two researchers then confirmed that Matsuda's receptor was in fact a cannabinoid receptor (Restak, 1993).

Subsequent work has isolated at least two types of receptors, both of which are coupled to second-messenger systems that use cyclic AMP as the second messenger. The CB_1 receptor, the one identified by Herkinham and Matsuda, is found primarily in the CNS; the CB_2 receptor is located mainly outside the nervous system altogether (Martin, 2000; Munro, Thomas, & Abu-Shaar, 1993).

CB_1 cannabinoid receptors are concentrated primarily in the cortex, hippocampus, cerebellum, and substantia nigra but also occur in the hypothalamus, brainstem, and spinal cord (Breivogel & Sim-Selley, 2009). CB_2 receptors are found primarily in the spleen and the immune system (Mechoulam et al., 1994). These receptors are structurally different from those found in the brain, and they seem to be associated with the effects of cannabinoids on immune functions. This peripheral cannabinoid receptor also appears to be affected by CBN. Recent studies have shown that the CB_2 receptor is found in the brain as well and that its activation may have a protective effect against destruction of neurons by the immune system (specifically cytotoxic T-lymphocytes), which occurs in certain diseases. This mechanism could be used to slow the progression of neurodegenerative disorders such as Huntington's disease and Alzheimer's disease (Fernández-Ruiz, Pazos, García-Arencibia, Sagredo, & Ramos, 2008).

Like the discovery of the opioid receptor, the discovery of the cannabinoid receptor has stimulated research into the nature of its endogenous ligands (substances that occur naturally in the body and activate the cannabinoid receptor). Such endogenous substances have been referred to as *endocannabinoids*. The first endocannabinoid was identified by William Devane and Raphael Mechoulam at the Hebrew University of Jerusalem. They called it *anandamide* after the Sanskrit word *ananda*, meaning "internal bliss" (Mechoulam et al., 1994; Restak, 1993). They also identified *2-arachidonyl glycerol*, more conveniently referred to as *2-AG*. Since then, three other endocannabinoids have been discovered: *N-arachidonoyl dopamine, 2-arachidonoyl glyceryl ether*, and *Virodhamine*. Compared to the endocannabinoids, THC is longer lasting and has a much greater effect on the cannabinoid receptors.

Cannabinoid receptors and their endogenous ligand appear to function more as neuromodulators of many different neurotransmitters than as neurotransmitters themselves. CB_1 receptors are located mostly in neurons on the terminal buttons. That is, they are presynaptic, and the enzyme that destroys the endocannabinoids is located in the cell body and dendrites of the postsynaptic cell. This indicates that the endocannabinoids are a signaling mechanism between the postsynaptic cell and the presynaptic cell. What seems to be happening is that when the membrane of the postsynaptic cell is depolarized, this triggers the release of an endocannabinoid that acts at the CB_1 receptors on the presynaptic membrane, causing ion channels to open and consequently blocking the action potentials as they arrive. The result is that the presynaptic neuron is disabled. Thus, the postsynaptic neuron is able to shut down the presynaptic neuron. If the neurotransmitter released by the presynaptic neuron is inhibitory, the result is depolarization-induced

suppression of inhibition (DSI). If the transmitter is excitatory, the result is depolarization-induced suppression of excitation (DSE). This effect lasts for tens of seconds and affects other synapses in the area.

When THC is administered, it would have the same effect of shutting down both excitatory and inhibitory transmission in neurons that have these CB_1 receptors in the entire brain for a much longer period of time than would the endocannabinoids.

DSI and DSE operate on neurons that use many different neurotransmitters, including norepinephrine (NE), dopamine (DA), serotonin (5-HT), acetylcholine (ACh), histamine, opioid peptides, GABA, and prostaglandins. In addition, cannabinoids are known to increase synthesis of NE, DA, 5-HT, and GABA. They can potentiate the actions of NE, ACh, GABA, and opioid peptides, and they can alter the functioning of receptors for NE, DA, and ACh. Not all of these effects, however, are likely to be mediated via the cannabinoid receptor; some may be achieved directly by other means (Pertwee, 1992).

Cannabinoid receptors are found in the nucleus accumbens, and THC increases dopamine levels and activity in the mesolimbic dopamine reward system. This likely occurs through potentiation of the effects of endogenous opioid peptides, which in turn function as neuromodulators of dopamine transmission. It has been suggested that this mechanism is responsible for the reinforcing effects of cannabinoids (Gardner, 1992; Tanda, Pontieri, & Chiara, 1997). However, a recent study found that release of dopamine in the human striatum was not significantly affected by administration of a capsule containing 10 mg of THC. This contradicts previous research and suggests that recreational doses of THC, specifically, may not increase dopamine levels in the brain. Because all participants in the study displayed marked behavioral effects, it is reasonable to conclude that a single cannabis joint may not have the potential to cause significantly elevated dopamine transmission (Stokes, Mehta, Curran, Breen, & Grasby, 2009).

Cannabinoid receptors are also found in the cerebellum and basal ganglia, other parts of the extrapyramidal motor system, and the hippocampus. These anatomical findings correspond with what we know about the effects of cannabinoids on movement and memory.

The endocannabinoid system within the central nervous system appears to contribute to many functions, particularly those involved in stress recovery. One review article concluded, "Thus, 'relax, eat, sleep, forget and protect' might be some of the messages that are produced by the actions of endocannabinoids, alone or in combination with other mediators" (Di Marzo, Melck, Bisogno, & De Petrocellis, 1998, p. 528). There is also evidence that CB_1 receptors are important to the reinforcing effects and the development of physical dependence on opioid drugs such as morphine and heroin (Ledent et al., 1999).

Few cannabinoid receptors are found in the medulla in the brain stem. This is not surprising since we know that they have little effect on the breathing reflex (Martin, 2000).

EFFECTS OF CANNABIS

Effects on the Body

Low and moderate doses of marijuana have predictable physiological effects. These are fully apparent a few minutes after smoking and usually last about 2 to 3 hours. The most common effect is bloodshot eyes, caused by the dilation of the small blood vessels in the whites of the eyes. This effect, which peaks about an hour after smoking, causes no discomfort to the user. Heavy marijuana use can sometimes be detected because the user looks stoned—an appearance marked by a slight droop in the eyelids.

Another effect is the sensation of dry mouth and a compulsion to drink, which frequently leads users to drink alcoholic beverages while smoking marijuana. An intense feeling of hunger, known as the *munchies*, is strongest about 3 hours after smoking, when other effects have declined. This increase in appetite eventually appears to show tolerance; after a few weeks of continuous marijuana use, appetite is actually depressed.

Smoking marijuana also causes a reliable increase in heart rate, which can go as high as 160 beats per minute in some individuals. Muscle relaxation usually occurs as well. There are also unpredictable fluctuations in blood pressure and body temperature. Nausea and vomiting sometimes result, especially after the user has been moving around.

In addition to somatic effects, subjective psychoactive effects are commonly present and can include alterations of perception, euphoria, feelings of well-being, and increased appreciation of humor.

Effects on Sleep

Marijuana causes drowsiness and increases sleeping time in humans, but higher doses can interfere with sleep, causing restlessness and insomnia (Tart & Crawford, 1970). Habitual users may in fact have difficulty getting to sleep (Paton & Pertwee, 1973). Low doses of marijuana cause slight changes in sleep-stage patterns, although some research has shown no effect on sleep. Recent studies have shown that Sativex, which contains naturally derived cannabinoids, helps individuals with chronic pain disorders achieve more regular and restful sleep even at relatively low doses: 2.7 mg THC and 2.5 mg CBD (Russo, Guy, & Robson, 2007). At higher doses, marijuana disrupts normal sleep stages, but when marijuana is discontinued, this does not cause poor quality of sleep or frequent wakening (Feinberg, Jones, Walker, Cavness, & Floyd, 1976).

Medically Useful Effects

Certain somatic effects of cannabis that are not normally noticed have medical usefulness. For example, *glaucoma*, a condition in which pressure in the eyes is too high, has been successfully treated with marijuana as THC reduces that pressure. In a rather famous case in the United States, a young man with glaucoma was prosecuted for growing marijuana but won his case by arguing that it was necessary to break the law in order to treat his glaucoma (Grinspoon, 1971; Grinspoon & Bakalar, 1993, 1997).

THC can act as an *antiemetic* (a drug that stops nausea and vomiting). Nabilone and Marinol are now frequently used to treat the nausea and sickness of people receiving chemotherapy for cancer.

THC has been shown to be effective in treating movement disorders and *spasticity* (Braude & Szara, 1976; Cohen & Stillman, 1976; Institute of Medicine, 1982). People with damaged spinal cords and people suffering from diseases like multiple sclerosis often experience uncontrollable muscle spasms, loss of motor control, and pain. Clinical studies clearly show that cannabinoids are an effective treatment for this spasticity (Earleywine, 2002). This effect has been applied to Tourette's syndrome as well. In a 2006 review it was reported that patients with Tourette's noticed a major reduction in uncontrolled muscle spasms or *tics* without adverse cognitive effects while taking THC in moderate oral doses (Ben Amar, 2006).

The effectiveness of cannabis in treating other disorders, such as Parkinson's disease, is the topic of extensive debate. It has been reported that patients experience a reduction in Parkinsonian symptoms after using cannabis, but a review of medical trials with cannabis reveals little overall objective or subjective effect (Ben Amar, 2006).

The cannabinoid system has been implicated in the modulation of pain responses. It has been found that CNS neurons in pain centers become less responsive to pain-inducing stimuli after administration of synthetic cannabinoids (Martin et al., 1976). Also, blockade of CB_1 receptors in the spinal cord increases sensitivity to pain as measured by the hot plate test (Richardson, Aanonsen, & Hargreaves, 1998). Lately, research has focused more on the ability of cannabis to improve subjective pain ratings. In this regard, patients suffering from HIV have reported decreases in muscle and nerve pain after using cannabis (Woolridge et al., 2005), and patients with neuropathic pain have reported similar improvements after administration of both a low THC (3.5%) and a high THC (7%) cannabis joint (Wilsey et al., 2008). Patients with spinal cord injuries also reported that marijuana led to a more effective reduction in pain than conventional medications (Cardenas & Jensen, 2006).

Cannabinoids have also been linked with appetite stimulation, and it has been shown that individuals suffering from HIV/AIDS or undergoing cancer treatment are able to slow chronic weight loss with the administration of oral THC or smoked cannabis (Ben Amar, 2006). In addition, studies have found that CBD is effective in reducing psychotic symptoms of schizophrenia, and the mechanism of action suggests it may be useful in treating other mental disorders such as bipolar disorder (Zuardi et al., 2006). Cannabinoids also have the potential for use as a treatment for anxiety, arthritis, dystonia, insomnia, microbial infections, seizures, and tumors.

Route of Administration for Medical Purposes

Many people who use cannabis for medicinal purposes inhale cannabis smoke. The rapid absorption of cannabinoids in the lungs allows patients to monitor the dose they administer and get immediate effects. For medicinal purposes, getting high is usually considered an undesirable side effect, and monitoring or titrating the dose of cannabis allows patients to get the maximum medicinal effect without side effects. Commercially manufactured cannabinoids such as Nabilone and Marinol are taken as pills and have a delayed effect, as they are absorbed slowly. This makes titration difficult and is one reason why many users of medicinal cannabis prefer smoking marijuana to taking pills. In an effort to overcome this problem, newer medicinal cannabinoid preparations like Sativex are administered as a spray under the tongue and are absorbed much faster, making titration easier. Cannabinoid inhalers with much faster effects are also being developed.

EFFECTS ON THE BEHAVIOR AND PERFORMANCE OF HUMANS

Historical Accounts

The first European writer to describe the effects of cannabis was Théophile Gautier, a member of Le Club des Hachichins of Paris in the middle of the nineteenth century (Gautier, 1966). Gautier was an artist, not a scientist, and his accounts must be considered with some skepticism because they were written primarily to entertain rather than inform. Gautier's experiences are, therefore, not typical of contemporary North American use, but much of what he reports is characteristic of the hallucinogenic effects of cannabis intoxication at high doses. Gautier's account is a classic, and in spite of its embellishments and inaccuracies, it has shaped the expectancies and prejudices of users and opponents through the years.

Later, Charles Baudelaire, another member of the club, published his accounts of the hashish experience. Other classical descriptions were written by Fitzhugh Ludlow, the American son of an abolitionist minister and friend of Mark Twain, and the American traveler and diplomat Baynard Taylor (Ebin, 1961; Solomon, 1966).

Mood Changes and Getting High

A typical experience with marijuana is characterized by swings of mood from euphoric gaiety with hilarious laughter to placid dreaminess. The experience is nearly always pleasant—a feeling of well-being and joyfulness is usually referred to as being high—but occasionally there are feelings of anxiety and foreboding, even at low doses in hospitable surroundings.

When cannabis is consumed socially, as it often is, there is frequent laughing and good humor. Almost anything seems funny, and the most innocent event or statement may ignite gales of contagious laughter. If the drug is taken alone or in a quiet setting, the user may spend time predominantly in a dreamy state reflecting on the subjective experience. It is frequently felt that perceptions are keener and that sensory effects are more intense and enjoyable. Just as slightly funny things seem hilarious, mundane thoughts and insights may take on great significance and importance. Artists and musicians frequently feel that their creativity is enhanced.

Although physical activity sometimes increases and users feel that their actions are effortless, they generally avoid tasks requiring effort and prefer instead to remain passive.

In spite of consistent reports from users that marijuana elevates mood, when subjective changes in feelings are measured systematically by a test like the POMS, findings are not at all clear-cut. Both positive and negative changes in mood have been reported (de Wit, Kirk, & Justice, 1998; Jones & Benowitz, 1976; Rossi, Babor, Meyer, & Mendelson, 1974), and the pattern of responding to mood scales appears to be unique. For example, in one study, smoking marijuana caused an increase in scales indicating stimulation and at the same time increased scores on scales associated with sedation. There were no changes in scales indicating euphoria or positive mood states (Chait et al., 1988). The subjective effects of smoked marijuana and oral THC are similar, except for their time course (Chait & Zacny, 1992) (refer back to Figure 14-1).

Many researchers believe that the reason for variability in subjective ratings between studies is that environment can have a considerable influence on how the drug changes mood. The effects of surroundings on mood have been investigated, but differences such as smoking in a neutral as opposed to a psychedelic environment or while watching television, listening to rock music, or carrying on a conversation had no effect on subjective self-ratings. One factor that does seem to be important, however, is the mood of others. In a 1978 experiment, mood self-ratings were not correlated with ratings of intoxication, but after subjects took marijuana, mood ratings were highly correlated with the mood of the other subjects in the experiment, whether they were

high or not. Thus, it would seem that after smoking marijuana, a person becomes more susceptible to being influenced by the mood of others (Rossi, Kuehnle, & Mendelson, 1978).

Mood changes have been studied extensively in experienced users, but almost no attempts have been made to study the subjective effects of marijuana in naive subjects, even though one's first experience with the drug seems to be an important determinant of later use. One study of college students showed that those who reported positive effects at first experience were more likely to use the drug sooner the second time and use it regularly later (Davidson & Schenk, 1994).

Perception

One of the subjective effects of the cannabinoids is an increased sensory sensitivity, but subjective testing of sensory thresholds has found only decreases in sensitivity or no change in auditory, visual, and tactile thresholds (Jones, 1978). Such cannabis-induced sensory distortions may be due to the physical distribution of CB_1 receptors as they are densely located in the inferior colliculus and posterior thalamus, both of which are involved in sensory processing (Skosnik, Krishnan, Vohs, & O'Donnell, 2006). The cannabinoids also cause a loss of sensitivity to pain, which indicates that the drug has analgesic properties.

The time-distorting effect of cannabis has been demonstrated experimentally (Domino, Rennick, & Pearl, 1976). Weil, Zinberg, and Nelson (1968) found that three subjects out of nine judged a 5-minute speech to be 10 minutes long. Distortions of time sense may be due to a decrease in cerebellar blood flow during cannabis use as the cerebellum is associated with the body's internal timing system (Mathew, Wilson, Turkington, & Coleman, 1998). Increases in subjective time rate (people experience time passing more quickly) is one of the most reliable behavioral effects of cannabis (Chait & Pierri, 1992).

Memory

Cannabis appears to have no effect on the ability to recall material already well learned or on recognition memory (the ability to recognize words or figures), but it does disrupt the ability to recall words or narrative material (Chait & Pierri, 1992). The problems occur primarily in short-term memory, in which information is held actively in the brain for short periods of time. While under the influence of cannabis, people frequently show what has been called *temporal disintegration*—they lose the ability to retain and coordinate information for a purpose. If they are required to hold information in the brain for any length of time, it frequently gets lost before it can be used. It is not unusual, for example, for people under the influence of cannabis to start a sentence and then stop halfway through because they forgot what they started to say. When such things happen, others who have been using the drug are not likely to remember the initial idea either, and some very disjointed conversations result. Some users have described this inability to hold things in short-term storage by saying that thoughts come so quickly that it is difficult to keep from being distracted by them. It is quite likely that the deficits in short-term memory and the distorted sense of time are related since memory helps with judging the passage of time.

It has been pointed out that the effects of cannabis on memory are similar to the symptoms of Korsakoff's psychosis, a neurological disorder seen in long-term alcoholics (see Chapter 6). Among the symptoms of Korsakoff's psychosis are a memory disorder and a disorientation in time that is caused by damage to the limbic system, especially the hippocampus. This is a likely hypothesis in light of the fact that cannabinoid receptors are found in high concentrations in the hippocampus. This similarity has been substantiated by the fact that smaller right hippocampus volume was found to be associated with high levels of cannabis use (5.8 joints/day) during adolescence (Ashtari et al., 2011). Such observed reductions in hippocampal volume may be due to the possible neurotoxic effects of THC (Demirakca et al., 2011). The relationship between cannabis and hippocampal volume is complex as CBD has been shown to have neuroprotective effects.

Creativity

One of the subjective effects of cannabis is that it helps to improve appreciation of art, even art produced by the user. The widespread belief that the drug increases the creativity of artists may have arisen largely because the drug was widely used by musicians and artists. There is little consistent evidence from objective research that creativity is enhanced (Chait & Pierri, 1992) or that artists who use marijuana are more successful than artists who are not users (Grinspoon, 1971). Research has shown that THC leads to bilateral hemispheric activation, but many studies have reported significantly greater right-hemisphere activity. It has been suggested that this differential hemispheric activation may relate to cannabis' tendency to promote creativity (Quickfall & Crockford, 2006).

Performance

Any attempt to summarize the effects of cannabis on the various measures of performance is nearly impossible. There is no doubt that certain tasks are impaired by high doses of the drug, but results are so variable due to the experience of subjects, instructions, motivation, setting, and dosage that it is difficult to be specific.

An example of this confusion can be found in experiments on hand–eye coordination where subjects are required to track a moving target manually. One early classic study found that marijuana impaired this ability in novice subjects, but the performance of experienced subjects actually improved with marijuana (Weil et al., 1968).

Certain simple reaction times appear to be unaffected by marijuana. In complex and choice-reaction-time tests, accuracy but not speed is likely to be affected. Marijuana is often reported to impair hand–eye coordination tasks such as the pursuit rotor and tasks that measure both psychomotor and memory tests (e.g., the digit symbol substitution test; de Wit et al., 1998).

Performance in a similar tracking task was measured after consuming high potency cannabis (13% THC). Hand–eye coordination and delays in visual motor response were found to be affected at both a low dose (250 micrograms/kg) and more significantly at a higher dose (500 micrograms/kg) (Ramaekers et al., 2006). It seems that the amount of THC consumed is directly related to the level of impairment in performance-based testing, therefore variability in the data may be due to a lack of dosage standardization in addition to other factors.

Driving

Numerous studies have been conducted on the effects of marijuana on driving and flying, and most have reported impaired performance, although such effects are not reported for all individuals (Chait & Pierri, 1992; Klonoff, 1974).

Studies in a driving simulator have shown that marijuana has little effect on the ability to control a car, but impairs the driver's ability to attend to peripheral stimuli. Thus, marijuana-intoxicated drivers might be able to stop a car as fast as they normally could, but they may not be as quick to notice things that they should stop for, probably because they are attending to internal events rather than to what is happening on the road (Moskowitz, Hulbert, & McGlothlin, 1976).

One study of the effects of THC on driving in real traffic showed moderate impairment caused by low doses of THC (100 and 200 micrograms/kg body weight). These effects were greatly amplified when small doses of alcohol were consumed as well (Ramaekers, Robbe, & O'Hanlon, 2000). In analyses of motor-vehicle accidents, it has been reported that alcohol is very often consumed with cannabis prior to driving. The combined effect of the two drugs seems to contribute significantly to driving fatalities, much more than cannabis alone. In fact, an observational study of motor-vehicle accident victims requiring hospitalization in the Netherlands reported no connection between cannabis use alone and vehicle trauma. Alcohol, benzodiazepines, and other combinations of drugs, predictably, were found to contribute significantly (Movig et al., 2004).

Performance Screening Tests

At this time, it is not possible to do a roadside screening test for individuals driving under the influence of THC in the same manner as the Breathalyzer tests for alcohol intoxication. Even blood samples that test positive for THC are not indicative of impaired driving because THC can be detected for several hours or even days since last use, long after any impairing effect has subsided (Skopp, Richter, & Pötsch, 2003). The State Police of Victoria in Australia have been developing a performance screening test for marijuana intoxication based on the test developed for alcohol in the 1970s called the *Standardized Field Sobriety Test*. It consists of tests of gaze nystagmus (involuntary eye movements as someone sights a moving object), the walk and turn test (where the individual walks heel to toe up and down

a line), and a one-legged stand (where the individual stands on one leg and counts aloud). Performance on all these tasks is scored using objective criteria. Evaluations of the test employed three groups of individuals: one that had been given a placebo, and two others that had smoked marijuana with low or high THC content. The test identified intoxication in 2.5% of the placebo group, 38.5% of the low-THC group, and 56.4% of the high-THC group. These results suggest that it should be possible to develop a reliable screening test for THC intoxication (Papafotiou, Carter, & Stough, 2005).

EFFECTS ON THE BEHAVIOR OF NONHUMANS

Unconditioned Behavior

THC has a biphasic effect on spontaneous motor activity (SMA); in many species, there is an increase in activity followed by a depression in behavior. The depressant effect is more powerful, appears in more species, lasts longer, and is more resistant to tolerance. Interestingly, the stimulatory effects appear to be an exaggerated response to environmental stimuli rather than a general increase in activity (de Wit et al., 1998). At high doses, the decrease in motion is called *ataxia* and is accompanied by a loss of motor control and by fine tremors—laboratory animals assume one posture without moving for long periods; monkeys stare into space or look at their hands and occasionally appear as though they are hallucinating (Paton & Pertwee, 1973).

One effect was noticed early in animal experimentation: a taming effect or a reduction in aggression. Animals that were normally aggressive and hard to handle became tame and placid after receiving THC. THC will reduce the attack behavior of the dominant member of a pair of rats and will also diminish the ability of a submissive rat to defend itself in a fight. Predatory attack behavior of several species is also reduced.

In rats, THC causes a decrease in food intake and a subsequent weight loss. THC is about half as potent as amphetamine in suppressing food intake, but unlike amphetamine, THC causes an increased preference for sweet sugar solutions. This may be related to the munchies effect observed in humans (Sofia, 1978).

A number of tests have shown that THC is as potent as morphine in reducing the response of rats to painful stimuli. CBN also has analgesic effects but is only as potent as aspirin. No analgesic effects were found for CBD (Sofia, 1978). The metabolites of THC are probably more potent than their parent compound. At one time, it was believed that the analgesic effects of THC were dependent on interactions with the opioid system, but it has since been shown that such effects are mediated through systems in the brain and spinal cord that act independently of opioid pain control (de Wit et al., 1998).

Conditioned Behavior

As with humans, THC appears to interfere with tasks that require short-term memory, such as the radial arm maze and the matching-to-sample test, in which the animal is required to remember a stimulus for a brief period of time. These deficits in memory are correlated with suppression of cell firing in the rat's hippocampus and can be caused by direct microinjection of THC into the hippocampus (Fadda, Robinson, Fratta, Pertwee, & Riedel, 2004). THC has also been shown to interfere with schedules and tasks that require timing. Nonhuman performance on other tasks appears normal until doses high enough to suppress all behavior are reached.

Like the barbiturates and the benzodiazepines, THC decreases avoidance responding at doses that do not alter escape responding in a discriminated avoidance task. Such decreases in avoidance responding is a common effect shared with the tranquilizers, anesthetics, and alcohol. One might expect that a drug that has both anxiolytic and analgesic effects would increase punished behavior, but neither delta-9-THC nor a similar cannabinoid, delta-8-THC, appears to increase behavior suppressed by punishment with electric shock (McMillan & Leander, 1976). In this regard, THC is very unlike the tranquilizers, anesthetics, and alcohol.

DISSOCIATION

Both delta-9-THC and delta-8-THC cause dissociation in rats. Rats were unable to transfer to a nondrug state what they had learned in a drug state, and there was a symmetrical inability to transfer to the drug state what they had learned in the nondrug state (Henricksson & Järbe, 1971). Dissociation has also been demonstrated in humans using marijuana. In one study, participants were asked to learn a list of words after taking a placebo and then to recall the list after smoking marijuana and vice versa. When the participants acquired information in one state, they had difficulty transferring it to the other state. This effect was not very powerful because the loss of recall could be overcome by prompting and cuing the participants by reminding them of word categories (Stillman, Eich, Weingartner, & Wyatt, 1976). In another study, only asymmetrical dissociation was found. Information acquired while the participants were not intoxicated was remembered after smoking marijuana, but information acquired during marijuana intoxication was not remembered when sober (Darley & Tinklenberg, 1974).

Dissociation has not been demonstrated for motor skill and perceptual tasks such as card sorting and tasks requiring hand–eye coordination, even though marijuana impaired performance on those tasks (Järbe & Mathis, 1992).

DRUG STATE DISCRIMINATION

Rats are easily able to discriminate THC from placebo when it is administered intravenously, intraperitoneally, or orally. The stimulus properties are evident as early as 7.5 minutes after injection and peak at 30 minutes but are still reliable at 60 minutes. A training dose of delta-9-THC would generalize to delta-8-THC and the 11-hydroxy metabolite but would not generalize to CBD (Balster & Ford, 1978), although some generalization occurs to CBN (Järbe & Mathis, 1992). Interesting interactions have been noted with these other naturally occurring cannabinoids; in some experiments, CBD has been shown to enhance and prolong the stimulus effects of THC (Järbe & Mathis, 1992).

Many other drugs have been tested to learn whether the THC response generalizes to them. There appears to be partial generalization to sedative drugs and no generalization to drugs of any other class, including stimulants, hallucinogens, and opioids. Cannabinoid discriminations can be blocked by the cannabinoid receptor antagonist, SR-414716A. Interestingly, animals trained to discriminate THC generalized poorly to anandamide and then only when anandamide was given in high doses (de Wit et al., 1998).

Experienced marijuana smokers can easily learn to distinguish marijuana cigarettes containing 0% THC from marijuana cigarettes containing 2.7% THC. In one study, individuals were able to make the discrimination within 90 seconds of taking the first puff. They were successful in identifying marijuana containing 1.7% THC, but they identified a sample with 0.09% THC as a placebo (Chait et al., 1988).

TOLERANCE

In laboratory animals, tolerance to the effects of THC on operant behavior develops rapidly. Depending on the dose and the route of administration, complete tolerance may develop after 5 or 6 days of repeated injections of THC (Abel, McMillan, & Harris, 1974). This tolerance lasts for more than a month, and there is cross-tolerance between delta-9-THC and its 11-hydroxy metabolite (Kosersky, McMillan, & Harris, 1974). Tolerance also develops within a few days to increases in motor activity, but the progress is much slower for the depression in activity. There is no tolerance at all to the anorexic effects or the discriminative stimulus effects. There is also tolerance to the lethal effects in pigeons; a dose of 180 mg/kg had no effect on tolerant animals but was lethal in naive pigeons (Martin, 2000). Tolerance does not appear to be due to alterations in absorption, metabolism, or distribution of the drug (Dewey et al., 1976). Instead, it is known that tolerance is associated with a decrease in the number of cannabinoid receptors in selected brain areas (Martin, 2000), as well as downregulation/desensitization of cannabinoid receptors (González, Cebeira, & Fernández-Ruiz, 2005).

There is some disagreement about the development of tolerance in humans. Many marijuana users have reported a sensitization or reverse tolerance to the drug—they become more sensitive to the effects, rather than less sensitive, with repeated use. Reverse tolerance has never been shown in laboratory studies with nonhumans or humans. For several reasons, reverse tolerance is observed only outside the laboratory. One likely reason is a matter of dosage. In laboratory studies, dosage is carefully measured. Outside the laboratory, users calculate their consumption in terms of the number of joints they smoke. With experience, users learn to inhale more efficiently so that they are able to get more drug into their

bodies from a given amount of marijuana. Therefore, they will require fewer joints to get high. In addition, experience may be required to learn not only how to get high but also the activities, situations, and company that contribute to the high. All these factors could contribute to the observation that over time, fewer joints are needed to get high.

Early experiments showed that tolerance to the subjective effects of THC and marijuana would develop only if the drug was given in high doses for an extended period of time (Frank, Lessin, Tyrrell, Hahn, & Szara, 1976; Jones & Benowitz, 1976). However, more recent studies have shown that the subjective effects of both high and low doses of orally administered THC and high-potency smoked marijuana administered four times a day showed a considerable drop over 4 consecutive days (Haney, Ward, Comer, Foltin, & Fischman, 1999a, 1999b). In the same experiment, no tolerance to increased food consumption was seen.

WITHDRAWAL

Withdrawal symptoms have been seen after prolonged administration of high doses in nonhumans. These symptoms are not severe and frequently appear as an increase in motor behavior. Recently, it has been reported that cessation of chronic cannabinoid injection causes a marked withdrawal in rodents, but this withdrawal is usually masked by the long half-life of THC and its metabolites. If animals receive high doses of a synthetic cannabinoid for 2 weeks, no withdrawal is seen after administration stops. If the animals receive an injection that blocks cannabinoid receptors, however, withdrawal does occur as measured by the release of stress hormones (Rodríguez de Fonseca Carrera, Navarro, Koob, & Weiss, 1997).

Withdrawal symptoms, without the use of cannabinoid blockers, have been reported with humans. In a 50-day outpatient study it was found that the onset of withdrawal symptoms typically occurred between days 1 and 3 of abstinence, peaked between days 2 and 6, and most symptoms remained until days 4 to 14 (Budney, Moore, Vandrey, & Hughes, 2003). Withdrawal symptoms with the greatest severity generally included appetite change, restlessness, and thoughts of and cravings for cannabis (Milin, Manion, Dare, & Walker, 2008).

SELF-ADMINISTRATION IN HUMANS AND NONHUMANS

THC is self-administered by humans, but, until the past decade, there were no demonstrations of nonhuman self-administration (Griffiths et al., 1980). Justinova, Tanda, Redhi, and Goldberg (2003) trained squirrel monkeys, with no history of exposure to other drugs, to self-administer THC via intravenous injections. Prior to this, success has been achieved only with water-soluble synthetic cannabinoids like WIN55212-2, which is self-administered by mice (Ledent et al., 1999).

It is seldom difficult to get humans to take cannabis. In a hospital ward setting, Mendelson, Kuehnle, Greenberg, and Mello (1976) conducted an experiment in which participants were required to press a button to gain points with which they could buy marijuana cigarettes. A joint could be earned for about 30 minutes of work. Extra points could be saved for money at the end of the experiment. In this experiment were two groups of participants: casual users and heavy users of marijuana. The number of joints smoked by each group was far less than the number available but showed a slight increase over the 26 days of the experiment. Casual users smoked about two joints per day at the beginning and increased to three by the end of the experiment. Heavy users started at four a day and ended at about seven. Apart from this slight increase, the amount consumed was fairly stable from day to day; no cyclic patterns or periods of abstinence were noted, although there was a big increase on the last day that marijuana was available. No evidence of withdrawal was seen when use was stopped. In this study, there seemed to be a level of high that most users tried to achieve, and they stopped when they achieved it. In other words, they appeared to titrate the dose.

Marijuana self-administration in humans in experimental settings has been demonstrated a number of times since then, but, curiously, it has not yet been shown that THC content is important. In one experiment (Kelly, Foltin, Mayr, & Fischman, 1994), marijuana cigarettes with 0 and 2.3% THC were smoked with equal frequency, even though self-reports of "high," "potency," and "liking" were higher for the THC-containing marijuana.

Titration

The ability of users to titrate a specific dose was studied in another experiment. Experienced marijuana users were given joints of different potencies and asked to smoke until they achieved a "nice high." To some extent, these experienced users did smoke fewer high-potency joints than low-potency joints before they stopped, but the compensation was far from perfect. The participants smoked 60% more of the weak marijuana than the strong marijuana, but even after this compensation, they administered a 250% higher dose to themselves when the strong joints were available (Cappell & Pliner, 1974). On the basis of this experiment, even experienced users seem unable to adjust their intake accurately in the face of variations in the potency of the marijuana they are smoking. Doubt is also cast on the notion that there is such a thing as a "social high" that can be determined on the basis of an administered dose. Factors other than dosage must control marijuana intake.

Even though people in experiments will smoke an equal number of marijuana cigarettes with 0 and 2.4% THC (Kelly et al., 1994), choice experiments have shown that the reinforcing effect of marijuana increases with higher THC content. In a preference study, experienced users sampled marijuana of two different potencies (0.63 and 1.95% THC). During the choice phase of the experiment, participants chose the high-potency marijuana much more often than the low-potency marijuana (Chait & Burke, 1994).

EPIDEMIOLOGY

In North America, cannabis is predominantly a social drug. In the 1970s, most marijuana was smoked in groups. The drug was consumed in an almost ritualistic manner and often in a circle with a pipe or joint passed around. More recently, however, solitary use of the drug has become more common, and the ritualism has declined.

The social nature of marijuana may also be responsible for initiation to marijuana use. A very small percentage of users first smoked marijuana alone. There can be no doubt that the strong social reinforcement and the feelings of shared pleasure and intimacy contribute considerably not only to the start of drug use but to its continuation as well.

In some countries where cannabis is a traditional drug with a long history, the pattern and extent of use is quite different from that in Europe and North America, where cannabis use is comparatively recent. In countries such as India, Egypt, Greece, Morocco, and Jamaica, the majority of cannabis users take extensive doses every day, and there is little casual use. In the United States, the vast majority of users are casual, and a smaller percentage uses it daily. Compared with other countries, relatively small amounts are consumed in North America. It has been estimated that a casual cannabis user can get "stoned" on 5 to 6 mg of THC, and the average daily user in the United States consumes about 50 mg of THC per day. The average daily user in Eastern countries consumes 200 mg per day. In addition, marijuana use is not as persistent in the United States as in other countries. Most westerners who start using cannabis eventually decrease their use and stop. In countries where use is more extensive, it may persist for 20 to 40 years.

According to the National Household Survey on Drug Abuse, between 1985 and 1992 the number of marijuana users in the United States declined from 9.3% of the population to 4.3%, and the number of frequent marijuana users (once a week or more) dropped from 4.6 to 2.4% (U.S. Department of Health and Human Services, 1994). This decline bottomed out between 1992 and 1994 (U.S. Department of Health and Human Services, 1995), and more recently in the United States, the use of cannabis has increased. The National Institute on Drug Abuse has reported that, in 2009, cannabis use increased among high school students from Grades 8 to 12. The increase was especially marked for Grade 12 students where use was at its highest since the 1980s at 6.1%. Perceived risk of cannabis use also declined, which suggests that the trend will continue upward. The situation in Canada appears different. According to the Canadian Alcohol and Drug Use Monitoring Survey, prevalence of last-year use in individuals 15 and older dropped from 14.1% in 2004 to 10.6% in 2009. Lifetime use decreased only slightly from 44.5% in 2004 to 42.4% in 2009. Similarly, in the United Kingdom it has been reported by Focal Point Annual Report on Drugs that last-year use has declined fairly significantly from 2007 (8.2%) to 2009 (6.6%).

HARMFUL EFFECTS

Cannabis is a drug of great controversy. Probably no other drug in recent times has generated more public concern and debate or stimulated more research into its safety (or lack thereof). This body of scientific literature is highly specialized, confusing, and often contradictory, and it is often misrepresented in the popular media, which has tended to publicize only selected research findings and to ignore others. Nonexperts have had difficulty keeping track of it all. People are generally confused, and those with particular biases have no trouble finding evidence to support their position.

The debate on the harmful effects of cannabis products has taken on a new dimension in recent times with the move to use cannabis as a medical treatment for numerous diseases and the tendency to "decriminalize" its use in countries like Holland, Portugal, and Spain.

Marijuana has been accused of having many harmful effects, some of which we shall discuss. It will be obvious to anyone who has read this section that cannabis, like any other drug, has a great number of effects on many systems of the body, some of which have the potential for great harm. It should also be obvious that even though the potential for harm exists, especially at high doses, there are very few hard data to show that the drug really does any harm. The lack of data may mean that there is no harm, but it may also mean that reliable data are difficult to collect.

Violence and Aggression

One of the oldest beliefs about cannabis is that it directly causes violence and aggression and is associated with crime, but there are absolutely no systematic data to support this myth. In long-term studies where marijuana was given to individuals in controlled hospital ward settings, increases in violence were never reported. In addition, mood rating scales generally show decreases in feelings of hostility and increases in friendliness. Myerscough and Taylor (1985) investigated marijuana's effect on aggression by administering low, medium, and high doses of THC and then subjecting participants to intense provocation. They discovered that greater doses of THC were associated with less aggressive behavior throughout the experimental session.

Numerous surveys and field studies, using a variety of techniques, have compared criminal behavior and crimes of violence in groups of marijuana users and nonusers, and in the vast majority of these studies no connection has been found. In fact, if there was a correlation, it showed a decrease in violence. For example, one study found that among a certain population of young criminal males, marijuana was used specifically to reduce aggression rather than to increase it (Tinklenberg, 1974). Although there may be isolated cases of idiosyncratic or unusually violent reactions among some individuals after taking marijuana, these ordinarily occur in people with a prior psychiatric disturbance or when other drugs are used at the same time.

Mental Disturbance

When the drug is taken in larger doses than usual, the user may be overcome with overwhelming anxiety and paranoid feelings. Such a state often leads to a trip to a hospital emergency department. At higher doses, THC can elicit an acute psychotic reaction, a panic that produces positive, negative, and cognitive symptoms. Users panic because they lose touch with reality and feel that they may be going insane. Such panic attacks are often referred to as *freak-outs* and usually occur when the drug is taken in unusual and stressful circumstances, if more drug is consumed than the user is accustomed to, or if the cannabis is mixed with other drugs. Freak-outs are much more common with hallucinogens, such as LSD, than with cannabis. Patients usually can be effectively treated by being quietly "talked down," but in severe cases, a benzodiazepine tranquilizer can be effective (Dinwiddie & Farber, 1995). As well, preliminary evidence indicates that CBD may counteract THC-elicited positive symptoms including hallucinations and visual distortions (Morrison, Kapur, & Murray, 2009).

What is not so clear is whether cannabis use can cause psychotic or schizophrenia-like illness in later life. A number of studies have shown that heavy cannabis users have an increased risk of suffering from schizophrenia in later life, but more recent research has suggested that this trend can be explained by the fact that cannabis may precipitate or speed up the emergence of schizophrenic symptoms in people who would have developed the disease in any case (Iverson, 2005). There is little evidence that cannabis by itself use will generate psychoses. It appears instead to be dependent on a combination of factors including age of first use, environmental risk factors, dosage, and genetic predisposition (Casadio, Fernandes, Murray, & Di Forti, 2011). An Australian study spanning a 30-year period has shown that the incidence of schizophrenia did not increase in spite of a drastic increase in cannabis use during that time (Degenhardt, Hall, & Lynskey, 2003).

Permanent Intellectual Impairment and Brain Damage

There is conflicting evidence from laboratory studies and experiments with nonhuman animals that exposure to high levels of cannabis might cause damage to nerve cells (Chan, Hinds, Impey, & Storm, 1998; Collins, Pertwee, & Davies, 1994; Silkker, Paule, Ali, Scarlett, & Bailey, 1992), but there is no evidence that heavy cannabis use causes any irreversible damage in humans.

In an exhaustive review of the literature, Iversen (2005) concluded that there is little evidence that long-term heavy use of cannabis by humans produces any severe or debilitating impairment of cognitive functioning. Long-term use of cannabis may produce subtle impairments in the higher cognitive functions of memory, attention, and the organization and integration of complex information; however, the nature and extent of cognitive deficits are related primarily to the amount of recent cannabis use. Pope, Gruber, Hudson, Huestis, and Yurgelun-Todd (2001) found that, although heavy cannabis users scored significantly below controls on cognitive tests on days 0, 1, and 7 of cannabis abstinence, by day 28 there were virtually no differences between the two groups on any cognitive tests.

Much of the research suggesting that cognitive effects of marijuana are reversible has been conducted in adults, but because marijuana is being widely consumed by teenagers and preteens, there is concern that marijuana use may have irreversible effects on a developing brain. Still, data suggest that these effects may be reversible. Fried, Watkinson, James, and Gray (2002) compared the IQ of a group of young people when they were 9 years old with their IQ at ages 17 to 19. Those who were using cannabis in their late teens showed a decline in IQ from when they were 9, but there was no decline in IQ in people who had previously been heavy users but who had, by their late teens, stopped taking the drug.

Amotivational Syndrome

It has sometimes been observed that when a young person starts smoking marijuana, systematic changes occur in that person's lifestyle, ambitions, motivation, and possibly personality. These changes have been collectively referred to as *amotivational syndrome.* Its symptoms are apathy, loss of effectiveness, and a diminished capacity or willingness to carry out complex long-term plans, endure frustration, concentrate for long periods, follow routines, or successfully master new material.

There is no doubt that many young individuals have changed from clean, aggressive, upwardly mobile achievers into the sort of person just described at about the same time as they started smoking marijuana. What is not clear, however, is whether a causal relationship exists between the loss of middle-class motivations and cannabis. There is considerable evidence showing that cannabis is correlated with reduced educational achievement. Furthermore, reduction in years of schooling depends largely on the age of first use, with the greatest decrease found for those who begin using cannabis before the age of 15 (Horwood et al., 2010).

Evidence for the existence of an amotivational syndrome was found in an experiment in which rhesus monkeys were exposed to the smoke from marijuana cigarettes every day for a year (Silkker et al., 1992). These monkeys pressed a lever for banana-flavored food pellets on a progressive ratio schedule. Each time the pellet was received, the ratio requirement increased, and more presses were required. Silkker and colleagues found that during exposure to marijuana smoke, breaking points were considerably lower than they were for controls, and they returned to normal when exposure to the smoke was discontinued. Thus, the monkeys exposed to marijuana smoke were not as willing to work hard for an attractive food as nonexposed monkeys. Because the animals responded normally on other tasks for the same food pellets, the researchers argued that this result was analogous to the amotivational syndrome seen in humans and was not a result of either loss of the ability to respond or loss of appetite.

Laboratory studies with humans have found conflicting effects of cannabis on motivation. In an early experiment by Mendelson et al. (1976), hospitalized volunteers worked on an operant task to earn money and marijuana for 26 days. Smoked marijuana did not influence the amount of work done by either the casual-user group or the heavy-user group; all remained motivated to earn and take home a significant amount of money in addition to the work they did for the marijuana. Likewise, Smucker-Barnwell, Earleywine, and Wilcox (2006) found no difference in motivation between individuals in a large sample (n = 487) of chronic, daily cannabis users versus abstinent controls.

This issue is clearly not settled. But even if there is no specific motivational effect, it is clear that cannabis affects attention and memory, and these are intellectual capacities necessary for success in educational and career endeavors.

Progression to Other Drugs

There are claims that marijuana is a *gateway drug* or a stepping-stone toward the use of more dangerous drugs. In support of this *gateway theory* are studies that show that virtually all heroin users had used marijuana before they adopted heroin (Golub & Johnson, 1994). In addition, studies have shown that the more a person uses marijuana, the greater the probability that the person will use other drugs as well (Mullins, Vitola, & Michelson, 1975).

These data suffer from the same difficulty as the research on amotivational syndrome: No causal relationship can be established. The fact that marijuana is used before heroin does not mean that marijuana use causes heroin use. Most people drink soda pop before they drink alcohol, but this fact does not mean that soda pop causes alcohol drinking.

Recently, an alternative hypothesis to gateway theory, known as *common factor model*, has been proposed that accounts for individuals' progression from using marijuana to using harder drugs. Common factor model relies on the following assumptions (as quoted from Morral, McCaffrey, & Paddock, 2002): (a) Individuals have a nonspecific random propensity to use drugs that is normally distributed in the population; (b) this propensity is correlated with the risk of having an opportunity to use drugs and with the probability of using them given an opportunity; and (c) neither use nor opportunity to use marijuana is associated with hard drug initiation after conditioning on drug use propensity. Common factor model is able to reproduce and account for each of the phenomena used to support claims of a so-called gateway effect, even though marijuana use has no direct relationship with the initiation of hard-drug use in the model. This theory is supported by a large study, carried out by Degenhardt and colleagues (2010) through the World Health Organization, that evaluated patterns of order and initiation of drug use in 17 countries. Results of this study indicate that an individuals' degree of drug exposure is a far more powerful predictor of hard-drug use than simple marijuana use. Alternative models have implications for drug policy as they indicate that it is not necessarily marijuana that creates a gateway effect, but rather the black market created by marijuana prohibition that indirectly exposes individuals to hard drugs and acquaints them with drug dealers.

Reproduction

Although not all researchers have been able to replicate this finding, marijuana seems to lower the levels of the sex hormone testosterone in both human and nonhuman males. Although decreases in testosterone are unrelated to inhibition of male sexual behavior, it is not yet apparent whether such decreases have any biological significance. The levels of testosterone vary greatly from one individual to another and within the same individual throughout the course of a day. We do not know as yet whether a marijuana-induced suppression of testosterone will make any difference in the face of this great natural variability. A reduction in testosterone levels could conceivably lead to a reduction in fertility; however, little reliable data have been collected to show that this occurs more frequently among chronic cannabis users.

The effects of cannabis on sexual behavior and arousability are generally dose dependent in males as well as females (Gorzalka, Hill, & Chang, 2010). In males, it has been found that although marijuana use increases sexual desire, it also has a detrimental effect on erectile functioning. In females, results are generally positive as research shows that marijuana consumption increases sexual desire as well as satisfaction, pleasure, and orgasm quality.

In a large-scale research project between 1984 and 1989, more than 7,000 pregnant women in the United States were studied, and their drug use histories were recorded. Of these women, 11% reported using marijuana during pregnancy. Marijuana use was not associated with low birth weight or prematurity. By comparison, 35% of the women smoked tobacco, and this history was associated with low birth weight (Shiono et al., 1995).

Some functional differences have been detected in children exposed prenatally to cannabinoids through maternal marijuana smoking. One study showed abnormal sleep patterns in newborns that persisted at least until the age of 3 years in cannabis-exposed children (Dahl, Scher, Williamson, Robles, & Day, 1995). There is some evidence that prenatal exposure to cannabis may have effects that do not show up for several years. These effects may include hyperactivity, impulsiveness, and learning disorders. The effects are small, however, and it is impossible to demonstrate any causal connection to marijuana use (Earleywine, 2002).

Immunity

It has been clearly established that cannabinoids modulate activity in the body's immune system, which fights invading microorganisms and infection. The function and level of different white blood cells is affected by cannabinoids in addition to the cytokine network, which is involved in inflammatory response. Previously, it was thought that the relationship between cannabinoids and the immune system was exclusively antagonistic, but lately it has become clear that the regulation of immune function is far too complex for this simple generalization. No conclusive evidence suggests that cannabis users are significantly more prone to disease or infection than nonusers. In addition to the medically useful effects mentioned earlier, the regulatory power of cannabinoids in the cytokine network may allow for the targeted treatment of inflammatory disorders such as Crohn's disease (Tanasescu & Constantinescu, 2010).

Cancer

Evidence is clear that tobacco smoke is associated with cancer. But what about marijuana smoke? Even though marijuana users typically inhale much less smoke than tobacco users, the smoke from marijuana contains 50 to 70% more carcinogenic material than tobacco smoke, and marijuana smokers typically inhale more deeply and hold the smoke in the lungs longer than tobacco smokers. Unfortunately, results in this area are frequently confounded by the fact that most marijuana smokers also smoke tobacco. It seems possible that marijuana accelerates the carcinogenic effects of tobacco smoke. Even though the median age for developing cancer is between 55 and 65, one study of people under age 45 with lung cancer found that almost all smoked both tobacco and marijuana (Sridhar et al., 1994).

On the other hand, there are reports that cannabidiol and delta-9-THC are potent antioxidants (Hampson, Grimaldi, M., Axelrod, J., & Wink, 1998). Antioxidants neutralize free radicals, which damage DNA and can increase the risk of cancer. More recent reviews of cannabis use and cancer prevalence have failed to show that there is any statistically significant relationship between cannabis and increased risk of cancer. Some studies have shown a link between cannabis and certain types of cancer, but when the data are combined and analyzed, many of these correlations disappear. As well, conflicting research sometimes suggests that cannabis greatly increases the risk for a certain type of cancer, while another study suggests it may be a treatment for the same type. Much more careful and selective research must be done to determine the role of cannabis use alone in cancer development.

CHAPTER

15

Hallucinogens, Phantasticants, and Club Drugs

A variety of drugs with different mechanisms of action are discussed in this chapter. At one time, they might have all been referred to as *hallucinogens*. While it may be true that many of these drugs can cause hallucinations, often they are not taken in high enough doses to do so—other effects seem to be important to the user.

Many of these drugs have profound subjective and emotional effects. They make the user feel in touch, either with others around them or with their inner selves; feel closer to God or the universe; or feel ecstatic. They can also enhance the enjoyment or appreciation of music and social situations. A variety of other names have been suggested that describe some of these other common effects, names that include *phantasticants*, *psychedelics* ("mind manifesters"), *entactogens* ("touching within"), and *empathogens* ("empathy enhancers"). The latter three were proposed in an attempt to describe the effect of these drugs on personal insights and empathy. Due to the nature of these subjective effects, it has been suggested that certain drugs of this type could be useful tools in psychotherapy (Metzner, 1993). Because the mental state created by some of these drugs is superficially similar (and sometimes almost identical) to certain forms of psychosis, the name *psychotomimetics* ("psychosis mimics") is also sometimes used. More recently, some of these drugs have become associated with the club scene and are used to enhance the pleasure of

music, dancing, and being with others. When used this way, they are referred to as *club drugs*.

LSD AND THE MONOAMINE-LIKE DRUGS

The molecular structure of many drugs with hallucinogenic and phantasticant properties bears a resemblance to the monoamine neurotransmitters: serotonin, dopamine, and norepinephrine. *LSD (lysergic acid diethylamide)* and many other drugs are similar to serotonin, which is an indoleamine. Mescaline has a structure similar to the catecholamines, dopamine and norepinephrine. Even though they differ somewhat in structure, there is a considerable overlap between the effects of these *indoleamine-like* and *catecholamine-like* drugs, so they can be discussed together. In the next section we will discuss MDMA (ecstasy), which has certain chemical properties of both mescaline and amphetamines as well as similar behavioral effects.

Indoleamine-like drugs have effects that are similar to LSD and differ mainly in potency and duration of action. These include *psilocybin*, the ingredient in magic mushrooms; *lysergic acid amide*, found in morning glory seeds; *DMT*, found in the bark of a tree in the jungles of South and Central America; *bufotenine*, found in plants and in the venom of toads from the *Bufo* genus;

and *harmine* and *harmaline*, which are found in a tropical vine that grows in South America and is used by the native peoples in the area to make an intoxicating drink (McKim, 2003).

Mescaline is a catecholamine-like drug. It too has many effects in common with LSD but is about 1/2,000th as potent. It is the active ingredient in a cactus known as the *peyote* (*Lephophora williamsii*), which is native to the deserts of Mexico and the southwestern United States. The peyote is a small, spineless cactus that barely sticks out of the ground and has a thick, tuberous root. It has been used for centuries by Native Americans in rituals and religious ceremonies.

Since LSD is the most widely used and studied member of the monoamine-like drugs, it will be discussed in detail as a representative of this class. In fact, it also shares some effects with ecstasy and other drugs in this chapter.

History of LSD

LSD is a synthetic drug; however, a number of similar chemicals occur naturally in the *ergot fungus* that infects grains, especially rye. During the Middle Ages in Europe, there were outbreaks of what is now called *ergotism*, a reaction caused by eating fungus-infected grain. There were two kinds of effects caused by different fungi. One kind severely constricted blood flow to the limbs and made the person feel excessively warm. This eventually led to gangrene, and the limb would fall off. In 1039, a religious order was formed in France to treat people afflicted with this kind of ergotism. The patron saint of this order was St. Anthony, and the disease became known as *St. Anthony's fire* because of the sensation of heat. The other type of ergotism was characterized by convulsions, delirium, and hallucinations. That these afflictions were caused by the fungus was not discovered until more than 700 years later, in 1777. In fact, St. Anthony's fire was caused by derivatives of lysergic acid in the ergot fungus.

The story of LSD begins in the twentieth century. One of the effects of the lysergic acid derivatives in ergot was contractions of the uterus, a fact that was known to midwives who used it to aid women in childbirth. This prompted Albert Hofmann of the Sandoz Laboratories in Basel, Switzerland, to experiment with the derivatives of lysergic acid in the hope of finding a new medicine. He had no inkling that he was dealing with a hallucinogen. In

1938, he synthesized a series of lysergic acid compounds but found none of them particularly interesting and went on to other things. Five years later, in 1943, Hofmann made a new batch of the twenty-fifth derivative (which he called LSD-25) and tried some new experiments, but he began to feel very peculiar and had to go home. He suspected that the reason for his strange sensations was that he had accidentally taken some of the LSD-25. To test this theory, a few days later he deliberately ingested 0.25 mg (250 micrograms, μg), which he thought was an extremely small dose. His plan was to start with a dose so small that it would have no effect and slowly work up, but he did not know the extreme potency of LSD. A quarter of a milligram is a rather large dose and is more than sufficient to cause a significant hallucinatory effect. Hofmann experienced the first LSD trip.

Sandoz Laboratories did not know what to do with LSD, so the drug was distributed for testing to laboratories in Europe and the United States. It was thought that it might be useful in the treatment of mental disorders and alcoholism or at least as a means of studying psychotic behavior. Some researchers, like Humphry Osmond at the University of Saskatchewan, believed that LSD offered the power to provide great personal insights and possessed considerable psychotherapeutic potential. LSD was used in experiments in mental hospitals and laboratories until the mid-1960s, when it broke out of the laboratory and into the street.

Timothy Leary, a research professor in the Department of Social and Human Relations at Harvard University, was always considered by his colleagues to be a bit unconventional and radical in his views. The psychedelic revolution began for Leary in 1960. While he was in Mexico, he ate some mushrooms containing psilocybin, which caused him to have a "full-blown conversion experience." When he returned to Harvard, he and his colleague, Richard Alpert, distributed psilocybin to as many people as they could convince to take it. In 1961, they tried LSD, started a new religion, and adopted LSD as a sacrament. In 1963, Leary and Alpert were dismissed from Harvard, a move that generated considerable publicity for them and the drug. They coined the phrase that was to become the philosophy of the hippie movement of the 1960s: "Turn on, tune in, drop out."

LSD had its heyday during the 1960s and early 1970s, the years of the hippie movement, which reached its peak at the Woodstock Music Festival in 1969. LSD has not vanished since then, but the pattern of its use is now somewhat different. In the 1960s, LSD was used as a true psychedelic—high doses were consumed in order to achieve vivid hallucinations and personal or cosmic insights. Using these high doses was not always a pleasurable experience. It has been suggested that drug users, since that time, are not as interested in insight as they are in pleasure (Baumeister & Placidi, 1983).

LSD is now taken in smaller doses and used more as a phantasticant or entactogen than as a hallucinogen. The effect is a euphoric high similar to that of marijuana, and powerful mind-altering states are neither desired nor achieved.

Dosage and Sources

LSD is sold as hits. In the 1970s, a typical hit contained about 100 μg of LSD with a range of 0 to 300 μg (James & Bhatt, 1972). The minimum dose required to produce a full psychedelic experience with visual hallucinations is often cited as 200 μg. Although the average dose does not appear to have changed much over time, there has always been great variation in the dosage available in a hit.

Hits of LSD have traditionally been absorbed in blotting paper, which may be plain or printed with various cartoons or mosaic patterns. More recent variations include the *gel tab*, LSD in gelatin that is set in molds of various shapes, or flat squares called *window panes*. LSD is also now available in candies or tiny pills called *microdots*. There is usually a larger dose of LSD in gelatin than in blotting paper because the gelatin protects the drug from deterioration caused by light and exposure to air. Mescaline is acquired from the dried *heads* of the peyote cactus and can be consumed orally or soaked in water to create an intoxicating drink. The typical effective dosage of mescaline is 200 to 400 μg.

Pharmacokinetics

LSD is usually taken orally and is effective between 30 and 90 minutes after ingestion. Only 1% of the drug ever reaches the brain. The half-life of LSD is approximately 175 to 300 minutes in humans (Aghajanian & Bing, 1964; Papac & Foltz, 1990). It is metabolized extensively in the liver, and its metabolites are secreted into the digestive system in the bile and excreted in feces.

Mescaline is also readily absorbed from the digestive system and has a similar half-life (Brown, 1972).

Effects on the Body

There are few consistent physical side effects of LSD; the most common is dilation of the pupils. Nausea, changes in body temperature, and increased heart rate have also been reported. Mescaline often causes a period of nausea during the early stages of its effect.

Neurophysiology

Even though LSD has been around for a long time and has been studied extensively, its effects on the nervous system are still not clear. While it acts as a serotonin receptor blocker in the peripheral nervous system, in the central nervous system it appears to be a selective agonist at some serotonin receptors, particularly the 5-HT_{2A} receptor. This is also true for other indoleamine-like and catecholamine-like hallucinogens. Their effects on 5-HT_{2A} receptors are one of the few that all these drugs have in common. It has been suggested that, in cortical neurons specifically, LSD and other hallucinogenic compounds trigger a particular intracellular signaling cascade that is distinct from other 5-HT_{2A} receptor agonists (González-Maeso et al., 2007). This appears to be one of the reasons these compounds can trigger hallucinations.

There are three regions of the brain that seem to be involved in the hallucinogenic effect: the locus coeruleus (LC), the cortex, and the raphe nuclei. The LC receives input from many sensory sources throughout the body, including the raphe nuclei. It sends axons to almost every area of the brain including the cortex, where it promotes the release of NE (see Chapter 4). It is involved in fear and emotional responses and appears to function as a novelty detector. Stimulation of 5-HT_{2A} receptors by both indoleamine- and catecholamine-like hallucinogens can suppress output of the LC, although it occurs through different mechanisms. In addition, these drugs enhance the response of the LC to novelty. This might explain the common effects of hallucinogenic drugs on perception. After taking mescaline, for example, people often report that it is like seeing things for the first time.

In the cortex, these drugs change the response of large glutamatergic neurons to synaptic input by increasing the duration of excitatory action potentials. This effect is mediated through serotonin synapses and is most prominent in the medial prefrontal cortex, where there is a large concentration of 5-HT_{2A} receptors. This area of the cortex is instrumental in information processing and perception.

The raphe nuclei are clustered in the brainstem and function to release serotonin in the rest of the brain. It has been found that LSD acts as a 5-HT_{1A} receptor agonist in the raphe system, where it inhibits neuronal firing and serotonin release (Passie, Halpern, Stichtenoth, Emrich, & Hintzen, 2008). Because the LC receives input from the raphe nuclei via serotonin neurons, suppression of the raphe system by hallucinogenic drugs may be the precursor to LC suppression and the resulting effects.

Subjective Effects

HALLUCINOGENIC EFFECT. How does a scientist go about studying hallucinations? Hallucinations are, by definition, in the realm of subjective experience, and one of the first principles of scientific inquiry is that all scientific data must be public and observable to anyone. It is, however, possible to study the verbal reports of people who are experiencing or have experienced hallucinations. Heinrich Kluver (1966) combined reports of subjects in his own experiments on mescaline and those of other researchers and noticed that there were consistencies. Mostly, these people described vivid visual images, and the researchers were aware that the images were not real. If they closed their eyes, they would see these images against a black background; if they opened their eyes, the images would be projected on whatever they were looking at. Kluver noticed that the images were frequently geometric, and he identified some common patterns: a grating or lattice; a cobweb; a tunnel, funnel, or cone; and a spiral. Kluver remarked that images of these types also appear in fever deliriums, insulin hypoglycemia, and states that occur just before drifting off to sleep (*hypnogogic states*). Unfortunately, what Kluver described was only the first of two stages of imagery; the second stage, described by others, is more complex and involves meaningful images of people, animals, and places. Even during this phase, there are some common elements among individuals. For example, 60 to 70% of all subjects report seeing small animal or human figures that are friendly and caricature-like, and 72% of all subjects report religious imagery.

Despite the great interest surrounding these observations, no comprehensive, systematic, or scientific work on them was attempted until the 1970s. The problem was tackled by Ronald Siegel (Siegel & Jarvik, 1975) from the University of California in Los Angeles (UCLA). Siegel adopted a variation of the technique of trained introspection, which had been used by the early German schools of psychology. Siegel trained his observers to use a code to describe their experiences. They were able to code images, colors, and movement by using a series of letters and numbers that could be quickly expressed. Following this training, Siegel gave participants a series of blind tests in which they were administered placebos or any of a number of drugs in random order and left in a darkened room to report their experiences. Neither the participants nor the researchers scoring the imagery codes knew what drug had been given.

Whereas the participants given placebos saw a predominance of random forms, those getting the hallucinogenic drugs saw far more lattice and tunnel forms, confirming the observations of Kluver. During control sessions, participants saw primarily black and violet forms, but in hallucinogenic sessions, they saw more colors, ranging into the yellow, orange, and red end of the spectrum. Finally, in all conditions, aimless and pulsating movement was reported, but in hallucinogenic sessions there was an increase in "explosive" movement.

After demonstrating that all of these drugs appeared to create similar types of images, Siegel was also able to show that, at higher doses, people sometimes go through a phase where they see themselves being swept up into their own hallucination. This is followed by a stage where the images lose their geometric quality and become meaningful pictures of real objects. These images can change rapidly, as fast as 10 times a second, but the changes are not without a pattern. Each image appears to be related to the one before it. Figure 15-1 illustrates this point. Siegel also noted that the images during this stage were related to the participant's surroundings; for example, sounds such as footsteps induced an image of someone walking. Another interesting finding was that the colors appeared to shift from the blue end of the spectrum to the red end as the effect of the drug increased in intensity.

FIGURE 15-1 This series of drawings (viewed from top to bottom, column by column) illustrates the systematic changes in complex meaningful imagery reported after taking mescaline. Note that each scene contains an element of the previous one. (Pen and ink drawings by David Sheridan. From Siegel & Jarvik, 1975)

Because all these drugs have such similar effects, Siegel wondered whether the similarities might be due to cultural factors since all his subjects came from a similar culture (UCLA). To answer this question, he visited a remote tribe of Huichol Indians in the Sierra Madre range of Mexico. These Indians make brightly colored pictures of their peyote visions from colored yarn. Siegel found that the experiences represented by the Huichols in their yarn pictures were very similar to those reported by the subjects in his laboratory.

Siegel postulated that the nature and structure of hallucinations must be determined by the nature and structure of the visual system and the brain, not by the drug, because (a) these hallucinatory experiences are similar among vastly different drugs; (b) the experiences resemble the effects produced by other nondrug hallucinations, such as those from fever, hypoglycemia, and migraine headaches; and (c) the experiences are similar between cultures. In other words, the hallucinations are a result of nonspecific interference in brain functioning; the drug intensifies what might be considered normal background noise in the perceptual systems, and this noise is then organized, by the normal processes of perception and cognition, into images and patterns (Siegel, 1977; Siegel & Jarvik, 1975).

Siegel's study addressed only the visual property of the hallucinogenic experience, but LSD can cause entactogenic and empathogenic effects as well. These experiences often have a profound effect on emotions, insights, and feelings, which are not as easily studied and can be conveyed only by less scientific modes of expression, as we shall see.

PHANTASTICANT AND PERCEPTUAL EFFECTS. Hallucinogenic drugs can cause users to feel that the experiences they are having are of great emotional or worldly significance. Often these experiences can be spiritual in nature. For this reason, drugs like LSD have been widely used in traditional religious ceremonies. The spiritual nature of the hallucinogenic experience is described here by R. Gordon Wasson (1972) in this account of his participation in a Mazatec Indian psilocybe mushroom rite:

> It permits you to see more clearly than our perishing mortal eyes can see, vistas beyond the horizons of this life, to travel backwards and forwards in time, to enter other planes of existence, even (as the Indians say) to know God. It is hardly surprising that your emotions are profoundly affected and you feel that an indissoluble bond unites you and the others who have shared in this sacred agape. All that you see during this night has a pristine quality; the landscape, the edifices, the carvings, the animals—they look as though they had come straight from the Maker's workshop. (p. 197)

Another commonly reported experience is the greatly enhanced pleasure derived from viewing art and, especially, listening to music:

> Ordinarily I am not particularly susceptible to music. This time, lying on the cot, I became acutely aware of the Montoya record playing. This was more than music: the entire room was saturated with sounds that were also feelings—sweet, delicious, sensual—that seemed to be coming from somewhere deep down inside me. I became mingled with the music, gliding along with the chords. Everything I saw and felt was somehow inextricably interrelated. This was pure synesthesia, and I was part of the synthesis. I suddenly "knew" what it was to be simultaneously a guitar, the sounds, the ear that received them, and the organism that responded, in what was the most profoundly consuming aesthetic experience I have ever had. (Richardson in Aanonsen & Osmond, 1970, p. 53)

ENTACTOGENIC AND EMPATHOGENIC EFFECTS. Another commonly reported effect is that the hallucinogens seem to provide insight into one's past and one's own mind, revealing repressed thoughts and unrecognized feelings. Such insights are similar to those that psychoanalysis attempts to achieve through psychotherapy. It was this effect that inspired Humphry Osmond to suggest that hallucinogens might be useful tools in psychotherapy and prompted the use of the term *entactogenic* ("touching within") to describe this effect. Here is a description of the experiences of psychologist Bernard Aaronson, who took LSD as part of an experiment:

> We sat on the bench under the trees and talked about the loneliness of being, and talked about how people are forever needing things they expect you to provide. For what seemed a long time, I cried as I have not cried since I was a baby, for all the people in the world who need things and whose needs cannot be met. I cried too for all the people around me that I botched in the giving or to whom I cannot give because I am depleted . . . . I expressed great hostility toward both my parents and with H.'s help analyzed my feelings as they derived from my relationship with each of them. I analyzed my relationship with my next older brother, and examined the meaning in my life of my relationship with that friend whom I love the most. (Aaronson & Osmond, 1970, pp. 47–48)

A more complete account of the subjective experiences of hallucinogens is beyond the scope of this book. A good selection of accounts of drug experiences may be found in Grinspoon and Bakalar (1979b).

Perception

As we have seen, people who use LSD frequently report that their perceptions are much keener and that their sight and hearing have become more acute. There have been a few studies of the effects of LSD on visual sensory thresholds, but their results are not consistent. In general, however, impairments of sensory functions attributable to LSD are reported more often than improvements (Hollister, 1978).

Although it is clear that LSD increases the enjoyment of music, it has not yet been established whether there are any changes in auditory thresholds. The perception of the passage of time is distorted in most individuals; however, the direction of distortion is not consistent. In most cases, time is perceived as slowing down (10 seconds seem more like 20), but in some experiments the reverse has been reported (Hollister, 1978).

Behavior and Performance

One of the difficulties with measuring human performance under the influence of hallucinogens is maintaining the motivation of the participant to cooperate. Like marijuana, hallucinogens frequently cause people to become inattentive to the task and so caught up in internal experiences that they lose their motivation to perform, as well as they are able, tasks that they may feel are irrelevant at the time. The available data show mostly that LSD impairs reaction time. Functioning on intellectual tasks is also impaired. Like THC, LSD causes a deficit in short-term, or working, memory. Other impairments are seen in problem-solving and cognitive functions such as mental addition and subtraction, color naming, concentration, and recognition (Hollister, 1978).

Claims have been made that LSD-like hallucinogens improve creativity, but again, as with THC, these are difficult to substantiate experimentally. There is little doubt that LSD changes the sort of work done by artists, but it is debatable whether these changes are improvements.

Tolerance

In humans, tolerance to the effects of LSD and related drugs develops rapidly. When LSD is taken repeatedly for 2 or 3 days, tolerance develops and the drug no longer produces the desired effect. This tolerance dissipates quickly, however, and sensitivity returns within a week. This is one reason why these drugs are seldom taken continually. The ability of LSD to disrupt the operant behavior of nonhumans also shows rapid tolerance. Cross-tolerance has been observed between LSD, psilocybin, and mescaline but not between LSD and d-amphetamine or THC (Brown, 1972). Such tolerance appears to be mediated by the downregulation of the serotonin 5-HT$_{2A}$ receptor (Gresch, Smith, Barrett, & Sanders-Bush, 2005).

Withdrawal

No withdrawal symptoms for LSD or any similar drugs have been documented. This may be because the drugs are seldom taken continuously for any period of time and do not lead to physical dependence. However, some issues can persist for a short time after use is stopped, such as flashbacks or residual perceptual distortions.

Self-Administration

NONHUMANS. It is widely accepted that LSD and similar monoamine-like hallucinogens are not self-administered by nonhumans. In fact, they appear to have aversive effects, and it has been demonstrated that laboratory animals will work to avoid being given LSD. In one experiment, rhesus monkeys learned to press a lever to turn off a stimulus that normally preceded an infusion of LSD and, thus, prevented the infusion (Hoffmeister & Wuttke, 1975). Nevertheless, a study done in 2004 did show transient self-administration of DMT, mescaline, and psilocybin in some monkeys with a history of self-administering MDMA (discussed later in this chapter; Fantegrossi, Woods, & Winger, 2004). This suggests that the occasional use of these drugs may be reinforcing in some individuals. This may explain why, outside the laboratory, there are reports that nonhumans will, from time to time, consume plants that contain LSD-like drugs.

HUMANS. The self-administration of hallucinogens like LSD in human cultures is almost universal and very ancient, but its use is different from the use of most other drugs. First, these drugs are never continuously consumed. They are indulged in sporadically and on special occasions. The use of hallucinogens in most cultures is usually associated with religious ceremonies. In many cultures, these drugs are taken only by priests and shamans for the purpose of divination, talking to the dead, or seeking direction from a deity. Even in modern Western culture, hallucinogens are usually taken episodically. Unlike other heavily used drugs such as alcohol, LSD use, for most people, does not increase over time. This may be due in part to the rapid development of tolerance that occurs when individuals use LSD continually.

LSD use among teenagers in the United States remained fairly high throughout the 1990s but has since been steadily declining. In 2009, 6.8% of individuals aged 18 to 25 reported lifetime use of LSD and 0.3% reported using LSD within the past 30 days (Substance Abuse and Mental Health Services Administration, 2010).

Harmful Effects

Psilocybin, LSD, and mescaline are not very toxic. There are no recorded cases of anyone dying from an overdose of any of these drugs. However, the media has focused attention on behaviors, which may be provoked by the acute effects of hallucinogenic drugs. For example, stories appear occasionally about LSD users who jump out of windows because they believe that they can fly or commit murders under the influence of the drug. These events undoubtedly occur, but they are extremely rare and probably occur with no greater frequency under the influence of LSD than alcohol or any other drug.

A common effect of less concern is the *acute psychotic reaction* or *psychedelic crisis*, which occurs when the user is having an unpleasant experience or bad trip. During a psychedelic crisis, the user often forgets that their experience is drug-induced. Consequently, they can undergo reactions ranging from vague anxiety to prolonged terror or panic. Panic reactions are not normally seen in experienced users, are frequently a result of an unusually high dose (or mixture) of drugs, and do not constitute a serious medical emergency. Panicked users can usually be calmed down if put in close contact with someone who talks to them and reassures them that their state is drug induced. If their attention can be concentrated on this fact, the panic can usually be dispelled.

Another adverse effect of many hallucinogens is that some of their effects may be briefly experienced long after the drug has worn off. These episodes are commonly known as *flashbacks*, and the condition is listed in the *DSM-IV-TR* (2000) as "Hallucinogen Persisting Perception Disorder (Flashbacks)" (HPPD). In a similar effect, called *trailing phenomena*, objects seem to move in a jerky, discontinuous fashion as though being illuminated by stroboscopic light. These symptoms may occur unpredictably after a single use of LSD and normally last only a few seconds or minutes. It has been suggested that stress or the use of other drugs such as caffeine, alcohol, or marijuana may trigger these perceptual distortions (Halpern & Pope, 2003). The prevalence of individuals who display HPPD symptoms after one-time, or even chronic, use is likely very small, and there is insufficient evidence to establish a cause–effect relationship between hallucinogen use and development of HPPD. Though the condition exists, its development is likely contingent on numerous other factors than just hallucinogen use alone.

ECSTASY AND SYNTHETIC MESCALINE-LIKE DRUGS

The structure of the mescaline molecule has been altered to form a family of drugs that is a combination of catecholamine-like hallucinogens and amphetamines. These drugs are all synthetic. Much of this research was done in the hope of finding drugs with medically useful properties, and many were created. So far, these substances have been used exclusively in the drug subculture. Perhaps the best known of these is ecstasy.

The term *ecstasy* usually refers to *MDMA* (3,4-methylenedioxymethamphetamine) but may also refer to a mixture of *MDMA*, *MDEA* (N-ethyl-3,4-methylenedioxyamphetamine), and *MDA* (3,4-methylenedioxyamphetamine), drugs with similar potencies and effects (Kalant, 2001). MDMA was originally synthesized by the Merck drug company and patented in 1914. It was never developed or used for any purpose until the late 1960s, when it first appeared on the drug scene (Siegel, 1986). MDMA may also be known on the street as *X*, *Adam*, *MDM*, *M&M*, and *e*.

During the 1960s, many other synthetics were invented and manufactured in clandestine labs in an attempt to circumvent the law, which identified only specific chemicals as illegal. At that time, slight changes in the molecule could make a drug legal until such time as there was specific legislation against it. Such drugs have become known as *designer drugs*, and they appeared on the street with a variety of names such as DMA, DOM, DOET, and so on. For the most part, these substances are more potent and considerably more toxic than mescaline, and they cause more unpleasant side effects, such as headaches and nausea. Unlike commercially developed drugs, many designer drugs were not screened for adverse effects, and some had extremely toxic effects and caused a number of deaths. Many of these designer drugs have virtually disappeared, but some, like ecstasy, are still around and are still widely used.

Prior to July 1985, when it was reclassified by the governments of the United States, the United Kingdom, and Canada, some psychiatrists gave MDMA to their patients because it seemed to enhance intimacy and communication between the patient and the therapist (the terms *entactogen* and *empathogen* were invented with ecstasy in mind; Adler, Abramson, Katz, & Hager, 1985; Verebey, Alrazi, & Jaffe, 1988). When it was reclassified in 1985, its use, even for psychotherapeutic purposes, was banned because it was discovered that the drug had neurotoxic effects; it was shown that a dose of about four times the normal effective dose causes a depletion of serotonin in the brains of rats 1 week after a single administration, a finding now confirmed in humans (Baggott, Jerome, & Stuart, 2001).

Ecstasy is sold in white or colored tablets that may or may not be marked with a symbol. Each pill may contain up to 100 mg or more of MDMA and may also contain varying amounts of MDEA, MDA, PMA (para-methyoxyamphetamine), and MBDB (3,4-methhlene-dioxy-phenyl-N-methylbutanamine). A review of the purity of ecstasy tablets showed that in the late 1990s, as many as 20% of tablets did not contain MDMA at all; many contained only drugs like caffeine, ephedrine, or ketamine. However, these purity problems have not persisted into the 2000s, and non-MDMA tablets are now infrequent (Parrott, 2004).

Pharmacokinetics

Ecstasy is typically taken orally and reaches a peak concentration in the bloodstream 2 hours after ingestion. The majority of the drug is either excreted unchanged in the urine or metabolized to MDA. It has a half-life of about 8 hours, thus taking about 40 hours for 95% of the drug to be eliminated. For this reason, many of its effects persist for several days after use.

Ecstasy is most often used by teens and young adults attending dance clubs or raves, although its use is associated with an increasing number of other activities such as sex. It produces a marked increase in wakefulness, endurance, energy, a sense of euphoria, an increased sense of well-being, sharpened sensory perception, greater sociability and extroversion, and a heightened sense of closeness to other people. As with LSD, these effects are subject to rapid acute tolerance, which generally means that ecstasy is unlikely to be used continuously. As with LSD, this tolerance dissipates within a few days.

Neurophysiology

Ecstasy and similar synthetics increase transmission at synapses that use serotonin, norepinephrine, and, to a lesser extent, dopamine. It works primarily by causing the release of the neurotransmitter and blocking transmitter reuptake. Ecstasy also affects the release of

oxytocin, a hormone involved in bonding and building trust (Dumont et al., 2009). This neurophysiological effect may be the cause of ecstasy's empathogenic and entactogenic properties.

Behavior and Performance

A dose of 75 to 100 mg of ecstasy induces a state similar to that caused by marijuana or low doses of phencyclidine (PCP), with no hallucinations, and an enhanced awareness of emotions and sensations— effects similar to the entactogenic effects described earlier in the section on LSD (Lamb & Griffiths, 1987; Siegel, 1986).

Short-term, physiological effects of ecstasy include increased body temperature, perspiration, headache, pupil dilation, and muscular tension, which causes jaw clenching and tooth grinding (*bruxism*). Once the acute effects of ecstasy have subsided, several after effects are often reported, including difficulty in concentration, irritability, insomnia, fatigue, and depression similar to the crash or comedown after the use of amphetamine and cocaine (see Chapter 10).

Discriminative Stimulus Properties

Although not as much is known about mescaline and the synthetic mescaline-like drugs, it appears that increased serotonin activity is important in their stimulus effects. Rats trained to discriminate saline from MDMA will generalize the response to a serotonin (5-HT_{1A}) agonist. MDMA stimulus properties do not generalize to cocaine or mescaline.

Tolerance

Similar to LSD, psilocybin, and mescaline, tolerance to the effects of ecstasy develops rapidly in humans.

Self-Administration

NONHUMANS. It has been shown that, unlike LSD, MDMA is readily self-administered by primates (Lamb & Griffiths, 1987) and mice (Trigo, Panayi, Soria, Maldonado, & Robledo, 2006). Research with rhesus monkeys has shown that the reinforcing effects of MDMA are strongest at moderate doses, with lower doses and higher doses being ineffective reinforcers (Fantegrossi, Ullrich, Rice, Woods, & Winger, 2002).

In this experiment, the reinforcing effects of MDMA could be eliminated by administration of a drug that selectively blocked 5-HT$_{2A}$ receptors, but this same drug did not eliminate the reinforcing effects of cocaine or methamphetamine. This suggests that the reinforcing effects of MDMA are mediated by a different mechanism than the psychomotor stimulants. Given this finding, it seems odd that other drugs that increase serotonin activity at 5-HT$_{2A}$ receptors, such as LSD and the selective serotonin reuptake inhibitors (SSRIs), tend not to be self-administered.

HUMAN EPIDEMIOLOGY. The use of ecstasy increased steadily among young people in the United States and Europe throughout the 1990s until 2000. In the United States, ecstasy use increased in high school students, and the number of mentions of ecstasy in emergency room admissions roughly doubled between 1994 and 1999 (NIDA, 2001). A similar trend was seen in the United Kingdom and Canada (Morgan, 2000). Following this peak in 2000, when 3.6% of grade 12 students in the United States reported using the drug in the previous 30 days, ecstasy use underwent a drastic decline. In 2004, that figure dropped to 1.2%. This decline was accompanied with a general increase in perceived risk of using the drug (Johnston, O'Malley, Bachman, & Schulenberg, 2005). There are signs, however, that ecstasy use may be resurging. Ecstasy use in Canada and the United States has increased over the last 5 years, according to the U.N. World Drug Report (2010), and the trend will likely continue to rise. In the United Kingdom, rates of ecstasy use dropped about 1.4% from 2002 to 2008, showing a gradual decline (UNODC, *World Drug Report*, 2010).

Withdrawal

Ecstasy is known to have negative aftereffects; however, due to rapid development of tolerance, it is not taken repeatedly, and withdrawal effects are not seen.

Harmful Effects of Ecstasy

Earlier reports of dopamine neurotoxicity have been shown to be in error, but there is good evidence that, after chronic use, there is depletion of serotonin in the brain that is in proportion to the extent and intensity of use. What is not clear at this time is whether serotonin depletion is irreversible or due to receptor downregulation.

There is considerable evidence from studies of chronic users that this depletion in serotonin plays out in behaviors known to be associated with serotonin. Chronic users show sleep disorders, persistent anxiety, impulsiveness, hostility, and selective impairment of memory and attention (Wareing, Fisk, & Murphy, 2000). The cognitive deficits seem to dissipate about 6 months after use is stopped, but the anxiety and hostility may remain for years. It is likely that any recovery is due to an upregulation of serotonin receptors or some other regulatory adjustment to compensate for the decreased serotonin activity in the brain (Morgan, 2000). The influence of ecstasy in precipitating depression is controversial, with some studies reporting a strong link and others not. In a review of the literature, Guillot (2007) found that, of the 22 studies reviewed, 11 reported increased depression scores associated with ecstasy use and the remaining 11 did not. Contributing to the confusion is the fact that ecstasy is rarely used in isolation; polydrug use tends to be the norm, making it difficult to attribute psychological symptoms to any particular drug. In addition, most users who demonstrated increased levels of depression reported that being diagnosed preceded their use of ecstasy (Guillot, 2007; Guillot & Greenway, 2006).

One of the more troubling and dangerous effects of ecstasy is the loss of heat regulation in the body, causing an increase in body temperature. This may not be serious in many circumstances, but at a rave where the user is dancing vigorously in a warm environment, it can cause symptoms similar to heatstroke, including muscle tissue damage, kidney failure, and liver damage. In addition, if one is dancing vigorously, this also causes profuse sweating, and the body can become dehydrated and lose large amounts of salt. Dancers often attempt to compensate by drinking water excessively, but doing this without replacing salt can dilute the blood and create an electrolyte imbalance. This in turn can cause organs, including the brain, to swell, resulting in seizures. In a 2009 review of the harmful effects of ecstasy, it was found that *hyperthermia* and *hyponatraemia* (electrolyte disturbance) were the most common causes of death related to ecstasy (Rogers et al., 2009).

Lethal Effects

The therapeutic index of ecstasy is about 15 (Gable, 2004); however, there is a great range of doses that have been known to cause death, some within the range of recreational drug use. Death may result from a number of different mechanisms. Hyperthermia and hyponatraemia are two causes. In one study of 87 ecstasy-related deaths, 8 were related to the heart or circulatory system, 4 were caused by liver damage, 9 were caused by swelling of the brain resulting from blood dilution, 30 were caused by overheating, 14 were caused by suicide or accident, and in 22 cases the cause could not be determined (Kalant, 2001).

A complicating factor is that there is nothing in the way of quality control in the clandestine labs that manufacture ecstasy, and the pills may also contain amphetamine, ephedrine, and other substances like *PMA*. PMA was developed in a clandestine lab in Canada in the early 1970s and was distributed in the illicit drug market in the United States and Canada. This drug is extremely potent, second only to LSD, but it is also very toxic and has a therapeutic index of 2.5, making it very dangerous to use (Schmidt, 1987). A number of deaths were attributed to PMA before warnings could be spread about it.

In many ecstasy-related fatalities, other drugs have been consumed such as alcohol, amphetamines, or other club drugs like GHB or PMA. Using data from the General Mortality Register, it was calculated that the risk of death per person, per tablet of ecstasy, is 1 in 39,000 when combined with other drugs, but only 1 in 1.8 million when ecstasy is the sole drug used (Noller, 2009).

SALVIA

Salvia dinorum is a psychoactive plant that produces visions and dissociative effects, much like LSD and other hallucinogens. The plant is native to Oaxaca, Mexico, and has a long history of use in tribal ceremonies, as with many naturally occurring hallucinogens. *Salvinorin A*, the active compound in *Salvia dinorum*, is unique as it is the first known *diterpene hallucinogen*. Salvinorin A does not chemically resemble other psychoactive compounds like LSD and mescaline as they are alkaloid and contain nitrogen. Dried *Salvia dinorum* usually contains about 0.18% Salvinorin A (Ott, 1995) and, by mass, is one of the most potent natural hallucinogens. The effects of the drug can be present in doses as small as 200 μg, which is somewhat comparable to the effective dose of synthetic psychoactive drugs like LSD. Despite its potency, Salvinorin A has an extremely low toxicity, and rats chronically exposed to doses far in excess of effective

human doses showed no harmful physiological damage (Mowry, Mosher, & Briner, 2003).

Neurophysiology

Salvinorin A has been identified as a highly selective kappa (κ)-opioid receptor agonist (Yan & Roth, 2004) and as a partial D_2 dopamine receptor agonist (Seeman, Guan, & Hirbec, 2009). Interestingly, it appears to have no action at the 5-HT_{2A} serotonin receptor, which is instrumental in the psychedelic response to the monoamine-like hallucinogens. It has been suggested that the hallucinogenic effects of Salvinorin A are modulated by its action at the κ-opioid receptor, though this is only speculation. Little research has been done in this regard, unlike with LSD.

Salvinorin A quickly crosses the blood–brain barrier and disperses throughout the central nervous system upon ingestion. The concentration of the drug is highest in the cerebellum as well as the visual cortex (Hooker et al., 2008), which may explain the hallucinogenic properties in addition to the problems integrating sensory experience and motor control while intoxicated.

Pharmacokinetics

After ingestion of salvia, the drug is effective only for a short time. The drug-induced experience can last anywhere from 5 to 30 minutes, which is extremely short in comparison to other common hallucinogens. The main metabolic product of Salvinorin A is *Salvinorin B*, which is an inert metabolite. The metabolism of Salvinorin A to Salvinorin B occurs very rapidly, which explains the brief duration of intoxication when salvia is ingested. Levels of Salvinorin B are undetectable in the urine of rhesus monkeys even shortly after ingestion, suggesting that the metabolite is either immediately cleared or stored in organs and tissue (Schmidt et al., 2005).

Behavioral Effects

Salvinorin A produces intense hallucinations, which are extremely subjective, and with that comes a host of varied behavioral and physiological effects. Some common effects include uncontrollable laughter, loss of motor coordination, changes in perception, emotional swings, and *synaesthesia* (where sensory pathways get crossed so that, for example, words are seen in color and music tastes good). There have been many personal accounts of salvia intoxication, but no systematic studies have been done in humans to observe the effects of the drug. A recent study attempted to remedy this by observing unaltered, full-length videos of salvia "trips" posted on YouTube. Despite the many flaws inherent in this method, certain effects were consistently noted such as *hypomovement* (relaxed or slumped body position), *hypermovement* (uncontrollable laughter or restlessness), speech deficits, and emotional changes (Lange, Daniel, Homer, Reed, & Clapp, 2010).

Tolerance and Withdrawal

Repeated exposure to salvia does not appear to lead to the development of tolerance. In fact, most users report that higher doses are required initially, and the amount needed decreases for a short time after. Few users seem to report needing an increased dose over time and indicate that at higher doses the drug effect simply continues to intensify. This is distinct from nearly all other drugs and suggests that the mechanism of action is especially different from other hallucinogens. Tolerance to LSD can become pronounced in as little as 2 days.

By all accounts, discontinuing salvia use does not lead to unpleasant physical withdrawal symptoms. Again, there has been little research done in this regard, but most users report mild adverse effects such as headache, insomnia, and irritability.

DISSOCIATIVE ANESTHETICS: PHENCYCLIDINE AND KETAMINE

Phencyclidine, also known as *PCP*, is a synthetic drug that was developed and marketed in 1963 as an analgesic and anesthetic by the Parke-Davis Company. For these purposes, it proved very effective and safe because it did not depress blood pressure or heart and respiration rates. It caused a trance-like state rather than a loss of consciousness and has been classified as a *dissociative anesthetic* because it seemed to separate people from sensory experience. In 1965, it was withdrawn from the market because patients reported that while they were recovering from the drug, they experienced a delirium, disorientation, and agitation referred to as *emergence delirium*. The use of PCP was then restricted to nonhumans. It started to be sold on the street in 1965 under the names *crystal*, *angel dust*, and *hob*, but it did not become popular until after the 1960s.

Ketamine was first synthesized in 1962 and marketed in 1969 as a safer alternative to PCP. It is a more potent anesthetic, has a shorter duration of action than PCP, and has milder emergence effects. Ketamine continues to be used as an anesthetic for children and as a veterinary anesthetic under the names *Ketaset* and *Vetalar*. Its street names include *K*, *Special K*, and *kitkat*, and it is widely used as a club drug at dance clubs or raves. It also has the reputation of being used as a date rape drug.

Ketamine sold on the street is probably diverted from legitimate veterinary use. It comes in liquid form and is colorless and tasteless. It may be swallowed or injected. Often the liquid is heated and turned to a white powder that is snorted.

Pharmacokinetics and Dose

PCP and ketamine are weak, lipid-soluble bases and can be inhaled, injected, or taken orally. A moderate dose of PCP is 5 to 10 mg. The effects of PCP are felt within a minute of inhalation or intravenous injection and from 20 to 40 minutes after oral administration. Peak effects usually occur between 10 and 90 minutes, and the effects may last from 4 to 8 hours. Drug levels fall rapidly at first as the drug is absorbed into body fat; however, low levels may persist in the body for several weeks as the drug is released from body fat (Gorelick & Balster, 2000).

During oral administration, ketamine is slowly absorbed and subject to first-pass metabolism, so the drug is often administered intranasally. Ketamine is rapidly absorbed, and effects last from 35 to 40 minutes. A normal dose of ketamine is called a *bump* and contains about 75 to 125 mg. A typical oral dose of ketamine is 175 mg, and a typical intranasal dose is 50 mg (Gable, 2004).

Neurophysiology

The dissociative anesthetics appear to alter the functioning of norepinephrine, dopamine, acetylcholine, and serotonin, but it is believed that the principal effect responsible for their reinforcing properties is that they block NMDA receptors for glutamate and aspartate, which are excitatory transmitters in many parts of the brain, including the cortex. PCP and ketamine have a binding site embedded in the ion channels normally activated by NMDA receptors. When the binding site is occupied by PCP or ketamine, the NMDA receptor ion channel is blocked, making these transmitters ineffective. This mechanism is thought to be similar to that of the alcohol molecule (Dinwiddie & Farber, 1995; Gorelick & Balster, 2000; see also Chapter 6). When the NMDA receptor is occupied by ketamine, especially in the frontal cortex, significant negative psychotic symptoms are present, as assessed by the Brief Psychiatric Rating Scale (Stone et al., 2008). These drugs appear to act as reinforcers by influencing glutamate activity, and thereby dopamine release, in the mesolimbic and mesocortical pathways in a manner similar to the barbiturates and benzodiazepines (see Chapter 7).

Behavior and Performance

The dissociative anesthetics are known to cause amnesia for events that occur while under the influence of the drug. Although no studies of the effects of PCP on memory in humans have been conducted, PCP does seem to be more disruptive of memory in nonhumans than LSD, THC, opioids, and other psychoactive drugs (Balster, 1987). It is known that NMDA receptors are vital in the formation of long-term memories, and so it is not surprising that NMDA antagonists like PCP and ketamine are powerful amnesic drugs. In addition, it has been demonstrated that PCP and ketamine induce a type of thought disorder very similar to that seen in schizophrenic patients (Gilmour et al., 2011).

PCP and ketamine are not hallucinogenic in the same sense as LSD. Taken at usual doses, the dissociative anesthetics cause relaxation, warmth, a tingling feeling, and a sense of numbness. There are euphoric feelings, distortions in body image, and a feeling of floating in space. When these effects wear off, they are sometimes followed by a mild depression that may last from 24 hours to a week. At higher doses, the user may become stuporous or even comatose. Psychotic behavior occurs frequently and may include anything from manic excitation to catatonia, in which the user assumes one position and does not move for a prolonged period of time. There may be sudden mood changes accompanied by laughing and crying; disoriented, confused, and delusional thought; drooling; and repetitive (stereotyped) actions. This psychotic state often disappears as drug levels decline, but sometimes the psychosis requires hospitalization and lasts for weeks.

Stimulus Properties

Dissociative anesthetics appear to have unique stimulus properties. Animals trained to discriminate PCP and ketamine do not generalize this response to any other class of drugs, including stimulants, depressants, and hallucinogens, and no drug has been shown to antagonize their stimulus properties. They generalize only to other drugs known to block NMDA receptors, such as dextromethorphan (see later in this chapter), indicating that this effect is likely the basis for their stimulus properties.

Tolerance

Like LSD, PCP is typically used sporadically. When the drug is used every day, tolerance develops, and there is some evidence of dependence and withdrawal symptoms (Grinspoon & Bakalar, 1979b). When users first try the drug, they need only a few puffs of a PCP-laced cigarette to get high, but within 2 to 6 weeks, they may require two joints to achieve the same effect. Tolerance also seems to develop to the analgesic effects in burn patients. Tolerance has also been demonstrated in nonhumans and appears to take place at physiological and behavioral levels rather than in pharmacokinetics (Balster, 1987; Gorelick & Balster, 2000). Rapid tolerance also develops to the reinforcing effects and discriminative stimulus properties of ketamine in rats (Rocha et al., 1996).

Withdrawal

Research with nonhumans has shown that there may be some withdrawal after continual use of PCP. The symptoms include vocalizations, grinding of the teeth, diarrhea, difficulty staying awake, anxiety, confusion, and tremors. No systematic studies of PCP withdrawal in humans have been done (Gorelick & Balster, 2000).

Self-Administration

NONHUMANS. PCP is self-administered by monkeys, dogs, baboons, and rats either by intravenous infusion or orally (Balster, 1987; Carroll, 1993; Griffiths et al., 1980). PCP injected directly into a part of the nucleus accumbens and the frontal cortex has been shown to be reinforcing, an effect that is not diminished by a dopamine antagonist, showing that this effect is independent of dopamine transmission (Carlezon & Wise, 1996). It has also been demonstrated that ketamine is self-administered intravenously by both rats and monkeys (Moreton, Meisch, Stark, & Thompson, 1977).

HUMAN EPIDEMIOLOGY. Patterns of PCP use are similar to LSD. Most use is experimental or occasional, but unlike LSD, some occasional users become heavy chronic users. Unfortunately, even though tolerance does develop to the reinforcing effects of dissociative anesthetics, the tolerance is not severe enough to discourage continuous use as is the case with LSD (Linder, Lerner, & Burns, 1981).

Not until the decline of LSD in the 1970s did PCP use start to increase. Before PCP became popular in its own right, it was more widely used than most people suspected because it was often mixed with other drugs or sold as something different. While its use has declined, it is still popular in some metropolitan areas and among certain groups who continue to take it by itself or mixed with marijuana or cocaine (Gorelick & Balster, 2000). The small percentage of users has continued to decrease. In 2004 and 2008, roughly 0.5% of high school students in the United States reported using PCP within the past 30 days (Johnston et al., 2005; Substance Abuse and Mental Health Services Administration (2010). In the United Kingdom and Canada, the trend has been fairly stable at low percentages over the last few years.

Ketamine was little used until it entered the club scene in the 1980s when its popularity expanded. Its use, however, appears to have leveled off. Ketamine use among high school students in the United States has shown little change since 2000 with about 2% of grade 12 students reporting use within the past 12 months (Johnston et al., 2005).

Harmful Effects

PCP and ketamine have an unfounded reputation for causing violence and uncontrollable behavior. An examination of the literature on the drug has not found any systematic evidence that these drugs specifically cause violent or criminal behavior. It is true, however, that the psychotic state induced by large doses of dissociative anesthetics causes disorientation, agitation, and hyperactivity, and that these effects have the potential for injury to the individual and others nearby. However, PCP and ketamine do not seem to turn normal, innocent people into dangerous and violent criminals (Brecher, Wang, Wong, & Morgan, 1988; Gorelick & Balster, 2000). Laboratory research even suggests that PCP may have a taming effect on normally aggressive animals (Balster, 1987).

As with many other drugs of abuse, it appears that chronic ketamine use is associated with long-term neurological changes. In a recent study of chronic ketamine users, researchers observed a significant reduction in gray matter volume in the left superior frontal gyrus and the right middle frontal gyrus (Liao et al., 2011). Reduction in gray matter volume was correlated with the duration of use for both of the affected brain regions.

Long-lasting psychotic behavior has been reported after PCP use, even in individuals without any psychotic tendencies. This PCP psychosis may last several months in some individuals and is indistinguishable from schizophrenia as it includes both positive and negative symptoms.

Acute behavioral effects of PCP and ketamine can sometimes be responsible for injury and death. For example, because the drugs are anesthetics, rather severe injuries have been tolerated or self-inflicted without pain or any effort at avoidance. Although the exact frequency of this sort of event has not been documented, it is probably more likely to happen with PCP than with LSD and the other serotonin-like and norepinephrine-like hallucinogens.

GENETIC DAMAGE AND REPRODUCTION. PCP has been shown to slow the growth of the fetus, precipitate labor, and cause fetal distress. Children born to mothers who use PCP often show muscle stiffness, tremor, irritability, and impaired attention and behavior control that may last for several years, although it is difficult to be sure that these effects are due specifically to PCP since other maternal drug use is common (Gorelick & Balster, 2000). Also, usage of PCP and ketamine has been linked to widespread cell death in the developing rat brain. Blockage of NMDA receptors by PCP or ketamine for even a few hours during prenatal development appears to induce significant neurodegeneration (Ikonomidou et al., 1999).

Lethal Effects

A lethal dose of the ketamine is 25 times the effective dose for intranasal administration (Gable, 2004). Although toxic effects may vary, high doses cause coma, convulsions, and respiratory arrest. Brain hemorrhage and kidney failure have also been reported. The lethal effects of PCP and ketamine are potentiated by the presence of depressant drugs, such as alcohol or barbiturates, in the body.

DEXTROMETHORPHAN

Dextromethorphan is a synthetic *antitussive* (cough-suppressant) drug, which is structurally similar to opioids. Many years ago, it was considered safe after research showed that it did not have as serious an abuse potential as opioids. However, more recently there have been numerous reports of people consuming large quantities of over-the-counter cough medicines such as Robitussin for their psychological effects, a practice sometimes called *roboing* (Darboe, Keenan, & Richards, 1996). This trend has led to more in-depth examination of dextromethorphan's behavioral pharmacology as well as *dextrorphan*, a metabolite of dextromethorphan.

Neurophysiology

Dextromethorphan and dextrorphan have been shown to be low-affinity NMDA receptor agonists, similar to PCP and ketamine. When bound, they act as ion channel blockers in a manner similar to alcohol and the dissociative anesthetics (see Chapter 4) and therefore have similar pharmacological properties. Dextrorphan has a greater affinity for the NMDA receptor than dextromethorphan and consequently has a much greater PCP-like effect. Dextromethorphan also affects the functioning of *sigma* receptors, a poorly understood class of receptors once believed to be a type of opioid receptor but later deemed to have no structural similarity to opioid receptors. Dextromethorphan is a Sigma-1 and Sigma-2 receptor agonist, though it appears to bind with higher affinity to the Sigma-1 receptor, which is found predominantly in the central nervous system (Weissman, Su, P., Hedreen, & London, 1988). Sigma-1 receptor activation has been linked with cough-suppression in guinea pigs (Brown, Fezoui, Selig, Schwartz, & Ellis, 2004), which may contribute to the antitussive effect of dextromethorphan. Interestingly, dextromethorphan has been used to decrease morphine-induced reward in rats through Sigma-1 receptor activity in the ventral tegmental area. These findings suggest that low doses of dextromethorphan could be used in the treatment of opioid addiction (Chen, Hsu, Huang, Lu, & Tao, 2011).

Pharmacokinetics

In most cases, dextromethorphan is converted rapidly to dextrorphan during first-pass metabolism through the liver. Because the effects of dextrorphan are greater than dextromethorphan, the most intense effects of consuming dextromethorphan may be delayed until this transformation occurs. Since first-pass metabolism is greatest after oral administration, oral consumption may be the most effective route of administration.

Population studies have shown that there is considerable individual variation in the ability to metabolize dextromethorphan to dextrorphan. Some individuals are rapid metabolizers and should be able to experience the effects of dextrorphan rapidly, but others are slow metabolizers, so the metabolite will not reach high levels, and the effects will be diminished. The cytochrome P450 enzyme plays a crucial role in the metabolism of dextromethorphan, and slow metabolizers tend to have low levels of this enzyme, specifically of the CYP2D6 variant. About 5 to 10% of Caucasians and 4% of African Americans are poor metabolizers (He, Daniel, Hajiloo, & Shockley, 1999). Such differences in metabolism can cause considerable individual variation in the effects of taking dextromethorphan.

Discriminative Stimulus Properties

Rats trained to discriminate dextromethorphan will generalize fully to PCP, though at a higher dose. Generalization is dose- and training-specific, and this has led researchers to believe that dextromethorphan and dextrorphan are not identical to PCP and other full NMDA receptor blockers (Holtzman, 1994).

Self-Administration

It appears that both rats and rhesus monkeys will readily self-administer both dextromethorphan and dextrorphan (Nicholson, Hayes, & Balster, 1999).

Behavioral Effects

NONHUMANS. The effects of dextromethorphan and dextrorphan have been investigated in rats. Dextromethorphan caused a decrease in locomotor activity, whereas dextrorphan caused an increase along with stereotyped behavior at higher doses. Some memory and learning impairment was seen with dextromethorphan but not with dextrorphan. The two drugs appear to have different behavioral effects with dextromethorphan closely mimicking sedatives and dextrorphan resembling PCP and ketamine (Morgan, Porritt, & Poling, 2006).

HUMANS. Dextromethorphan has been used as a cough suppressant for over 30 years. At normal therapeutic doses it has few side effects and no PCP-like effects. However, selective serotonin reuptake inhibitors and monoamine oxidase inhibitors seem to increase the likelihood of unpleasant side effects (Ziaee et al., 2005). At higher doses, its effects are similar to PCP and ketamine; these include ataxia, dizziness, euphoria, tactile and visual hallucinations, altered time perception, and increased perceptual awareness.

GHB

GHB (gamma-hydroxybutyrate) occurs naturally in the body as a metabolite of gamma-aminobutyric acid (GABA) and acts as a neurotransmitter or neuromodulator (Castelli, 2008). When administered as a drug, it is rapidly absorbed, easily crosses the blood–brain barrier, and, in increasing doses, produces anxiolysis (anxiety reduction), sedation, and anesthesia (Castelli, 2008). The sodium salt of GHB, *sodium oxybate*, is sold under the trade name *Xyrem* as a treatment for narcolepsy. GHB has also been marketed in Italy as *Alcover*, a treatment for alcoholism. When sold on the street, it has many names, including *liquid X*, *GBH* (*grievous bodily harm*), *scoop*, *cherry meth*, *blue nitro*, *easy lay*, and more than 30 others (O'Connell, Kaye, & Plosay, 2000).

Initially, GHB was widely used in Europe as a medicine and in the United States as a dietary supplement. It received little attention from public health officials until the early 1990s, when its use became more widespread as a growth promoter among bodybuilders, as a sedative, and as a recreational drug used alongside ecstasy and ketamine as a club drug. GHB has also been identified as a date rape drug. In 1990, the U.S. Food and Drug Administration declared GHB unsafe and banned it from public sale.

The legal status of GHB remains unclear. In 2000, the U.S. attorney general was voted authority by the U.S. Congress to make GHB a Schedule I drug; that is, it has abuse potential but no medical use. However, when sold as Xyrem, GHB is classed as Schedule III drug. This is similar to the classification of Marinol, a

preparation containing THC that has medical use (see Chapter 14). This ambiguity has not yet been resolved. In the United Kingdom, GHB was made a Class C drug (thought to have the least capacity for harm) as of 2003.

Pharmacokinetics and Dose

GHB and its precursor, *GBL*, are considered to be pharmacologically equivalent, except that GBL is more readily absorbed. When taken orally, GHB produces effects within 15 to 30 minutes and peak effects are reached between 25 and 45 minutes. It has a half-life of 30 to 50 minutes. Endogenous GHB is taken into cells via an active reuptake mechanism from the synaptic cleft, where it is rapidly metabolized. A minimum dose is about 10 mg/kg body weight and will produce muscle relaxation. A therapeutic dose for sleep is in the range of 15 to 30 mg/kg, and a high dose of 60 mg/kg will cause unarousable sleep or coma lasting for 1 to 5 hours. A lethal dose may be anywhere between 300 and 900 mg/kg. This gives it a therapeutic index of between 20 and 60.

In a recent review of 226 GHB-associated deaths, 94% were due to cardiorespiratory arrests and 65% involved coadministration of another drug (Zvosec, Smith, Porrata, Strobl, & Dyer, 2011).

Neuropharmacology

GHB binds to at least two receptor types in the CNS: the GHB receptor and, at high concentrations (higher than those that occur naturally in the body), the $GABA_B$ receptor. However, the GHB binding site on the $GABA_B$ receptor is distinct from that of GABA itself (Castelli, 2008; Wu et al., 2004). GABA does not bind to the GHB binding site on the $GABA_B$ receptor complex. The GHB receptor is part of a complex that has its effect by releasing a second messenger inside the membrane. Even though there are high levels of endogenous GHB outside the CNS, all GHB receptors appear to be inside the CNS. The highest densities of GHB receptors are found in the hippocampus and regions of the cortex, whereas the highest concentrations of GHB molecules are found in the substantia nigra and hypothalamus (Castelli, 2008). GHB also appears to have a modulatory effect on GABA levels, in some cases decreasing GABA, and, because it is also a GABA precursor, it can also increase GABA levels.

GHB acts both presynaptically and postsynaptically to modulate activity of other neurotransmitters. Its main effect seems to be on dopamine synapses, where it inhibits dopamine release and causes the accumulation of excess dopamine in the presynaptic neuron. It has also been reported that after a period of inhibition or at higher doses, there is a surge in dopamine activity.

Effects on Behavior

NONHUMANS. There are significant differences between GHB and the other drugs discussed in this chapter. GHB has sedative properties and, at high doses, acts as an anesthetic. The anesthetic state it induces appears to be more similar to a cataleptic state than anesthesia; brainwaves show seizure-like activity that can be blocked with anticonvulsant drugs. The nonresponsive state achieved at high levels of GHB is more similar to a petit mal seizure than anesthesia. At higher doses, jerks and seizure-like activity can be seen.

Cognitive deficits after prolonged GHB use have been observed in nonhumans that are distinct from amnesia during and after drug use. Deficits in spatial learning and memory were observed in adolescent rats that were thought to be due to a decrease in NMDA receptor expression after chronic administration (Sircar, Wu, Reddy, Sircar, & Basak, 2011).

HUMANS. Users report that GHB causes alcohol-like intoxication without a hangover. They report increased feelings of relaxation and euphoria. GHB is sometimes used in conjunction with alcohol and various club drugs like ketamine and ecstasy to enhance their effects. It is also reputed to be an aphrodisiac, increasing libido and enhancing sexual pleasure; however, such effects may be due to a reduction in sexual inhibition rather than a true aphrodisiac quality.

Amnesia for events both during and after drug use has also been reported (Miotto et al., 2001). At higher doses, before passing out, people show many of the signs of alcohol intoxication, they appear confused, speech is incoherent, and they have poor balance and coordination. Driving ability is clearly impaired (Couper & Logan, 2001).

EFFECTS ON SLEEP. Unlike the barbiturates and benzodiazepines (or almost any other drug, for that matter), GHB normalizes sleep patterns and increases stages 3 and 4 and REM sleep. This effect is the basis for its development as a treatment for narcolepsy. In narcolepsy, normal sleep does not occur at night, so the narcoleptic falls into uncontrollable sleep during the day. The benzodiazepine and barbiturate hypnotics alter normal nighttime sleep patterns and are consequently not useful, but GHB appears to be an effective treatment.

ANXIOLYTIC PROPERTIES. There is conflicting evidence in the literature that GHB has anxiolytic effects. Drugs that increase punished behavior are often subject to abuse. A recent study showed that GHB increases punished responding to an extent comparable to pentobarbital, suggesting that it does indeed have antianxiety effects that might contribute to its abuse liability (Frawly & McMillan, 2008).

Drug State Discrimination

Animals trained to discriminate GHB from saline only partially generalize to morphine, LSD, and chlordiazepoxide; generalize even less to amphetamine and ethanol; and do not generalize at all to barbital and PCP-like compounds, indicating a unique subjective effect.

Any generalization to other drugs seems to be highly dose specific. At high training doses of GHB, animals will generalize to drugs that are $GABA_B$ agonists, suggesting that this effect is probably responsible for its subjective effect, but at low doses, the subjective effect appears to be mediated by its activity at its own receptor. Similarly, alcohol-trained rats generalize only to GHB at a very narrow range of intermediate doses.

Self-Administration

GHB will create a place preference in rats, but this learning requires more trials than with cocaine. In nonhuman primates, GHB has been shown to have abuse potential, but a history of self-administration may be important (Goodwin, Kaminski, Griffiths, Ator, & Weerts, 2011). On the other hand, there is evidence that GHB will reduce the self-administration of alcohol in both rats and humans, with humans reporting a reduction in craving for alcohol. This may be a result of the dopamine-blocking effect of GHB, but this effect needs further study.

Human Epidemiology

While there are little data available on the extent of GHB use, a 2002 survey of 16- to 23-year olds revealed that the prevalence of overall lifetime use is approximately 0.05%

(Wu, Schlenger, & Galvin, 2006). The Drug Abuse Warning Network is a system that tracks drug use by the number of times it is mentioned in cases seen in hospital emergency rooms in the United States and Canada. In 1992, there were 20 mentions of GHB, but in 1998 it was mentioned on nearly 1,300 occasions. This cannot be taken as an indication of how often the drug is used, but it does suggest a drastic increase in use. Prevalence of GHB use among high school students in the United States does not appear to have changed much since legislation was introduced in 2000 to make it a Schedule I drug.

Tolerance and Withdrawal

Tolerance develops to the motor-impairing effects of GHB in rats following high doses for 9 days. These rats were cross-tolerant with alcohol on the same effect. Tolerance has also been demonstrated to the sedating and anesthetic effects of GHB.

In humans, continual GHB use several times a day can lead to tolerance and dependence, after which a sudden reduction in use can lead to withdrawal symptoms including anxiety, tremor, agitation, delirium, and hallucinations (van Noorden, Kamal, de Jong, Vergouwen, & Zitman, 2010).

GHB will alleviate alcohol withdrawal symptoms in humans and nonhumans and has been used therapeutically in Italy to treat alcohol withdrawal and dependence. GHB is also effective in reducing withdrawal effects from opiates.

MEPHEDRONE

Mephedrone, or *4-methylephedrone*, is a synthetic stimulant and empathogenic drug that belongs to the amphetamine and cathinonine classes. Mephedrone is a relatively new drug and did not gain popularity until 2007 when it began to be sold and distributed online. The intended effects of mephedrone are similar to those of khat, MDMA, cocaine, and amphetamines as it creates a feeling of euphoria, increased energy, confidence, elevated mood, and decreased hostility. Users can swallow, snort, smoke, or inject the drug. Although the exact neurological method of action is not known, it appears that mephedrone interacts with dopamine and serotonin transporters and blocks the reuptake of these neurotransmitters (Martínez-Clemente, Escubedo, Pubill, & Camarasa, 2011).

Similar to other drugs in its class, mephedrone is most popular among young adults (18 to 25 years),

especially those involved in the club scene. In a survey by a British clubbing magazine, *Mixmag*, mephedrone was the fourth most popular drug among the over 2,200 readers who were surveyed. Possible reasons for the rapid increase in popularity include the convenience of online purchase and a decrease in purity and availability of drugs with similar intended effects. Because of its popularity among young clubbers, it is likely to be used alongside alcohol and other stimulant drugs.

Harmful Effects

The toxicology of mephedrone has not been fully established. As of January 2011, the LD_{50} of mephedrone was not known. Because of the lack of scientific testing and short history of use, the long-term effects are also not known. Les King, former drug advisor to the British government, has said, "All we can say is [mephedrone] is probably as harmful as ecstasy and amphetamines. . ." (reported by Reed, 2010). An analysis of patients admitted to the ER for medical reasons related to self-reported mephedone use revealed that 53.3% of patients experienced anxiety, 40% tachycardia, and 20% seizures (Wood, Greene, & Dargan, 2011).

Legal Status

Since 2008, many countries have passed legislation making the sale, possession, and manufacture of mephedrone illegal. As of December 2010, the European Union made the drug illegal across Europe. In Australia and New Zealand, it is controlled indirectly as it is treated as an analog of other controlled substances. Drugs controlled in this fashion are substantially similar to, and thereby treated as if, they are in fact another illegal substance intended for sale, possession, or manufacture for human consumption. Until recently, similar means of enforcement existed in the United States; however, many individuals exploited this loophole and legally sold mephedrone as plant food or bath salts. The U.S. Drug Enforcement Administration (DEA) declared an emergency scheduling authority as of September 2011 that will make mephedrone and two other synthetic substances (MDPV and methylone) illegal for a minimum of 1 year. During this time, the DEA will perform further studies to determine if mephedrone should be made permanently illegal, and if so, how it should be scheduled.

REFERENCES

Aaronson, B., & Osmond, H. (1970). *Psychedelics: The uses and implications of hallucinogenic drugs*. Garden City, New York: Anchor Books/Doubleday.

Abel, E. L., McMillan, D. E., & Harris, L. S. (1974). Delta-9-tetrahydrocannabinol: Effects of route of administration on onset and duration of activity and tolerance development. *Psychopharmacologia, 35*, 29–38.

Abel, E. L., & Sokol, R. J. (1989). Alcohol consumption during pregnancy: The dangers of moderate drinking. In H. W. Goode & D. P. Agarwal (Eds.), *Alcoholism: Biomedical and genetic aspects* (pp. 216–227). New York: Pergamon Press.

Adams, I. B., & Martin, B. R. (1996). Cannabis: Pharmacology and toxicology in animals and humans. *Addiction, 91*, 1585–1614.

Adler, J., Abramson, P., Katz, S., & Hager, M. (1985, April 15). Getting high on "Ecstasy." *Newsweek*, p. 96.

Advokat, C. (2005). Differential effects of clozapine versus other antipsychotics on clinical outcome and dopamine release in the brain. *Essential Psychopharmacology, 6*, 73–90.

Aghajanian, G. K., & Bing, O. H. (1964). Persistence of lysergic acid diethylamide in the plasma of human subjects. *Clinical Pharmacology and Therapeutics, 5*, 611–614.

Agurell, S., Lindgren, J., Ohlsson, A., Gillespie, H. K., & Hollister, L. (1984). Recent studies in the pharmacokinetics of delta-1-tetrahydrocannabinol in man. In S. Agurell, W. L. Dewey, & R. E. Willett (Eds.), *The cannabinoids: Chemical, pharmacological, and therapeutic aspects* (pp. 165–184). Orlando, FL: Academic Press.

Ahima, R. S., & Harlan, R. E. (1990). Charting of type II glucocorticoid receptor-like immunoreactivity in the rat central nervous system. *Neuroscience, 39*, 579–604.

Ahmed, S. H., & Koob, G. F. (1998). Transition from moderate to excessive drug intake: Change in hedonic set point. *Science (New York, N.Y.), 282*, 298–300.

Alcoholics Anonymous. (1980). *Dr. Bob and the good oldtimers*. New York: Author.

Alcoholics Anonymous. (2012). Retrieved April 3, 2012, from http://www.aa.org/en_pdfs/f-165_aaaroundtheworld_fall10.pdf

Aldrich, A., Aranda, J. V., & Neims, A. H. (1979). Caffeine metabolism in the newborn. *Clinical Pharmacology and Therapeutics, 25*, 447–453.

Aldrich, M. R., & Baker, R. W. (1976). Historical aspects of cocaine use and abuse. In S. J. Mule (Ed.), *Cocaine: Chemical, biological, clinical, social and treatment aspects* (pp. 1–12). Boca Raton, FL: CRC Press.

Alexander, B. K., & Schweighofer, A. R. F. (1988). Defining "addiction." *Canadian Psychology, 29*, 151–162.

Ambermoon, P., Carter, A., Hall, W. D., Dissanayaka, N. N., & O'Sullivan, J. D. (2011). Impulse control disorders in patients with Parkinson's disease receiving dopamine replacement therapy: Evidence and implications for the addictions field. *Addiction (Abingdon, England), 106*, 283–293.

Amed, S., & Koob, G. (1998). Transition from moderate to excessive drug intake: Change in hedonic set point. *Science, 282*, 298–300.

American Cancer Society. (2011). *Cancer facts and figures*. Atlanta, GA: American Cancer Society.

American Lung Association. (2004). *Trends in tobacco use*. Retrieved from http://www.lungusa.org/site/pp.asp?c=dvLUK9O0E&b=33347

American Lung Association. (2006). *Trends in tobacco use 2006*. Retrieved from http://www.lungusa.org/site/pp.asp?c=dvLUK900OE&b=33309#latest

American Psychiatric Association. (1987). *Diagnostic and statistical manual of mental disorders* (3rd ed., Revised). Washington, DC: Author.

American Psychiatric Association. (1994). *Diagnostic and statistical manual of mental disorders* (4th ed.). Washington, DC: Author.

American Psychiatric Association. (2000). *Diagnostic and statistical manual of mental disorders* (4th ed., Text Revision). Washington, DC: Author.

American Society of Hospital Pharmacists. (1987). *Drug information '87*. Bethesda, MD: Author.

Andrews, M. M., Meda, S. A., Thomas, A. D., Potenza, M. N., Krystal, J. H., Worhunsky, P., et al. (2011). Individuals family history positive for alcoholism show functional magnetic resonance imaging differences in reward sensitivity that are related to impulsivity factors. *Biological Psychiatry, 69*, 675–683.

Angrist, B., & Sudilovsky, A. (1978). Central nervous system stimulants. In L. L. Iverson, S. D. Iverson, & S. H. Snyder (Eds.), *Handbook of psychopharmacology* (Vol. 11, pp. 95–165). New York: Plenum Press.

Anonymous. (1955). An autobiography of a schizophrenic experience. *Journal of Abnormal and Social Psychology, 512*, 677–689.

Arber, E. (1895). *English reprints: A counterblaste to tobacco (by James I of England)*. Westminster, MD: A. Constable.

Arendt, M., Munk-Jørgensen, P., Sher, L., & Jensen, S. O. (2011). Mortality among individuals with cannabis, cocaine, amphetamine, MDMA, and opioid use disorders: A nationwide follow-up study of danish substance users in treatment. *Drug and Alcohol Dependence, 114,* 134–139.

Armitage, A. K. (1973). Some recent observations relating to the absorption of nicotine from tobacco smoke. In W. L. Dunn (Ed.), *Smoking behavior: Motives and incentives* (pp. 83–91). Washington, DC: Winston.

Armor, D. J., Polach, J. M., & Stambul, H. B. (1978). *Alcoholism and treatment.* New York: Wiley.

Arnaud, M. J. (1993). Metabolism of caffeine and other components of coffee. In S. Garattini (Ed.), *Caffeine, coffee and health* (pp. 43–95). New York: Raven Press.

Arnaud, M. J. (2011). Pharmacokinetics and metabolism of natural methylxanthines in animal and man. *Handbook of Experimental Pharmacology, 200,* 33–91.

Ascherio, A., Zhang, S. M., Hernan, M. A., Kawachi, I., Colditz, G. A., Speizer, F. E., et al. (2001). Prospective study of caffeine consumption and risk of Parkinson's disease in men and women. *Annals of Neurology, 50,* 56–63.

Asfar, T., Ebbert, J. O., Klesges, R. C., & Relyea, G. E. (2011). Do smoking reduction interventions promote cessation in smokers not ready to quit? *Addictive Behaviors, 36,* 764–768.

Ashtari, M., Avants, B., Cyckowski, L., Cervellione, K. L., Roofeh, D., Cook, P., et al. (2011). Medial temporal structures and memory functions in adolescents with heavy cannabis use. *Journal of Psychiatric Research, 45,* 1055–1066.

Ashton, C. H. (1984). Benzodiazepine withdrawal: An unfinished story. *British Medical Journal, 288,* 1135–1140.

Ator, N., & Griffiths, R. R. (1992). Oral self-administration of triazolam, diazepam and ethanol in the baboon: Drug reinforcement and benzodiazepine physical dependence. *Psychopharmacology, 108,* 301–312.

Ator, N. A., Atack, J. R., Hargreaves, R. J., Burns, H. D., & Dawson, G. R. (2010). Reducing abuse liability of GABAA/benzodiazepine ligands via selective partial agonist efficacy at alpha1 and alpha2/3 subtypes. *Journal of Pharmacology and Experimental Therapeutics, 332,* 4–16.

Ator, N. A., Griffiths, R. R., & Weerts, E. M. (2005). Self-injection of flunitrazepam alone and in the context of methadone maintenance in baboons. *Drug and Alcohol Dependence, 78,* 113–123.

Atweh, S. F., & Kuhar, M. J. (1983). Distribution and physiological significance of opioid receptors in the brain. *British Medical Bulletin, 39,* 47–52.

Austin, G. A. (1985). *Alcohol in Western society from antiquity to 1800.* Santa Barbara, CA: ABC-Clio Information Services.

Axelrod, J., & Reisenthal, J. (1953). The fate of caffeine in man and a method for its estimation in biological materials. *Journal of Pharmacology and Experimental Therapeutics, 107,* 519–523.

Azorlosa, J. L., Greenwald, M. K., & Stitzer, M. L. (1995). Marijuana smoking, effects of varying puff volume and breathhold duration. *Journal of Pharmacology and Experimental Therapeutics, 272,* 560–569.

Babor, T. F., Berglas, S., Mendelson, J. H., Ellingboe, J., & Miller, K. (1983). Alcohol: Effect on the disinhibition of behavior. *Psychopharmacology, 80,* 53–60.

Badaiani, A., & Robinson, T. E. (2004). Drug-induced neurobehavioral plasticity: The role of environmental context. *Behavioral Pharmacology, 15,* 327–339.

Baekeland, F. (1977). Evaluation of treatment methods in chronic alcoholism. In B. Kissen & H. Begleiter (Eds.), *The biology of alcoholism* (Vol. 5, pp. 385–440). New York: Plenum Press.

Baggott, M., Jerome, L., & Stuart, R. (2001). *3,4-methylenedioxymethamphetamine (MDMA): A review of the English-language scientific and medical literature.* Retrieved from http://www.maps.org/research/mdma/protocol/litreview.html

Bagnardi, V., Zatonski, W., Scotti, L., La Vecchia, C., & Corrao, G. (2008). Does drinking pattern modify the effect of alcohol on the risk of coronary heart disease? Evidence from a meta-analysis. *Journal of Epidemiology and Community Health, 62,* 615–619.

Baird, D. D. (1992). Evidence for reduced fecundity in female smokers. In D. Poswillio & E. Alberman (Eds.), *Effects of smoking on the fetus, neonate and child* (pp. 5–22). Oxford, England: Oxford University Press.

Baldessarini, R. J. (1985). *Chemotherapy in psychiatry: Principles and practice.* Cambridge, MA: Harvard University Press.

Ball, J. C., & Snarr, R. W. (1969). A test of the maturation hypothesis with respect to opiate addiction. *United Nations Bulletin on Narcotics, 21,* 9–13.

Balodis, I. M., Potenza, M. N., & Olmstead, M. C. (2009). Binge drinking in undergraduates: Relationships with sex, drinking behaviors, impulsivity, and the perceived effects of alcohol. *Behavioural Pharmacology, 20,* 518–526.

Balster, R. L. (1987). The behavioral pharmacology of phencyclidine. In H. Y. Meltzer (Ed.), *Psychopharmacology: The third generation of progress* (pp. 1573–1579). New York: Raven Press.

Balster, R. L., & Ford, R. D. (1978). The discriminative stimulus properties of cannabinoids: A review. In B. T. Ho, D. W. Richards, & D. L. Chute (Eds.), *Drug discrimination and state dependent learning* (pp. 131–147). Orlando, FL: Academic Press.

Bareggi, S., Ferini-Strambi, L., Pirola, R., & Smirne, S. (1998). Impairment of memory and flunitrazepam levels. *Psychopharmacology, 140,* 157–163.

Barker, M. J., Greenwood, K. M., Jackson, M., & Crowe, S. F. (2004). Cognitive effects of long-term benzodiazepine use: A meta-analysis. *CNS Drugs, 18,* 37–48.

Barnes, G., & Elthrington, L. G. (1973). *Drug dosage in laboratory animals: A handbook.* Berkeley, CA: University of California Press.

Barone, J. J., & Roberts, H. (1984). Human consumption of caffeine. In P. B. Dews (Ed.), *Caffeine: Perspectives from recent research* (pp. 59–73). Berlin: Springer-Verlag.

Barrett, R. J., Caul, W. F., & Smith, R. L. (2004). Evidence for bidirectional cues as a function of time following treatment with amphetamine: Implications for understanding tolerance and withdrawal. *Pharmacology, Biochemistry, and Behavior, 79,* 761–771.

Barrett, R. J., & Smith, R. L. (2005). Evidence for PTZ-like cues as a function of time following treatment with chlordiazepoxide: Implications for understanding tolerance and withdrawal. *Behavioural Pharmacology, 16,* 147–153.

Barrett, S. P., Boileau, I., Okker, J., Pihl, R. O., & Dagher, A. (2004). The hedonic response to cigarette smoking is proportional to dopamine release in the human striatum as measured by positron emission tomography and [11C]raclopride. *Synapse, 54,* 65–71.

Barrows, S., & Room, R. (1991). Social history and alcohol studies. In S. Barrows & R. Room (Eds.), *Drinking: Behavior and belief in modern history* (pp. 1–25). Berkeley, CA: University of California Press.

Barry, H., III., & Kubina, R. K. (1972). Discriminative stimulus characteristics of alcohol, marijuana and atropine. In J. M. Singh, L. Miller, & H. Lal (Eds.), *Drug addiction: Experimental pharmacology* (Vol. 1, pp. 3–16). Mt. Kisco, NY: Futura.

Barry, H., III., McGuire, M. S., & Krimmer, E. C. (1982). Alcohol and meprobamate resemble phenobarbital rather than chlordiazepoxide. In F. C. Colpaert & J. F. Slangen (Eds.), *Drug discrimination: Applications in CNS pharmacology* (pp. 219–233). Amsterdam, NY: Elsevier Biomedical.

Bass, C. E., Jansen, H. T., & Roberts, D. C. (2010). Free-running rhythms of cocaine self-administration in rats held under constant lighting conditions. *Chronobiology International, 27,* 535–548.

Baumeister, R. F., & Placidi, K. S. (1983). A social-history and analysis of the LSD controversy. *Journal of Humanistic Psychology, 23,* 25–60.

Bear, M. F., Conners, B. W., & Paradiso, M. A. (2007). *Neuroscience: Exploring the brain* (3rd ed.). Baltimore, MD: Lippincott Williams & Wilkins.

Beautrais, A. L., Joyce, P. R., Mulder, R. T., Fergusson, D. M., Deavoll, B. J., & Nightingale, S. K. (1996). Prevalence and comorbidity of mental disorders in persons making serious suicide attempts: A case-control study. *The American Journal of Psychiatry, 153,* 1009–1014.

Becker, H. C. (2008). Alcohol dependence, withdrawal, and relapse. *Alcohol Research and Health, 31,* 348–361.

Bellville, J. W., Forrest, W. H., Shroff, P., & Brown, B. W. (1971). The hypnotic effects of codeine and secobarbital and their interactions in man. *Clinical Pharmacology and Therapeutics, 2,* 607–612.

Ben Amar, M. (2006). Cannabinoids in medicine: A review of their therapeutic potential. *Journal of Ethnopharmacology, 105,* 1–25.

Benedetti, F., Amanzio, M., & Maggi, G. (1995). Potentiation of placebo analgesia by proglumide. *Lancet, 346,* 1231.

Benet, S. (1975). Early diffusion and folk use of hemp. In V. Rubin (Ed.), *Cannabis and culture* (pp. 31–50). The Hague: Mouton.

Benowitz, N. L., & Henningfield, J. E. (1994). Establishing a nicotine threshold for addiction. *New England Journal of Medicine, 331,* 123–125.

Benzodiazepine/Driving Collaborative Group. (1993). Are benzodiazepines a risk for road accidents? *Drug and Alcohol Dependence, 33,* 19–22.

Bergman, J., & Johanson, C. E. (1985). The reinforcing properties of diazepam under several conditions in rhesus monkeys. *Psychopharmacology, 86,* 108–113.

Berridge, K. C. (2000). Measuring hedonic impact in animals and infants: Microstructure of affective taste reactivity patterns. *Neuroscience and Biobehavioral Reviews, 24,* 173–198.

Berridge, K. C. (2007). The debate over dopamine's role in reward: The case for incentive salience. *Psychopharmacology, 191,* 391–431.

Berridge, K. C., & Robinson, T. E. (1998). What is the role of dopamine in reward: Hedonic impact, reward learning, or incentive salience? *Brain Research: Brain Research Reviews, 28,* 309–369.

Berridge, V., & Edwards, G. (1981). *Opium and the people.* London: St. Martin's Press.

Berthou, F., Guillois, B., Riche, C., Dreano, Y., Jacqz-Aigrain, E., & Beaune, P. H. (1992). Interspecies variations in caffeine metabolism related to cytochrome P4501A enzymes. *Xenobiotica; the Fate of Foreign Compounds in Biological Systems, 22,* 671–680.

Besser, G. (1967). Some physical characteristics of auditory flicker fusion in man. *Nature, 214,* 17–19.

Bickerdyke, J. (1971). *The curiosities of ale and beer.* New York: Blom.

Birnbaum, I., & Parker, E. (1977). Acute effects of alcohol on storage and retrieval. In I. M. Birnbaum & E. S. Parker (Eds.), *Alcohol and human memory* (pp. 99–107). Hillsdale, NJ: Erlbaum.

Blandini, F., Nappi, G., Tassorelli, C., & Martignoni, E. (2000). Functional changes of the basal ganglia circuitry in Parkinson's disease. *Progress in Neurobiology, 62,* 63–88.

Bocca, M., Le-Doz, F., Ftard, O., Pottier, M., L'Hoste, J., & Denise, P. (1999). Residual effects of zolpidem, 10 mg and zopiclone, 7.5 mg versus flunitrazepam, 1 mg and placebo on driving performance and ocular saccades. *Psychopharmacology, 143*, 373–379.

Boer, G. J., Feenstra, M. G. P., Mirmiran, M., Swaab, D. F., & Van Haaren, F. (1988). *The biochemical basis of functional teratology: Progress in brain research* (Vol. 73). Amsterdam, NY: Elsevier.

Boffetta, P., & Hashibe, M. (2006). Alcohol and cancer. *The Lancet Oncology, 7*, 149–156.

Boileau, I., Dagher, A., Leyton, M., Gunn, R. N., Baker, G. B., Diksic, M., et al. (2006). Modeling sensitization to stimulants in humans: An [11C]raclopride/positron emission tomography study in healthy men. *Archives of General Psychiatry, 63*, 1386–1395.

Boileau, I., Dagher, A., Leyton, M., Welfeld, K., Booij, L., Diksic, M., et al. (2007). Conditioned dopamine release in humans: A positron emission tomography [11C]raclopride study with amphetamine. *Journal of Neuroscience, 27*, 3998–4003.

Bolwig, T. G. (2011). How does electroconvulsive therapy work? Theories on its mechanism. *Canadian Journal of Psychiatry. Revue Canadienne De Psychiatrie, 56*, 13–18.

Bonati, M., & Garattini, S. (1984). Interspecies comparison of caffeine disposition. In P. B. Dews (Ed.), *Caffeine: Perspectives from recent research* (pp. 48–56). Berlin: Springer-Verlag.

Bonnet, M. H., & Arand, D. L. (1992). Caffeine use as a model of acute and chronic insomnia. *Sleep, 15*, 526–536.

Borgwardt, S., McGuire, P., & Fusar-Poli, P. (2011). Gray matters!—Mapping the transition to psychosis. *Schizophrenia Research, 133*, 63–67.

Bostwick, J. M., & Pankratz, V. S. (2000). Affective disorders and suicide risk: A reexamination. *The American Journal of Psychiatry, 157*, 1925–1932.

Bowers, M. B., Jr. (1987). The role of drugs in the production of schizophreniform psychosis and related disorders. In H. Y. Meltzer (Ed.), *Psychopharmacology: A third generation of progress* (pp. 819–823). New York: Raven Press.

Bows, H. A. (1965). The role of diazepam (Valium) in emotional illness. *Psychosomatics, 6*, 336–340.

Boyer, W. F., & Feighner, J. P. (1991). Side effects of the selective serotonin re-uptake inhibitors. In J. P. Feighner & W. F. Boyer (Eds.), *Selective serotonin re-uptake inhibitors* (pp. 133–152). Chichester, England: Wiley.

Bozarth, M. A., & Wise, R. A. (1984). Anatomically distinct opiate receptor fields mediate rewards and physical dependence. *Science, 244*, 516–517.

Brabant, C., Alleva, L., Quertemont, E., & Tirelli, E. (2010). Involvement of the brain histaminergic system in addiction and addiction-related behaviors: A comprehensive review with emphasis on the potential therapeutic use of histaminergic compounds in drug dependence. *Progress in Neurobiology, 92*, 421–441.

Brady, J. V., Griffiths, R. R., Heinz, R. D., Ator, N. A., Lucas, S. E., & Lamb, R. J. (1987). Assessing drugs for abuse liability and dependence potential in laboratory primates. In M. A. Bozarth (Ed.), *Methods of assessing the reinforcing properties of abused drugs* (pp. 45–86). New York: Springer-Verlag.

Braude, M. C., & Szara, S. (1976). *Pharmacology of marijuana* (2 vols.). Orlando, FL: Academic Press.

Brauer, L., Ambre, J., & de Wit, H. (1996). Acute tolerance to the subjective but not cardiovascular effects of d-amphetamine in normal, healthy men. *Journal of Clinical Psychopharmacology, 16*, 72–76.

Brecher, E. M., & the Editors of *Consumer Reports*. (1972). *Licit and illicit drugs*. Mt. Vernon, NY: Consumers Union.

Brecher, E. M., Wang, B. W., Wong, H., & Morgan, J. P. (1988). Phencyclidine and violence: Clinical and legal issues. *Journal of Clinical Psychopharmacology, 8*, 397–401.

Breivogel, C. S., & Sim-Selley, L. J. (2009). Basic neuroanatomy and neuropharmacology of cannabinoids. *International Review of Psychiatry (Abingdon, England), 21*, 113–121.

Brenesova, V., Oswald, I., & Loudon, J. (1975). Two types of insomnia: Too much waking or not enough sleep. *British Journal of Psychiatry, 126*, 439–445.

Brewer, C. (1992). Controlled trials of antabuse in alcoholism: The importance of supervision and adequate dosage. *Acta Psychiatrica Scandinavica. Supplementum, 369*, 51–58.

Bridge, J. A., Iyengar, S., Salary, C. B., Barbe, R. P., Birmaher, B., Pincus, H. A., et al. (2007). Clinical response and risk for reported suicidal ideation and suicide attempts in pediatric antidepressant treatment, a meta-analysis of randomized controlled trials. *Journal of the American Medical Association, 297*, 1683–1696.

Britton, D. R., El-Wardany, Z. S., Brown, C. P., & Bianchine, J. R. (1978). Clinical pharmacokinetics of selected psychotropic drugs. In L. L. Iverson, S. D. Iverson, & S. H. Snyder (Eds.), *Handbook of psychopharmacology* (Vol. 13, pp. 299–344). New York: Plenum Press.

Broadwater, M., Varlinskaya, E. I., & Spear, L. P. (2011). Chronic intermittent ethanol exposure in early adolescent and adult male rats: Effects on tolerance, social behavior, and ethanol intake. *Alcoholism, Clinical and Experimental Research, 35*, 1392–1403.

Brookes, L. G. (1985). Central nervous system stimulants. In S. D. Iverson (Ed.), *Psychopharmacology: Recent advances and future prospects* (pp. 264–277). Oxford, England: Oxford University Press.

Brookhuis, K., Volkerts, E., & O'Hanlon, J. (1990). Repeated dose effects of lormetrazepam and flurazepam upon driving performance. *European Journal of Clinical Pharmacology, 39,* 83–87.

Brooks, J. E. (1952). *The mighty leaf: Tobacco through the centuries.* Boston, MA: Little, Brown.

Brown, F. C. (1972). *Hallucinogenic drugs.* Springfield, IL: Thomas.

Brown, C., Fezoui, M., Selig, W. M., Schwartz, C. E., & Ellis, J. L. (2004). Antitussive activity of sigma-1 receptor agonists in the guinea-pig. *British Journal of Pharmacology, 141,* 233–240.

Brust, J. C. (2010). Ethanol and cognition: Indirect effects, neurotoxicity and neuroprotection: A review. *International Journal of Environmental Research and Public Health, 7,* 1540–1557.

Budney, A. J., Moore, B. A., Vandrey, R. G., & Hughes, J. R. (2003). The time course and significance of cannabis withdrawal. *Journal of Abnormal Psychology, 112,* 393–402.

Burg, A. W. (1975). Physiological disposition of caffeine. *Drug Metabolism Reviews, 4,* 199–228.

Bushnell, P. J., Kavlock, R. J., Crofton, K. M., Weiss, B., & Rice, D. C. (2010). Behavioral toxicology in the 21st century: Challenges and opportunities for behavioral scientists. Summary of a symposium presented at the annual meeting of the neurobehavioral teratology society, June, 2009. *Neurotoxicology and Teratology, 32,* 313–328.

Busto, U., Bendayan, R., & Sellers, E. (1989). Clinical pharmacokinetics of non-opiate abused drugs. *Clinical Pharmacokinetics, 16,* 1–26.

Butschky, M. F., Bailey, D., Henningfield, J. E., & Pickworth, W. B. (1994). Smoking without nicotine delivery decreases withdrawal in 12-hour abstinent smokers. *Pharmacology, Biochemistry and Behavior, 50,* 91–96.

Caggiula, A. R., Donny, E. C., Palmatier, M. I., Liu, X., Chaudhri, N., & Sved, A. F. (2009). The role of nicotine in smoking: A dual-reinforcement model. *Nebraska Symposium on Motivation, 55,* 91–109.

Caggiula, A. R., Donny, E. C., White, A. R., Chaudhri, N., Booth, S., Gharib, M. A., et al. (2001). Cue dependency of nicotine self-administration and smoking. *Pharmacology, Biochemistry and Behavior, 70,* 515–530.

Caldwell, J. (1976). Physiological aspects of cocaine usage. In S. J. Mule (Ed.), *Cocaine: Chemical, biological, clinical, social and treatment aspects* (pp. 187–200). Boca Raton, FL: CRC Press.

Calhoun, V. D., & Pearlson, G. D. (2012). A selective review of simulated driving studies: Combining naturalistic and hybrid paradigms, analysis approaches, and future directions. *NeuroImage, 59,* 25–35.

Calhoun, V. D., Pekar, J. J., & Pearlson, G. D. (2004). Alcohol intoxication effects on simulated driving: Exploring alcohol-dose effects on brain activation using functional MRI. *Neuropsyhopharmacology, 29,* 2097–2107.

California Environmental Protection Agency, Office of Environmental Health Hazard Assessment. (2005). *Proposed identification of environmental tobacco smoke as a toxic air contaminant: Part B health effects.* Retrieved from http://www.arb.ca.gov/regact/ets2006/ets2006.htm

Callahan, M. M., Robertson, R. S., Branfman, A. R., McCormish, M. F., & Yesair, D. W. (1983). Comparison of caffeine metabolism in three nonsmoking populations after oral administration of radio-labelled caffeine. *Drug Metabolism and Disposition, 11,* 211–217.

Callahan, P. M., De La Garza, R., 2nd., & Cunningham, K. A. (1997). Mediation of the discriminative stimulus properties of cocaine by mesocorticolimbic dopamine systems. *Pharmacology, Biochemistry and Behavior, 57,* 601–607.

Campbell, J. C., & Seiden, L. S. (1973). Performance influence on the development of tolerance to amphetamine. *Pharmacology, Biochemistry and Behavior, 1,* 703–708.

Cannon, C. M., & Palmiter, R. D. (2003). Reward without dopamine. *Journal of Neuroscience,* (Nov. 26), 10827–10831.

Cappell, H., & Pliner, P. (1974). Cannabis intoxication: The role of pharmacological and psychological variables. In L. L. Miller (Ed.), *Marijuana: Effects on human behaviour* (pp. 233–264). Orlando, FL: Academic Press.

Cardenas, D. D., & Jensen, M. P. (2006). Treatments for chronic pain in persons with spinal cord injury: A survey study. *The Journal of Spinal Cord Medicine, 29,* 109–117.

CARE Study Group. (2008). Maternal caffeine intake during pregnancy and risk of fetal growth restriction: A large prospective observational study. *BMJ (Clinical Research Ed.), 337,* a2332.

Carek, P. J., Laibstain, S. E., & Carek, S. M. (2011). Exercise for the treatment of depression and anxiety. *International Journal of Psychiatry in Medicine, 41,* 15–28.

Carlezon, W. A., & Wise, R. A. (1996). Rewarding actions of phencyclidine and related drugs in nucleus accumbens shell and frontal cortex. *Journal of Neuroscience, 16,* 3112–3122.

Carlson, N. R. (2011). *Foundations of Behavioral Neuroscience* (8th ed.). Boston, MA: Pearson Education, Inc.

Carlsson, A. (1994). The search for the ideal medications: Developing a rational neuropharmacology. In N. C. Andreasen (Ed.), *Schizophrenia: From mind to molecule* (pp. 161–172). Washington, DC: American Psychiatric Press.

Carney, J. M. (1982). Effects of caffeine, theophylline and theobromine on schedule controlled responding in rats. *British Journal of Pharmacology, 75,* 451–454.

Caroline, D. (2011). Amy Winehouse inquest records verdict of misadventure. (2011). *The Guardian.* Retrieved from http://www.guardian.co.uk/music/2011/oct/26/amy-winehouse-verdict-misadventure

Carroll, M. E. (1993). The economic context of drug and non-drug reinforcers affects acquisition and maintenance of drug reinforced behavior and withdrawal effects. *Alcohol and Drug Dependence, 33,* 201–210.

Carroll, M. E. (1998). Psychological and psychiatric consequences of caffeine. In R. E. Tarter, R. T. Ammerman, & P. J. Ott (Eds.), *Handbook of substance abuse: Neurobehavioral pharmacology* (pp. 97–110). New York: Plenum Press.

Carroll, M. E., & Bickel, W. (1998). Behavioral-environmental determinants of the reinforcing effect of cocaine. In S. T. Higgins & J. L. Katz (Eds.), *Cocaine abuse: Behavior, pharmacology and clinical applications* (pp. 81–106). San Diego, CA: Academic Press.

Carroll, M. E., & Meisch, R. A. (1984). Increases in food reinforced behavior due to food deprivation. In T. Thompson, P. B. Dews, & J. E. Barrett (Eds.), *Advances in behavioral pharmacology* (Vol. 4, pp. 47–88). Orlando, FL: Academic Press.

Carvalho, L. P., de Greckshk, G., Chapouthier, G., & Rossier, J. (1983). Anxiogenic and non-anxiogenic benzodiazepine antagonists. *Nature, 301,* 64–66.

Casadio, P., Fernandes, C., Murray, R. M., & Di Forti, M. (2011). Cannabis use in young people: The risk for schizophrenia. *Neuroscience and Biobehavioral Reviews, 35,* 1779–1787.

Caspi, A., Hariri, A. R., Holmes, A., Uher, R., & Moffitt, T. E. (2010). Genetic sensitivity to the environment: The case of the serotonin transporter gene and its implications for studying complex diseases and traits. *The American Journal of Psychiatry, 167,* 509–527.

Caspi, A., Sugden, K., Moffitt, T. E., Taylor, A., Craig, I. W., Harrington, H., et al. (2003). Influence of life stress on depression: Moderation by a polymorphism in the 5-HTT gene. *Science (New York, N.Y.), 301,* 386–389.

Castelli, M. P. (2008). Multi-faceted aspects of Gamma-hydroxybutyric acid: A neurotransmitter, therapeutic agent and drug of abuse. *Mini Reviews in Medicinal Chemistry, 8,* 1188–1202.

Centers for Disease Control and Prevention. (1999). Determination of nicotine, pH, and moisture content of six US commercial moist snuff products—Florida, January–February 1999. *The Journal of the American Medical Association, 281,* 2279–2280.

Centers for Disease Control and Prevention. (2012). Retrieved April 4, 2012, from http://www.cdc.gov/tobacco/basic_information/health_effects/heart_disease/.

Chait, L. D., & Burke, K. A. (1994). Preference for high- versus low-potency marijuana. *Pharmacology, Biochemistry and Behavior, 49,* 643–647.

Chait, L. D., Evans, S. M., Grant, K. A., Kamien, J. B., Johanson, C. E., & Schuster, C. R. (1988). Discrimina-tive stimuli and subjective effects of smoked marijuana in humans. *Psychopharmacology, 94,* 206–212.

Chait, L. D., & Griffiths, R. R. (1982). Differential control of puff duration and interpuff interval in cigarette smokers. *Pharmacology, Biochemistry and Behavior, 17,* 155–158.

Chait, L. D., & Pierri, J. (1992). Effects of smoked marijuana on human performance: A critical review. In L. Murphy & A. Bartke (Eds.), *Marijuana/cannabinoids: Neurobiology and neurophysiology* (pp. 387–424). Boca Raton, FL: CRC Press.

Chait, L. D., Uhlenhuth, E. H., & Johanson, C. E. (1986). The discriminative stimulus and subjective effects of d-amphetamine, phenmetrazine and fenfluramine in humans. *Psychopharmacology, 89,* 301–306.

Chait, L. D., & Zacny, J. P. (1992). Reinforcing and subjective effects of oral Δ9-THC and smoked marijuana in humans. *Psychopharmacology, 107,* 255–262.

Chan, G. C. -K., Hinds, T. R., Impey, S., & Storm, D. R. (1998). Hippocampal neurotoxicity of Δ9-tetrahydrocannabinol. *Journal of Neuroscience, 18,* 5322–5332.

Chandler M. A., & Rennard, S. (2010). Smoking cessation. *Chest, 137,* 428–435.

Chang, S. M., Hahm, B. J., Lee, J. Y., Shin, M. S., Jeon, H. J., Hong, J. P., et al. (2008). Cross-national difference in the prevalence of depression caused by the diagnostic threshold. *Journal of Affective Disorders, 106,* 159–167.

Chapman, S., & MacKenzie, R. (2010). The global research neglect of unassisted smoking cessation: Causes and consequences. *PLoS Medicine, 7,* e1000216.

Chen, S. L., Hsu, K. Y., Huang, E. Y., Lu, R. B., & Tao, P. L. (2011). Low doses of dextromethorphan attenuate morphine-induced rewarding via the sigma-1 receptor at ventral tegmental area in rats. *Drug and Alcohol Dependence, 117,* 164–169.

Cheney, R. H. (1925). *Coffee.* New York: New York University Press.

Childress, A. R., Ehrman, R. N., Wang, Z., Li, Y., Sciortino, N., Hakun, J., et al. (2008). Prelude to passion: Limbic activation by "unseen" drug and sexual cues. *PLoS One, 3,* e1506.

Childs, E., & de Wit, H. (2006). Subjective, behavioral, and physiological effects of acute caffeine in light, nondependent caffeine users. *Psychopharmacology, 185,* 514–523.

Cho, A., Coalson, D., Klock, P., Klafta, J., Marks, S., Toledano, A., et al. (1997). The effects of alcohol history on the reinforcing, subjective and psychomotor effects of nitrous oxide in healthy volunteers. *Drug and Alcohol Dependence, 46,* 63–70.

Choudhuri, S., & Valerio, L. G. (2005). Usefulness of studies on the molecular mechanism of action of herbals/botanicals: The case of St. John's wort. *Journal of Biochemical and Molecular Toxicology, 19,* 1–11.

Christoph, M., Ebner, B., Stolte, D., Ibrahim, K., Kolschmann, S., Strasser, R. H., et al. (2010). Broken heart syndrome: Tako tsubo cardiomyopathy associated with an overdose of the serotonin-norepinephrine reuptake inhibitor venlafaxine. *European Neuropsychopharmacology: The Journal of the European College of Neuropsychopharmacology, 20,* 594–597.

Chutuape, M. A., Mitchell, S., & de Wit, H. (1994). Ethanol preloads increase ethanol preference under concurrent random ratio schedules in social drinkers. *Experimental and Clinical Psychopharmacology, 2,* 310–318.

Ciccarone, D. (2011). Stimulant abuse: Pharmacology, cocaine, methamphetamine, treatment, attempts at pharmacotherapy. *Primary Care, 38,* 41–58, v–vi.

Clarke, S., Dargan, P., & Jones, A. (2005). Naloxone in opioid poisoning: Walking the tightrope. *Emergency Medicine Journal, 22,* 612–616.

Cobb, N. K., & Abrams, D. B. (2011). E-cigarette or drug-delivery device? Regulating novel nicotine products. *The New England Journal of Medicine, 365,* 193–195.

Cochran, S. V., & Rabinowitz, F. E. (2000). *Men and depression: Clinical and empirical perspectives.* San Diego, CA: Academic Press.

Cocteau, J. (1968). *Opium: The diary of a cure* (M. Crossland & S. Road, Trans.). London: Peter Owen.

Cohen, S., & Stillman, R. C. (1976). *The therapeutic potential of marijuana.* New York: Plenum Press.

Coldwell, S., Kaufman, E., Milgrom, P., Kharasch, E., Chen, P., Mautz, D., et al. (1998). Acute tolerance and reversal of the motor control effects of midazolam. *Pharmacology, Biochemistry and Behavior, 52,* 537–545.

Cole-Harding, S., & Michels, V. J. (2007). Does expectancy affect alcohol absorption? *Addictive Behaviors, 32,* 194–198.

Collins, D. R., Pertwee, R. G., & Davies, S. N. (1994). The action of synthetic cannabinoids on the induction of long-term potentiation in the rat hippocampal slice. *European Journal of Pharmacology, 259,* R7–R8.

Colloca, L., & Benedetti, F. (2005). Placebos and painkillers: Is mind as real as matter? *Nature Reviews/Neuroscience, 6,* 545–552.

Colpaert, F. C. (1977). Discriminative stimulus properties of benzodiazepines and barbiturates. In H. Lal (Ed.), *Discriminative stimulus properties of drugs* (pp. 93–106). New York: Plenum Press.

Colvin, M. (1983). A counselling approach to outpatient benzodiazepine detoxification. *Journal of Psychoactive Drugs, 15,* 105–108.

Comer, S. D., Sullivan, M. A., Yu, E., Rothenberg, J. L., Kleber, H. D., Kampman, K., et al. (2006). Injectable, sustained-release naltrexone for the treatment of opioid dependence: A randomized, placebo-controlled trial. *Archives of General Psychiatry, 63,* 210–218.

Conger, J. (1951). The effect of alcohol on conflict behavior in the albino rat. *Quarterly Journal of Studies on Alcohol, 12,* 1–29.

Conley, K. M., Toledano, A. Y., Apfelbaum, J. L., & Zacny, J. P. (1997). Modulating effects of a cold water stimulus on opioid effects in volunteers. *Psychopharmacology, 131,* 313–320.

Consroe, P., & Sandyk, R. (1992). Potential role for cannabinoids for therapy of neurological disorders. In L. Murphy & A. Bartke (Eds.), *Marijuana/cannabinoids neurology and neurophysiology* (pp. 459–524). Boca Raton, FL: CRC Press.

Corbani, M., Gonindard, C., & Meunier, J. C. (2004). Ligand-regulated internalization of the opioid receptor-like 1: A confocal study. *Endocrinology, 145,* 2876–2885.

Corbett, A. D., Henderson, G., McKnight, A. T., & Paterson, S. J. (2006). 75 years of opioid research: The exciting but vain quest for the Holy Grail. *British Journal of Pharmacology 147,* S153–S162. Retrieved from http://www.ncbi.nlm.nih.gov/pmc/articles/PMC1760732/

Cornelis, M. C., El-Sohemy, A., Kabagambe, E. K., & Campos, H. (2006). Coffee, CYP1A2 genotype, and risk of myocardial infarction. *The Journal of the American Medical Association, 295,* 1135–1141.

Cornuz, J., Zwahlen, S., Jungi, W. F., Osterwalder, J., Klingler, K., van Melle, G., et al. (2008). A vaccine against nicotine for smoking cessation: A randomized controlled trial. *PLoS One, 3,* 2547.

Costa, E. (1985). Preface. In D. Kemali & G. Racagni (Eds.), *Chronic treatments in neuropsychiatry: Advances in biochemical pharmacology* (Vol. 40, pp. 5–6). New York: Raven Press.

Couper, F., & Logan, B. (2001). GHB and driving impairment. *Journal of Forensic Sciences, 26,* 919–923.

Courvoisier, S., Fournel, J., Ducrot, R., Kolsky, M., & Koetschet, P. (1953). Propriétés pharmacodynamiques du chlor-hydrate de chloro-3 (diméthylamino-3' Propyl)-10-phenorthiazine (4.560 R. P.). *Archives Internationales de Pharmacodynamie et de Thérapie, 92,* 305–361.

Cox, B. M., Borsodi, A., Caló, G., Chavkin, C., Christie, M. J., Civelli, O., et al. *Opioid receptors, introductory chapter.* Last modified on 2009-10-13. IUPHAR database (IUPHAR-DB), Retrieved November 23, 2011, from http://www.iuphar-db.org/DATABASE/FamilyIntroductionForward?familyId=50

Cozzi, N. V., Sievert, M. K., Shulgin, A. T., Jacob, P., 3rd., & Ruoho, A. E. (1999). Inhibition of plasma membrane monoamine transporters by beta-ketoamphetamines. *European Journal of Pharmacology, 381,* 63–69.

Crawford, R. J. M. (1981). Benzodiazepine dependency and abuse. *New Zealand Medical Journal, 94,* 195.

Creasey, W. A. (1979). *Drug disposition in humans.* New York: Oxford University Press.

Cree, J. E., Meyer, J., & Hailey, D. K. (1973). Diazepam in labor: Its metabolism and effect on clinical condition and thermogenesis of the newborn. *British Medical Journal, 4,* 251–255.

Creese, I. (1983). Receptor interactions of neuroleptics. In J. T. Coyle & S. J. Enna (Eds.), *Neuroleptics: Neurochemical, behavioral, and clinical perspectives* (pp. 183–222). New York: Raven Press.

Crews, F. T., & Nixon, K. (2009). Mechanisms of neurodegeneration and regeneration in alcoholism. *Alcohol and Alcoholism (Oxford, Oxfordshire), 44,* 115–127.

Cromer, J. R., Cromer, J. A., Maruff, P., & Snyder, P. J. (2010). Perception of alcohol intoxication shows acute tolerance while executive functions remain impaired. *Experimental and Clinical Psychopharmacology, 18,* 329–339.

Crowley, T. J. (1987). Clinical issues in cocaine abuse. In S. Fisher, A. Raskin, & E. H. Uhlenhuth (Eds.), *Cocaine: Clinical and behavioral aspects* (pp. 193–211). New York: Oxford University Press.

Curran, C., Byrappa, N., & McBride, A. (2004). Stimulant psychosis: Systematic review. *British Journal of Psychiatry, 185,* 196–2004.

Curtis, M. A., Kam, M., Nannmark, U., Anderson, M. F., Axell, M. Z., Wikkelso, C., et al. (2007). Human neuroblasts migrate to the olfactory bulb via a lateral ventricular extension. *Science, 315,* 1243–1249.

Czyrak, A., Mackowiak, M., Chocyk, A., Fijal, K., & Wedzony, K. (2003). Role of glucocorticoids in the regulation of dopaminergic neurotransmission. *Polish Journal of Pharmacology, 55,* 667–674.

Dackis, C. A., Kampman, K. M., Lynch, K. G., Pettinati, H. M., & O'Brien, C. P. (2005). A double-blind, placebo-controlled trial of modafinil for cocaine dependence. *Neuropsychopharmacology: Official Publication of the American College of Neuropsychopharmacology, 30,* 205–211.

Daglish, M. R., Weinstein, A., Malizia, A. L., Wilson, S., Melichar, J. K., Britten, S., et al. (2001). Changes in regional cerebral blood flow elicited by craving memories in abstinent opiate-dependent subjects. *The American Journal of Psychiatry, 158,* 1680–1686.

Dahl, R. E., Scher, M. S., Williamson, D. E., Robles, N., & Day, N. (1995). A longitudinal study of prenatal marijuana use: Effects on sleep and arousal at age three years. *Archives of Pediatric and Adolescent Medicine, 149,* 145–150.

Damsa, C., Kosel, M., & Moussally, J. (2009). Current status of brain imaging in anxiety disorders. *Current Opinion in Psychiatry, 22,* 96–110.

Dani, J. A., & Balfour, D. J. (2011). Historical and current perspective on tobacco use and nicotine addiction. *Trends in Neurosciences.* doi:10.1016/j.tins.2011.05.001

Daniell, H. W. (1971). Smoker's wrinkles: A study in the epidemiology of "crow's feet." *Annals of Internal Medicine, 75,* 873–880.

Darboe, M., Keenan, G., & Richards, T. (1996). The abuse of dextromethorphan-based cough syrup: A pilot study of the community of Waynesboro, Pennsylvania. *Adolescence, 31,* 633–644.

Darke, S. (2011). *Life of the heroin user: Typical beginnings, trajectories and outcomes.* New York: Cambridge University Press.

Darley, C. F., & Tinklenberg, J. R. (1974). Marijuana and memory. In L. L. Miller (Ed.), *Marijuana: Effects on human behavior* (pp. 73–102). Orlando, FL: Academic Press.

Darwin, C. (1882). *The descent of man.* New York: Appleton.

Dassanayake, T., Michie, P., Carter, G., & Jones, A. (2011). Effects of benzodiazepines, antidepressants and opioids on driving: A systematic review and meta-analysis of epidemiological and experimental evidence. *Drug Safety: An International Journal of Medical Toxicology and Drug Experience, 34,* 125–156.

Davidson, E. S., & Schenk, S. (1994). Variability in subjective responses to marijuana: Initial experiences of college students. *Addictive Behaviors, 19,* 531–538.

Davis, D. L. (1962). Normal drinking in recovered alcohol addicts. *Quarterly Journal of Studies on Alcohol, 23,* 94–104.

Davis, T. R. A., Kensler, C. J., & Dews, P. B. (1973). Comparison of behavioral effects of nicotine, d-amphetamine, caffeine and dimethylheptyltetra-hydrocannabinol in squirrel monkeys. *Psychopharmacologia, 32,* 51–65.

Day, N. L., Leech, S. L., Richardson, G. A., Cornelius, M., Robles, N., & Larkby, C. (2002). Prenatal alcohol exposure predicts continued deficits in offspring size at 14 years of age. *Alcohol: Clinical and Experimental Research, 26,* 1584–1591.

De Quincey, T. (1901). *The confessions of an English opium-eater.* London: Macmillan.

de Wit, H. (1996). Priming effects with drugs and other reinforcers. *Experimental and Clinical Psychopharmacology, 4,* 5–10.

de Wit, H., & Chutuape, M. A. (1993). Increased ethanol choice in social drinkers following ethanol preload. *Behavioural Pharmacology, 4,* 29–36.

de Wit, H., Clark, M., & Brauer, L. (1997). Effects of d-amphetamine in grouped versus isolated humans. *Pharmacology, Biochemistry and Behavior, 57,* 333–340.

de Wit, H., Enggasser, J. L., & Richards, J. B. (2002). Acute administration of d-amphetamine decreases impulsivity in healthy volunteers. *Neuropsychopharmacology: Official*

Publication of the American College of Neuropsychopharmacology, 27, 813–825.

de Wit, H., & Griffiths, R. R. (1991). Testing the abuse liability of anxiolytic and hypnotic drugs in humans. *Drug and Alcohol Dependence, 28,* 83–111.

de Wit, H., & Johanson, C. E. (1987). A drug preference procedure for use with human volunteers. In M. A. Bozarth (Ed.), *Methods of assessing the reinforcing properties of abused drugs* (pp. 559–572). New York: Springer-Verlag.

de Wit, H., Johanson, C. E., & Uhlenhuth, E. H. (1984). Reinforcing properties of lorazepam in normal volunteers. *Drug and Alcohol Dependence, 13,* 31–41.

de Wit, H., Kirk, J., & Justice, A. (1998). Behavioral pharmacology of cannabinoids. In R. E. Tarter, R. T. Ammerman, & P. J. Ott (Eds.), *Handbook of substance abuse: Neurobehavioral pharmacology* (pp. 131–146). New York: Plenum Press.

de Wit, H., & McCracken, S. G. (1990). Ethanol self-administration in males with and without an alcoholic first-degree relative. *Alcoholism: Clinical and Experimental Research, 14,* 63–70.

de Wit, H., Uhlenhuth, E. H., & Johanson, C. E. (1987). The reinforcing properties of amphetamine in overweight subjects and subjects with depression. *Clinical Pharmacology and Therapeutics, 42,* 127–136.

de Wit, H., & Zacny, J. (1995). Abuse potential of nicotine replacement therapies. *CNS Drugs, 4,* 456–468.

Dean, O., Giorlando, F., & Berk, M. (2011). N-acetylcysteine in psychiatry: Current therapeutic evidence and potential mechanisms of action. *Journal of Psychiatry & Neuroscience, 36,* 78–86.

Degenhardt, L., Dierker, L., Chiu, W. T., Medina-Mora, M. E., Neumark, Y., Sampson, N., et al. (2010). Evaluating the drug use "gateway" theory using cross-national data: Consistency and associations of the order of initiation of drug use among participants in the WHO world mental health surveys. *Drug and Alcohol Dependence, 108,* 84–97.

Degenhardt, L., Hall, W., & Lynskey, M. (2003). Testing hypotheses about the relationship between cannabis use and psychosis. *Drug and Alcohol Dependence, 71,* 37–48.

Dekeyne, A., & Millan, M. (2003). Discriminative stimulus properties of antidepressant agents: A review. *Behavioural Pharmacology, 14,* 391–407.

Deminiére, J. M., Piazza, P. V., Guegan, G., Abrous, N., Maccari, S., Le Moal, M., et al (1992). Increased locomotor response to novelty and propensity to intravenous amphetamine self-administration in adult offspring of stressed mothers. *Brain Research, 586,* 135–139.

Demir, B., Ulug, B., Lay Ergun, E., & Erbas, B. (2002). Regional cerebral blood flow and neuropsychological functioning in early and late onset alcoholism. *Psychiatry Research, 115,* 115–125.

Demirakca, T., Sartorius, A., Ende, G., Meyer, N., Welzel, H., Skopp, G., et al. (2011). Diminished gray matter in the hippocampus of cannabis users: Possible protective effects of cannabidiol. *Drug and Alcohol Dependence, 114,* 242–245.

Deneau, G. A., Yanagita, T., & Seevers, M. H. (1969). Self-administration of psychoactive substances by the monkey: A measure of psychological dependence. *Psychopharmacologia, 16,* 30–48.

Depoortere, R. Y., Li, D. H., Lane, M. W., & Emmett-Oglesby, M. W. (1993). Parameters of self-administration of cocaine in rats under a progressive-ratio schedule. *Pharmacology, Biochemistry and Behavior, 45,* 539–548.

Desai, R. I., Barber, D. J., & Terry, P. (2003). Dopaminergic and cholinergic involvement in the discriminative stimulus effects of nicotine and cocaine in rats. *Psychopharmacology, 167,* 335–343.

Desmond, P. V., Patwardham, R. V., Schenker, S., & Hoyumpa, A. M. (1980). Short-term ethanol administration impairs the elimination of chlordiazepoxide (Librium) in man. *European Journal of Clinical Pharmacology, 18,* 275–278.

DeVane, C. L. (1998). Differential pharmacology of newer antidepressants. *Journal of Clinical Psychiatry, 59*(Suppl. 20), 85–93.

Dewey, W. L., Martin, B. R., & Harris, L. S. (1976). Chronic effects of delta-9-THC in animals: Tolerance and biochemical changes. In M. C. Braude & S. Szara (Eds.), *Pharmacology of marijuana* (Vol. 2, pp. 585–594). Orlando, FL: Academic Press.

Dews, P. B. (1955). Differential sensitivity to pentobarbital of pecking performance in pigeons depending on the schedule of reward. *Journal of Pharmacology and Experimental Therapy, 113,* 393–401.

Dews, P. B. (1958). Studies on behavior: 4. Stimulant actions of methamphetamine. *Journal of Pharmacology and Experimental Therapeutics, 122,* 137–147.

Dews, P. B. (1962). A behavioral output enhancing effect of imipramine in pigeons. *International Journal of Neuropharmacology, 1,* 265–272.

Dews, P. B., O'Brien, C. P., & Bergman, J. (2002). Caffeine: Behavioral effects of withdrawal and related issues. *Food and Chemical Toxicology, 40,* 1257–1261.

Dews, P. B., & Wenger, G. R. (1977). Rate dependency of the behavioral effects of amphetamine. In T. Thompson & P. B. Dews (Eds.), *Advances in behavioral pharmacology* (Vol. 1, pp. 167–227). Orlando, FL: Academic Press.

Di Chiara, G., Bassareo, V., Fenu, S., De Luca, M. A., Spina, L., Cadoni, C., et al. (2004). Dopamine and drug addiction: The nucleus accumbens shell connection. *Neuropharmacology, 47*(Suppl. 1), 227–241.

Di Chiara, G., & Imperato, A. (1988). Drugs abused by humans preferentially increase synaptic dopamine concentrations in the mesolimbic system of freely moving rats. *Proceedings of the National Academy of Sciences of the United States of America, 85*, 5274–5278.

Di Marzo, V., Melck, D., Bisogno, T., & De Petrocellis, L. (1998). Endocannabinoids: Endogenous cannabinoid receptor ligands with neuromodulatory action. *Trends in Neuroscience, 21*, 521–528.

di Tomaso, E., Beltramo, M., & Piomelli, D. (1996). Brain cannabinoids in chocolate. *Science, 382*, 677–678.

DiMascio, A. (1973). The effects of benzodiazepines on aggression: Reduced or increased? In S. Garattini, E. Musi, & L. O. Randall (Eds.), *The benzodiazepines* (pp. 433–440). New York: Raven Press.

Dinwiddie, S. H., & Farber, N. B. (1995). Pharmacological therapies of cannabis, hallucinogens, phencyclidine and volatile solvent addiction. In N. S. Miller & M. S. Gold (Eds.), *Pharmacological therapies for alcohol and drug addiction* (pp. 213–216). New York: Marcel Dekker.

DiPadova, C., Roine, R., Frezza, M., Gentry, R. T., Baraona, E., & Lieber, C. S. (1992). Effects of ranitidine on blood alcohol levels after ethanol ingestion. Comparison with other H2-receptor antagonists. *The Journal of the American Medical Association, 267*, 83–86.

DiPadova, C., Worner, T. M., Julkunnen, R. J. K., & Lieber, C. S. (1987). Effects of fasting and chronic alcohol consumption on the first-pass metabolism of ethanol. *Gastroenterology, 92*, 1169–1173.

Ditmar, E. A., & Dorian, V. (1987). Ethanol absorption after bolus ingestion of an alcoholic beverage: A medico-legal problem: Part II. *Canadian Society of Forensic Sciences Journal, 20*, 61–69.

Doetsch, F., Caillé, I., Lim, D. A., Garcí-a-Verdugo, J. M., & Alvarez-Buylla, A. (1999). Subventricular zone astrocytes are neural stem cells in the adult mammalian brain. *Cell, 97*, 703–716.

Doherty, J., O'Donovan, M., & Owen, M. (2011). Recent genomic advances in schizophrenia. *Clinical Genetics.* doi:10.1111/j.1399-0004.2011.01773.x; 10.1111/j.1399-0004.2011.01773.x

Dole, V. P. (1980). Addictive behavior. *Scientific American, 234*, 138–154.

Domino, E. F. (1973). Neuropsychopharmacology of nicotine and tobacco smoking. In W. L. Dunn (Ed.), *Smoking behavior: Motives and incentives* (pp. 5–32). Washington, DC: Winston.

Domino, E. F., Rennick, P., & Pearl, J. H. (1976). Short-term neuropsychopharmacological effects of marijuana smoking in experienced male users. In M. C. Braude & S. Szara (Eds.), *Pharmacology of marijuana* (Vol. 1, pp. 585–594). Orlando, FL: Academic Press.

Domjan, M. (2010). *The principles of learning and behavior* (6th ed.). Belmont, CA: Wadsworth Cengage Learning.

Drevets, W. C., Thase, M. E., Moses-Kolko, E. L., Price, J., Frank, E., Kupfer, D. J., et al. (2007). Serotonin-1A receptor imaging in recurrent depression: Replication and literature review. *Nuclear Medicine and Biology, 34*, 865–877.

Drummer, O. H., Gerostamoulos, J., Batziris, H., Chu, M., Caplehorn, J., Robertson, M. D., et al. (2004). The involvement of drugs in drivers of motor vehicles killed in Australian road traffic crashes. *Accident; Analysis and Prevention, 36*, 239–248.

Drummer, O., & Ransom, D. (1996). Sudden death and benzodiazepines. *American Journal of Forensic Medicine and Pathology, 17*, 336–342.

Dubowski, K. M. (1985). Absorption, distribution and elimination of alcohol: Highway safety aspects. *Journal of Studies on Alcohol, 10*(Suppl.), 98–108.

Dudley, R. (2000). Evolutionary origins of human alcoholism in primate frugavory. *Quarterly Review of Biology, 75*, 3–15.

Dudley, R. (2002). Fermenting fruit and the historical ecology of ethanol ingestion: Is alcoholism in modern humans an evolutionary hangover? *Addiction, 97*, 381–388.

Dumont, G. J., Sweep, F. C., van der Steen, R., Hermsen, R., Donders, A. R., Touw, D. J., et al. (2009). Increased oxytocin concentrations and prosocial feelings in humans after ecstasy (3,4-methylenedioxymethamphetamine) administration. *Social Neuroscience, 4*, 359–366.

Dunlop, M., & Court, J. M. (1981). Effects of maternal caffeine ingestion on neonatal growth in rats. *Biology of the Neonate, 39*, 178–184.

Dwyer, A. V., Whitten, D. L., & Hawrelak, J. A. (2011). Herbal medicines, other than St. John's wort, in the treatment of depression: A systematic review. *Altern Med Rev, 40*–49.

Dykstra, L. A., Preston, K. L., & Bigelow, G. E. (1997). Discriminative stimulus and subjective effects of opioids with mu and kappa activity: Data from laboratory animals and human subjects. *Psychopharmacology, 130*, 14–27.

Earleywine, M. (2002). *Understanding marijuana.* New York: Oxford University Press.

Easterbrook, J. A. (1959). The effect of emotion on cue utilization and the organization of behavior. *Psychological Review, 66*, 183–201.

Ebin, D. (1961). *The drug experience.* New York: Orion Press.

Edwards, S., & Koob, G. F. (2010). Neurobiology of dysregulated motivational systems in drug addiction. *Future Neurology, 5*, 393–401.

Egashira, T., Yamamoto, T., & Yamanaka, Y. (1987). Effects of d-methamphetamine on monkey brain monoamine oxidase, in vivo and in vitro. *Japanese Journal of Pharmacology, 45*, 79–88.

Eikelboom, R., & Stewart, J. (1982). Conditioning of drug-induced physiological responses. *Psychological Reviews, 89*, 529–572.

El-Alfy, A. T., Ivey, K., Robinson, K., Ahmed, S., Radwan, M., Slade, D., et al. (2010). Antidepressant-like effect of delta9-tetrahydrocannabinol and other cannabinoids isolated from cannabis sativa L. *Pharmacology, Biochemistry and Behavior, 95,* 434–442.

Elie, R., Ruther, E., Farr, I., Emilien, G., & Salinas, E. (1999). Sleep latency is shortened during 4 weeks of treatment with zaleplon, a novel nonbenzodiazepine hypnotic. *Journal of Clinical Psychiatry, 60,* 536–544.

Ellenwood, E. H., Linnoila, M., Angle, H. V., Moore, J. W., Skinner, J. T., III., Easler, M., et al. (1981). Use of simple tasks to test for impairment of complex skills by a sedative. *Psychopharmacologia, 73,* 350–354.

ElSohly, M. A., & Salamone, S. J. (1999). Prevalence of drugs used in cases of alleged sexual assault. *Journal of Analytical Toxicology, 23,* 141–146.

Emonson, D. L., & Vanderbeek, R. D. (1995). The use of amphetamines in U.S. air force tactical operations during desert shield and storm. *Aviation, Space, and Environmental Medicine, 66,* 260–263.

Enna, S. J., & Coyle, J. T. (1983). Neuroleptics. In J. T. Coyle & S. J. Enna (Eds.), *Neuroleptics: Neurochemical, behavioral, and clinical perspectives* (pp. 1–14). New York: Raven Press.

Eriksson, P. S., Perfilieva, E., Björk-Eriksson, T., Alborn, A., Nordborg, C., Peterson, D. A., et al. (1998). Neurogenesis in the adult human hippocampus. *Nature Medicine, 4,* 1313–1317.

Erlenmeyer-Kimling, L., Rock, D., Roberts, S. A., Janal, M., Kestenbaum, C., Cornblatt, B., et al. (2000). Attention, memory, and motor skills as childhood predictors of schizophrenia-related psychoses: The new york high-risk project. *The American Journal of Psychiatry, 157,* 1416–1422.

Eros, E., Czeizel, A., Rockenbauer, M., Sorensen, H., & Olsen, J. (2002). A population-based case-control teratogenic study of nitrazolam, medazepam, tofisopam, alprazolam and clonazepam treatment during pregnancy. *European Journal of Obstetrics and Gynecology and Reproductive Biology, 101,* 147–154.

Ersche, K. D., Barnes, A., Jones, P. S., Morein-Zamir, S., Robbins, T. W., & Bullmore, E. T. (2011). Abnormal structure of frontostriatal brain systems is associated with aspects of impulsivity and compulsivity in cocaine dependence. *Brain: A Journal of Neurology, 134,* 2013–2024.

Ersche, K. D., Fletcher, P. C., Lewis, S. J. G., Clark, L., Stocks-Gee, G., London, M., et al. (2005). Abnormal frontal activations related to decision-making in current and former amphetamine and opiate dependent individuals. *Psychopharmacology, 180,* 612–623.

Evans, A. H., Pavese, N., Lawrence, A. D., Tai, Y. F., Appel, S., Doder, M., et al. (2006). Compulsive drug use linked to sensitized ventral striatal dopamine transmission. *Annals of Neurology, 59,* 852–858.

Evans, S. M., & Griffiths, R. R. (1992). Caffeine tolerance and choice in humans. *Psychopharmacology, 108,* 51–59.

Evans, S. M., Griffiths, R. R., & de Wit, H. (1996). Preference for diazepam, but not buspirone, in moderate drinkers. *Psychopharmacology, 123,* 145–163.

Fadda, P., Robinson, L., Fratta, W., Pertwee, R. G., & Riedel, G. (2004). Differential effects of THC- or CBD-rich cannabis extracts on working memory in rats. *Neuropharmacology, 47,* 1170–1179.

Falek, A., Madden, J. J., Shafer, D. A., & Donahoe, R. M. (1982). Opiates as modulators of genetic damage and immunocompetence. *Advances in Alcohol and Substance Abuse, 1,* 5–20.

Fant, R. V., Henningfield, J. E., Nelson, R. A., & Pickworth, W. B. (1999). Pharmacokinetics and pharmacodynamics of moist snuff in humans. *Tobacco Control, 8,* 387–392.

Fantegrossi, W., Ullrich, T., Rice, K., Woods, J., & Winger, G. (2002). 3,4-methylenedioxymethamphetamine (MDMA, "ecstasy") and its stereoisomers as reinforcers in rhesus monkeys: Serotonergic involvement. *Psychopharmacology, 161,* 356–364.

Fantegrossi, W., Woods, J., & Winger, G. (2004). Transient reinforcing effects of phenylisopropylamine and indolealkylamine hallucinogens in rhesus monkeys. *Behavioural Pharmacology, 15,* 149–157.

Farris, C., Treat, T. A., & Viken, R. J. (2010). Alcohol alters men's perceptual and decisional processing of women's sexual interest. *Journal of Abnormal Psychology, 119,* 427–432.

Faure, A., Richard, J. M., & Berridge, K. C. (2010). Desire and dread from the nucleus accumbens: Cortical glutamate and subcortical GABA differentially generate motivation and hedonic impact in the rat. *PLoS One, 5,* e11223.

Feinberg, I., Jones, R., Walker, J., Cavness, C., & Floyd, T. (1976). Effects of marijuana extract and tetrahydrocannabinol on electroencephalographic sleep patterns. *Clinical and Pharmacological Therapy, 19,* 782–794.

Ferguson, J. A., Suelzer, C. J., Eckert, G. J., Zhou, X. H., & Dittus, R. S. (1996). Risk factors for delirium tremens development. *Journal of General Internal Medicine, 11,* 410–414.

Fernández-Ruiz, J., Pazos, M. R., García-Arencibia, M., Sagredo, O., & Ramos, J. A. (2008). Role of CB2 receptors in neuroprotective effects of cannabinoids. *Molecular and Cellular Endocrinology, 286*(Suppl. 1), S91–S96.

Ferre, S. (2008). An update on the mechanisms of the psychostimulant effects of caffeine. *Journal of Neurochemistry, 105,* 1067–1079.

Field, M., Mogg, K., Zetteler, J., & Bradley, B. P. (2004). Attentional biases for alcohol cues in heavy and light social drinkers: The roles of initial orienting and maintained attention. *Psychopharmacology, 176,* 88–93.

Field, M., & Quigley, M. (2009). Mild stress increases attentional bias in social drinkers who drink to cope: A replication and extension. *Experimental and Clinical Psychopharmacology, 17,* 312–319.

Fillmore, M., & Vogel-Sprott, M. (1992). Expected effect of caffeine on motor performance predicts the type of response to placebo. *Psychopharmacology, 106,* 209–214.

Fillmore, M., & Vogel-Sprott, M. (1998). Behavioral impairment under alcohol: Cognitive and pharmacokinetic factors. *Alcoholism: Clinical and Experimental Research, 22,* 1476–1482.

Finagrette, H. (1988). *Heavy drinking: The myth of alcoholism as a disease.* Berkeley, CA: University of California Press.

Finnegan, L. P. (1982). Outcome of children born to women dependent on narcotics. *Advances in Alcohol and Substance Abuse, 1,* 55–101.

Fiorino, D. F., & Phillips, A. G. (1999). Facilitation of sexual behavior and enhanced dopamine efflux in the nucleus accumbens of male rats after D-amphetamine-induced behavioral sensitization. *The Journal of Neuroscience: The Official Journal of the Society for Neuroscience, 19,* 456–463.

Fischman, M. W., & Schuster, C. R. (1982). Cocaine self-administration in humans. *Federation Proceedings, 41,* 204–209.

Fischman, M. W., Schuster, C. R., Resnekov, L., Shick, J. F. E., Krasnegor, N. A., Fennell, W., et al. (1976). Cardiovascular and subjective effects of intravenous cocaine administration in humans. *Archives of General Psychiatry, 33,* 983–989.

Fitton, A., Faulds, D., & Goa, K. L. (1992). Moclobemide: A review of its pharmacological properties and therapeutic use in depressive illness. *Drugs, 43,* 561–596.

Fleischhacker, W. W. (2009). Second-generation antipsychotic long-acting injections: Systematic review. *The British Journal of Psychiatry, 52*(Suppl.), S29–S36.

Fleming, K., Bigelow, L. B., Weinberger, D. R., & Goldberg, T. E. (1995). Neuropsychological effects of amphetamine may correlate with personality characteristics. *Psychopharmacology Bulletin, 31,* 357–362.

Ford, R. D., & Balster, R. L. (1977). Reinforcing properties of intravenous procaine in monkeys. *Pharmacology, Biochemistry and Behavior, 6,* 289–296.

Forman, S. D., Dougherty, G. G., Casey, B. J., Siegle, G. J., Braver, T. S., Barch, D. M., et al. (2004). Opiate addicts lack error-dependent activation of rostral anterior cingulate. *Biological Psychiatry, 55,* 531–537.

Forrest, D. (1973). *Tea for the British.* London: Chatto & Windus.

Forrest, W. H., Jr., Bellville, J. W., & Brown, B. W., Jr. (1972). The interaction of caffeine with pentobarbital as a nighttime hypnotic. *Anesthesiology, 36,* 37–41.

Fournier, J. C., DeRubeis, R. J., Hollon, S. D., Dimidjian, S., Amsterdam, J. D., Shelton, R. C., et al. (2010). Antidepressant drug effects and depression severity: A patient-level meta-analysis. *The Journal of the American Medical Association, 303,* 47–53.

Fowler, C. D., Arends, M. A., & Kenny, P. J. (2008). Subtypes of nicotinic acetylcholine receptors in nicotine reward, dependence, and withdrawal: Evidence from genetically modified mice. *Behavioural Pharmacology, 19,* 461–484.

Frank, I. M., Lessin, P. J., Tyrrell, E. D., Hahn, P. M., & Szara, S. (1976). Acute and cumulative effects of marijuana smoking on hospitalized subjects: A 36-day study. In M. C. Braude & S. Szara (Eds.), *Pharmacology of marijuana* (Vol. 2, pp. 673–680). Orlando, FL: Academic Press.

Frascella, J., Potenza, M. N., Brown, L. L., & Childress, A. R. (2010). Shared brain vulnerabilities open the way for nonsubstance addictions: Carving addiction at a new joint? *Annals of the New York Academy of Sciences, 1187,* 294–315.

Frawly, K., & McMillan, D. E. (2008). Effects of gamma-hydroxybutyrate on punished responding in pigeons. *Behavioural Pharmacology, 19,* 77–79.

Fredholm, B. B. (1995). Adenosine, adenosine receptors and the actions of caffeine. *Pharmacology and Toxicology, 76,* 93–101.

Fredholm, B. B., Bättig, K., Holmén, J., Nehlig, A., & Zvartau, E. E. (1999). Actions of caffeine in the brain with special reference to factors that contribute to its widespread use. *Pharmacological Review, 51,* 83–133.

Freeman, N., Friedman, R. S., Bartholow, B. D., & Wulfert, E. (2010). Effects of alcohol priming on social disinhibition. *Experimental and Clinical Psychopharmacology, 18,* 135–144.

French, R. V. (1884). *Nineteen centuries of drink in England.* London: Longman.

Frezza, M., DiPadova, C., Pozzato, G., Terpin, M., Baraona, E., & Leiber, C. S. (1990). High blood alcohol levels in women: The role of decreased gastric alcohol dehydrogenase activity and first-pass metabolism. *New England Journal of Medicine, 322,* 95–99.

Fried, P., Watkinson, B., James, D., & Gray, R. (2002). Current and former marijuana use: Preliminary findings of a longitudinal study of effects on IQ in young adults. *Canadian Medical Association Journal, 166,* 887–891.

Fujiwara, H., Hirao, K., Namiki, C., Yamada, M., Shimizu, M., Fukuyama, H., et al. (2007). Anterior cingulate pathology and social cognition in schizophrenia: A study of gray matter, white matter and sulcal morphometry. *NeuroImage, 36,* 1236–1245.

Fuxe, K., Marcellino, D., Guidolin, D., Woods, A. S., & Agnati, L. F. (2008). Heterodimers and receptor mosaics of different types of G-protein-coupled receptors. *Physiology (Bethesda, Md.), 23,* 322–332.

Gable, R. (2004). Acute toxic effects of club drugs. *Journal of Psychoactive Drugs, 36,* 303–313.

Garattini, S., Mussini, E., Marcucci, F., & Guaitani, A. (1973). Metabolic studies on benzodiazepines in various animal species. In S. Garattini, E. Mussini, & L. O. Randall (Eds.), *The benzodiazepines* (pp. 75–97). New York: Raven Press.

Garbutt, J. C. (2009). The state of pharmacotherapy for the treatment of alcohol dependence. *Journal of Substance Abuse Treatment, 36,* S15–S23.

Gardner, E. L. (1992). Cannabinoid interactions with brain reward systems: The neurobiological basis of cannabinoid abuse. In L. Murphy & A. Bartke (Eds.), *Marijuana/cannabinoids neurology and neurophysiology* (pp. 275–336). Boca Raton, FL: CRC Press.

Garfield, E. (1983). Current comments. *Current Contents, 18,* 5–14.

Garrett, B. E., & Griffiths, R. R. (1997). The role of dopamine in the behavioral effects of caffeine in animals and man. *Pharmacology Biochemistry and Behavior, 57,* 533–541.

Garrett, B. E., & Griffiths, R. R. (1998). Physical dependence increases the relative reinforcing effects of caffeine versus placebo. *Psychopharmacology, 138,* 195–202.

Gasior, M., Jaszyna, M., Munzar, P., Witkin, J. M., & Goldberg, S. R. (2002). Caffeine potentiates the discriminative-stimulus effects of nicotine in rats. *Psychopharmacology, 162,* 385–395.

Gautier, T. (1966). The hashish club. In D. Solomon (Ed.), *The marijuana papers* (pp. 163–178). New York: New American Library.

Gauvin, D. V., Cheng, E. Y., & Holloway, F. A. (1993). Behavioral correlates. In M. Galanter (Ed.), *Recent developments in alcoholism* (Vol. 11, pp. 281–300). New York: Plenum Press.

Gauvin, D. V., Harland, R. D., Michaelis, R. C., & Holloway, F. A. (1989). Caffeine-phenylethylamine combinations mimic the cocaine discriminative cue. *Life Sciences, 44,* 67–73.

Gawin, F. H., & Kleber, H. (1987). Issues in cocaine abuse treatment research. In S. Fisher, A. Raskin, & E. H. Uhlenhuth (Eds.), *Cocaine: Clinical and behavioral aspects* (pp. 174–192). New York: Oxford University Press.

Gay, G. R., & Inaba, D. S. (1976). Acute and chronic toxicology of cocaine abuse: Current sociology, treatment and rehabilitation. In S. J. Mule (Ed.), *Cocaine: Chemical, biological, clinical, social and treatment aspects* (pp. 245–252). Boca Raton, FL: CRC Press.

Gazdzinski, S., Durazzo, T. C., & Meyerhoff, D. J. (2005). Temporal dynamics and determinants of whole brain tissue volume changes during recovery from alcohol dependence. *Drug and Alcohol Dependence, 78,* 263–273.

Geller, I., Bachman, E., & Seifter, J. (1963). The effects of reserpine and morphine on behavior suppressed by punishment. *Life Sciences, 4,* 226–231.

George, F. R. (1997). The behavioral genetics of addiction. In B. A. Johnson & J. D. Roache (Eds.), *Drug addiction and treatment: Nexus of neuroscience and behavior* (pp. 187–204). Philadelphia, PA: Lippincott-Raven Press.

George, F. R., & Goldberg, S. R. (1989). Genetic approaches to the analysis of addiction processes. *Trends in Pharmacological Science, 10,* 78–83.

George, F. R., Ritz, M. C., & Elmer, G. I. (1991). The role of genetics in vulnerability to drug dependence. In J. Pratt (Ed.), *The biological basis of drug tolerance and dependence* (pp. 265–295). London: Academic Press.

George, W. H., Davis, K. C., Heiman, J. R., Norris, J., Stoner, S. A., Schacht, R. L., et al. (2011). Women's sexual arousal: Effects of high alcohol dosages and self-control instructions. *Hormones and Behavior, 59,* 730–738.

Gerak, L. R., Woolverton, W. L., Nader, M. A., Patrick, G. A., Harris, L. S., Winger, G., et al. (2001). Behavioral effects of flunitrazepam: reinforcing and discriminative stimulus effects in rhesus monkeys and prevention of withdrawal signs in pentobarbital-dependent rats. *Drug and Alcohol Dependence, 63,* 39–49.

Gerostamolous, J., Staikos, V., & Drummer, O. H. (2001). Heroin-related deaths in Victoria: A review of cases for 1997 and 1998. *Drug and Alcohol Dependence, 61,* 123–127.

Giannini, A. J., Burge, H., Shaheen, J. M., & Price, W. A. (1986). Khat: Another drug of abuse. *Journal of Psychoactive Drugs, 18,* 155–158.

Giannini, A. J., Miller, N. S., & Turner, C. E. (1992). Treatment of khat addiction. *Journal of Substance Abuse Treatment, 9,* 379–382.

Gibbons, R. D., Brown, C. H., Hur, K., Marcus, S. M., Bhaumik, D. K., Erkens, J. A., et al. (2007). Early evidence on the effects of regulators' suicidality warnings on SSRI prescriptions and suicide in children and adolescents. *The American Journal of Psychiatry, 164,* 1356–1363.

Gilbert, R. M. (1976). Caffeine: A drug of abuse. In R. J. Gibbins, Y. Israel, H. Kalant, R. E. Popham, W. Schmidt, & R. G. Smart (Eds.), *Research advances in alcohol and drug problems* (Vol. 3, pp. 49–176). New York: Wiley/Interscience.

Gill, H. S., DeVane, C. L., & Risch, S. C. (1997). Extrapyramidal symptoms associated with cyclic antidepressant treatment: A review of the literature and consolidating hypotheses. *Journal of Clinical Psychopharmacology, 17,* 377–389.

Gilmour, G., Dix, S., Fellini, L., Gastambide, F., Plath, N., Steckler, T., et al. (2011). NMDA receptors, cognition and schizophrenia-testing the validity of the NMDA receptor hypofunction hypothesis. *Neuropharmacology.*

Gitlin, M. J. (1993). Pharmacotherapy for personality disorders: Conceptual framework and clinical strategies. *Journal of Clinical Psychopharmacology, 13,* 343–353.

Glennon, R. A. (1987). Psychoactive phenylisopropylamines. In H. Y. Meltzer (Ed.), *Psychopharmacology: A third generation of progress* (pp. 1627–1634). New York: Raven Press.

Glennon, R. A., Young, R., Martin, B. R., & Dal Cason, T. A. (1995). Methcathinone ("cat"): An enantiometric potency comparison. *Pharmacology, Biochemistry and Behavior, 50,* 601–606.

Glick, S. D., Maisonneuve, I., Raucci, J., & Archer, S. (1995). Kappa opioid inhibition of morphine and cocaine self-administration in rats. *Brain Research, 681,* 147–152.

Goas, J. A., & Boston, J. E. (1978). Discriminative stimulus properties of clozapine and chlorpromazine. *Pharmacology, Biochemistry and Behavior, 8,* 235–241.

Goldberg, L. (1943). Quantitative studies on alcohol tolerance in man: The influence of ethyl alcohol on sensory, motor, and psychological functions referred to blood alcohol in normal and habituated individuals. *Acta Physiologica Scandanavica, 16*(Suppl.), 5.

Goldberg, S. R. (1976). The behavioral analysis of drug addiction. In S. D. Glick & J. Goldfarb (Eds.), *Behavioral pharmacology* (pp. 283–316). St. Louis, MO: Mosby.

Goldberg, S. R., Spealman, R. D., & Goldberg, D. M. (1981). Persistent behavior at high rates maintained by intravenous self-administration of nicotine. *Science, 214,* 573–575.

Goldstein, A., Kaizer, S., & Warren, R. (1965). Psychotropic effects of caffeine in man: 2. Alertness, psychomotor coordination and mood. *Journal of Pharmacology and Experimental Therapeutics, 150,* 146–151.

Goldstein, A., Kaizer, S., & Whitby, O. (1969). Psychotropic effects of caffeine in man: 4. Quantitative and qualitative differences associated with habituation to coffee. *Clinical Pharmacology and Therapeutics, 10,* 489–497.

Goldstein, R. Z., Craig, A. D., Bechara, A., Garavan, H., Childress, A. R., Paulus, M. P., et al. (2009). The neurocircuitry of impaired insight in drug addiction. *Trends in Cognitive Sciences, 13,* 372–380.

Goldstein, R. Z., Leskovjan, A. C., Hoff, A. L., Hitzemann, R., Bashan, F., Khalsa, S. S., et al. (2004). Severity of neuropsychological impairment in cocaine and alcohol addiction: Association with metabolism in the prefrontal cortex. *Neuropsychologia, 42,* 1447–1458.

Goldstone, S., Boardman, W., & Lhamon, W. (1958). The effects of quintal barbitone, dextroamphetamine, and placebo on apparent time. *British Journal of Psychology, 49,* 324–328.

Golub, A., & Johnson, B. D. (1994). The shifting of importance of alcohol and marijuana as gateway substances among serious drug abusers. *Journal of Studies on Alcohol, 55,* 507–514.

González, S., Cebeira, M., & Fernández-Ruiz, J. (2005). Cannabinoid tolerance and dependence: A review of studies in laboratory animals. *Pharmacology, Biochemistry and Behavior, 81,* 300–318.

González-Maeso, J., Ang, R. L., Yuen, T., Chan, P., Weisstaub, N. V., López-Giménez, J. F., et al. (2008). Identification of a serotonin/glutamate receptor complex implicated in psychosis. *Nature,* 93–97.

González-Maeso, J., Weisstaub, N. V., Zhou, M., Chan, P., Ivic, L., Ang, R., et al. (2007). Hallucinogens recruit specific cortical 5-HT(2A) receptor-mediated signaling pathways to affect behavior. *Neuron, 53,* 439–452.

Goodwin, A. K., Kaminski, B. J., Griffiths, R. R., Ator, N. A., & Weerts, E. M. (2011). Intravenous self-administration of gamma-hydroxybutyrate (GHB) in baboons. *Drug and Alcohol Dependence, 114,* 217–224.

Gorelick, D. A., & Balster, R. L. (2000). Phencyclidine (PCP). In F. E. Bloom & D. J. Kupfer (Eds.), *Psychopharmacology: The fourth generation of progress.* New York: Raven Press. Retrieved from http://www.acnp.org/g4/GN401000171/Default.htm

Gorzalka, B. B., Hill, M. N., & Chang, S. C. (2010). Male-female differences in the effects of cannabinoids on sexual behavior and gonadal hormone function. *Hormones and Behavior, 58,* 91–99.

Goth, A. (1984). *Medical pharmacology: Principles and concepts.* St. Louis, MO: Mosby.

Graham, H. N. (1984). Tea: The plant and its manufacture: Chemistry and consumption of the beverage. In G. A. Spiller (Ed.), *The methylxanthine beverages and foods: Chemistry, consumption and health effects* (pp. 29–74). New York: Liss.

Grant, K. A., & Barrett, J. E. (1991). Blockade of the discriminative stimulus effects of ethanol with 5-HT3, receptor antagonists. *Psychopharmacology, 104,* 451–456.

Grattan-Miscio, K. E., & Vogel-Sprott, M. (2005). Effects of alcohol and performance incentives on immediate working memory. *Psychopharmacology, 181,* 188–196.

Green, A. S., & Grahame, N. J. (2008). Ethanol drinking in rodents: Is free-choice drinking related to the reinforcing effects of ethanol? *Alcohol (Fayetteville, N.Y.), 42,* 1–11.

Greenberg, J. A., Boozer, C. N., & Geliebter, A. (2006). Coffee, diabetes, and weight control. *The American Journal of Clinical Nutrition, 84,* 682–693.

Greenblatt, D. J., & Shader, R. I. (1974). *The benzodiazepines in clinical practice.* New York: Raven Press.

Greenlees, D. (2005). Philip Morris makes $5.2 billion bid in Asia. *International Herald Tribune.* Retrieved from http://www.iht.com/articles/ 2005/03/14/business/tobacco.html

Gresch, P. J., Smith, R. L., Barrett, R. J., & Sanders-Bush, E. (2005). Behavioral tolerance to lysergic acid diethylamide is associated with reduced serotonin-2A receptor signaling in rat cortex. *Neuropsychopharmacology: Official Publication of the American College of Neuropsychopharmacology, 30*, 1693–1702.

Griffiths, R. R., Bigelow, G. E., & Henningfield, J. E. (1980). Similarities in animal and human drug taking behavior. In N. K. Mello (Ed.), *Advances in substance abuse* (Vol. 1, pp. 1–90). Greenwich, CT: JAI Press.

Griffiths, R. R., Bigelow, G. E., & Lieberson, I. (1979). Human drug self-administration: Double-blind comparison of pentobarbital, diazepam, chlorpromazine and placebo. *Journal of Pharmacology and Experimental Therapeutics, 210*, 301–310.

Griffiths, R. R., Evans, S. M., Heishman, S. J., Preston, K. L., Sannerud, C. A., Wolf, B., et al. (1990). Low dose caffeine physical dependence in humans. *Journal of Pharmacology and Experimental Therapeutics, 225*, 1123–1132.

Griffiths, R. R., Lamb, R. J., Sannerud, C. A., Ator, N., & Brady, J. V. (1991). Self-injection of barbiturates and benzodiazepines. *Psychopharmacology, 103*, 154–161.

Griffiths, R. R., Lucas, S. E., Bradford, L. K., Brady, J. V., & Snell, J. D. (1981). Self-injection of barbiturates and benzodiazepines in baboons. *Psychopharmacology, 75*, 101–109.

Griffiths, R. R., & Mumford, G. K. (1995). Caffeine: A drug of abuse? In F. E. Bloom & D. J. Kupfer (Eds.), *Psychopharmacology: The fourth generation of progress*. New York: Raven Press. Retrieved from www.acnp.org/g4/GN401000/65/Default.htm

Griffiths, R. R., & Sannerud, C. A. (1987). Abuse and dependence on benzodiazepines and other anxiolytic/sedative drugs. In H. Y. Meltzer (Ed.), *Psychopharmacology: The third generation of progress* (pp. 1535–1542). New York: Raven Press.

Griffiths, R. R., & Woodson, P. (1988). Caffeine physical dependence: A review of human and laboratory animal studies. *Psychopharmacology, 94*, 437–451.

Grino, M., Guillaume, V., Castanas, E., Boudouresque, F., Conte-Devolx, B., & Oliver, C. (1987). Effect of passive immunization against corticotropin-releasing factor (CRF) on the postadrenalectomy changes of CRF binding sites in the rat anterior pituitary gland. *Neuroendocrinology, 45*, 492–497.

Grinspoon, L. (1971). *Marihuana reconsidered*. Cambridge, MA: Harvard University Press.

Grinspoon, L., & Bakalar, J. B. (1976). *Cocaine*. New York: Basic Books.

Grinspoon, L., & Bakalar, J. B. (1979a). The amphetamines: Medical uses and health hazards. In D. R. Smith (Ed.), *Amphetamine use, misuse and abuse* (pp. 260–274). Boca Raton, FL: CRC Press.

Grinspoon, L., & Bakalar, J. B. (1979b). *Psychedelic drugs reconsidered*. New York: Basic Books.

Grinspoon, L., & Bakalar, J. B. (1993). *Marijuana, the forbidden medicine*. New Haven, CT: Yale University Press.

Grinspoon, L., & Bakalar, J. B. (1997). *Marijuana, forbidden medicine* (Rev. and Exp. Ed.). New Haven, CT: Yale University Press.

Grinspoon, L., & Hedblom, P. (1975). *The speed culture*. Cambridge, MA: Harvard University Press.

Guillot, C. (2007). Is recreational ecstasy (MDMA) use associated with higher levels of depressive symptoms? *Journal of Psychoactive Drugs, 39*, 31–39.

Guillot, C., & Greenway, D. (2006). Recreational ecstasy use and depression. *Journal of Psychopharmacology (Oxford, England), 20*, 411–416.

Gunne, L. M., & Anggard, E. (1972). *Pharmacokinetic studies with amphetamines: Relationship to neuropsychiatric disorders*. Paper presented at the International Symposium on Pharmacological Kinetics, Washington, DC.

Gunzerath, L., Faden, V., Zakhari, S., & Warren, K. (2004). National Institute on Alcohol Abuse and Alcoholism report on moderate drinking. *Alcoholism: Clinical and Experimental Research, 28*, 829–847.

Gupta, S., & Warner, J. (2008). Alcohol-related dementia: A 21st-century silent epidemic? *The British Journal of Psychiatry: The Journal of Mental Science, 193*, 351–353.

Gutjahr, E., Gmel, G., & Rehm, J. (2001). Relation between average alcohol consumption and disease: An overview. *European Addiction Research, 7*, 117–127.

Hackshaw, A., Rodeck, C., & Boniface, S. (2011). Maternal smoking in pregnancy and birth defects: A systematic review based on 173 687 malformed cases and 11.7 million controls. *Human Reproduction Update, 17*, 589–604.

Haddad, P. M., Lambert, T., & Lauriello, J. (2011). *Antipsychotic long-acting injections*. New York: Oxford University Press.

Haertzen, C. A. (1970). Subjective effects of narcotic antagonists cyclazocine and nalorphine on the addiction research center inventory (ARCI). *Psychopharmacologia, 18*, 366–377.

Haglund, B., & Cnattingius, L. (1990). Cigarette smoking as a risk factor for sudden infant death syndrome. *American Journal of Public Health, 80*, 29–32.

Hajak, G. (1999). A comparative assessment of the risks and benefits of zopiclone: A review of 15 years' clinical experience. *Drug Safety, 21*, 457–469.

Hall, K. M., Irwin, M. M., Bowman, K. A., Frankenberger, W., & Jewett, D. C. (2005). Illicit use of prescribed stimulant medication among college students. *Journal of American College Health, 53*, 167–174.

Hallstrom, C., & Lader, M. H. (1981). Benzodiazepine withdrawal phenomenon. *International Pharmacopsychiatry, 16*, 235–244.

Halpern, J. H., & Pope, H. G., Jr. (2003). Hallucinogen persisting perception disorder: What do we know after 50 years? *Drug and Alcohol Dependence, 69,* 109–119.

Hampson, A. J., Grimaldi, M., Axelrod, J., & Wink, D. (1998). Cannabidiol and (-)Δ9-tetrahydrocannabinol are neuroprotective antioxidants. *Proceedings of the National Academy of Sciences USA, 95,* 8268–8273.

Han, D. D., & Gu, H. H. (2006). Comparison of the monoamine transporters from human and mouse in their sensitivities to psychostimulant drugs. *BMC Pharmacology, 6,* 6.

Hanchar, H. J., Chutsrinopkun, P., Meera, P., Supavilai, P., Sieghart, W., Wallner, M., et al. (2006). Ethanol potently and competitively inhibits binding of the alcohol antagonist Ro15-4513 to alpha4/6beta3delta GABAA receptors. *Proceedings of the National Academy of Sciences of the United States of America, 103,* 8546–8551.

Haney, M., Comer, S., Fischman, M., & Foltin, R. (1997). Alprazolam increases food intake in humans. *Psychopharmacology, 123,* 311–314.

Haney, M., Ward, A., Comer, S., Foltin, R., & Fischman, M. (1999a). Abstinence symptoms following oral THC administration to humans. *Psychopharmacology, 141,* 385–394.

Haney, M., Ward, A., Comer, S., Foltin, R., & Fischman, M. (1999b). Abstinence symptoms following smoked marijuana in humans. *Psychopharmacology, 141,* 395–404.

Hanson, H. M., Witloslawski, J. J., & Campbell, E. H. (1967). Drug effects in squirrel monkeys trained on a multiple schedule with a punishment contingency. *Journal of the Experimental Analysis of Behavior, 10,* 565–569.

Harrell, P. T., & Juliano, L. M. (2009). Caffeine expectancies influence the subjective and behavioral effects of caffeine. *Psychopharmacology, 207,* 335–342.

Harris, R. T., Glaghorn, J. L., & Schoolar, J. C. (1968). Self-administration of minor tranquilizers as a function of conditioning. *Psychopharmacologia, 13,* 81–88.

Harris, S., & Dawson, H. (1994). Caffeine and bone loss in healthy post menopausal women. *American Journal of Clinical Nutrition, 60,* 573–578.

Harrison, E. L., & Fillmore, M. T. (2011). Alcohol and distraction interact to impair driving performance. *Drug and Alcohol Dependence, 117,* 31–37.

Harrison, W. M., Rabkin, J. G., Erhardt, A. A., Stewart, J. W., McGrath, T. J., Ross, D., et al. (1986). Effects of antidepressant medication on sexual function: A controlled study. *Journal of Clinical Psychopharmacology, 6,* 144–148.

Haskell, C. F., Kennedy, D. O., Wesnes, K. A., & Scholey, A. B. (2005). Cognitive and mood improvements of caffeine in habitual consumers and habitual non-consumers of caffeine. *Psychopharmacology, 179,* 813–825.

Hazekamp, A., Ruhaak, R., Zuurman, L., van Gerven, J., & Verpoorte, R. (2006). Evaluation of a vaporizing device (volcano) for the pulmonary administration of tetrahydrocannabinol. *Journal of Pharmaceutical Sciences, 95,* 1308–1317.

He, N., Daniel, H., Hajiloo, L., & Shockley, D. (1999). Dextromethorphan O-demethylation polymorphism in an African-American population. *European Journal of Clinical Pharmacology, 55,* 475–479.

Heatherley, S. V. (2011). Caffeine withdrawal, sleepiness, and driving performance: What does the research really tell us? *Nutritional Neuroscience, 14,* 89–95.

Heckman, M. A., Weil, J., & Gonzalez de, M. E. (2010). Caffeine (1, 3, 7-trimethylxanthine) in foods: A comprehensive review on consumption, functionality, safety, and regulatory matters. *Journal of Food Science, 75,* R77–R87.

Heikkinen, A. E., Möykkynen, T. P., & Korpi, E. R. (2009). Long-lasting modulation of glutamatergic transmission in VTA dopamine neurons after a single dose of benzodiazepine agonists. *Neuropsychopharmacology: Official Publication of the American College of Neuropsychopharmacology, 34,* 290–298.

Heinz, A., Siessmeier, T., Wrase, J., Hermann, D., Klein, S., Grusser-Sinopoli, S. M., et al. (2004). Correlation between dopamine D2 receptors in the ventral striatum and central processing of alcohol cues and craving. *American Journal of Psychiatry, 161,* 1783–1789.

Heise, G. A., & Boff, E. (1962). Continuous avoidance as a baseline for measuring the behavioral effects of drugs. *Psychopharmacology, 3,* 264–282.

Heishman, S. J., Kleykamp, B. A., & Singleton, E. G. (2010). Meta-analysis of the acute effects of nicotine and smoking on human performance. *Psychopharmacology, 210* 453–469.

Heishman, S. J., Taylor, R. C., & Henningfield, J. E. (1994). Nicotine and smoking: A review of effects on human performance. *Experimental and Clinical Psychopharmacology, 2,* 345–395.

Hemby, S., Co, C., Koves, T., Smith, J., & Dworkin, S. (1997). Differences in extracellular dopamine concentrations in the nucleus accumbens during response-dependent and response-independent cocaine administration in the rat. *Psychopharmacology, 133,* 7–16.

Henningfield, J. E., Johnson, R., & Jasinski, D. (1987). Clinical procedures for the assessment of abuse potential. In M. A. Bozarth (Ed.), *Methods of assessing the reinforcing properties of abused drugs* (pp. 573–590). New York: Springer-Verlag.

Henningfield, J. E., Lucas, S. E., & Bigelow, G. E. (1986). Human studies of drugs as reinforcers. In S. R. Goldberg & I. P. Stollerman (Eds.), *Behavioral analysis of drug dependence* (pp. 69–122). Orlando, FL: Academic Press.

Henningfield, J. E., Miyasato, K., & Jasinski, D. R. (1985). Abuse liability and pharmacodynamic characteristics of intravenous and inhaled nicotine. *Journal of Pharmacology and Experimental Therapeutics, 234,* 1–12.

Henningfield, J. E., Miyasato, K., Johnson, R. E., & Jasinski, D. R. (1983). Rapid physiological effects of nicotine in humans and selective blockade of effects by mecamylamine. In *Problems of drug dependence* (NIDA Monograph No. 43). Washington, DC: U.S. Government Printing Office.

Henningfield, J. E., Radzius, A., & Cone, E. J. (1995). Estimation of available nicotine content of six smokeless tobacco products. *Tobacco Control, 4*, 57–61.

Henricksson, B. G., & Järbe, T. U. (1971). The effect of two tetrahydrocannabinols (delta-9-THC and delta-8-THC) on conditioned avoidance learning in rats and its transfer to normal state conditions. *Psychopharmacologia, 22*, 23–30.

Herning, R. I., Jones, R. T., & Bachman, J. (1983). EEG changes during tobacco withdrawal. *Psychophysiology, 20*, 507–512.

Herrera-Guzmán, I., Gudayol-Ferre, E., Herrera-Guzman, D., Guardia-Olmos, J., Hinojosa-Calvo, E., & Herrera-Abarca, J. E. (2009). Effects of selective serotonin reuptake and dual serotonergic-noradrenergic reuptake treatments on memory and mental processing speed in patients with major depressive disorder. *Journal of Psychiatric Research, 43*, 855–863.

Heyman, G. M. (1996). Resolving the contradictions of addiction. *Behavioral and Brain Sciences, 19*, 561–610.

Hicks, M. J., De, B. P., Rosenberg, J. B., Davidson, J. T., Moreno, A. Y., Janda, K. D., et al. (2011). Cocaine analog coupled to disrupted adenovirus: A vaccine strategy to evoke high-titer immunity against addictive drugs. *Molecular Therapy: The Journal of the American Society of Gene Therapy, 19*, 612–619.

Higgitt, A. C., Lader, M. H., & Fonagy, P. (1985). Clinical management of benzodiazepine dependence. *British Medical Journal, 291*, 688–690.

Hiltunen, A. J. (1997). Acute alcohol tolerance in cognitive and psychomotor performance: Influence of the alcohol dose and prior alcohol experience. *Alcohol (Fayetteville, N.Y.), 14*, 125–130.

Hirsh, K. (1984). Central nervous system pharmacology of the dietary methylxanthines. In G. A. Spiller (Ed.), *The methylxanthine beverages and foods: Chemistry, consumption and health effects* (pp. 235–301). New York: Liss.

International Coffee Organization (2012). Retrieved from http://dev.ico.org/profiles_e.asp

Ho, A. K. S., & Allen, J. P. (1981). Alcohol and the opiate receptor: Interactions with the endogenous opiates. *Advances in Alcohol and Substance Abuse, 1*, 53–75.

Hoffmeister, F. H., & Wuttke, W. (1969). On the actions of psychotropic drugs on the attack and aggressive-defensive behavior of mice and cats. In S. Garattini & E. G. Sigg (Eds.), *Aggressive behavior* (pp. 273–280). New York: Wiley/Interscience.

Hoffmeister, F. H., & Wuttke, W. (1973). Self-administration of acetylsalicylic acid and combinations with codeine and caffeine in rhesus monkeys. *Journal of Pharmacology and Experimental Therapeutics, 186*, 266–275.

Hoffmeister, F. H., & Wuttke, W. (1975). Psychotropic drugs as negative reinforcers. *Pharmacological Reviews, 27*, 419–428.

Holdstock, L., & de Wit, H. (1998). Individual differences in the biphasic effect of alcohol. *Alcoholism: Clinical and Experimental Research, 22*, 1903–1911.

Hollister, L. E. (1978). Psychotomimetic drugs in man. In L. L. Iverson, S. D. Iverson, & S. H. Snyder (Eds.), *Handbook of psychopharmacology* (Vol. 11, pp. 389–425). New York: Plenum Press.

Hollister, L. E. (1983). The pre-benzodiazepine era. *Journal of Psychoactive Drugs, 15*, 9–13.

Hollister, L. E., Gillespie, H. K., Ohlsson, A., Lindgren, J. E. Wahlen, A., & Agurell, S. (1981). Do plasma concentrations of delta 9-tetrahydrocannabinol reflect the degree of intoxication? *Journal of Clinical Pharmacology, 21*, 171S.

Hollister, L. E., Motzenbecker, F. P., & Degan, R. O. (1961). Withdrawal reactions from chlordiazepoxide ("Librium"). *Psychopharmacologia, 2*, 63–68.

Holtzman, S. G. (1994). Discriminative stimulus effects of dextromethorphan in the rat. *Psychopharmacology, 116*, 249–254.

Hommer, D. W., Skolnick, P., & Paul, S. M. (1987). The benzodiazepine/GABA receptor complex and anxiety. In H. Y. Meltzer (Ed.), *Psychopharmacology: The third generation of progress* (pp. 977–983). New York: Raven Press.

Hooker, J. M., Xu, Y., Schiffer, W., Shea, C., Carter, P., & Fowler, J. S. (2008). Pharmacokinetics of the potent hallucinogen, salvinorin A in primates parallels the rapid onset and short duration of effects in humans. *NeuroImage, 41*, 1044–1050.

Horger, B. A., Wellman, P. J., Morien, A., Davies, B. T., & Schenk, S. (1994). Caffeine exposure sensitizes to the reinforcing effects of cocaine. *Motivation, Emotion, Feeding, Drinking, Sexual Behavior, 2*, 53–56.

Horwood, L. J., Fergusson, D. M., Hayatbakhsh, M. R., Najman, J. M., Coffey, C., Patton, G. C., et al. (2010). Cannabis use and educational achievement: Findings from three australasian cohort studies. *Drug and Alcohol Dependence, 110*, 247–253.

Hser, Y., Hoffman, V., Grella, C., & Anglin, M. (2001). A 33-year follow-up of narcotics addicts. *Archives of General Psychiatry, 58*, 503–508.

Hu, W., Saba, L., Kechris, K., Bhave, S. V., Hoffman, P. L., & Tabakoff, B. (2008). Genomic insights into acute alcohol tolerance. *Journal of Pharmacology and Experimental Therapeutics, 326*, 792–800.

Huang, J., & Ho, B. T. (1974). Discriminative stimulus properties of d-amphetamine and related compounds in rats. *Pharmacology, Biochemistry and Behavior, 2,* 669–673.

Hughes, J. R., Gust, S. W., Skoog, K., Keenan, R. M., & Fenwick, J. W. (1991). Symptoms of tobacco withdrawal: A replication and extension. *Archives of General Psychiatry, 48,* 52–59.

Hughes, J. R., Higgins, S. T., & Bickel, W. K. (1994). Nicotine withdrawal versus other drug withdrawal syndromes: Similarities and differences. *Addiction, 89,* 1461–1470.

Hughes, J. R., Higgins, S. T., Bickel, W. K., & Hunt, W. K. (1989). *Caffeine is a reinforcer in humans.* Paper presented to the Behavioral Pharmacology Society, Annapolis, MD.

Hughes, J. R., Higgins, S. T., Gulliver, S., & Mireault, G. (1987, June 6). *Dependence on caffeine in moderate coffee drinkers.* Paper presented to the International Study Group Investigating Drugs as Reinforcers, Philadelphia, PA.

Hughes, J. R., Higgins, S. T., & Hatsukami, D. (1990). Effects of abstinence from tobacco: A critical review. In L. T. Kozlowski (Ed.), *Advances in alcohol and drug problems* (Vol. 10, pp. 317–398). New York: Plenum Press.

Hughes, K. C., & Shin, L. M. (2011). Functional neuroimaging studies of post-traumatic stress disorder. *Expert Review of Neurotherapeutics, 11,* 275–285.

Hukkanen, J., Jacob, P., 3rd., & Benowitz, N. L. (2005). Metabolism and disposition kinetics of nicotine. *Pharmacological Reviews, 57,* 79–115.

Hutchison, A., Smith, P., & Darlington, C. (1996). The behavioral and neuronal effects of the chronic administration of benzodiazepine anxiolytic and hypnotic drugs. *Progress in Neurobiology, 48,* 73–97.

Ikonomidou, C., Bosch, F., Miksa, M., Bittigau, P., Vockler, J., Dikranian, K., et al. (1999). Blockade of NMDA receptors and apoptotic neurodegeneration in the developing brain. *Science (New York, N.Y.), 283,* 70–74.

Institute of Medicine. (1982). *Marijuana and health.* Washington, DC: National Academy Press.

International Coffee Organization. (2012). Retrieved April 19, 2012, from www.ico.org/profilese.asp.

Inturrisi, C. G., Schultz, M., Shin, S., Umas, J. G., Angel, L., & Simon, E. J. (1983). Evidence from opiate binding studies that heroin acts through its metabolites. *Life Sciences, 33*(Suppl. 1), 773–776.

Isbister, G. K., Bowe, S. J., Dawson, A., & Whyte, I. M. (2004). Relative toxicity of selective serotonin reuptake inhibitors (SSRIs) in overdose. *Journal of Toxicology. Clinical Toxicology, 42,* 277–285.

Ito, C. (2009). Histamine H3-receptor inverse agonists as novel antipsychotics. *Central Nervous System Agents in Medicinal Chemistry, 9,* 132–136.

Iversen, L. (2005). Long-term effects of exposure to cannabis. *Current Opinion in Pharmacology, 5,* 69–72.

Jaffe, J. H. (1987). Pharmacological agents in the treatment of drug dependence. In H. Y. Meltzer (Ed.), *Psychopharmacology: The third generation of progress* (pp. 1605–1616). New York: Raven Press.

James, J. J. (1991). *Caffeine and health.* London: Academic Press.

James, J. J. (1994). Caffeine, health and commercial interests [Review]. *Addiction, 89,* 1595–1599.

James, S. H., & Bhatt, S. (1972). Analysis of street drugs. *Journal of Drug Education, 2,* 197–210.

Janicak, P. G., Davis, J. M., Preskorn, S. H., & Ayd, F. J., Jr. (1993). *Principles and practice of pharmacology.* Baltimore, MD: Williams & Wilkins.

Janke, W., & DeBus, G. (1968). In H. E. Efron (Ed.), *Experimental studies on antianxiety agents with normal subjects: Methodological considerations and a review of the main effects, 1957–1967* (pp. 205–208). Washington, DC: U.S. Government Printing Office.

Jansson-Fröjmark, M., & Lindblom, K. (2008). A bidirectional relationship between anxiety and depression, and insomnia? A prospective study in the general population. *Journal of Psychosomatic Research, 64,* 443–449.

Järbe, T. U. C., & Mathis, D. A. (1992). Dissociative and discriminative stimulus functions of cannabinoids/cannabinometics. In L. Murphy & A. Bartke (Eds.), *Marijuana/cannabinoids neurology and neurophysiology* (pp. 425–458). Boca Raton, FL: CRC Press.

Jarvik, M. E. (1973). Further observations on nicotine as the reinforcing agent in smoking. In W. L. Dunn (Ed.), *Smoking behavior: Motives and incentives* (pp. 33–50). Washington, DC: Winston.

Jarvik, M. E. (1979). Biological influences on cigarette smoking. In N. E. Krasnegor (Ed.), *The behavioral aspects of smoking* (pp. 7–45) (NIDA Research Monograph No. 26). Washington, DC: U.S. Government Printing Office.

Jasinski, D. R., Johnson, R. E., & Nenningfield, J. E. (1984). Abuse liability assessment in human subjects. *Trends in Pharmacological Science, 5,* 196–200.

Javaid, J. I., Musa, M. N., Fischman, M., Schuster, C. R., & Davis, J. M. (1983). Kinetics of cocaine in humans after intravenous and intranasal administration. *Biopharmaceutics and Drug Disposition, 4,* 9–18.

Jayaram-Lindström, N., Hammarberg, A., Beck, O., & Franck, J. (2008). Naltrexone for the treatment of amphetamine dependence: A randomized, placebo-controlled trial. *The American Journal of Psychiatry, 165,* 1442–1448.

Jellinek, E. M. (1960). *The disease concept of alcoholism.* New Haven, CT: Hillhouse Press.

Johanson, C. E., & Uhlenhuth, E. H. (1980). Drug preference and mood in humans: Diazepam. *Psychopharmacology, 71,* 269–273.

Johnson, H. J. (1965). A case history: A surgeon's cure of tobacco habituation. *Medical Times, 93,* 437.

Johnston, K. D., & Timney, B. (2008). Effects of acute ethyl alcohol consumption on a psychophysical measure of lateral inhibition in human vision. *Vision Research, 48,* 1539–1544.

Johnston, L. D., O'Malley, P. M., Bachman, J. G., & Schulenberg, J. E. (2005). *Monitoring the future national results on adolescent drug use: Overview of key findings, 2004* (NIH Publication No. 05-5726). Bethesda, MD, MI: National Institute on Drug Abuse.

Johnston, L. D., O'Malley, P. M., Bachman, J. G., & Schulenberg, J. E. (2011). *Monitoring the future national survey results on drug use, 1975–2010: Volume II: College students and adults ages 19–50.* Ann Arbor, MI: Institute for Social Research, the University of Michigan.

Jones, B. C., Jones, B., Blundell, L., & Bruce, G. (2002). Social users of alcohol and cannabis who detect substance-related changes in a change blindness paradigm report higher levels of use than those detecting substance-neutral changes. *Psychopharmacology, 165,* 93–96.

Jones, B. T., Jones, B., Smith, H., & Copley, N. (2003). A flicker paradigm for inducing change blindness reveals alcohol and cannabis information processing bias in social users. *Addiction, 98,* 235–244.

Jones, C. (2005). Senior drug addicts increasing. *USA Today.* Retrieved from http://www.usatoday.com/news/health/2005-01-21-senior-addicts_x.htm

Jones, E. (1953; 1957). *The life and work of Sigmund Freud* (1st ed.). New York: Basic Books.

Jones, K. L., & Smith, D. W. (1975). The fetal alcohol syndrome. *Teratology, 12,* 1–10.

Jones, R. T. (1978). Marijuana: Human effects. In L. L. Iverson, S. D. Iverson, & S. H. Snyder (Eds.), *Handbook of psychopharmacology* (Vol. 12, pp. 373–412). New York: Plenum Press.

Jones, R. T. (1987). Tobacco dependence. In H. Y. Meltzer (Ed.), *Psychopharmacology: The third generation of progress* (pp. 1589–1595). New York: Raven Press.

Jones, R. T., & Benowitz, N. (1976). The 30-day trip: Clinical studies of cannabis tolerance and dependence. In M. C. Braude & S. Szara (Eds.), *Pharmacology of marijuana* (Vol. 2, pp. 627–642). Orlando, FL: Academic Press.

Jowett, B. (1931). *The dialogues of Plato* (3rd ed., Vol. 5). London: Oxford University Press.

Judd, L. J., Squire, L. R., Butters, N., Salmon, D. P., & Paller, K. A. (1987). Effects of psychotropic drugs on cognition and memory in normal humans and animals. In H. Y. Melt-

zer (Ed.), *Psychopharmacology: A third generation of progress* (pp. 1467–1475). New York: Raven Press.

Juergens, S. M. (1993). Benzodiazepines and addiction. *Psychiatric Clinics of North America, 16,* 75–86.

Juliano, L. M., & Griffiths, R. R. (2004). A critical review of caffeine withdrawal: Empirical validation if symptoms and signs, incidence, severity, and associated features. *Psychopharmacology, 176,* 1–29.

Julien, R. (2001). *A primer of drug action* (9th ed.). New York: Worth Publishers.

June, H. L., Colker, R. E., Domanagu, K. R., Perry, L. E., Hicks, L. H., June, P. L., et al. (1992). Ethanol self-administration in deprived rats: Effects of RO-4513 alone and in combination with flumazenil (RO 15 1788). *Alcoholism: Clinical and Experimental Research, 16,* 11–16.

Justinova, Z., Tanda, G., Redhi, G. H., & Goldberg, S. R. (2003). Self-administration of delta 9-tetrahydrocannabinol (THC) by drug naive squirrel monkeys. *Psychopharmacology, 169,* 135–140.

Kahlig, K. M., & Galli, A. (2003). Regulation of dopamine transporter function and plasma membrane expression by dopamine, amphetamine, and cocaine. *European Journal of Pharmacology, 479,* 153–158.

Kahlig, K. M., Binda, F., Khoshbouei, H., Blakely, R. D., McMahon, D. G., Javitch, J. A., et al. (2005). Amphetamine induces dopamine efflux through a dopamine transporter channel. *Proceedings of the National Academy of Sciences of the United States of America, 102,* 3495–3500. doi:10.1073/pnas.0407737102

Kalant, H. (2001). The pharmacology and toxicology of "ecstasy" (MDMA) and related drugs. *Canadian Medical Association Journal, 165,* 917–928.

Kalant, H., LeBlanc, E., & Gibbins, R. J. (1971). Tolerance to, and dependence on, ethanol. In Y. Israel & J. Mardonez (Eds.), *Biological basis of alcoholism* (pp. 235–269). New York: Wiley/Interscience.

Kalivas, P. W., & Volkow, N. D. (2005). The neural basis of addiction: a pathology of motivation and choice. *American Journal of Psychiatry, 162,* 1403–1413.

Kalix, P. (1994). Khat, an amphetamine-like stimulant. *Journal of Psychoactive Drugs, 26,* 69–74.

Kallman, W. M., Kallman, M. J., Harry, G. J., Woodson, P. P., & Rosecrans, J. A. (1982). Nicotine as a discriminative stimulus in human subjects. In F. C. Colpaert & J. L. Slangen (Eds.), *Drug discrimination: Applications in CNS pharmacology* (pp. 211–218). Amsterdam, NY: Elsevier Biomedical.

Kan, C. C., Breteler, M. H., van der Ven, A. H., Timmermans, M. A., & Zitman, F. G. (2001). Assessment of benzodiazepine dependence in alcohol and drug dependent outpatients: A research report. *Substance Use & Misuse, 36,* 1085–1109.

Kaplan, G. B., Greenblatt, D. J., Ehrenberg, B. L., Goddard, J. E., Cotreau, M. M., Harmatz, J. S., et al. (1997). Dose-dependent pharmacokinetics and psychomotor effects of caffeine in humans. *Journal of Clinical Pharmacology, 37*, 693–703.

Kareken, D. A., Claus, E. D., Sabri, M., Dzemidzic, M., Kosobud, A. E. K., Radnovich, A. J., et al. (2004). Alcohol-related olfactory cues activate the nucleus accumbens and ventral tegmental area in high-risk drinkers: Preliminary findings. *Alcoholism: Clinical and Experimental Research, 28*, 550–557.

Karila, L., Weinstein, A., Aubin, H. J., Benyamina, A., Reynaud, M., & Batki, S. L. (2010). Pharmacological approaches to methamphetamine dependence: A focused review. *British Journal of Clinical Pharmacology, 69*, 578–592.

Katz, G. (2011). Tachyphylaxis/tolerance to antidepressants in treatment of dysthymia: Results of a retrospective naturalistic chart review study. *Psychiatry and Clinical Neurosciences, 65*, 499–504.

Katz, J., & Goldberg, S. R. (1987). Second order schedules of drug injection. In M. A. Bozarth (Ed.), *Methods of assessing the reinforcing properties of drugs* (pp. 105–115). New York: Springer-Verlag.

Kay, D. C., Eisenstein, R. B., & Jasinski, D. R. (1969). Morphine effects on human REM state, waking state and NREM sleep. *Psychopharmacologia, 14*, 404–416.

Kaye, S., & Haag, H. B. (1957). Terminal blood alcohol concentration in ninety-four fatal cases of acute alcoholism. *Journal of the American Medical Association, 165*, 451–452.

Keenan, R. M., Henningfield, J. E., & Jarvik, M. E. (1995). Pharmacological therapies: Nicotine addiction. In N. S. Miller & M. S. Gold (Eds.), *Pharmacological therapies for alcohol and drug addiction* (pp. 239–264). New York: Marcel Dekker.

Keith, D. E., Anton, B., Murray, S. R., Zaki, P. A., Chu, P. C., Lissin, D. V., et al. (1998). Mu-opioid receptor internalization: Opiate drugs have differential effects on a conserved endocytic mechanism in vitro and in the mammalian brain. *Molecular Pharmacology, 53*, 377–384.

Kelleher, R. T. (1976). Characteristics of behavior controlled by scheduled injections of drugs. *Pharmacological Reviews, 27*, 307–323.

Kelleher, R. T., & Morse, W. H. (1964). Escape behavior and punished behavior. *Federation Proceedings, 22*, 808–817.

Kellogg, C. K. (1988). Benzodiazepines: Influence on the developing brain. In G. R. Boer, M. G. P. Feenstra, M. Mirmiran, D. F. Swaab, & F. Van Haaren (Eds.), *Biochemical basis of functioning neuroteratology: Permanent effects of chemicals on the developing brain* (Vol. 73, pp. 207–228). Amsterdam, NY: Elsevier Biomedical.

Kellogg, C. K., Tervo, D., Ison, J., Paisi, T., & Miller, R. K. (1980). Prenatal exposure to diazepam alters behavioral development in rats. *Science, 207*, 205–207.

Kelly, T. H., Foltin, R. W., Mayr, M. T., & Fischman, M. W. (1994). Effects of delta-9-tetrahydrocannabinol and social context on marijuana self-administration by humans. *Pharmacology, Biochemistry and Behavior, 49*, 763–768.

Kelm, M. K., Criswell, H. E., & Breese, G. R. (2011). Ethanol-enhanced GABA release: A focus on G protein-coupled receptors. *Brain Research Reviews, 65*, 113–123.

Kendler, K. S., Myers, J., & Zisook, S. (2008). Does bereavement-related major depression differ from major depression associated with other stressful life events? *The American Journal of Psychiatry, 165*, 1449–1455.

Kenny, P. J., Chen, S. A., Kitamura, O., Markou, A., & Koob, G. F. (2006). Conditioned withdrawal drives heroin consumption and decreases reward sensitivity. *The Journal of Neuroscience: The Official Journal of the Society for Neuroscience, 26*, 5894–5900.

Kessler, R. C., Berglund, P., Demler, O., Jin, R., Merikangas, K. R., & Walters, E. E. (2005). Lifetime prevalence and age-of-onset distributions of DSM-IV disorders in the national comorbidity survey replication. *Archives of General Psychiatry, 62*, 593–602.

Kessler, R. C., Chiu, W. T., Demler, O., Merikangas, K. R., & Walters, E. E. (2005). Prevalence, severity, and comorbidity of 12-month DSM-IV disorders in the national comorbidity survey replication. *Archives of General Psychiatry, 62*, 617–627.

Khanna, J., Kalant, H., Chau, A., & Shah, G. (1998). Rapid tolerance and cross tolerance to motor impairment effects of benzodiazepines, barbiturates and ethanol. *Pharmacology, Biochemistry and Behavior, 59*, 511–519.

Kihlman, B. A. (1977). *Caffeine and chromosomes*. Amsterdam, NY: Elsevier.

Kimura, M., & Higuchi, S. (2011). Genetics of alcohol dependence. *Psychiatry and Clinical Neurosciences, 65*, 213–225.

King, D. J. (1993). Measures of the neuroleptic effects on cognition and psychomotor performance in healthy volunteers. In I. Hindmarch & P. D. Stonier (Eds.), *Human psychopharmacology: Measures and methods* (Vol. 4, pp. 195–209). Chichester, England: Wiley.

Kirk, J., & de Wit, H. (2000). Individual differences in the priming effect of ethanol in social drinkers. *Journal for Studies on Alcohol, 61*, 64–71.

Kirsch, I., Deacon, B. J., Huedo-Medina, T. B., Scoboria, A., Moore, T. J., & Johnson, B. T. (2008). Initial severity and antidepressant benefits: A meta-analysis of data submitted to the food and drug administration. *PLoS Medicine, 2*, e45.

Kirshenbaum, A. P., Jackson, E. R., Brown, S. J., Fuchs, J. R., Miltner, B. C., & Doughty, A. H. (2011). Nicotine-induced impulsive action: Sensitization and attenuation by mecamylamine. *Behavioural Pharmacology, 22*, 207–221.

Kleber, H. D. (1974). Clinical experiences with narcotic antagonists. In S. Fisher & A. M. Freeman (Eds.), *Opiate addiction: Origins and treatment* (pp. 211–220). New York: Wiley.

Kleven, M., & Koek, W. (1999). Effects of benzodiazepine agonists on punished responding in pigeons and their relationship with clinical doses in humans. *Psychopharmacology, 141*, 206–212.

Kling, M. A., Carson, R. E., Borg, L., Zametkin, A., Matochik, J. A., Schluger, J., et al. (2000). Opioid receptor imaging with positron emission tomography and [18F]cyclofloxy in long-term, methadone-treated former heroin addicts. *Journal of Pharmacology and Experimental Therapeutics, 295*, 1070–1076.

Klonoff, H. (1974). Effects of marijuana on driving in a restricted area and on city streets: Driving performance and physiological changes. In L. L. Miller (Ed.), *Marijuana: Effects on human behavior* (pp. 359–397). Orlando, FL: Academic Press.

Kluver, H. (1966). *Mescal and mechanisms of hallucinations.* Chicago, IL: University of Chicago Press.

Knight, C. A., Knight, I., Mitchell, D. C., & Zepp, J. E. (2004). Beverage caffeine intake in US consumers and subpopulations of interest: Estimates from the share of intake panel survey. *Food and Chemical Toxicology, 42*, 1923–1930.

Kobler, J. (1973). *Ardent spirits: The rise and fall of prohibition.* New York: Putnam.

Kolata, G. (1991, January 1). Temperance: An old cycle repeats itself. *New York Times*, pp. 35, 40.

Koob, G. (2000). Drug addiction. *Neurobiology of Disease, 7*, 543–545.

Koob, G., & Le Moal, M. (2001). Drug addiction, dysregulation of reward and allostasis. *Neuropsychopharmacology, 24*, 97–129.

Koob, G. F., & Le Moal, M. (2008). Addiction and the brain antireward system. *Annual Review of Psychology, 59*, 29–53.

Koob, G. F., Sanna, P. P., & Bloom, F. E. (1998). Neuroscience of addition. *Neuron, 21*, 467–476.

Korkosz, A., Taracha, E., Plaznik, A., Wrobel, E., Kostowski, W., & Bienkowski, P. (2005). Extended blockade of the discriminative stimulus effects of nicotine with low doses of ethanol. *European Journal of Pharmacology, 512*, 165–172.

Kosersky, D. S., McMillan, D. E., & Harris, L. S. (1974). Delta-9-tetrahydrocannabinol and 11-hydroxydelta-9-tetrahydrocannabinol: Behavioral effects and tolerance development. *Journal of Pharmacology and Experimental Therapeutics, 189*, 61–65.

Kozlowski, L. T., & Henningfield, J. E. (1995). Thinking the unthinkable: The prospect of regulation of nicotine in cigarettes by the United States government. *Addiction, 90*, 165–167.

Kramer, M. S. (1987). Determinants of low birth weight: Methodological assessment and meta-analysis. *Bulletin of the World Health Organization, 65*, 663–737.

Kramer, P. D. (1993). *Listening to prozac.* New York: Viking.

Kranzler, H. R., & Gage, A. (2008). Acamprosate efficacy in alcohol-dependent patients: Summary of results from three pivotal trials. *The American Journal on Addictions/American Academy of Psychiatrists in Alcoholism and Addictions, 17*, 70–76.

Kreek, M. J. (1982). Opioid disposition and effects during chronic exposure in the perinatal period in man. *Advances in Alcohol and Substance Abuse, 1*, 21–53.

Kubicki, M., McCarley, R., Westin, C. F., Park, H. J., Maier, S., Kikinis, R., et al. (2007). A review of diffusion tensor imaging studies in schizophrenia. *Journal of Psychiatric Research, 41*, 15–30.

Kumor, K., Sherer, M., Muntaner, C., Jaffe, J. H., & Herning, R. (1988). Pharmacological aspects of cocaine rush. In L. S. Harris (Ed.), *Problems of drug dependence, 1988* (NIDA Research Monograph No. 90). Washington, DC: U.S. Government Printing Office.

Lader, M. (2011). Benzodiazepines revisited—Will we ever learn? *Addiction (Abingdon, England), 106*, 2086–2109.

Laisi, U., Linnoila, T., Seppala, J. J., & Mattila, M. J. (1979). Pharmacokinetic and pharmacodynamic interactions of diazepam with different alcoholic beverages. *European Journal of Clinical Pharmacology, 16*, 263–270.

Lamb, R. J., & Griffiths, R. R. (1987). Self-injection of d,1-3,4-methylenedioxy-methamphetamine (MDMA) in the baboon. *Psychopharmacology, 91*, 268–272.

Lamb, R. J., Preston, K., Schindler, C., Meisch, R. A., Davis, F., Katz, J. L., et al. (1991). The reinforcing and subjective effects of morphine in post-addicts: A dose response study. *Journal of Pharmacology and Therapeutics, 259*, 1165–1173.

Landwehrmeyer, B., Mengod, G., & Palacios, J. M. (1993). Dopamine D3 receptor mRNA and binding sites in human brain. *Brain Research: Molecular Brain Research, 18*, 187–192.

Lane, J. D. (1997). Effects of brief caffeinated-beverage deprivation on mood, symptoms, and psychomotor performance. *Pharmacology, Biochemistry and Behavior, 58*, 203–208.

Lane, R., & Baldwin, D. (1997). Selective serotonin reuptake inhibitor-induced serotonin syndrome [Review]. *Journal of Clinical Psychopharmacology, 17*, 208–221.

Lange, J. E., Daniel, J., Homer, K., Reed, M. B., & Clapp, J. D. (2010). Salvia divinorum: Effects and use among YouTube users. *Drug and Alcohol Dependence, 108*, 138–140.

Lankester, E. R. (1889). Mithradatism. *Nature, 40*, 149.

Lara, D. R. (2010). Caffeine, mental health, and psychiatric disorders. *Journal of Alzheimer's Disease, 20*(Suppl. 1), S239–S248.

Lasagana, L., Felsinger, J. M., & Beecher, H. K. (1955). Drug-induced mood changes in man. *Journal of the American Medical Association, 157*, 1006–1020.

Laties, V. G. (1986). Lessons from the history of behavioral pharmacology. In N. K. Krasenegor, D. B. Gray, & T. Thompson (Eds.), *Developmental behavioral pharmacology: Advances in behavioral pharmacology* (Vol. 5, pp. 21–42). Hillsdale, NJ: Erlbaum.

Ledent, C., Valverde, O., Cossu, G., Petitet, F., Aubert, J. F., Beslot, F., et al. (1999). Unresponsiveness to cannabinoids and reduced addictive effects of opiates in CB1 knockout mice. *Science, 283*, 401–404.

Lee, N. K., & Rawson, R. A. (2008). A systematic review of cognitive and behavioural therapies for methamphetamine dependence. *Drug and Alcohol Review, 27*, 309–317. doi:10.1080/09595230801919494

Leiber, C. S. (1977). Metabolism of alcohol. In C. S. Leiber (Ed.), *Metabolic aspects of alcoholism* (pp. 1–30). Baltimore, MD: University Park Press.

Leiber, C. S., & De Carli, L. M. (1977). Metabolic effects of alcohol on the liver. In C. S. Leiber (Ed.), *Metabolic aspects of alcoholism* (pp. 31–80). Baltimore, MD: University Park Press.

Lejoyeux, M. (1996). Use of serotonin (5-hydroxy-tryptamine) reuptake inhibitors in the treatment of alcoholism. *Alcohol, 31*(Suppl. 1), 69–75.

Lelas, S., Gerak, L., & France, C. (1999). Discriminative stimulus effects of triazolam, and midazolam in rhesus monkeys. *Behavioral Pharmacology, 10*, 39–50.

Lemberger, L., Schildcrout, S., & Cuff, G. (1987). Drug delivery systems: Applicability to neuropsychopharmacology. In H. Y. Meltzer (Ed.), *Psychopharmacology: A third generation of progress* (pp. 1285–1295). New York: Raven Press.

Lemmens, V., Oenema, A., Knut, I. K., & Brug, J. (2008). Effectiveness of smoking cessation interventions among adults: A systematic review of reviews. *European Journal of Cancer Prevention, 17*, 535–544.

Leonard, B. E. (1993). The comparative pharmacology of new antidepressants. *Journal of Clinical Pharmacology, 54*(Suppl.), 3–15.

Lesch, K. P., Aulakh, C. S., Wolozin, B. L., Tolliver, T. J., Hill, J. L., & Murphy, D. L. (1993). Regional brain expression of serotonin transporter mRNA and its regulation by reuptake inhibiting antidepressants. *Brain Research. Molecular Brain Research, 17*, 31–35.

Lester, D. B., Rogers, T. D., & Blaha, C. D. (2010). Acetylcholine-dopamine interactions in the pathophysiology and treatment of CNS disorders. *CNS Neuroscience & Therapeutics, 16*, 137–162.

Leucht, S., Kissling, W., & Davis, J. M. (2009). Second-generation antipsychotics for schizophrenia: Can we resolve the conflict? *Psychological Medicine, 39*, 1591–1602.

Levin, E. D. (1992). Nicotinic systems and cognitive function. *Psychopharmacology, 108*, 417–431.

Levine, H. G. (1981). The vocabulary of drunkenness. *Journal of Studies on Alcohol, 42*, 1038–1051.

Lewis, D. A., Hashimoto, T., & Volk, D. W. (2005). Cortical inhibitory neurons and schizophrenia. *Nature Reviews Neuroscience, 6*, 312–324.

Li, H. (1975). The origin and use of cannabis in eastern Asia. In V. Rubin (Ed.), *Cannabis and culture* (pp. 51–62). The Hague: Mouton.

Li, T. K., Hewitt, B. G., & Grant, B. F. (2004). Alcohol use disorders and mood disorders: A national institute on alcohol abuse and alcoholism perspective. *Biological Psychiatry, 56*, 718–720.

Liao, Y., Tang, J., Corlett, P. R., Wang, X., Yang, M., Chen, H., et al. (2011). Reduced dorsal prefrontal gray matter after chronic ketamine use. *Biological Psychiatry, 69*, 42–48.

Lickey, M. E., & Gordon, B. (1991). *Medicine and mental illness: The use of drugs in psychiatry*. New York: Freeman.

Liguori, A., & Robinson, J. H. (2001). Caffeine antagonism of alcohol-induced driving impairment. *Drug and Alcohol Dependence, 63*, 123–129.

Linder, R. L., Lerner, S. E., & Burns, R. S. (1981). *PCP: The devil's dust*. Belmont, CA: Wadsworth.

Lindgren, M., Osterberg, K., Orbaek, P., & Rosen, I. (1997). Solvent-induced toxic encephalopathy: Electrophysiological data in relation to neurophysiological findings. *Journal of Clinical and Experimental Neuropsychology, 19*, 772–783.

Ling, W., Rawson, R. A., & Compton, M. A. (1994). Substitution pharmacotherapies for opioid addiction: From methadone to LAAM and buprenorphine. *Journal of Psychoactive Drugs, 26*, 119–128.

Linnoila, M., & Hakkinen, T. (1974). Effects of diazepam and codeine alone and in combination with alcohol, on simulated driving. *Clinical Pharmacology and Therapeutics, 15*, 368–373.

Lobmaier, P., Gossop, M., Waal, H., & Bramness, J. (2010). The pharmacological treatment of opioid addiction—a clinical perspective. *European Journal of Clinical Pharmacology, 66*, 537–545.

Logan, B. K. (1996). Methamphetamine and driving impairment. *Journal of Forensic Sciences, 41*, 457–464.

Lombardo, J. A. (1986). Stimulants and athletic performance (part 1 of 2): Amphetamines and caffeine. *The Physician and Sportsmedicine, 14*, 128–140.

London, E. D., Cascella, N. G., Wong, D. F., Phillips, R. L., Dannals, R. F., Links, J. M., et al. (1990). Cocaine induced reduction of glucose utilization in human brain: A study using positron emission tomography and (fluorine 18)-fluorodeoxyglucose. *Archives of General Psychiatry, 47*, 567–574.

Longo, M., Wickes, W., Smout, M., Harrison, S., Cahill, S., & White, J. M. (2010). Randomized controlled trial of dexamphetamine maintenance for the treatment of methamphetamine dependence. *Addiction (Abingdon, England), 105,* 146–154.

López, J. F., Chalmers, D. T., Little, K. Y., & Watson, S. J. (1998). A.E. Bennett Research Award. Regulation of serotonin1A, glucocorticoid, and mineralocorticoid receptor in rat and human hippocampus: Implications for the neurobiology of depression. *Biological Psychiatry, 43,* 547–573.

Lopez-Garcia, E., van Dam, R. M., Li, T. Y., Rodriguez-Artalejo, F., & Hu, F. B. (2008). The relationship of coffee consumption with mortality. *Annals of Internal Medicine, 148,* 904–914.

Lopez-Garcia, E., van Dam, R. M., Willett, W. C., Rimm, E. B., Manson, J. E., Stampfer, M. J., et al. (2006). Coffee consumption and coronary heart disease in men and women: A prospective cohort study. *Circulation, 113,* 2045–2053.

López-Muñoz, F., Ucha-Udabe, R., & Alamo, C. (2005). The history of barbiturates a century after their clinical introduction. *Neuropsychiatric Disease Treatment, 1,* 329–343.

Lorrain, D., Arnold, G., & Vezina, P. (2000). Previous exposure to amphetamine increases incentive to obtain the drug: Long-lasting effects revealed by the progressive ratio schedule. *Behavioural and Brain Research, 107,* 9–21.

Lukas, S. E. (1991). Topographic brain mapping during cocaine-induced intoxification and self-administration. In G. Racagni, N. Brunello, & T. Fukuda (Eds.), *Biological psychiatry* (Vol. 2, pp. 25–29). New York: Excerpta Medica.

Luppi, P., & Fort, P. (2011). What are the mechanisms activating the sleep-active neurons in the preoptic area? *Sleep and Biological Rhythms, 9,* 59–64.

Lussier, J. P., Heil, S. H., Mongeon, J. A., Badger, G. J., & Higgins, S. T. (2006). A meta-analysis of voucher-based reinforcement therapy for substance use disorders. *Addiction (Abingdon, England), 101,* 192–203.

Maher, A. R., Maglione, M., Bagley, S., Suttorp, M., Hu, J. H., Ewing, B., et al. (2011). Efficacy and comparative effectiveness of atypical antipsychotic medications for off-label uses in adults: A systematic review and meta-analysis. *The Journal of the American Medical Association, 306,* 1359–1369.

Mahler, S. V., Smith, K. S., & Berridge, K. C. (2007). Endocannabinoid hedonic hotspot for sensory pleasure: Anandamide in nucleus accumbens shell enhances 'liking' of a sweet reward. *Neuropsychopharmacology: Official Publication of the American College of Neuropsychopharmacology, 32,* 2267–2278.

Maier, S. E., & West, J. R. (2001). Drinking patterns and alcohol-related birth defects. *Alcohol Research & Health, 25,* 168–174.

Malcolm, R., Brady, K. T., Johnston, A. L., & Cunningham, M. (1993). Types of benzodiazepines abused by chemically dependent inpatients. *Journal of Psychoactive Drugs, 25,* 315–319.

Malison, R. T., Price, L. H., Berman, R., van Dyck, C. H., Pelton, G. H., Carpenter, L., et al. (1998). Reduced brain serotonin transporter availability in major depression as measured by [123I]-2 beta-carbomethoxy-3 beta-(4-iodophenyl)tropane and single photon emission computed tomography. *Biological Psychiatry, 44,* 1090–1098.

Maltzman, I. (1994). Why alcoholism is a disease. *Journal of Psychoactive Drugs, 26,* 13–31.

Mann, K., Agartz, I., Harper, C., Shoaf, S., Rawlings, R. R., Momenan, R., et al. (2001). Neuroimaging in alcoholism: Ethanol and brain damage. *Alcoholism, Clinical and Experimental Research, 25,* 104S–109S.

Mann, L. B., & Folts, J. D. (2004). Effects of ethanol and other constituents of alcoholic beverages on coronary heart disease: A review. *Pathophysiology: The Official Journal of the International Society for Pathophysiology, 10,* 105–112.

Mansour, A., Fox, C., Burke, S., Meng, F., Thompson, R. C., Akil, H., et al. (1994). Mu, delta and kappa opioid receptor mRNA expression in rats CNS: An in situ hybridization study. *Journal of Comparative Neurology, 350,* 412–438.

Mariscal, M., Palma, S., Llorca, J., Perez-Iglesias, R., Pardo-Crespo, R., & Delgado-Rodriguez, M. (2006). Pattern of alcohol consumption during pregnancy and risk for low birth weight. *Annals of Epidemiology, 16,* 432–438.

Mark, L. C. (1971). Pharmacokinetics of barbiturates. In H. Matthew (Ed.), *Acute barbiturate poisoning* (pp. 75–84). Amsterdam, NY: Excerpta Medica.

Markou, A., Weiss, F., Gold, L. H., Caine, S. B., Schulteis, G., & Koob, G. (1993). Animal models of drug craving. *Psychopharmacology, 112,* 163–182.

Marlatt, G. A., & Rohsenow, D. J. (1980). Cognitive processes in alcohol use: Expectancy and the balanced placebo design. In N. K. Mello (Ed.), *Advances in substance abuse: Behavioral and biological research* (pp. 159–199). Greenwich, CT: JAI Press.

Marsden, C. D. (1977). Neurological disorders induced by alcohol. In G. Edwards & M. Grant (Eds.), *Alcoholism: New knowledge and new responses* (pp. 189–198). London: Croom Helm.

Martell, B. A., Orson, F. M., Poling, J., Mitchell, E., Rossen, R. D., Gardner, T., et al. (2009). Cocaine vaccine for the treatment of cocaine dependence in methadone-maintained patients: A randomized, double-blind, placebo-controlled efficacy trial. *Archives of General Psychiatry, 66,* 1116–1123.

Martin, B. (2000). Marijuana. In *Psychopharmacology: The fourth generation of progress.* Retrieved from http://www.acnp.org/g4/GN401000170

Martin, E. R., Eades, C. G., Thompson, J. A., Huppler, R. F., & Gilbert, P. E. (1976). The effects of morphine- and morphine-like drugs in the non-dependent and morphine-dependent chronic spinal dog. *Journal of Pharmacology and Experimental Therapeutics, 197,* 517–532.

Martin, G. E., Hendrickson, L. M., Penta, K. L., Friesen, R. M., Pietrzykowski, A. Z., Tapper, A. R., et al. (2008). Identification of a BK channel auxiliary protein controlling molecular and behavioral tolerance to alcohol. *Proceedings of the National Academy of Sciences of the United States of America, 105,* 17543–17548.

Martin, R., & Acre, A. (1996). Benxodiazepine receptors increase induced by stress and maze learning performance in chick forebrain. *Pharmacology, Biochemistry and Behavior, 53,* 581–584.

Martínez-Clemente, J., Escubedo, E., Pubill, D., & Camarasa, J. (2011). Interaction of mephedrone with dopamine and serotonin targets in rats. *European Neuropsychopharmacology: The Journal of the European College of Neuropsychopharmacology.*

Maskos, U., Molles, B. E., Pons, S., Besson, M., Guiard, B., Guilloux, J. -P., et al. (2005). Nicotine reinforcement and cognition restored by targeted expression of nicotinic receptors. *Nature, 436,* 103–107.

Masuki, K., & Iwamoto, T. (1966). Development of tolerance to tranquilizers in the rat. *Japanese Journal of Pharmacology, 16,* 191–197.

Mathew, R. J., Wilson, W. H., Turkington, T. G., & Coleman, R. E. (1998). Cerebellar activity and disturbed time sense after THC. *Brain Research, 797,* 183–189.

Maxwell, M. A. (1984). *The alcoholics anonymous experience: A close up view for professionals.* New York: McGraw-Hill.

McCarthy, R. G. (1959). *Drinking and intoxication.* New York: Free Press.

McCracken, S., de Wit, H., Uhlenhuth, E. H., & Johanson, E. (1990). Preference for diazepam in anxious adults. *Journal of Clinical Psychopharmacology, 10,* 190–196.

McEwan, B., & Lashley, E. (2002). *The end of stress as we know it.* Washington, DC: Joseph Henry Press.

McGovern, P. E., Zhang, J., Tang, J., Zhang, Z., Hall, G. R., Moreau, R. A., et al. (2004). Fermented beverages of pre- and proto-historic China. *Proceedings of the National Academy of Sciences USA, 101,* 17593–17598.

McGregor, C., Srisurapanont, M., Jittiwutikarn, J., Laobhripatr, S., Wongtan, T., & White, J. M. (2005). The nature, time course and severity of methamphetamine withdrawal. *Addiction (Abingdon, England), 100,* 1320–1329.

McKim, W. (2003). *Drugs and behavior* (5th ed.). Upper Saddle River, NJ: Prentice Hall.

McKim, W. A. (1980). The effects of caffeine, theophylline and amphetamine on the operant responding of the mouse. *Psychopharmacology, 68,* 135–138.

McKim, W. A., & Mishara, B. L. (1987). *Drugs and aging.* Toronto, ON: Butterworths.

McKim, W. A., & Quinlan, L. T. (1991). Changes in alcohol consumption with age. *Canadian Journal of Public Health, 82,* 231–234.

McLellan, A. T., Weinstein, R. L., Shen, Q., Kendig, C., & Levine, M. (2005). Improving continuity of care in a public addiction treatment system with clinical case management. *American Journal of Addiction, 14,* 426–440.

McMillan, D. E., & Leander, J. D. (1976). Effects of drugs on schedule-controlled behavior. In S. D. Glick & J. Goldfarb (Eds.), *Behavioral pharmacology* (pp. 85–139). St. Louis, MO: Mosby.

McNeil, J. J., Piccenna, L., & Ioannides-Demos, L. L. (2010). Smoking cessation-recent advances. *Cardiovascular Drugs and Therapy/Sponsored by the International Society of Cardiovascular Pharmacotherapy, 24,* 359–367.

Meaney, M. (2001). Maternal care, gene expression, and the transmission of individual differences in stress reactivity across generations. *Annual Review of Neuroscience, 24,* 1161–1192.

Mechoulam, R., Hanus, L., & Martin, B. (1994). The search for endogenous ligands of the cannabinoid receptor. *Biochemical Pharmacology, 48,* 1537–1544.

Mechoulam, R., McCallum, N. K., Lander, N., Yagen, B., Ben Zvi, Z., & Levy, S. (1976). Aspects of cannabis chemistry and metabolism. In M. C. Braude & S. Szara (Eds.), *Pharmacology of marijuana* (Vol. 1, pp. 39–46). Orlando, FL: Academic Press.

Mehta, S., Chen, H., Johnson, M., & Aparasu, R. R. (2011). Risk of serious cardiac events in older adults using antipsychotic agents. *The American Journal of Geriatric Pharmacotherapy, 9,* 120–132.

Meisch, R. A. (1977). Ethanol self-administration in infra-human species. In T. Thompson & P. B. Dews (Eds.), *Advances in behavioral pharmacology* (Vol. 1, pp. 35–84). Orlando, FL: Academic Press.

Mellinger, G. D., Balter, M. B., & Uhlenhuth, E. H. (1984). Prevalence and correlates of long-term regular use of anxiolytics. *Journal of the American Medical Association, 25,* 375–379.

Mello, N. K. (1978). Alcoholism and the behavioral pharmacology of alcohol, 1967–1977. In M. A. Lipton, A. Di Mascio, & K. F. Killam (Eds.), *Psychopharmacology: A generation of progress* (pp. 1619–1637). New York: Raven Press.

Mello, N. K. (1987). Alcohol abuse and alcoholism. In H. Y. Meltzer (Ed.), *Psychopharmacology: The third generation of progress* (pp. 1515–1520). New York: Raven Press.

Mello, N. K., & Mendelson, J. H. (1972). Drinking patterns during work-contingent and non-contingent alcohol acquisition. *Psychosomatic Medicine, 34,* 139–164.

Mello, N. K., & Mendelson, J. H. (1987). Operant analysis of human drug self-administration: Marijuana, alcohol, heroin, and polydrug use. In M. A. Bozarth (Ed.),

Methods for assessing the reinforcing properties of abused drugs (pp. 525–558). New York: Springer-Verlag.

Melnik, T., Soares, B. G., Puga, M. E., & Atallah, A. N. S. (2010). Efficacy and safety of atypical antipsychotic drugs (quetiapine, risperidone, aripiprazole and paliperidone) compared with placebo or typical antipsychotic drugs for treating refractory schizophrenia: Overview of systematic reviews. *Sao Paulo Medical Journal, 128*, 141–166.

Meltzer, H. Y. (1990). Clozapine: Pattern of efficacy in treatment resistant schizophrenia. In H. Y. Meltzer (Ed.), *Novel antipsychotic drugs* (pp. 33–46). New York: Raven Press.

Meltzer, H. Y. (1994). An overview of the mechanism of action of clozapine. *The Journal of Clinical Psychiatry, 55*(Suppl. B), 47–52.

Melzack, R. (1990). The tragedy of needless pain. *Scientific American, 262*, 27–33.

Mendelson, H. H., Kuehnle, J. C., Greenberg, I., & Mello, N. K. (1976). The effects of marijuana use on human operant behavior: Individual data. In M. C. Braude & S. Szara (Eds.), *Pharmacology of marijuana* (Vol. 2, pp. 643–653). Orlando, FL: Academic Press.

Meng, Y., Lichtman, A. H., Bridgen, D. T., & Martin, B. R. (1997). Inhalation studies with drugs of abuse. In Rao S. Rapaka, Nora Chiang, & Billy R. Martin (Eds.), *Pharmacokinetics, metabolism, and pharmaceutics of drugs of abuse*, (pp. 201–224) (NIDA monograph 173). Retrieved from http://archives.drugabuse.gov/pdf/monographs/monograph173/201-224_Meng.pdf

Meredith, C. W., Jaffe, C., Ang-Lee, K., & Saxon, A. J. (2005). Implications of chronic methamphetamine use: A literature review. *Harvard Review of Psychiatry, 13*, 141–154.

Metzner, R. (1993). Letter to MAPS. *Newsletter of the Multidisciplinary Association for Psychedelic Studies, 4*. Retrieved from http://www.maps.org/news-letters/v04n1/04143met.html

Meyer, M. R., Wilhelm, J., Peters, F. T., & Maurer, H. H. (2010). Beta-keto amphetamines: Studies on the metabolism of the designer drug mephedrone and toxicological detection of mephedrone, butylone, and methylone in urine using gas chromatography-mass spectrometry. *Analytical and Bioanalytical Chemistry, 397*, 1225–1233.

Meyer, R. E., & Mirin, S. M. (1979). *The heroin stimulus*. New York: Plenum Press.

Meyer, U., van Kampen, M., Isovich, E., Flügge, G., & Fuchs, E. (2001). Chronic psychosocial stress regulates the expression of both GR and MR mRNA in the hippocampal formation of tree shrews. *Hippocampus, 11*, 329–336.

Miczek, K. A., & Barry, H., III. (1976). Pharmacology of sex and aggression. In S. D. Glick & J. Goldfarb (Eds.), *Behavioral pharmacology* (pp. 176–257). St. Louis, MO: Mosby.

Milin, R., Manion, I., Dare, G., & Walker, S. (2008). Prospective assessment of cannabis withdrawal in adolescents with cannabis dependence: A pilot study. *Journal of the American Academy of Child and Adolescent Psychiatry, 47*, 174–178.

Millan, M. J. (1986). Kappa-opioid receptors and analgesia. *Trends in Pharmacological Sciences, 11*, 70–76.

Millan, M. J. (1990). Multiple opioid systems and pain. *Pain, 27*, 303–337.

Minifie, B. W. (1970). *Chocolate, cocoa and confectionary science and technology*. Westport, CT: Avi.

Mintzer, M., & Griffiths, R. (1998). Flurazepam and triazolam: A comparison of behavioral effects and abuse liability. *Drug and Alcohol Dependence, 53*, 49–66.

Mintzer, M., Stoller, K., & Griffiths, R. (1999). A controlled study of flunazemil-precipitated withdrawal in chronic low-dose benzodiazepine users. *Psychopharmacology, 147*, 200–209.

Miotto, K., Darakjian, J., Basch, J., Murray, J., Zogg, J., & Rawson, R. (2001). Gamma-hydroxybutyric acid: Patterns of use, effects and withdrawal. *American Journal on the Addictions, 10*, 232–241.

Mirsky, I. A., Piker, P., Rosebaum, M., & Lederer, H. (1945). "Adaptation" of the central nervous system to various concentrations of alcohol in the blood. *Quarterly Journal of Studies on Alcohol, 2*, 35.

Mitchell, M. C. (1985). Alcohol-induced impairment of central nervous system function: Behavioral skills involved in driving. *Journal of Studies on Alcohol, 10*(Suppl.), 109–116.

Mitchell, S., Laurent, C., & de Wit, H. (1996). Interaction of expectancy and the pharmacological effects of d-amphetamine: Subjective effects and self-administration. *Psychopharmacology, 125*, 371–378.

Miyata, H., Ando, K., & Yanagita, T. (2002). Brain regions mediating the discriminative stimulus effects of nicotine in rats. *Annals of the New York Academy of Sciences, 965*, 354–363.

Modrow, H. E., Holloway, F. A., & Carney, J. M. (1981). Caffeine discrimination in the rat. *Pharmacology, Biochemistry and Behavior, 14*, 683–688.

Moghaddam, B., & Javitt, D. (2012). From revolution to evolution: The glutamate hypothesis of schizophrenia and its implication for treatment. *Neuropsychopharmacology: Official Publication of the American College of Neuropsychopharmacology, 37*, 4–15.

Möhler, H., Fritschy, J. M., Crestani, F., Hensch, T., & Rudolph, U. (2004). Specific GABA(A) circuits in brain development and therapy. *Biochemical Pharmacology, 68*, 1685–1690.

Moncrieff, J., Wessely, S., & Hardy, R. (2004). Active placebos versus antidepressants for depression. *Cochrane Database of Systematic Reviews (Online)*, CD003012.

Money, K. E., & Miles, W. S. (1974). Heavy water nystagmus and the effects of alcohol. *Nature, 247,* 404–405.

Monteiro, W. O., Noshirvani, I. M., Marks, I. M., & Lelliott, P. T. (1987). Anorgasmia from clomiprimine in obsessive-compulsive disorder: A controlled trial. *British Journal of Psychiatry, 151,* 107–112.

Mora, M. S., Nestoriuc, Y., & Rief, W. (2011). Lessons learned from placebo groups in antidepressant trials. *Philosophical Transactions of the Royal Society of London. Series B, Biological Sciences, 366,* 1879–1888.

Moreau, J. J. (1973). *Hashish and mental illness.* H. Peters, G. G. Nahas (Eds.), & G. J. Barnett (Trans.). New York: Raven Press. (Original work published 1845)

Moreno, J. L., Holloway, T., Albizu, L., Sealfon, S. C., & González-Maeso, J. (2011). Metabotropic glutamate mGlu2 receptor is necessary for the pharmacological and behavioral effects induced by hallucinogenic 5-HT2A receptor agonists. *Neuroscience Letters, 493,* 76–79.

Moreton, J. E., Meisch, R. A., Stark, L., & Thompson, T. (1977). Ketamine self-administration in the rhesus monkey. *Journal of Pharmacology and Experimental Therapeutics, 203,* 303–309.

Morgan, J. (2000). Ecstasy (MDMA): A review of its possible persistent psychological effects. *Psychopharmacology, 152,* 230–248.

Morgan, T., Porritt, M., & Poling, A. (2006). Effects of dextromethorphan on rats' acquisition of responding with delayed reinforcement. *Pharmacology, Biochemistry and Behavior, 85,* 637–642.

Morral, A. R., McCaffrey, D. F., & Paddock, S. M. (2002). Reassessing the marijuana gateway effect. *Addiction (Abingdon, England), 97,* 1493–1504.

Morrison, C. F. (1967). The effects of nicotine on operant behavior of rats. *International Journal of Neuropharmacology, 6,* 229–240.

Morrison, C. F. (1969). The effects of nicotine on punished behavior. *Psychopharmacologia, 14,* 221.

Morrison, C. F. (1974). The effects of nicotine and its withdrawal on the performance of rats on signalled and unsignalled avoidance schedules. *Psychopharmacologia, 38,* 25–35.

Morrison, C. F., & Stephenson, J. A. (1969). Nicotine injections as the conditioned stimulus in discrimination learning. *Psychopharmacologia, 15,* 351–360.

Morrison, C. F., & Stephenson, J. A. (1972a). Effects of stimulants on observed behavior of rats on six operant schedules. *Neuropharmacology, 12,* 297–310.

Morrison, C. F., & Stephenson, J. A. (1972b). The occurrence of tolerance to a central nervous system depressant effect of nicotine. *British Journal of Pharmacology, 45,* 315–320.

Morrison, P., Kapur, S., & Murray, R. (2009). The phenomenology of acute THC-psychosis. *European Psychiatry, 24,* S146.

Moskowitz, J., Hulbert, S., & McGlothlin, W. H. (1976). Marijuana: Effects on simulated driving performance. *Accident Analysis and Prevention, 8,* 45–50.

Movig, K. L., Mathijssen, M. P., Nagel, P. H., van Egmond, T., de Gier, J. J., Leufkens, H. G., et al. (2004). Psychoactive substance use and the risk of motor vehicle accidents. *Accident; Analysis and Prevention, 36,* 631–636.

Mowry, M., Mosher, M., & Briner, W. (2003). Acute physiologic and chronic histologic changes in rats and mice exposed to the unique hallucinogen salvinorin A. *Journal of Psychoactive Drugs, 35,* 379–382.

Mullins, C. J., Vitola, B. M., & Michelson, A. E. (1975). Variables related to cannabis use. *International Journal of Addictions, 10,* 481–502.

Mumford, G. K., Evans, S. M., Kamiski, B. J., Preston, K. L., Sannerud, C. A., Silverman, K., et al. (1994). Discriminative stimulus and subjective effects of theobromine and caffeine in humans. *Psychopharmacology, 115,* 1–8.

Mundy, A., & Etter, L. (2009, June 12). Senate passes FDA tobacco bill historic measure limits ads, packaging; smokeless products affected. *Wall Street Journal.* Retrieved from http://online.wsj.com/article/SB124474789599707175.html

Munro, S., Thomas, K. L., & Abu-Shaar, M. (1993). Molecular characterization of a peripheral receptor for cannabinoids. *Nature, 365,* 61–65.

Muskowitz, H., & Burns, M. (1981). The effects of alcohol and caffeine alone and in combination, on skilled performance. In L. Goldberg (Ed.), *Alcohol, drugs and traffic safety* (Vol. 3, pp. 969–983). Stockholm: Almqvist & Wiksell.

Murphy, S. L., Janquan, X., Kochanek, M. A. (2012). Deaths: Preliminary data for 2010. *National Vital Statistics Reports, 60*(4). Retrieved from http://www.cdc.gov/nchs/data/nvsr/nvsr60/nvsr60_04.pdf

Myerscough, R., & Taylor, S. (1985). The effects of marijuana on human physical aggression. *Journal of Personality and Social Psychology, 49,* 1541–1546.

Myerson, R. M. (1971). Effects of alcohol on cardiac and muscular function. In Y. Israel & J. Mardones (Eds.), *Biomedical basis of alcoholism* (pp. 183–208). New York: Wiley/Interscience.

Nagai, F., Nonaka, R., & Satoh Hisashi Kamimura, K. (2007). The effects of non-medically used psychoactive drugs on monoamine neurotransmission in rat brain. *European Journal of Pharmacology, 559,* 132–137.

Naimi, T. S., Brown, D. W., Brewer, R. D., Giles, W. H., Mensah, G., Serdula, M. K., et al. (2005). Cardiovascular risk factors and confounders among nondrinking and moderate-drinking U.S. adults. *American Journal of Preventive Medicine, 28,* 369–373.

Naranjo, C. A., & Sellers, E. M. (1986). Clinical assessment and pharmacology of the alcohol withdrawal syndrome. In M. Galanter (Ed.), *Recent developments in alcoholism* (Vol. 4, pp. 265–281). New York: Plenum Press.

National Cancer Institute. (2011). Retrieved November 2, 2011, from http://www.cancer.gov/cancertopics/factsheet/Tobacco/cessation. Accessed November 2, 2011.

National Drug Intelligence Center. (2009, July). Domestic cannabis cultivation assessment. Retrieved from http://www.justice.gov/ndic/pubs37/37035/index.htm

National Institute on Alcohol Abuse and Alcoholism. (2004). *Alcohol's damaging effects on the brain.* Bethesda, MD: Author.

National Institute on Drug Abuse. National Institutes of Health. U.S. Department of Health and Human Services. Principles of drug addiction treatment: A research-based guide. Second edition NIH Publication No. 09–4180, Revised April 2009

National Institutes of Health. (2007). *Morbidity and mortality chart book on cardiovascular blood and lung diseases 2007.* Retrieved from http://www.nhlbi.nih.gov/resources/docs/07a-chtbk.pdf

Nehlig, A., Daval, J. -L., & Debry, G. (1992). Caffeine and the central nervous system: Mechanisms of action, biochemical, metabolic and psychostimulant effects. *Brain Research Reviews, 17*, 139–170.

Neims, A. H., Bailey, J., & Aldrich, A. (1979). Disposition of caffeine during and after pregnancy. *Clinical Research, 20*, 236A.

Nesse, R., & Berridge, K. (1997). Psychoactive drug use in evolutionary perspective. *Science, 278*, 63–66.

Niccols, A. (2007). Fetal alcohol syndrome and the developing socio-emotional brain. *Brain and Cognition, 65*, 135–142.

Nicholl, J., & O'Cathain, A. (1992). Antenatal smoking, postnatal passive smoking and sudden infant death syndrome. In D. Poswillio & E. Alberman (Eds.), *Effects of smoking on the fetus, neonate and child* (pp. 138–170). Oxford, England: Oxford University Press.

Nicholson, K. L., Hayes, B. A., & Balster, R. L. (1999). Evaluation of the reinforcing properties and phencyclidine-like discriminative stimulus effects of dextromethorphan and dextrorphan in rats and rhesus monkeys. *Psychopharmacology, 146*, 49–59.

Nicolson, R., Lenane, M., Singaracharlu, S., Malaspina, D., Giedd, J. N., Hamburger, S. D., et al. (2000). Premorbid speech and language impairments in childhood-onset schizophrenia: Association with risk factors. *The American Journal of Psychiatry, 157*, 794–800.

NIDA. (2001, June). *Epidemiologic trends in drug abuse advance report.* Retrieved from http://www.nida.nih.gov/CEWG/AdvancedRep/601ADV/601adv.html

Niemi, L. T., Suvisaari, J. M., Tuulio-Henriksson, A., & Lönnqvist, J. K. (2003). Childhood developmental abnormalities in schizophrenia: Evidence from high-risk studies. *Schizophrenia Research, 60*, 239–258.

Noller, G. (2009). Literature review and assessment report on MDMA/ecstasy. *National Drug Policy, Ministry of Health (Wellington)*, 1–104.

Nriagu, J. O. (1983). Saturnine gout among the Roman aristocrats. *New England Journal of Medicine, 308*, 660–663.

Nutt, D. J., & Stahl, S. M. (2010). Searching for perfect sleep: The continuing evolution of GABAA receptor modulators as hypnotics. *Journal of Psychopharmacology (Oxford, England), 24*, 1601–1612.

Nyswander, M. (1967). The methadone treatment of heroin addiction. *Hospital Practice, 2*, 27–33.

O'Brien, C. (2010). Addiction and dependence in the DSM-5. *Addiction, 106*, 866–867.

O'Brien, C. P. (1976). Experimental analysis of conditioning factors in human narcotic addiction. *Pharmacological Reviews, 27*, 533–543.

O'Brien, C. P. (2008). Review: Evidence-based treatments of addiction. *Philosophical Transactions of the Royal Society of London. Series B, Biological Sciences, 363*, 3277–3286.

O'Connell, T., Kaye, L., & Plosay, J. (2000). Gamma-hydroxybutyrate (GHB): A newer drug of abuse. *American Family Physician, 62*, 2478–2482.

O'Malley, S. S., Cooney, J. L., Krishnan-Sarin, S., Dubin, J. A., McKee, S. A., Cooney, N. L., et al. (2006). A controlled trial of naltrexone augmentation of nicotine replacement therapy for smoking cessation. *Archives of Internal Medicine, 166*, 667–674.

O'Neil, S., Tipton, K. F., Prichard, J. S., & Quinlan, A. (1984). Survival after high blood alcohol levels: Association with first order elimination kinetics. *Archives of Internal Medicine, 144*, 641–642.

Ogbourne, A. C., & Glaser, F. B. (1981). Characteristics of affiliates of alcoholics anonymous. *Journal of Studies on Alcohol, 42*, 661–675.

Olds, J., & Milner, P. (1954). Positive reinforcement produced by electrical stimulation of septal area and other regions of rat brain. *Journal of Comparative and Physiological Psychology, 47*, 419–427.

Olson, V. G., & Nestler, E. J. (2007). Topographical organization of GABAergic neurons within the ventral tegmental area of the rat. *Synapse (New York, N.Y.), 61*, 87–95.

Opland, D. M., Leininger, G. M., & Myers, M. G., Jr. (2010). Modulation of the mesolimbic dopamine system by leptin. *Brain Research, 1350*, 65–70.

Ordway, G. A., Klimek, V., & Mann, J. J. (2002). Neurocircuitry of mood disorders. In K. L. Davis, D. Cherney, J. T. Coyle, & C. Nemeroff (Eds.), *Psychopharmacology: A fifth generation of progress* (pp. 1052–1065). Nashville, TN: American College of Neuropsychopharmacology.

Organization for Economic Cooperation and Development. (1978, September). *Road research: New research on the role of alcohol and drugs in road accidents.* Paris: Author.

Orson, F. M., Kinsey, B. M., Singh, R. A., Wu, Y., Gardner, T., & Kosten, T. R. (2008). Substance abuse vaccines. *Annals of New York Academy of Sciences, Oct,* 257–269.

Oster-Aaland, L., Lewis, M. A., Neighbors, C., Vangsness, J., & Larimer, M. E. (2009). Alcohol poisoning among college students turning 21: Do they recognize the symptoms and how do they help? *Journal of Studies on Alcohol and Drugs, 16*(Suppl.), 122–130.

Oswald, I., Lewis, S. A., Tangey, J., Firth, H., & Haider, I. (1973). Benzodiazepines and human sleep. In S. Garattini, E. Mussini, & L. O. Randall (Eds.), *The benzodiazepines* (pp. 613–625). New York: Raven Press.

Otis, L. S. (1964). Dissociation and recovery of a response learned under the influence of chlorpromazine or saline. *Science, 143,* 1347–1348.

Ott, J. (1995). Ethnopharmacognosy and human pharmacology of salvia divinorum and salvinorin A, *Curare, 18,* 103–129.

Overall, J. E. (1987). Introduction: Methodology in psychopharmacology. In H. Y. Meltzer (Ed.), *Psychopharmacology: A third generation of progress* (pp. 995–996). New York: Raven Press.

Overton, D. A. (1972). State-dependent learning produced by alcohol and its relevance to alcoholism. In B. Kissen & H. Begleiter (Eds.), *The biology of alcoholism* (Vol. 2, pp. 193–217). New York: Plenum Press.

Overton, D. A. (1973). State-dependent learning produced by addicting drugs. In S. Fisher & A. M. Freeman (Eds.), *Opiate addiction: Origins and treatment* (pp. 61–67). New York: Wiley.

Overton, D. A. (1982). Comparison of the degree of discriminability of various drugs using the T-maze drug discrimination paradigm. *Psychopharmacology, 76,* 385–395.

Overton, D. A. (1987). Applications and limitations of the drug discrimination method for the study of drug abuse. In M. A. Bozarth (Ed.), *Methods of assessing the reinforcing properties of abused drugs* (pp. 291–340). New York: Springer-Verlag.

Overton, D. A., & Batta, S. K. (1977). Relationship between abuse liability of drugs and their degree of discriminability in the rat. In T. Thompson & K. R. Unna (Eds.), *Predicting dependence liability of stimulant and depressant drugs* (pp. 125–135). Baltimore, MD: University Park Press.

Owen, R. T., & Tyrer, P. (1983). Benzodiazepine dependence: A review of the evidence. *Drugs, 25,* 385–398.

Paez-Pereda, M., Hausch, F., & Holsboer, F. (2011). Corticotropin releasing factor receptor antagonists for major depressive disorder. *Expert Opinion on Investigational Drugs, 20,* 519–535.

Palmer, J., Rosenberg, L., Rao, R., & Shapiro, S. (1995). Coffee consumpton and myocardial infarction in women. *American Journal of Epidemiology, 141,* 724–731.

Palmiter, R. D. (2008). Dopamine signaling in the dorsal striatum is essential for motivated behaviors: Lessons from dopamine-deficient mice. *Annals of the New York Academy of Sciences, 1129,* 35–46.

Paolini, M., & De Biasi, M. (2011). Mechanistic insights into nicotine withdrawal. *Biochemical Pharmacology, 82*(8), 996–1007.

Papac, D. I., & Foltz, R. L. (1990). Measurement of lysergic acid diethylamide (LSD) in human plasma by gas chromatography/negative ion chemical ionization mass spectrometry. *Journal of Analytical Toxicology, 14*(3), 189–190.

Papafotiou, K., Carter, J. D., & Stough, C. (2005). An evaluation of the sensitivity of the Standardized Field Sobriety Tests (SFSTs) to detect impairment due to marijuana intoxication. *Psychopharmacology, 180,* 107–114.

Parada, M., Corral, M., Caamano-Isorna, F., Mota, N., Crego, A., Holguin, S. R., et al. (2011). Binge drinking and declarative memory in university students. *Alcoholism, Clinical and Experimental Research, 35,* 1475–1484.

Parasrampuria, D. A., Schoedel, K. A., Schuller, R., Gu, J., Ciccone, P., Silber, S. A., et al. (2007). Assessment of pharmacokinetics and pharmacodynamic effects related to abuse potential of a unique oral osmotic-controlled extended-release methylphenidate formulation in humans. *Journal of Clinical Pharmacology, 47,* 1476–1488.

Parolaro, D., & Rubino, T. (2008). The role of the endogenous cannabinoid system in drug addiction. *Drug News Perspective, 21,* 149–157.

Parrott, A. C. (2004). Is ecstasy MDMA? A review of the proportion of ecstasy tablets containing MSMA, their dosage levels and changing perceptions of purity. *Psychopharmacology, 173,* 234–241.

Parsons, W. D., & Neims, A. H. (1978). Effects of smoking on caffeine clearance. *Clinical Pharmacology and Therapy, 24,* 40–45.

Passie, T., Halpern, J. H., Stichtenoth, D. O., Emrich, H. M., & Hintzen, A. (2008). The pharmacology of lysergic acid diethylamide: A review. *CNS Neuroscience & Therapeutics, 14,* 295–314.

Pastuszak, A., Schick-Boschetto, B., Zuber, C., Feldkamp, M., Pinelli, M., Sihn, S., et al. (1993). Pregnancy outcome following first-trimester exposure to fluoxetine (Prozac). *Journal of the American Medical Association, 269,* 2246–2248.

Paton, W. D. M., & Pertwee, R. C. (1973). The actions of cannabis in animals. In R. Mechoulam (Ed.), *Marijuana* (pp. 192–287). Orlando, FL: Academic Press.

Paul, S. M., Marangos, P. J., Goodwin, F. K., & Skolnick, P. (1980). Brain-specific benzodiazepine receptors and putative endogenous benzodiazepine-like compounds. *Biological Psychiatry, 15,* 407–428.

Paulozzi, L. J., Budnitz, D. S., & Xi, Y. (2006). Increasing deaths from opioid analgesics in the United States. *Pharmacoepidemiology and Drug Safety, 15,* 618–627.

Paulus, M. P., Hozack, N. E., Zauscher, B. E., Frank, L., Brown, G. G., Braff, D. L., et al. (2002). Behavioral and functional neuroimaging evidence for prefrontal dysfunction in methamphetamine-dependent subjects. *Neuropsychopharmacology, 26,* 53–63.

Pavlov, I. (1927). *Conditioned reflexes.* New York: Dover.

Pearson, T. A., & Terry, P. (1994). What to advise patients about drinking alcohol. *Journal of the American Medical Association, 272,* 967–968.

Peciña, S. (2008). Opioid reward 'liking' and 'wanting' in the nucleus accumbens. *Physiology & Behavior,* 675–680.

Pecina, S., & Berridge, K. C. (2005). Hedonic hot spot in nucleus accumbens shell: Where do mu-opioids cause increased hedonic impact of sweetness? *The Journal of Neuroscience: The Official Journal of the Society for Neuroscience, 25,* 11777–11786.

Peciña, S., Berridge, K. C., & Parker, L. A. (1997). Pimozide does not shift palatability: Separation of anhedonia from sensorimotor suppression by taste reactivity. *Pharmacology Biochemistry & Behavior, 58,* 801–811.

Peciña, S., Cagniard, B., Berridge, K. C., Aldridge, J. W., & Zhuang, X. (2003). Hyperdopaminergic mutant mice have higher "wanting" but not "liking" for sweet rewards. *The Journal of Neuroscience: The Official Journal of the Society for Neuroscience, 23,* 9395–9402.

Peck, J. D., Leviton, A., & Cowan, L. D. (2010). A review of the epidemiologic evidence concerning the reproductive health effects of caffeine consumption: A 2000–2009 update. *Food and Chemical Toxicology: An International Journal Published for the British Industrial Biological Research Association, 48,* 2549–2576.

Peluso, M. A., Glahn, D. C., Matsuo, K., Monkul, E. S., Najt, P., Zamarripa, F., et al. (2009). Amygdala hyperactivation in untreated depressed individuals. *Psychiatry Research, 173,* 158–161.

Perkins, K. A. (2009). Discriminative stimulus effects of nicotine in humans. *Handbook of Experimental Pharmacology, 192,* 369–400.

Perkins, K. A., Fonte, C., Blakesley-Ball, R., Stolinski, A., & Wilson, A. S. (2005). The influence of alcohol pre-treatment on the discriminative stimulus, subjective, and relative reinforcing effects of nicotine. *Behavioural Pharmacology, 16,* 521–529.

Perry, P. J., Argo, T. R., Barnett, M. J., Liesveld, J. L., Liskow, B., Hernan, J. M., et al. (2006). The association of alcohol-induced blackouts and grayouts to blood alcohol concentrations. *Journal of Forensic Sciences, 51,* 896–899.

Pertwee, R. G. (1992). In vivo interactions between psychotropic cannabinoids and other drugs involving central and peripheral neurochemical mediators. In L. Murphy & A. Bartke (Eds.), *Marijuana/cannabinoids: Neurobiology and neurophysiology* (pp. 165–218). Boca Raton, FL: CRC Press.

Peters, J. M. (1967). Caffeine-induced haemorrhagic automutilation. *Archives Internationales de Pharmacodynamie et de Therapie, 169,* 139–146.

Peters, R., Peters, J., Warner, J., Beckett, N., & Bulpitt, C. (2008). Alcohol, dementia and cognitive decline in the elderly: A systematic review. *Age and Ageing, 37,* 505–512.

Peterson, M. (2011). *Tobacco companies must get review by U.S. regulators for product changes.* New York: Bloomberg Press.

Petursson, H., & Lader, M. H. (1981). Withdrawal from long-term benzodiazepine treatment. *British Medical Journal, 283,* 643–645.

Pfaus, J. G., & Pinel, P. J. (1988). *Alcohol inhibits and disinhibits sexual behavior in the male rat.* Unpublished manuscript.

Phillips-Bute, B. G., & Lane, J. D. (1998). Caffeine withdrawal symptoms following brief caffeine deprivation. *Physiology and Behavior, 63,* 35–39.

Phillis, J. W., & O'Regan, M. H. (1988). The role of adenosine in the central actions of the benzodiazepines. *Progress in Neuro-Psychopharmacology and Biological Psychiatry, 12,* 384–404.

Pianezza, M., Sellers, E., & Tyndale, R. (1998). Nicotine metabolism defect reduces smoking. *Nature, 393,* 750.

Piazza, P. V., & Le Moal, M. (1998). The role of stress in drug self-administration. *Trends in Pharmacological Science, 19,* 67–74.

Pickens, R., & Thompson, T. (1968). Cocaine-reinforced behavior in rats: Effects of reinforcement magnitude and fixed-ratio size. *Journal of Pharmacology and Experimental Therapeutics, 161,* 122–129.

Pierce, I. H. (1941). Absorption of nicotine from cigarette smoke. *Journal of Laboratory and Clinical Medicine, 26,* 1322–1325.

Pierce, R. C., & Kalivas, P. W. (1997). A circuitry model of the expression of behavioral sensitization to amphetamine-like psychostimulants. *Brain Research: Brain Research Reviews, 25,* 192–216.

Pijlman, F. T., Rigter, S. M., Hoek, J., Goldschmidt, H. M., & Niesink, R. J. (2005). Strong increase in total delta-THC in cannabis preparations sold in dutch coffee shops. *Addiction Biology, 10,* 171–180.

Pinel, J. P. J. (2011). *Biopsychology* (8th ed.). Boston, MA: Pearson Education, Inc.

Pira, L., Mongeau, R., & Pani, L. (2004). The atypical antipsychotic quetiapine increases both noradrenaline and dopamine release in the rat prefrontal cortex. *European Journal of Pharmacology, 504,* 61–64.

Pirec, V., Coalson, D. W., Lichtor, J. L., Klafta, J., Young, C., Rupani, G., et al. (1995). Cold water immersion modulates the reinforcing effects of nitrous oxide in healthy volunteers. *Experimental and Clinical Pharmacology, 3,* 148–155.

Pirich, C., O'Grady, J., & Sinzinger, H. (1993). Coffee, lipoproteins and cardiovascular disease. *Weiner Klinische Wochenschrsft, 105,* 306.

Platt, D. M., & Bano, K. M. (2011). Opioid receptors and the discriminative stimulus effects of ethanol in squirrel monkeys: Mu and delta opioid receptor mechanisms. *European Journal of Pharmacology, 650,* 233–239.

Pomerleau, C. S., & Pomerleau, O. F. (1992). Euphoriant effects of nicotine in smokers. *Psychopharmacology, 108,* 460–465.

Pompéia, S., Gorenstein, C., & Curran, H. (1996). Benzodiazepine effects on memory tests: Dependence on retrieval cues? *International Clinical Psychopharmacology, 11,* 229–236.

Pompili, M., Serafini, G., Innamorati, M., Möller-Leimkühler, A. M., Giupponi, G., Girardi, P., et al. (2010). The hypothalamic-pituitary-adrenal axis and serotonin abnormalities: A selective overview for the implications of suicide prevention. *European Archives of Psychiatry and Clinical Neuroscience, 260,* 583–600.

Pope, H. G., Jr., Gruber, A. J., Hudson, J. I., Huestis, M. A., & Yurgelun-Todd, D. (2001). Neuropsychological performance in long-term cannabis users. *Archives of General Psychiatry, 58,* 909–915.

Popke, E. J., Mayorga, A. J., Fogle, C. M., & Paule, M. G. (2000). Effects of acute nicotine on several operant behaviors in rats. *Pharmacology, Biochemistry and Behavior, 65,* 247–254.

Porcu, P., & Grant, K. A. (2004). Discriminative stimulus effects of ethanol in rats using a three-choice ethanol-midazolam-water discrimination. *Behavioral Pharmacology, 15,* 555–567.

Porjesz, B., & Begleiter, H. (1987). Evoked brain potentials and alcoholism. In O. A. Parsons, N. Butters, & P. E. Nathan (Eds.), *Neuropsychology of alcoholism* (pp. 45–63). New York: Guilford Press.

Porsolt, R. D., Pawelec, C., & Jalfre, M. (1982). Use of a drug discrimination procedure to detect amphetamine-like effects of antidepressants. In F. C. Colpaert & J. L. Slangen (Eds.), *Drug discrimination: Applications in CNS pharmacology* (pp. 193–210). Amsterdam, NY: Elsevier Biomedical.

Post, R. M., Weiss, S. R. B., Pert, A., & Uhde, T. W. (1987). Chronic cocaine administration: Sensitization and kindling effects. In S. Fisher, A. Raskin, & E. H. Uhlenhuth (Eds.), *Cocaine: Clinical and behavioral aspects* (pp. 109–173). New York: Oxford University Press.

Poulos, C. X., & Cappell, H. (1991). Homeostatic theory of drug tolerance: A general model of physiological adaptation. *Psychological Review, 98,* 390–408.

Pradhan, S. N. (1970). Effects of nicotine on several schedules of behavior in rats. *Archives Internationale de Pharmacodynamie, 183,* 127–138.

Pravetoni, M., Keyler, D. E., Raleigh, M. D., Harris, A. C., Lesage, M. G., Mattson, C. K., et al. (2011). Vaccination against nicotine alters the distribution of nicotine delivered via cigarette smoke inhalation to rats. *Biochemical Pharmacology, 81,* 1164–1170.

Preskorn, S. H. (1993). Pharmacokinetics of antidepressants: Why and how they are relevant to treatment. *Journal of Clinical Psychiatry, 54*(Suppl. 9), 14–33.

Preston, K. L., Griffiths, R. R., Clone, E. J., Darwin, W. D., & Gorodetzky, C. W. (1986). Diazepam and methadone blood levels following concurrent administration of diazepam and methadone. *Alcohol and Drug Dependence, 18,* 195–202.

Price, D. D., Finniss, D. G., & Benedetti, F. (2008). A comprehensive review of the placebo effect: Recent advances and current thought. *Annual Review of Psychology, 59,* 565–590.

Price, R. K., Risk, N. K., & Spitznagel, E. L. (2001). Remission from drug abuse over a 25-year period: Patterns of remission and treatment use. *American Journal of Public Health, 91,* 1107–1113.

Primus, R. J., Thurkauf, A., Xu, J., Yevich, E., McInerney, S., Shaw, K., et al. (1997). II. Localization and characterization of dopamine D4 binding sites in rat and human brain by use of the novel, D4 receptor-selective ligand [3H] NGD 94-1. *Journal of Pharmacology and Experimental Therapy, 282,* 1020–1027.

Quickfall, J., & Crockford, D. (2006). Brain neuroimaging in cannabis use: A review. *The Journal of Neuropsychiatry and Clinical Neurosciences, 18,* 318–332.

Quinn, P. D., & Fromme, K. (2011). Subjective response to alcohol challenge: A quantitative review. *Alcoholism, Clinical and Experimental Research, 35,* 1759–1770.

Rabe, K. F., Hurd, S., Anzueto, A., Barnes, P. J., Buist, S. A., Calverley, P., et al. (2007). Global strategy for the diagnosis, management, and prevention of chronic obstructive pulmonary disease: GOLD executive summary. *American Journal of Respiratory and Critical Care Medicine, 176,* 532–555.

Ramaekers, J., Robbe, H., & O'Hanlon, J. (2000). Marijuana, alcohol and actual driving performance. *Human Psychopharmacology (Clinical and Experimental), 15,* 551–558.

Ramaekers, J. G., Kauert, G., van Ruitenbeek, P., Theunissen, E. L., Schneider, E., & Moeller, M. R. (2006). High-potency marijuana impairs executive function and inhibitory motor control. *Neuropsychopharmacology: Official Publication of the American College of Neuropsychopharmacology, 31,* 2296–2303.

Ramchandani, V. A., Kwo, P. Y., & Li, T. (2001). Effect of food and food composition on alcohol elimination in healthy men and women. *Journal of Clinical Pharmacology, 41,* 1345–1350.

Rasmussen, H., Erritzoe, D., Andersen, R., Ebdrup, B. H., Aggernaes, B., Oranje, B., et al. (2010). Decreased frontal serotonin 2A receptor binding in antipsychotic-naive patients with first-episode schizophrenia. *Archives of General Psychiatry, 67,* 9–16.

Ravina, B., Elm, J., Camicioli, R., Como, P. G., Marsh, L., Jankovic, J., et al. (2009). The course of depressive symptoms in early Parkinson's disease. *Movement Disorders: Official Journal of the Movement Disorder Society, 24,* 1306–1311.

Reed, J. (2010). "What is legal high mephedrone." *BBC Newsbeat.*

Rehm, J., & Sempos, C. T. (1995). Alcohol consumption and all-cause mortality. *Addiction, 90,* 471–480.

Reid, R. L. (1957). The role of the reinforcer as a stimulus. *British Journal of Psychology, 49,* 292–299.

Reinhold, J. A., Mandos, L. A., Rickels, K., & Lohoff, F. W. (2011). Pharmacological treatment of generalized anxiety disorder. *Expert Opinion on Pharmacotherapy, 12,* 2457–2467.

Reinisch, J. M., & Sanders, S. A. (1982). Early barbiturate exposure: The brain, sexually dimorphic behavior and learning. *Neuroscience and Biobehavioral Reviews, 6,* 311–319.

Rementiria, J. L., & Bhatt, K. (1977). Withdrawal symptoms in neonates from intrauterine exposure to diazepam. *Journal of Pediatrics, 90,* 123–126.

Remington, B., Roberts, P., & Glautier, S. (1997). The effect of drink familiarity on tolerance to alcohol. *Addictive Behaviors, 22,* 45–53.

Restak, R. (1993, September/October). Brain by design. *The Sciences,* 27–33.

Reynolds, K., Lewis, B., Nolen, J. D., Kinney, G. L., Sathya, B., & He, J. (2003). Alcohol consumption and risk of stroke: A meta-analysis. *The Journal of the American Medical Association, 289,* 579–588.

Rezvani A. H., & Levin, E. (2001). Cognitive effects of nicotine. *Biological Psychiatry, 49,* 258–267.

Richards, C. D. (1980). In search of the mechanisms of anesthesia. *Trends in Neuroscience, 3,* 9–13.

Richardson, J. D., Aanonsen, L., & Hargreaves, K. M. (1998). Hypoactivity of the spinal cannabinoid system results in NMDA-dependent hyperalgesia. *Journal of Neuroscience, 18,* 451–457.

Richardson, N. J., Rogers, P. J., Elliman, N. A., & O'Dell, R. J. (1995). Mood and performance effects of caffeine in relation to acute and chronic caffeine deprivation. *Pharmacology, Biochemistry and Behavior, 52,* 313–320.

Richelson, E. (2001). Pharmacology of antidepressants. *Mayo Clinic Proceedings, 76,* 511–527.

Richey, S. M., & Krystal, A. D. (2011). Pharmacological advances in the treatment of insomnia. *Current Pharmaceutical Design, 17,* 1471–1475.

Rickels, K. (1983). Benzodiazepines in emotional disorders. *Journal of Psychoactive Drugs, 15,* 49–54.

Rickels, K., Downing, R. W., & Winokur, A. (1978). Antianxiety drugs: Clinical use in psychiatry. In L. L. Iverson, S. D. Iverson, & H. S. Snyder (Eds.), *Handbook of psychopharmacology* (Vol. 13, pp. 395–430). New York: Plenum Press.

Riedel, W. J., Klaassen, T., & Schmitt, J. A. (2002). Tryptophan, mood, and cognitive function. *Brain, Behavior, and Immunity, 16,* 581–589.

Riley, E. P., Infante, M. A., & Warren, K. R. (2011). Fetal alcohol spectrum disorders: An overview. *Neuropsychology Review, 21,* 73–80.

Ritchie, M. J. (1975). The xanthines. In L. S. Goodman & A. Gillman (Eds.), *The pharmacological basis of therapeutics* (pp. 367–378). London: Collier-Macmillan.

Roache, J. D., & Griffiths, R. R. (1987). Lorazepam and meprobamate dose effects in humans: Behavioral effects and abuse liability. *Journal of Pharmacology and Experimental Therapeutics, 243,* 978–988.

Robert, J. C. (1967). *The story of tobacco in America.* Chapel Hill, NC: University of North Carolina Press.

Roberts, D. C., Brebner, K., Vincler, M., & Lynch, W. J. (2002). Patterns of cocaine self-administration in rats produced by various access conditions under a discrete trials procedure. *Drug and Alcohol Dependence, 67,* 291–299.

Roberts, D. C., Morgan, D., & Liu, Y. (2007). How to make a rat addicted to cocaine. *Progress in Neuro-Psychopharmacology & Biological Psychiatryis, 31,* 1614–1624.

Robinson, D. (1977). Factors influencing alcohol consumption. In G. Edwards & M. Grant (Eds.), *Alcoholism: New knowledge and new responses* (pp. 60–77). London: Croom Helm.

Robinson, S., Sandstrom, S. M., Denenberg, V. H., & Palmiter, R. D. (2005). Distinguishing whether dopamine regulates liking, wanting, and/or learning about rewards. *Behavioral Neuroscience, 119,* 5–15.

Robinson, T. E., & Berridge, K. C. (1993). The neural basis of drug craving: An incentive-sensitization theory of drug addiction. *Brain Research Reviews, 18,* 274–291.

Robinson, T. E., & Berridge, K. C. (2000). The psychology and neurobiology of addiction: An incentive-sensitization view. *Addiction, 95,* S91–S117.

Robinson, T. E., & Berridge, K. C. (2008). Review. The incentive sensitization theory of addiction: Some current issues. *Philosophical Transactions of the Royal Society of London. Series B, Biological Sciences, 363,* 3137–3146.

Rocha, B. A., Ward, A. S., Egilmez, Y., Lutle, U., & Emmett-Ogelsby, M. (1996). Tolerance to the discriminative stimulus and reinforcing effects of ketamine. *Behavioural Pharmacology, 7,* 160–168.

Rodgers, R. J., Holch, P., & Tallett, A. J. (2010). Behavioural satiety sequence (BSS): Separating wheat from chaff in the behavioural pharmacology of appetite. *Pharmacology, Biochemistry and Behavior, 97,* 3–14.

Rodríguez de Fonseca, F., Carrera, M. R. A., Navarro, M., Koob, G. F., & Weiss, F. (1997). Activation of corticotropin-releasing factor in the limbic system during cannabinoid withdrawal. *Science, 276,* 2050–2054.

Roffman, M., & Lal, H. (1972). Role of brain amines in learning association with "amphetamine state." *Psychopharmacology, 25,* 196–204.

Rogers, G., Elston, J., Garside, R., Roome, C., Taylor, R., Younger, P., et al. (2009). The harmful health effects of recreational ecstasy: A systematic review of observational evidence. *Health Technology Assessment (Winchester, England), 13,* iii–iv, ix–xii, 1–315.

Rogers, P. J., & Dernoncourt, C. (1998). Regular coffee consumption: A balance of adverse effects and beneficial effects for mood and psychomotor performance. *Pharmacology, Biochemistry and Behavior, 59,* 1039–1045.

Rogers, P. J., Heatherley, S. V., Hayward, R. C., Seers, H. E., Hill, J., & Kane, M. (2005). Effects of caffeine and caffeine withdrawal on mood and cognitive performance degraded by sleep restriction. *Psychopharmacology, 179,* 742–751.

Rogers, R. D., Moeller, F. G., Swann, A. C., & Clark, L. (2010). Recent research on impulsivity in individuals with drug use and mental health disorders: Implications for alcoholism. *Alcoholism, Clinical and Experimental Research, 34,* 1319–1333.

Rojas, P. S., Fritsch, R., Rojas, R. A., Jara, P., & Fiedler, J. L. (2011). Serum brain-derived neurotrophic factor and glucocorticoid receptor levels in lymphocytes as markers of antidepressant response in major depressive patients: A pilot study. *Psychiatry Research, 189,* 239–245.

Romeo, J., Warnberg, J., Nova, E., Diaz, L. E., Gomez-Martinez, S., & Marcos, A. (2007). Moderate alcohol consumption and the immune system: A review. *The British Journal of Nutrition, 98*(Suppl. 1), S111–S115.

Room, R. (1983). Sociological aspects of the disease concept of alcoholism. In R. G. Smart, F. B. Glassier, Y. Israel, H. Kalant, R. E. Popham, & W. Schmidt (Eds.), *Research advances in alcoholism and drug problems* (Vol. 7, pp. 47–91). New York: Plenum Press.

Rorabaugh, W. J. (1979). *The alcoholic republic.* New York: Oxford University Press.

Rose, J. E. (2006). Nicotine and nonnicotine factors in cigarette addiction. *Psychopharmacology, 184,* 274–285.

Rose, J. E., Mukhin, A. G., Lokitz, S. J., Turkington, T. G., Herskovic, J., Behm, F. M., et al. (2010). Kinetics of brain nicotine accumulation in dependent and nondependent smokers assessed with PET and cigarettes containing 11C-nicotine. *Proceedings of the National Academy of Sciences of the United States of America, 107,* 5190–5195.

Rose, J. S., Branchey, M., Buydens-Branchey, L., Stapleton, J. M., Chasen, K., Werrell, A., et al. (1996). Cerebral perfusion in early and late opiate withdrawal: A technetium-99m-HMPAO SPECT study. *Psychiatry Research: Neuroimaging, 67,* 39–47.

Rose, M. E., & Grant, J. E. (2008). Pharmacotherapy for methamphetamine dependence: A review of the pathophysiology of methamphetamine addiction and the theoretical basis and efficacy of pharmacotherapeutic interventions. *Annals of Clinical Psychiatry: Official Journal of the American Academy of Clinical Psychiatrists, 20,* 145–155.

Rosner, S., Hackl-Herrwerth, A., Leucht, S., Lehert, P., Vecchi, S., & Soyka, M. (2010). Acamprosate for alcohol dependence. *Cochrane Database of Systematic Reviews (Online),* CD004332.

Rossi, A. M., Babor, T. F., Meyer, R. E., & Mendelson, J. H. (1974). Mood states. In J. H. Mendelson, A. M. Rossi, & R. E. Meyer (Eds.), *The use of marijuana: A psychological and physiological inquiry* (pp. 115–133). New York: Plenum Press.

Rossi, A. M., Kuehnle, J. C., & Mendelson, J. H. (1978). Marijuana and mood in human volunteers. *Pharmacology, Biochemistry and Behavior, 8,* 447–453.

Rossi, S., De Chiara, V., Musella, A., Mataluni, G., Sacchetti, L., Siracusano, A., et al. (2010). Effects of caffeine on striatal neurotransmission: Focus on cannabinoid CB1 receptors. *Molecular Nutrition & Food Research, 54,* 525–531.

Rothman, K., & Keller, A. (1972). The effects of a joint exposure to alcohol and tobacco on risk of cancer of the mouth and pharynx. *Journal of Chronic Diseases, 25,* 711–716.

Rothman, R. B., & Baumann, M. H. (2003). Monoamine transporters and psychostimulant drugs. *European Journal of Pharmacology, 479,* 23–40.

Rothschild, A. J., & Locke, C. A. (1991). Reexposure to fluoxetine after serious suicidal attempts by three patients: The role of akathesia. *Journal of Clinical Psychiatry, 52,* 491–493.

Rowlett, J. K., & Lelas, S. (2007). Comparison of zolpidem and midazolam self-administration under progressive-ratio schedules: Consumer demand and labor supply analyses. *Experimental and Clinical Psychopharmacology, 15,* 328–337.

Rowlett, J. K., Massey, B. W., Kleven, M. S., & Woolverton, W. L. (1996). Parametric analysis of cocaine self-administration under a progressive ratio schedule in rhesus monkeys. *Psychopharmacology, 125,* 361–370.

Rowlett, J. K., Platt, D. M., Lelas, S., Atack, J. R., & Dawson, G. R. (2005). Different GABAA receptor subtypes mediate the anxiolytic, abuse-related, and motor effects of benzodiazepine-like drugs in primates. *Proceedings of the National Academy of Sciences of the United States of America, 102*, 915–920.

Rubin, H. B., & Henson, D. B. (1976). Effects of alcohol on male sexual responding. *Psychopharmacologia, 47*, 123–134.

Rubinstein, M. L., Benowitz, N. L., Auerback, G. M., & Moscicki, A. B. (2008). Rate of nicotine metabolism and withdrawal symptoms in adolescent light smokers. *Pediatrics, 122*, e643–7.

Rudgley, R. (1995). The archaic use of hallucinogens in Europe: An archaeology of altered states. *Addiction, 90*, 63–64.

Rudolph, U., & Knoflach, F. (2011). Beyond classical benzodiazepines: Novel therapeutic potential of GABAA receptor subtypes. *Nature Reviews. Drug Discovery, 10*, 685–697.

Rudorfer, M. V., & Potter, W. Z. (1987). Pharmacokinetics of antidepressants. In H. Y. Meltzer (Ed.), *Psychopharmacology: A third generation of progress* (pp. 1353–1363). New York: Raven Press.

Rumbaugh, C. L., Bergeron, C. L., Fang, H. C., & McCormick, R. (1971). Cerebral anginographic changes in the drug abuse patient. *Radiology, 101*, 335–344.

Rush, A. J., & Ryan, N. D. (2002). Current and emerging therapeutics for depression. In K. Davis, D. Charney, J. Coyle, & C. Nemeroff (Eds.), *Neuropsychopharmacology: The fifth generation of progress* (pp. 1082–1096). New York: Raven Press.

Rush, C. (1998). Behavioral pharmacology of zolpidem relative to benzodiazepines: A review. *Pharmacology, Biochemistry and Behavior, 61*, 253–269.

Rush, C. R., Sullivan, J. T., & Griffiths, R. R. (1995). Intravenous caffeine in stimulant drug abusers: Subjective reports and physiological effects. *Journal of Pharmacology and Experimental Therapeutics, 273*, 351–358.

Russell, C. S., Taylor, R., & Law, C. E. (1968). Smoking in pregnancy: Maternal blood pressure, pregnancy outcome, baby weight and growth, and other related factors. *British Journal of Preventive Social Medicine, 22*, 119.

Russell, M. A. H. (1976). Tobacco smoking and nicotine dependence. In R. J. Gibbins, Y. Israel, H. Kalant, R. E. Popham, W. Schmidt, & R. G. Smart (Eds.), *Research advances in alcohol and drug problems* (Vol. 1, pp. 1–48). New York: Wiley.

Russo, E. B., Guy, G. W., & Robson, P. J. (2007). Cannabis, pain, and sleep: Lessons from therapeutic clinical trials of sativex, a cannabis-based medicine. *Chemistry & Biodiversity, 4*, 1729–1743.

Ryback, R. S. (1970). Alcohol amnesia: Observations in seven drinking inpatient alcoholics. *Quarterly Journal of Studies on Alcohol, 31*, 616–632.

Rylander, G. (1969). Clinical and medico-criminological aspects of addiction to central stimulating drugs. In F. Sjoquist & M. Tottie (Eds.), *Abuse of central stimulants* (pp. 251–274). Stockholm: Almqvist & Wiksell.

Ryu, S., Choi, S. K., Joung, S. S., Stjh, H., Cha, Y. S., Lee, S., et al. (2001). Caffeine as a lipolytic food component increases endurance performance in rats and athletes. *Journal of Nutritional Science and Vitaminology, 47*, 139–147.

Saal, D., Dong, Y., Bonci, A., & Malenka, R. C. (2003). Drugs of abuse and stress trigger a common synaptic adaptation in dopamine neurons. *Neuron, 37*, 577–582.

Saario, I., & Linnoila, M. (1976). Effects of subacute treatment with hypnotics, alone and combination with alcohol, on psychomotor skills related to driving. *Acta Pharmacologica et Toxicologica, 38*, 382–392.

Salamone, J. D., Correa, M., Mingote, S. M., & Weber, S. M. (2005). Beyond the reward hypothesis: Alternative functions of nucleus accumbens dopamine. *Current Opinion in Pharmacology, 5*, 34–41.

Samson, H. H. (1987). Initiation of ethanol-maintained behavior: A comparison of animal models and their implication to human drinking. In T. Thompson, P. B. Dews, & J. E. Barrett (Eds.), *Advances in behavioral pharmacology: Vol. 6. Neurobehavioral pharmacology* (pp. 221–248). Hillsdale, NJ: Erlbaum.

Sanchis-Segura, C., & Spanagel, R. (2006). Behavioural assessment of drug reinforcement and addictive features in rodents: An overview. *Addiction Biology, 11*, 2–38.

Sandridge, J., Zylstra, R., & Adams, S. (2004). Alcohol consumption: An overview of benefits and risks. *Southern Medical Journal, 97*, 664–672.

Sanna, E., & Harris, A. (1993). Neuronal ion channels. In M. Galanter (Ed.), *Recent developments in alcoholism* (Vol. 11, pp. 169–186). New York: Plenum Press.

Santhakumar, V., Wallner, M., & Otis, T. S. (2007). Ethanol acts directly on extrasynaptic subtypes of GABAA. *Alcohol, 41*, 211–221.

Sasco, A. J., Secretan, M. B., & Straif, K. (2004). Tobacco smoking and cancer: A brief review of recent epidemiological evidence. *Lung Cancer (Amsterdam, Netherlands), 45*(Suppl. 2), S3–S9.

Schechter, M. (1998). Rohypnol ("roofies") control of drug discrimination: Effect of coadministered ethanol or flumenazil. *Pharmacology, Biochemistry and Behavior, 59*, 19–25.

Schechter, M. D., & Glennon, R. A. (1985). Cathinone, cocaine and methamphetamine: Similarity of behavior effects. *Pharmacology, Biochemistry and Behavior, 22*, 913–916.

Schiffman, J., Sorensen, H. J., Maeda, J., Mortensen, E. L., Victoroff, J., Hayashi, K., et al. (2009). Childhood motor coordination and adult schizophrenia spectrum disorders. *The American Journal of Psychiatry, 166*, 1041–1047.

Schiffman, J., Walker, E., Ekstrom, M., Schulsinger, F., Sorensen, H., & Mednick, S. (2004). Childhood video-taped social and neuromotor precursors of schizophrenia: A prospective investigation. *The American Journal of Psychiatry, 161*, 2021–2027.

Schmauss, C., & Yaksh, T. L. (1984). In vivo studies on spinal opiate receptor systems mediating antinociception: II. Pharmacological profiles suggesting a differential association of mu, delta and kappa receptors with visceral chemical and cutaneous thermal stimuli in the rat. *Journal of Pharmacology and Experimental Therapeutics, 228*, 1–12.

Schmidt, C. J. (1987). Psychedelic amphetamine, methylendioxymethamphetamine. *Journal of Pharmacology and Experimental Therapeutics, 240*, 1–7.

Schmidt, M. D., Schmidt, M. S., Butelman, E. R., Harding, W. W., Tidgewell, K., Murry, D. J., et al. (2005). Pharmacokinetics of the plant-derived kappa-opioid hallucinogen salvinorin A in nonhuman primates. *Synapse (New York, N.Y.), 58*, 208–210.

Schmiterlow, C., & Hanson, E. (1965). The distribution of C-14 nicotine. In E. S. Von Euler (Ed.), *Tobacco alkaloids and related compounds* (pp. 75–86). New York: Macmillan.

Schneier, F. R. (2011). Pharmacotherapy of social anxiety disorder. *Expert Opinion on Pharmacotherapy, 12*, 615–625.

Schörring, E., & Hecht, A. (1979). Behavioral effects of low, acute doses of morphine in nontolerant groups of rats in an open-field test. *Psychopharmacology, 64*, 67–71.

Schottenfield, R., Parkes, J., O'Conner, P., Chewarski, M., Oliveto, A., & Kostenet, T. (2000). Thrice weekly versus daily buprenorphine maintenance. *Biological Psychiatry, 47*, 1072–1079.

Schuckit, M. A. (1987). Biology of risk for alcoholism. In H. Y. Meltzer (Ed.), *Psychopharmacology: The third generation of progress* (pp. 1527–1533). New York: Raven Press.

Schuckit, M. A. (1992). Advances in understanding the vulnerability to alcoholism. In C. E. O'Brien & J. H. Jaffe (Eds.), *Addictive states* (pp. 93–108). New York: Raven Press.

Schuckit, M. A. (2009). An overview of genetic influences in alcoholism. *Journal of Substance Abuse Treatment, 36*, S5–S14.

Schultes, R. E. (1987). Coca and other psychoactive plants: Magico-religious roles in primitive societies of the world. In S. Fisher, A. Raskin, & E. H. Uhlenhuth (Eds.), *Cocaine: Clinical and behavioral aspects* (pp. 212–250). New York: Oxford University Press.

Schultz, W., Dayan, P., & Montague, P. R. (1997). A neural substrate of prediction and reward. *Science (New York, N.Y.), 275*, 1593–1599.

Schuster, C. R. (1970). Psychological approaches to opiate dependence and self-administration by laboratory animals. *Federation Proceedings, 29*, 1–5.

Schuster, C. R. (2004). Conversation with Charles R. Schuster. *Addiction (Abingdon, England), 99*, 667–676.

Schuster, C. R., Dockens, W. S., & Woods, J. H. (1966). Behavioral variables affecting the development of amphetamine tolerance. *Psychopharmacologia, 9*, 170–182.

Schuster, R. M., & Thompson, T. (1969). Self-administration and behavioral dependence on drugs. *Annual Review of Pharmacology, 9*, 483–502.

Schwartz, J. (1994, June 27–July 3). Smoking under siege. *Washington Post* (National Weekly Edition) pp. 6–9.

Schweizer, T. A., & Vogel-Sprott, M. (2008). Alcohol-impaired speed and accuracy of cognitive functions: A review of acute tolerance and recovery of cognitive performance. *Experimental and Clinical Psychopharmacology, 16*, 240–250.

Science News. (1992). And you thought you hated mornings. *Science News, 141*, 28.

Scott, C. C., & Chen, K. K. (1944). Comparison of the action of l-thyl theobromine and caffeine in animals and man. *Journal of Pharmacology and Experimental Therapeutics, 82*, 89–97.

Scott, J. C., Woods, S. P., Matt, G. E., Meyer, R. A., Heaton, R. K., Atkinson, J. H., et al. (2007). Neurocognitive effects of methamphetamine: A critical review and meta-analysis. *Neuropsychology Review, 17*, 275–297.

Searles, J. S. (1988). The role of genetics in the pathogenesis of alcoholism. *Journal of Abnormal Behavior, 97*, 153–167.

Seeman, P. (2002). Atypical antipsychotics: Mechanism of action. *Canadian Journal of Psychiatry, 47*, 27–38.

Seeman, P., Guan, H. C., & Hirbec, H. (2009). Dopamine D2high receptors stimulated by phencyclidines, lysergic acid diethylamide, salvinorin A, and modafinil. *Synapse (New York, N.Y.), 63*, 698–704.

Seeman, P., Lee, T., Chau-Wong, M., & Wong, K. (1976). Antipsychotic drug dose and neuroleptic/dopamine receptors. *Nature, 261*, 717–718.

Seiden, L. S., & Dykstra, L. A. (1977). *Psychopharmacology: A biochemical and behavioral approach.* New York: Van Nostrand-Reinhold.

Seifert, S. M., Schaechter, J. L., Hershorin, E. R., & Lipshultz, S. E. (2011). Health effects of energy drinks on children, adolescents, and young adults. *Pediatrics, 127*, 511–528.

Sellers, E. M., Ciraulo, D. A., DuPont, R. L., Griffiths, R. R., Kosten, T. R., Romach, M. K., et al. (1993). Alprazolam and benzodiazepine dependence. *Journal of Clinical Psychiatry, 54*(Suppl.), 64–75.

Sevak, R. J., Stoops, W. W., Hays, L. R., & Rush, C. R. (2009). Discriminative stimulus and subject-rated effects of methamphetamine, d-amphetamine, methylphenidate, and triazolam in methamphetamine-trained humans. *Journal of Pharmacology and Experimental Therapeutics, 328*, 1007–1018.

Sharpley, C. F. (2010). A review of the neurobiological effects of psychotherapy for depression. *Psychotherapy (Chic), 47,* 603–615.

Sheehan, J. J., Sliwa, J. K., Amatniek, J. C., Grinspan, A., & Canuso, C. M. (2010). Atypical antipsychotic metabolism and excretion. *Current Drug Metabolism, 11,* 516–525.

Shiono, P. H., Klebanoff, M. A., Nugent, R. P., Cotch, M. F., Wilkins, D. E., & Rollins, D. E. (1995). The impact of cocaine and marijuana use and low birthweight and preterm birth: A multicenter study. *American Journal of Obstetrics and Gynecology, 172,* 19–27.

Shiovitz, T. M., Welke, T. L., Tigel, P. D., Anand, R., Hartman, R. D., Sramek, J. J., et al. (1996). Cholinergic rebound and rapid onset psychosis following abrupt clozapine withdrawal. *Schizophrenia Bulletin, 22,* 591–595.

Shirani, A., Paradiso, S., & Dyken, M. E. (2011). The impact of atypical antipsychotic use on obstructive sleep apnea: A pilot study and literature review. *Sleep Medicine, 12,* 591–597.

Shoptaw, S. J., Kao, U., Heinzerling, K., & Ling, W. (2009). Treatment for amphetamine withdrawal. *Cochrane Database of Systematic Reviews Online, 15,* CD003021.

Siegel, R. K. (1977). Hallucinations. *Scientific American, 237,* 132–140.

Siegel, R. K. (1982). Cocaine and sexual dysfunction: The curse of Mama Coca. *Journal of Psychoactive Drugs, 14,* 71–74.

Siegel, R. K. (1986). MDMA: Medical use and intoxication. *Journal of Psychoactive Drugs, 18,* 349–353.

Siegel, R. K., & Jarvik, M. E. (1975). Drug-induced hallucinations in animals and man. In R. K. Siegel & L. J. West (Eds.), *Hallucinations: Behavior, experience, and theory* (pp. 81–162). New York: Wiley.

Siegel, S. (1975). Evidence from rats that morphine tolerance is a learned response. *Journal of Comparative and Physiological Psychology, 89,* 489–506.

Siegel, S. (1983). Classical conditioning, drug tolerance and drug dependence. In Y. Israel, F. B. Graser, H. Kalant, W. Popham, W. Schmidt, & R. G. Smart (Eds.), *Research advances in alcohol and drug problems* (Vol. 7). New York: Plenum Press.

Siegel, S., Hinson, R. E., Krank, M. D., & McCully, J. (1982). Heroin "overdose" death: Contribution of drug-associated environmental cues. *Science, 216,* 436–437.

Siemens, A. J., Kalant, H., & deNie, J. C. (1976). Metabolic interactions between delta-9-tetrahydrocannabinol and other cannabinoids in rats. In M. C. Braude & S. Szara (Eds.), *Pharmacology of marijuana* (Vol. 1, pp. 77–92). Orlando, FL: Academic Press.

Sienkiewicz-Jarosz, H., Scinska, A., Kuran, W., Ryglewicz, D., Rogowski, A., Wrobel, E., et al. (2005). Taste responses in patients with Parkinson's disease. *Journal of Neurology, Neurosurgery, and Psychiatry, 76,* 40–46.

Silber, B. Y., Papafotiou, K., Croft, R. J., Ogden, E., Swann, P., & Stough, C. (2005). The effects of dexamphetamine on simulated driving performance. *Psychopharmacology, 179,* 536–543.

Silkker, W., Jr., Paule, M. G., Ali, S. F., Scarlett, A. C., & Bailey, J. R. (1992). Behavioral, neurochemical and neurophysiological effects of chronic marijuana smoke on the nonhuman primate. In L. Murphy & A. Bartke (Eds.), *Marijuana/ cannabinoids neurology and neurophysiology* (pp. 219–274). Boca Raton, FL: CRC Press.

Silverman, K., Kirby, K. C., & Griffiths, R. R. (1994). Modulation of drug reinforcement by behavioral requirements following drug ingestion. *Psychopharmacology, 114,* 243–247.

Silverman, K., Mumford, G. K., & Griffiths, R. R. (1994). Enhancing caffeine reinforcement by behavioral requirements following drug ingestion. *Psychopharmacology, 114,* 424–432.

Silverman, P. B., & Bonate, P. L. (1997). Role of conditioned stimuli in addiction. In B. A. Johnson & J. D. Roache (Eds.), *Drug addiction and treatment: Nexus of neuroscience and behavior* (pp. 115–133). Philadelphia, PA: Lippincott-Raven Press.

Simon, E. J. (1981). Opiate receptors and endorphins: Possible relevance to narcotic addiction. *Advances in Alcohol and Substance Abuse, 1,* 13–31.

Simonson, E., & Brozek, J. (1952). Flicker fusion frequency. *Physiological Review, 32,* 349–378.

Simpson, G. M., & Singh, H. (1990). Tricyclic antidepressants. In J. D. Amsterdam (Ed.), *Pharmacotherapy of depression* (pp. 75–91). New York: Marcel Dekker.

Singletary, K. W., & Gapstur, S. M. (2001). Alcohol and breast cancer. *Journal of the American Medical Association, 286,* 2143–2151.

Sircar, R., Wu, L. C., Reddy, K., Sircar, D., & Basak, A. K. (2011). GHB-induced cognitive deficits during adolescence and the role of NMDA receptor. *Current Neuropharmacology, 9,* 240–243.

Skopp, G., Richter, B., & Pötsch, L. (2003). Serum cannabinoid levels 24 to 48 hours after cannabis smoking. [Cannabinoidbefunde im Serum 24 bis 48 Stunden nach Rauchkonsum]. *Archiv Fur Kriminologie, 212,* 83–95.

Skosnik, P. D., Krishnan, G. P., Vohs, J. L., & O'Donnell, B. F. (2006). The effect of cannabis use and gender on the visual steady state evoked potential. *Clinical Neurophysiology: Official Journal of the International Federation of Clinical Neurophysiology, 117,* 144–156.

Small, E. (1979). *The species problem in cannabis.* Toronto, ON: Corpus.

Smith, A. (2009). Effects of caffeine in chewing gum on mood and attention. *Human Psychopharmacology, 24,* 239–247.

Smith, C. G. (1964). Effects of d-amphetamine upon operant behavior of pigeons: Enhancement of reserpine. *Journal of Pharmacology and Experimental Therapeutics, 146*, 167–174.

Smith, D. (1998). Review of the American Medical Association Council on Scientific Affairs report on medical marijuana. *Journal of Psychoactive Drugs, 30*, 127–136.

Smith, D. E., & Wesson, D. R. (1983). Benzodiazepine dependency syndromes. *Journal of Psychoactive Drugs, 15*, 85–96.

Smith, D. E., Buxton, M. E., & Dammann, G. (1979). Amphetamine abuse and sexual dysfunction: Clinical and research considerations. In D. R. Smith (Ed.), *Amphetamine use, misuse and abuse* (pp. 228–248). Boca Raton, FL: CRC Press.

Smith, G. M., & Beecher, H. K. (1959). Amphetamine sulfate and athletic performance. *Journal of the American Medical Association, 170*, 542.

Smith-Kielland, A., Skuterud, B., & Mørland, J. (1999). Urinary excretion of 11-nor-9-carboxy-Δ9-tetrahydrocannabinol and cannabinoids in frequent and infrequent users. *Journal of Analytical Toxicology, 23*, 323–332.

Smucker-Barnwell, S. S., Earleywine, M., & Wilcox, R. (2006). Cannabis, motivation, and life satisfaction in an internet sample. *Substance Abuse Treatment, Prevention, and Policy, 1*, 2.

Smyth, B., Hoffman, V., Fan, J., & Hser, Y. I. (2007). Years of potential life lost among heroin addicts 33 years after treatment. *Preventive Medicine, 44*, 369–374.

Sneader, W. (1985). *Drug discovery: The evolution of modern medicines.* Chichester, England: Wiley.

Snyder, S. H. (1977). Opiate receptors and internal opiates. *Scientific American, 236*, 44–56.

Snyder, S. H. (1984). Adenosine as a mediator of the behavioral effects of caffeine. In P. B. Dews (Ed.), *Caffeine: Perspectives from recent research* (pp. 129–141). Berlin: Springer-Verlag.

Snyder, S. H. (1986). *Drugs and the brain.* New York: Scientific American Library.

Soares, S. R., & Melo, M. A. (2008). Cigarette smoking and reproductive function. *Curr Opin Obstet Gynecol, 20*, 281–291.

Society for Neuroscience; website of booklet: http://www.sfn.org/skins/main/pdf/brainfacts/2008/brain_facts.pdf. Illustration can be found on page 7 of booklet.

Sofia, R. D. (1978). Cannabis: Structure-activity relationships. In L. L. Iverson, S. D. Iverson, & S. H. Snyder (Eds.), *Handbook of psychopharmacology* (Vol. 12, pp. 319–371). New York: Plenum Press.

Soldatos, C., Dikeos, D., & Whitehead, A. (1999). Tolerance and rebound insomnia with rapidly eliminated hypnotics: A meta-analysis of sleep laboratory studies. *International Clinical Psychopharmacology, 14*, 287–303.

Solinas, M., Ferre, S., Antoniou, K., Quarta, D., Justinova, Z., Hockemeyer, J., et al. (2005). Involvement of adenosine A1 receptors in the discriminative-stimulus effects of caffeine in rats. *Psychopharmacology, 179*, 576–586.

Solomon, D. (1966). *The marijuana papers.* Indianapolis, IN: Bobbs-Merrill.

Solomon, R. L., & Corbit, J. D. (1974). An opponent-process theory of motivation: I. Temporal dynamics of affect. *Psychological Review, 81*, 119–145.

Spear, L. P. (1997). Neurobehavioral abnormalities following exposure to drugs of abuse during development. In B. A. Johnson & J. D. Roache (Eds.), *Drug addiction and its treatment: The nexus of neuroscience and behavior* (pp. 233–255). Philadelphia, PA: Lippincott-Raven Press.

Spiegel, R., & Aebi, H. J. (1981). *Psychopharmacology: An introduction.* Chichester, England: Wiley.

Spiga, R., & Roache, J. D. (1997). Human drug self-administration: A review and methodological critique. In B. A. Johnson & J. D. Roache (Eds.), *Drug addiction and treatment: Nexus of neuroscience and behavior* (pp. 39–71). Philadelphia, PA: Lippincott-Raven Press.

Spitzer, W. O., Lawrence, V., Dales, R., Gill, G., Archer, M. C., Clarke, P., et al. (1990). Links between passive smoking and disease: A best evidence synthesis. *Clinical and Investigative Medicine, 13*, 17–42.

Sporer, K. (1999). Acute heroin overdose. *Annals of Internal Medicine, 130*, 584–590.

Sporer, K. (2003). Strategies for preventing heroin overdose. *British Medical Journal, 22*, 442–444.

Squires, R. F., & Braestrup, C. (1977). Benzodiazepine receptors in the brain. *Nature, 266*, 732–734.

Sramek, J. J., & Pi, E. H. (1996). Ethnicity and antidepressant response. *Mount Sinai Journal of Medicine, 63*, 320–325.

Sridhar, K. S., Ruab, W. A., Weatherby, N. L., Metsch, L. R., Jurratt, H. L., Inciardi, J. A., et al. (1994). Possible role of marijuana smoking as a carcinogen in development of lung cancer at a young age. *Journal of Psychoactive Drugs, 26*, 285–288.

Srisurapanont, M., Arunpongpaisal, S., Wada, K., Marsden, J., Ali, R., & Kongsakon, R. (2011). Comparisons of methamphetamine psychotic and schizophrenic symptoms: A differential item functioning analysis. *Progress in Neuro-Psychopharmacology & Biological Psychiatry, 35*, 959–964.

Starmer, G. A. (1990). Alcohol and car driving: Impairment and per se limits for drivers. In I. Hindmarch & P. D. Stonier (Eds.), *Human psychopharmacology: Measures and methods* (Vol. 3, pp. 183–201). Chichester, England: Wiley Ltd.

Stavric, B., & Gilbert, S. G. (1990). Caffeine metabolism: A problem in extrapolating results from animal studies to humans. *Acta Pharmacologica Jugoslavica, 40*, 475–489.

Stephenson, F. A. (1987). Benzodiazepines in the brain. *Trends in Neuroscience, 10*, 185–186.

Sternback, L. H. (1973). Chemistry of the 1,4-benzodiazepines and some aspects of the structure-activity relationship. In S. Garattini, E. Mussini, & L. O. Randall (Eds.), *The benzodiazepines* (pp. 1–26). New York: Raven Press.

Stevenson, G. W., Folk, J. E., Rice, K. C., & Negus, S. S. (2005). Interactions between delta and mu opioid agonists in assays of schedule-controlled responding, thermal nociception, drug self-administration, and drug versus food choice in rhesus monkeys: Studies with SNC80 [(+)-4-[(alphaR)-alpha-((2S,5R)-4-allyl-2,5-dimethyl-1-piperazinyl)-3-methoxybenzyl]-N,N-diethylbenzamide] and heroin. *Journal of Pharmacology and Experimental Therapeutics, 314,* 221–231.

Stewart, B. S., Lamaire, G. A., Roche, J. D., & Meisch, R. A. (1994). Establishing benzodiazepines as oral reinforcers: Midazolam and diazepam self-administration in rhesus monkeys. *Journal of Pharmacology and Experimental Therapeutics, 271,* 200–211.

Stewart, J. (1962). Differential responses based on the physiological consequences of pharmacological agents. *Psychopharmacologia, 3,* 132–138.

Stewart, J., & Badiani, A. (1993). Tolerance and sensitization to the behavioral effects of drugs. *Behavioral Pharmacology, 4,* 289–312.

Stewart, J., & de Wit, H. (1987). Reinstatement of drug-taking behavior as a method of assessing incentive motivational properties of drugs. In M. A. Bozarth (Ed.), *Methods of assessing the reinforcing properties of abused drugs* (pp. 211–227). New York: Springer-Verlag.

Stewart, R., Besset, A., Bebbington, P., Brugha, T., Lindesay, J., Jenkins, R., et al. (2006). Insomnia comorbidity and impact and hypnotic use by age group in a national survey population aged 16 to 74 years. *Sleep, 29,* 1391–1397.

Stillman, R., Eich, J. E., Weingartner, H., & Wyatt, R. J. (1976). Marijuana-induced state-dependent amnesia and its reversal by cuing. In M. C. Braude & S. Szara (Eds.), *Pharmacology of marijuana* (Vol. 4, pp. 453–456). Orlando, FL: Academic Press.

Stokes, P. R., Mehta, M. A., Curran, H. V., Breen, G., & Grasby, P. M. (2009). Can recreational doses of THC produce significant dopamine release in the human striatum? *NeuroImage, 48,* 186–190.

Stolerman, I. P., Fink, R., & Jarvik, M. E. (1973). Acute and chronic tolerance to nicotine as measured by activity in rats. *Psychopharmacologia, 30,* 329–342.

Stolerman, I. P., Pratt, J. A., & Garcha, H. S. (1982). Further analysis of the nicotine cue in rats. In F. C. Colpaert & J. L. Slangen (Eds.), *Drug discrimination: Applications in CNS pharmacology* (pp. 203–210). Amsterdam, NY: Elsevier Biomedical.

Stone, J. M., Erlandsson, K., Arstad, E., Squassante, L., Teneggi, V., Bressan, R. A., et al. (2008). Relationship between ketamine-induced psychotic symptoms and NMDA receptor occupancy: A [(123)I]CNS-1261 SPET study. *Psychopharmacology, 197,* 401–408.

Strain, E. C., Mumford, G. K., Silverman, K., & Griffiths, R. R. (1995). Caffeine dependence syndrome, evidence from case histories and experimental evaluations. *Journal of the American Medical Association, 272,* 1043–1048.

Strang, J., Griffiths, P., & Gossop, M. (1997). Heroin smoking by 'chasing the dragon': Origins and history. *Addiction, 92,* 673–683; discussion 685–695.

Stripling, J. S., & Ellinwood, E. H., Jr. (1976). Cocaine: Physiological effects of acute and chronic administration. In S. J. Mule (Ed.), *Cocaine: Chemical, biological, clinical, social and treatment aspects* (pp. 165–186). Boca Raton, FL: CRC Press.

Substance Abuse and Mental Health Services Administration. (2010). *Results from the 2009 national survey on drug use and health: Volume I. Summary of national findings* (Office of Applied Studies, NSDUH Series H-38A, HHS Publication No. SMA 10-4586 Findings). Rockville, MD.

Sutherland, G., Stapleton, J. A., Russell, M. A., Jarvis, M. J., Hajek, P., & Belcher, M. (1992). Randomized control trial of nasal nicotine spray. *Lancet, 340,* 324–329.

Swanson, J. R., Jones, G. R., Krasselt, W., Denmark, L. N., & Ratti, F. (1997). Death of two subjects due to imipramine and desipramine metabolite accumulation during chronic therapy: A review of the literature and possible mechanisms. *Journal of Forensic Science, 42,* 335–339.

Takahashi, A., Kwa, C., Debold, J. F., & Miczek, K. A. (2010). GABA(A) receptors in the dorsal raphe nucleus of mice: Escalation of aggression after alcohol consumption. *Psychopharmacology, 211,* 467–477.

Tanasescu, R., & Constantinescu, C. S. (2010). Cannabinoids and the immune system: An overview. *Immunobiology, 215,* 588–597.

Tanda, G., Manzar, P., & Goldberg, S. R. (2000). Self-administration behavior is maintained by the psychoactive ingredient of marijuana in squirrel monkeys. *Nature Neuroscience, 3,* 1073–1074.

Tanda, G., Pontieri, F., & Chiara, G. (1997). Cannabinoid and heroin activation of mesolimboc dopamine transmission by a common 1 opioid receptor mechanism. *Science, 276,* 2048–2050.

Tapert, S. F., Cheung, E. H., Brown, G. G., Frank, L. R., Paulus, M. P., Schweinsburg, A. D., et al. (2003). Neural response to alcohol stimuli in adolescents with alcohol use disorder. *Archives of General Psychiatry, 60,* 727–735.

Tarnopolsky, M. A. (1994). Caffeine and endurance performance. *Sports Medicine, 18,* 109–125.

Tart, C. T., & Crawford, H. J. (1970). Marijuana intoxication: Reported effects on sleep. *Psychophysiology, 7,* 348.

Tatum, A. L., & Seevers, M. H. (1931). Theories of drug addiction. *Physiological Review, 11*, 107–120.

Taylor, J. L., & Tinklenberg, J. R. (1987). Cognitive impairment and benzodiazepines. In H. Y. Meltzer (Ed.), *Psychopharmacology: The third generation of progress* (pp. 1449–1454). New York: Raven Press.

Teicher, M. H., Glod, C. C., & Cole, J. O. (1990). Emergence of intense suicidal preoccupation during fluoxetine treatment. *American Journal of Psychiatry, 147*, 207–210.

Thompson, T., & Schuster, C. R. (1964). Morphine self-administration, food reinforced and avoidance behaviour in rhesus monkeys. *Psychopharmacologia, 5*, 87–94.

Thompson, T., & Schuster, C. R. (1968). *Behavioral pharmacology*. Englewood Cliffs, NJ: Prentice Hall.

Thompson, T., Trombley, J., Luke, D., & Lott, D. (1970). Effects of morphine on behavior maintained by four simple food reinforcement schedules. *Psychopharmacologia, 17*, 182–192.

Ticku, M. K., & Olsen, R. W. (1978). Interaction of barbiturates with dihydropicrotoxin binding sites related to the GABA receptor-ionophore system. *Life Sciences, 22*, 1643–1652.

Tindell, A. J., Berridge, K. C., Zhang, J., Pecina, S., & Aldridge, J. W. (2005). Ventral pallidal neurons code incentive motivation: Amplification by mesolimbic sensitization and amphetamine. *The European Journal of Neuroscience, 22*, 2617–2634.

Tinklenberg, J. R. (1974). Marijuana and human aggression. In L. L. Miller (Ed.), *Marijuana: Effects on human behavior* (pp. 339–358). Orlando, FL: Academic Press.

Tollefson, G. D. (1993). Adverse drug reactions/interactions in maintenance therapy. *Journal of Clinical Psychiatry, 54*, 48–58.

Tomberg, C. (2010). Alcohol pathophysiology circuits and molecular mechanisms. *Journal of Psychophysiology, 24*, 215–230.

Torres, G. E., Gainetdinov, R. R., & Caron, M. G. (2003). Plasma membrane monoamine transporters: Structure, regulation and function. *Nature Reviews. Neuroscience, 4*, 13–25.

Torry, J. M. (1976). A case of suicide with nitrazepam and alcohol. *Practitioner, 217*, 648–649.

Trevitt, J., Kawa, K., Jalali, A., & Larsen, C. (2009). Differential effects of adenosine antagonists in two models of parkinsonian tremor. *Pharmacology, Biochemistry and Behavior, 94*, 24–29.

Trigo, J. M., Panayi, F., Soria, G., Maldonado, R., & Robledo, P. (2006). A reliable model of intravenous MDMA self-administration in naïve mice. *Psychopharmacology (Berl), 184*, 212–220.

Trivedi, M. H., Rush, A. J., Wisniewski, S. R., Nierenberg, A. A., Warden, D., Ritz, L., et al. (2006). Evaluation of outcomes with citalopram for depression using measurement-based care in STAR*D: Implications for clinical practice. *The American Journal of Psychiatry, 163*, 28–40.

Tuesta, L. M., Fowler, C. D., & Kenny, P. J. (2011). Recent advances in understanding nicotinic receptor signaling mechanisms that regulate drug self-administration behavior. *Biochemical Pharmacology, 82*, 984–995.

Turk, M. W., Yang, K., Hravnak, M., Sereika, S. M., Ewing, L. J., & Burke, L. E. (2009). Randomized clinical trial of weight loss maintenance. *Journal of Cardiovascular Nursing, 24*, 58–80.

U.S. Department of Health and Human Services. (1989). *Reducing the health consequences of smoking: 25 years of progress: A report of the surgeon general*. Rockville, MD: U.S. Department of Health and Human Services, Centers for Disease Control, Center for Chronic Disease Prevention and Promotion.

U.S. Department of Health and Human Services. (1990). *Alcohol, tobacco, and other drugs may harm the unborn*. Rockville, MD: U.S. Department of Health and Human Services, Public Health Service, Alcohol, Drug Abuse, and Mental Health Administration, Office for Substance Abuse Prevention.

U.S. Department of Health and Human Services. (1994). *Preliminary estimates from the 1993 national household survey on drug abuse* (Advance report number 7). Washington, DC: U.S. Department of Health and Human Services, Substance Abuse and Mental Health Services Administration.

U.S. Department of Health and Human Services. (1995). *Preliminary estimates from the 1994 national household survey on drug abuse* (Advance report number 10). Washington, DC: U.S. Department of Health and Human Services, Substance Abuse and Mental Health Services Administration.

U.S. Department of Health and Human Services, Centers for Disease Control and Prevention, Coordinating Center for Health Promotion, National Center for Chronic Disease Prevention and Health Promotion, Office on Smoking and Health. (2006). *The health consequences of involuntary exposure to tobacco smoke: A report of the surgeon general*. U.S. Department of Health and Human Services.

U.S. Department of Health and Human Services, Centers for Disease Control and Prevention, National Center for Chronic Disease Prevention and Health Promotion, Office on Smoking and Health. (2004). *The health consequences of smoking: A report of the surgeon general*.

U.S. Department of Health and Human Services, Centers for Disease Control and Prevention, National Center for Chronic Disease Prevention and Health Promotion, Office on Smoking and Health. (2010). *How tobacco smoke causes disease: The biology and behavioral basis for smoking-attributable disease: A report of the surgeon general*. U.S. Department of Health and Human Services.

U.S. Department of Justice. (2011). Retrieved November 16, 2011, from http://www.deadiversion.usdoj.gov/drugs_concern/meth.htm

U.S. Environmental Protection Agency. (1992). *Respiratory health effects of passive smoking: Lung cancer and other disorders*. Washington, DC: Office of Research and Development, Office of Health and Environmental Assessment.

Üçok, A., & Gaebel, W. (2008). Side effects of atypical antipsychotics: A brief overview. *World Psychiatry, 7,* 58–62.

Uher, R., Caspi, A., Houts, R., Sugden, K., Williams, B., Poulton, R., et al. (2011). Serotonin transporter gene moderates childhood maltreatment's effects on persistent but not single-episode depression: Replications and implications for resolving inconsistent results. *J Affect Disord.*

Uhlenhuth, E. H., de Wit, H., Balter, M. B., Johanson, C. E., & Mellinger, G. D. (1988). Risks and benefits of long-term benzodiazepine use. *Journal of Clinical Pharmacology, 8,* 161–167.

Ungless, M. A., Whistler, J. L., Malenka, R. C., & Bonci, A. (2001). Single cocaine exposure in vivo induces long-term potentiation in dopamine neurons. *Nature, 411,* 583–587.

United Nations. (1980). Special issue devoted to Catha edulis (khat). *Bulletin on Narcotics, 32.*

UNODC. (2010). World drug report 2010. *United Nations Publication, 10.*

United States National Library of Medicine, National Institutes of Health (2011). *Drug Portal Generic Name Stem showing Activity.* http://druginfo.nlm.nih.gov/drugportal/jsp/drugportal/DrugNameGenericStems.jsp, accessed December 7, 2011.

Uppal, A., Singh, A., Gahtori, P., Ghosh, S. K., & Ahmad, M. Z. (2010). Antidepressants: Current strategies and future opportunities. *Current Pharmaceutical Design, 16,* 4243–4253.

Uusi-Oukari, M., & Korpi, E. R. (2010). Regulation of GABA(A) receptor subunit expression by pharmacological agents. *Pharmacological Reviews, 62,* 97–135.

Vaillant, G. E. (1992). Is there a natural history of addiction? In C. E. O'Brien & J. H. Jaffe (Eds.), *Addictive states* (pp. 41–56). New York: Raven Press.

Van Dam, N. T., & Earleywine, M. (2010). Pulmonary function in cannabis users: Support for a clinical trial of the vaporizer. *The International Journal on Drug Policy, 21,* 511–513.

van Dam, R. M., & Hu, F. B. (2005). Coffee consumption and risk of type 2 diabetes: A systematic review. *The Journal of the American Medical Association, 294,* 97–104.

van der Kooy, D. (1987). Place conditioning: A simple and effective method for assessing the motivational properties of drugs. In M. A. Bozarth (Ed.), *Methods of assessing the reinforcing properties of abused drugs* (pp. 229–240). New York: Springer-Verlag.

Van Laar, M., Volkerts, E., & Verbaten, M. (2001). Subchronic effects of the GABA-agonist lorazepam and the 5-HT2A/2C antagonist ritanserin on driving performance, slow wave sleep and daytime sleepiness in healthy volunteers. *Psychopharmacology, 154,* 189–197.

Van Laar, M., Volkerts, E., & Willigenberg, A. (1992). Therapeutic effects on actual driving performance of chronically administered buspirone and diazepam in anxious outpatients. *Journal of Clinical Psychopharmacology, 12,* 86–95.

Van Lancker, J. L. (1977). Smoking and disease. In M. E. Jarvik, J. W. Cullen, E. R. Gritz, T. M. Vogt, & L. J. West (Eds.), *Research on smoking behavior* (pp. 230–280) (NIDA Research Monograph No. 17, DHEW Pub. No. ADM 78 581). Washington, DC: U.S. Government Printing Office.

van Noorden, M. S., Kamal, R., de Jong, C. A., Vergouwen, A. C., & Zitman, F. G. (2010). Gamma-hydroxybutyric acid (GHB) dependence and the GHB withdrawal syndrome: Diagnosis and treatment [GHB-afhankelijkheid en-onthoudingssyndroom: Diagnostiek en behandeling]. *Nederlands Tijdschrift Voor Geneeskunde, 154,* A1286.

van Ree, J. M., Gerrits, M. A., & Vanderschuren, L. S. (1999). Opioid reward and addiction: An encounter of biology, psychology and medicine. *Pharmacological Reviews, 51,* 341–396.

Vansickel, A. R., Hays, L. R., & Rush, C. R. (2006). Discriminative-stimulus effects of triazolam in women and men. *The American Journal of Drug and Alcohol Abuse, 32,* 329–349.

Veilleux, J. C., Colvin, P. J., Anderson, J., York, C., & Heinz, A. J. (2010). A review of opioid dependence treatment: Pharmacological and psychosocial interventions to treat opioid addiction. *Clinical Psychological Review, 30,* 155–166.

Verebey, K., Alrazi, J., & Jaffe, J. H. (1988). The complications of "ecstasy" (MDMA) [Letter]. *Journal of the American Medical Association, 259,* 1649–1650.

Verster, J., Volkerts, E., Schreuder, A., Eijken, E., van Heuckelum, J., Veldhuijzen, D., et al. (2002). Residual effects of middle-of-the-night administration of zaleplon and zolpidem on driving ability, memory functions, and psychomotor performance. *Journal of Clinical Psychopharmacology, 22,* 576–584.

Victor, M., Adams, R. D., & Collins, G. H. (1971). *The Wernicke-Korsakoff syndrome.* Philadelphia, PA: Davis.

Villemagne, V., Yuan, J., Wong, D. F., Dannals, R. F., Hatzidimitriou, G., Mathews, W. B., et al. (1998). Brain dopamine neurotoxicity in baboons treated with doses of methamphetamine comparable to those recreationally abused by humans: Evidence from [11C]WIN-35,428 positron emission tomography studies and direct in vitro determinations. *Journal of Neuroscience, 18,* 419–427.

Vitiello, B., & Swedo, S. (2005). Antidepressant medication in children. *New England Journal of Medicine, 350,* 1489–1491.

Vitiello, M. V., & Woods, S. C. (1975). Caffeine: Preferential consumption by rats. *Pharmacology, Biochemistry and Behavior, 3,* 147–149.

Vogel, G. (1997). Cocaine wreaks subtle damage on developing brains. *Science, 287,* 38–39.

Vogel, J. R. (1979). Objective measurement of human performance changes produced by antianxiety drugs. In S. Fielding & H. Lal (Eds.), *Anxiolytics* (pp. 343–374). Mt. Kisco, NY: Futura.

Vogel-Sprott, M. (1984). Response measures of social drinking: Research implications and application. *Journal of Studies on Alcohol, 44,* 817–836.

Vogel-Sprott, M. (1992). *Alcohol tolerance and social drinking: Learning and the consequences.* New York: Guilford Press.

Vogel-Sprott, M., Easdon, G., Fillmore, M., Finn, P., & Justus, A. (2001). Alcohol and behavioral control: Cognitive and neural mechanisms. *Alcoholism: Clinical and Experimental Research, 25,* 117–121.

Volk, D. W., & Lewis, D. A. (2010). Prefrontal cortical circuits in schizophrenia. *Current Topics in Behavioral Neurosciences, 4,* 485–508.

Volkow, N. D., Fowler, J. S., Wang, G. J., Swanson, J. M., & Telang, F. (2007). Dopamine in drug abuse and addiction: Results of imaging studies and treatment implications. *Archives of Neurology, 64,* 1575–1579.

Volkow, N. D., Fowler, J. S., Wolf, A. P., Hitzemann, R., Dewey, S., Bendriem, B., et al. (1991). Changes in brain glucose metabolism in cocaine dependence and withdrawal. *American Journal of Psychiatry, 148,* 621–626.

Volkow, N. D., Mullani, N., Gould, L., Adler, S., & Krajeswski, K. (1988). Effects of acute alcohol intoxication on cerebral blood flow measured by PET. *Psychiatry Research, 24,* 201–209.

Volkow, N. D., Wang, G. J., & Baler, R. D. (2011). Reward, dopamine and the control of food intake: Implications for obesity. *Trends in Cognitive Sciences, 15,* 37–46.

Volkow, N. D., Wang, G. J., Fischman, M. W., Foltin, R. W., Fowler, J. S., Abumrad, N. N., et al. (1997). Relationship between subjective effects of cocaine and dopamine transporter occupancy. *Nature, 386,* 827–830.

Volkow, N. D., Wang, G. J., Fischman, M. W., Foltin, R., Fowler, J. S., Franceschi, D., et al. (2000). Effects of route of administration on cocaine induced dopamine transporter blockade in the human brain. *Life Sciences, 67,* 1507–1515.

Volkow, N. D., Wang, G. J., Fowler, J. S., Tomasi, D., Telang, F., & Baler, R. (2010). Addiction: Decreased reward sensitivity and increased expectation sensitivity conspire to overwhelm the brain's control circuit. *BioEssays: News and Reviews in Molecular, Cellular and Developmental Biology, 32,* 748–755.

Volkow, N. D., Wang, G. J., Ma, Y., Fowler, J., Zhu, W., Maynard, L., et al. (2003). Expectation enhances the regional brain metabolic and reinforcing effects of stimulants in cocaine abusers. *Journal of Neuroscience, 23,* 11461–11468.

von Zastrow, M. (2010). Regulation of opioid receptors by endocytic membrane traffic: Mechanisms and translational implications. *Drug and Alcohol Dependence, 108,* 166–171.

Vree, T. B., & Henderson, P. T. (1980). Pharmacokinetics of amphetamines: In vivo and in vitro studies of factors governing their elimination. In J. Caldwell (Ed.), *Amphetamines and related stimulants: Chemical, biological, clinical and sociological aspects* (pp. 47–68). Boca Raton, FL: CRC Press.

Waldorf, D., Murphy, S., Renarman, C., & Joyce, B. (1977). *Doing coke: An ethnography of cocaine users and sellers.* Washington, DC: Drug Abuse Council.

Wallner, M., & Olsen, R. W. (2008). Physiology and pharmacology of alcohol: The imidazobenzodiazepine alcohol antagonist site on subtypes of GABAA receptors as an opportunity for drug development? *British Journal of Pharmacology, 154,* 288–298.

Walsh, M. -T., & Dinan, T. (2001). Selective serotonin reuptake inhibitors and violence: A review of available evidence. *Acta Psychiatrica Scandanavica, 104,* 84–91.

Walsh, T., McClellan, J. M., McCarthy, S. E., Addington, A. M., Pierce, S. B., Cooper, G. M., et al. (2008). Rare structural variants disrupt multiple genes in neurodevelopmental pathways in schizophrenia. *Science (New York, N.Y.), 320,* 539–543.

Wang, G. J., Volkow, N. D., Fowler, J. S., Franceschi, D., Wong, C., Peppas, N., et al. (2003). *Alcohol intoxication induces greater reductions in brain metabolism in male than in female subjects. Alcoholism: Clinical and Experimental Research, 27,* 909–917.

Ward, B. W., Barnes, P. M., Freeman, G., & Schiller, J. S. (National Center for Health Statistics, December). *Early release of selected estimates based on data from the January–June 2010 national health interview survey. National Center for Health Statistics.*

Wareing, M., Fisk, J., & Murphy, P. (2000). Working memory deficits in current and previous users of MDMA ("ecstasy"). *British Journal of Psychology, 91,* 181–188.

Wasson, R. G. (1972). The divine mushroom of immortality. In P. T. Furst (Ed.), *Flesh of the gods* (pp. 185–200). New York: Praeger.

Watkins, R. L., & Adler, E. V. (1993). The effect of food on alcohol absorption and elimination patterns. *Journal of Forensic Sciences, 38,* 285–291.

Wax, P., Becker, C., & Curry, S. (2003). Unexpected "gas" casualties in Moscow: A medical toxicology perspective. *Annals of Emergency Medicine, 41,* 700–705.

Wayner, M. J., Jolicoeur, F. B., Rondeau, D. B., & Barone, F. C. (1976). Effects of acute and chronic administration of caffeine on schedule dependent and schedule induced behavior. *Pharmacology, Biochemistry and Behavior, 5*, 343–348.

Weddington, W. W. (1995). Methadone maintenance for opioid addiction. In N. S. Miller & M. S. Gold (Eds.), *Pharmacological therapies for alcohol and drug addiction* (pp. 411–418). New York: Marcel Dekker.

Wee, S., & Koob, G. F. (2010). The role of the dynorphin-kappa opioid system in the reinforcing effects of drugs of abuse.*Psychopharmacology, 210*, 121–135.

Wee, S., & Woolverton, W. L. (2006). Self-administration of mixtures of fenfluramine and amphetamine by rhesus monkeys. *Pharmacology, Biochemistry and Behavior, 84*, 337–343.

Weil, A. T., & Rosen, W. (1983). *Chocolate to morphine: Understanding mind-acting drugs.* Boston, MA: Houghton Mifflin.

Weil, A. T., Zinberg, N. E., & Nelson, J. M. (1968). Clinical and psychological effects of marijuana in man. *Science, 192*, 1234–1242.

Weiss, B. (1969). Enhancement of performance by amphetamine-like drugs. In F. Sjoquist & M. Tottie (Eds.), *Abuse of central stimulants* (pp. 31–60). Stockholm: Almqvist & Wiksell.

Weissman, A. D., Su, T. P., Hedreen, J. C., & London, E. D. (1988). Sigma receptors in post-mortem human brains. *Journal of Pharmacology and Experimental Therapeutics, 247*, 29–33.

Wenger, J. R., Tiffany, T. M., Bombardier, C., Nicoins, K., & Woods, S. C. (1981). Ethanol tolerance in the rat is learned. *Science, 213*, 575–576.

West, R. (1993). Beneficial effects of nicotine: Fact or fiction. *Addiction, 88*, 589–590.

West, R. (2001). Theories of addiction. *Addiction, 96*, 3–15.

White, A. M., Hingson, R. W., Pan, I. J., & Yi, H. Y. (2011). Hospitalizations for alcohol and drug overdoses in young adults ages 18–24 in the United States, 1999–2008: Results from the nationwide inpatient sample. *Journal of Studies on Alcohol and Drugs, 72*, 774–786.

Whitfield, J. B., & Martin, N. G. (1994). Alcohol consumption and alcohol pharmacokinetics: Interaction within the normal population. *Alcoholism: Clinical and Experimental Research, 18*, 238–243.

Wickelgren, I. (1997). Getting the brain's attention. *Science, 278*, 35–37.

Wiersma, D., Nienhuis, F. J., Slooff, C. J., & Giel, R. (1998). Natural course of schizophrenic disorders: A 15-year followup of a dutch incidence cohort. *Schizophrenia Bulletin, 24*, 75–85.

Wikler, A. (1980). *Opioid dependence: Mechanisms and treatment.* New York: Plenum Press.

Wilder, B. J., & Bruni, J. (1981). *Seizure disorders: A pharmacological approach to treatment.* New York: Raven Press.

Willett, W., Stampfer, M., Manson, J., Colditz, G., Rosner, B. A., Speizer, F. E., et al. (1996). Coffee consumption and coronary disease in women. A ten-year follow-up. *Journal of the American Medical Association, 275*, 458–462.

Williams, G. D., Clem, D., & Dufour, M. C. (1993). *Surveillance report #27. Apparent per capita alcohol consumption: National, state, and regional trends, 1977–1991.* Rockville, MD: National Institute on Alcohol Abuse and Alcoholism, Division of Biometry and Epidemiology.

Wilsey, B., Marcotte, T., Tsodikov, A., Millman, J., Bentley, H., Gouaux, B., et al. (2008). A randomized, placebo-controlled, crossover trial of cannabis cigarettes in neuropathic pain. *Journal of Pain, 9*, 506–521.

Wilson, D. (2010). Cigarette Giants in global fight on tighter rules. *New York Times.* Retrieved from http://www.nytimes.com/2010/11/14/business/global/14smoke.html

Wingen, M., Ramaekers, J. G., & Schmitt, J. A. (2006). Driving impairment in depressed patients receiving long-term antidepressant treatment. *Psychopharmacology, 188*, 84–91.

Winger, G., Stitzer, M. L., & Woods, J. H. (1975). Barbiturate-reinforced responding in rhesus monkeys: Comparisons of compounds with different durations of actions. *Journal of Pharmacology and Experimental Therapeutics, 195*, 505–514.

Winick, C. (1962). Maturing out of narcotic addiction. *Bulletin on Narcotics, 14*, 1–8.

Wise, R. A. (1980). The dopamine synapse and the notion of 'pleasure centers' in the brain. *Trends of Neuroscience, 3*, 91–95.

Wolfe, S. M., & Victor, M. (1972). The physiological basis of the alcohol withdrawal syndrome. In N. K. Mello & J. H. Mendelson (Eds.), *Recent advances in the study of alcoholism* (pp. 188–199). Washington, DC: U.S. Government Printing Office.

Wood, D. M., Greene, S. L., & Dargan, P. I. (2011). Clinical pattern of toxicity associated with the novel synthetic cathinone mephedrone. *Emergency Medicine Journal, 28*, 280–282.

Wood, R. I. (2004). Reinforcing aspects of androgens. *Physiology and Behavior, 83*, 279–291.

Woods, J., & Winger, G. (1997). Abuse liability of flunitrazepam. *Journal of Clinical Psychopharmacology, 17*(Suppl. 2), 1S–57S.

Woods, N. F. (1984). *Human sexuality in health and illness.* St. Louis, MO: Mosby.

Woolridge, E., Barton, S., Samuel, J., Osorio, J., Dougherty, A., & Holdcroft, A. (2005). Cannabis use in HIV for pain and other medical symptoms. *Journal of Pain and Symptom Management, 29*, 358–367.

World Health Organization. (1993). *The international statistical classification of diseases and related health problems (ICD-10).* Geneva: Author.

Worley, C. M., Valdez, A., & Schenk, S. (1994). Reinforcement of extinguished cocaine-taking by cocaine and caffeine. *Pharmacology, Biochemistry and Behavior, 48*, 217–221.

Wu, L. T., Schlenger, W. E., & Galvin, D. M. (2006). Concurrent use of methamphetamine, MDMA, LSD, ketamine, GHB, and flunitrazepam among american youths. *Drug and Alcohol Dependence, 84*, 102–113.

Wu, Y., Ali, S., Ahmadian, G., Liu, C. C., Wang, Y. T., Gibson, K. M., et al. (2004). Gamma-hydroxybutyric acid (GHB) and gamma-aminobutyric acidB receptor (GABABR) binding sites are distinctive from one another: Molecular evidence. *Neuropharmacology, 47*, 1146–1156.

Wyvell, C. L., & Berridge, K. C. (2000). Intra-accumbens amphetamine increases the conditioned incentive salience of sucrose reward: Enhancement of reward "wanting" without enhanced "liking" or response reinforcement. *The Journal of Neuroscience: The Official Journal of the Society for Neuroscience, 20*, 8122–8130.

Xu, H., Li, S. -J., Bodurka, J., Zhao, X., Xi, Z. X., & Stein, E. A. (2000). Heroin-induced neuronal activation in rat brain assessed by functional MRI. *Neuroreport, 11*, 1085–1092.

Xu, J., Mendrek, A., Cohen, M. S., Monterosso, J., Rodriguez, P., Simon, S. L., et al. (2005). Brain activity in cigarette smokers performing a working memory task: Effects of smoking abstinence. *Biological Psychiatry, 58*, 143–150.

Yamaguchi, T., Sheen, W., & Morales, M. (2007). Glutamatergic neurons are present in the rat ventral tegmental area. *The European Journal of Neuroscience, 25*, 106–118.

Yan, F., & Roth, B. (2004). Salvinorin a: A novel and highly selective κ-opioid receptor agonist. *Life Sciences, 75*, 2615–2619.

Yanagita, T. (1987). Prediction of drug abuse liability from animal studies. In M. A. Bozarth (Ed.), *Methods for assessing the reinforcing properties of abused drugs* (p. 189). New York: Springer-Verlag.

Yin, H. H., Zhuang, X., & Balleine, B. W. (2006). Instrumental learning in hyperdopaminergic mice. *Neurobiology of Learning and Memory, 85*, 283–288.

Yokel, R. A. (1987). Intravenous self-administration: Response rates, the effects of pharmacological challenges, and drug preferences. In M. A. Bozarth (Ed.), *Methods of assessing the reinforcing properties of abused drugs* (pp. 1–34). New York: Springer-Verlag.

Young, A. M., & Goudie, A. J. (1995). Adaptive processes regulating tolerance to the behavioral effects of drugs. In F. E. Bloom & D. J. Kupfer (Eds.), *Psychopharmacology: The fourth generation of progress* (pp. 733–742). New York: Raven Press.

Young, A. M., Steigerwald, E., Makhay, M., & Kapitsopoulos, G. (1991). Onset of tolerance to discriminative stimulus effects of morphine. *Pharmacology, Biochemistry and Behavior, 39*, 487–493.

Zack, M., & Vogel-Sprott, M. (1995). Behavioral tolerance and sensitization to alcohol in humans: The contribution of learning. *Experimental and Clinical Psychopharmacology, 3*, 396–401.

Zacny, J., Cho, A., Coalson, D., Rupani, G. G., Young, C., Klafta, J., et al. (1996). Differential acute tolerance development to the effects of nitrous oxide in humans. *Neuroscience Letters, 209*, 73–76.

Zacny, J., Cho, A., Tolendano, A., Galinkin, J., Coalson, D., Klock, P., et al. (1997). Effects of information on the reinforcing and psychomotor effects on nitrous oxide in health volunteers. *Alcohol and Drug Dependence, 48*, 85–95.

Zacny, J. P. (1995). A review of the effects of opioids on psychomotor and cognitive functioning in humans. *Experimental and Clinical Psychopharmacology, 3*, 432–466.

Zacny, J. P., Hill, J., Black, M., & Sadeghi, P. (1998). Comparing the subjective, psychomotor and physiological effects of intravenous pentazocine and morphine in normal volunteers. *Journal of Pharmacology and Experimental Therapeutics, 286*, 1197–1207.

Zacny, J. P., Stitzer, M. L., Brown, F. J., Yingling, F. E., & Griffiths, R. R. (1987). Human cigarette smoking: Effects of puff and inhalation parameters on smoke exposure. *Journal of Pharmacology and Experimental Therapeutics, 240*, 554–564.

Zacny, J. P., & Walker, E. A. (1998). Behavioral pharmacology of opiates. In R. E. Tarter, R. T. Ammerman, & P. J. Ott (Eds.), *Handbook of substance abuse* (pp. 343–362). New York: Plenum Press.

Zajecka, J., Tracy, K., & Mitchell, S. (1997). Discontinuation symptoms after treatment with serotonin reuptake inhibitors: A literature review. *Journal of Clinical Psychiatry, 58*, 291–297.

Ziaee, V., Akbari Hamed, E., Hoshmand, A., Amini, H., Kebriaeizadeh, A., & Saman, K. (2005). Side effects of dextromethorphan abuse, a case series. *Addictive Behaviors, 30*, 1607–1613.

Zuardi, A. W., Crippa, J. A., Hallak, J. E., Moreira, F. A., & Guimarães, F. S. (2006). Cannabidiol, a cannabis sativa constituent, as an antipsychotic drug. *Brazilian Journal of Medical and Biological Research = Revista Brasileira De Pesquisas Medicas e Biologicas / Sociedade Brasileira De Biofisica ... [Et Al.], 39*, 421–429.

Zuckerman, B., & Frank, D. A. (1994). Prenatal cocaine exposure: Nine years later. *Journal of Pediatrics, 124*(5, Pt. 1), 731–733.

Zvosec, D. L., Smith, S. W., Porrata, T., Strobl, A. Q., & Dyer, J. E. (2011). Case series of 226 gamma-hydroxybutyrate-associated deaths: Lethal toxicity and trauma. *The American Journal of Emergency Medicine, 29*, 319–332.

CREDITS

PHOTO CREDITS

Chapter 1

p. 18: vectomart/Shutterstock.

Chapter 4

p. 71: Alila Sao Mai/Shutterstock.

Chapter 6

p. 155: Courtesy of the National Institute on Alcohol Abuse and Alcoholism, www.niaaa.nih.gov.

Chapter 8

p. 183: Interfoto/Alamy.

Chapter 11

p. 255: Pics-xl/Shutterstock (left); Adrian Sherratt/Alamy (right).

Chapter 15

p. 336: Pen and ink drawings by David Sheridan. Siegel, R. K., & Jarvik, M. E. (1975).

TEXT CREDITS

Chapter 1

p. 3: Adapted from United States National Library of Medicine, National Institutes of Health, 2011; available online at: http://druginfo.nlm.nih.gov/drugportal/jsp/drugportal/DrugNameGenericStems.jsp; p. 5: With kind permission from Springer Science+Business Media: Psychopharmacology, "The effects of caffeine, theophylline and amphetamine on the operant responding of the mouse," 68 (1980)pp. 135–138, W.A. McKim; p. 14: "The Fluid Model of the Structure of Cell Membranes," Science, Vol. 175, February 1972, pp. 720–731; p. 22: "The case of SJW (St. John's wort) serves as a prototypical . . ." from Choudhuri, S., & Valerio, L. G. (2005). sefulness of studies on the

molecular mechanism of action of herbals/botanicals: The case of St. John's wort. Journal of Biochemical and Molecular Toxicology, 19, 1–11, p. 9. Reproduced with permission of John Wiley & Sons, Inc.

Chapter 2

p. 27: Peter B. Dews, Studies on Behavior. I. Differential Sensitivity to Pentobarbital of Pecking Performance in Pigeons Depending on the Schedule of Reward, Journal of Pharmacology and Experimental Therapeutics, April 1955 113:393–401; p. 44: Adapted from Solomon, R. L., & Corbit, J. D. (1974). An opponent-process theory of motivation: I. Temporal dynamics of affect. Psychological Review, 81, 119–145; p. 47: Adapted from Solomon, R. L., & Corbit, J. D. (1974). An opponent-process theory of motivation: I. Temporal dynamics of affect. Psychological Review, 81, 119–145.

Chapter 3

pp. 44, 47: Adapted from Solomon, R. L., & Corbit, J. D. (1974). An opponent-process theory of motivation: I. Temporal dynamics of affect. Psychological Review, 81, 119–145; p. 49: C. P. O'Brien, Experimental Analysis of Conditioning Factors in Human Narcotic Addiction, Pharmacological Reviews December 1975 27:533–543; p. 54: Reprinted from the Lancet, 346(8984), 1231, Benedetti, F., Amanzio, M., & Maggi, G. (1995). Potentiation of Placebo Analgesia by Proglumide, with permission from Elsevier.

Chapter 4

p. 57: "A prototypical nerve cell" adapted from Society for Neuroscience Brain Facts, 2008, p. 7; p. 58: Pearson Education; p. 60: Pearson Education; p. 61: Pearson Education; p. 65: Pearson Education; p. 69: Pearson Education; p. 77: Pearson Education; p. 79: Pearson Education; p. 82: Pearson Education;

Color Plates

Color Plate A: "Four major neurotransmitter systems" adapted from Bear, Connors, & Paradiso, Neuroscience: Exploring the Brain, Third edition, 2007; figures 15-12 [p. 500], 15-13 [p. 501], 15-14 [p. 503], 15-15 [p. 504], used with permission from Wolters Kluwer Health.

Color Plate B: From Heinz, A., Siessmeier, T., Wrase, J., Hermann, D., Klein, S., Grusser-Sinopoli, S. M., et al. (2004). Correlation between Dopamine D2 Receptors in the Ventral Striatum and Central Processing of Alcohol Cues and Craving. American Journal of Psychiatry, 2004; 161: 1783–1789. Reprinted with permission from the American Journal of Psychiatry, (Copyright ©2004). American Psychiatric Association.

Color Plate C: Reprinted from Biological Psychiatry, 58, "Brain activity in cigarette smokers performing a working memory task: Effects of smoking abstinence,"143–150, (2005), with permission from Elsevier.

Color Plate D: Adapted from Villemagne, V., Yuan, J., Wong, D. F., Dannals, R. F., Hatzidimitriou, G., Mathews, W. B., et al. (1998). Brain dopamine neurotoxicity in baboons treated with doses of methamphetamine comparable to those recreationally abused by humans: Evidence from [11C]WIN-35,428 positron emission tomography studies and direct in vitro determinations. Journal, Society for Neuroscience, 1998, p. 421.

Chapter 5

p. 98: "Substance Dependence and Substance Abuse criteria" from DSM-IV-TR, 2000, American Psychiatric Association; p. 101: Archives.drugabuse.gov; p. 107: "The similarity between the patterns of self-administration of ethanol in a human and a rhesus monkey under continuous drug availability" adapted from Griffiths, R. R., Bigelow, G. E., Henningfield, J. E. (1980). Similarities in animal and human drug taking behavior. In N. K. Mello (Ed.), Advances in substance abuse (Vol. 1, pp. 1–90), p. 19. Jessica Kingsley Publishers, Inc.; p. 124: Solomon, R. L., & Corbit, J. D. (1974). An opponent-process theory of motivation: I. Temporal dynamics of affect. Psychological Review, 81, 119–145; p. 133: Plato, Laws I, 649a–b; translation in Jowett, B. (1931). The dialogues of Plato (Vol. 5, 3rd ed.). London: Oxford University Press., p. 28.

Chapter 6

p. 135: Williams, G. D., Clem, D., & Dufour, M. C. (1993). Surveillance report #27. Apparent per capita alcohol consumption: National, state, and regional trends, 1977–1991. Rockville, MD: National Institute on Alcohol Abuse and Alcoholism, Division of Biometry and Epidemiology; pp. 145, 146: OECD (1978) Road research: New research on the role of alcohol and drugs in road accidents; p. 153: Plato, The Dialogues, Symposium 176a–b, translation in Jowett, B. (1931). The dialogues of Plato (Vol. 5, 3rd ed.). London: Oxford University Press; p. 155: National Institute on Alcohol Abuse and Alcoholism, 2004; http://pubs.niaaa.nih.gov/publications/aa63/aa63.htm; p. 158: Data from Reynolds, K., Lewis, B., Nolen, J. D., Kinney, G. L., Sathya, B., & He, J. (2003). Alcohol consumption and risk of stroke: A meta-analysis. JAMA : The Journal of the American Medical Association, 289(5), 579–88.

Chapter 7

p. 167: Mikko Uusi-Oukari and Esa R. Korpi, Regulation of GABAA Receptor Subunit Expression by Pharmacological Agents, Pharmacological Reviews March 2010 62:97–135; p. 176: "Benzodiazepine dependency syndromes," D.E. Smith and D.R. Wesson, Journal of Psychoactive Drugs, 15 (1983) pp. 85–96. Reprinted by permission from Taylor & Francis Ltd., http://www.tandf.co.uk/journals; p. 179: Data from Johnston, L. D., O'Malley, P. M., Bachman, J. G., & Schulenberg, J. E. (2011). Monitoring the future national survey results on drug use, 1975–2010: Volume II, college students and adults ages 19–50. Ann Arbor: Institute for Social Research, the University of Michigan.

Chapter 8

p. 188: From de Wit, H., & Zacny, J. (1995). Abuse potential of nicotine replacement therapies. CNS Drugs, 4, 456–468. p. 459; p. 189: Reprinted from Trends in Neurosciences, 34/7, Dani, John A., Balfour, David J.K., Historical and current perspective on tobacco use and nicotine addiction, p. 383, (2011), with permission from Elsevier; p. 198: Reprinted from Pharmacology, Biochemistry, and Behavior, 70(4), Chaudhri, N., Booth, S.,

Gharib, M. A., Sved, A. F. , Cue dependency of nicotine self-administration and smoking, pp. 515–530, (2001), with permission from Elsevier; p. 202: Van Lancker, J. L. (1977). Smoking and disease. In M. E. Jarvik, J. W. Cullen, E. R. Gritz, T. M. Vogt, & L. J. West (Eds.), Research on smoking behavior (pp. 230–280) (NIDA Research Monograph No. 17, DHEW Pub. No. ADM 78 581), p. 252. Washington, DC: U.S. Government Printing Office; p. 207: Valery Lemmens, Anke Oenema, Inge Knut, et al, Effectiveness of smoking cessation interventions among adults: A systematic review of reviews, European Journal of Cancer Prevention, 17(6), 535–4.

Chapter 9

p. 209: Anonymous, 1650; p. 201: Sources: Barone & Roberts (1984); Gilbert (1976); Heckman et al. (2010); Mumford et al. (1994); www.espinet.org/new/cafchart.htm (accessed Sept 2011); http://www.energy-fiend.com/ (accessed Sept 2011); p. 222: R R Griffiths, S M Evans, S J Heishman, K L Preston, C A Sannerud, B Wolf, and P P Woodson, Low-dose caffeine physical dependence in humans, Journal of Pharmacology and Experimental Therapeutics December 1990 255:1123–32; p. 223: "Intravenous self-injection rates of caffeine for a baboon with a history . . .," from Griffiths, R. R., & Mumford, G. K. (1995). Caffeine: A drug of abuse? In F. E. Bloom & D. J. Kupfer (Eds.), Psychopharmacology: The fourth generation of progress.

Chapter 10

p. 237: Rajkumar J. Sevak, William W. Stoops, Lon R. Hays, and Craig R. Rush, Discriminative Stimulus and Subject-Rated Effects of Methamphetamine, d-Amphetamine, Methylphenidate, and Triazolam in Methamphetamine-Trained Humans, Journal of Pharmacology and Experimental Therapeutics, March 2009 328:1007–1018; pp. 238–239: Rylander, G. (1969). Clinical and medico-criminological aspects of addiction to central stimulating drugs. In F. Sjoquist & M. Tottie (Eds.), Abuse of central stimulants (pp. 251–274). Stockholm: Almqvist & Wiksell, p. 263; p. 243: Rajkumar J. Sevak, William W. Stoops, Lon R. Hays, and Craig R. Rush, Discriminative Stimulus and Subject-Rated Effects of Methamphetamine,

d-Amphetamine, Methylphenidate, and Triazolam in Methamphetamine-Trained Humans, Journal of Pharmacology and Experimental Therapeutics, March 2009 328:1007–1018; p. 245: Reprinted from Pharmacology, Biochemistry, and Behavior, 79(4), Barrett, R. J., Caul, W. F., & Smith, R. L., Author(s), Evidence for bidirectional cues as a function of time following treatment with amphetamine: Implications for understanding tolerance and withdrawal, p. 765 (2004), with permission from Elsevier; p. 246: Johnston, L. D., O'Malley, P. M., Bachman, J. G., & Schulenberg, J. E. (2011). Monitoring the Future national survey results on drug use, 1975–2010. Volume II: College students and adults ages 19–50 Ann Arbor: Institute for Social Research, The University of Michigan; p. 247: With kind permission from Springer Science+Business Media: Adapted from "Self-administration of psychoactive substances by the monkey: A measure of psychological dependence" Psychopharmacologia, 16 (1969) pp. 30–48, Gerald Deneau, T. Yanagita, M.H. Seevers.

Chapter 11

p. 254: Opium by Jean Cocteau translated by Margaret Crosland/Peter Owen Ltd., London; pp. 262–263: De Quincey, T. (1901). The confessions of an English opium-eater. London: Macmillan, pp. 169–170, 224; p. 263: Opium by Jean Cocteau translated by Margaret Crosland/Peter Owen Ltd., London; p. 266: "Daily intake of morphine and heroin in a human and a rhesus monkey . . ." adapted from Griffiths, R. R., Bigelow, G. E., & Henningfield, J. E. (1980). Similarities in animal and human drug taking behavior. In N. K. Mello (Ed.), Advances in substance abuse (Vol. 1, pp. 1–90). Jessica Kingsley Publishers, Inc.; p. 274: Reprinted from Preventive Medicine, 44(4), Smyth, B., Hoffman, V., Fan, J., Hser, Y. I., Years of potential life lost among heroin addicts 33 years after treatment, pp. 369–374, (2007), with permission from Elsevier.

Chapter 12

p. 277: William Shakespeare, Macbeth; p. 278: Reprinted with permission from the Diagnostic and Statistical Manual of Mental Disorders, Fourth Edition, Text Revision (©2000). American Psychiatric Association; pp. 278–279: The Journal of Abnormal and Social

Psychology, Vol. 51(3), Nov 1955, 677–689; p. 288: Seeman P. Atypical Antipsychotics: Mechanism of Action. Can J Psychiatry. 2002, 47 (1): 27–38. Figure 4A and 4B. 3 Theories of Atypical Action; p. 33.

Chapter 13

p. 295: Reprinted with permission from the Diagnostic and Statistical Manual of Mental Disorders, Fourth Edition, Text Revision, (Copyright © 2000). American Psychiatric Association; p. 312: Charles Baudelaire.

Chapter 14

p. 316: S Agurell, M Halldin, J E Lindgren, A Ohlsson, M Widman, H Gillespie, and L Hollister, Pharmacokinetics and metabolism of delta 1-tetrahydrocannabinol and other cannabinoids with emphasis on man, Pharmacological Reviews, March 1986 38:21–43.

Chapter 15

p. 337: From Wasson, R. G. (1972). The divine mushroom of immortality. In P. T. Furst (Ed.), Flesh of the Gods (pp. 185–200). New York: Praeger, p. 197; p. 337: Aaronsen & Osmond, Psychedelics: The Uses and Implications of Hallucinogenic Drugs, Anchor Books/Doubleday, 1970, p. 53; p. 337: Aaronson & Osmond, Psychedelics: The Uses and Implications of Hallucinogenic Drugs, Anchor Books/Doubleday, 1970, pp. 47–48.

INDEX

Pages on which there is a definitive discussion of each concept are indicated in boldface type

11-hydroxy-delta-9-THC, 317
12-step facilitation therapy, **129**
12-step program, 181
2-AG, **318**
2-arachidonyl glycerol, **318**
4-ABP, 204
5-H1AA, 296
5-HT, 296–300, 302–6
5-HT$_{1A}$ receptors, 297, 299–300, 355
5-HT$_{2A}$–mGlu receptor complex, 287
5-HT$_{2A}$ receptors, 287, 289, 334, 335, 338
5-HT$_3$ receptors, 147
5-hydroxytryptamine, 80 (*see also* serotonin;
   serotonin receptors)

abruptio placentae, 250
absorption, 7, 10, 215
abstinence-focused intervention, 276
abstinence syndrome, **102**
abuse liability, 34, **110**
abuse potential, **110**
acamprosate, 160
acetaldehyde, **21**, 139
acetaminophen, 255–56, 269
acetophenazine, 286
acetylcholine, 80, 83–85, 189, 318, 343
acetylcholinesterase, 83
acetyl-coenzyme A, 139
acetylsalicylic acid (*see* ASA)
ACh (*see* acetylcholine)
action potential, 59–60
active placebo, 307
acute administration, harmful effects of,
   152–54
acute psychotic reaction, 328, **339**
acute tolerance, **41**–42, 174
Adam, **339**
adaptation
   hedonic dysregulation, 123–25
addiction, **97**–100, 120–21
addicts, 122
additive effect, 7
adenosine, 89
adenosine receptors, 216
adolescents
   behavioral treatments for, 129–30
adrenaline, 69, 81
adrenergic neurons, 85
adrenergic receptors, 85
adrenocorticotropic hormone (ACTH), 125

affective flattening, 278–79
age, **21**, 150
aggression, 173
agranulocytosis, 290
AIDS, 315
akathisia, **290**, 308, **310**
alcohol, 111, **132**, 173–74, 178, 203, 315,
   323, 324, 338
   absorption, 136–37
   acute tolerance, 147
   behavioral tolerance, 147–48
   chronic tolerance, 147
   discriminative stimulus properties, 146–47
   disinhibition, 145–46
   distribution, 137–38
   driving, 51–52, 145
   elimination, 139
   ethanol, 132
   ethyl, 132
   excretion, 136
   first-pass metabolism, **136**
   hand–eye coordination, 143
   history, 133–35
   isopropyl, 132
   memory, 144–45
   metabolic tolerance, 147
   methanol, 132
   methyl, 132
   neuropharmacology, 139–40
   perception, 143
   performance, 143–44
   rubbing, 132
   self-administration, 148–49
   sleep, 143
   specific gravity, 138
   subjective effects, 143
   tolerance, 51–52, 139
   withdrawal, 148
   wood, 132
alcohol absorption rates
   beer, 137
   concentration, 137
   sparkling wines, 137
alcohol-avoiding strains, 111
alcohol blackout
   en block, **144**
   fragmentary, **144**
alcohol consumption, benefits of, 156–59
alcohol dehydrogenase, **19**, **21**, 136

alcoholics, 122
Alcoholics Anonymous, 159–60
alcohol-induced behavior, 153
Alcoholism
   pharmacotherapies for, 160–61
alcoholism, **100**, 150
   genetics of, 150–51
alcohol-preferring strains, **110**
alcohol withdrawal
   early minor syndrome, 147
aldehyde dehydrogenase, 139
Alexander the Great, 231
Alles, Gordon, 230
all-or-none law, 61
allostatic process, 123
alogia, 278–79
alpha2-adrenergic receptor agonists, 274
alprazolam, 165, 178
Alzheimer's disease, 193
Amed, S., 113
American Association for the Cure of
   Inebriates, **100**
American Medical Association, 230, 314
American Psychiatric Association, 294
amethysts, **142**
amineptine, 251
amino acid neurotransmitters, 87–89
amisulpride, 286
amitriptyline, 306, 310
amnesia, 348
AMPA receptor hyperactivity, 283
AMPA receptors, 283
amphetamine, 91, 111, 121, 181, 192, **228**,
   230–46, 249–53, 332, 338
   absorption, 231–32
   ADHD, treatment of, 240
   athletic performance, 240–41
   conditioned behavior, 241–42
   depression, 243–44
   distribution, 232
   excretion of, 232
   half-life, 232
   harmful effects, 249–50
   neurophysiology, 232–35
   performance, 239–40
   pKa, 231
   psychosis, 238
   reproduction, 249–50
   self-administration, 231–32

sensitization, 242–43
sleep, 236
sources, 228–29
stereotyped behavior, 238, 241
subjective effects, 236–38
tolerance, 50, 242–43
treatment, 251–53
unconditioned behavior, 241
violence, 238–39
withdrawal, 243–44
amphetamine discrimination, 242
amphetamine lever, 244–45
amphetamine withdrawal depression, 244
amygdala, 86, **115**
anabolic steroids, 106
Anacin, 210
analgesia, **30**, 254, 261, 324
tolerance, 48
anandamide, **318**, 324
Andean Indians, 249
angel dust, 343
anhedonia, 279, 294
anorectic drugs, 235
anorexia
tolerance, 43
Antabuse, **21**, 131, 160
anterograde amnesia, 171
antianxiety drugs, 291–92
anticholinergic drugs, 69
antipsychotics, 69
atropin, 68
tricyclic antidepressants, 68
anticonvulsants, 171, 174
antidepressants, 206, 234, 252, 296–98,
300–310
absorption, 303
alcohol, 303–4
children and adolescents, 307, 309–10
compliance, 309
conditioned behavior, 307–8
discriminative stimulus properties, 308
distribution, 303
effectiveness, 306–7
effects on sleep, 305–6
effects on the body, 304–5
excretion, 303–4
first generation, 301–3
first-pass metabolism, 303, 309
half-life, 303–5
harmful effects, 309–10
history, 300–302
MAOIs, 300–306, 308–10
overdose, 310
performance, 306
personality, 306
punishment-suppressed behavior, 308

reproduction, 309
second generation, 300–301, 303
self-administration, 308
SNRIs, 301, 303, 306–10
SSRIs, 296–97, 301, 303–10
subjective effects, 306
suicide, 309–10
TCAs, 300–303, 305–8
teratogenic effect, 309
therapeutic index, 310
third-generation, 301–3
tolerance, 308
tricyclic, 300–305
violence, 309–10
withdrawal, 308
antidotes, 277
antiemetics, 293, **319**
antipsychotic drugs, **277**–78, 281–82, 287,
289, 291–93
absorption/distribution, 289
atypical, 286–89
compliance, 291–92
conditioned behavior, 291–92
discovery of, 285–86
dissociation, 292
drug state discrimination, 292
effects on performance, 291
effects on sleep, 291
effects on the body, 290–91
examples of, 286
excretion, 289–90
harmful effects, 293
history, 285–86
lethal effects, 291
reproduction, 293
routes of administration, 289
self-administration, 292
sexual activity, 293
subjective effects, 291
therapeutic effects, 293
tolerance, 292
typical, 286–89
typical and atypical dissociation constants,
288
typical vs. atypical, 286–89
unconditioned behavior, 291
withdrawal, 292
anxiety, 111, 168, 174, 320, 328
anxiolytics, 163
aqua vitae, **157**
ARCI, **36**
aripiprazole, 286, 287, 289, 291, 293
arousal level, 191
arthritis, 320
artificial hibernation, 285
ASA, 257 (see also aspirin)

aspirin, 254–55, 257
Assyrian medical tablets, 256
athletic performance, 218
attention, **37**
atypical antipsychotics, **286**, 288, 292
atypicals (see third-generation antidepressants)
automutilation, 241
autonomic nervous system, 68
autoreceptor, 82
autoreceptors, 67
availability, **120**
aversive stimuli, 109
Avicenna, 256
avoidance–escape task, **33**
avolition, 278–79
axo-axonal synapses, 68
axon hillock, **58**, 61

Badaiani, A., 121
bad trip, 339
BAL
balanced placebo design, **29**
calculation, 138–39
balanced placebo design, **29**
BAL time course, 136
absorption phase, 136
excretion phase, 136
plateau phase, 136
Ban Drowz, 210
barbiturates, 89, **163**–80, 265, 267, 270,
344, 346, 348
harmful effects, 180–81
history, 164–67
neurophysiolog, 167–69
overdose, 180–81
performance, 171–73
self-administration, 177–80
sleep, 171
subjective effects, 171
treatment, 181
withdrawal, 175, 324
Barger, G., 230
basal ganglia, 73–74, **115**, 318
bath salts, 231
Bayer Company, 257
BDNF, 311
beer, 133, 137
behavior
using physiology to, 27
behavioral couples therapy (BCT), **129**
behavioral neuroscience, 27
behavioral pharmacology, **25**, 31
in Europe, 27
history of, 25–26
behavioral treatments, 129
Benedetti, F., 53

benzodiazepines, 89, 111, 163–80, 348
  discriminative stimulus properties, 173–74
  driving, 172–73
  half-life, 170
  harmful effects, 180–81
  history, 164–67
  memory, 172
  neurophysiology, 167–69
  overdose, 180–81
  performance, 171–73
  self-administration, 177–80
  sleep, 171
  subjective effects, 171
  tolerance, 174
  treatment, 171, 180–81
  withdrawal, 175–77
benzodiazepine withdrawal symptoms, 175
  low-dose withdrawal, **175**
  sedative-hypnotic withdrawal, **175**
Bergman, J., 111
bhang, **315**
bicuculline, 89
binding potential, 297
biogenic amine, 84
biogenic amines, 85
birth defects, 180, 203
black box warning, 307, 309
Blackman, D. E., 27
blood-brain barrier, **17**, 317
blue nitro, 347
Boff, E., 173
BOLD imaging, 196
Bolshevik bombings, 258
bone density, 226
bong, **316**
bowman's capsule, **19**
B process, **44**, 123
Brady, Joseph, 26
brain, **69**, 70–71
brain control circuits
  disruption of, 125–26
brain derived neurotopic factor (see BDNF)
brain imaging
  of drug effects, 91
brain stem, 319
brandy, 133
breaking point, **113**, 329
breathalyzer, 137, 144
brief strategic family therapy (BSFT), **130**
British Parliament, 257
bromides, 164
bronchitis, 202
bronchodilation, 235
bronchodilators, 241
bruxism, **340**
buccal membranes, **13**

bufotenine, **332**
buprenorphine, 256, 274–76
bupropion, 205–6, 229, 251–52, 303, 305, 308
buspirone, 21, 166
butyrophenones, 281, 286

cacao, **211**
caffeine, 112, 142, 195
  anxiety, 226
  automutilation, 219
  effects of, 217–20
  fetal growth, 225
  half-life, 216
  headache, 217
  headache remedies, 217
  LD_{50}, 219
  lethal dose, 226
  mood, 222
  physical dependence, 222
  pregnancy, 225
  spontaneous motor activity, 219
  tolerance, 221
  withdrawal, 221–23
caffeinism, 226
caine reaction, **250**
Calhoun, V. D., 145
California Civil Addict Program, 273
Cambridge risk task, 272
Camellia sinensis, 211
cAMP (see cyclic AMP)
Campbell, J. C., 50, 51
cancer, 155
cannabidiol (see CBD)
cannabinoid blockers, 325
cannabinoid receptors, 317
cannabinoids, **314** (see also CBD; CBN; THC)
  antagonist, 324
  breathing reflex, 319
  medicinal purposes, 316
  memory, 318
  pain, 317
  receptor site, 317
  synthetic, 314–15
cannabinol (see CBN)
cannabis, 178, 312–31
  creativity, 322
  hand-eye coordination, 322
  history, 312–14
  inhalers, 316
  narcotic, 314
  phenotypes, 312
  preparations, 315
  reaction time, 322
  Standardized Field Sobriety Test, **323**

Cannabis indica, **312**
Cannabis sativa, **312**
capillary, **10**
Cappell, Howard, 43
carbon monoxide, **80**, 202
cardiac disease, 226
carfentanil, **271**
  potency, 271
  therapeutic index (TI), 271
carphenazine, 286
cassina, 212
catalepsy, **265**
catecholamine-like hallucinogens, 334, 339
catecholamines, 85
catheter, **10**, 105, 106
cathinone, **229**, 231–32, 234–35, 238, 242
  half-life, 232
  neurophysiology, 232–35
  psychosis, 231, 238
  route of administration, 231–32
  sources, 229
CB_1 receptors, 318–21
CB_2 receptors, 317
CBD, **314**, 317, 319, 322, 324
CBN, **314**, 318, 324
cell body, 58, 68
centers, **68**
central gray, 267
cerebellum, 72, 318, 321
cerebral blood flow, 122
c-fos, **65**
"chasing the dragon" smoking, 258
Chechen rebels, 271
cheese effect, **304**
chemical name, **2**
chemoreceptor trigger zone, 262
Chen Nung, 230
cherry meth, 347
China White, 256
chipping (see ice cream habit)
chloral hydrate, 164
chlordiazepoxide, **45**, 165, 174, 180, 195, 348
chloride ion channel, 89
chlorpromazine, **26**, 106, 281, 285–86, 291–92, 332–49
chlorprothixene, 286
chocolate, 212
cholinergic neurons, **81**
cholinergic receptors, **83**
  muscarinic, **83**
  nicotinic, **83**
chronic consumption
  harmful effects of, 154–56
chronic tolerance, **51**, 174
Ciba Company, 230
cilia, 202

cimetidine, 137
circadian rhythms, 247
circularity, 110
citalopram, 308, 310
citric acid cycle, 139
Civil War, 257
clandestine labs, 231
classical conditioning, **31**
    of compensatory responses, 47–48
    of drug stimuli and responses, 46–47
    of drug tolerance, 48
    of Withdrawal, 48–50
classic heroin withdrawal, 267
clock test, **240**
clonazepam, 165, **165**
clozapine, 286–88, 290–92
CNS, 68, **69–71**, 89, 317, 320
Coca-Cola, 230
cocaine, 108, 113, **228–39**, 241–53, 340, 341
    conditioned behavior, 241–42
    distribution, 232
    half-life, 232
    harmful effects, 249–50
    LD50, 250
    neurophysiology, 232–35
    overdose, 250
    pharmacokinetics, 232
    physical dependence, 251
    pKa, 231
    psychosis, 238
    reproduction, 249–50
    self-administration in humans, 244–45
    self-administration in nonhumans,
        246–48
    sensitization, 242–43
    sources, 228–29
    subjective effects, 236–38
    tolerance, 242–43
    treatment, 251–53
    unconditioned behavior, 241
    withdrawal, 243–44
cocaine bugs, 238
cocaine HCl, 231–32
cocaine hydrochloride (see cocaine HCl)
cocaine-induced euphoria, 236–38
cocaine sudden-death syndrome, 250
cocoa, 211–12
    caffeine, 211
    fermentation, 211
    history, 213–14
    theobromine, 212
    tree, 211
Cocteau, Jean, 254, 263
codeine, 255–56, 258–59
Coffeacanephora, **209**
robusta, **209**

coffee, 209–11
    history, 213
cognitive behavioral therapy (CBT), **129**, 251
cognitive deficits, 279–80
coke-out, **242**
Coleridge, Samuel Taylor, 263
Colloca, L., 53
coma, 72
comedown, **236**, 243
"common cold of mental illness," 295
complex reaction time (CRT), **36**
compliance, **291–92**
COMT, **85**
conditional tolerance, **48**
conditioned behavior, 173
conditioned compensatory responses
    withdrawal, 48–50
conditioned place preference (CPP), **35**,
        110, 114
conditioned reinforcement, 114
conditioned response, **31**, **47**
conditioned stimulus, **31**, **47**
conditioned tolerance, **114**
conditioning
    classical, **31**
    operant, **31**
    Pavlovian, **31**
    respondent, **31**
Confessions of an English Opium-Eater, 262
Conger, J., 146
constant blood level theory, 199
context, **53**
contingency, 129
contingency management, 251
contingency management interventions, 129
control
    placebo effect, 53
Controlled Substances Act, 314
convulsions, 26, 30
Cook, Len, 27
cortex, **76–78**, **115**, 195, 317, 334, 335
cortical dysfunction, 126
corticotropin-releasing hormone (see CRH)
cosmetic psychopharmacology, 306
cosmos, 231, 236
A Counterblaste to Tobacco, **184**
Courvousier, Simone, 291
CPP, **35**
CR, **47**
Crack, **232**
crank bugs, 238
crash, **236**, 243, 245
craving, 121, **122**, 131, 200
    incentive sensitization and, 121–23
CREB, **65**
CRH, 299

cross sensitization, **52**
cross-tolerance, **41**, 174, 325, 338
crystal, 343
CS, **47**
cued recall, **37**
culture, 149
curare, **83**, 189
cyclic AMP, 64, 260, 267, 317
    second-messenger, 260
CYP1A2 enzyme, 216
cytochrome P450 enzymes, 290
cytochrome P4503A4, 21, 22

D1 receptors, 281
D2 receptor blockers, 286
D_2 receptor blockers, 147
D2 receptors, 281–82, 286–90, 293
D_2 receptors, 126
D3 receptors, 282, 287, 289
D4 receptors, 282, 287, 289
DA, 191, 194, 287, 289, 296, 299, 302–3
    (see also dopamine)
dagga, 313
Dale, Henry, 50
Dale's law, **80**
d-amphetamine, 111
DATs, 232–35, 251
declarative memory, **37**
deep brain stimulation, 311
Degenhardt, L., 329
delirium tremens or the DTs, 148
delta-8-THC, 324 (see also THC)
delta-9-THC, **314**, 317, 324 (see also THC)
Demerol, 256 (see also meperidine)
dendrites, 58, 76
Deneau, G. A., 246
dependence, 43–44, **43–44**
dependence model, **103**
dependent variable, 28
depolarization, 59, 61
depolarization-induced suppression of
        excitation (DSE), 67, 318
depolarization-induced suppression of
        inhibition (DSI), 67, 318
depot injection, 289, 292
depressant, **26**
depression, 294–300, 305, 307, 309, 311
    anhedonia, 294
    characteristics of, 294–95
    DSM-IV-TR criteria for major depressive
        episode, 294–95
    glucocorticoid theory, 298–99
    hypothalamic–pituitary–adrenal (HPA)
        axis, 298–99
    monoamine theory, 296–98
    mortality, 295

depression (*continued*)
  nature of, 294–95
  symptoms of, 294–95
depressive disorders, 294 (*see also* depression)
De Quincey, Thomas, 262–63
descending reticular formation, **71**
design, 28
  between-subject, **28**
  within-subject, **28**
designer drugs, 256, 339
detoxification, **19**, 128, 274–76
de Wit, H., 111, 113
Dews, Peter, 26, 27
dextromethorphan, 346
  behavioral effects, 346–47
  cough suppressant, 347
  discriminative stimulus properties, 346
  first pass, 346
  locomotor activity, 346
  metabolism, 346
  neurophysiology, 346
  oral consumption, 346
  pharmacokinetics, 346
  self-administration, 346
  stereotyped behavior, 346
diacetylmorphine (*see* heroin)
diamorphine (*see* heroin)
Diana, Princess, 51
diazepam, 76, 111, 172, 175, 176
diffusion, **59**
digit symbol substitution test, 239
discounting of delay, 121
discriminative stimuli, 33–34
disease, **98**
disease model, **100**
  exposure, 101
  predisposition, 101
disinhibition, **37**, 145–46
disorder, **102**
dissociation, **33**
dissociation constants, 281, 287–88
dissociative anesthetics, **343–46**
  anesthetic, 343
  depression, 344
  harmful effects, 345
  lethal effects, 345–46
  neurophysiology, 346
  performance, 340
  pharmacokinetics, 343
  psychotic behavior, 345
  reproduction, 345–46
  self-administration, 344
  stereotyped actions, 344
  stimulus properties, 344
  taming effect, 345

tolerance, 344
  withdrawal, 344–45
distillation, 132–33
distribution, **8**, 137–38, 215
  lipid solubility, **16**
distribution, benzodiazepine, 170
disulfiram, **21**
DMA, 339
DMT, **332**, 338
DNA, 66, 272
DOET, **339**
do-it-again system, 119
dolophine (*see* methadone)
DOM, **339**
dopamine, 73, 85–86, **142**, 169, 296, 299, 301, 306, 318, 341–45, 348 (*see also* DA)
  role of, 117–18
dopamine hypothesis, **281–82**
dopamine receptor blockers, 220
dopamine transporters (*see* DATs)
dorsal horn, 70
dorsolateral prefrontal cortex, 196
dose–effect curve, **4**
dose–response curve, 4–5
double-blind procedure, **30**
downers, **164**
downregulation, **42**
DRC, 4–5
Dreser, Heinrich, 257
driving, **38**, 111, 172–73
DRL, **50**
dronabinol, 315
Drug Abuse Warning Network, 349
drug addiction
  effective treatment, principles of, 126–28
drug effects
  conditioning of, 46
  operant analysis of, 26–27
drugs (*see also* specific drugs)
  reinforcing properties of, 34
drug self-administration, 106–7
drug state discrimination, 36
drug vaccines, 252
DSM (DSM-III), **100**
DSM (DSM-IV), 97–100
  substance abuse, **97**
  substance dependence, **97**
DSM-5, 277, 294
DSM-IV-TR, 222, 244, 248
DSST (*see* digit symbol substitution test)
Dworkin, S., 54
dysfunctional glutamate neurotransmission, 280
dysphoria, 123
dysthymic disorder, 294
dystonia, 320

e, 339
Earleywine, M., 329
easy lay, 347
Ebers Papyrus, 256
ecstasy, **339–42** (*see also* MDMA)
  acute tolerance, 340
  alcohol withdrawal, 339
  aphrodisiac, 348
  cognitive deficits, 341
  craving for alcohol, 348
  depletion in serotonin, 341
  discriminative stimulus properties, 340
  driving, 348
  electrolyte imbalance, 341
  entactogenic effects, 340
  epidemiology, 348–49
  half-life, 340
  harmful effects, 341
  heat regulation, 341
  lethal effects, 341–42
  narcolepsy, 347
  neurophysiology, 340
  opiates withdrawal, 349
  performance, 338
  pharmacokinetics, 340
  place preference, 348
  raves, 340
  REM sleep, 348
  self-administration, 338
  tolerance, 340
  withdrawal, 341
ECT, 310–11
ED$_{50}$, **5**, **33**
Edeleano, L., 230
EEG, 237
effectiveness, **6**
effective treatment programs, 126–28
electroconvulsive therapy (*see* ECT)
electroencephalographic (*see* EEG)
electrostatic charge, **59**
elevated plus maze, **30**
emergence delirium, **343**
Emergency Scheduling Act, 231
empathogen, **332**
empathogenic effects, 336
emphysema, 202
endocannabinoids, 89–90, **318**, 319
endocytosis, 260, 266
endogenous, 259
endogenous benzodiazepine, 169
endogenous opiate system, 147
endogenous opioid peptides, **318**
endogenous opioids, 259
endorphins, 73, **83**, **259**
energy drinks, 212
enkephalins, 73, 87, 259

entactogen, 332
entactogenic effects, 340
enzyme, **19**
enzyme induction, **21**
ephedrine, **220**
epidermis, **16**
epinephrine, 228, **230**, 235
episodic memory, **37**
EPS, 281, 286–87, 289, –290, 292
ergot fungus, 333
ergotism, 333
ethanol, 106, 113, 348 (*see also* alcohol)
ETS, 204
euphoria, 191
Europe, behavioral pharmacology in, 27
European Behavioral Pharmacology Society,
     27
Excedrin, 210
excipients, **4**
excitatory postsynaptic potential, 61
excitotoxicity, 283
excretion, 215
excretion, benzodiazepine, 170
exercise, 311
expectancy, **53–54**
expectation mechanism, **53**
experimental control, **28**
experimenter bias, **29–30**
explicit memory, **37**, **172**
extended amygdala, 125
extrapyramidal signs and symptoms
     (*see* EPS)

FDA, 287, 290
fear, 75
fenfluramine, **241**
fentanyl, 256, 268, 271
fermentation, **132**
fetal abnormalities, 250
fever, 335, 336
FHN
     vs. FHP, 151
FHP
     vs. FHN, 151
FI (*see* fixed interval (FI))
fight-or-flight response, **68**
firing, 60
first-generation antidepressants, **300**,
     302–3
first-generation antipsychotic medications
     (*see* typical antipsychotics)
first-pass metabolism, **19**
fixed interval (FI), **32**, **50**, 241
fixed ratio (FR), **32**, 33
fixed ratio schedule (*see* FR)
flashbacks, **339**

flumazenil, 172, **176**, 181
fluoxetine, 84, 85, 301 (*see also* Prozac)
     dreams, 305–6
     half-life, 304
     personalities, 306
     sleep, 305
     teenagers and children, 310
     violence and suicide, 309–10
fluphenazine, 286
fMRI, 94, 122, 145, 244, 261, 272
fMRI BOLD, 261
formication, 238
formulation, **4**
fortified wines, 133
FR, 109, 114, 146, 241, 246, 248
freak-out, **328**
free recall, **37**
freeze, **236**
French Wine of Cola, Ideal Tonic, 230
Freud, Sigmund, 204
Fried, P., 328
frontal cortex, 344
frozen addict, 256
Fry, S. J., 214
functional magnetic resonance imaging
     (*see* fMRI)

GABA, 80, **83**, 87, 140–41, 174, 259, 261,
     280, 283, 285, 287, 318, 347
GABA$_A$ receptor, 140, 164–69
GABA$_B$ receptor, 347
GABAergic interneurons, 283
GABAergic neurons, 283
GABA-receptor-ionophore complex, **140**
GABA receptors, 88–89
     GABA$_A$, **88**
     GABA$_B$, **88**
GABA receptor subunits, **168**
     alpha, 167, 168
     beta, 167
     gamma, 167
gamma-aminobutyric acid, 88–89
ganglia, 73
ganja, **315**
Garrett, B. E., 223
gated ion channel, 64
gateway drug, 329
gaze nystagmus, 323
GBH, 347
GBL, 347
gel tab, 334
gender, 150
gene expression, 66
general anesthetics, 164
genes, 66
genetic predisposition, 111

GHB, **164**, **347–49**
     anesthetic, 346
     anxiolytic properties, 348
     behavior, 346–47
     cataleptic state, 348
     dose, 348
     drug state discrimination, 348
     epidemiology, 348–49
     half-life, 347
     lethal dose, 347
     narcolepsy, 347
     neurophysiology, 346
     pharmacokinetics, 346
     self-administration, 346
     sleep, 347
     therapeutic index, 347
     tolerance, 349
     withdrawal, 349
GHB receptors, 347
glaucoma, 321
glial cells, 67
glomerulus, **19**
glucocorticoid theory, 298–99
glutamate, 73, 87–88
glutamate hypothesis, **282–83**
glutamate NMDA receptor, 282
glutamatergic neurons, 281–83
glycine, 89
Goldberg, D. M., 197
Goldberg, S. R., 197, 326
Goldstein, A., 217
go pills, 239 (*see also* amphetamine)
go–stop task, 146
G-protein-coupled receptors, 259 (*see also*
     opioid receptors)
grapefruit, **21**
Gray, R., 328
gray matter, 94
Greenberg, I., 326
Griffiths, R. R., 111, 223
Grinspoon, L., 337
growth hormone, 80
Gruber, A. J., 328
Guarana, 212
Guillot, C., 341

H$_2$-receptor antagonists, 136
Haag, H. B., 152
habit-forming drugs, 254
habituation, 106
halcion (*see* triazolam)
Hallstrom, C., 175
hallucinations, 277–78, 287, **332–49**
hallucinogen PCP, 259
hallucinogens, 97, **332–49**

haloperidol, 148, 244–45, 281, 286, 289, 291–92
Halstead, William Stewart, 264–65
hand–eye coordination, 143
hangover, 153, 348
hard liquor, 133
harmaline, **333**
Harrison Narcotic Act, 230, 254, 257, 258
Harvey, William, 213
hashish, 313–16
hash oil, **315**, 316
headaches, 336, 339
heart disease, 156
Hebb, Donald, 33
hedonic dysregulation, 123–**25**, 125
hedonism, **118**
Heise, G. A., 173
Hemby, S., 54
hemp, **312**, 313
heptoxdiazines, **165**
heroic, 257
heroin, 121, 125, 181, **255**, 257–58,
    261–64, 267–76, 319, 329
  addicts, 263–64, 267–68, 273, 275
  antagonist therapies, 276
  history, 257–58
  overdose, 271–73
  withdrawal, 49, 267
heroin-addicted criminal offenders, 273
heroin-addicted seniors, 268
heroisch, 257
heteroreceptors, 67
Hinson, R. E., 49
hippocampus, 70, **70**, **74**, **115**, 322, 324
Hippocrates, 256
histamine, **80**, 318
HIV/AIDS, 249, 273, 275
hob, **343**
homeostasis, **42**, **123**
hormones, **80**
hot plate (HP), **48**
Hudson, J. I., 328
Huestis, M. A., 328
Huichol Indians, 336
human testing, **38**
  phase 1, **38**
  phase 2, **38**
  phase 3, **39**
  phase 4, **39**
Huntington's chorea, 293
hydrocodone, **256**, 269
hyperalgesia, **47**
hyperfortin, **22**
hyperpolarization, 59
hypnogogic states, **335**
hypoactivity, 126
hypoglycemia, 335, 336

hypothalamic–pituitary–adrenal (HPA)
    axis, 298
hypothalamus, **75**–76, 317
hypothermia
  tolerance, 43

iatrogenic use, 177–78
ICD-10, **98**–99
ice cream habit, 267
illicit drug market, 231
imipramine, 106, 300–301
immune system, 317, 318, 330
immunization, 207–8
implicit memory, **37**, **172**
incentive salience, **117**, 123
incentive sensitization
    and craving, 121–23
incentive sensitization theory, **121**
inclined plane test, **30**
independent variable, 28
Indians of the Andes, 231
indoleamine, 85
inebriety, **100**
inhalation, 12
  smoke, **13**
inhibition, 61–62
inhibitory postsynaptic potential, **62**
inhibitory tone, **167**, 169
initial screening tests, 38–39
insomnia, 294, 319, 320, 340, 343
Institute of France, 255
insulin, 81
international treaties, 230
Internet, 231
interval schedules, **32**
intracranial administration, **109**
intramuscular injection, **9**
intranasal administration, **13**
intraperitoneal injection, **9**
intrathecal injection, **10**
intravenous injection, **9**
intraventricular injection, 109
introspection, **35**
  systematic, **35**–36
  unstructured, **35**
inverse agonists, **169**
ion, 83
ion channels
  gated, **59**
  nongated, **59**
  voltage gated ion channels, **59**
iproniazid, 300–301
Iversen, L., 328
Iverson, Susan, 27

James, D., 328
Jee-cocktail, 231

jeff, 231
Jellinek, E. M., 100, 150
Johanson, C. E., 111, 112
Johns Hopkins Medical School, 264
Johnson, H. J., 191
joint, **316**
Joplin, Janis, 272
"joy plant," 256
jugular vein, 105, 108
Juliano, L. M., 223
Justinova, Z., 326

K, 343
Kaizer, S., 217
Kaye, S., 152
keratin, 16
Kessler, D., 205
ketamine, 282–83, 343–48 (see also
    dissociative anesthetics; Special K)
khat psychosis, 231
kicking the habit, 267
kidneys, **19**–20
  pH, **20**
kinase, 65, **65**
Kirby, K. C., 111
kitkat, **343**
Kluver, Heinrich, 335
Ko Kuei Chen, 230
Koob, G., 113, 123, 125
Korsakoff's psychosis, **322**
Koves, T., 54
Kramer, Peter, 306
Krank, M. D., 49
Kubla Khan (poem), 263
Kuehnle, J. C., 326
Kwo, P. Y., 139

LAAM, 256, 259, 275
laboratory animals, 106
Laborit, Henri, 285, 291, 293
Lader, M. H., 175
Largactil, 285–86
laudanum, **257**
LD$_{50}$, **5**, **38**
L-DOPA, **74**
lead poisoning, 133
Le Club des Hachichins, 313, 320
Le Moal, M., 125
Lephophora williamsii, 333
Leshner, Alan, 101
lethal effects, 226
levo-c-acetylmethadol (see LAAM)
levorphanol, 256
Li, T., 139
limbic system, 74–75, 322
Lindesmith, A. R., 104
Linnaeus, Carolus, 312

lipid, **14**, 59
lipid bilayer, **14**
lipid solubility, 170
liquid X, 347
liver, **19**
liver function
    age, 21
    species, 22
locus coeruleus, **72**, 296, 299, 334
long-term memory, **37**
long-term residential treatment, **128**
lorazepam, 172
loss of control, 151–52
low-dose withdrawal, 175–76
loxapine, 286
LSD, 106, 328, **332–39**
    acute psychotic reaction, 339
    cognitive functions, 338
    creativity, 338
    cross-tolerance, 338
    discriminative stimulus properties, 340
    effects on the body, 334
    empathogenic effects, 336
    entactogenic effects, 340
    half-life, 334
    harmful effects, 338–39
    history, 333–34
    hits, 334
    neurophysiology, 334–35
    performance, 338
    pharmacokinetics, 334
    self-administration, 338
    sources, 334
    subjective effects, 335–37
    thresholds, 337
    tolerance, 338
    withdrawal, 338
LSD-25, 333
lysergic acid amide, 332

MA (*see* monoamines)
ma, 313
Macbeth, 277
Macht, David, 26, 33
mackworth clock test, **37**
MADD, 135
magic mushrooms, 332
magnetic resonance imaging (MRI) (*see* MRI)
main effect, **6**
mainlining, **9**
mainstream smoke, **204**
major depressive disorder, 294–95, 299, 300
major depressive episode, 294–95
major tranquilizer, 285
MAO, **85**, 232–33, 242, 302–3
MAO-A, **302**

MAO-B, **302**
MAOIs, 300–303 (*see also* antidepressants)
MA psychosis, **238**, 249
marijuana, 122, 230–31, **313**
    cigarettes, 325–26
    cognitive functioning, 321
    decriminalization, 314
    IQ, 328
    National Household Survey on Drug
        Abuse, 327
    schizophrenia, 328
Marinol, 315, 319, 320
Marlatt, George, 29
Maskos, U., 191
MATs (*see* monoamine transporters)
maturing out, 268
MBDB, **340**
McCully, J., 49
MDA, **339**
MDEA, **339**
MDMA, **339** (*see also* ecstasy)
mecamylamine, 192, 194
medial forebrain bundle, 72, **72**, 73, 296, 298
median effective dose, **5**
median lethal dose, **5**
medicines, 212
medulla, 71
Mello, Nancy, 105
Mendelson, H. H., 326, 329
Mendelson, Jack, 105
MEOS, 147
meow meow (*see* mephedrone)
meperidine, **256**, 259
mephedrone, 229, **231–32**, 234
meprobamate, **163**
mescaline, 173, 334–39
mesolimbic dopaminergic synapses, 280
mesolimbic dopamine system, 53, 86, **115**,
    117–19, 118, 121, 124
mesolimbic pathway, 281–83, 289
mesoridazine, 286
metabolism, **19**
metabolites, **19**
metabotropic glutamate (mGlu) receptors, 287
methadone, 178, 256, 258–59, 262, 265,
    271, 273–76
methadone-maintained mothers, 273
methadone maintenance, 178
methamphetamine, 341
methaqualone, **163**
methylxanthine
    athletic performance, 218
    conditioned behavior, 219–20
    consumption, 213, 215, 218, 227
    dependence syndrome, 224–25
    discriminative stimulus properties, 220

effects of, 217–20
    extent of, 214–15
    harmful effects, 225–26
    human performance, 217–18
    lethal effects, 226
    neurophysiology, 217–18
    pKa, 215
    routes of administration, 215
    self-administration, 223–24
    sleep, 218–19
    sources, 209–12
    subjective effects, 220–21
    tolerance, 221
    unconditioned behavior, 219
    withdrawal, 221–23
Mexican Valium, **166**
Meyer, Roger, 263
microdots, 334
midazolam, 170, **170**, 174
migraine, 336
millivolts, 58
minor tranquilizers, 285
Mirin, Steven, 263
Misuse of Drugs Act, 231
Mithridatism, **40**
mixed agonist, **260–61**, 264, 270, 274
mixed opioid agonist–antagonist (*see* partial
    agonist)
M&M, **339**
modafinil, 251–52
modern psychiatry, 277
moist snuff, **182**
molindone, 286
Monitoring the Future Survey, 269
monoamine-like hallucinogens, 338, 342
monoamine oxidase (*see* MAO)
monoamine oxidase inhibitors (*see* MAOIs)
monoamine psychosis (*see* MA psychosis)
monoamines, 85
monoamine theory, 296–98
monoamine transporters, 232
mood disorder, 294–96, 298 (*see also* major
    depressive disorder)
Moreau de Tours, J. J., 313
morning glory seeds, 332
morphine, 90, 192, 254–65, 268, 270–71,
    319, 323, 346, 348
    conditioned behavior, 265
    drug state discrimination, 265
    first-pass metabolism, 258
    half-life, 259
    overdose, 49
    pKa, 258
    self-administration in nonhumans, 270
    subjective effects, 262–64

morphine (*continued*)
    tolerance, **47**
    unconditioned behavior, 264–65
morphine sulfate (*see* morphine)
morphium (*see* morphine)
Morrison, Jim, 272
motivational enhancement therapy (MET), **129**
motivational incentives, 129
motoneurons, **70**
motor cortex, 74
motor loop, **115**
motor performance, **36**
MPTP, 256
MRI, 92–94, 122, 280
multidimensional family therapy (MDFT), **130**
multiple sclerosis, 170, 314, 319
Mumford, G., 221
munchies, 319, 323
muscarinic receptors, **189**
myelin, 60, 68
myelinated axons, 60
myelin sheath, 60
Myerscough, R., 327

nabidiolex, 314
Nabilone, 315, 319, 320
Na+/Cl– dependent substrate-specific
    neuronal membrane transporters, 233
Naimi, T. S., 158
nalorphine, 256, 258, 260–61, 265, 270
naloxone, 256, **258–59**, 261, 270–71, 274, 276
naltrexone, 160–61, 252, 270, 276
narcotic analgesics, **254**
Narcotic Control Act, 254, 314
narcotics (*see* narcotic analgesics)
National Survey on Drug Use and Health
    (2010), 269
natural reinforcers, 119
nausea, 315, 316, 319
N-back test, **37**
NE, 194, 296, 298–99, 301–3
negative GABA$_A$ modulators, **169**
negative symptoms, **278–79**
Nelson, J. M., 321
NE neurons, 275
Neolithic burial sites, 256
NE receptors, 87
    alpha, 87
    beta, 87
nerves, 68
nervous system, 67–68, 154
    development of, 78–79
NETs, 232–35, 251

neuroanatomy
    motivation, 114–15
neurohormone, 86
neuroleptic, **286**, 291 (*see also* antipsychotic
    drugs)
neuromodulator, 91
neurons, 63
neuropharmacology, 139–40
neurophysiology, 167–69, 216–17
    nature and, 162–63
neurotic depression, 294
neurotransmitter, 42, 63, 91
neurotransmitters, 79–81
    drugs and, 81–83
Newsweek, 306
Nicot, J., 183
Nicotiana, **182**
    rustica, **182**
    tabacum, **182**
nicotine
    bolus, 186
    CNS effects, 191–92
    conditioned behavior, 194–95, 195–96
    discovery, 182
    distribution, 188
    drug state discrimination, 195
    excretion, 188–89
    gum, 188
    harmful effects, 201–4
    inhaler, 205
    memory, 193
    nasal spray, 205
    neurophysiology, 189–90
    patch, 188
    performance, 192–93
    pKa, 186
    PNS effects, 189
    reproduction, 203–4
    routes of administration, 200
    self-administration, 196–201
    sleep, 195–96
    subjective effects, 192–93
    tolerance, 191
    unconditioned behavior, 193–94
    withdrawal, 195–96
nicotine-1'-N-oxide, 188
nicotine bolus theory, 199–200
nicotine delivery systems, 185
nicotine replacement therapy, **205**
nicotinic receptors, **189**, 196
nitrazepam, **165**
nitric oxide, **80**, 90
nitrous oxide, 112
NMDA glutamate receptor, 259
NMDA receptor blockers, 147, 346
NMDA receptor hypoactivity, 283

NMDA receptors, 87, 141, 282–83, 343, 344
nocebo effect, 54, **54**
nod, 245, 263
No-Doz, 210
nonexperimental research, **30**
non-narcotic analgesics, 254
nonproprietary name, **4**
noradrenergic, **81**
norepinephrine, 72, 86–87, 318, 332, 340, 343
norepinephrine transporters (*see* NETs)
novel environments, 55
novocaine, 235
nuclei, 68
nucleus accumbens, **115**, 119, 122, 169, 191, 318, 344

obsessive-compulsive personality, 306
odds ratio (OR), 203
off-label use, **39**
olanzapine, 286
olive oil partition coefficients, **14**
operant analysis
    of drug effects, 26–27
operant behavior, **31**
operant chamber, 106
operant conditioning, **31**
    behavioral tolerance, 50
    of drug tolerance, 50–52
operant techniques, 27
opiates, **111**, 112, 254 (*see also* opioids)
opioid analgesic poisonings, 271
opioid metabolism, 266
opioid peptides, **90**, 318
    delta, **90**
    kappa, **90**
    mu, **90**
opioid receptors, 259–61, 265–66, 275
    delta, 259–61, 266, 270
    kappa, 259–61, 264–67, 270
    mu, 259–61, 265–67, 270, 275
    "opioid receptor–like" receptor, 259
opioids, **254–76**
    agonists, 258, 260–61
    antagonist therapies, 276
    body, effects on, 262
    conditioned behavior, 265
    distribution, 258
    drug state discrimination, 265
    excretion, 259
    harmful effects, 270–73
    history, 256–58
    lifestyle effects, 273
    maintenance therapies, 275–76
    mood, 263–64
    natural, 254–56
    neurophysiology, 259–62

origins, 254–56
performance, 264
pharmacokinetics, 258
pharmacological treatment, 274–76
pregnancy, 272–73
receptors, 259–60
reproduction, 272–73
routes of administration, 258
rushes, 263
self-administration in humans, 267–69
self-administration in nonhumans, 270
semisynthetic, 254–56
sleep, effects on, 262
subjective effects, 262–64
synthetic, 256
tolerance, 265–66, 272
unconditioned behavior, 264–65
withdrawal, 264, 267
opium, 165, **254–57**, 262–63, 270
opium poppy, 255–56
opponent process theory, 44–46
Opponent Process Theory of Solomon and
    Corbit, 244
oral administration, **13**, **104**
orbitofrontal cortex, 122
O'Shaughnessy, W. B., 313
outpatient treatment programs, 128
over-the-counter painkillers, 255
Overton, Donald, 33, 146
oxazepam, 165
oxycodone, **255**, 269
OxyContin, 255–56, 269 (*see also*
    oxycodone)
OxyContin OP, 256 (*see also* OxyContin)
OxyNEO, 256 (*see also* OxyContin)

pain, 87, 112, 256, 261–62, 264, 267–68
    mechanical, 261
    phantom limb, 261
    thermoceptive, 261
    visceral nociception, 261
paliperidone, 286
panic disorder, 163
Papaver somniferum, **254**
Paracelsus, 257
paramorphine (*see* thebaine)
parasympathetic nervous system, **68**
Parkinson's disease, 170, 256, 281, 286, 290,
    296
partial agonist, 261, 264–65, 270
patellar reflex, 191
Pavlov, I., 219
paw lick latency, **30**
paw lick test, **48**
PCP, 87, 112, 131, 282–83, 343–46 (*see also*
    dissociative anesthetics)

peak user, **245**
Pearlson, G. D., 145
pentazocine, 256, 261, 264
pentobarbital, 112, 195
    administration of, 26
    dose-effect curves for, 27
pentylenetetrazol, **45**
peptides, 81, 90–91
perception, **36**
Percocet, 255 (*see also* thebaine)
Percodan, 255 (*see also* thebaine)
performance, **36**
periaqueductal gray (PAG), 73, 91
peripheral nervous system, **67**
perphenazine, 286
PET, 91–92, 122, 143, 191, 235–36, 249,
    272, 275
pethidine, 256 (*see also* meperidine)
peyote, **333**
pH, **15**, 231–32
phagocytes, 202
phantasticants, **333–49**
pharmacokinetics, 7–8
pharmacological interventions, 206–7
pharmacotherapies, 160–61
pharmacotherapy
    future of, 131
Pharmacy Act, 257
phenazocine, 256
phencyclidine (*see* hallucinogen PCP; PCP)
phenmetrazine, 238
phenobarbital, 175
phenothiazines, 281, 286
phenylpropanolamine, **220**
Phoenix, River, 272
physical dependence, **44**, 103, 106–7, 113,
    150, 180, 196
physical/psychological dependence theory,
    98, 103, 125
physiological dependence, 98
physiological psychology, **27**
physiological saline, **9**
Pickens, R., 109, 246
pimizide, 286
pinpoint pupils, 262, 270
pKa, **15**
placebo, 53, **177**, 335
placebo control, **28**
placebo effects, **28**, 53–54
    in medical treatment, 54
placebo response rates, 307
placental barrier, **18**
plant food, 231
plastic immobility, 291
pleasure, **123**
pleasure centers, 76, **117**

PMA, 342
PNS, **67**, 68
POMS, 321
PONS, 71–72
Pope, H. G., Jr., 328
pores, **10**
positive GABA$_A$ modulator, 147, 167
positive reinforcement model, **108**
    circularity, 110
    neurological mechanisms, 110
    problems, 109–10
positive symptoms, **277–78**
positron emission tomography
positron emission tomography (PET)
    (*see* PET)
Posselt, L., 182
postsynaptic potentials, 61
postural hypotension, **304**
potency, **6**
potential years of life lost (*see* PYLL)
potentiation, **7**
Poulos, Constantine, 43
PR (*see* progressive ratio)
Preventative Medicine, 273
previous experience, 112
priming, **113–14**
    craving, 113
    loss of control, 113
    mesolimbic dopamine system, 113
    relapse, 113
    ventral tegmental area, 113
procaine (*see* novocaine)
procedural memory, **37**
prochlorperazine, 286
Profile of mood states (POMS), **36**
progressive ratio, **35**, 112, 113, 248, 323
Prohibition, 135
prolactin, 81, 235
promazine, 286
promethazine, 285
promoter region, 297
proof, 157
propoxyphene, 256, 264, 267–68
proprietary name, **4**
prostaglandins, 318
protein binding, **17**–18
proteins, 64
Prozac, 301 (*see also* fluoxetine)
    induced violence, 309–10
    personality, 306
    suicide, 309–10
psychedelics, 332
psychoanalysis, 341
psychological dependence, **44**
psychological withdrawal, 125, **125**
psychopharmacology, **25**

psychosis, 277, 279, 285–87, 290, 294
    negative symptoms, 279
    positive symptoms, 277, 279
psychostimulant withdrawal, 244
psychotherapeutic drugs, **38**
    development and testing of, 38–39
Psychotherapeutic revolution, 26
    chlorpromazine, 26
psychotic disorders, 277
psychotomimetics, 332
punding, **238**, 241, 245, 249
punishing, 109
punishment, **32**
pursuit rotor, **36**
pusher, 268
PXR, **22**
PYLL, 273 (*see also* YPLL)

quetiapine, 286
quinine, 272

raclopride, 286
radioisotopes, 91
Raleigh, Walter, 313
Ramchandani, V. A., 149
ranitidine, 136, 137
Raphé nuclei, 334, 335
raphe system, 296
rate dependency effect, **241**
ratio schedules, **32**
raves, 340, 343
rebound effect, 171
rebound insomnia, 171
recall, 172
receptor gated ion channel, 64
receptor mosaics, 216
receptor sites, 64, 91
recognition sites, 88
Redhi, G. H., 326
reducing drug reward, 131
Reimann, F. A., 182
reinforcement, **31**–32
    liking in, 118–19
    wanting in, 119
reinforcing value, **110**
    dose size, 110
    genetic differences, 110
    hunger, 112
    physical dependence, 113
    previous experience, 112
    self-medication, 111
    stress, 112
    task demands, 111
reinstatement, 113–14
relaxation task, 111
REM deprivation, 305
remoxipride, 286

REM rebound, 171
REM sleep, 262, 291, 305
reproduction, 153–54, 155–56
reserpine, 286, 296
residual effects, 172
respiratory center, 71
response inhibition
    tests of, 37–38
resting potential, 59, 87
reticular activating system, 72, 191
reticular formation, 72–73
reuptake, **67**
reverse tolerance, **52**, 325
rhesus monkey, 106
Rhöne-Poulenc company, 285, 291
risperidone, 286
RO 5-0690, 165
RO 15-4513, 142
roaches, **170**
Robbins, Trevor, 27
Roberts, David, 248
Robinson, T. E., 121
Robiquet, Pierre J., 255
Robitussin, 346
roboing, 346
Romberg sway test, 146
roofies, **166**
Rose, J. E., 186
route of administration, **8**, 215
    and absorption, 169–70
    inhalation, 12
    intramuscular (i.m.), **9**
    oral, 13
    parenteral, **8**
    subcutaneous, **9**
    transdermal, 16
Royal College of Physicians of London, 184
run-abstinence cycle, **245**, 247
runs, 242, 245, 249
Rush, Benjamin, 134
rushes, 87, 192, **236**, 238, 242, 252
Russian security forces, 271
Rylander, Gosta, 238

salicylic acid, 257
Sanger, David, 27
Sativex, 314, 316, 319, 320
Schedule-1 substance, 231
schedule of reinforcement, **32**
schizophrenia, 277–83, 285–87, 289
    antipsychotic medications, 285–93
    brain structural and functional
        abnormalities in, 280–81
    case study, 278–79
    catatonic, 277–79
    dopamine hypothesis, 281–82

DSM-IV-TR diagnostic criteria for,
    277–78
etiology of, 280
glutamate–dopamine interactions, 283–85
glutamate hypothesis, 282–83
incidence of, 279
nature of, 277–80
paranoid, 278
symptoms of, 277–79
theories of, 280–85
Schmidt, C. F., 230
Schuckit, M. A., 152
Schuster, Bob, 252
Schuster, Charles, 25, 265, 270
scoop, 347
scopolamine, 85
Scythians, 312, 313
secondary sex characteristics, 262, 272
second-generation antidepressants, 301
second-generation antipsychotic medications
    (*see* atypical antipsychotics)
second-messenger, 65
second-order schedules, 114, **114**, 197
sedative abusers, 112
sedative-hypnotics, **163**–81
    withdrawal, 175
Seiden, L. S., 50, 51
selective serotonin reuptake inhibitors
    (*see* SSRIs)
selegiline, 302
self-administration, 54, 106–8, 177–80
    humans, 105–6
    in humans, 177–78
    nonhumans, 105–6
    in nonhumans, 178–79
sensitization, **52**, 52–53, 114, 121, 122, 325
    alcohol, 52
    amphetamine, 52
    cocaine, 52
    conditioning, 52
    duration, 53
    mesolimbic dopamine system, 53
    nicotine, 52
    novel environments, 55
    opiates, 53
    phencyclidine, 52
septum, 75
serotonergic neurons, 85
serotonin, 72, 87, 206, 209, 318, 332, 334,
    335, 340
serotonin and norepinephrine reuptake
    inhibitors (*see* SNRIs)
serotonin receptors, **87**
    5-HT_1, **87**
    5-HT_2, **87**
    5-HT_3, **87**

5-HT$_4$, **87**
5-HT$_5$, **87**
serotonin syndrome, **304–5**, 310
serotonin transporters (*see* SERTs)
sertindole, 286
SERTs, 232–35, 251
Serturner, Frederick, 255
set point, **42**, **123**
sherry, 133
shock avoidance, 194
shooting up, 273, 275
short-term memory, **37**, 172, 322, 324
short-term residential treatment, **128**
side effect, **6**
sidestream smoke, **204**
SIDS, **204**
Siegel, S., 49
Siegel, Shepard, 48
Silverman, K., 111
Simon, Eric J., 259
simple reaction time, **36**
single photon emission computed
    tomography, 92
sinsemilla, 315
Sion, Amda, 231
sites of action, **8**
SI units, 136
Skinner, B. F., 26, 27, 33, 34
Skinner box, **31**, 244–45
skin popping, **9**
sleep, 87, 218–19
Slovak, Hillel, 272
SMA (*see* spontaneous motor activity)
Smith, D. W., 175, 176
Smith, J., 54
Smith, Kline, and French, 230
smoking
    birth weight, 204
    cancer, 203
    compulsion, 205–6
    genetics, 191
    immunization, 207–8
    pregnancy, 203
    social class, 196
    treatment, 205–6
Smucker-Barnwell, S. S., 329
Smyth, Breda, 273
SNC80, 270
SNRIs, 301, **303**
snuff, 187
Snyder, Solomon, 260–61
soda fountains, 230
soft drinks, 212
Solomon, R. L., 44
solvents, 164
somatic nervous system, **68**

somatostatin, 81
spasticity, **319**
Spealman, R. D., 197
Special K, 343
SPECT, 92, 272, 296
speed ball, **245**
speed freak, **245**
spinal cord, **70**–71, 317, 319, 320
spin–spin relaxation time, **94**
spleen, 317
spontaneous motor activity, **30**, 193, 264–65
SSRIs, 85, 297, 301, **301**, 303–5 (*see also*
    antidepressants)
St. Anthony's fire, **333**
stereotyped behaviors, **30**, **52**
Sternback, L. H., 165
Stewart, J., 113
stimulant psychosis, 238
stimulants, **26**
stimulus properties, **33**
    generalization, **34**
St.-John's-wort, **22**, 310
Stolerman, Ian, 27
stress, 112, 125, 169, 172, 298–300
    reinforcement, 120
striated muscles, **68**
striatum, 191
substance abuse, **97**
Substance Abuse and Mental Health
    Services Administration, 269
substance dependence, **97**
substance P, 81
substantia nigra, 73
substrate-type monoamine transporter
    blockers, 234–35
substrate-type releasers, 233–34
Sumerian idiogram, 256
summation, **62–63**
    spatial, **62**
    temporal, **62**
superadditive effect, **7**
surgical shock, 285
Sydenham, John, 257
sympathetic nervous system, **68**
sympathomimetic, **228**
symptom reemergence, 176
synapses, 63
synaptic cleft, 63, 90
synaptic pruning, **280–81**, 283
synaptic vesicles, 63, 90
synthetic mescaline-like drugs, **339–42**

tachyphylaxis, **40**
tactile hallucination, 238
"taking care of business or scoring," 267
talked down, 328

taming effect, 173
Tanda, G., 326
tardive dyskinesia, **290**, 293
Taylor, S., 327
TCAs, 300–303 (*see also* antidepressants)
tea, 211
    black, 211
    cassina, 212
    fermented, 211
    green Chinese, 211
    history, 213
    jasmine, 211
    oolong, 211
    semifermented, 211
    theobromine, 211
    theophylline, 211
temazepam, **165**
temperance movement, 134
temporal lobe, 74, 75, 77
teratogens, **78**
terminal buttons, **63**, 67
terminating synaptic action, 67
testosterone, 272, 330
tetranabinex, **314**
thalamus, 75, 115, **115**, 163, 260
thalidomide, **78**
THC, 67, 106, **314**, 338, 344
    absorption, 315–16
    amotivational syndrome, 328–29
    analgesic effects, 324
    ataxia, 323
    attention, 313, 328
    avoidance responding, 324
    conditioned behavior, 324
    content, 315, 323
    dissociation, 324
    distribution, 317
    driving, 326
    drug state discrimination, 324–25
    effects on the body, 319
    epidemiology, 326–27
    excretion, 317
    first-pass metabolism, 315
    half-life, 315, 317
    harmful effects, 327
    high, 326
    immunity, 330
    inhalation, 316
    I.V. administration, 316
    lethal effects, 325
    matching-to-sample test, 324
    memory, 324
    mood, 320–21
    motor activity, 325
    neuropharmacology, 317–19
    oral, 320

THC (*continued*)
oral administration, 315–16
perception, 321
performance, 322
punished behavior, 324
reproduction, 330
screening test, 323
self-administration, 326
sleep, 319
spontaneous motor activity (SMA), 323
subjective effects, 321–23
taming, 323
titration, 326
tolerance, 325
unconditioned behavior, 323–24
violence, 327–28
withdrawal, 326
thebaine, **255–56**
Theobroma cacao, 211
theobromine, 209, 212, 215
theophylline, 22, 89, 209, 212, 215, 217, 219, 220
therapeutic index (TI), **5**
therapeutic testing, 38–39
therapeutic window, **23–24**
thioridazine, 286
thiothixene, 286
third-generation antidepressants, **301**–3, 305
Thompson, T., 109
Thompson, Travis, 25, 246, 265, 270
Thorazine (*see* chlorpromazine)
three-groups design, **29**
threshold, 59
absolute, **36**
difference, **36**
time course, **23**
routes of administration, 23
titration, 326
tobacco
air-cured, 186
bright, 184
chewing, 184
cigarettes, 184
curing, 183
flue-cured, 184
history, 183–85
legal status, 185
preparations, 182–83
smoke, 186–87
smokeless, 185
snuff, 186, 187
vaccine, 208
tolerance, **40**
acute tolerance, **41**–42
behavioral tolerance, **43**
cellular tolerance, **42**

cross-tolerance, **41**
dependence, 98
functional disturbances, **43**
metabolic tolerance, **42**
operant conditioning, **50**
pharmacodynamic tolerance, **42**–43
physiological tolerance, **51**
practice, 51
tachyphylaxis, **40**
tooting, **231**
topiramate, 252
Tourette's syndrome, 293, 319
toxins, **1**
trade name, 2–4
trailing phenomena, 339
tranquilizers, 178
transcranial magnetic stimulation, 311
transcription factors, 65
transdermal administration, 16
transmitter, 57
transport mechanisms, **59**
active, **17**
passive, **17**
treatment programs, 128
triazepam, 170, **170**
triazolam, 111, 236, 242
tricyclic antidepressants (*see* TCAs)
trifluoperazine, 286
triflupromazine, 286
triiazolam, 174
tryptophan, 85, 296, 304
tuberculosis, 300
tuberoinfundibular pathway, 293
tunnel vision, 239–40
turkey drugs, 220
typical antipsychotics, **286**–92
tyramine, 304
tyrosine, 85

UCR (*see* unconditioned response)
UCS (*see* unconditioned stimulus)
unconditioned behavior, 173, 219
unconditioned response, **31, 47**
unconditioned stimulus, **31, 47**
unintentional injuries, 273–74
University of Michigan, 246
University of Minnesota, 246
unpleasant symptoms, relief of, 111
upper, **230**
upregulation, **42**
U.S. Congress, 257–58
U.S. Food and Drug Administration, 185, 307, 309, 347
U.S. Surgeon General's Report, 184

valproic acid, 161
Vanquish, 210

varenicline, 206
variable interval schedule, **32**
variable ratio schedule, **32**
variables
dependent, **28**
independent, **28**
VAS, **36**
vasodilation, 235
vasopressin, 81
vehicle, **9**
venlafaxine, 234
ventral horn, 70
ventral tegmental area (VTA), 73, 115, 121, 296, 299
ventrolateral preoptic nucleus (VLPO), 219
vesicular monoamine transporter (*see* VMAT)
VI (*see* variable interval schedule)
Vicodin, 256, 269 (*see also* hydrocodone)
Vietnam War veterans, 268
vigilance, **37**
vigilance task, 111
visual analog scale (VAS), **36**
vitamin D deficiency, 280
Vivarin, 210
VMAT, 233–34
Vogel-Sprott, M., 50, 51, 52
Volkow, N. D., 53
vomiting, 316, 319
vomiting center, 71, 191
von Fleischl-Marxow, Ernst, 238
VR (*see* variable ratio schedule)
VTA (*see* ventral tegmental area (VTA))

Wake Forest University, 248
Wake Ups, 210
walk and turn test, 323
wanting system, 119
Warren, R., 217
washout time, **304**
Wasson, R. Gordon, 337
Watkinson, B., 328
Weil, A. T., 321
Wellbutrin, 251, 303, 308 (*see also* bupropion)
Wernicke–Korsakoff syndrome, 154
Wesson, D. R., 175, 176
white matter, **68**
Wilcox, R., 329
WIN 55212-2, 315
window panes, **334**
withdrawal, **43**, 102, 113, 175, 195–96
withdrawal rebound, 171
withdrawal symptoms, **43**, 113, 222
"word salad," 279
World Anti-Doping Agency, 251
World Health Organization, 98, 100, **166**, 295

World War II, 230, 236, 239, 295

X, **339**, **347**
Xyrem, **347**

Yanagita, T., 113
years of potential life lost (*see* YPLL)
yeasts, 132
yen sleep, 267

YPLL, 273–74 (*see also* PYLL)
Yurgelun-Todd, D., 328

zaleplon, **164**, 168, 170, 171
z-axis, **93**
Z drugs, **164**, 168
  neurophysiology, 164
  performance, 171–72

pharmacokinetics, 166
  sleep, 168
Zinberg, N. E., 321
ziprasidone, 286
zolpidem, **164**, 168, 171, 173
zopiclone, **164**, 168, 171, 173
zotepine, 286
Zyban, 251, 303, 308 (*see also* bupropion)